AF768723

# Database Programming with Visual J++™

WITHDRAWN

que®

# Database Programming with Visual J++™

*Written by Christopher S. Lester with*

*Daniel Brookshier • Randy Curnutt • Loren D. Eidahl*
*• Nelson Howell • Stephen Wynkoop*

Que®

# Database Programming with Visual J++™

**Copyright© 1997 by Que® Corporation.**

All rights reserved. Printed in the United States of America. No part of this book may be used or reproduced in any form or by any means, or stored in a database or retrieval system, without prior written permission of the publisher except in the case of brief quotations embodied in critical articles and reviews. Making copies of any part of this book for any purpose other than your own personal use is a violation of United States copyright laws. For information, address Que Corporation, 201 W. 103rd Street, Indianapolis, IN 46290. You may reach Que's direct sales line by calling 1-800-428-5331.

Library of Congress Catalog No.: 97-67473

ISBN: 0-7897-1015-3

This book is sold *as is*, without warranty of any kind, either express or implied, respecting the contents of this book, including but not limited to implied warranties for the book's quality, performance, merchantability, or fitness for any particular purpose. Neither Que Corporation nor its dealers or distributors shall be liable to the purchaser or any other person or entity with respect to any liability, loss, or damage caused or alleged to have been caused directly or indirectly by this book.

99 98 97 6 5 4 3 2 1

Interpretation of the printing code: the rightmost double-digit number is the year of the book's printing; the rightmost single-digit number, the number of the book's printing. For example, a printing code of 97-1 shows that the first printing of the book occurred in 1997.

All terms mentioned in this book that are known to be trademarks or service marks have been appropriately capitalized. Que cannot attest to the accuracy of this information. Use of a term in this book should not be regarded as affecting the validity of any trademark or service mark.

Screen reproductions in this book were created using Collage Plus from Inner Media, Inc., Hollis, NH.

# Contents at a Glance

# Table of Contents

# Credits

**PRESIDENT**
Roland Elgey

**SENIOR VICE PRESIDENT/PUBLISHING**
Don Fowley

**PUBLISHER**
Stacy Hiquet

**PUBLISHING MANAGER**
Fred Slone

**GENERAL MANAGER**
Joe Muldoon

**EDITORIAL SERVICES DIRECTOR**
Elizabeth Keaffaber

**MANAGING EDITOR**
Caroline Roop

**ACQUISITIONS EDITOR**
Kelly Marshall

**PRODUCT DIRECTOR**
Erik Dafforn

**PRODUCTION EDITOR**
Juliet MacLean

**EDITOR**
Sean Dixon

**STRATEGIC MARKETING MANAGER**
Barry Pruett

**WEB MASTER**
Thomas H. Bennett

**PRODUCT MARKETING MANAGER**
Kristine R. Ankney

**ASSISTANT PRODUCT MARKETING MANAGER/DESIGN**
Christy M. Miller

**ASSISTANT PRODUCT MARKETING MANAGER/SALES**
Karen Kincaid

**TECHNICAL EDITOR**
Craig Olague

**MEDIA DEVELOPMENT SPECIALIST**
Brandon Penticuff

**TECHNICAL SUPPORT SPECIALIST**
Nadeem Muhammed

**ACQUISITIONS COORDINATOR**
Carmen Krikorian

**SOFTWARE RELATIONS COORDINATOR**
Susan D. Gallagher

**SOFTWARE COORDINATOR**
Andrea Duvall

**BOOK DESIGNER**
Ruth Harvey

**COVER DESIGNER**
Aaron Moore

**PRODUCTION TEAM**
DiMonique Ford
Trey Frank
Nicole Ruessler
Lisa Stumpf

**INDEXER**
Chris Wilcox

Composed in *Century Old Style* and *ITC Franklin Gothic* by Que Corporation.

*To my daughter, Mariah, and my wife, Dawn, for making it possible to come this far...*

# About the Authors

**Christopher S. Lester** is currently a member of the Microsoft Exchange Debug team. He has dabbled in UNIX-based databases, Xbase, dBASE, and data design (as well as several programming languages). He has extensive experience with LAN-based messaging systems and Microsoft Exchange in particular. When Chris is not working, he can be found eating, sleeping, or racing his '96 Impala SS.

**Randy Curnutt** is president of Solutions Plus, Inc., a software consulting company, specializing in providing comprehensive solutions by applying leading-edge technology. He has been in the computer industry for nearly fourteen years and has focused on client/server solutions and object-oriented technology during the past six years. He has experience with Smalltalk, C, C++, and numerous other development languages. In addition, he has in-depth experience with relational database management systems. He enjoys projects that push his technical and business skills, providing an opportunity to add value. Randy received a B.S. in computer science and applied mathematics degree from Purdue University in 1984. He enjoys spending time with his family, reading, writing, and engaging in outdoor activities such as golfing, swimming, and fishing. Randy can be reached via the Internet at **solplus@iquest.net**.

**Loren D. Eidahl** is currently the president of CTS, Inc., based in Minneapolis, Minnesota. CTS is an Internet consulting company that specializes in Internet-based business solutions. He has been involved with computers for over fourteen years, since the early days of the PC when 16K was quite a bit of RAM. Over the years, he has been involved in many projects, ranging from satellite communications to the marketing of point-of-sale products. For the past eight years, he has been a consultant to a wide range of industries. Currently, Loren devlops software in several languages, including Visual Basic, Java, PowerBuilder, and Delphi. In addition, he enjoys multimedia and virtual reality development. Loren's free time finds him with his wife, two children, and two dogs. He also enjoys walleye and trout fishing in northern Minnesota and Canada. You can reach him at **leidahl@cornerstonetech.com** or visit his Web page at **http://www.cornerstonetech.com**.

**Nelson Howell** is a veteran of the computer industry. Starting with IBM mainframes in 1967, he has survived the changes from mainframes to minis to microcomputers. In addition to writing, he provides support to users of software for Icon Technology Solutions. Now at home in Tucson, Arizona, he is surrounded by his family of four sons and a very tolerant wife.

**Stephen Wynkoop** is an author and lecturer working extensively with Microsoft-based products and technologies, with emphasis on Internet and client/server technologies. Stephen has been developing applications and consulting in the computer industry for more than fourteen years. He is a coauthor of *Special Edition Using Microsoft SQL Server 6.5*, as well as a contributor to other Que titles on the Internet and *Special Edition Using Windows NT Server 4.0*. Stephen is a regular speaker at Microsoft's Technical conferences and has written books on Microsoft Access and Microsoft Office 95 integration. Stephen is also a Microsoft Certified Professional (MCP) for both Windows for Workgroups and Windows NT technologies. Reach Stephen via the Internet at **swynk@pobox.com**, or visit his Web site at **http://www.pobox.com/~swynk**.

# Acknowledgments

As you know, a book such as this is not written alone. In addition to the authors whose help we enlisted to round out the content of this book, I'd like to thank Kelly Marshall for granting me the opportunity to write this book, Juliet MacLean for helping finalize the results, and the Que production staff who helped make this book a reality.

I also want to thank my family for putting up with me working twenty-four hours a day for a few months without too many complaints. And to all my friends and relatives up north in Oklahoma—I'm not dead; I was only hibernating.

## We'd Like to Hear from You!

As part of our continuing effort to produce books of the highest possible quality, Que would like to hear your comments. To stay competitive, we *really* want you to let us know what you like or dislike most about this book or other Que products.

Please send your comments, ideas, and suggestions for improvement to:

The Expert User Team
E-Mail: **euteam@que.mcp.com**
CompuServe: 105527, 745
Fax: (317) 581-4663

Our mailing address is:

Expert User Team
Que Corporation
201 West 103rd Street
Indianapolis, IN 46290-1097

You can also visit our team's home page on the World Wide Web at:

**http://www.mcp.com/que/developer_expert**

Thank you in advance. Your comments will help us to continue publishing the best books available in today's market.

Thank You,

*The Expert User Team*

# Introduction

Java is becoming a more mature language. With maturity, however, comes a need to move beyond simple applets and animated gifs. So far we have used Java's capabilities as a network programming language to create re-directs, active image maps, and other interesting, but small, projects.

With the entry of Microsoft into the Java development arena, this is changing. Object wrappers for ODBC access enable Java developers to extend their client's investments in data storage and warehousing. Soon, with the Application Foundation Classes, Java will be on an even par with C with respect to GUI enhancements, enabling sophisticated client front-ends for databases and more commercial data management applications.

Along with the prospects for data access with Java there are potential pitfalls as well. This book covers the aspects of data design and security issues that will evolve as Java becomes a more mainstream development language.

Integration issues will become more pressing as well, and with several chapters devoted to exploring the different options for publishing your data, your most difficult choice will be choosing the method.

# Who Should Use This Book

This book is written for developers familiar with the Java language. It covers database design and the SQL language as well as integrating Java with ODBC data sources and Data Warehousing. It can also serve as a reference for users at any experience level. You'll find links to tools, articles, and other resources on the Web at **http://www.microsoft.com/visualj**, Microsoft's site, or at the Que Publishing site, **http://www.mcp.com/que**, where you can find additional books online, as well.

# How to Use This Book

This book is divided into four sections that present database design and programming as a logical series of steps in the order in which the reader would most likely begin developing a database application. Ideally, you will go through the sections and their chapters in sequence. However, because you might not read the text in this order, we have localized the content as much as possible so that you can understand the content of each chapter without memorizing the information that is not relevant to the task at hand.

### Part I: Foundations for Database Programming with Visual J++

Part I presents the basic concepts of data design and an overview of current technologies. In this section, you'll learn about necessary information that is related to developing and designing a database. The background information about data design is recommended for anyone designing data tools.

Chapter 1, "Java, Visual J++, and Databases," introduces you to all of the concepts you'll see later in the book. Also, you will discover how Visual J++ fits into the database development scheme.

Chapter 2, "Database Design Concepts," covers the design process in depth, including an introduction to several different design methodologies and a thorough tutorial on data normalization.

In Chapter 3, "Creating a Simple Database Application," you'll be introduced to a simple contact manager to illustrate the most basic meaning of a database. You'll also get a peek at some more advanced uses of Java and database design.

### Part II: A New Look at Database Programming

Part II introduces you to the foundations of database programming, beginning with the SQL standard. From the SQL standard you will explore ODBC, DAO, and RDO to gain a complete understanding of the options available to Visual J++ developers.

Chapter 4, "The SQL Standard: A Language for Data Access," provides you with a complete reference on the most important SQL-92 concepts and usage, allowing you to incorporate its advanced feature into your designs.

Chapter 5, "ODBC," explores the ODBC interface and the technologies that make up Microsoft's foundations for database connectivity solution.

Chapter 6, "Data Access Objects," leads you through an in-depth look at the new DAO3.5 and the ODBCDirect capabilities of the new API.

Chapter 7, "Remote Data Objects," continues the instruction on data access technologies and illustrates Microsoft's fastest remote data interface for use with Visual J++.

### Part III: Microsoft Visual InterDev

Microsoft Visual InterDev provides a powerful new integrated development environment in which the developer is free to design the Web site without the hassle of continually coding the HTML.

Chapter 8, "Introducing Microsoft Visual InterDev," introduces you to Microsoft's new integrated Internet development environment.

In Chapter 9, "Microsoft Visual InterDev Web Site Design," you learn to harness the power of Microsoft Visual InterDev to speed the design process and create active content with the Web Wizards.

In Chapter 10, "Database Development with Microsoft Visual InterDev," you learn how to use the database wizard and the design time controls to easily integrate database content on the Internet. In addition, you'll learn to use the Active Database Object using active scripting.

### Part IV: Publishing Your Data to the Web

Chapter 11, "Understanding SQL Server and the Internet," provides an in-depth look at how SQL Server 6.5 can be used to publish your data on the Internet.

Chapter 12, "IIS Internet Database Connector," provides a complete tour of the new IDC, and takes a look under the hood to give you an idea of what is going on behind the scenes of the IDC.

### Part V: Advanced Issues with Visual J++

Chapter 13, "Security Issues," takes a good look at the technologies available today to protect your data from theft and malicious intent.

Chapter 14, "Dealing with Disaster Before It Happens," provides you with the information necessary to arm yourself with the knowledge to protect your data from disaster before it happens.

Chapter 15, "Distributing Java Applications," tells you how to extend the capabilities included in transactions across servers. This chapter explains the setup, use, and troubleshooting associated with these extended transaction capabilities.

Chapter 16, "Implementing Data Warehousing with Visual J++," provides you with information about how to keep data consistently available to the users of client systems. Availability of data from a database is ensured by a combination of fault-tolerant mechanisms and the duplication of data before it's lost.

Chapter 17, "Building a Web Crawler with DAO," completes the circle begun in Chapter 3 by transforming the specifications into a working Web Crawler.

Chapter 18, "The Client/Server Quandary," introduces you to the concept of client/server and how this concept affects the way you design and develop applications.

**Part VI: Appendixes**

The appendixes provide detailed references for DAO and RDO. These references are the most comprehensive coverage of these APIs, as of this writing.

**ON THE WEB**

For additional information, visit this book's Web site at **http://www.quecorp.com/dpvj**.

## Conventions Used in This Book

Que has over a decade of experience writing and developing the most successful computer books available. With that experience, we've learned what special features help readers the most. Look for these special features throughout the book to enhance your learning experience.

The following font conventions are used in this book to help make reading it easier.

- *Italic type* is used to introduce new terms.
- Screen messages, code listings, and command samples appear in `monospace type`. For more details about syntax, see the following section, "Syntax Guidelines."
- Code that you are instructed to type appears in **bold**.
- Shortcut keys are denoted with underscores. For example, "choose File, Edit" means that you can press Alt+F, and then press E to perform the same steps as clicking the File menu and then clicking Edit.

**TIP** Tips present short advice on quick or often-overlooked procedures and shortcuts.

**NOTE** Notes present interesting or useful information that isn't necessarily essential to the discussion. A note provides additional information that might help you avoid problems or offers advice that relates to the topic.

**CAUTION**

Cautions warn you about potential problems that a procedure might cause, unexpected results, or mistakes to avoid.

### Syntax Guidelines

It's important to have a clearly defined way of describing Transact-SQL commands. In this book, the following rules apply:

- Anything in *italics* means that you have to substitute the italicized text with your own text.
- Anything placed inside square brackets "[...]" means that it can be optionally left out of the command.
- Anything placed inside curly braces "{...}" means that one of the values must be chosen to complete the syntax.
- The available values are separated by the bar (or pipe) character "|" (meaning "OR"). Consider the following example:

  ```
  {DISK ¦ TAPE ¦ DISKETTE}
  ```

  It would be translated as "DISK or TAPE or DISKETTE."
- Finally, if you see "..." after any bracketed block in a Transact-SQL statement, it means that section can be repeated as many times as is appropriate.

PART I

# Foundations for Database Programming with Visual J++

CHAPTER 1

# Java, Visual J++, and Databases

**Java**

Consider an overview of the Java language and its uses.

**Visual J++**

Examine Microsoft's implementation of Java.

**Microsoft InterDev**

Learn to use Microsoft InterDev for Database Development.

**Data warehousing**

Explore the concept of data warehousing.

During the past two or three years, the world has seen the rise of the Internet and intranets, increasingly faster and more powerful computers, and a newly formed language called Java, which promises to revolutionize the way we develop applications. If you had looked at the market before this period, you would have noticed that a number of companies were becoming overwhelmed by the ever increasing amounts of information. Where some companies viewed the onslaught nervously and attempted to shut the chaos out, a few reveled in the emerging opportunities. These pioneers led the way in creating an informational revolution.

Companies such as SAP, Microsoft, Oracle, and Sybase began providing extensive data management services in addition to their base products. As a result, companies now have the capability to use the mass of information to make intelligent, strategic business decisions.

A second crisis, however, is appearing on the horizon. Although more and more companies are attempting to take advantage of its growing popularity, the Internet has resisted efforts aimed at commercialization. The cost involved in implementing these solutions over a wide variety of architectures and operating systems have prevented commercial ventures from succeeding; this is beginning to change as companies grow accustomed to using this new medium, and as a means of getting information from one place to another, the Internet has no equal.

Now that there are browsers capable of streaming information in a more esthetically pleasing format, and new feature sets are being added every day, you'll see the trend toward commercialization continue. This has both advantages and disadvantages. On one hand, more information than ever will be available to us in an accessible mechanism. However, as soon as newer communications technologies such as Asynchronous Digital Subscriber Lines (ADSL) and Cable Modems become available, quite a few people probably will suffer from information overload.

Applying the lessons learned developing data warehousing for the corporate environment can prevent a recurrence of the information crisis of the mid 1980's. Allowing information to be placed into our data environments without any constraints or structure is perhaps more destructive than not having the data in the first place. Instead of uninformed decisions, you'll end up with misinformed business decisions based on irrelevant data or misinformation.

Imagine the opportunity—all of this data, no one to manage it, and no way to integrate it into companies' existing data warehouses. As developers in a language that is well suited to the Internet, you can take advantage of Java's client/server architecture to create scalable tools for data mining and data warehousing via the Internet. Those should be enough to pique your interest, so take a quick look at what you'll see in this book. ■

# Reviewing Java

Java is a language that will revolutionize application development in the same manner as roads revolutionized interstate travel. That is a fact. You probably don't need to be reminded of the platforms that Java will run on, or an explanation of "secure," "robust," and "portable." Java has a cool name, does a lot of stuff we like, and is an easy development tool to work with. What more could you ask for? Well, quite a lot, and for the most part, Sun has filled our basic need—a language that isn't filled with ten thousand different ways to do the same thing, massive memory allocation headaches, or a severe case of multiple personalities.

This is not to say that C/C++ isn't a good development platform; in fact, many appreciate what C/C++ offers. When you spend hours tracking down memory leaks in an application because you didn't release a pointer properly, however, it's time for a change. Have you ever crashed a system because you wrote off the end of the stack or had someone read into your application's memory space? You won't see these problems developing in Java. Debugging is something that we deal with every day, but it is one task that Java makes much easier.

It is very easy to write multithreaded applications for Java, making it a natural for the Web, and, because network programming is simple in Java and databases are well supported, client/server database programming is also a natural for Java. There is a problem with Java, however—the graphical toolkit is too generic, making it difficult to develop applications that look professional. That aside, you can create servers in Java very easily, and the client can be written in any language, including Java.

Some other caveats of advanced programming in Java: Java doesn't provide inherent support for object persistence or keep the state information of the object between sessions. You'll have to create your own object persistence. When you become more familiar with using the standard I/O classes, you'll discover that using streams to read and write entire classes to binary storage can be done rather easily. The ways in which different platforms behave under the same circumstances is also an issue; that can be very disconcerting in the debugging process. Read the following sections to refresh your Java knowledge before heading into the dark reaches of database programming.

## Threading in Java

Threading is both simple and complex at the same time. Because Java has a level of abstraction between the application and the system, you can use the existing model on the client's operating system (OS). This would usually be "Green Threads" for Solaris and UNIX models and the Win32 Threading models (Apartment and Free threading) for Win32 platforms. The Mac threading model is the cooperative Threading model, much like Windows 3.1, at least until Copeland ships. This can lead to inconsistencies across platforms, but dealing with cross-platform issues is simply a fact of life with Java.

Another caveat is that all of the threads run in the same process space as the virtual machine. This means that security is enhanced, but you can't spin off new threads in their own processes. We can work around this, however, by using ActiveX components. For the most part, threading in Java works very well. Simply extend the Thread class, or implement the Runnable interface.

At the moment, there is a running debate in the computer newsgroups concerning the best way to create a thread. Extending the Thread class has struck some people like the `goto` statement of C. Both methods work well enough for this debate to be one of semantics, not actual performance. Each thread has several methods that directly control its execution, as you'll see listed in Table 1.1. For a complete reference, consult the Visual J++ Books Online included with Visual J++.

**Table 1.1 Java.Lang.Thread Partial Method Reference**

| Method | Description |
|---|---|
| `Thread.join()` | Sits around and waits for the thread to die. |
| `Thread.interrupt()` | Interrupts the thread's execution. |
| `Thread.resume()` | Starts execution after the thread is suspended. |
| `Thread.run()` | Overload this method to do the work if you've extended Thread. |
| `Thread.start()` | Calls the `Run()` method of the thread to begin thread execution. |
| `Thread.sleep()` | Suspends the thread for a specified amount of time. |
| `Thread.stop()` | Stops execution of the current thread. |
| `Thread.yield()` | Forces the thread to yield to other threads. |

## Networking

Networking is something that Java does well. Although some of the lower-level options in C aren't included (such as Remote Procedure Calls), the Sockets implementation is very clean and easy to use. With Visual J++, you have the capability to use ActiveX/COM within your application. These components handle the networking elements internally, freeing you to concentrate on the application code.

Java uses three kinds of socket: a ServerSocket, a client Socket, and a datagram Socket. A ServerSocket listens on a port for incoming connections and returns a client Socket when a connection is detected. The client Socket is then used for the actual communication. The datagram Socket is exactly what you think it is, a Socket that uses only datagrams. A datagram Socket does not guarantee delivery of the packet, although the loss of reliability is offset by removing the overhead associated with TCP handshaking. You can get away with using datagrams in cases where losing packets wouldn't greatly affect the application, such as BOOTP agents or Trivial FTP (TFTP), but use normal (TCP) Sockets for other applications.

## Using Streams

C programmers are familiar with streams: Istream, ostream, ifstream, ofstream. However, this is one place in which Java is more complex than C. There are 22 streams in Java, which means that you need to have a very clear idea why you want to use a particular stream, unless you want to be limited to the use of two or three. You can use streams for a variety of tasks in Java, from object persistence to mime encoding. You can do this by extending the existing stream classes, much like derived classes in C. Table 1.2 lists these streams and what they can be used for.

**Table 1.2 Java Streams Reference**

| Stream | Description |
|---|---|
| `Java.io.BufferedInputStream` | Provides for buffered input |
| `Java.io.BufferedOutputStream` | Provides for buffered output |
| `Java.io.ByteArrayInputStream` | Treats input as an array of bytes |
| `Java.io.ByteArrayOutputStream` | Treats output as an array of bytes |
| `Java.io.DataInputStream` | Generic stream for reading data |
| `Java.io.DataOutputStream` | Generic stream for writing data |
| `Java.io.FileInputStream` | Byte level read on a file object |
| `Java.io.FileOutputStream` | Byte level write to a file object |
| `Java.io.FilterInputStream` | Filters incoming stream of data |
| `Java.io.FilterOutputStream` | Filters outgoing data from a stream |
| `Java.io.InputStream` | Abstract class for Input streams, extend this class |

| Stream | Description |
|---|---|
| `Java.io.LineNumberInputStream` | Keeps track of the lines read in |
| `Java.io.Outputstream` | Writes a single byte or an array of bytes |
| `Java.io.PipedInputStream` | Implements incoming half of a pipe |
| `Java.io.PipedOutputStream` | Implements outgoing half of a pipe |
| `Java.io.Printstream` | Implements a variety of printing methods, used to output ASCII text |
| `Java.io.PushbackInputStream` | Enables us to read ahead one byte and then push that byte back on the stream |
| `Java.io.SequenceInputStream` | Joins two streams |
| `Java.io.StringBufferInputStream` | Reads data from a `String` object |
| `Java.io.StreamTokenizer` | Breaks input stream up into tokens delimited by a character |

## Client/Server Issues

Building Java applets can be fun, and they can spruce up a Web site. However, applets don't provide much access to system resources. The issue of host access—you can only access the host that loaded the applet—is also a problem. This puts a damper on single-tier applications; those applications that provide both the interface and the implementation of the transaction must find some other way to access another host. Java's ease of network support helps overcome the security limitation by including robust support for the client/server model. The user interface and data gathering can be split off to a client, enabling the server to perform the real work. The client will be an applet, and the server can be a stand-alone application capable of accessing anything a native C application can. Not only does the client/server model make sense, but the complexity is on both sides by separating the processes.

# Getting to Know Visual J++

Java and the Internet: A cross-platform solution to all of our problems. Just run a browser on your desk and away you go. You might be asking yourself "Is this the end of Windows as we know it?" It might have seemed that way a year ago, but since then, a dazzling array of products developed specifically for the Internet has streamed out of Redmond, and one of particular interest is Microsoft's implementation of the Java language.

We all know how portable Java is, but few acknowledge the fact that Java is a young language. This is evident if you've ever tried to make a decent Java GUI application that doesn't scream "X-Windows" to all who see it, not to mention the added disadvantage of having to learn how to build your own classes to handle simple things like dialog boxes. This situation has resulted in the growth of dozens of add-in classes and Integrated Development Environments to handle this need.

As it stands now, there are few development environments on the market that won't remind you of the "good" old days of the first efforts into the C tools market. By adding database and ActiveX support to Visual J++, Microsoft has brought a new level of complexity to the Java language. This is a good thing, however, enabling you to build distributed applications by using a variety of languages, linking them all through ODBC or ActiveX. Visual J++ is also the newest entry in the Developer Studio series. With integrated support for ActiveX and native database support, as well as Developer Studio's tools, Visual J++ promises to be a very powerful Java development environment. Here's a list of the new features found in Visual J++:

- ActiveX integration
- Database connectivity
- DirectX Api support
- Registry access (with Microsoft's Java SDK)

## ActiveX Integration

Microsoft's Visual J++ has provided what many were asking for—more power. By providing Java with COM support, thousands of existing components can now be used with Java. Although the capability to support instancing ActiveX controls in our Java applications hasn't been implemented, the IDispatch interface of ActiveX components are exposed to Java developers in Visual J++. In addition to support for using ActiveX components, Microsoft added the capability to create your own ActiveX components with Visual J++ in the release version. Creating your own ActiveX component is fairly simple with Visual J++. Simply do the following:

1. Create the class.
2. Use the guidgen utility to retrieve a unique identifier for the component.
3. With the MIDL compiler, create the interface definition for the Java class by using the unique identifier returned by guidgen.

## DirectX Support

Most developers have probably heard of DirectX but have not bothered to play with it. After all, that's for game graphics, and you design real applications. That might be true, but those graphics are what initially interest most end users. Usually, the meat of an application is mostly rudimentary and boring to them, so if you can make your front-ends more appealing with graphics, why not do so?

The foundation of the DirectX libraries lies with Microsoft's intention to open the Windows platform to more serious gaming and publishing developments. Previously, the hardware accelerations that made the dedicated graphics workstations a must for real publishing or graphics development were unknown to the Intel platforms. Microsoft has worked to change this and to provide what is essentially a backdoor to the hardware.

What does this mean for you? If you've tried your hand at Java's graphics, you know what slow really means. Even double buffering the graphics and rendering the primitives beforehand results in only mediocre speed levels. DirectX gives Java a needed boost in performance. By using the routines in DirectX, you no longer have to wring your hands with the Java.awt.graphics classes. Instead, you can rely on DirectX for your drawing needs. For more information on DirectX, check the documentation on the Microsoft Web site (**http://www.microsoft.com/visualj**), or the Visual J++ Books Online (included with Microsoft Visual J++).

## Database Support in Visual J++

By using Visual J++, you can access hundreds of existing databases. Microsoft has included *RDO* and *DAO* support in Visual J++. What is RDO and DAO? They are simply a means of accessing a database without having to know the specifics of each individual database engine. This enables you to write code that will not suddenly become obsolete or need to be totally rewritten because a client changes data sources.

**Remote Data Objects** To answer the "What is RDO?" question a little more thoroughly before going on, Remote Data Objects are what are called an *object wrapper* around the ODBC application programming interface. Microsoft took the most ODBC APIs and created functions enabling you to access them and then exported these as public functions. In this way, languages such as Visual Basic and Java, which cannot access those APIs directly, now have the means to do so.

Because RDO has been so tightly wrapped to ODBC, it is natural to assume that you can take full advantage of ODBC's power. In fact, you can take it one step further and access some databases directly, such as Microsoft's SQL Server Data Transaction Control (used to control replication and submission of data to multiple data sources, which is very helpful with data warehousing).

Using RDO with Visual J++ creates a unique role in the client/server database integration market. You now have a tool that is conceptually easier to develop with and that can be used to create powerful data monitors and online analytical tools. Chapter 7, "Remote Data Objects," covers using RDO within the Visual J++ development environment. You'll see many of the techniques of using RDO while following the development of a back-end to a Search Engine.

**Data Access Objects** Data Access Objects are a set of methods rolled up into an OLE DLL, originally designed to enable access to the power of the Microsoft Jet database engine. Similar in function to RDO, Data Access Objects are mainly used to access a local ISAM database, (indexed sequential access method), usually a relational database management system such as Microsoft Foxpro or Microsoft Access. Data Access Objects have been optimized to work with the Jet Engine though, and until this release, would load the Jet Engine no matter which database was accessed.

Fortunately, there is now a way around this; using ODBCDirect you can send queries directly to an ODBC data source without loading the Microsoft Jet Engine. And Microsoft isn't the only one you can use DAO to access because other vendors have added support for them as well, giving you access to a wide variety of database engines.

# Publishing Data with Microsoft InterDev

A possible alternative to using Visual J++, Microsoft InterDev is an extremely powerful set of tools. It is interesting that it, too, integrates with Developer Studio. Microsoft InterDev presents us with somewhat of a quandary concerning where to start. On one hand, you can design your entire Web site with Microsoft InterDev. On the other hand, there are the multiple views and wizards to cover. Because dealing with information effectively is your major concern, however, this book focuses on the database tools that you can find in Microsoft InterDev.

One of the problems developers face most often is how to get data back to the client in a usable form—preferably in a form that enables you to tailor the information to the specific transaction. Microsoft InterDev provides a rich set of tools with which you can accomplish this, from the Data View, in which you can see the actual structure of each data source in your site, to the Database Wizard, which takes care of scripting what you design. All of these tools, coupled with the capability to design queries across multiple databases visually, as well as to execute data definition language directly, make this a powerful solution to your information needs. Here's a quick overview of the components covered in this book.

## The Active Server

With the tight integration of ActiveX components through the Active Server pages, Microsoft InterDev enables you to use your ActiveX and OLE controls with an even wider distribution. Because Visual J++ gives you the capability to create ActiveX controls, it would be natural to integrate those with Microsoft InterDev's database development capabilities. The Active Server works through the use of client-side scripting (VBSript and JScript) and server-side scripting (Active Data Objects and the Internet Database Connector, for example), eliminating the usual overhead when using single-integrated database applications.

## The Data View

You will use the Data View to browse the Web site's data sources. It provides you with an interactive view of the data by using the database tools included with Microsoft InterDev, making the transition from browsing to actually changing the data source structure or data an easy task. The layout of the Data View (illustrated in Figure 1.1) is much like that of Windows Explorer or the Class View from Developer Studio; the data sources are viewed in the left pane, and the details describing the data sources, such as structure, are viewed on the right.

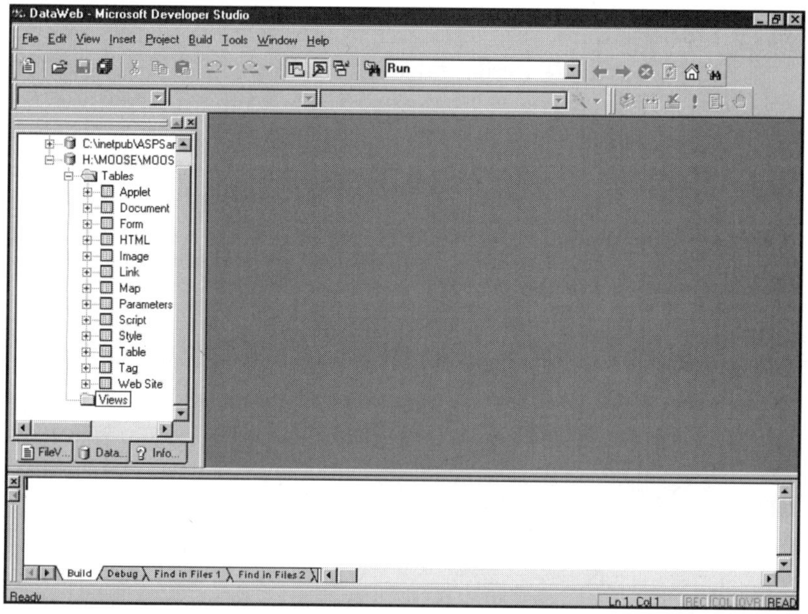


**FIG. 1.1**
This is Microsoft InterDev's Data View.

## Design Time ActiveX Data Controls

These controls, such as the Data Command Control and the Data Range Control, enable you to manipulate the presentation and collection methods during design time. These controls give you much better control over how the client interface will look and feel. These controls are the muscle behind the wizards in Microsoft InterDev. They generate server-side scripting according to what you've designed, making your job much easier.

## Database Wizards

Database Wizards won't help create databases as their name suggests; instead, they enable you to create complex interfaces to your data sources without having to worry about scripting the IDC files and their HTML templates. You can design the application visually, such as an interactive search, and then use the Database Wizards to create the scripting for it.

## Database Designer

This component enables you to visually design a database. You've probably done this with Access or another RDBMS, but not with SQL Server. The Database Designer enables redefinition of the structure of the SQL database without going through complex DDL statements. What you design with the Database Designer is written out as a series of DDL and ASP scripts that you can either execute now or review for accuracy.

## Query Designer

What the Database Designer does for you with databases, the Query Designer does with queries. If you've worked with a desktop RDBMS, you've probably run across query by example or visual query builders. The Query Designer is very similar, enabling you to build queries visually that scale across multiple data sources from many different vendors. You might also decide to make a change to one of the data sources, and you can execute DDL and SQL directly against the data source. After you're finished designing the query, this wizard creates all the necessary Active Server Pages to do the work of displaying and navigating through the data.

# Database Concepts and Technologies

Before diving into the more advanced implementation topics, refresh your memory a little on the basics of database design and some of the newer concepts being used today.

## Current Database Topologies

In the ever-changing world of technology, databases have seemed to remain fairly static, moving at a snail's pace compared to new processor designs and languages. Now we are seeing some hint of a push to update our thinking regarding the actual architecture of the databases we use. Take a brief look at the most prevalent of these.

**Relational Databases** Although they have only recently begun overtaking the flat file databases that were common in the mainframe environment, relational databases have been around for two and a half decades. E.F. Codd is credited with being responsible for creating the relational database theory, which is based on algebraic set theory, and an outgrowth of Codd's work was relational algebra and relational calculus. These mathematical models were designed to enable you to embed database commands into existing programming languages.

Codd defined twelve rules in order for a database to be "truly relational." Although it is beyond the scope of this book to delve deeply into relational theory and the implementation of these rules, it is in your interest to see what a relational database actually is.

The actual idea of a relational database can be broken into two components: relations and keys. *Relations* define the context and links between the keys, and the *keys* are used for creating uniqueness in the database. This uniqueness is what enables the relations defined between the *tuples* (a small set of data pertaining to a single row in a relation) to work correctly. This is the simple, yet powerful concept behind the relational database.

**Object-Oriented Relational Databases** A database model based on the object-oriented design theory that helped produce Java, object-oriented databases are still in their infancy. The concept of an object-oriented relational database is a fairly simple one: Take everything that can be uniquely identified with a particular object and filter everything else up to a higher level, where again you find what is unique. Continue this process until you have defined all of the entities in your database. Then you can add the concept of relations between objects of the same or different types much in the same manner as a relational database.

**Multidimensional Databases** Multidimensional databases have arisen in the last few years to handle the challenge of scaling queries to massive sets of data. Their roots are in mathematical arrays, which contributes to their speed when retrieving and storing data. Multidimensional databases use a model that is akin to a cube of data. Each attribute is represented by one column in the cube. In this manner, the query is executed and the database engine only needs to search through those attributes contained in the query rather than the entire database. If you look at the actual data in a multidimensional database, you would see what appeared to be clusters of arrays laid out in a haphazard fashion. Because a multidimensional database stores the data in array-like cubes, there is no need for massive indexing or normalization of the model. In fact, less than 2-4 percent of the entire database is used for indexing because the only location the database engine needs to know about is where to find the data cube closest to the query target.

There is a large debate going on between people who prefer relational models and those who prefer the multidimensional model. These two models were fairly separate until recently with the advent of the large data warehouse and online analytical processing (OLAP).

▶ **See** "Understanding the Concept of Data Warehousing" for additional information on the benefits of using either model in the discussion on data warehousing and the technology used to implement it, **p. 450**

# ODBC

Open Database Connectivity (ODBC) is an open standard that defines a series of interfaces so that you can write applications without cringing every time vendors upgrade their drivers or convince your clients that they need to "upsize." Now it's okay to upsize and add all of the features that you want to a driver.

# Database Design

Database design is a sticky issue, and we hope that, being the developer, you won't have to deal with the actual implementation of the customer's data strategy. However, just in case the most advanced database in the company sits beside someone's desk and comes with multiple shelving, we'll cover some basic design issues like modeling, normalization, and referential integrity.

**Data Models** Data models are the bread and butter of the highly paid, often elusive, consultants. They are used to map out a logical view of the data and to determine the metadata from these views to build a longlasting database. Of the many data models, perhaps three are most relevant to you:

- The entity relationship model
- The semantic model
- The object-oriented model

These models are most often seen in the development of online transaction processing (OLTP) applications. One other, the dimensional model, might be of interest to you if you're designing an OLAP application. Sometimes called the star or snowflake schema, the dimensional model provides a way to abstract the data and deal effectively with multidimensional views of the data.

**Normalization** Normalization is the foundation for the physical design of the tables in a database so that you can prevent error from creeping in. There are six forms of normalization that can be performed on data, including the Boyce-Codd algorithm. Most people stop after the third normal form; however, due to scaling and mission- critical issues (such as online banking), it might be necessary to go further at times.

**Referential Integrity** You can use built-in measures against these types of errors. This is called referential integrity, or simply *rules* and *triggers*. There are generally three types of rules, and a trigger can be executed by nearly any action on the database. Table 1.3 describes the most common rule types.

**Table 1.3 Referential Integrity: Some Common Rules Found in Databases**

| Type | Description |
|---|---|
| Insert | An insert rule is checked when an operation attempts to add new items to the database. |
| Delete | Delete rules force a certain set of circumstances to be met before enabling deletion of an item. |
| Update | Update rules check a set of conditions before enabling an update to take place. |

# Data Warehousing and Visual J++

Data warehousing is the key of IS. Although this is a huge topic, this book covers it in as much detail as possible. However, this is not meant to be the source of your data warehousing strategy. Our coverage of this issue is aimed at familiarizing you with the terminology and architecture, what to look for in the tools, and the issues arising from such a large undertaking. We'll also cover implementing a data warehouse in the simplest sense. We'll discuss ways to fit Visual J++ and Microsoft InterDev into the overall scheme of a data warehouse, such as a data transformer or extractor. These components manage the process of converting the information for the online, transaction-oriented databases and extracting summarized data to feed into the data warehouse. Using Visual J++ to develop front-end tools is discussed, and we'll also cover some of the components that go into the data warehousing strategy and how they relate to both Visual J++ and Microsoft InterDev. Here are a few of the concepts that this book covers at length.

## Data Sources

In choosing the data source for your data warehouse, you'll probably already have several data sources in place. This is what makes moving to a data warehouse a daunting and often unattainable goal. When you examine the multitudes of departmental and even group-level data stores, you probably will see a lot of redundancy and little thought as to how to integrate these data stores unless the company has an effective data strategy in place. Of the data gathering systems your clients will have in place, the Online Transaction Processing system is the most common.

OLTP, or OnLine Transaction Processing, has become another buzzword thrown around the past few years, and its use in applications on the Web is increasing. From its use in simple grocery cart applications that exist now, you should see the use of OLTP evolve to a more mature stage in the next year or two. Most OLTP applications are still outside the realm of the Internet, such as manufacturing or point of sale transactions (POS). Still, it is in this area that you will see the greatest growth for database applications on the Internet. You'll see the implementation of customer tracking, POS and marketing implementations using a Web browser as the client, which, when tied into the overall strategic data warehouse will give a much better tool to use for forecasting and business decisions. This will bring about the elimination of many of the buggy applications seen on the market today, and reduce the complexity of the operating systems used (i.e., no more XENIX terminals with proprietary software, just Windows 95 with a browser).

## Data Marts

The term *data mart* defines a place in which information is pulled from the data warehouse and is summarized or rearranged into a form appropriate for the data mart's purpose. You will find that as the size of a data warehouse increases, it becomes more difficult to cull the data to fit a specific report or need. Resource utilization also becomes a problem, with all processing done at the warehouse level. Transferring summarized data to a data mart can be an elegant solution to this problem. With the capability to customize the data as needed and to use any type of reporting and analyzing tools necessary, the data mart becomes a natural extension of the data warehouse.

## Extraction Tools and Transformers

Extraction tools and transformers refer to a group of tools responsible for moving the data from the data warehouse into the data marts. They are also responsible for maintaining the metadata about those data marts, such as

- What is included
- How the aggregation was performed
- Why the particular data exists
- Where the source came from

Implementing an extraction or transformer requires a thorough knowledge of both the business needs for the tools and of the underlying data. You'll see a simple extractor when you look at the search engine developed in this book. Transformers are inherently more complex than an extractor, mainly because of the complexity in designing a gateway between formats. Transformers are used in an environment such as the data warehouse to transform the data from the relational, detail-oriented databases to more multidimensionally based storage with information in a summarized form.

## The Data Warehouse

The actual data warehouse can be implemented in several ways. The most common is the traditional view of a data warehouse: All of the data from the OLTPs is summarized and assimilated into the data warehouse, which then transfers the data to data marts for further summarization. A second implementation could be to have multiple data warehouses feeding the data marts, reducing the number of replications required when feeding to a data mart. Whichever way you design it, building the data warehouse is never what you expect it to be. Basically, you can throw out traditional relational design methods, for they really don't apply to a large pool of summarized data.

▶ **See** "Introduction to Database Models" for more information on performance issues associated with particular database types, **p. 26**

**The Target Database—Relational or Multidimensional** Although relational databases have been the standard for database implementation for the last ten years, the theory has been around for about twenty-five. This has led to numerous changes or additions in the theory, such as entity-relations, semantic data models, and most recently, object-oriented relational databases. With the increasing amount of data flowing into these data stores, though, there are concerns that retrieving that data is becoming increasingly difficult.

This is where the multidimensional database comes into play. Some think of the multidimensional database management system (MDBMS) as the next generation in database technology. Solution providers who implement MDBMS claim dramatic increases in performance and the capability to organize the data quickly. The performance increases are attributed to the way the MDBMS stores its data internally. Instead of using indexes and keys as with a relational database, the data is stored in a multidimensional array. So instead of performing a row by row search with a SQL statement, the database engine already knows where to look, reducing the target set of data to query.

**The Front-End** The front-end of a data warehouse is the management-reporting tool. These tools can be developed in any language or even with something like Microsoft InterDev, which can provide access to data sources with Web scripting. These tools should be optimized so that the end user doesn't have to know SQL or any other language to use them.

# From Here...

You've had a quick glimpse into database design and development. Long books can be written about all of the topics mentioned, and indeed have been. From the development of Java comes an opportunity to exploit its rich set of features to make our jobs easier. Design techniques will help bring you closer to understanding data and how to create efficient support systems. Using both enables the focus on the Internet to be about more than power outages and slow response times.

- Chapter 2, "Database Design Concepts," provides a good background in database terminology and theory, introducting you to several design techniques and focusing on relational database theory.

- Chapter 3, "Creating a Simple Database Application," contrasts the development of a simple registry access database with a much more advanced sample to give you an idea of the range of database applications.
- Chapter 5, "ODBC," gives you a close look at the technology that is responsible for RDO and DAO, giving you a solid understanding of how those two object models were implemented.
- Chapter 6, "Data Access Objects," covers the version 3.5 of the DAO API from Microsoft, including the new ODBCDirect interfaces that enable DAO programming without the Jet Engine.
- Chapter 10, "Database Development with Microsoft Visual InterDev," takes a tour of the new database development environment by Microsoft and explains the many new tools and API's found in Microsoft InterDev.
- Chapter 16, "Implementing Data Warehousing with Visual J++," explains the concepts behind data warehousing and details some of the implementation issues.

CHAPTER 2

# Database Design Concepts

**Introduction to databases**

You will look at four main forms of databases: flat file, relational, object-oriented, and multidimensional.

**Data analysis**

Sifting through the flood of data for real information can be an awesome task; learn some methods to decrease the difficulty of data analysis.

**Normalization**

After you have decided what to include as data, you learn to create a structure that makes maintaining and upsizing the database easier.

**The physical design**

Learn how to deal with the gritty implementation issues of database design, like performance and referential integrity.

**Implementation**

You will take an idea, a Web search engine, and follow the steps to create a database that suits your needs.

Database design has been a difficult subject for most developers to grasp. Database design doesn't really fit anywhere in the "How many lines have you done today?" mentality, and when you are involved in a large project, the analysis stage seems to drag on forever. Good design is essential, however, to ensure that you don't end up with an incredible mess. Understanding the design process helps you find your bearings in what can become an overwhelming task. Designing a large data warehouse or data mart, as well as the tools that go along with them, is a task for an entire team. You might be leading that team, however, and knowing how the overall design phase works is crucial. Many companies are implementing a data strategy for the first time or have very inefficient designs in place, and you will have to design the database to build the reporting and collection tools that make databases effective. The worst thing that you can do when designing a database is to build it without looking at how the data flows through the organization and how it will be used. So, take a look at the world of database design, and see what you've been missing. ■

# Introduction to Database Models

First, familiarize yourself with some of the most popular types of databases:

- Flat-file
- Relational
- Object-oriented
- Multidimensional

You should be comfortable with the first two models, flat-file and relational, as they have been in circulation for over 25 years. Of these four models, the two that you will use most often are probably the relational and the multidimensional.

## Flat-File Model

The flat-file model has been around for many years. It was a natural extension of the file cabinets people were used to. A very simple model, all of the data is stored in a single table. The flat-file database is falling out of use, however, except by COBOL programmers, and unfortunately, on the Internet—because it doesn't scale well, performance degrades harshly when many records are placed into a flat format. Often, changing a single piece of data requires changing several hundred or thousand records. So, unless you want to support a single database for a while, don't use this model for anything but test purposes.

## Relational Model

We have E.F. Codd to thank for relational database models. His theory on relational databases has been the foundation for nearly every model since. You will probably choose to use a relational database model if you want to use Visual J++ or Microsoft InterDev, at least until more object-oriented or other types of database vendors begin supporting Open Database Connectivity standards or Data Access Objects. This is not a disadvantage, however, because most current database technology is relational and has been optimized to a point that performance under most loads is well within the acceptable range.

If you look at a single relational table, you probably will wonder how it differs from a flat-file model. What makes a relational database relational? Well, relations do. In truth, while relating individual pieces of data is the hallmark of the relational database, there are other benefits to using this model. It is simplest to think of a relational model as a series of links between unique objects. These objects can have any number of attributes. In Figure 2.1, for example, the Page database is linked to the Site database with the `SiteID` attribute.

**FIG. 2.1**
This is a visual look at relationships in a database.

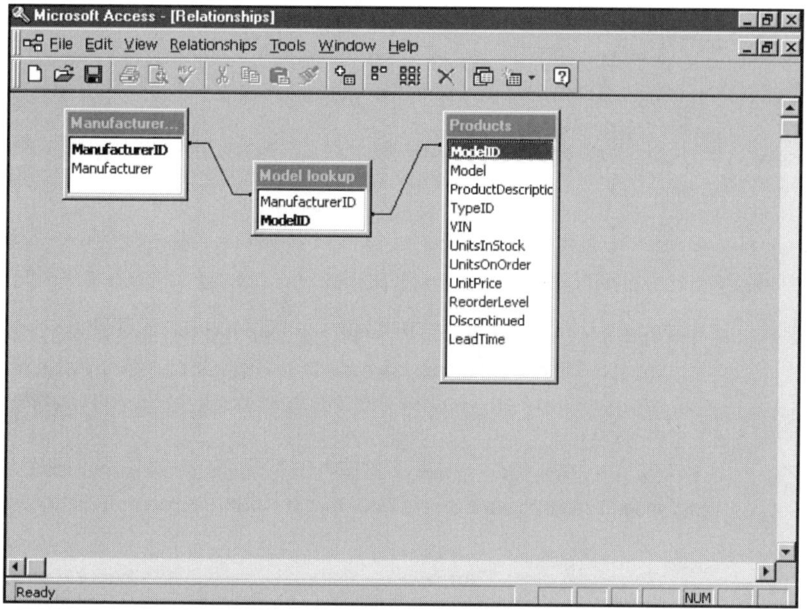


As you can see in Figure 2.1, a relational database is a simple concept. To be complete, a list of Codd's relational rules follows. Although only Rule 1 directly pertains to the actual relational model, the rest benefit the end user of a system that is based on the relational model.

- *Rule 0* Any system that is advertised as, or claims to be, a relational database management system must be able to manage databases entirely through its relational capabilities.
- *Rule 1: Information Representation* All information in a relational database is represented explicitly at the logical level and in exactly one way—by values in tables.
- *Rule 2: Guaranteed Access* Each datum (atomic value) in a relational database is guaranteed to be logically accessible by using a combination of table name, primary key, and column name.
- *Rule 3: Systematic Treatment of Null Values* Null values (distinct from the empty character string or a string of blank characters and distinct from zero or any other number) are supported for representing missing information and inapplicable information in a systematic way, independent of data type.
- *Rule 4: Dynamic Online Catalog, Based on Relational Model* The database schema (description of a database's internal structures) must be stored in the same manner as "normal" data to allow each one access through the same relational query language.

- *Rule 5: Comprehensive Data Sublanguage* At least one of the data manipulation languages supported by a relational database must enable the following operations:

  Data definitions

  View definitions

  Data manipulation (interactive and by program)

  Integrity constraints

  Authorization

  Transaction boundaries (begin, commit, rollback)

- *Rule 6: View Updating* When an update (insert, delete, or update) takes place in the view and is clearly derived from the base tables of the view (not a calculated column), the database must also enable the update to effect the same change in the base tables of the view.
- *Rule 7: High-Level Insert, Update, and Delete* The capability for handling updates, inserts, and deletes as set operations (multiple relations and/or views) must be supported.
- *Rule 8: Physical Data Independence* Changes to the access methods or the storage methods of a database are transparent to the operations performed against the data.
- *Rule 9: Logical Data Independence* Any change to the database that does not involve a loss of data will not affect the operations being performed on the database at that time.
- *Rule 10: Integrity Independence* Integrity constraints specific to a particular relational database must be definable in the relational data sublanguage and storable in the catalog, not in the application program.
- *Rule 11: Distribution Independence* The level and type of distribution will be transparent to the data manipulation languages supported by this database engine.
- *Rule 12: Nonsubversion* All languages supported by a relational database must base all operations solely on the schema; no operations can be allowed to bypass these definitions and constraints.

## Object-Oriented Model

The object-oriented model developed from our fascination with objects in the past decade. The concept of an object-oriented database is very much the same as the one Java embraces: Conceptualize the object and find those properties that belong solely to that object and nothing else; if you find properties that can belong to something else, then they must belong to a parent. This is similar to having several filters, one on top of another; what doesn't filter out on one level drops to the next. As you probably know, there is an added complexity in the object-oriented model, for the child objects inherit the data contained in the parent objects.

## Multidimensional Model

This is a relatively new database model that was developed from mathematical array theories. Although most databases are based on arrays, the multidimensional database is actually structured to mimic an array. The multidimensional model is better suited to an environment in which massive amounts of summarized data are stored. Multidimensional views are made much easier when the database engine supports the concept of dimensions directly, unlike databases based on relational models. Query times also can be reduced dramatically in the multidimensional model due to its array-like structure. Because a normal database iterates through each record during a query, the overhead becomes substantially higher when moving a cursor of large amounts of records.

A method that vendors of relational databases have used to minimize the query times is indices into the data. Usually called indexes, these structures are simply pointer offsets into the database for certain data items. The MDBMS stores the data in a format that is already conducive to queries because the engine knows the general location of the data you are looking for. Because it is actually stored in an array structure, the Multidimensional Database Management System (MDBMS) doesn't have to iterate through each row. Instead, it selectively chooses the columns of the array it needs, sometimes cutting search times exponentially. The need for keys has been removed as well, because the primary purpose of the key is to provide an easy means of looking up the data desired.

Most of the functions that you would expect to perform by hand, such as creating the schema, are performed automatically by the MDBMS engine. Databases that are based on this model generally perform much faster calculations than SQL-based alternatives simply because the proprietary nature of the MDBMS enables the vendor to build in the analytic capabilities that need a second or third tier when using SQL-based databases.

When deciding whether or not to use this type of database, you must understand the business needs of the system you are building. A multidimensional database system is designed for advanced calculations and queries against summarized data that will not be in normalized form, most likely in OLAP applications or data warehouse environments. These databases do not usually have the industrial strength multiuser capabilities of SQL databases, and would not be a good choice for use in a heavily transacted environment or one requiring detail at the atomic level.

# Data Analysis

The field of data analysis has grown a great deal, especially since people discovered that they could pay someone else to do this job for them. Data analysis is really just the task of sifting the information until it is useful data and then transforming the data into a manageable form. Normalization helps, of course, but it isn't absolutely necessary.

## Some Ideas and Definitions

Next, we'll review some of the terms that you'll see if you take on a design project, and then we'll explore the process you might take to complete it.

We've included some explanations on some of the concepts touched on lightly in this book, which you might run into in the field.

**Views** Think of a view as a query. If you send a query to determine how many servers have the same monitor, the result is a view. A view can span multiple databases, or just one database. Think of a view as a logical entity, not a physical one.

**Relations** Relations can be taken to have two different (and somewhat related) meanings. Taken in the sense of the relational model, every row in a table is called a relation. This is due to the fact that only data that is related to one another is some manner can be said to exist in the same relation after normalization (discussed later in this chapter). The other definition, also used in the context of relational theory, is the link between a column from one table and a column from another. These types of relations are constraints placed upon the two tables between these two columns (referred two as `REFERENCES` in Structured Query Language).

**Data Models** Data models are simply a logical way to view the data. Usually you will use them to set up the data flows or to flesh out the relations between the objects.

**Relational Algebra** Relational algebra was an outgrowth of Codd's work on relational databases. He needed something that could be inserted into a program to execute relational statements. You're probably familiar with some of the relational algebraic concepts, such as the SQL language.

## The Lost Art of Data Modeling

Lost Art? Indeed, there are thousands of people who design databases without touching a data model. You can call it the wizard approach to database design or one-button wonders. There is a definite shift in database vendors toward taking the pain out of data design. This is good, but it doesn't help much when you are working on large projects due to the fact that most wizards oversimplify the design and do not enable you to tailor the design to the situation (unless, of course, you push the button and then redesign the pieces specific to this situation).

**Entity Relationship Model** An entity relationship (E-R) diagram is a sketch showing how your data is used. Do you have several of those to only one of these? How is this data related? These are the types of questions that an E-R diagram answers. E-R models, as the diagrams have come to be called, offer a significant advantage by enabling you to visually define relationships among the data. For example, take a look at the simple E-R diagram in Figure 2.2.

Notice that there are several types of relations. These relations do not flow in only one direction, as you might be used to seeing in normal flowcharts. They can and do go both ways. Let's look into the types of relations that you can have.

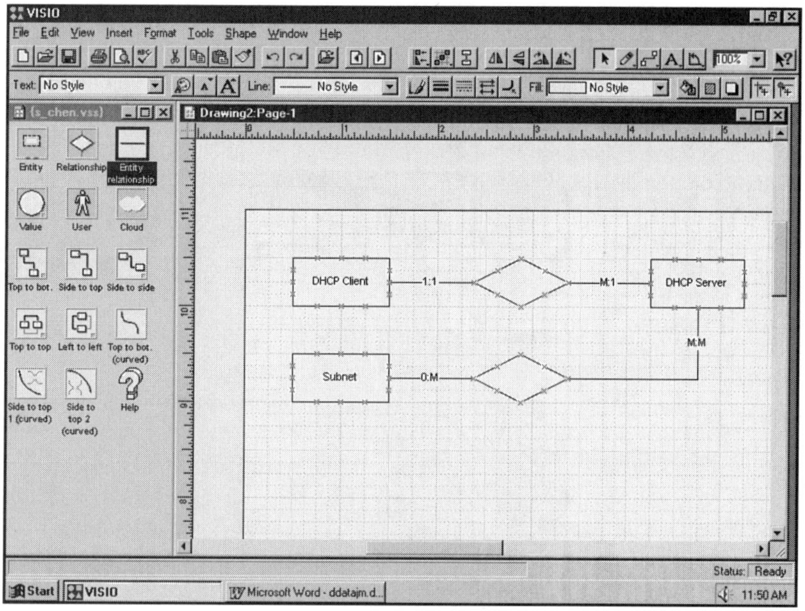


**FIG. 2.2**
This displays an E-R model used to diagram the relations of a DHCP server on a network.

***1:1 (One-to-One)*** This simply means that the relationship is one-to-one. For example, examine the relationship of the server to its IP address in Figure 2.3. Basically, having a one-to-one relationship means that there can be only one IP address for each server. We'll assume that your client isn't layering IP addresses or is using more than one NIC.

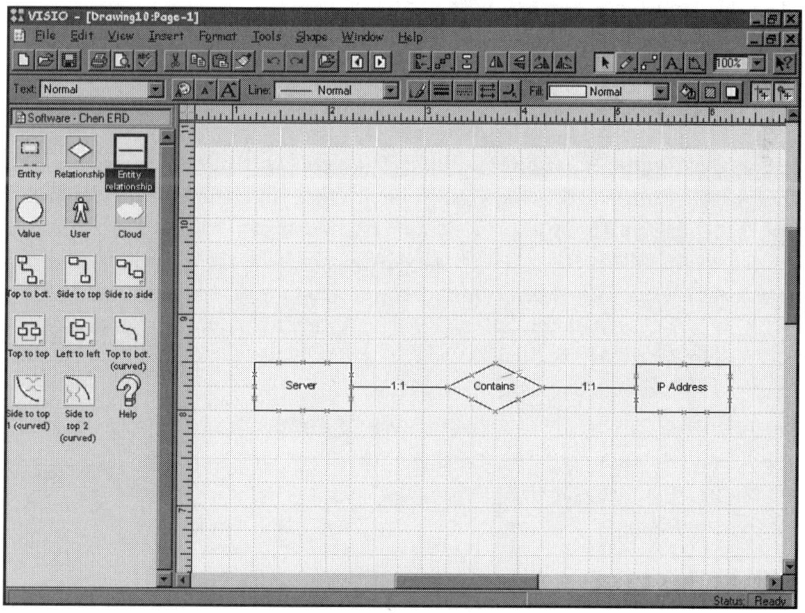


**FIG. 2.3**
A 1:1 relationship between Server and IP Address ensures that for each Server there is one and only one IP Address.

***1:M (One-to-Many)*** This is, perhaps, the most common type of relation. For example, in Figure 2.4, there is one Web site with many pages; however, the reverse is not true: An HTML page has one and only one Web site. This is an example of a one-to-many relationship of Web sites to HTML pages.

**FIG. 2.4**
A 1:M relationship shows that for each Web site multiple HTML pages are allowed; however, there can be only one Web site for each HTML page.

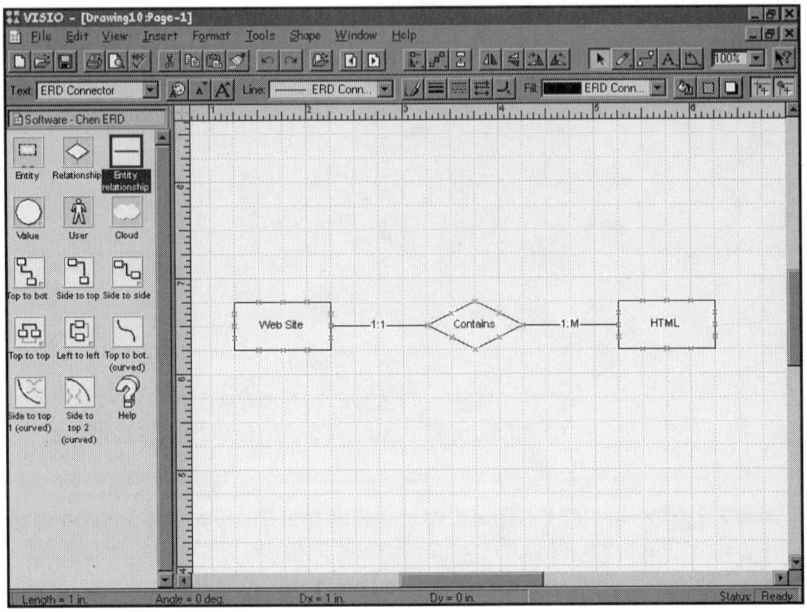


***M:M (Many-to-Many)*** An example of a many-to-many relationship is the one from the ActiveX objects to an HTML page shown in Figure 2.5. In this instance, it is possible for an HTML page to have many ActiveX objects, and conversely, for an ActiveX object to exist on many HTML pages.

**Conditional Relations** Although the concepts just discussed are helpful in modeling the data, it isn't realistic to always have one or more relations for every object in your data model. What if there aren't any users viewing a particular page? What about the ActiveX to HTML page relation? This can go either way—you can have HTML pages without an ActiveX object and visa versa. This type of ambiguous situation is where the idea of conditional relationships arose. Conditional relationships add functionality to your model by enabling you to state that there is a 1:M relationship or a 1:1 relationship or no relationship at all. This is modeled on a diagram as 0:M, as shown in Figure 2.6.

**FIG. 2.5**
A M:M relationship shows that several ActiveX objects can be placed on a single HTML page, and that one ActiveX object can appear in several HTML pages.

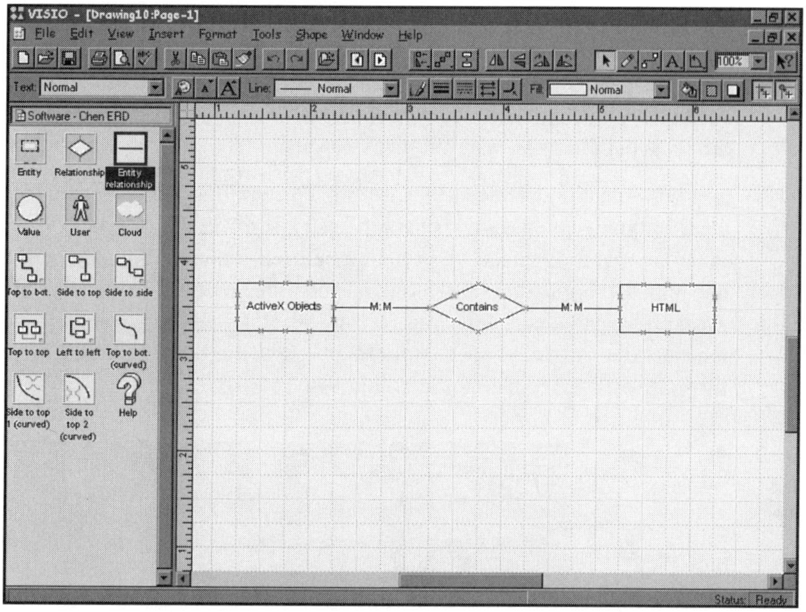


**FIG. 2.6**
Conditional Relationships can show more than a single relational state, and thus, enhance the value of the data model.

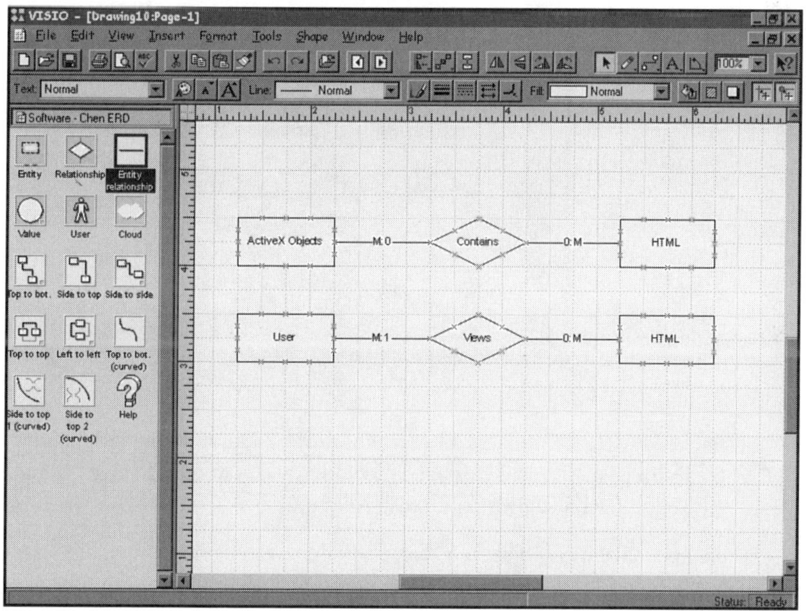

**Relational** The concept of the relational model is similar to that of the entity relationship model, as most of the terminology and processes are similar. Whereas most other data models discuss relations in abstract terms, however, the relational model refers to the actual tables as relations. This might help some people conceptually, which is probably why the relational model is popular with programmers.

The relational model uses the concepts of the primary key and the candidate key, and includes another type—*the cross-reference key* (also known as the *foreign* key). This key is found in more than one relation. Similar to a relation in the E-R model, this key relates the individual tables to one another. Figure 2.7 illustrates the relational model. It is very similar to the E-R model, and it has been stated that it is simply a different take on the E-R model; however, the creators of the relational model argue that there are significant differences. The differences lie mainly in the mathematical implementation of these models.

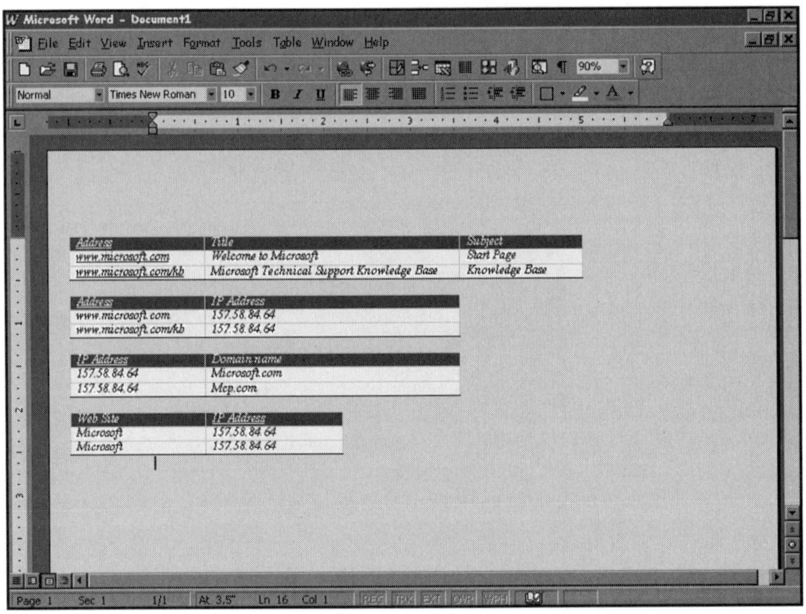


**FIG. 2.7**
This is the relational model.

In Figure 2.7, the primary keys are underlined, and the foreign keys are *italicized* to distinguish these columns. The reason for doing so is to enable an explanation of why these were chosen and what they mean to the relation.

The primary keys in each of these relations were chosen because the data in each of the relations depends fully on that column, and the column is unique. There can be no other primary keys with the same value.

The cross-reference keys were chosen according to the primary key of the referencing table. For example, we needed a way to attach HTML pages to their respective Web sites, so we placed a constraint on the `HTML.SiteID` and the `Web Sites.SiteID` so that one and only one `Web Site.SiteID` exists for each `HTML.SiteID`.

Last, each and every one of these columns was at one point a candidate key (which is not always the case). The primary and cross-reference keys were drawn from the pool of candidate keys according to the strategic value of each.



**Semantic Model** The Semantic model is an object-oriented data model designed to deal with the ever-increasing amount of information and to encapsulate it within the database itself. When glanced at, this model looks similar to the relational model because both are programmatic rather than visual. The Semantic data model holds definitions for a wide range of attributes and class definitions. It also tries to store descriptions and state information and other metadata with the database definition itself. Because this is not a model that is used often with relational databases, the implementation of it is not included here.

**Object-Oriented Model** As you probably know, the object-oriented model is also based on the object model, in which each object carries with it the information that it needs to exist. This information is passed on to every child of the object, plus a unique set of information relating to that child object, ad infinitum. The main difference between the semantic and the object-oriented data models is that the object-oriented model is a visual model. This makes the object-oriented model somewhat easier to comprehend because you can "see" what the data looks like.

# Normalization

Normalization is a process that prevents errors from cropping up in your data model after implementing the physical database schema. These errors can range from simple integrity concerns such as removing a salesman when the model he sold is discontinued, or more complex scalability problems as we increase the load on the database. Normalization is based on analyzing the dependencies, or relationships, between attributes. We're going to take a quick look into this process, and in Chapter 17, "Building a Web Crawler with DAO," you will actually use the data design developed in this chapter to base a Web Crawler. We begin by analyzing what a dependency is and how it relates to the data that we have.

▶ **See** "Examining a Sample Database Application" to develop some sample applications by using what you've learned here, **p. 54**

## Dependencies

Dependencies are simple relationships between different pieces of data. That said, there are several types of dependencies that you analyze when determining your keys for the database. The first kind of dependency that you encounter is the *functional dependency*. A functional dependency describes a relation in which A determines B. Usually this will be a M:1 relationship in which there are several As to one B, but not the reverse (see Figure 2.8).

**FIG. 2.8**
This is a functional dependency diagram.

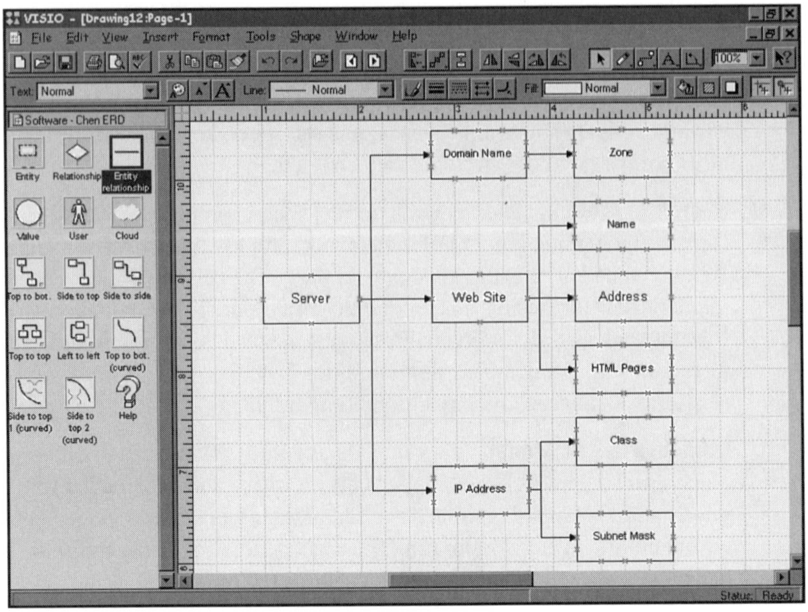


The data listed on the left side in Figure 3.8 is called *determinants*—those values that determine what the right side will be.

There are three other types of dependencies: ***transitive***, ***multivalued***, and ***join***.

- The transitive dependency describes a condition in which one non-key is dependent on another non-key in a relation.
- The multivalued dependency is a situation in which two or more keys are dependent upon one key; however, the dependent keys have nothing to do with each other. An example of this would be where the address is the key, and you have both Server and Web site within the same relation.
- The join dependency occurs when you attempt to break a relation into two smaller ones and create a situation in which they cannot be rejoined to create the original.

By analyzing these dependencies, you can determine what bits of data would make good primary and candidate keys. For an attribute to become a primary key, it must uniquely identify all the other attributes in the relation, and the attribute must be functionally dependent on the primary key. A candidate key is also a determinant for items, is unique, and defines a set of values for the relation. In fact, the primary key is a candidate key. There can be several candidate keys in a relation, such as a relation that contains a machine's attributes. It contains a hostname, network address, and serial number; each of these are unique and can define the machine. So, we call them candidate keys.

# First Normal Form (1NF)

Placing the data into first normal form simply gets the obvious out of the way. Doing so requires that you place the data into separate rows. In the case of re-engineering an existing relational database, this will be a step that does not need to be done. However, for most businesses, the trusty file cabinet is the database of choice. Transforming this paper data into logical columns and rows of information can be tedious, but it is obviously a step that you take (see Figure 2.9).



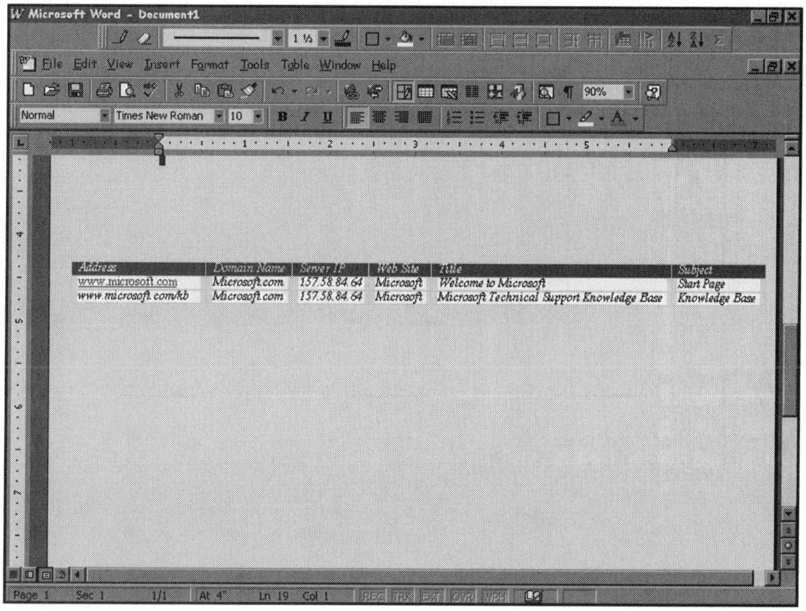


**FIG. 2.9**
Placing the data into 1NF means sifting through the existing information for groups of related information.

# Second Normal Form (2NF)

To transform your data into 2NF (see Figure 3.10), you need to remove all partial dependencies on the keys for the relation. This means that any data held in a single relation must depend fully on the primary key; if it does not, then move the data into a separate table.

# Third Normal Form (3NF)

When transforming the data into 3NF, look for any anomalies that might be present in the data, such as having to update more than one row when changing a value. A database is said to be in 3NF if no transitive dependencies exist (illustrated in Figure 3.11). This refers to an item that is not a key depending on the values of one or more items that are also not keys.

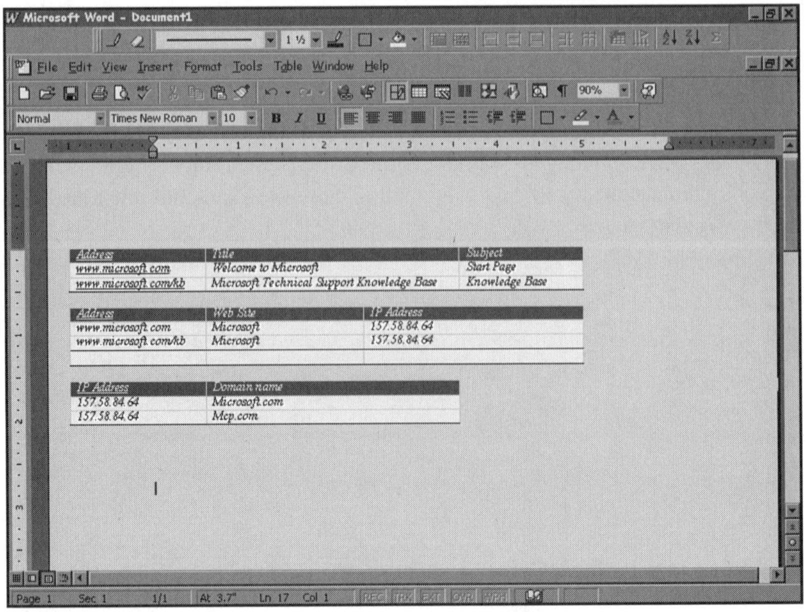


**FIG. 2.10**
Placing data into 2NF entails removing the repeating groups into separate tables and filling in any sparse columns.

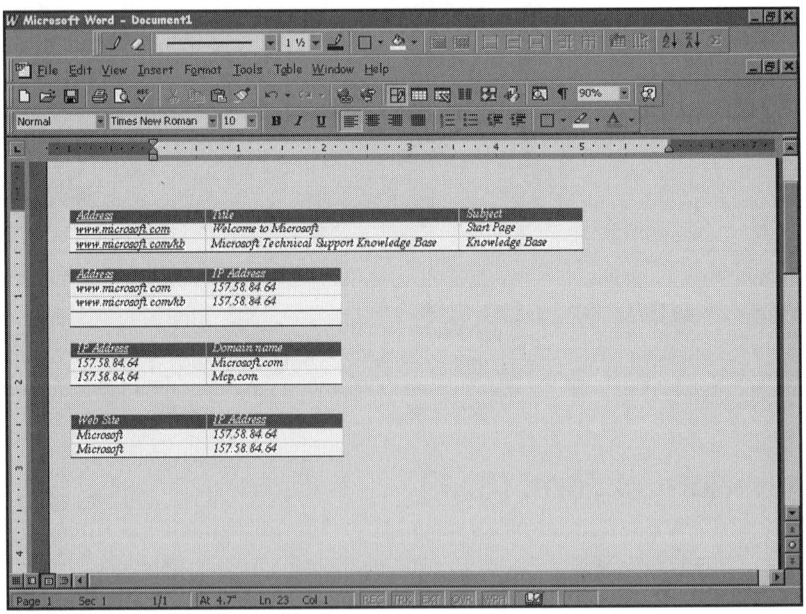


**FIG. 2.11**
Moving to 3NF removes all transitive dependencies.

## Boyce-Codd Normal Form (BCF)

Boyce-Codd normal form was devised to deal with the problems resulting from having more than one candidate key in a relation. The explicit meaning of Boyce-Codd normal form is to remove any remaining anomalies that result from functional dependencies. When you place a relation into BCF, however, make sure that every item that is a determinant is also a candidate key. In our situation, we are already in BCNF simply because the model is not that complex.



## Fourth Normal Form

In transforming a relation into 4NF (see Figure 2.12), you take all of the multivalued dependencies out of the relation. Multivalued dependencies can introduce unexpected results occurring from updates made to the database.

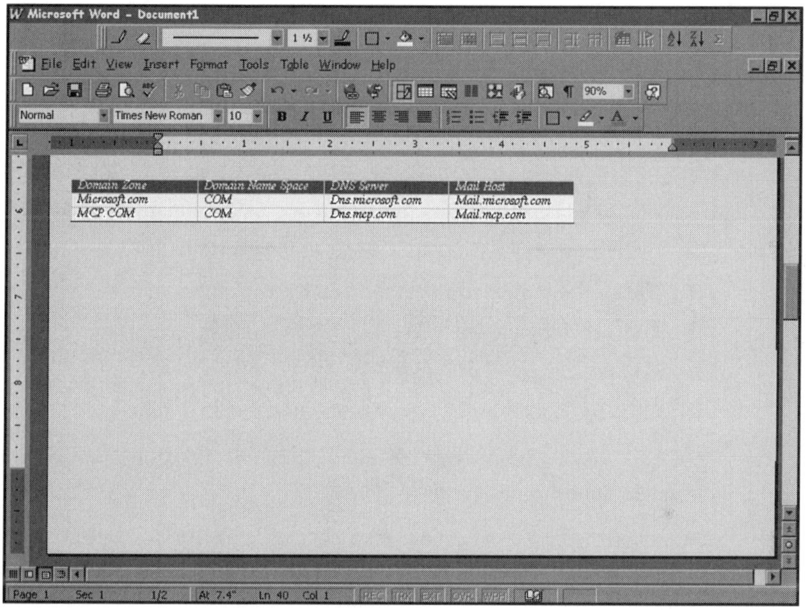


**FIG. 2.12**
This showcases a multivalued dependency in action.

Although all of these attributes are arguably dependent on the domain zone, notice that none are actually dependent on one other. This situation creates update anomalies in which you would have to change a value several times if you wanted to update any part of the relation. This is true even though it is in BCNF.

## Fifth Normal Form

Placing the data into fifth normal form means removing any *join dependencies*. Join dependencies are created when data that is separated into two tables can no longer be joined to create the original relation. These instances are so rare and hard to discover that many in our industry refer to people who transform data into fifth normal form as "obsessed."

# The Physical Design

Now you must attend to the physical design of the database. After you normalize the relations, you can begin the process of placing these relations in a physical structure. During this phase, you also must consider several factors that can make or break your implementation. These factors are as follows:

- Metadata
- Optimization of your data for queries
- Query optimization for slowly changing data
- Security
- Scalability

## Metadata

Metadata is knowledge about the data rather than the data itself. Having designed in metadata gives you control and a means to sort through the information that you gather. You need information about:

- Where the information came from (as in a summarized database)
- How the data was filtered
- How the data was organized
- Which relations and keys were defined in the database

This helps a data administrator visualize the logical structure of the data environment, making changes or future planning much easier.

There are three different cases in which we'll make good use of the metadata we collect, and each can demand different requirements. In the first case, a single database environment, you should include:

- Information about the schema
- Logical relations
- Relevant administrative information

The second type of environment is the enterprise view, a collection of several different data stores that are tightly integrated, such as a data warehouse (although a data warehouse has properties of a data flow environment, as well). In addition to the information required in the single database environment, the enterprise view needs:

- Definitions of the data boundaries
- Values that were aggregated
- Fields that were aggregated
- Filters applied to the data
- Logical views that were constructed



The third type is a situation in which you attempt to combine several loosely organized environments (often referred to as a heterogenous system), such as a merger. In this case, metadata can be used to gain a full understanding so that reverse engineering of the existing system can be done and a new one can be created. This case requires information concerning:

- The means used to extract and transform the data
- The types of referential integrity employed
- The constraints placed on the data

This metadata is also crucial for a series of heterogeneous views from a group of interrelated databases.

In every case, you want to store information about the objects and the data itself. A well-thought-out plan for metadata can save you a great deal of trouble later on when someone wants to change what you built.

## Optimizing Your Database for Queries

Performance comes into play when you decide which database type and which engine of that type to use. Take a look at how your data will be accessed, track a user's path through the data, and then design the database schema so that information can be accessed quickly and efficiently. Employing different methods of physical structures can have a dramatic effect on performance. If some of the tables in your database have few records or fields, try running them without indexing—most database engines can snap up a thousand rows in a single access. There's no need for an index in this case, for it just creates more overhead.

In some applications, you might want to create your own database to store data that is specific to a single use. This is the case with object persistence in Java. When there isn't an easy way to store structures, you have to create one. In this case, think about the access method before designing it. For instance, binary trees are an obvious choice for large tables, but what about smaller ones? A generically indexed, sequential type of table would actually be faster if the tables remain small, as they probably would for custom-built databases. These tables can be built in memory when you initialize the database, although you can certainly store the b-tree or indexes in the header of the database, making the database initialization easier to deal with than building these when you load the file into memory.

While you optimize the tables, take a look at the data flow. It is fairly simple, by observing the data flow, to make sure that you're not creating more work during optimization. You can decide which data to keep in front-end databases by observing the data flows, as well. If data isn't used frequently—archive it. This speeds up access and queries if the database views don't become too large for an individual user. Try to do this with as many user views as possible. Making the data easy to use is one of the most important aspects of database design (aside from preventing anomalies from creeping into your design). If this is a system database, check the load on the network and test replication scenarios during peak traffic on the network. See if something breaks. Several vendors supply testing tools to simulate load on a server that you can use. It's no fun to lock up your network because bandwidth is saturated. In the next section, you'll find some types of optimizations that you can apply depending on how the data is used and how often the data is updated.

**Query Optimization for Slowly Changing Data** If you can determine that the data does not change often and that the updates can be controlled, you might "denormalize" the database structure for query optimizations. A schema that is gaining popularity for query optimizations is the *star schema*. A star schema attempts to optimize the database for queries by placing a summary of all facts in one location and spreading out dimensions of summary tables from the fact table. This schema is used in environments such as data warehouses, in which the data is held static and the changes come from a few sources. Using a schema such as the star with online transaction processing (OLTP) isn't recommended for the same reasons for using normalization on OLTP databases and not in a data warehouse—the optimizations would yield poor performance.

▶ **See** "De-Normalizing the Data" for more infromation about the star schema, **p. 463**

**Optimizing for Data Throughput** Although the star schema does an admirable job of structuring a database for queries, optimizing for data input is quite different. In this case, use the 3NF or higher normal forms to generate a relational schema optimized for incoming transactions. Implement the physical structure with a relational database due to the good multiuser capabilities and the proven data handling capacity of these types of databases.

## Security

Security is a factor in the physical implementation, as well. At the least, most databases provide user security, and most provide for group security as well; this is in addition to the operating system you place the database on. Most of the security issues you'll deal with in database design are needed to ensure that unauthorized people can't access sensitive reports.

Security can be dealt with in several ways with Visual J++. Data Access Objects and ODBC both enable user and group access to the database. If you set this up correctly, there will be a decent means of ensuring that security is in place. Another alternative is to develop a link to the network security built into the operating system and allow security permissions to be placed on specific objects in the database, as well.

## Scalability

Scalability refers to the capability of a database to sustain its original performance and to grow without introducing errors, while remaining easy to maintain. You will find that if your data model is good, you structured the database correctly, and you've got a good set of metadata, then scalability becomes a product feature. At that point, you can compare how well one product scales with the next over thousands, millions, billions, and soon, trillions of transactions. Most vendors would love to show you how fast and reliably they can work.

# Implementation



Now that you're familiar with the components of data analysis, it's time to implement it. In this book, we need a database to work with, which, we hope, will culminate in something useful. For our purposes, Company X needs a Java-based search engine. This search engine is going to act much like the ones you see on the Web, eating up terabytes of HTML pages in search of links. You might also find it beneficial to store the text and pictures, maybe even the ActiveX controls. Before writing any code, however, you must determine the needs of the engine and what it will be designed to do. Then you can chart a data flow through this beast, and get on the road to greatness.

## What a Search Engine Does

A search engine searches, right? Actually, it does much more than just search. Let's try parsing HTML documents and categorizing their contents, following any links found in those documents, and repeating the process. At the same time, there is another side to a search engine—the user interface. Making the engine technically interesting is only half of the battle; the user interface is the other. What are you going to provide visitors to your Web site that they can't find elsewhere? You can enable users to query anything that might be in the database, giving them options for searching for different kinds of objects, such as documents, pictures, ActiveX objects, and VB and Java script. Has that been done? Then pull the data locally instead of storing links to the servers where the data resides and present your new search engine as an Object-Oriented Directory Service for the Internet. Sure, X.500 might be out of your reach right now, but if you provide users with data so that they never have to leave your Web site to retrieve something, then you will accomplish the same thing.

### X.500

For those of you who are unfamiliar with the *X.500*, this term is used widely to refer to any system that treats every item in the system as an object and has a single access point for any object existing inside the *X.500* directory. This standard is the basis for the emerging (yet less functional) Lightweight Directory Access (LDA) standards, which can be found via the Internic as RFC1782. X.500 is an International Telegraph and Telephone Consultative Committee (better known as CCITT) standard and publicly available from **http://sunsite.doc.ic.ac.uk/computing/ccitt/ccitt-standards/1992/X/**.

## Data Definition for the Search Engine Database

You've identified several types of data that need to be collected and the entities dealing with those pieces of data. Table 2.1 lists all of the individual pieces of data that you'll be dealing with and what you should do with them.

**Table 2.1 Entities in the Search Engine Example**

| Entity | Use |
|---|---|
| HTML Page | The HTML page is parsed for links and the database stores the contents. |
| HTML Tags | The search engine looks at tags to determine what action to take. |
| Objects | The `<OBJECT> </OBJECT>` tag pair will be used to denote the beginning and end of an object, which will be stored in the database. |
| Pictures | The various `<IMG>` tags will be parsed for several reasons, including the actual pictures and to break down image maps. |
| JScript & VBScript | Store scripts as possible repositories for a code wizard or application generator. |
| Documents | Links can be parsed to determine if the link is referring to a known document type. If so, the document can be downloaded and stored in the database as an OLE object. |
| Code Listings | Code listings can serve as part of a repository, as well. |
| Users | You might want to store the user settings and search patterns for their convenience and useful statistics (marketing). |
| Servers | Use these as a possible way to categorize the data. |

It might seem ridiculous to try for so much, but at least it will be fun. So, let's start with just keeping the Server, User, and Link information. We won't actually add the document storage until we've covered more ground. We've introduced several entities in this scenario; however, the data flow of this model will be fairly easy. Our data flow model for this project will have four flows:

- Parsing and categorizing the data
- The flow of the data being collected
- Processing the user request
- Sending back the results

These data flows are represented visually in Figure 2.13.

Notice how this process breaks your task into smaller pieces. By charting the data flow, you are prepared to place the data into the data model. You can choose any model that suits you, but we find the object-oriented model easier to conceptualize and view the entire set of relations.

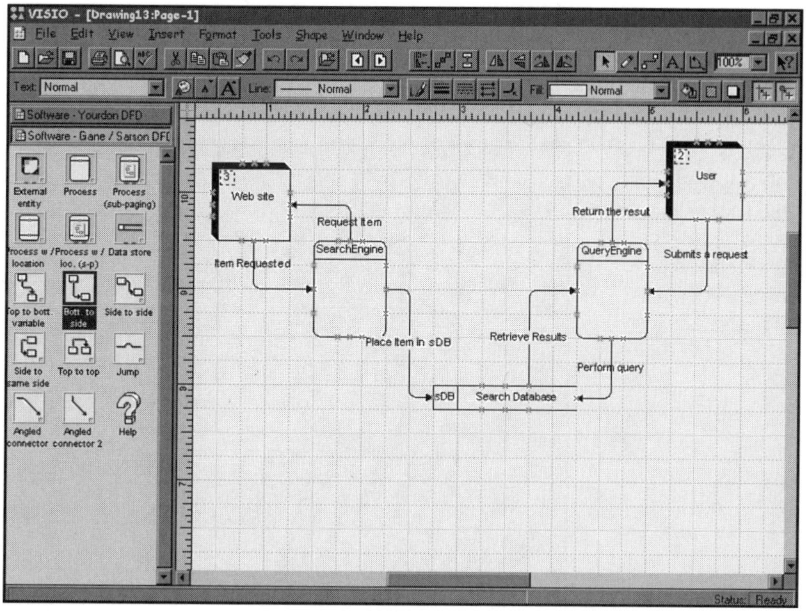


**FIG. 2.13**
This displays the three data flows shown for the search engine.

## The Data Model

E-R diagrams are, for the most part, pretty clumsy to develop. You spend a lot of time drawing and very little time actually defining the relations among the objects. They are visual, however, which contributes to their popularity. Beginning with the data flow diagrams in Figure 2.13, there exists several entities to place into our model: the server, the user, the HTML page, HTML tags, and objects (in other words, whatever lies behind the links—pictures, scripts, and so on). Creating the object-oriented design requires:

- Defining the objects' attributes and data
- Determining what makes them unique
- Placing the attributes and data into a model

Consider the server object, for example—what are the defining characteristics of the server? the IP Address? the host name? The process of determining which attributes to apply to the server object but not to the child objects is the same process that will be done on each of the children, as well. As a general rule, with object-oriented methodologies, you should take each attribute and ask yourself whether that attribute is unique to a particular object or whether it can be used for several objects. If the attribute can be used in several instances, then it should be placed in a parent object. After you've decided which object attributes to place with each individual object, you can begin the process of placing the attributes in relations and normalizing those relations. Finding the relations in the object-oriented model simply requires remembering which attributes were left at the parent level because they were shared by several objects. An example of a simple object-oriented model is shown in Figure 2.14.

**FIG. 2.14**
The OO diagram for the MOOSE displays the attributes for only the first three objects (a complete diagram has a depth of several more levels).

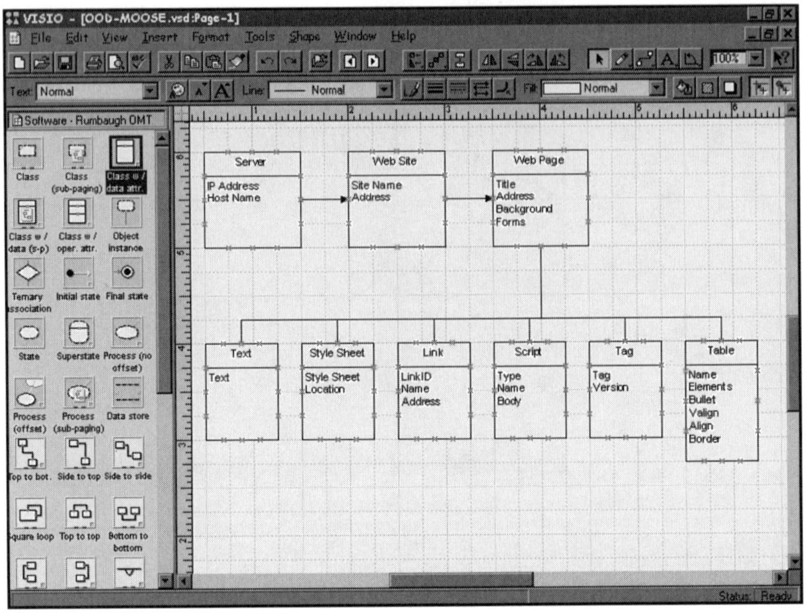


Now that the diagram is done, you can start the transformation of this model to the functional dependencies and begin normalizing the relations. There probably will be several databases here, some organized rather differently to speed up query times. Those issues will be covered in the section on physical design in this chapter.

▶ **See** "Understanding the Concept of Data Warehousing" for more information about building a data warehouse, **p. 450**

## Normalizing the MOOSE Data Model

After the transformation of the data model to a relational table format is complete, you can begin the long road to normalization. In Figure 2.15, take a look at a loosely constructed table, which is, essentially, 0NF. These are your building blocks.

We will eventually be placing this data into fourth normal form. The fourth normal form was chosen as our target in an effort to minimize the amount of work required during design because the point of diminishing returns is reached with respect to the real benefits of further normalization for this particular application.

There are many problems with the relations at this point. Start resolving these problems by moving to first normal form, removing the repeating groups, and making sure there is a value for each cell in the row.

**FIG. 2.15**
This is the HTML relation in non-normalized form.

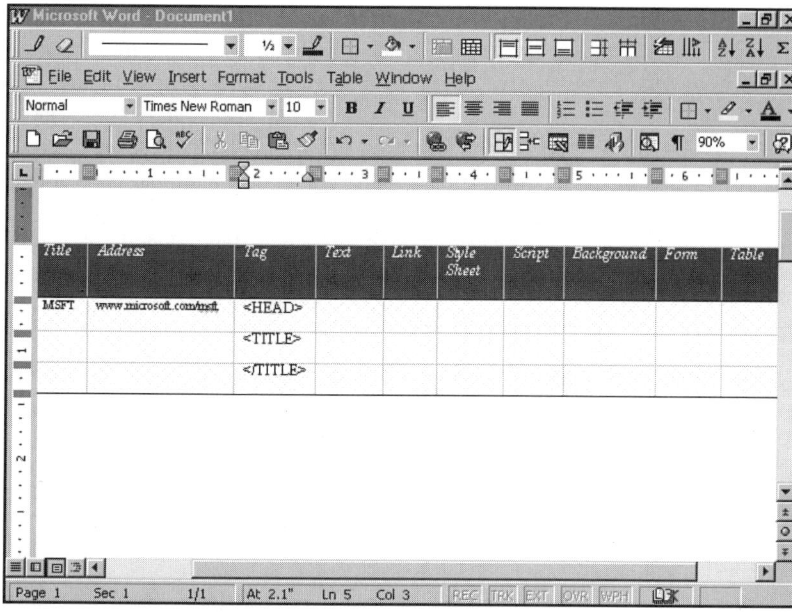


To bring the data into compliance with 1NF, as shown in Figure 2.16, we have filled out the columns of the table so that each cell has a value. This guarantees no "holes" in the relational tables.

**FIG. 2.16**
Place the MOOSE data design into 1NF.

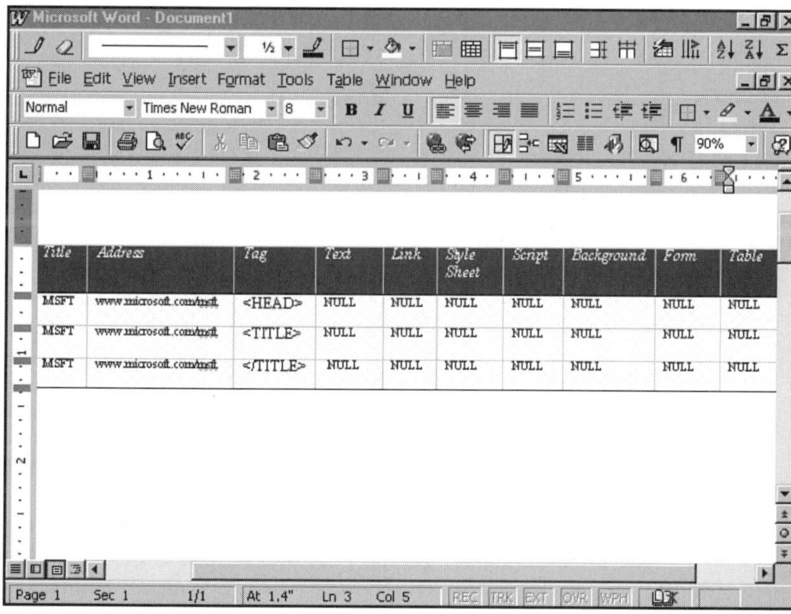

The model is starting to look more like a database now, with rows and columns instead of loosely organized data. There are several problems still unresolved, however. What if you want to update the location of a server? With the current data structure, the update would have to be done for each row containing the location in the database. That's bad, but what if a row is deleted? The Web crawler checks the page again and a picture is gone. You could lose any one of several things, including the server itself! Update anomalies are still in the database, as well as the sparse data in each row. To eliminate these problems, the relation must be broken into several distinct tables, getting rid of the partial dependencies in the process. The results of placing the data into 2NF are illustrated in Figure 2.17. You might also want to generate unique IDs to use as primary keys to conserve space and eliminate the need to update multiple tables.

**FIG. 2.17**
This is the HTML relation as it looks in 2NF.

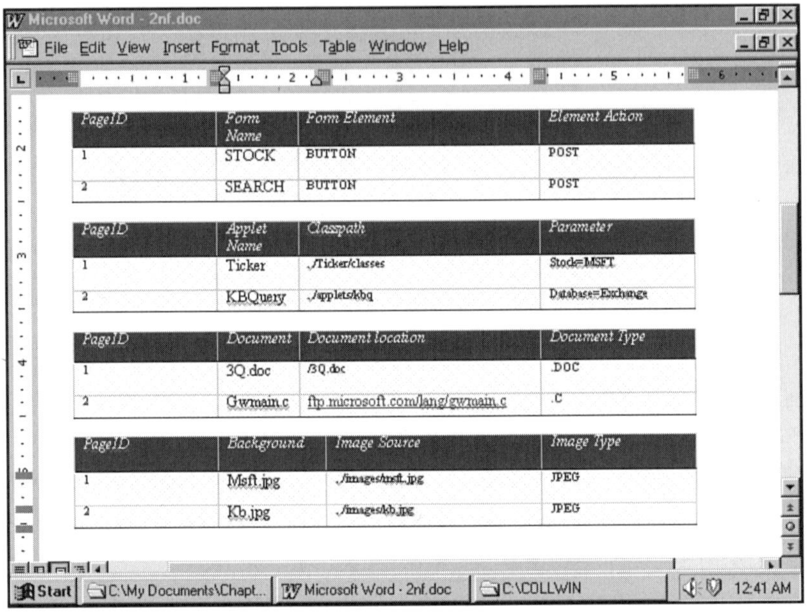

| PageID | Form Name | Form Element | Element Action |
|---|---|---|---|
| 1 | STOCK | BUTTON | POST |
| 2 | SEARCH | BUTTON | POST |

| PageID | Applet Name | Classpath | Parameter |
|---|---|---|---|
| 1 | Ticker | ./Ticker/classes | Stock=MSFT |
| 2 | KBQuery | ./applets/kbq | Database=Exchange |

| PageID | Document | Document location | Document Type |
|---|---|---|---|
| 1 | 3Q.doc | /3Q.doc | .DOC |
| 2 | Gwmain.c | ftp.microsoft.com/lang/gwmain.c | .C |

| PageID | Background | Image Source | Image Type |
|---|---|---|---|
| 1 | Msft.jpg | ./images/msft.jpg | JPEG |
| 2 | Kb.jpg | ./images/kb.jpg | JPEG |

Here's a summary of the actions taken to move the HTML relation into 2NF.

- Move the form data item into a separate relation.
- Move the applet data item into a separate relation.
- Move the document data item into a separate relation.
- Move the background data item into a separate relation.

Now that the relation has been broken into several relations without any partial dependencies, you'll notice that there still are update, delete, and insertion problems. Although, not as great as before, these problems are still serious ones to have in a production environment. To eliminate these problems, move everything into third normal form, as shown in Figure 2.18. Continue using the same process by breaking up the existing relations until the only data left in a relation with each other depend on the key.

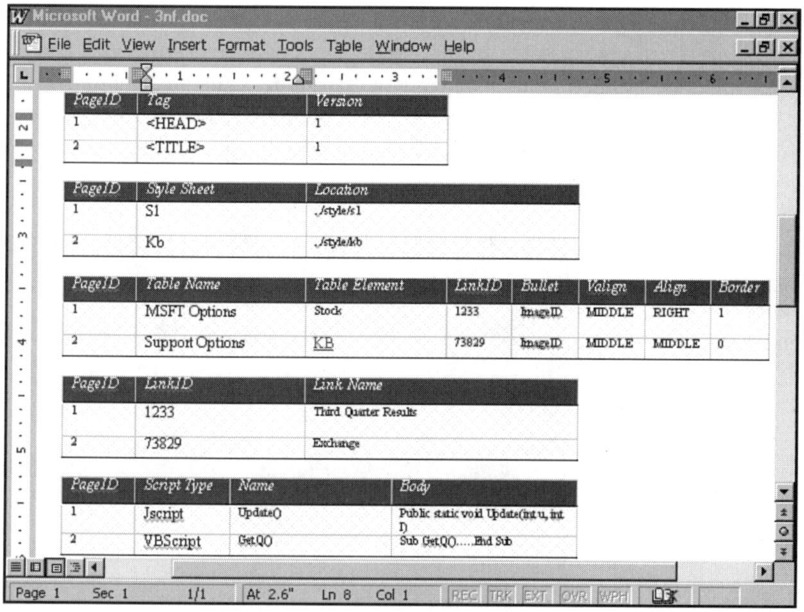

| PageID | Tag | Version |
|---|---|---|
| 1 | <HEAD> | 1 |
| 2 | <TITLE> | 1 |

| PageID | Style Sheet | Location |
|---|---|---|
| 1 | S1 | ./style/s1 |
| 2 | Kb | ./style/kb |

| PageID | Table Name | Table Element | LinkID | Bullet | Valign | Align | Border |
|---|---|---|---|---|---|---|---|
| 1 | MSFT Options | Stock | 1233 | ImageID | MIDDLE | RIGHT | 1 |
| 2 | Support Options | KB | 73829 | ImageID | MIDDLE | MIDDLE | 0 |

| PageID | LinkID | Link Name |
|---|---|---|
| 1 | 1233 | Third Quarter Results |
| 2 | 73829 | Exchange |

| PageID | Script Type | Name | Body |
|---|---|---|---|
| 1 | Jscript | Update() | Public static void Update(int u, int I) |
| 2 | VBScript | GetQ() | Sub GetQ()....End Sub |

**FIG. 2.18**
The HTML relation is shown in 3NF.

Here's a summary of the actions that move MOOSE into the third normal form:

- Move the Tag data into another relation to avoid update, insert, and deletion anomalies.
- Create new relations for the Link data, avoiding several possible anomalies.
- Create a new relation for the Style Sheet data.
- Move Table data into a separate relation, which prevents issues with multiple operations to update or change the data.
- Move Script data into separate relations to eliminate an update anomaly and an insertion anomaly.

By putting the MOOSE data into third normal form, you have arrived at a state in which the data is considered normalized. Abnormalities can still crop up, however, so you must go one step further and try for Boyce-Codd normal form to avoid translating these problems to your physical implementation. By transforming your data into the Boyce-Codd normal form, you gain the benefit of eliminating problems resulting from the use of candidate keys that overlap one another. In the following example, all candidate keys are in italics:

Server (**`IP`**, *Hostname, Some Attribute,* Some other Attribute)

If the candidate keys are not determinants, problems could arise. Boyce-Codd normal form specifies that all candidate keys must also be determinants for a given relation. The HTML relation is already in BCNF because only one candidate key is in the relation.

Because of your functional dependencies, you can now feel confident that no update, deletion, or insertion anomalies exist. That doesn't mean problems won't occur if two or more keys exist in a multivalued relationship in which each depends on "A" but neither key is related to the other. For example, in the HTML relation, the Text dependency isn't related to the Title dependency. Moving the relation to fourth normal form, however, (see Figure 2.19) eliminates these types of problems.

**FIG. 2.19**
Transfer multivalued dependencies from the HTML relation into 4NF.

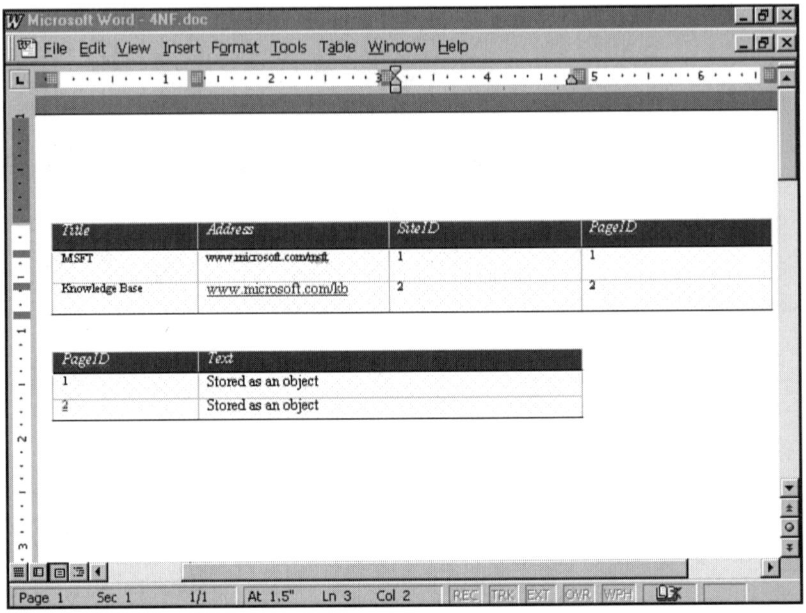


Only a single change was required to bring the HTML relation into fourth normal form: Move the Text data to another relation to avoid all three anomalies.

Now that you have come this far, there is no need to hunt around for join dependencies. Those can be very difficult to find and have no real benefit because of their rarity. After your relations are in fourth normal form, the data model is a relatively straightforward port to the physical model. Table 2.2 provides a quick recap of normalized relations.

**CAUTION**

While merging the relations from various views, be careful to recognize that attributes with the same name can have different meanings, and the reverse holds true as well.

**Table 2.2 Complete Normalized Relations for MOOSE in Fourth Normal Form**

| Relation | Primary Key | Foreign Key | Other Elements |
|---|---|---|---|
| Server | IP Address | | Host name, Domain name |
| Web site | SiteID | IP Address | Address, Name |
| HTML | PageID | SiteID | Address |
| Text | PageID | | Text |
| Form | PageID | | Form Name, Form element |
| Applet | ObjectID | PageID | Classpath |
| ParameterValue | ParameterID | ObjectID | Parameter Value |
| ParameterName | ParameterID | | Name |
| Document | LinkID | | DocType, DocObject |
| Image | LinkID | | ImageType, Image |
| Style | PageID | | Style Sheet, Location |
| Link | LinkID | PageID | Link Name, Address |
| Script | PageID | | Script Type, Name, Body |
| Tag | PageID | | Tag, Version |
| Table | PageID | LinkID | Table Name, Element, Bullet, Valign, Align, Border |

# Converting the Relations to Database Structures

After you have the normalized relations in a suitable form for conversion, you need to consolidate the views you've generated during the design process. Consolidation of the views is fairly straightforward, with a few exceptions. When consolidating, remember that several users might be referring to the same object, using different terminology. In addition, keep in mind that any caveat of the English language also applies here—one user might think of PC as politically correct, and the other as personal computer. Both usages are correct, and users will assume that you know this fact. Don't assume anything. If there is vagueness about whether the two relational attributes are in fact the same, ask. Don't make educated guesses simply because you think you should "know" what the object is supposed to be.

In addition, remember that determining what users need usually means asking, "What's wrong with the current product that you want improved?" This question is not the same as, "What kind of system would make you more productive?" Be careful to separate the gripes from the actual needs.

## From Here...

You've run through the basic concepts of data analysis and design, helped design and build a database for the Web search engine named MOOSE, and were introduced to many of the terms and ideas in the data modeling field. Now that you've got the design fundamentals behind you, it is time to learn what the client/server environment means to you by delving into the theory and reality behind client/server programming.

- Chapter 3, "Creating a Simple Database Application," explores the basics of creating a working database application.
- Chapter 4, "The SQL Standard: A Language for Data Access," offers an introduction to the world standard for database access languages and explains how to use this powerful tool.

CHAPTER 3

# Creating a Simple Database Application

**Exploring what database applications do**

Most database applications perform common functions.

**Examining a sample database application**

Take an in-depth look at what the Database Wizard for Java generates.

**Comparing RDO and DAO database access**

DAO and RDO code is shown and compared.

This chapter examines the key pieces of a database application that Visual J++ generates when using the Database Wizard for Java. Although this is a bare-bones code, it does show several techniques that will be used repeatedly when designing your own database applications.

Because the wizard is capable of generating code for DAO and RDO, we show both examples. The differences between DAO code and RDO will be compared so that you can understand what to look for in each type.

The code in this chapter is very simple and basically just consists of the code that is automatically generated by the wizard. There is a lot of code left out of the listings in this chapter, mainly so that we can concentrate on the database sections in which we are interested. ■

# Exploring What Database Applications Do

Database applications are rarely as simple as the sample in this chapter, but they do contain the same components as shown here. Every database application developer will have to use these same methods to set up the connection to the database and to perform operations on the database. Most of the actual coding of database applications is repetitive, and you will find the DAO access to the database is made up of simple, easy-to-follow steps. You will spend the greatest portion of your development efforts deciding exactly what to do rather than performing the operations.

Inside a database application, three distinct operations are performed. First, the session with the database and any initialization code must be initiated. Second, the application needs to perform the operation against the database. Third, the application retrieves the result and handles the return from the operation performed. Take an in-depth look at these operations as they relate to our sample application.

# Examining a Sample Database Application

By using the Database Wizard, you quickly can generate a database application for many simple tasks. The code generated for you with the Database Wizard for Java is surprisingly complete (for simple access). You will find error handling, threading, and data encapsulation built into the sample. Consequently, you can use the code listed here and change the portions that you do not need. If your intent is for a much larger application, you should strip the useful information generated by the wizard and add it to your larger application. Figure 3.1 shows the user interface generated for our sample application.

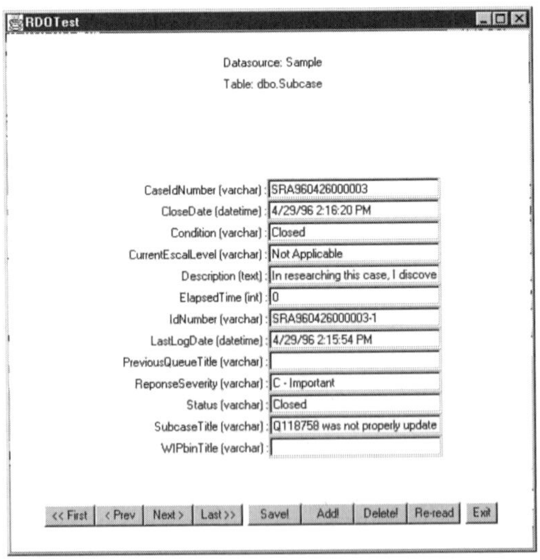


**FIG. 3.1**
The user interface for our sample application is generated as well, although you can modify it to suit your needs.

The code that the Database Wizard generated is not very complex. The wizard-generated code is lumped into the applet's initialization method, and there is no workable interface. You might want to consider using the Java Resource Wizard for more involved custom forms, although you will notice that the more advanced controls, such as Tree controls and List View controls, are still not converted to be database-aware. These will need to be converted with the Application Foundation Classes. Listing 3.1 sets up the user interface for the applet and dynamically creates the labels from the `Recordset` object.

The tasks of this section of code are simple. To start, the listing starts with a loop that iterates through each of the fields. For each of the fields, there are operations. First, the database field is retrieved by looking up the field name in the hash that maps to our database. The result of the lookup is a `DBField` object.

Next, the `rdoColumn` object is created by creating a name object and using it to look up the column. As soon as the column is available, we can now retrieve the column attributes. The column attributes are copied to the `DBField` object.

Now we start linking to the user interface by creating a `TextField` object and adding it to the `DBField` object. The next task is to set up the `DBField` object to the default column attributes. These attributes are used to set the behavior of the `DBField` to match information from the column description. The attributes set in this example include the editability of the field and the auto increment nature of the field. The last thing that occurs to each database field is that its label and field objects are added to the display.

After all of the fields have been processed, the rest of the wizard-generated code is for building the user interface. Basically, the code adds tool bars and other widgets to enable a user to move through and edit the database.

The last line in Listing 3.1 is a call to the `updateUI()` method. Method `updateUI()` causes the database to be accessed and the display to be updated with data.

Part I Ch 3

**Listing 3.1 RDOTEST.JAVA—Creating the User Interface for the Database Application by Using a *TextField* for Each Database Field and a Toolbar to Support Actions**

```
//Non UI specific code cut out for clarity.
for (int i = 0; i < field.length; i++)
        {


            DBField df = (DBField)hashField.get(field[i].strName);
            vName.putString(field[i].strName);
            rdoColumn rdoCol = rdoCols.getItem(vName);
            df.attributes    = rdoCol.getAttributes();
            String attribs   = new String();
            df.field         = new TextField(textFieldWidth);
            if (!readOnly && ((df.attributes &
                        AttributeConstants.rdUpdatableColumn) == 0))
            {
```

*continues*

**Listing 3.1 Continued**

```
                attribs += " (ReadOnly)";
                df.field.disable();
            }
            if ((df.attributes &
                        AttributeConstants.rdAutoIncrColumn)!=0)
            {
                attribs += " (Auto)";
                df.field.disable();
            }
            if (readOnly)
            {
                df.field.disable();
            }
            dbcolumn[col++].add(df.label);
            dbcolumn[col++].add(df.field);
            col %= columns;
        }
        // Set the layout of the toolbar panel
        toolbar.setLayout(new GridLayout(1, 0));
        toolbar.add(buttonFirst);
        toolbar.add(buttonPrev);
        toolbar.add(buttonNext);
        toolbar.add(buttonLast);

        // Set the layout of the update tools panel
        updatetools.setLayout(new GridLayout(1, 0));
        updatetools.add(buttonUpdate);
        updatetools.add(buttonAdd);
        updatetools.add(buttonDelete);
        updatetools.add(buttonReread);

        // Combine the tools together
        tools.setLayout(new FlowLayout());
        tools.add(toolbar);
        if (!readOnly)
        {
            tools.add(updatetools);
        }
            if (frame != null)
              tools.add(buttonExit);

        // Set layout for feedback panel
        feedback.setLayout(new GridLayout(0, 1));
        feedback.add(labelDatabase);
        feedback.add(labelRecordset);
        feedback.add(labelPosition);
            feedback.add(labelStatus);

        // Lay out the component groups vertically
        GridBagLayout gb = new GridBagLayout();
        setLayout(gb);
        GridBagConstraints c = new GridBagConstraints();
        c.insets = new Insets(20, 30, 20, 30);
```

```
        c.gridx = 0;
        add(feedback);
        gb.setConstraints(feedback, c);
        add(db);
        gb.setConstraints(db, c);
        add(tools);
        gb.setConstraints(tools, c);

        // Update fields based on current record
        updateUI();
```

## Initiating the Connection

The connection to the database is initiated through DAO by using the `DBEngine` object to create a connection object that will contain the information such as username, password, and default connection options. Listing 3.2 details how this is done in the sample DAO application generated with the Java Database Wizard.

If you are familiar with Microsoft database programming with Visual C++ or Visual Basic, you should find the following code very familiar. The only difference between the Java version and others is that the Variant type is used to pass data into the calls that initialize and set up the connection to the database.

The primary section of code in Listing 3.2 is the call to the `createWithLic()` method, which takes the license ID and the server as parameters. This establishes the connection to the server. The last line is then used to connect to a particular database that resides on the database server.



**Listing 3.2 DAOTEST.JAVA—Creating a New Instance of the *DBEngine* Object and Opening a Workspace**

```
public void init()
    {
        //--------------------------------------------------------------
        //DAO SUPPORT: Open the database and set up field info
        // Initialize database engine through license manager
        //------------------------------------------------------------
        //  Use a global empty variant for optional variant args

        varEmpty = new Variant();
        varEmpty.putEmpty();

        ILicenseMgr mgr = new LicenseMgr();
        _DBEngine idbengine = (_DBEngine)mgr.createWithLic
        (
                  "mbmabptebkjcdlgtjmskjwtsdhjbmkmwtrak",
                  "{00000010-0000-0010-8000-00AA006D2EA4}",
                 null,
                 ComContext.INPROC_SERVER
         );
```

continues

**Listing 3.2 Continued**

```
// Open database
 Variant vExclusive = new Variant();
 Variant vReadOnly = new Variant();
 Variant vConnect = new Variant();
 vExclusive.putBoolean(false);
 vReadOnly.putBoolean(readOnly);
 vConnect.putString("");
 database = idbengine.OpenDatabase(strDatabase,
                                   vExclusive,
                                   vReadOnly,
                                   vConnect);
```

After an application has opened a database, it is free to manipulate the data or change the structure of the database, assuming that the user has permission to do so.

## Performing the Database Operations

Although there are multitudes of operations to perform on a database, all of them go through similar procedures to accomplish the desired results. In Listing 3.3, the database is queried for its data with what amounts to as a SQL `SELECT` statement in DAO.

As was mentioned previously, if you have done DAO work before, the code is very similar. Like Listing 3.2, the code in Listing 3.3 uses the Variant type to pass data into the DAO method call to the database's `OpenRecordset()` method. The record set is now available for processing.

**Listing 3.3 DAOTEST.JAVA—Returning the Entire Database as a Result Set to the Application by Opening a Recordset on a Database**

```
// Create a new recordset
     Variant vOpenType = new Variant();
     Variant vOptions = new Variant();
     Variant vLockType = new Variant();
     vOpenType.putShort((short)RecordsetTypeEnum.dbOpenDynaset);
     vOptions.putShort((short)(readOnly ?
            RecordsetOptionEnum.dbReadOnly : 0));
      vLockType.putInt(LockTypeEnum.dbOptimistic);
     recordset = database.OpenRecordset(strRecordset,
                                        vOpenType,
                                        vOptions,
                                        vLockType);
```

If you were writing the application with RDO, the syntax remains much the same. RDO operations differ only because an RDO object needs to open a connection to the data source instead of directly opening the database, as shown in Listing 3.4.

**Listing 3.4 RDOTEST.JAVA—Initializing and Opening a Connection by Using RDO**

```
//----------------------------------------------------------------// Use a
global empty variant for optional variant args

varEmpty = new Variant();
varEmpty.putEmpty();

// Use the runtime key to get the engine interface
ILicenseMgr mgr = new LicenseMgr();
m_IEngine = (_rdoEngine)mgr.createWithLic(
                "B1692F60-23B0-11D0-8E95-00A0C90F26F8",
                "{5E71F04C-551F-11CF-8152-00AA00A40C25}",
                null,
                ComContext.INPROC_SERVER);

m_IEnvironment = m_IEngine.rdoCreateEnvironment("", "", "");

Variant varPromptOption = new Variant();
Variant varReadOnly = new Variant();
Variant varConnectString = new Variant();
Variant varOptions = varEmpty;

// Set the OpenConnection parameters
varPromptOption.putInt(PromptConstants.rdDriverComplete);
varReadOnly.putBoolean(readOnly);
varConnectString.putString(m_strConnect);

// Open a connection
m_IConnection = m_IEnvironment.OpenConnection("",
                                              varPromptOption,
                                              varReadOnly,
                                              varConnectString,
                                              varOptions);
```



## Retrieving the Result

Now that the database has returned a result (the `Recordset` object), you need a method to do something with it. This is perhaps the most common database operation because we either process data and/or present the data to the user. The following section of the example demonstrates three different operations that can be performed on the result set returned to the application.

- Inserting
- Updating
- Deleting
- Reading
- Scrolling

Look at the previous list of operations, and their relationship to a database application. First, consider scrolling, which provides the means for moving through the result set's records. Without scrolling (also known as a database cursor), you can access multiple records, as opposed to a single record. DAO implements scrolling through the `Recordset.Move()` methods. RDO uses similar terminology, as well. These `Move()` methods simply move the record pointer—the cursor—a set number of records ahead or back. Listing 3.5 provides an example of the `Move` methods being used to scroll through the result set when the user presses the first, next, or previous buttons. The code is simply calling the `MoveFirst()`, `MoveNext()`, and `MovePrevious()` methods of the `Recordset` object. After each of these method calls, the `updateUI()` method is called to cause the display to be populated with the contents of the current row of data fetched by the `Move` command.

**Listing 3.5 DAOTEST.JAVA—Scrolling Through the Recordset by Using the *Move()* Methods**

```
if (evt.target == buttonFirst)
        {
            recordset.MoveFirst();
            updateUI();
            return true;
        }
        else if (evt.target == buttonPrev)
        {
            recordset.MovePrevious();
            updateUI();
            return true;
        }
        else if (evt.target == buttonNext)
        {
            recordset.MoveNext();
            updateUI();
            return true;
        }
```

RDO is almost a carbon copy of these. Because RDO is much more SQL dependent, however, you need to send the SQL statement to the data source before attempting to pull back the result set, as shown in Listing 3.6.

The first task of the following code is to create a Select statement that will be used to create a query that in turn will be used to populate the result set. The Select statement that is created here is done by simply concatenating the keyword `SELECT`, the field names to access, the keyword `FROM`, and the name of the table. The Select statement is simply specifying a select of the specified fields from the specified table. It should be noted here that although the example uses the `String` type, if many SQL statements are built, the `StringBuffer` type should be used instead. The `StringBuffer` requires less time to execute because it does not create a new `String` object after each concatenation.

**Listing 3.6 RDOTEST.JAVA—Initiating the SQL Query and Handling the Returned Result Set with RDO**

```
// Set the SQL
String strSQL = "SELECT ";
for (int nField = 0; nField < field.length; nField++)
{
      strSQL += field[nField].strName;
      if (nField + 1 < field.length)
           strSQL += ", ";
}
strSQL += " FROM " + m_strTable;
Variant varSQL = new Variant();
varSQL.putString(strSQL);

// Set the prepared statement
m_IPreparedStatement =
m_IConnection.CreatePreparedStatement(m_strDummyQueryName, varSQL);


// Get a resultset, setting cursor type and concurrency
Variant varType = new Variant();
Variant varConcurrency = new Variant();
varOptions = varEmpty;
varType.putInt(ResultsetTypeConstants.rdOpenKeyset);
varConcurrency.putInt(LockTypeConstants.rdConcurRowVer);
m_IResultset = m_IConnection.OpenResultset(m_strDummyQueryName,
                            varType,
                            varConcurrency,
                            varOptions);

// Don't count records, just set nonzero if not empty
if (!m_IResultset.getEOF()) recordCount = 1;
```

The preceding RDO code does look quite a bit different from the DAO example of Listing 3.4. Notice that we are doing the same thing as before, simply pulling the data back from the data source through a result set. This is the normal operation for any application, whether it uses ODBC, DAO, RDO, or even JDBC. All methods of data access use similar methods of gathering data. Indeed, underneath the COM wrappers (or abstraction layer, in the case of JDBC) you will find pure ODBC function calls being made.

The next method in Listing 3.7 shows how the application retrieves the data from the result set returned by the database. Notice that we use `getCollect()` and `putCollect()` for brevity (you need to pass only the column name and the value to this method). These methods are fine for smaller chunks of data. A more granular level is required when you need to control the amount of data flowing across the wire at one time (see Chapter 6, "Data Access Objects," and Chapter 7, "Remote Data Objects," for more information). You should always be careful not to move large amounts of data, especially when accessing the server with slow Internet communication.

**Listing 3.7 DAOTEST.JAVA—Manipulating and Viewing the Contents of a Field with the *putCollect* and *getCollect* Methods**

```
/*
*
* Updates the contents of the TextField associated with a given field
* using the current record.
* @param f Field to update
*/
    void updateTextField(DBField f)
    {
        if (recordset != null)
        {
            String strValue;
            try
            {
                // Get the field's value at the current record
                vName.putString(f.strName);

                // Attempt to get the value
                Variant vValue;
                vValue = recordset.getCollect(vName);

                // We want booleans to be 'true' and 'false'
                if (f.vt == Variant.VariantBoolean)
                {
                    Boolean b = new Boolean(vValue.getBoolean());
                    strValue = b.toString();
                }
                else
                {
                    strValue = vValue.toString();
                }
            }

          // Converting a variant of type VT_NULL to a String can cause
          // this exception to be thrown.
            catch (ClassCastException c)
            {
                // Choose "" as the String representation for null.
                strValue = "";
            }

            // Set the text of the TextField associated with the field
            f.field.setText(strValue);
        }
    }
```

RDO uses similar conventions for reading from the database field, from using the same input parameters to using the `getCollect()` method. Setting up the read is the same as DAO, which means much less work to create generic methods (or to implement interface overloading to achieve the same effect). Reading from the database is shown in Listing 3.8.

**Listing 3.8 RDOTEST.JAVA—Reading from the Database in RDO**

```
/*
*
* Updates the contents of the TextField associated with a given field
* using the current record.
* @param f Field to update
*/

    void updateTextField(DBField f)
    {
            if (m_IResultset != null)
        {
            String strValue;
            try
            {
                // Get the field's value at the current record
                vName.putString(f.strName);

                // Attempt to get the value
                Variant vValue;
                        vValue = m_IResultset.getCollect(vName);

                // We want booleans to be 'true' and 'false'
                if (f.strType.toUpperCase() == "BIT")
                {
                    Boolean b = new Boolean(vValue.getBoolean());
                    strValue = b.toString();
                }
                else
                {
                    strValue = vValue.toString();
                }
            }

        // Converting a variant of type VT_NULL to a String can cause
        // this exception to be thrown.
           catch (ClassCastException c)
           {
        // Choose "" as the String representation for null.
               strValue = "";
           }

        // Set the text of the TextField associated with the field
           f.field.setText(strValue);
        }
    }
```

Notice that in both DAO and RDO, you set up the read operation in the exact same way, although through different interfaces—whereas DAO uses the `Recordset` interface, RDO uses the `Resultset` interface.

Inserts, updates, and deletes all use the same methodology to perform the read operation, as well. Listing 3.9 shows the three operations as they exist in the DAO sample.

**Listing 3.9 DAOTEST.JAVA—Performing Updates on the Data by Using Several of the Same Techniques as Reading the Data**

```
/*
*
* Updates the field in the database based on the associated TextField.
* @param df Field to update.
*/
    void updateDatabaseField(DBField df) throws Exception
    {
        if (recordset != null)
        {
            try
            {
                // Convert field value to the right variant type
                String strValue = df.field.getText();
                vValue.putString(strValue);
                vName.putString(df.strName);
                 // We want booleans to be 'true' and 'false'
                if (df.vt == Variant.VariantBoolean)
                {
                    if (strValue.equals("true"))
                    {
                        vValue.putBoolean(true);
                    }
                    else
                    if (strValue.equals("false"))
                    {
                        vValue.putBoolean(false);
                    }
                    else
                    {
                     throw new Exception(df.strName + " must be
                            either  true' or 'false' in lowercase.");
                   }
               }
               else
               {
                   // Convert to variant type
                   vValue.changeType(df.vt);
               }

               // Write to database unless the original value was null
               // and the text field is empty.
               vOriginalValue = recordset.getCollect(vName);
               if (!((vOriginalValue.getvt() == Variant.VariantNull) &&
                       (strValue.equals(""))))
                {
                    recordset.putCollect(vName, vValue);
                }
            }
```

```
// Converting a variant of type VT_NULL can cause this exception
            catch (ClassCastException c)
            {
            }
        }
    }
```

This method will take the `DBField` object and extract the name and value from the class, which are then used to perform the update. As you will see from comparing the RDO and DAO versions, you can make a generic method out of the `UpdateDatabase` and `UpdateTextField` methods. You can accomplish this by passing the object to the method, where the method will perform type checking on the class and then cast the object to the proper interface. Listing 3.10 details the RDO version and uses the same syntax.



**Listing 3.10 RDOTEST.JAVA—Using RDO to Perform the Update to the Data Source**

```
/*
*
* Updates the field in the database based on the associated TextField.
* @param df Field to update.
*/
    void updateDatabaseField(DBField df) throws Exception
    {
            if (m_IResultset != null)
        {
            try
            {
                // Convert field value to the right variant type
                String strValue = df.field.getText();
                vValue.putString(strValue);
                vName.putString(df.strName);

                // We want booleans to be 'true' and 'false'
                if (df.strType.toUpperCase() == "BIT")
                {
                    if (strValue.equals("true"))
                    {
                        vValue.putBoolean(true);
                    }
                    else
                    if (strValue.equals("false"))
                    {
                        vValue.putBoolean(false);
                    }
                    else
                    {
                        throw new Exception(df.strName +
                    " must be either 'true' or 'false' in lowercase.");
                    }
                }
```

continues

**Listing 3.10 Continued**

```
                    // Write to database unless the original value was null
                    // and the text field is empty.
                    vOriginalValue = m_IResultset.getCollect(vName);
                    if (!((vOriginalValue.getvt() == Variant.VariantNull)
                          &&(strValue.equals(""))))
                    {
                          m_IResultset.putCollect(vName, vValue);
                    }
                }

// Converting a variant of type VT_NULL can cause this exception
                catch (ClassCastException c)
                {
                }
            }
        }
```

## Error Handling and Gracefully Shutting Down

Most applications call functions (or methods) with return values that the application can check to determine whether or not the function succeeded. All data access methods available to Java programs have error handlers in place that enable the application to determine what happened on the last method call. Listing 3.11 details how this is done with DAO.

**Listing 3.11 DAOTEST.JAVA—Method to Convert COM Exceptions for Humans to Read**

```
/*
*
* Converts an exception into a human readable string possibly involving * the
DBField structure and the HRESULT value if it's a COM exception.
*/
    protected String getExceptionMessage(Exception e, DBField f)
    {
        if (e instanceof ComFailException)
        {
            int h = ((ComFailException)e).getHResult();
            switch (h)
            {
            case 0x800a0c5b:
                return "Field value is too long";

            case 0x800a0cf4:
                if ((f == null) || f.strValidation.equals(""))
                {
                    return "Validation rule failed";
```

```
                }
                else
                {
                    return f.strValidation;
                }

            default:
                return "DAO COM Exception " + e.getMessage();
            }
        }
        return e.getMessage();
    }
```

Catching exceptions when they occur is also an important part of designing "graceful" exits in your application. In Listing 3.12, we are attempting to update the database and definitely need to know if this update has failed so that we can cancel the update, inform the user, and reposition the database cursor.



**Listing 3.12 RDOTEST.JAVA—Methods for Applications to Handle Exceptions and COM Errors**

```
try
{
// Try to update the field.
       updateDatabaseField(field[i]);
}
catch (Exception e)
{
// If the update failed, alert the user and cancel the update
      String strError;
      strError = "Error updating " + field[i].strName + " : " +
                  getExceptionMessage(e, field[i]);
      if (frame != null)
            new Alert(frame, "Save failed!", strError);
     else
             labelStatus.setText(strError);

     recordset.CancelUpdate(UpdateTypeEnum.dbUpdateRegular);
     break;
}
```

As in normal development, use the `try{...}catch {}` to recover or to report to the user that an error has occurred. If the code does not handle the exception in this method, the exception needs to be handled at a higher level. In Listing 3.12 we are catching any errors that may have occurred during the call to the `updateDatabaseField()` method. If the exception occurs, the catch is able to clean up and notifies the user that the update did not succeed.

# From Here...

In this chapter, you examined the sample database applications for both RDO and DAO. You should now understand the basics for building simple database applications. In the next few chapters, you look at the basics of data access protocols, including ODBC, SQL, DAO, and RDO.

- Chapter 5, "ODBC," examines the base upon which all Microsoft data access classes are built.
- Chapter 6, "Data Access Objects," teaches you how to use DAO in your applications.
- Chapter 7, "Remote Data Objects," explores RDO, which has been developed as the fastest means of accessing ODBC data sources without calling the ODBC APIs directly. Learn how this can be used within the Java environment.

PART II

# A New Look at Database Programming

CHAPTER 4

# The SQL Standard: A Language for Data Access

SQL was first standardized in 1986 to provide a standard means of accessing relational database engines. This first draft gave us the means to define tables and to use the SELECT statement to retrieve data. Since that time, the American National Science Institute has produced two additional versions. SQL-89, as it is known, is what ODBC SQL conformance standards were initially targeted to. SQL-89 also added extensions for referential integrity and for using constraints. The newest published version is SQL-92, which provides several new features for schema manipulation and data definition.

SQL (Structured Query Language) has been the standard for data access languages for nearly a decade now, and its importance has only increased in the last few years. Now, with DAO and RDO, the Java developer has a means of using this language.

What does this language do for the Java developer? SQL enables cross-platform solutions and easier development because most database vendors support at least a basic set of SQL. The SQL standards benefit all language platforms. For Java developers, adding SQL capabilities means Java can now be seen as a more serious development platform,

**Exploring the SQL language**

Learn the programming syntax and concepts behind the SQL language.

**Creating prepared statements**

Learn how to maximize query performance with prepared statements

**Using referential integrity with SQL**

Referential constraints ensure the conistency of your database. Learn how to implement and use constraints in SQL.

**Controlling transaction processing with SQL**

SQL transactions can isolate your changes from the rest of the data source until you have completed your transaction. This enables you to ensure the results before the changes are made.

**Using the new schema definitions**

SQL-92 has added several new statements, including a group of statements aimed at enabling an information schema.

**SQL 3—a glimpse into the evolving standard**

SQL is a growing language that is constantly being updated for today's technology. Find out how the next generation of SQL is shaping up.

which is something Java needs if it is to become more than a niche language (as BASIC was before Visual Basic, or as FORTRAN is now).

SQL is a very good language for manipulating and accessing data. With it, you can define tables, create new schemas, and retrieve and modify data. You can also create references, indexes, and constraints to protect your data's integrity. ■

▶ **See** "Exploring ODBC" for more information on SQL, **p. 104**

# Exploring the SQL Language

The SQL-92 standard was developed to give more functionality to schema definitions and data connection enhancements (the capability to actually connect to a data source). ANSI (the America National Institute of Standards) has broken SQL-92 into three different levels of conformance, which enables vendors to implement the level of support they feel is necessary and to expand it to include their own constructs.

The first level of SQL conformance is ***Entry Level SQL***. This is the minimal conformance level required by ANSI. Entry Level SQL was defined to enable the basic database functionality expected by an application, such as:

- Check constraints
- Colons preceding parameter names
- Commas and parentheses in parameter lists
- Data Manipulation Language
- Direct execution of data manipulation statements
- Embedded interfaces to seven languages
- Module language definitions
- Renaming of columns in the `SELECT` statement
- Referential integrity
- SQL-89's default clause
- Statements for defining schemas
- Usage of the `SQLSTATE` parameter
- `WITH CHECK OPTION` statement

You will find that most vendors, with the exception of the SQL databases, will only support Entry level SQL. The larger SQL vendors like Microsoft and Oracle support Intermediate level, but we don't know of one that has completely supported Full SQL yet.

*Intermediate Level SQL* has been defined to provide database developers with a target for mainstream database functionality and to enable more advanced operations, such as:

- Cascaded deletes on referential actions
- `CASE` expression

- Casting between data types
- Diagnostics management
- Domain creation
- Dynamic SQL
- Isolation levels for transactions
- Join enhancements such as the `UNION JOIN`
- Multiple Module support
- Multiple character sets
- New data types (Interval and simplified `DateTime` types)
- Schema redefinition statements
- Table Intersection

*Full SQL* is the term given to the most advanced functionality defined by ANSI. However, nothing says that you can't go out on a limb and create new features. Full SQL adds complete support for the information schema, advanced operations on data types, scrolling cursors, and many other features.

The capabilities described in Full SQL are not supported fully by any database vendor that we know of at this time, although this situation will certainly change as the market demands the capabilities listed as follows:

- Additional options defining data and time data types
- Assertions
- `BIT` string data type
- Cascaded updates on referential actions
- Character set translation
- Deferred constraint checks
- Named constraints
- Scrolling cursors
- Self-referencing updates and deletes
- Subqueries in check constraints
- Temporary table creation



## SQL Keywords

Like any language, SQL has its list of keywords. They are actually quite extensive, even when compared to traditional languages. Sometime soon you will probably get to revive the PL/1 pastime of entering your initials and pressing enter. It is good to have a SQL reference around unless you decide to memorize the entire standard. Without one, most of us would be using guesswork when it comes to what is actually supported by SQL, especially with more advanced usage. The reserved words for the SQL-92 standard are listed and defined in Table 4.1.

**Table 4.1 SQL-92 Reserved Words**

| Keyword | Description |
|---|---|
| ABSOLUTE | Used to specify an absolute position within the FETCH statement. |
| ACTION | Used to indicate that NO ACTION will be taken during a referential integrity check if the integrity is violated. |
| ADD | Used to add a definition. |
| ALL | Returns every record, including duplicates. |
| ALLOCATE | Specifies which cursor or descriptor to use with a statement. |
| ALTER | Specifies that the following statement will change some data structure. Used in ALTER TABLE, ALTER VIEW, and so on. |
| AND | Used in logical statements to specify that both conditions must be met. |
| ANY | Returns all rows in the result set. |
| ARE | Used in the SQL NAME ARE statement. |
| AS | Used in a variety of manners, including AS <column>, AS <reference>, AS <data type>. |
| ASC | Specifies ascending sort order. |
| ASSERTION | Ensures referential integrity in truth tests for updates made to data. |
| AT | Used in time zone expressions to set the time zone. |
| AUTHORIZATION | Used with the Information schema definitions to denote the authorization of the object. |
| AVG | Returns the average of an expression. A mathematical set function. |
| BEGIN | Begins a transaction. |
| BETWEEN | Finds a range of values. |
| BIT | Denotes a BIT data type. |
| BIT_LENGTH | Returns the number of bits in a particular string. |
| BOTH | Used in the TRIM specification to trim all blanks from a column. |
| BY | Usually used with ORDER BY or GROUP BY statements. |
| CASCADE | Sets the referential action. |
| CASCADED | Used within a View definition to define the level of CHECK OPTION. |
| CASE | Denotes the CASE expression test for a condition, taking action based on the results of the test. |

| Keyword | Description |
|---|---|
| CAST | Casts one variable type to another. |
| CATALOG | Used in the SET CATALOG statement. |
| CHAR | Denotes a character data type. |
| CHARACTER | Denotes a character data type. |
| CHAR_LENGTH | Returns the number of characters in the string. |
| CHARACTER_LENGTH | Returns the number of characters in the string. |
| CHECK | Used in the CHECK OPTION statement. |
| CLOSE | Closes an object. |
| COALESCE | Tests each value in a list for truth until one satisfies the condition. Similar to the CASE statement. |
| COLLATE | Specifies a collating sequence. |
| COLLATION | Creates a named collation. |
| COLUMN | Denotes a column of data. |
| COMMIT | Ends a transaction by committing the updates. |
| CONNECT | Connects to a data source. |
| CONNECTION | Denotes the current connection to the data source. |
| CONSTRAINT | Denotes a condition any operation that changes data must meet if there are domain, table, or column constraints. |
| CONSTRAINTS | Denotes a group of such conditions. |
| CONTINUE | Continues the operation after an error has occurred. |
| CONVERT | Converts a character expression. |
| CORRESPONDING | Used in a query expression; the query columns correspond to the given column list. |
| COUNT | Returns the number of records. |
| CREATE | Creates new SQL data structures. |
| CROSS | Denotes a CROSS JOIN. |
| CURRENT | Used with a cursor to make changes WHERE CURRENT OF the cursor. |
| CURRENT_DATE | Returns the current date in a function. |
| CURRENT_TIME | Returns the time in a function. |
| CURRENT_TIMESTAMP | Returns the currents timestamp. |

*continues*

**Table 4.1 Continued**

| Keyword | Description |
|---|---|
| CURRENT_USER | Returns the current user. |
| CURSOR | Denotes a method of moving through a result set. |
| DATE | Denotes a data type. |
| DAY | DateTime field. |
| DEALLOCATE | Deallocates a descriptor or prepared statement. |
| DEC | Denotes a decimal data type. |
| DECIMAL | Denotes a SQL data type. |
| DECLARE | Creates cursors and local temporary tables. |
| DEFAULT | Specifies defaults. |
| DEFERRABLE | Specifies that the constraint is allowed to be deferred. |
| DEFERRED | Specifies that the constraint check time is initially deferred. |
| DELETE | Deletes a number of rows meeting the DELETE statement's criteria. |
| DESC | Specifies a descending sort order. |
| DESCRIBE | Discovers information about prepared statements columns. |
| DESCRIPTOR | Sets or returns the descriptors for columns. |
| DIAGNOSTICS | Returns information about a statement or a condition. |
| DISCONNECT | Disconnects a data source. |
| DISTINCT | Specifies that the result set should contain only unique values. |
| DOMAIN | Used with the CREATE statement to create a SQL domain. |
| DOUBLE | Denotes a data type. |
| DOUBLE PRECISION | Denotes a data type. |
| DROP | Deletes an object created with the CREATE statement. |
| ELSE | Used in a CASE statement to specify an alternative execution sequence. |
| END | Used with a CASE statement to specify the end of the statement. |
| END-EXEC | Signals the end of the embedded SQL statements. |
| ESCAPE | Used in a MATCH or LIKE predicate to choose the escape character. |
| EXCEPT | Used with a SELECT query to return all results except the query term to the right of the EXCEPT keyword. |

| Keyword | Description |
|---|---|
| EXCEPTION | Used with the SQL diagnostics statement to retrieve information about an exception by its number. |
| EXEC SQL | Used in an embedded SQL statement to denote that this is the beginning of a SQL phrase. |
| EXECUTE | Executes a SQL statement directly. |
| EXISTS | Determines whether or not a particular expression exists. |
| EXTERNAL | Sets the COLLATION sequence. |
| EXTRACT | Extracts certain portions of a DateTime data type. |
| FALSE | Tests a logical condition. |
| FETCH | Used with a cursor to retrieve a row of records into variables. |
| FIRST | Sets the FETCH orientation. |
| FLOAT | Denotes a data type. |
| FOR | Depends on the context; can mean FOR(10), FOR <Column>, FOR <SELECT> |
| FOREIGN KEY | Used in CONSTRAINT definition to specify that this is a Table Constraint. |
| FOUND | Used in embedded exception declarations to determine whether or not the condition was found. |
| FROM | Used with the SELECT statement to specify the source of the result set. |
| FULL | Specifies the range of records to return in a clause. |
| GET | Retrieves information about character set, diagnostics, and many other items. |
| GLOBAL | Defines the scope of a table. |
| GO | Used with GO TO, an alternative spelling of GOTO. |
| GOTO | Enables the execution to jump out of sequence to a named procedure or module. |
| GRANT | Sets security and permissions on SQL objects. |
| GROUP | Used in a SELECT statement as GROUP BY. This enables the logical grouping of the results. |
| HAVING | Used in a SELECT statement to filter out results from a query. |
| HOUR | DateTime field. |

*continues*

**Table 4.1 Continued**

| Keyword | Description |
|---|---|
| IDENTITY | Used in a character translation expression to denote that this translation makes no changes to the characters. |
| IMMEDIATE | Used with a statement identifier to state that the action should occur immediately. |
| IN | Specifies which database the tables are in within the FROM clause. |
| INDICATOR | Denotes a descriptor. |
| INITIALLY | Specifies the constraint check time. Either IMMEDIATE or DEFERRED. |
| INNER | Specifies the type of JOIN. |
| INPUT | Specifies that a parameter is an input direction. |
| INSENSITIVE | Used in a DECLARE...CURSOR statement to work off of a copy of the data so that the cursor is insensitive to changes. |
| INSERT | Inserts the specified data into a table. |
| INT | Denotes a data type. |
| INTEGER | Denotes a data type. |
| INTERSECT | Used in an outer join to specify all intersecting rows should be included with the result set. |
| INTERVAL | Denotes a data type. |
| INTO | Specifies where the data will be inserted. |
| IS | Specifies that the expression is a Boolean test. |
| ISOLATION LEVEL | Specifies an isolation level for the transaction. |
| JOIN | Joins two or more tables in a single result set. |
| KEY | Used in a constraint definition, such as PRIMARY KEY or FOREIGN KEY. |
| LANGUAGE | Denotes the programming language. |
| LAST | Specifies the FETCH orientation. |
| LEADING | Used with the TRIM specification to denote that leading white space is to be removed. |
| LEFT | Denotes a type of OUTER JOIN that retrieves every record from the left side of the join, whether or not there is a match with the right side. |
| LIKE | Determines whether or not an expression matches another, even partially. |

| Keyword | Description |
|---|---|
| LOCAL | Determines the scope of the operation. |
| LOWER | Used in a fold expression to convert all characters to lowercase. |
| MATCH | Denotes a predicate type that compares a list of values for matching attributes. |
| MAX | Denotes an aggregate function. |
| MIN | Denotes an aggregate function. |
| MINUTE | Denotes a `DateTime` field. |
| MODULE | Denotes a block of SQL code with a named reference. |
| MONTH | Denotes a `DateTime` field. |
| NAMES | Gives names to certain objects (in schema definitions) and character sets (in module definitions). |
| NATIONAL | Denotes a character data type that specifies that a localized version of this data type is in use. |
| NATURAL | Specifies that the `Join` type has no specification and that all columns containing equal value shall be included in the `Join`. |
| NCHAR | Denotes National Character String data type. |
| NEXT | Specifies the `FETCH` orientation. |
| NO ACTION | Used with referential integrity to specify that no action will be taken. |
| NOT | Excludes values to the right of this keyword from the result set. |
| NULL | Specifies a `NULL` value. |
| NULLIF | Denotes a case abbreviation to determine whether or not a statement is `NULL` and then takes an action. |
| NUMERIC | Denotes a data type. |
| OCTET_LENGTH | Returns the octets (bytes) found in the string. |
| OF | Used in the `WHERE CURRENT OF` statement; also used in PASCAL to denote the type specification and in the `DECLARE CURSOR` statement to specify the scope of the updatable range of the cursor. |
| ON | Specifies which table reference will be used in a `JOIN`. |
| ONLY | Used with `READ` to specify a read-only operation. |
| OPEN | Opens a cursor. |
| OPTION | Used with `CHECK OPTION` or `GRANT OPTION` statements. |
| OR | Denotes the logical `OR`. |

*continues*

**Table 4.1 Continued**

| Keyword | Description |
|---|---|
| ORDER | Used in an ORDER BY statement.The values to the right of the ORDER BY statement are used to control the sorting order of a result set. |
| OUTER | Specifies the type of Join. |
| OUTPUT | Specifies the parameter direction with procedures. |
| OVERLAPS | Denotes a predicate that tests for overlap between two expressions. |
| PAD | Adds white space to a value. |
| PARTIAL | Defines the scope of a matching expression. |
| POSITION | Used in a numeric value expression to determine the position of a character within a block of characters. |
| PRECISION | Used to determine the accuracy of a date or time data type; also used to denote the number of decimal places in a numeric data type. |
| PREPARE | Creates a prepared statement. |
| PRESERVE | Used in the ON COMMIT {DELETE¦PRESERVE} ROWS statement. |
| PRIMARY KEY | Used with the CONSTRAINT statement to specify that the constraint refers to a PRIMARY KEY. |
| PRIOR | Sets the FETCH orientation. |
| PRIVILEDGES | Used with DDL statements to specify priviledges set on an object. |
| PROCEDURE | Creates a procedure. |
| PUBLIC | Used in the GRANT statement to enable public access to a resource. |
| READ | Determines the isolation level or the transaction type. |
| REAL | Denotes a data type. |
| REFERENCES | Creates column references. |
| RELATIVE | Specifies the FETCH orientation. |
| RESTRICT | Used with the GRANT statement. |
| REVOKE | Revokes a right that you've granted to someone. |
| RIGHT | Used with the GRANT statement to specify which rights will be given. |
| ROLLBACK | Used with transactions to restore the transaction to its initial state. |

| Keyword | Description |
|---|---|
| ROWS | Used in the ON COMMIT <action> ROWS statement. |
| SCHEMA | Denotes the logical representation of your data source, including structural and environmental information. |
| SCROLL | Determines the scrolling attribute of a cursor. |
| SECOND | Denotes a DateTime field. |
| SECTION | Used in embedded SQL statements. |
| SELECT | Specifies that this query returns a result set. |
| SESSION | Used in the SET SESSION AUTHORIZATION statement to set the authorization ID for the session. |
| SESSION_USER | Used to denote the SQL session authorization identifier (the account name in NT terms). |
| SET | Assigns a value to a SQL object—SET CURSOR, SET MODE. |
| SIZE | Used in the DIAGNOSTICS SIZE statement to retrieve the number of diagnostics. |
| SMALLINT | Denotes a data type. |
| SOME | Denotes a scope specifier. |
| SPACE | Determines the pad attribute: PAD SPACE |
| SQL | Reserved, not used. |
| SQLCODE | Used in a parameter declaration. |
| SLQERROR | Tests for an error condition. |
| SUBSTRING | A type of string value function used to find a subset of a character string. |
| SUM | Denotes a SQL algebraic set function. |
| SYSTEM_USER | Holds the operating system identifier that executed the module; this is implementation specific. |
| TABLE | Used in a CREATE statement to create a table structure. |
| TEMPORARY | Denotes that the object is a temporary object. |
| THEN | Used with CASE expressions to perform an action when a condition is fulfilled. |
| TIME | Denotes a subtype of the DateTime data types. |
| TIMESTAMP | Denotes a data type. |
| TIMEZONE_HOUR | Denotes a part of the TIMESTAMP data type. |

*continues*

**Table 4.1 Continued**

| Keyword | Description |
|---|---|
| TIMEZONE_MINUTE | Denotes a part of the TIMESTAMP data type. |
| TO | Used in an interval qualifier statement to specify the precision of a DATE data type. |
| TRAILING | Used in a TRIM statement to specify which characters will be trimmed. |
| TRANSACTION | Used to denote a SQL statement affecting a transaction, such as SET TRANSACTION, or END TRANSACTION. |
| TRANSLATE | Used in character set translation. |
| TRANSLATION | Specifies a character set translation. |
| TRIM | Trims white space from columns. |
| TRUE | Specifies a true value. |
| UNION | Joins the results of two or more SELECT statements. |
| UNIQUE | Specifies that only unique values are to be returned. |
| UNKNOWN | Denotes a truth value. |
| UPDATE | The UPDATE statement makes changes to the data. |
| UPPER | Used in a fold expression to convert all characters to uppercase. |
| USAGE | Used with embedded SQL statements in COBOL. |
| USER | Sets the username for a connection. |
| USING | Used with the JOIN statement to denote a derived column list. |
| VALUE | Denotes a descriptor that is used to get and set descriptor values. |
| VALUES | Specifies a number of tables. |
| VARCHAR | Denotes a SQL data type. |
| VARYING | Specifies that the data type can vary in length. |
| VIEW | Used in a CREATE statement to denote that you are creating a view. |
| WHEN | Used in a CASE statement. |
| WHENEVER | Used in embedded SQL statements. |
| WHERE | Denotes the search condition in a SELECT statement. |
| WITH | Sets extended conditions on an expression, such as WITH TIME ZONE. |
| WORK | Used with COMMIT and ROLLBACK. |

| Keyword | Description |
|---|---|
| WRITE | Used with READ, it sets the level of access to READ WRITE. |
| YEAR | Denotes a DateTime field. |
| ZONE | Used in SET TIME ZONE, or TIME ZONE to return and set the time zone information for a statement. |

## SQL Lexical Constructs

Every language will also have a set of lexical constructs to deal with various logical and numerical evaluations on statements. SQL's set of logical constructs is not as extensive as you might think, and they function exactly as you would expect them to in Java. Table 4.2 describes the mathematical operators available in SQL.

**Table 4.2 SQL Operators**

| Operator | Function |
|---|---|
| = | Assignment operator |
| > | Greater than |
| < | Less than |
| >= | Greater than or equal to |
| <= | Less than or equal to |
| != | Not equal to |



## SQL Data Types

SQL-92 has attempted to standardize several data types by defining them. At this time, most vendors still use ODBC drivers to map these types to their actual data types in the base tables. Still, these are the data types that you will use as a Visual J++ developer.

**SQL-92 Character Data Types** SQL-92 has defined three different ways to deal with character (or text) data. The first, CHARACTER, deals with known lengths of data. CHARACTER VARYING and VARCHAR both deal with varying amount of data unknown at the compile time.

Essentially, the length of all character strings varies when you declare them. The main difference between the two character data types concerns how they deal with blank space in the column. The CHAR (or CHARACTER) data type simply pads the field with the required amount of space. In contrast, the VARCHAR or CHARACTER VARYING types truncate the free space to maximize storage efficiency.

**NOTE** For any of the data types that are varying in length, the server usually stores at least one byte of overhead for each column of data (and perhaps two). Essentially, this means that you must use CHAR-type columns for anything less than three characters in length. In reality, use CHAR whenever the number of entries is always static, and use VARCHAR whenever the entries vary in length.

**SQL-92 Binary Data Types** SQL-92 defines two data types to deal with binary data. These data types are called BIT and BIT VARYING.

The binary data types are essentially the same as the character data types: The BIT data type stores fixed length fields of binary data, while the BIT VARYING stores variable lengths of binary data and truncates the column to the length of the data.

**SQL-92's Numeric Data Types** Your choices become more complex when choosing the data type for Numeric data. SQL-92 defines many numeric types, including one labeled NUMERIC. Table 4.3 details the different numeric data types and their storage requirements.

**Table 4.3 SQL-92 Numeric Data Types**

| Data Type | Size (in Bytes) | Stores |
|---|---|---|
| DECIMAL | 2–17 | Exact numeric data |
| DOUBLE | 8 | Range: 15 significant digits |
| DOUBLE PRECISION | 8 | Range: 15 significant digits |
| FLOAT | 4 | Range: 7 significant digits |
| INTEGER | 4 | Range: –2,147,483,648 to 2,147,483,648 |
| INTERVAL | Variable | |
| NUMERIC | 2-17 | Exact numeric data |
| SMALLINT | 2 | Range: –32,767 to 32,767 |
| REAL | 8 | Range: machine-dependent |

When you use numeric data, it is important to store as little of it as possible. If the data source that you are using supports the DECIMAL or NUMERIC data types, you might use them. You can control the length of the fields and, thus, control the amount of storage needed to use the NUMERIC or DECIMAL data types.

**NOTE** The lengths of these two data types are based purely on their representations on an Intel 32-bit platform as translated by SQL Server; on other platforms or products, the storage requirements for each variable would change.

**SQL-92 Date and Time Data Types** SQL-92 also defines several date and time data types for use with SQL that serve many purposes. For example, having a defined DATE data type enables you to construct time-based analysis tools much more easily than converting the data into integer format. The DATE and TIME data types are shown in Table 4.4.

**Table 4.4 SQL-92 *DATE* Data Types**

| Data Type | Size (in Bytes) |
|---|---|
| DATE | 10 |
| TIME | 8 |
| TIME WITH TIMEZONE | 14 |
| TIMESTAMP | 19 |
| TIMESTAMP WITH TIMEZONE | 25 |

**NOTE** The DATE data types will use at least 10 bytes. Only DATE is fixed at 10, the rest depend on the precision of the fractions of a second you that are using.



## SQL Predicates

*Predicates* are a mathematical term used in calculus to describe truth-valued functions that return either true or false. SQL-92 defines several different types of predicates for use with the SQL language. Using predicates in SQL enables you to perform logical operations that evaluate true for some data that you want to affect. All predicates have the same general syntax and usage and can be used almost anywhere in a SQL statement. The most common use, however, is inside the WHERE clause of the SELECT statement.

SQL predicates can use several constructs for each value that is being evaluated. A list of the types of constructs allowed in the predicates follows:

- *Unsigned value* A string literal or numeric quantity
- *Column reference* The name of a column
- *Set function* AVG, MAX, MIN—algebraic set functions
- *Scalar subqueries* A SELECT statement
- *Case expressions* The CASE (some expression), WHEN (some other expression or statement), THEN (another value expression)
- *Value expressions* Column references, Scalar subqueries, Set functions, Cast specifications, Case expressions, unsigned values, value expressions
- *Cast specifications* Casts one data type into another one, which is useful for mapping native data types to SQL data types

The following statement illustrates an example of a Scalar subquery and of using a BETWEEN predicate in the WHERE clause of this SELECT statement:

```
SELECT * FROM SomeTable WHERE
(SELECT * FROM SomeOtherTable) BETWEEN SomeVal_1 AND SomeVal_2;
```

**Comparison Predicates** Comparison predicates are used to compare two values and to determine a result. The syntax is

```
Value1 <operator> Value2.
```

This simple definition can be deceiving, however, if you know what could get put into a comparison. Using some of the constructs at your disposal might yield something like the next statement:

```
(SELECT * FROM Table1 WHERE Capacity >= 25)  != AVG(SELECT DISTINCT * FROM Table2
➥WHERE Capacity >=25)
```

As you can tell, the operation could become quite complex.

***BETWEEN* Predicate** The `BETWEEN` predicate supports nearly the same syntax as the comparison predicates, with the exception of the comparison operator. It looks like this:

```
[NOT] BETWEEN Value1 AND Value2
```

The `BETWEEN` statement can also use any form of a SQL expression that can be evaluated, on both sides of the predicate.

***IN* Predicate** Compared to the `BETWEEN` and Comparison predicates, the `IN` predicate is relatively simple. To the right of the `IN` keyword, you can specify one value expression or table subquery to denote the data that retrieves the result set.

```
[NOT] IN <SELECT statement>¦ <Value Expression 1, Value Expression 2>
```

The number of expressions is not limited, but they must be separated by a comma.

***LIKE* Predicate** Use the `LIKE` predicate to find values that have something in common. For example, by using `LIKE`, you can return each value in which at least some part of that value matches a given pattern. Here's the syntax for the `LIKE` predicate:

```
Value1 [NOT] LIKE <character pattern>
```

You can use the escape character "^" to use special SQL characters in your pattern matching, similar to Java and C.

***NULL* Predicate** The `NULL` predicate is useful for determining whether or not an expression has a value. You can use this to determine whether or not a returned query is empty. The syntax is

```
<Some expression> IS [NOT] NULL
```

***QUANTIFIED* Predicate** A `QUANTIFIED` predicate is useful for performing differential algorithms on sets of data. With it, you can easily determine if two sets of data meet your criteria. The syntax is

```
<Some expression> <operator> ALL ¦ SOME ¦ ANY <Table subquery>
```

***EXISTS* Predicate** An `EXISTS` predicate determines whether or not an item exists. When used on a query, the `EXISTS` predicate performs many of the same functions as the `NULL` predicate. Its syntax is

```
EXISTS <Table subquery>
```

***UNIQUE* Predicate** This predicate is useful for determining whether or not every row of the subquery is both unique and not null. This predicate returns TRUE if every row meets that condition and FALSE if they do not. The syntax is

```
UNIQUE <Table subquery>
```

***MATCH* Predicate** The MATCH predicate tests for a match between two different result sets. You can specify whether you want a full, partial, or unique match between the two. If a match is found, the statement will return TRUE; otherwise the MATCH predicate returns FALSE. The syntax is

```
<Some expression> MATCH [UNIQUE][PARTIAL¦FULL] <Table subquery>
```

***OVERLAPS* Predicate** The OVERLAPS predicate returns TRUE if the results of two expressions overlap. The syntax is

```
<Expression 1> OVERLAPS <Expression 2>
```

## Retrieving Your Data with the *SELECT* Statement

You probably are most familiar with the SELECT statement. There are many ways to use the SELECT statement to retrieve your data. Generally, the form of the SELECT statement is



```
SELECT <Column 1, Column 2...> FROM <Table 1, Table 2...>
```

This simple SELECT statement returns all of the columns from each of the tables listed in the FROM clause.

The SELECT statement is composed of several different clauses and constructs. Even if you have had experience using the SELECT statement, you've probably used only a few of the constructs available. Here is the syntax of the SELECT statement, with the individual clauses indicated:

- SELECT [DISTINCT¦ALL] <Columns> [AS <Columns>]
- FROM clause
- WHERE clause
- GROUP BY clause
- HAVING clause

**The *FROM* Clause** In its simple form, the FROM clause is a table name. In its complex form, it could be anything from joins to views to derived tables that make up the set of data that you pull from. The syntax of a FROM clause is

```
FROM <Table Name>¦ <Derived Table>¦<Joined Table>
```

This is deceptively simple, as all SQL constructs are when you first see them. This syntax implies that you can place a table name, derive one, or use a joined table for the tables list in a FROM clause.

Actually you can go further, for each method of determining the table name also has a qualifier, a correlation name for the table, and a list of derived column names.

These options are not clear from your normal usage of the FROM clause, which is usually just a group of table names. This actually means

- *<correlation name>* An identifier for the table or column, similar to an object name
- *<derived table>* A SELECT subquery that results in a temporary table
- *<derived column>* Another way to say "column name"
- *<Joined table>* The result of a join performed on a set of tables

The resulting FROM clause might look like this one:

```
SELECT * FROM (SELECT Column1, Column2 FROM
(SELECT Column1 FROM Table1
LEFT JOIN TempTable
ON Table2.Column1 = Table3.Column2))
```

**The *WHERE* Clause** The WHERE clause is one of the most frequently used clauses, simply because it helps you filter the data and specify search criteria for your queries. The syntax of the WHERE clause is:

```
WHERE <search expression>
```

with <search expression> being a value, expression, query, or a predicate. By using the search expression, you can tailor your queries to match your exact needs. Using predicates or a subquery are two ways to easily satisfy most queries.

**The *GROUP BY* Clause** The GROUP BY clause enables you to aggregate a list of columns and collate the data in those columns before presenting the resulting set to your application. Its syntax is

```
GROUP BY <Column1 [COLLATE <name>]>
```

**The *HAVING* Clause** The HAVING clause enables you to limit the amount of data returned to the application after the query has been executed. Most vendors implement this as a WHERE clause unless it is used with the GROUP BY clause for performance reasons. The syntax is

```
HAVING <search expression>
```

**The *ORDER BY* Clause** The ORDER BY clause enables you to specify the return order of the result set. This is very useful because it eliminates having to use bubblesorts or qsort on the result set. The syntax is

```
ORDER BY <Column [COLLATE <name>]>
```

## SQL-92 Methods for Joining Two or More Tables

SQL offers several means of combining the results of one or more tables. The types of joins that you are probably most familiar with are the INNER JOIN and the OUTER JOIN.

- INNER JOIN
- OUTER JOIN
- FULL

- Union
- CREATE VIEW
- SELECT Statement
- SELECT...INTO Statement

## The SQL *JOIN* Statement

The SQL JOIN statement comes in three forms: INNER, OUTER and FULL.

An INNER JOIN is useful if there is data in two or more tables that you need, and you want to pull data that meets a certain condition. The syntax is

```
SELECT * FROM SomeTable
INNER JOIN TempTable
ON SomeTable.CustID = SomeOtherTable.CustID
```

This returns a result set with every record that matches the INNER JOIN condition.

An OUTER JOIN, on the other hand, returns all data from a table, whether or not it meets your search conditions. This would be useful if you need to determine whether or not you have unassigned resources, or, in the case of a help desk, to determine whether or not any help requests remain unfulfilled in addition to the help requests that have been taken.



## SQL-92 *LEFT JOIN* Statement

A LEFT JOIN is an OUTER JOIN that returns every record from the left side of the join. The syntax is

```
SELECT * FROM SomeTable LEFT JOIN HrDB ON SrNum.EmployeeID =
➥SomeTable.EmployeeID;
```

This query returns all service requests regardless of whether or not an employee is assigned to them.

## SQL-92 *RIGHT JOIN* Statement

A RIGHT JOIN is an OUTER JOIN that returns all records from the right side of the join. Its syntax is

```
SELECT * FROM SomeTable RIGHT JOIN SrNum ON SomeTable.EmployeeID =
➥SrNum.EmployeeID;
```

This query does the same thing as the LEFT JOIN, but notice that the syntax is now backward; the right side of the join is the one pulling every row.

**Using the *UNION* Statement to Join Tables** The UNION statement is similar in concept to an INNER JOIN with one distinct difference. The UNION statement joins SELECT statements, not tables. The result is a single view on multiple SELECT queries, useful if you automatically generate SELECTS and simply need to join them for a user request. The syntax is simple:

```
SELECT * FROM SomeTable
UNION [ALL]
SELECT * FROM SomeOtherTable
```

If you specify `UNION ALL`, then duplicates will returned. The default action in a `UNION` is to skip duplicate rows in the result set returned to your application.

**The *CREATE VIEW* Statement** SQL has defined a unique concept that you probably haven't dealt with unless you've programmed extensively with SQL or perhaps with FoxPro or Oracle—*views*. Views are a logically constructed view on multiple tables that appear as a single table. Views are special because, unlike `SELECT` statements, which do the same thing, you can create a permanent view and use it by name, so you don't have to construct the `SQL SELECT` statement every time. Views act much like a stored procedure. The syntax for a `CREATE VIEW` is somewhat different from the other procedures that you have seen.

```
CREATE VIEW SomeView(Col1, Col2, Col3...)
AS SELECT [WITH CASCADED¦LOCAL CHECK OPTION] <Column List>
```

Listing 4.1, is a more complicated example of creating a view. In the example, we create a view using a version of the `SELECT` statement that contains a join. This is done simply to point out that a view can contain anything that a `SELECT` statement can return.

**Listing 4.1 VIEWS.JXX—Creating a View to See Only the Postoffices Where Gateways Are Defined**

```
CREATE VIEW GATEWAYS
 AS SELECT DISTINCT
           GatewayDB.Type, NetworkDB.NETWORK, NetworkDB.POSTOFFICE
      FROM NetworkDB, GatewayDB
      RIGHT JOIN ServerDB AS GWServ
      ON ( ( ServerDB.Server) = ( GatewayDB.Server) )
     WHERE EXISTS(GatewayDB.PO)
```

SQL-92 standards use views for a variety of things, but most important is the new schemata information schema. ANSI has defined several views to be used in conjunction with the information schema to return metadata about the structure and environment of the data. Any user can use these views (they are read-only); they were implemented to help define a standard for information schema and to make it easier for you to plan ahead and to look at the global view. By using these tools, you will not be forced to manage your data in a reactive manner because you will be able to design the solutions before the problems occur.

Creating such views is not a simple job, but the ANSI committee has put together several default views that you can use if your data source supports `CREATE SCHEMA` and several other of the SQL-92 constructs.

## Filtering and Transforming Your Data

SQL also simplifies the task of creating a result set that looks as the user expects it to. By using search conditions and predicates, you can achieve the ultimate goal—useful data.

Most of the data that you receive from a data source is in raw form. Until you use some of the SQL procedures, the data that you receive needs to be transformed into information. SQL can help you do this. If you use the SELECT statement wisely, the data will appear in a form that doesn't require transforming before you give that data to the users.

You can take more advantage of the power of the SQL SELECT statement by using the WHERE clause. Your filter can be any expression represented in the data, and with the WHERE clause you can use predicates to evaluate the data before your application has a chance to look at it.

Using views is another example of transforming or filtering data. By creating a view, you can enable users to select the most interesting data and give them the opportunity to save their workspaces. If you want, you can even set security on the views. The important thing is that users will not have to worry about finding the data that they need—it will be right there for them.

## Creating and Modifying Tables with SQL

You can create and modify tables with SQL in a variety of ways—from using the SELECT statement to create new tables from existing data, to creating relationships between tables with the CREATE CONSTRAINT and ALTER TABLE statements.



**The *SELECT...INTO* Statement** The SELECT...INTO statement enables you to use the same syntax as a SELECT statement, except that the result set is used to create a new permanent table. For example,

```
SELECT Col1, Col2, Col3 FROM Table1, Table2 INTO Table3;
```

This creates a third table, with columns 1, 2, and 3 making up the structure and contents of that table.

**The *DELETE* Statement** The DELETE statement is used to mark a row, or set of rows, for deletion from the data source. The syntax of the DELETE statement is

```
DELETE FROM <table name> [ WHERE <search condition> ]
```

**CAUTION**

The DELETE statement is a fairly simple one, which makes it a bit dangerous. You can use this procedure to perform searched deletes on a table, but if you fail to give this command any arguments, you can lose the entire table. This happens because the DELETE statement considers a lack of arguments as a license to kill, dutifully deleting every record in the table.

**The *UPDATE* Statement** The UPDATE statement is much like the DELETE statement except that the UPDATE statement enables you to perform what are referred to as *positioned updates.* A positioned update is an update operation in which you place the cursor to a specific row and cause an update to occur on that row only. This is accomplished by using a special syntax for the UPDATE statement:

```
UPDATE SomeTable SET <column =  value, col2 = val2...> WHERE CURRENT OF My_Cursor
```

This statement updates all records in which the cursor is current. You can also specify *searched updates* in addition to positioned ones. A searched update is simply using a SQL SELECT query to select the rows to be updated. The syntax for searched updates is almost exactly the same as the searched DELETE statement:

```
UPDATE SomeTable SET <Col1 = DEFAULT, Col2 = Value...) WHERE <condition>
```

**Inserting Data with the *INSERT INTO* Statement** Inserting data with the INSERT statement actually inserts results of an entire query into the target table, not just single rows of items. The syntax of the INSERT INTO statement is

```
INSERT INTO Table1 [(Column List)] <SELECT Statement>
```

**Designing Tables with the *CREATE TABLE* Statement** SQL has defined many methods to create tables, including the CREATE TABLE statement, which enables you to create the structure of your tables.

The CREATE TABLE statement also enables you to define temporary tables and to set the scope of the tables. Its sytnax is

```
CREATE [(GLOBAL¦LOCAL) TEMPORARY] TABLE TableName (ColumnName {DataType¦Domain}
➥[default clause][column constraint definition][collation sequence]),
➥(ColumnName....) [ON COMMIT {
DELETE ¦ PRESERVE } ROWS]
```

You are able to create two different types of tables: permanent and temporary. The following syntax creates a permanent table:

```
CREATE GLOBAL TABLE SomeTable
(Col1 VARCHAR(5) CONSTRAINT My_Constraints COLLATE My_Collation), (Col2
➥NUMERIC(4) CONSTRAINT My_Constraints COLLATE My_Collation), (CONSTRAINT
➥My_TableConstraint);
```

This syntax creates a table called SomeTable with two columns, Col1 and Col2, and specifies their constraints and collation sequence in addition to the data type. Notice that a table constraint snuck in—that's okay. Table constraints are a valid table element. The next example creates a simple temporary table.

```
CREATE GLOBAL TEMPORARY TABLE SomeTable
(Col1 VARCHAR(5)),(Col2 NUMERIC(4)), (CONSTRAINT My_TableConstraints)
ON COMMIT DELETE ROWS;
```

This syntax creates a temporary table with two columns. The last clause in this statement deletes the table when the transaction is processed. If you want to preserve the table through several transactions, simply use the PRESERVE keyword instead of the DELETE keyword.

**Creating Relations by Using SQL References** It is interesting that the word ***relation*** is not defined anywhere in the standard SQL language. Instead, SQL uses references to denote a relation in a table. Using these references is fairly easy, as shown in the following syntax:

```
ALTER TABLE WebSites ADD CONSTRAINT relation FOREIGN KEY (ServerID) REFERENCES
Server(ServerID);
```

This statement alters the table WebSite by adding a table constraint that creates a relation between the WebSite.ServerID and the Server.ServerID columns. You can also use the CREATE TABLE statement to set up what are referred to as column constraints (as shown in the code snippet that follows), which specify a single column relation or key. In contrast, you can use the table and domain constraints with multiple columns.

```
CREATE GLOBAL TABLE ServerIP
(ZONE VARCHAR(255) COLLATE My_Collation), (IP NUMERIC(16) CONSTRAINT IPConstraint
PRIMARY (IP) REFERENCES InterNic(IP) COLLATE My_Collation);
```

This statement creates a table with only two columns, one of which is the primary key (hence the word primary), and that key references the column IP in the table `InterNic`. This ensures that no two values in those columns will be duplicated or will be null.

▶ **See** "Introduction to Database Models" for more information about relations and relational theory, **p. 26**

## Performing Calculations with SQL

Generally, SQL has been lousy at mathematical calculations. This has been improved somewhat, but you still have to implement most of the more advanced functions. This doesn't mean, however, that using SQL set functions is any slower than collating the data yourself and performing permutations on it when the data gets to your applet or application.

The SQL-92 specifications define several algebraic set functions. Most people have come to call these set functions *aggregates* simply because they return a result that is an aggregate of the data. You can also use *scalar expressions* to perform logical calculations on your data. Although it would be nice to see more advanced statistical functions in SQL3, using aggregates and scalar expressions together is sufficient for most of the operations that you will perform.



**Using SQL Set Functions** SQL's set functions are easy to use and can save you a bit of programming because you can use each of these functions to perform simple calculations on your result sets. SQL-92 defines the six set functions, as shown in Table 4.5.

**Table 4.5 SQL-92's Set Functions**

| Function | Description |
|---|---|
| `AVG()` | Averages a set of values |
| `COUNT()` | Counts the number of non-null expressions |
| `COUNT(*)` | Returns the number of rows in a result set |
| `MAX()` | Returns the highest number, latest date, or the string highest in the sort order in a set |
| `MIN()` | Returns the lowest number, earliest date, or the string lowest in the sort order in a set |
| `SUM()` | Returns the total numeric value for the column(s) |

The `AVG()` function is useful if you are trying to determine time deviations or other statistical methods. The following syntax takes the average temperature for each season in the last three decades and computes the average temperature.

```
SELECT avg(temp) "Average Spring Temperature" FROM WeatherData
WHERE Season = "Spring"
UNION
```

```
SELECT avg(temp) "Average Summer Temperature" FROM WeatherData
WHERE Season = "Summer"
UNION
SELECT avg(temp) "Average Fall Temperature" FROM WeatherData
WHERE Season = "Fall"
UNION
SELECT avg(temp) "Average Winter Temperature" FROM WeatherData
WHERE Season = "Winter"
```

You can also use the `count(*)` function to determine the number of records that met your search criteria. For example, if you want to know how many days of 100+ degree heat Texas had last year, you use the following syntax:

```
SELECT count(*) "Days over One Hundred" FROM WeatherData
WHERE State = "TX" AND Temp >= 100;
```

# Creating Prepared Statements in SQL

By using prepared statements, you can gain execution time if you are going to execute the query several times. A prepared statement sets up the statement in advance, creating the action plan on the server—sending the query across. Everything but the actual execution is done before you execute the query. To create a prepared statement, use the `PREPARE` statement:

```
PREPARE My_SQL FROM SELECT * FROM SomeTable;
```

To execute a prepared statement, simply use the `EXECUTE` statement with the prepared statement's name:

```
EXECUTE My_SQL;
```

# Using Parameters with Your Statements

You can specify parameters for use with your prepared statements. These parameters enable you to change portions of the `SELECT` statement at runtime. You won't be able to change the actual statement; however, this limitation is alleviated somewhat because most queries are simply changes in the data sent or the data retrieved.

To use a parameter, you first need to create one. Creating dynamic parameters, ones that you specify at runtime, is simple. Put a question mark wherever you need a parameter:

```
SELECT ? FROM ?,? WHERE ?=?
```

Doing this lets you fill in those parameters without creating more code. Alternatively, you can define parameters with the `PARAMETER` statement and then use the parameters in your prepared statements. The syntax is

```
PARAMETER : SomeParam
```

This is useful if you prefer dealing with names instead of ordinals.

Now consider using the dynamic parameters with a prepared statement. First, you need the prepared statement that follows. Then, you will need to define the parameters and set the direction.

```
PREPARE My_Stmnt FROM "INSERT INTO WebDB VALUES (?, ?)"

PARAMETER :SiteName
PARAMETER :ServerID
PARAMETER :SiteID
PARAMETER :SiteAddress

ALLOCATE DESCRIPTOR :SiteName
ALLOCATE DESCRIPTOR :ServerID
ALLOCATE DESCRIPTOR :SiteID
ALLOCATE DESCRIPTOR :SiteAddress

SET DESCRIPTOR :SiteName VALUE DATA="Microsoft"
SET DESCRIPTOR :ServerID VALUE DATA="206.157.58.221"
SET DESCRIPTOR :SiteID VALUE DATA=3000""
SET DESCRIPTOR :SiteAddress VALUE DATA="www.microsoft.com"

EXECUTE My_Stmnt USING :SiteName, :ServerID,:SiteID, :SiteAddress
```

Thus, you could use the query again by simply setting the descriptors to different values.



# Using Referential Integrity with SQL

Referential integrity is a nice big word with lots of thought behind it—the thought was to make something very simple sound very complex. Referential integrity is simply the capability to ensure that your tables will not become denormalized. SQL does this through the judicious use of references and constraints.

You have three types of constraints at your disposal, two of which you've already seen: the Table constraint and the Field constraint. The third is the *Domain* constraint, the use of which is dependent on whether or not your data source supports SQL Domains.

A Domain constraint enables your constraints to be specific to a data type, which is what a domain is. By creating Domain constraints, you can enforce accounting rules, timestamp rules, and other type-specific rules that are only available on a Field constraint level unless you're using Domain constraints.

# Using Cursors with SQL

Cursors are a means of fetching data. In SQL, unlike most SQL libraries based on the call level interfaces, you can define your own cursors. If you need to create a calculated result and need that calculation on more than a single row, you might decide to design a cursor for that particular session.

There are two different kinds of cursors: static and dynamic. The static cursor is created with the `DECLARE...CURSOR` statement. The dynamic cursor is created from the `ALLOCATE...CURSOR` and uses a prepared statement for its source.

Designing a static cursor is done by designing your `SELECT` statement and then compiling it into a cursor (which is done when the `DECLARE...CURSOR` statement is executed). The syntax is

```
DECLARE Cursor_Name [INSENSITIVE][SCROLL] CURSOR FOR <query expression> [ORDER BY
<sorting spec>][FOR {READ ONLY¦UPDATE [OF <columns>]}]
```

An example of creating a cursor using the `DECLARE...CURSOR` statement is

```
DECLARE Cursor_Name SCROLL CURSOR FOR SELECT DISTINCT city, avg(temp),
➥avg(rainfall) FROM SomeTable WHERE avg(rainfall)>=30.5 ORDER BY city FOR READ
➥ONLY

OPEN Cursor_Name

FETCH FIRST FROM Cursor_Name INTO :city, :temp, :rainfall
FETCH NEXT FROM Cursor_Name INTO :city, :temp, :rainfall
...
CLOSE Cursor_Name
```

**CAUTION**

Remember to close a cursor after use, or it will continue to use server resources. Leaving cursors open is basically creating a memory leak on purpose. It will eventually take down the server that you are accessing.

It is a little easier to use a dynamic cursor, and it offers the benefits of using prepared statements and dynamic parameters. To create a dynamic cursor, simply create the prepared statement (which we'll call `sp_prepare`) and allocate the cursor for it:

```
ALLOCATE My_Cursor CURSOR FOR sp_prepare;

OPEN Cursor_Name

FETCH FIRST FROM Cursor_Name INTO :city, :temp, :rainfall
FETCH NEXT FROM Cursor_Name INTO :city, :temp, :rainfall
...
CLOSE Cursor_Name
```

# Controlling Transaction Processing with SQL

Transaction processing is the hallmark of the Database community right now. SQL implements transaction processing by enabling you to use `BEGIN`, `COMMIT`, and `ROLLBACK` to control the transaction process.

- `BEGIN` Begins a SQL transaction.
- `COMMIT` Ends a SQL transaction by committing the changes.
- `ROLLBACK` Ends a SQL transaction by restoring the data to the transaction's initial state.

You are also given control of isolation levels and access modes. These can be set using the `SET TRANSACTION` statement. You can specify two types of access: read-only or read-write. However, there are four isolation levels, and they require some explaining.

Isolation levels in SQL-92 are defined in terms of the events that they allow to take place and how those events affect your transactions. These events are

- *Dirty read* Transaction A modifies a row. Transaction B then reads that row before A performs a `COMMIT`. If A then performs a `ROLLBACK`, B will have read a row that was never committed and that might be considered to never have existed.
- *Non-repeatable read* Transaction A reads a row. Transaction B then modifies or deletes that row and performs a `COMMIT`. If A then attempts to reread the row, it might receive the modified value or discover that the row has been deleted. Thus, the data is different than what was read the first time.
- *Phantom* Transaction A reads the set of rows N that satisfy some <search condition>. Transaction B then executes an INSERT that generates one or more rows that satisfy the <search condition> used by Transaction A. If Transaction A then repeats the initial read with the same <search condition>, it obtains a different collection of rows.

The four isolation levels enable for varying levels of interference from these events:

- *Read Uncommitted isolation level* Permits all three events to occur.
- *Read Committed isolation level* Ensures that you won't get a dirty read, but it enables the other transactions to affect your application.
- *Repeatable Read isolation level* Ensures that the application will be able to assume that no non-repeatable reads occur.
- *Serializable isolation level* Enables your applications to assume that none of these events will occur. If the transaction is left at defaults, an isolation level of Serializable will be chosen.



The other isolation levels are relatively self-explanatory, but Serializable is not. Serializable means that the multiple concurrent SQL statements that execute on a server are guaranteed to act like a set of SQL statements that execute one at a time.

Dealing with schema data is somewhat different than dealing with normal transactions (unless you need to modify the schema within a transaction). All changes that you make to the schema within the same session are seen by your transaction. They are also seen by those transactions with a Read Uncommitted isolation level. The actions taken against the schema to support normal statement execution are deemed to be at an isolation level of Serializable. This means that when someone changes the schema while you are inserting a column of data with referential constraints on the column, the automatic checking of the constraints will not be affected.

If the data source detects an inability to guarantee two or more Serializable transactions, the data source might throw an exception and the transactions roll back implicitly. This is dependent on the implementation of the SQL language on the data source. The data source might also implicitly roll back your transactions when it encounters fatal errors.

An example of setting up the transaction environment is

```
SET TRANSACTION
ISOLATION LEVEL READ UNCOMMITTED
READ WRITE
DIAGNOSTICS SIZE 10
```

# Using the New Schema Definitions

SQL-92 provides a new capability for database administrators: You can now manipulate and change the schema definitions within SQL. Information such as in-place constraints, the tables, types of data, references between columns, and domains can be accessed and changed with SQL.

## Creating the Schema

You are already familiar with some of the schema definition statements: the `ALTER TABLE`, `GRANT`, `CREATE VIEW`, and `CREATE TABLE` statements. There are also a few other statements that you might like to know about, the most obvious one being the schema definition itself. The syntax for the `CREATE SCHEMA` is

```
CREATE SCHEMA <schema name clause>
      [DEFAULT CHARACTER SET <character set specification>]
      [ <schema element>... ]
```

The schema name clause is simply the name of the schema and an optional authorization identifier. The schema element can contain any one, or more, of the following:

- Assertion definition
- Character set definition
- Collation definition
- Domain definition
- Grant statement
- Table definition
- Translation definition
- View definition

The Assertion definition functions similarly to the C languages Assert functions. It simply checks that the value of the constraint meets a given condition. You can use these in situations in which the reliability of references and constraints is not ensured. The syntax for the Assertion definition is

```
CREATE ASSERTION <constraint name> CHECK (<search expression>)
```

The `character set` definition simply defines new character sets for use with your schema. This is useful in the emerging multinational environment of the Internet. The syntax for creating a `character set` is

```
CREATE CHARACTER SET <character set name>
        [AS] GET <existing character set name>
      [COLLATE <collation name> ¦ COLLATION FROM <collation source>]
```

The Collation source can be any of these values:

- `COLLATION NAME`
- `DEFAULT`

- DESC (collation name)
- EXTERNAL (external collation name)
- TRANSLATION <Translation name> [THEN COLLATION <collation name>]

SQL enables you to define your own collating schemes with the CREATE COLLATION statement. With this, you can define a standard set of collations to use for the schema and apply them to objects at runtime. The syntax of the CREATE COLLATION statement is

```
CREATE COLLATION <collation name> FOR <character set name>
      FROM <collation source> [NO PAD ¦ PAD SPACE]
```

The Collation source for this statement is the same as the preceding bulleted list.

Next on the list are the Domain definitions. By using Domains, you can logically group the columns of the same type in your schema's tables into a single manageable unit. This enables you to do things not possible on the Table level and prevents you from having to set constraints at the Field level. The syntax is

```
CREATE DOMAIN <domain name> [AS ] <data type> [ DEFAULT <default option> ]
➥[ CONSTRAINT <constraint name>] [COLLATE <collation name> ]
```



The Domain constraint must be created in the same manner as other constraints, and the DEFAULT clause can be one of the following types:

- Literal
- DateTime value function
- USER
- CURRENT_USER
- SESSION_USER
- SYSTEM_USER
- NULL

---

### What Are SQL Domains and How Do They Get Used?

SQL Domains were created to enable a broader scope than normal tables, and for more specialization than SQL views can easily offer. A Domain is nothing more than a grouping of columns from different tables that share a common data type. This unique trait enables the administrator to have specific control of every data type. You can set constraints, enforce rules, and keep the database schema additions consistent by using SQL Domains.

---

There is also an ALTER DOMAIN statement, which changes the attributes of an existing domain or drops it. Its syntax is

```
ALTER DOMAIN <domain name> < action>
Where <action> can be setting the defaults, dropping the domain, adding
➥constraints, and dropping constraints.
```

The last unfamiliar definition is the TRANSLATION definition statement, which defines the character set translations from one character set to another. The syntax is

```
CREATE TRANSLATION <translation name> FOR <character set name>
        TO <character set name> FROM <translation source>
```

The Translation source can be

- Character set name
- EXTERNAL("Some character set name")
- IDENTITY: means nothing will be done to the characters

There are several other statements you should be familiar with if you are going to be using the schema definitions, besides the new connection and session statements, which as a user of ODBC, you won't need. The only schema-based statement that you haven't seen is the DROP statement. Its syntax is

```
DROP <Object Name>
```

This statement effectively deletes references to the object.

## Managing Security in Your Schema

From protecting yourself from the competition to protecting yourself from your own employees, security is a hot issue. This is very true regarding your data as well. SQL-92 provides permissions management with the GRANT statement. By using the GRANT statement, you can set security privileges on both operations and objects. The syntax of the GRANT statement is

```
GRANT <privileges> ON <object name> TO <grantee> [ { <comma> <grantee> }... ]
➥[ WITH GRANT OPTION ]
```

You can set privileges for actions on tables, domains, collations, character sets, and translations. The types of privileges you can set are listed in Table 4.6.

**Table 4.6 Privileges that You Can Set on SQL Actions**

| Privilege | Description |
|---|---|
| INSERT | The capability to use the INSERT statement; you can also specify a column list. |
| UPDATE | The capability to use the UPDATE statement; you can also specify a column list. |
| DELETE | The capability to use the DELETE statement. |
| SELECT | The capability to use the SELECT statement. |
| REFERENCES | The capability to set and use REFERENCES. |
| USAGE | The capability to use an object, such as the schema views. |

You can revoke a privilege with the `REVOKE` statement:

```
REVOKE [ GRANT OPTION FOR ] <privileges> ON <object name> FROM <grantee> [ {
➥<comma> <grantee> }... ] <drop behavior>
```

# SQL3—A Glimpse into an Evolving Standard

SQL-92 was developed to add the capability to maintain and use the informational schema effectively. With the growth of object-oriented programming and data design, however, the next SQL standard needed to address these concerns and to help guide the industry's future path.

The SQL language has been broken into several components for the next version, which is known as SQL3. These components are

- *Encompassing Transactions* Supports the X/Open XA interface
- *Framework* A non-technical overview of the proposed standard
- *Foundation* Includes abstract data types and Object SQL
- *Language Bindings* Specifies how SQL3 maps data types and objects to and from native SQL
- *Persistent SQL Modules* Defines a method for optimizing SQL procedures executing against multiple servers
- *Remote Database Access* SQL companion standard for accessing remote databases
- *SQL Call Level Interface* Provides interfaces for binding to SQL



**ON THE WEB**

For a much more thorough introduction into SQL3 and a copy of the SQL3 specifications, contact ANSI at

**http://www.ansi.org**

## SQL3 Framework—Part 1

The SQL Framework is a non-technical document describing the various parts of SQL3. This document contains references to other standards affected by SQL3, definitions and notations of SQL3, and concepts defined by SQL3.

## SQL3 Foundations—Part 2

The SQL Foundations document holds most of the new functionality of SQL3. This portion of the standard is where the language concepts and terminology, as well as its uses, are specified.

## SQL3 Call Level Interface—Part 3

The Call Level Interface is an application programming interface enabling access to the SQL language without embedding SQL into the application. The Call Level Interface contains several functions for an application to use. These functions fall into five general categories:

- Allocating resources
- Handling connection control to the SQL server
- Executing SQL statements
- Gathering diagnostic information
- Controlling transaction termination

## SQL3 Persistent SQL Modules—Part 4

The Persistent SQL Modules document (part 4 of the SQL3 standard) specifies the syntax and the semantics for declaring and maintaining database language procedures and executing these procedures from standard programming languages. The specifications for the following procedures are included with this document:

- Flow of control statements and behavior
- Declarations of local cursors
- Declarations of local variables
- Declarations of local temporary tables
- Definitions for the tables in the Information Schema, describing persistent SQL modules

## SQL3 Language Bindings—Part 5

This part of the SQL3 standard simply defines the syntax and mechanisms used to embed SQL into existing programming languages, which includes specifications on how the data type conversions and object conversions are accomplished. Handling of dynamic SQL statements within embedded SQL is also discussed.

# From Here...

Now that you've been through a crash course in SQL, you'll discover how to use the SQL language in the next three chapters. Beginning with a foundation in ODBC, you will learn to use Microsoft's two implementations of data access with Visual J++, Data Access Objects, and Remote Data Objects.

- Chapter 5, "ODBC," leads you through the Open Database Connectivity architecture and its APIs.
- Chapter 6, "Data Access Objects," explains how you can use Data Access Objects to access more than just Microsoft Jet databases.
- Chapter 7, "Remote Data Objects," shows you how to use the power and speed of Remote Data Objects to access ODBC data sources.
- Chapter 10 "Database Development with Microsoft Visual InterDev," explains how Microsoft's Visual InterDev can shorten the product lifecycle and increase productivity.
- Chapter 12, "IIS Internet Database Connector," explores building database applications with two text files and a little SQL.

CHAPTER 5

# ODBC

**Exploring ODBC**

Discover some of the architecture that ODBC encompasses.

**Learning about cursors**

Learn what a cursor is and how cursors can be used to optimize your applications.

**Exploring ODBC conformance levels**

Discover what your solution calls for in this detailed explanation of ODBC conformance levels.

In every part of our industry, there has long been a search for a standard set of APIs to code to, and database programming is no exception. For years, database developers recompiled whenever the customer decided to upgrade the database behind the application. Now, there is common ground from which you can design an application that achieves cross-platform support for the backend.

ODBC is part of Microsoft's Windows Open Services Architecture. Based on the X\Open Call Level Interface standards, ODBC is designed to provide seamless access to multiple backend database providers and to ease the burden on you. This standard has become one of Microsoft's better achievements. With ODBC 2.5 widely available and ODBC 3.0 recently released, the interface appears to be gathering a good following among the relational database vendors, although support from vendors of object-oriented and multidimensional models is somewhat lacking.

The driving force behind the success of ODBC is the architecture. Microsoft created an extensible client/server architecture, consisting of the ODBC API, the Driver Manager, the DBMS driver, and the data source itself. This architecture enables DBMS vendors to focus on creating a driver without worrying about the entire path to the application. The real benefit, of course, is for developers, who no longer need to rewrite when the database needs to be upsized. Figure 5.1 gives a simplified view of the ODBC architecture. ■

**FIG. 5.1**
The ODBC architecture is based on the client/server model and is presented to the developer as a set of function level interfaces.

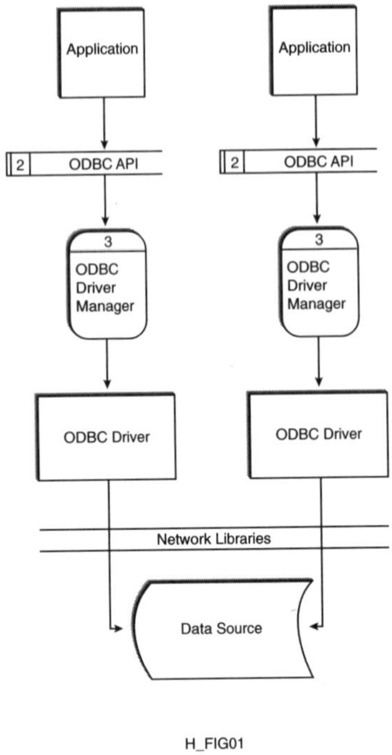


# Exploring ODBC

As mentioned previously, ODBC is essentially a client/server architecture. The ODBC interface, or API, is the part closest to your application. Calls through the API from your application cause the Driver Manager to load and unload the drivers and act as a mediator for responses to the calls from the application. The DBMS driver is responsible for processing these API calls, converting them to the appropriate dialect of SQL and interpreting the results passed back from the data source. Two other pieces also fit into this puzzle, your application and the database that is actually being used.

## The ODBC Administrator

The ODBC administrator is the area with which most end users deal, unless you are kind enough to register your data source for them. Installing the administrator and setting up data sources can be perplexing to someone who has no experience with them, so the following takes you step-by-step through the process of setting up a data source, describing the buttons and features along the way.

Installing the ODBC administrator is simple—run setup. ODBC setup prompts you for the information that it needs, such as the drivers that you want to install, and enables you to set up any data sources for the drivers that are to be installed. Figure 5.2 shows the Data Source Administrator after you set it up.

**FIG. 5.2**
The ODBC 32 Bit Administrator is a convenient method of registering and tracking data sources without resorting to code.

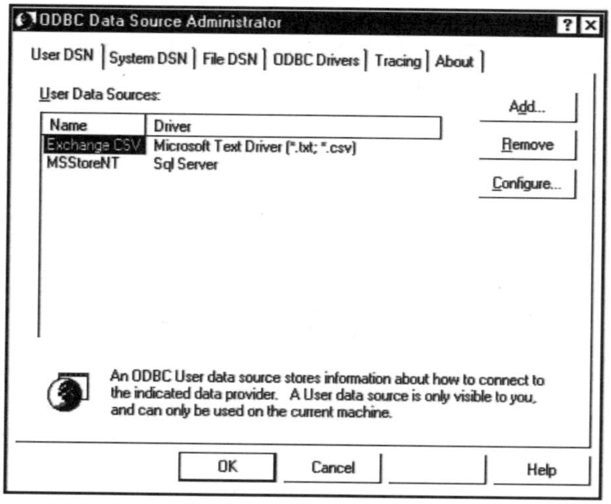


The installed data sources are seen under three different tabs—User DSN (Data Source Name), System DSN, and File DSN. The only difference between the User and System DSNs are the way in which the data source is treated when installed under these tabs. For example, whereas a User DSN is visible only to the user who created it, a System DSN can be visible to any user on the machine, including NT services. Both User and System DSNs are referred to as machine data sources. A File DSN, on the other hand, is not registered to any one user or machine. It is simply the connection information to a machine data source. You can create a File DSN and share it on the network to enable others to use the same data source. Table 5.1 describes each of the DSNs and what they are used for.

**Table 5.1 ODBC Data Source Types**

| Type | When to use |
|---|---|
| Machine—User | Use for individual projects, such as your personal contact database. |
| Machine—System | Create a system data source name when you want everyone with an account on this computer to be able to use the data source. |
| File | Enables multiple users to use the same data source; streamlines the connection process by enabling `SQLDriverConnect` to specify the File DSN for connection strings. |

To create a data source, decide what type of data source you want, as shown in Figure 5.3. The first thing you must provide is the driver type for your data source, which, in this example, is Microsoft Access.

**FIG. 5.3**
Choose a driver for your data source.

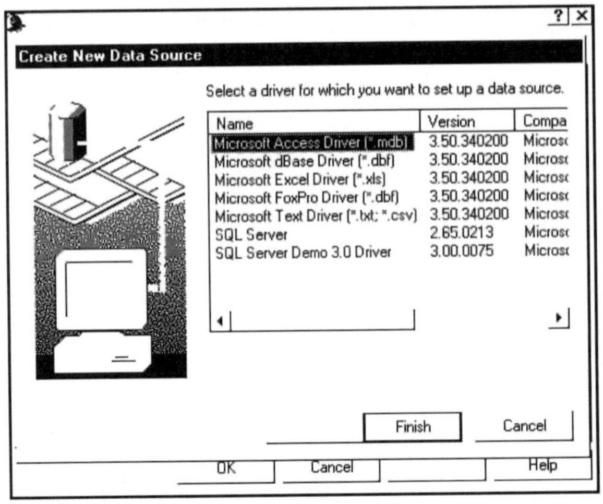


After you've decided which driver to use, a screen appears in which you can configure data source options such as the name, comments, and several other options that depend on the driver that you've chosen (see Figure 5.4). In our example, you can perform database operations and use the advanced features specific to Microsoft Access.

**FIG. 5.4**
Configure your data source.

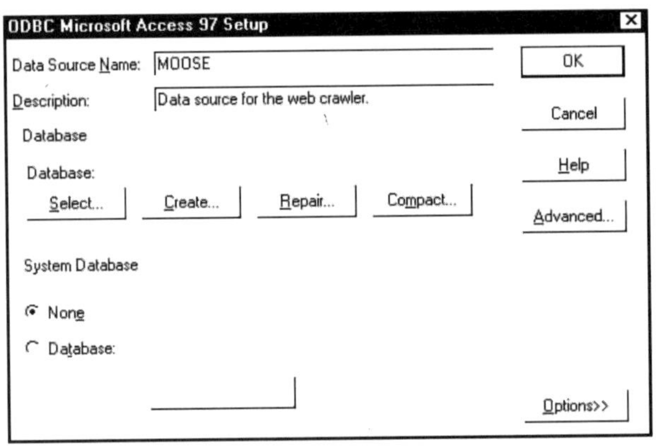


After you have given your DSN a name and have added some comments, you need to either create a database or choose an existing one (see Figure 5.5).

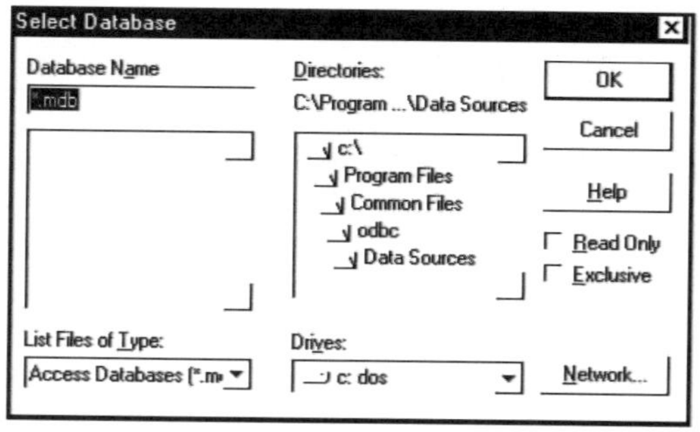


**FIG. 5.5**
When selecting a database, some drivers (such as the Microsoft Access driver) enable you to create an empty database instead of choosing an existing one.

After you've chosen the target database for your data source, you can specify any of the options available to you. Because the driver chosen is Microsoft Access, you are presented with several options, including whether or not to use a system database. Choose the Options button, and you will be presented with more configuration options. For this example, we've set the default Page Timeout to 15 minutes (see Figure 5.6).

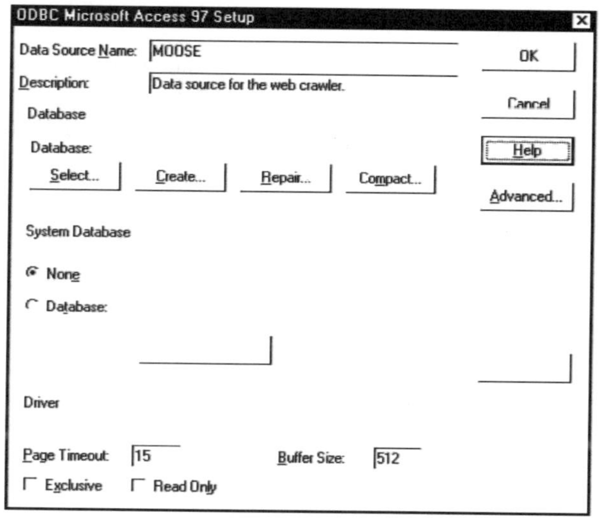


**FIG. 5.6**
Options for the data source are dependent on the database driver that you've chosen to implement.

The advanced options enable you to set even more details, such as the default directory. An example of this is shown in Figure 5.7.

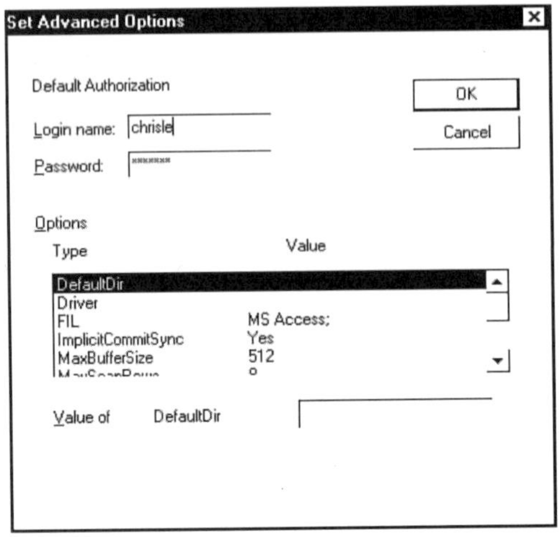


**FIG 5.7**
Advanced options for a data source offer the opportunity to fine-tune the driver to this particular implementation.

Depending on the type of driver you are using, the options for the data source will change. The default text driver, shown in Figure 5.8, illustrates this. You can see that compared to the Microsoft Access driver, this particular text driver has somewhat limited functionality.

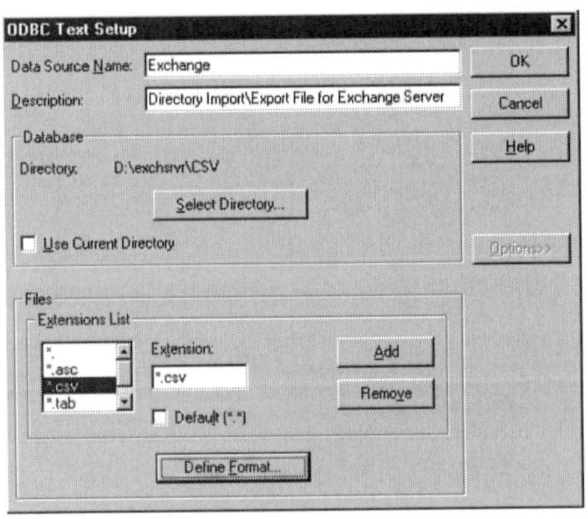


**FIG. 5.8**
The ODBC default text driver setup is incredibly simple when compared to the configurations of most other drivers. The only options you are allowed to choose are the default extension and the default directory.

The default text driver is fairly simple: You can specify a data source name, some comments, and the default directory. The only options available are deciding what file types this driver will use. Now take a look at the SQL Server data source in Figure 5.9, which exhibits quite a difference from the default text driver. You now have several tabs of configuration information, including network connection information and the choice of a backup server.

**FIG. 5.9**
SQL Server Demo driver allows options for login information, network transport, fallback servers, default databases, and many other interesting options.

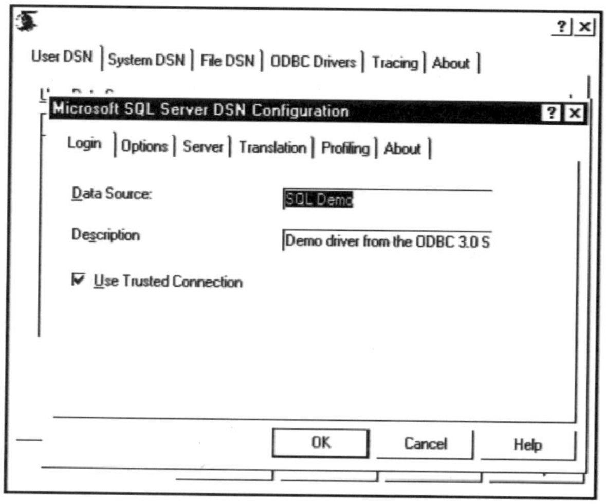


Because the setup is quite complex, ODBC has functions that enable you to automatically register and configure data sources and drivers. These functions, called `ConfigDriver` and `ConfigDSN`, enable you to create, delete, or modify the settings for your driver or data source.

You're probably also wondering how you can support all of these different drivers if they do not have the same options. ODBC has defined sets for functions to query information about the driver, the data source, and the SQL support, as covered in the following section.



## ODBC API

The ODBC API is implemented in many ways: As a Visual J++ programmer, you will usually use the RDO or DAO interface. This does not mean, however, that you can't write your own custom DLL for ODBC functions. In C++, you have many alternatives for accessing ODBC, from direct calls to the Driver Manager to indirect calls into the ODBC DLL. Though Visual J++ doesn't enable you to make direct calls to the ODBC Driver Manager, by using the Remote Data Object interface or the Data Access Objects exposed through the Microsoft Jet database engine, you still have much of the same functionality.

There are sixty different functions with hundreds of calling conventions in the ODBC 3.0 API, so covering all of them is beyond the scope of this book. However, we will examine what a typical C++ application does when accessing a database, the basic idea of which is illustrated in Figure 5.10.

## ON THE WEB

If you would like more information on the ODBC API, check out the ODBC 3.0 SDK, the Microsoft Developer Network, or the Platform SDK documentation. All of these (and more) can be found on the Microsoft Site Builder Network Web site:

**(http://www.microsoft.com/intdev/default.htm)**

**FIG. 5.10**
This is the logical flow of an ODBC application, illustrating what is actually happening in each step.

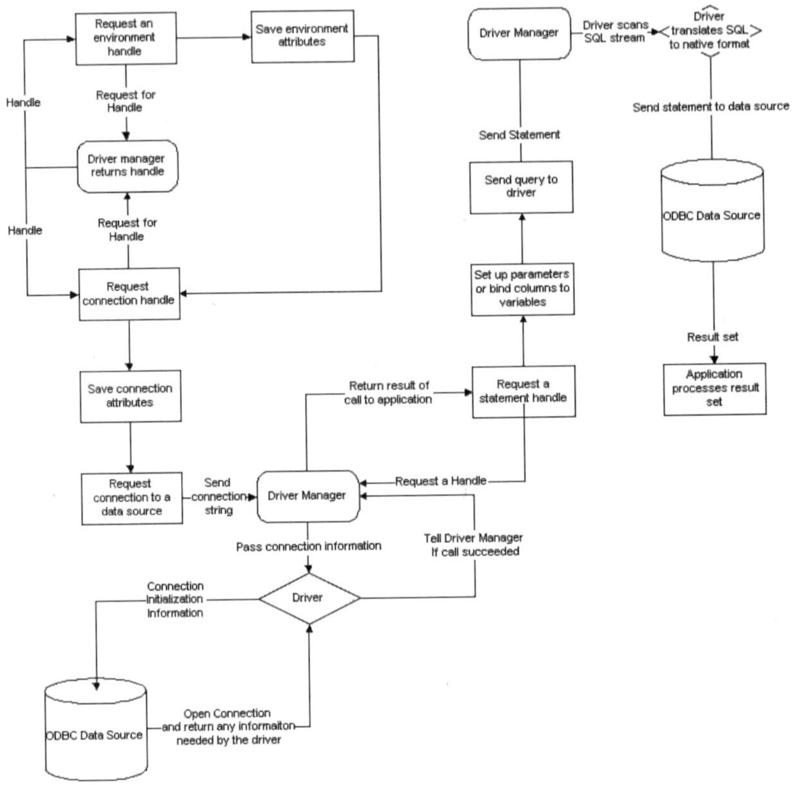


Notice that the Driver Manager's role in this process is mainly secretarial, as follows:

1. The application allocates the memory for the ODBC environment and connection information (via `SQLAllocHandle`) and then requests the connection.
2. The Driver Manager receives the request (actually a `SQLDriverConnect` call) and reads the configuration information from the registry to obtain the information specific to the data source named in the request.
3. As soon as the Driver Manager finds the driver (a DLL), the driver is loaded into memory; if the driver is already in memory, the Driver Manager increases the reference count for the driver. During the initialization, the driver allocates memory for the ODBC handle and environment information.

4. The Driver Manager calls the entry point in the driver for the connection routine. As shown in Figure 5.10, the actual routine that the Driver Manager calls displays a dialog box for more information, such as login ID and password.
5. The Driver Manager then opens a connection to the data source. You will usually see the driver initialize connection-specific data at this point. The actual data that the DBMS is queried for varies among vendors.

When a connection is established, control is returned to your application. To determine whether or not the call succeeded, you can verify the result of the connection attempt by checking the error returned (which should be `SQL_SUCCESS_WITH_INFO`) by using the `SQLError` function.

After the connection is established successfully, you can begin using the data source. Before plunging headfirst into SQL statements, however, it is a good idea to check the Driver Manager's capabilities by calling `SQLGetInfo`. You can find out what types of joins are supported, if asynchronous execution is available, as well as approximately 30 other pieces of information from the driver and data source. By using the information returned, you can tailor your application to take advantage of whatever enhanced features are present.

Not only can you decipher the capabilities of the driver, but you also can gain access to the metadata of the data source. Information such as the number of columns and the type of data held in each one can be gleaned by using the `SQLGetTypeInfo` function. This is a very useful function when writing applications that you expect to be used against several different vendors' database engines.

After the connection is established, you have as much information as you can possibly want about the driver and the data source. The application can execute SQL queries or stored procedures against the data source. Sending a simple SQL statement, as in Figure 5.10, is accomplished by using `SQLExecDirect`. The `SQLExecDirect` function is fine for ad hoc queries or queries in which setting up the prepared statement would result in poorer response times.



For statements that will be executed several times, however, the prepared statement is the best method of execution, even if the parameters change for the statement. Simply call the `SQLPrepare` function to set up the access plan on the server, and use the `SQLExecute` function to execute the query. Using prepared statements means that the SQL statement is not sent multiple times, and the access plan built when `SQLPrepare` is called is reused for each call to `SQLExecute`. The only datum that actually goes across the wire during the `SQLExecute` call is a reference to the access plan generated in the call to `SQLPrepare`.

Regardless of the method you use to send the query to the data source, the data must still be "fetched" back. Although for a simple application the `SQLGetData` function call that loops through the entire result set can suffice, there are more efficient ways to do this. By using a process called binding, the application can eliminate the need to call the `SQLGetData` function in a loop. Binding refers to the process of associating variables to the columns of the result set by using the `SQLBindCol` function, after which you can use the `SQLFetch` function to loop through all rows of the result set, storing the values in the bound variables as you go.

When you finish with the data source, free all of your handles and disconnect from the data source. This procedure is usually much simpler than using database-specific libraries and will work with any database that supports ODBC. Listing 5.1 is a short example of the C++ code that reads from a SQL Server, using the results of the query to create e-mail messages. This example is similar to any ODBC C++ application if it were stripped to the bare bones. In Chapter 6, “Data Access Objects,” and Chapter 7, “Remote Data Objects,” you get a look at DAO and RDO code in Visual J++. In those chapters, you will see many similarities between raw ODBC function calls and those used by RDO and DAO.

**Listing 5.1 Ex2PCM.CPP—ODBC C++ Example Using a Microsoft Exchange Directory Export File as the Data Source**

```
//Windows specific (of course, isn't C++ always platform specific <g>)

#include <windows.h>
#include <stdio.h>
#include <mapi.h>
#include <sql.h>
#include <sqlext.h>
#include <string.h>

#define     CONNSTR \
       "DSN=CompServ;Server=Compwest"
#define CONNLEN (sizeof(CONNSTR)-1)


int WINAPI WinMain(HINSTANCE d1, HINSTANCE d2, LPSTR d3, int d4)
{
       SQLHENV hEnv       =     0;
       SQLHDBC      hDBC  =     0;
       SQLHSTMT hStmt     =     0;
       UCHAR szConnStr[255];
       char szStmt[255];
       SQLCHAR      szFirstName[30];
       SQLCHAR      szLastName[30];
       SQLCHAR szIdNumber[32];
       SWORD cbConnStr;
       SDWORD       sdwLNLen;
       SDWORD       sdwFNLen;
       SDWORD sdwNative;
       SWORD swMsgLen;

       char buf[255];
       unsigned char szState[6];
       unsigned char szMsg[255];
       int          i;
       RETCODE      rc;
       char szResult[1000];

       LHANDLE lphSession;
       HANDLE       hMAPILib;
       LPMAPILOGON lpfnMAPILogon;
       LPMAPISENDMAIL lpfnMAPISendMail;
```

```
	LPMAPILOGOFF lpfnMAPILogoff;

	MapiRecipDesc recipient =
		{
			0, MAPI_TO, "X400:c=US;a=
;p=Microsoft;o=Quarantine;s=Lester;g=Chris;i=S;", 0, NULL
		};

	MapiMessage message =
	{
		0, "Test", "Hello Mr. Man\n", "IPM.NOTE.Compost", NULL, NULL, 0
➥,NULL, 1,
		&recipient, 0 , NULL
	};

	if(SQLAllocEnv(&hEnv)!=SQL_SUCCESS)
	{
		SQLError(hEnv, hDBC, hStmt, szState, &sdwNative,szMsg,
sizeof(szMsg),&swMsgLen);
		wsprintf(buf, "Error %d performing %s\nSQLState = %s\nSQL message =
%s",rc,"SQLAllocEnv",szState,szMsg);
		MessageBox(NULL,buf,"Error",MB_OK¦MB_ICONSTOP);
		goto Terminate;
	}

	if(SQLAllocConnect(hEnv, &hDBC))
	{
		SQLError(hEnv, hDBC, hStmt, szState, &sdwNative,szMsg,
sizeof(szMsg),&swMsgLen);
		wsprintf(buf, "Error %d performing %s\nSQLState = %s\nSQL message =
%s",rc,"SQLAllocConnect",szState,szMsg);
		MessageBox(NULL,buf,"Error",MB_OK¦MB_ICONSTOP);
		goto Terminate;
	}
	if(SQLDriverConnect(hDBC, NULL,szConnStr, CONNLEN,
➥szConnStr,sizeof(szConnStr), &cbConnStr,

	SQL_DRIVER_NOPROMPT)!=SQL_SUCCESS)
	{
		SQLError(hEnv, hDBC, hStmt, szState, &sdwNative,szMsg,
sizeof(szMsg),&swMsgLen);
		wsprintf(buf, "Error %d performing %s\nSQLState = %s\nSQL message =
%s",rc,"SQLDriverConnect",szState,szMsg);
		MessageBox(NULL,buf,"Error",MB_OK¦MB_ICONSTOP);
		goto Terminate;
	}
	if(SQLAllocStmt(hDBC, &hStmt)!=SQL_SUCCESS)
	{
		SQLError(hEnv, hDBC, hStmt, szState, &sdwNative,szMsg,
sizeof(szMsg),&swMsgLen);
		wsprintf(buf, "Error %d performing %s\nSQLState = %s\nSQL message =
%s",rc,"SQLAllocStmt",szState,szMsg);
		MessageBox(NULL,buf,"Error",MB_OK¦MB_ICONSTOP);
		goto Terminate;
	}
```



*continues*

**Listing 5.1 Continued**

```
      wsprintf(szStmt, "SELECT Employee.FirstName,
➥Employee.LastName,Cases.IdNumber \
                              from Employee, Cases Where Employee.Email =
➥Cases.OwnerEmail AND WHERE \
                              Cases.Status = 'Closed'");

      if(SQLBindCol(hStmt, 1, SQL_C_CHAR,(PTR)szLastName, sizeof(szLastName),
&sdwLNLen)!=SQL_SUCCESS)
      {
            SQLError(hEnv, hDBC, hStmt, szState, &sdwNative,szMsg,
sizeof(szMsg),&swMsgLen);
            wsprintf(buf, "Error %d performing %s\nSQLState = %s\nSQL message =
%s",rc,"SQLBindCol",szState,szMsg);
            MessageBox(NULL,buf,"Error",MB_OK¦MB_ICONSTOP);
            goto Terminate;
      }

      if(SQLBindCol(hStmt, 1, SQL_C_CHAR,(PTR)szFirstName, sizeof(szFirstName),
&sdwFNLen)!=SQL_SUCCESS)
      {
            SQLError(hEnv, hDBC, hStmt, szState, &sdwNative,szMsg,
sizeof(szMsg),&swMsgLen);
            wsprintf(buf, "Error %d performing %s\nSQLState = %s\nSQL message =
%s",rc,"SQLBindCol",szState,szMsg);
            MessageBox(NULL,buf,"Error",MB_OK¦MB_ICONSTOP);
            goto Terminate;
      }

      if(SQLBindCol(hStmt, 1, SQL_C_CHAR,(PTR)szIdNumber, sizeof(szIdNumber),
&sdwLNLen)!=SQL_SUCCESS)

      {
            SQLError(hEnv, hDBC, hStmt, szState, &sdwNative,szMsg,
sizeof(szMsg),&swMsgLen);
            wsprintf(buf, "Error %d performing %s\nSQLState = %s\nSQL message =
%s",rc,"SQLBindCol",szState,szMsg);
            MessageBox(NULL,buf,"Error",MB_OK¦MB_ICONSTOP);
            goto Terminate;
      }

      if(SQLExecute(hStmt)!=SQL_SUCCESS)
      {
            SQLError(hEnv, hDBC, hStmt, szState, &sdwNative,szMsg,
sizeof(szMsg),&swMsgLen);
            wsprintf(buf, "Error %d performing %s\nSQLState = %s\nSQL message =
%s",rc,"SQLExecute",szState,szMsg);
            MessageBox(NULL,buf,"Error",MB_OK¦MB_ICONSTOP);
            goto Terminate;
      }

      for( i=1;(rc = SQLFetch(hStmt)) == SQL_SUCCESS; i++)
      {
            wsprintf(szResult, "Record #%d\nLast Name: %s\nFirst Name:"
```

```
                    " %s\nCase Number: %s", i , szLastName, szFirstName,
➥szIdNumber);
            MessageBox(NULL, szResult, "Data", MB_OK¦MB_ICONSTOP);

            hMAPILib = LoadLibrary("MAPI32.DLL");
            lpfnMAPILogon =
                  (LPMAPILOGON)GetProcAddress(hMAPILib, "MAPILogon");
            lpfnMAPISendMail =
                  (LPMAPISENDMAIL)GetProcAddress(hMAPILib, "MAPISendMail");
            lpfnMAPILogoff =
                  (LPMAPILOGOFF)GetProcAddress(hMAPILib, "MAPILogoff");
            (*lpfnMAPILogon)(0,NULL,NULL,MAPI_LOGON_UI,0, &lphSession);
            (*lpfnMAPISendMail)(lphSession, 0, &message, 0, 0);
            (*lpfnMAPILogoff)(lphSession, 0,0,0);
            printf("Message sent.\n");
      }

      MessageBox(NULL,"Successfully completed.", "Success", MB_OK);

      FreeLibrary(hMAPILib);

Terminate:
      if(hStmt) SQLFreeStmt(hStmt, SQL_CLOSE);
      if(hDBC) SQLDisconnect(hDBC);
      if(hDBC) SQLFreeConnect(hDBC);
      if(hEnv) SQLFreeEnv(hEnv);

      FreeLibrary(hMAPILib);
return (rc);
}
```



The ODBC API consists of over 60 functions, most of which are grouped into specific tasks, such as connecting to a data source or allocating ODBC handles. In the following sections, you receive a useful picture of API by approaching API as though you are designing an application.

**Discovering the Data Source and Driver Capabilities** ODBC provides several functions designed to help application developers take advantage of the full functionality of the driver or to determine whether or not backup data sources exist if the preferred one is inaccessible. Information about the data source is also available, such as the data dictionary information.

Determining the type of driver that you're dealing with can help your application eek out the last bit of performance or take measures if some expected functionality isn't available. For example, if your application depends on being able to alter the schema of the data source and the driver doesn't support it; this would be good to know before you attempt to do so. The `SQLGetInfo` function can return just about everything an application could ask for, including ODBC support level and SQL conformance levels. This function can probably retrieve whatever you are looking for.

`SQLGetInfo` can return hundreds of bits of information about the driver, data source, and the target DBMS. Tables 5.2 and 5.3 describe the types of information you can determine about the driver and data sources from `SQLGetInfo`, beginning with the driver information.

**Table 5.2 Driver Information Available Through SQLGetInfo**

| Flag | Return Value |
|---|---|
| SQL_ACTIVE_ENVIRONMENTS | Maximum number of active environments that the driver can support |
| SQL_ASYNC_MODE | Driver support for Asynchronous Execution |
| SQL_BATCH_ROW_COUNT | Support level for SQLGetRowCount |
| SQL_BATCH_SUPPORT | Driver support for Batches |
| SQL_DATA_SOURCE_NAME | The data source name for this driver |
| SQL_DRIVER_HDBC | The driver's connection handle |
| SQL_DRIVER_HDESC | The driver's descriptor handle |
| SQL_DRIVER_HENV | The driver's environment handle |
| SQL_DRIVER_HLIB | The handle returned from load library when the Driver Manager called the routine to load the driver |
| SQL_DRIVER_HSTMT | The driver's statement handle |
| SQL_DRIVER_NAME | The driver's file name |
| SQL_DRIVER_ODBC_VER | The driver ODBC version support |
| SQL_DRIVER_VER | The driver version |
| SQL_DYNAMIC_CURSOR_ATTRIBUTES1 | Returns the first subset of the features in the driver's dynamic cursor library |
| SQL_DYNAMIC_CURSOR_ATTRIBUTES2 | Returns the second subset |
| SQL_FILE_USAGE | The way that the single tier driver treats files: as a file, catalog, or a table |
| SQL_FORWARD_ONLY_CURSOR_ATTRIBUTES1 | First subset of features available in the driver's forward-only cursor, such as concurrency and locking attributes |
| SQL_FORWARD_ONLY_CURSOR_ATTRIBUTES2 | Returns the second subset |
| SQL_GETDATA_EXTENSIONS | Bitmask telling you the features available when using SQLGetData with this driver |
| SQL_INFO_SCHEMA_VIEWS | Bitmask returning the views supported in the informational schema, such as the character sets available |

| Flag | Return Value |
|---|---|
| SQL_KEYSET_CURSOR_ATTRIBUTES1 | First subset of features available in the driver's keyset-driven cursor |
| SQL_KEYSET_CURSOR_ATTRIBUTES2 | Returns the second subset |
| SQL_MAX_ASYNC_CONCURRENT_STATEMENTS | Maximum number of asynchronous statements that can execute simultaneously |
| SQL_MAX_CONCURRENT_ACTIVITIES | Maximum number of statements supported for a single connection |
| SQL_MAX_DRIVER_CONNECTIONS | Maximum number of connections a driver can support |
| SQL_ODBC_INTERFACE_CONFORMANCE | Integer returning the level of ODBC conformance |
| SQL_ODBC_STANDARD_CLI_CONFORMANCE | Denotes whether the driver conforms to XOPEN CLI 1 or ISO92 CLI |
| SQL_ODBC_VER | ODBC version of the Driver Manager |
| SQL_PARAM_ARRAY_ROW_COUNTS | Denotes whether or not row counts are available for each parameter in a parameterized query |
| SQL_PARAM_ARRAY_SELECTS | Availability of result sets when using parameterized execution |
| SQL_ROW_UPDATES | Detects any updates made to a row since the row was last fetched |
| SQL_SEARCH_PATTERN_ESCAPE | The escape character, permitting the use of pattern matching underscore (_) and percent sign (%) in search patterns |
| SQL_SERVER_NAME | A character string containing the server name used in the `SQLConnect`, `SQLDriverConnect`, or `SQLBrowseConnect` call |
| SQL_STATIC_CURSOR_ATTRIBUTES1 | The first feature subset available in the driver's static cursor |
| SQL_STATIC_CURSOR_ATTRIBUTES2 | Flag returning the second subset |

The data source also contains a great deal of information, as shown in Table 5.3, that can help you decide whether or not to use specific features that you know exist in some, but not all, of your clients' environments.

**Table 5.3 Data Source Information Available with SQLGetInfo**

| Flag | Return Value |
|---|---|
| SQL_ACCESSIBLE_PROCEDURES | Denotes whether or not you can execute the procedures returned by SQLProcedures |
| SQL_ACCESSIBLE_TABLES | Denotes whether or not you have SELECT permissions on all tables |
| SQL_BOOKMARK_PERSISTENCE | Bitmask identifying operations where bookmarks persist |
| SQL_CATALOG_TERM | String representing the term used for "catalog" |
| SQL_COLLATION_SEQ | The name of the collation sequence |
| SQL_CONCAT_NULL_BEHAVIOR | Denotes how the data source handles the concatenation of NULL values in character columns with non-NULL values in character columns |
| SQL_CURSOR_COMMIT_BEHAVIOR | Indicates how a COMMIT operation affects cursors and prepared statements in the data source |
| SQL_CURSOR_ROLLBACK_BEHAVIOR | Indicates how a ROLLBACK operation affects cursors and prepared statements in the data source |
| SQL_CURSOR_SENSITIVITY | Indicates how sensitive the cursor is to changes in the result set |
| SQL_DATA_SOURCE_READ_ONLY | Denotes whether or not the data source itself is read-only |
| SQL_DEFAULT_TXN_ISOLATION | An integer representing the default transaction isolation level |
| SQL_DESCRIBE_PARAMETER | Denotes whether or not parameters can be described |
| SQL_MULT_RESULT_SETS | Denotes whether or not the data source supports multiple result sets |
| SQL_MULTIPLE_ACTIVE_TXN | Denotes whether or not multiple active transactions are supported |
| SQL_NEED_LONG_DATA_LEN | Denotes whether or not the data source needs to know the length of a long data type before sending |
| SQL_NULL_COLLATION | Specifies where NULL values appear in the result set |
| SQL_PROCEDURE_TERM | Denotes the vendor's name for "procedure" |
| SQL_SCHEMA_TERM | Denotes the vendor's name for the schema |
| SQL_SCROLL_OPTIONS | Bitmask of the scroll options supported by this data source, such as forward-only |

| Flag | Return Value |
|---|---|
| SQL_TABLE_TERM | Denotes the vendor name for a table |
| SQL_TXN_CAPABLE | Denotes what operations transactions can contain and how the data source deals with data definition language within a transaction |
| SQL_TXN_ISOLATION_OPTION | Isolation levels available from the data source |
| SQL_USER_NAME | The username associated with the database |

The information that you can determine about the DBMS is limited to the name, the version, and the database management system name. As you can tell, `SQLGetInfo` can be used in a number of ways to determine information about the driver and the data source. You can also use `SQLGetInfo` to return detailed information about the SQL statements that the driver and data source support, SQL conversion done by the driver, and the limits imposed on the SQL data types. You can even determine the types of scalar functions available to the application.

**Getting a Connection** Connecting to a data source is something that every ODBC application must do. As the sample code in Listing 5.1 shows, an application allocates the environment and connection handles and then opens a connection to the data source. The following list summarizes the steps needed to open an ODBC connection.

1. Call `SQLAllocHandle` with `SQL_HANDLE_ENV` as the first argument for a handle to the ODBC environment.
2. Call `SQLSetEnvAttr` to set the environment attributes given the handle returned in `SQLAllocHandle`.
3. Call `SQLAllocHandle` a second time with `SQL_HANDLE_HDBC` as the first argument to receive a connection handle.
4. Use `SQLSetConnectAttr` to set the attributes for the open connection handle.



As soon as you've set the connection attributes, your application can call one of three connection functions to tell the Driver Manager to open a connection to the data source. The three connection functions are described in Table 5.4.

**Table 5.4 SQL Connection Functions**

| Function | Description |
|---|---|
| SQLConnect | Use this to pass the connection parameters yourself. |
| SQLDriverConnect | This function displays a standard dialog box to connect to a data source. |
| SQLBrowseConnect | Call with information you receive from custom dialogs to connect. |

When deciding which connection function to use, your best bet is `SQLConnect` or `SQLBrowseConnect`, unless you trust your users to always choose the correct data source. The only time that the user might need a choice of data sources would be for database administration functions. Otherwise, you can have a user log on to a database that you aren't set up to handle (of course, you can also check for this before executing any SQL statements).

**Preparing Statements for Execution** There are several things that need to be done before you can execute any operation against a data source. The following summarizes the steps required, including where the optional functions can be used.

1. Allocate the statement handles by using `SQLAllocHandle` with the first parameter set to `SQL_HANDLE _STMT`.
2. (Optional) Call `SQLGetStmnt` or `SQLSetStmnt` to tailor the statement transaction to your needs; for example, specify that you don't want a row to be fetched after positioning the cursor.
3. (Optional) Use `SQLSetDescReq` or `SQLSetDescField` (and their `Get` counterparts) to change or retrieve information about the descriptors for the table.
4. (Optional) Use `SQLBindParameters` to set up variables that will hold the parameters for a parameterized query.
5. (Optional) Create a unique cursor name for positioned updates and deletes by calling `SQLSetCursorName` and using `WHERE CURRENT OF <%Cursor Name%>`.
6. (Optional) Set the cursor options by using `SQLSetScrollOptions`.
7. (Optional) Create a prepared statement by using `SQLPrepare`, which generates an active access plan on the data source; this is advantageous because executing the statement only requires referencing the statement handle, not sending the entire statement across to the data source.

Most of the functions dealing with statement preparation and execution are optional, the only one required being `SQLAllocHandle` to create a handle to the statement. The other functions, however, can change the behavior of the entire statement, cursor, and query. You'll probably find the most useful function to be `SQLPrepare`, which enables you to generate the access plan once on the server and then use it multiple times.

**Executing the Statement** As you can tell, you spend most of your coding time setting up the execution rather than sending the query. To send the SQL statement or execute a stored procedure on the data source, simply use `SQLExecDirect`. To execute a prepared statement, use `SQLExecute`.

Several functions are also available to enable you to obtain information about parameterized statements, such as `SQLNumParams`, which returns the number of parameters in a prepared statement, and `SQLDescribeParam`, which returns a description of the parameters that follow.

- `SQLDescribeParam` Use to determine information about your parameters, such as their data types.
- `SQLNumParams` Call to determine the number of parameters in your parameterized query.

If your application wants to verify the SQL code before execution, use `SQLNativeSql`. This function returns the exact SQL statement the driver would be sending to the data source.

After you've called `SQLExecute` to execute the prepared statement, the function might return `SQL_NEED_DATA`. This is where `SQLParamData` and `SQLPutData come in`. These two functions are used to determine what type of data is needed (`SQLParamData`) and to send the data needed (`SQLPutData`). You can take advantage of lower network bandwidth with these functions by passing incomplete parameters with the statement and waiting for the return of `SQL_NEED_DATA`. Of course, using these functions with a single statement doesn't lessen the network utilization much (if any) from shrinking the amount of data passed each time.

**Result Set Operations** After you've issued a statement to the data source, you must determine the results of your statement. You have a plethora of functions for retrieving results and information about results in ODBC. Most of your metadata can be gained from the result set, and all of the transaction-oriented functions operate off of the result set.

Determining information about the metadata in your result set can help you decide what to do with the results. You can discover many things about your result set, such as the number and data types of the columns returned or the number of rows in the result set. Consider what an application can do with the information gleaned from the functions that follow:

- `SQLColAttribute` Retrieves a single field descriptor of a column, such as whether or not the column is auto-incrementing
- `SQLDescribeCol` Gives you information such as the column name, data type, column size, number of decimal digits, and whether or not the column can contain null values
- `SQLGetDiagField` Returns a single field of additional diagnostic information
- `SQLGetDiagRec` Returns several fields of additional diagnostic information
- `SQLMoreResults` Determines whether or not there are more result sets available and, if so, initializes processing for the next result set
- `SQLNumResultCols` Returns the number of columns in the result set
- `SQLRowCount` Gives you the row count affected by an insert, update, or delete



The functions retrieving information from the columns of result sets can be very useful for setting up to receive the result set and determining what to do with it after your application retrieves it. Most can be called either before or after you've executed the SQL statement. However, with functions dependent on the result set returning (`SQLMoreResulst`, `SQLNumResultCols`, and `SQLRowCount`) you would not call on these functions until you've either called `SQLExecDirect` or `SQLPrepare` to set up the statement.

Now that you are able to determine information about the result set, take a look at the functions that manipulate result sets. The functions that follow are listed in the order that you would call them to provide you with a clear picture of how these functions are meant to be used.

1. Call `SQLBindCol` to use row-wise or column-wise binding of the result set data to a set of variables, eliminating the need for multiple `SQLGetData` calls.

2. Call `SQLGetData` to return part or all of a column in a result set. This is the only function that can break up a single column of data into several pieces, easing the retrieval of large amounts of data. If you're using bound columns, skip to Step 3.
3. Call `SQLFetch` to scroll forward through the result set, or use `SQLFetchScroll` to return rows with which you can scroll both directions through the result set. Both functions place the data into the variables specified in the `SQLBindCol` calls if available; otherwise use `SQLGetData` to retrieve each row.
4. Use `SQLSetPos` to move the cursor within the rowset returned by `SQLFetch` or `SQLFetchScroll`. After this is set, you can then perform positioned updates, inserts, or deletes. When you change the data of a result set, be aware that the rowset contents won't change until you refresh the data by fetching it again; the attributes, however, will change to reflect the deleted items.
5. Create batch deletions, updates, or inserts by using bookmarks with `SQLBulkOperations`.

**Closing the Transaction** As soon as you've done everything you wanted to do with the transaction, it's time to close it down and free all the handles that you've been allocated. These functions are fairly simple and are as follows:

1. Use `SQLCancel` to cancel a SQL statement before it is completed.
2. Use `SQLEndTran` to commit or roll back your transaction.
3. Close any cursors open on your statements by calling `SQLCloseCursor`.
4. Close any open statement handles and processing, discarding all results and freeing the resources associated with the handle by calling `SQLFreeStmt`.
5. Release the connection by using `SQLDisconnect`.
6. Free the connection handle and its associated resources by calling `SQLFreeHandle`.

## The Driver Manager

The Driver Manager is responsible for passing the ODBC calls made by the applications through to the driver. This component also tracks which drivers are loaded in memory, which applications are using those drivers, and when to load and unload the driver. This rather complicated task used to be done by the application—consider the array complexity of loading multiple DLLs with duplicate function names and referencing those with multiple connections. Fortunately, you don't have to manage this on your own.

**NOTE** So, what if you do have to manage these by yourself? Well, managing the pointer table of a single DLL's function entry points (and names) wouldn't be so bad. Although more complex, managing several could be done by setting up tables for each and mapping those tables to another root table for convenience. The real benefit is not being forced to code to a single vendor/single version. You have a choice.

The Driver Manager is also responsible for error checking and verification of the calling order of function parameters before passing the call through to the driver. It does not check the driver's capability to complete the request, however; error checking of that type is done at the driver level.

## DBMS Drivers

The driver is the most complex portion of the ODBC triangle and is responsible for almost everything associated with accessing the database engine. All drivers perform the conversion of SQL to a native form or API. Every driver supports the "Core" level ODBC and is highly influenced (by their customer base) to write a driver that conforms, at the least, to "Minimum" SQL standards (covered in Chapter 4, "The SQL Standard: A Language for Data Access"). These support levels at least guarantee that your application can expect to perform basic database functions using any driver.

In general, drivers conform to the client/server model, and either two or three components are involved in the process of connecting and querying the DBMS (Database Management System). The lone exceptions are the text drivers and some ISAM (Indexed Sequential Access Method) drivers, which are meant to be used locally. In these cases, the driver usually is the DBMS. The other two cases are both client/server models, both two-tier and three-tier. Figure 5.11 shows the architecture of the three models.

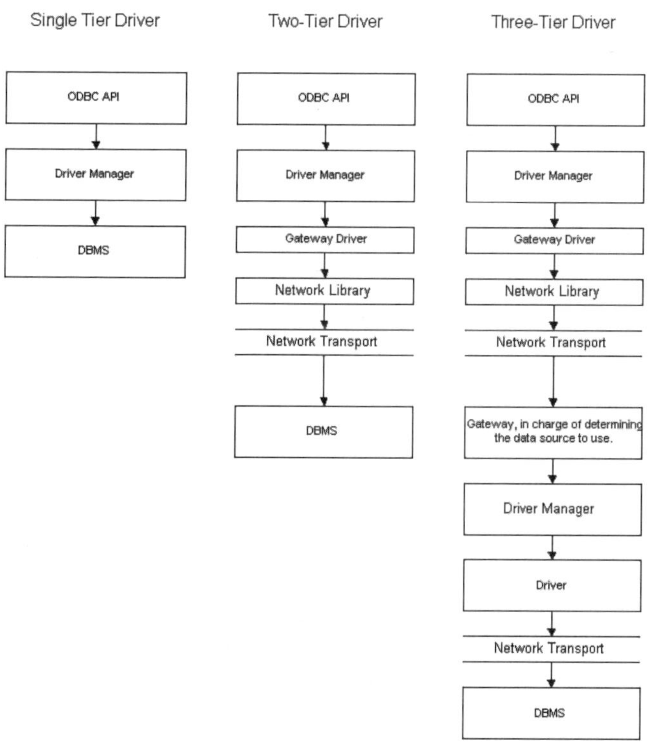


**FIG. 5.11**
ODBC driver architectures vary in form, but all follow the client/server implementation.

## Data Sources

Data sources are the reason you went to the trouble of learning ODBC in the first place. The data source is the DBMS. ODBC's Driver Manager gives the data source a name, which is mapped back to the real database behind the DSN. A data source can be nearly anything: text data sources, Excel spreadsheets, the registry; you can turn anything that can hold data into a data source. You might have to develop the driver, but it can be done.

The data source is responsible for processing the commands that the driver passes to it and for returning the result. Although that might sound simple, recall that the data source is the place in which your functions acquire real responsibilities such as record locking, indexing, multi-user access, security, and many other variables that go into a modern database management system.

# Cursors

A cursor is simply the pointer to the current record in a result set, much like the cursor in a word processing program. Why, then, are there so many different types of cursors? Well, the function of each cursor varies, as follows:

- A static cursor, which ODBC refers to as a snapshot, is a cursor that cannot be moved, very much like a photograph.
- A scrolling cursor works similarly to the way in which you would want to handle data—by moving through it. Of the two types of scrolling cursors, the forward-only cursor is perhaps the easiest to implement. As its name suggests, this cursor simply scrolls forward through a result set. There are other types of scrollable cursors, but you should think of them simply as being capable of moving through a result set.
- A scrollable, updateable cursor updates records as you move through them. This is useful, for you wouldn't be able to write very good multi-user applications without it.

## Understanding ODBC Cursors

The ODBC cursor library provides each one of the generic cursors discussed in the previous section. Although the names are somewhat different, and in the case of the dynamic cursors, the methods of scrolling and result set retrieval vary, the basic concept is based on static and scrolling cursors.

**Static** The static cursor is exactly what you think it is, static. ODBC provides the static cursor for viewing data when the user does not require immediate updates, such as when viewing an end-of-the-month report. After the data is retrieved, the data becomes outdated as soon as it is retrieved and the cursor must be closed and reopened to refresh the result set. A practical application of static cursors would involve a retail environment in which the data does not need to be updated frequently. Instead, you can cache the information until the next cycle is passed.

When implementing a static cursor, though, be aware that some databases—depending on the locking level—will hold open a lock on a result set until the last row is fetched. As a result, a user can go for a cup of coffee and inadvertently lock out every other user. To avoid this problem, use the client/server model when designing the application. Keep the ODBC code in the server and feed the clients data that you refresh from the server periodically. Then you can minimize the amount of time that the records (or pages) remain locked.

**Keyset-Driven** Think of keyset-driven cursors as being able to change the values but not the field of the data returned in your result set. You are able to retrieve rows based on a certain key, but as soon as they are retrieved, your result set is not updated except when you insert information. If someone else inserts, deletes, or alters a record, the keyset-driven cursor will not reflect this change and must be closed and reopened for the new data to be seen.

**Dynamic** With a dynamic cursor, data is presented as it exists in the database and is most effective in places in which real-time evaluation of the data is needed. A practical example involves a stock market scenario in which your clients want current information about market fluctuations. The simplest and most convenient method to achieve frequent updates would be to use dynamic cursors. In contrast, continually refreshing a static or keyset-driven cursor would be too much of a performance.

When you look at the result set returned by the dynamic cursor, you should see a reflection of all committed transactions in the database, as well as your own uncommitted transactions. This reflection should also be updated to include changes affecting some of the selection criteria such as Group By or the Where clause (covered in Chapter 4, "The SQL Standard: A Language for Data Access"). Your data might not have changed, but if your selection criteria's value does, you need to know about it.

**Mixed** A mixed keyset-type cursor is a cross between keyset-driven cursors and dynamic cursors. When using this type of cursor, you will see keyset-driven behavior when scrolling through the result sets. When your application scrolls outside of the result set, however, a new keyset is generated and filled with current data, much like a dynamic cursor.



## ODBC Scrolling Functions

ODBC provides two functions to retrieve rows returned from a result set: `SQLFetch` and `SQLExtendedFetch`. `SQLFetch` is used to retrieve result sets from forward-only cursors, and as you might have guessed, `SQLExtendedFetch` retrieves either one or more rows from scrollable cursors.

## Concurrency Control in ODBC

Generally speaking, there are two types of concurrency control: optimistic and *pessimistic* locking. Essentially, optimistic locking means that whatever you write to is not locked until the moment just before you commit the transaction. In contrast, pessimistic locking means that when you attempt any operation on an object, you will attempt to gain exclusive access to the object before the operation proceeds. This prevents other users from accessing the information until you are done with it. If you are updating the same information frequently, better performance will be seen by pessimistically locking the data.

If you don't expect to have concurrent transactions updating the same data, optimistic locking reduces the overhead required to maintain a lock on the data and enables users to access the data up until the moment of the update. Also consider the level of locking provided by the database vendor—you might access one data source in which the database locks data in 2K pages (like Microsoft's SQL Server), and another that allows for cell-level locking. If you're aware of these, you can structure reads and writes to accommodate (or optimize) for them, such as when you're accessing two different data sources with different locking granularities and need to do updates to views that contain both.

**ODBC Concurrency** ODBC has defined a set of concurrency levels that an application can use regardless of the data source involved, although only Level 2 conformance requires anything other than `SQL_CONCUR_READ_ONLY`.

**Transaction Isolation Levels** The data source itself can also enable various transaction isolation levels, which are more inclusive and varied than concurrency controls offered by ODBC. You can determine the isolation levels available in the driver and the data source by using the `SQLGetInfo` function.

Transaction isolation levels indicate how much a particular transaction is affected by three types of events, which are defined as follows:

- *Dirty Reads* This event describes what happens when one transaction is able to read uncommitted data from another transaction. For example, you perform an update but don't issue a commit. Another user's transaction reads from that update, and you roll back the transaction instead of committing it. As a result, the other user has read in data that doesn't exist anymore.
- *Non-repeatable Reads* A non-repeatable read occurs when a transaction reads the same row twice but gets different data each time. This can occur when your transaction reads a row once and then another transaction deletes the row and inserts a new row in the original position. You read the row again, obtaining different data that results in a non-repeatable read.
- *Phantoms* This is simply a row that matches your search criteria but, for some reason, doesn't show up until you refresh the query. This can happen when another transaction performs an update or insert after you issue the query, and the information matches your transaction's search criteria.

The SQL-92 specification defines four transaction isolation levels based on how certain events affect your transactions. The SQL-92 transaction isolation levels are defined as follows:

- *Read Uncommitted* This is level 0. Your application is unprotected from any of the events that can occur.
- *Read Committed* This enables the application to assume that no dirty reads will affect the transaction.
- *Repeatable Read* An application requesting this level of isolation is telling the data source that it expects to be isolated from dirty reads and non-repeatable reads.
- *Serializable* A serializeable transaction isolation level means that none of the events listed previously can affect the state of the transaction.

# ODBC Conformance Levels

All database engines are not built alike—if they were, the ODBC standard would be pointless. The difference in database engines and the competition in the marketplace has created a need for a certain level of guaranteed performance that you can build to and expect any ODBC-compliant database to support. Conformance levels were invented for this reason.

The architects of ODBC felt the need to establish a minimal set of features and to enable extensibility by defining two other levels of extended feature sets. The base level is referred to as the *Core* conformance level, which includes everything deemed necessary by the creators of ODBC to support a database application.

The next level up is the Level 1 conformance level. This level of conformance is the minimum level recommended by Microsoft due to its support of `SQLGetTypeInfo` and its added functionality for retrieving information about the capabilities of the driver itself.

Level 2 conformance provides everything else that the architects of ODBC could think of: scrollable cursors, extended catalog functions, and several other miscellaneous features.

## Core API

The Core API is a set of functions that developers must support when building database drivers. The Core API set has been expanded considerably with the advent of ODBC 3.0. All functionality that was once a part of Level 1 in ODBC 2.0 specification has now been moved into the Core conformance level. The new requirements for Core level support are as follows:

- Allocate and free handles by using `SQLAllocHandle` and `SQLFreeHandle`
- Full use of the `SQLFreeStmt` function
- The capability to use `SQLBindCol` to produce bound result sets
- Handle dynamic parameters with `SQLBindParameter` and `SQLNumParams`, but only in an input direction
- Enable the application to specify a binding offset
- Support for data-at-execution by using `SQLParamData` and `SQLPutData`
- Support for `SQLSetCursorName`, `SQLGetCursorName`, and `SQLCloseCursor`
- Access result set metadata with `SQLColAttribute`, `SQLDescribeCol`, `SQLNumResultCols`, and `SQLRowCount`
- Access the data dictionary by using `SQLColumns`, `SQLGetTypeInfo`, `SQLStatistics`, and `SQLTables`
- Support for `SQLConnect`, `SQLDriverConnect`, `SQLDisconnect`, and `SQLDataSources`
- Support `SQLExecDirect`, `SQLPrepare`, and `SQLExecute` for statement execution
- Enable fetching of one or many rows of a result set in a forward-only direction
- Support for `SQLGetData` to break a column's data into pieces
- Retrieve and set all connection, environment, and statement attributes

- Manipulate descriptor fields
- Retrieve diagnostic information
- Use `SQLGetInfo` and `SQLGetFunctions` to discover information about drivers and data sources
- Find out about any SQL substitutions made by the driver by using `SQLNativeSql`
- Use `SQLEndTran` to commit transactions, although a driver might or might not support transactions
- Use `SQLCancel` to cancel the data-at-execution dialogs and ODBC functions executing in other threads
- Use `SQLSpecialColumns` to get the `SQL_BEST_ROWID` special column handle, used to return the column that uniquely identifies the rowset

The Core Level API doesn't provide for asynchronous execution, or canceling of asynchronous functions through `SQLCancel`. The driver must also provide a way to specify a binding offset.

## Level 1 API

The Level 1 API includes everything defined in the Core API set plus extra functionality designed to enable the use of more powerful database applications. Most databases support the functions listed as follows natively (in other words, through their own specific API sets), and because Level 2 defines the "ultimate" driver, this is the recommended support level for ODBC drivers. The following features are added to the Level 1 API:

- Use scrollable cursors by calling `SQLFetchScroll`
- Asynchronous execution of ODBC functions
- Find the primary key of a table by calling `SQLPrimaryKeys`
- Use stored procedures through the ODBC escape sequence for procedure calls
- Retrieve information on the data dictionary regarding stored procedures by calling `SQLProcedureColumns` and `SQLProcedures`
- Browse the servers available for connection by calling `SQLBrowseConnect`
- Use ODBC functions instead of SQL statements to perform certain database operations
- Call `SQLMoreResults` to return the contents of multiple result sets generated by batches and stored procedures
- Delimit transactions spanning several ODBC functions, with true atomicity, which is the capability to guarantee the result or the return to the state previous of the operation
- Roll back a transaction with `SQLEndTran`

## Level 2 API

The Level 2 API contains the ODBC developer wish list—functions that the best drivers should be able to perform, including better concurrency control, the capability to use the full power of stored procedures, better access to metadata about the data source, and much more. As always, the Level 2 API includes the Core and Level 1 API requirements. The functions included in the Level 2 API are as follows:

- Enable three-part names of database tables and views
- Describe dynamic parameters by calling `SQLDescribeParam`
- Use the input/output parameters and the result values of stored procedures
- Support bookmarks
- Call `SQLColumnPrivileges`, `SQLForeignKeys`, and `SQLTablePrivileges` to access even more of the data dictionary
- Asynchronous execution of ODBC functions for specified individual statements
- The `SQL_ROWVER` row-identifying column to detect changes in the tables by calling `SQLSpecialColumns`
- Use of concurrency types other than read-only
- Enable you to time out logon request and SQL queries
- Change the default isolation level and execute transactions by using a serializable level of isolation

# SQL Conformance Levels in ODBC

SQL conformance levels were designed to provide a basic level of functionality that applications can expect. Although the SQL language is the *de facto* standard in the database industry at this point in time, every vendor supports its own version or subset of the SQL language. No two vendor's database management systems support the exact same SQL, not even Microsoft's own database engines. Therefore, the designers of ODBC felt that a certain level of SQL adherence was necessary in addition to the differing levels of driver support. Those levels are the minimum, core, and extended SQL.



## Minimum SQL

Minimum SQL conformance is the level that provides the least amount of support for SQL while still being functional. Text file drivers and some (not all) ISAM database drivers fall into this category. The actual SQL commands supported in this level are:

- `CREATE TABLE`
- `DROP TABLE`
- `SELECT`
- `INSERT`
- `UPDATE`
- `DELETE`
- `CHAR`, `VARCHAR`, and `LONG VARCHAR` data types

## Core SQL

Core SQL basically grew out of the SQL-92 standard that was evolving at the time that ODBC 1.0 was developed. This is the set of SQL that most DMBS vendors decided to support. You'll notice improved support for data definition, select statements, and several extra data types, as shown in the following list:

- `ALTER TABLE`
- `CREATE INDEX`
- `DROP INDEX`
- `CREATE VIEW`
- `DROP VIEW`
- `GRANT`
- `REVOKE`
- Full functionality of the `SELECT` statement
- `NUMERIC`, `DECIMAL`, `SMALLINT`, `INTEGER`, `FLOAT`, `REAL`, and `DOUBLE PRECISION` data types

## Extended SQL

Extended SQL added ODBC-specific functionality to SQL by specifying that escape characters could be used. This enables ODBC to generalize the many different formats of SQL statements found in different database management systems. This provides cross-platform support for things like the Date/Time functions. The driver developer must scan the SQL statements for the special characters and transform the "escaped" SQL statement into native format.

# From Here...

You have been taken on a journey through ODBC and survived—congratulations. You've seen the architecture of ODBC, the way in which a program would use ODBC, and the depths of the API layer. The purpose of this chapter was to give you the background needed to take on the interfaces Microsoft has opened up with Visual J++ rather than make you learn to deal with ODBC itself. Both Data Access Objects (DAO) and Remote Data Objects (RDO) rely heavily on the ODBC standards, RDO more so than DAO. Knowing what these interfaces cover provides a greater understanding of what you can do with them, and you won't need to spend time learning their basic concepts and terms. Now that you've been immersed in the depths of ODBC, it is time to learn to use this powerful API through Visual J++.

- Chapter 6, "Data Access Objects," explains how to use the Microsoft Data Access objects to perform operations on Jet databases and to harness the new `ODBCDirect` interface now included with DAO 3.5.
- Chapter 7, "Remote Data Objects," covers the Microsoft Remote Data Objects interface, which is directly abstracted from the ODBC J++ interfaces.

CHAPTER 6

# Data Access Objects

**Exploring the history of DAO**

Learn about the origin of Microsoft's Data Access Object interface.

**Examining a primer for Data Access Objects**

Explore an overview of the objects and interfaces available to the Visual J++ programmer.

**Learning about how DAO objects interact**

Take an in-depth look at the objects and collections that make up the Data Access Object interface.

**Exploring ODBC programming with DAO**

Learn to use the power of ODBC through the DAO interface.

**Learning about database replication with DAO**

Discover how to make Jet database replication a reality with DAO.

Data Access Objects have become the most popular of Microsoft's database solutions. This is mainly due to the ease of use and the fact that DAO was the only data access solution for users of the immensely popular Visual Basic language until Microsoft released Visual Basic version 4.0, which included Remote Data Objects, as well.

DAO is used in many different products not only because of its simplicity but also because of the nature of the API. DAO isn't really an API at all, but is instead a set of defined interfaces that map to ODBC function calls. Microsoft wrapped the ODBC calls into a COM object that publishes the set of interfaces that we know as the DAO "object model." Because DAO is a COM object, other vendors are able to exploit that fact, incorporating DAO into their products. ■

# Exploring the History of DAO

Microsoft was actually working on prototypes of the Jet database engine as early as 1988. Although this "engine" was mainly a stopgap measure to cover network administration until SMS (Microsoft Systems Management Server) arrived, the Jet Engine became popular through its inclusion as the relational database engine in Access 1.0. Soon after the Jet Engine's inclusion, DAO version 1.1 was introduced with Visual Basic 3.0 and Access 1.1. With the inclusion of the data definition language to the capabilities of DAO in version 1.1, developers began to see Data Access Objects as a workable, although certainly still limited, interface with which to design.

When version 1.0 of the Jet Engine shipped with Microsoft Visual Basic 2.0, version 0 of the DAO interface was also included, although the interface didn't have an actual name or version number. Using version 0 of DAO was quite limiting for Visual Basic programmers who were trying to access the Jet Engine, because the only access was to ODBC. Even then, programmers were restricted to using forward-only cursors, and many of the advanced features that made ODBC such a rich interface were missing.

Fortunately, with Microsoft Access 1.0, DAO 1.0 was introduced. DAO 1.0 added objects to deal with result sets (snapshot, dynaset, and table), as well as interfaces to the actual tables and queries. Users of Visual Basic were not as lucky, however, at least not until DAO 1.1 was released. With DAO 1.1, Visual Basic users gained the benefit of enhanced data definition language support, as well as the following three objects:

- `Tabledef` *objects* Enables users to view table structures, create fields, perform operations on links, and open a cursor on the table
- `Querydef` *objects* Enables users to store queries in a temporary database to be retrieved later or manipulated
- `Field` *objects* An object representing the column of data

Released with Microsoft Access 2.0, DAO 2.0 extended the idea of objects and added the idea of collections to the hierarchy of objects. In doing so, Microsoft greatly enhanced the DAO interface by including methods and objects, representing almost everything you could do with the Jet database engine.

A version of DAO 2.5, which shipped with the ODBC Drivers Pack 2.0, included better support of ODBC and was intended for use with the ODBC Drivers Pack. Both 16-bit and 32-bit versions were developed.

DAO version 3.0 was shipped with Visual Basic 4.0 32-bit, Visual C++ 4.0, and Microsoft Office 95. Although this version added little in the way of new collections or objects, it was intended to move closer to becoming a stand-alone interface that would be free of Microsoft Access and similar to ODBC in implementation.

This historical background brings us to DAO 3.5, which is in SDK form on Microsoft's Web site and ships with Microsoft Visual Basic 5.0 and Microsoft's Visual C++ 4.0. Microsoft has added several features to DAO 3.5, as shown in in the following list.

- There is now a `SetOption` method for the `DBEngine` object, so you don't have to change individual registry settings on each client.
- Jet 3.5 resolves a previous problem with Netware's 10,000-lock limit by introducing a new registry setting called `MaxLocksPerFile`. By default, this setting will split transactions when 9500 locks have been placed, enabling large rowset operations to complete.
- A new option has been added to the `DBEngine.Idle` method that enables you to refresh Jet's internal cache on demand.
- A new `CommitTrans` method that forces a flush to the disk of the transaction rather than waiting on possible lazy writes from the operating system has been added.
- Implicit transactions are no longer used with SQL data manipulation language statements such as `INSERT`, `UPDATE`, and `DELETE`.
- There are performance improvements due to enhanced caching and locking capabilities when dealing with large amounts of concurrent users.
- More predicates can now be utilized for Rushmore Optimization.
- The new `MaxRecords` property enables the user to specify a maximum number of records to retrieve from an ODBC server, regardless of the size of the result set.
- There is a new property called `FailOnError`, which enables you to specify whether or not you want the entire query sent to the server; this enables you to fail the entire query instead of issuing a partial failure.
- DAO has improved ODBC access with the ODBCDirect interfaces, which no longer loads the Jet Engine to access ODBC directly.

# Learning About a Primer for Data Access Objects

Data Access Objects are all derived from a single root object, the `DBEngine` object. If you're familiar with C++, think of the `DBEngine` object as your DLL entry point. This is the object that you will use as a reference when using other DAO objects and methods.

The DAO object hierarchy isn't very large. In fact, compared to most APIs, it is quite small. Also, as you can see from Figure 6.1, the DAO hierarchy is conceptually fairly simple for such a powerful interface.

When you instance a `DBEngine` object, you can create several different objects from it. These objects (the top level below the `DBEngine` object in Figure 6.1) then expose interfaces to manipulate them with, which we know as methods. The objects can also return new objects (shown beneath them in the graph) to clients of the DAO object.

Notice the redundancy with several of the objects and collections. Organizing the DAO model in this way helps you stay with object-oriented design methods when designing to this interface because the code will be the same when dealing with any collection or any `Field` object. You can move the methods dealing with those objects out into generic classes.

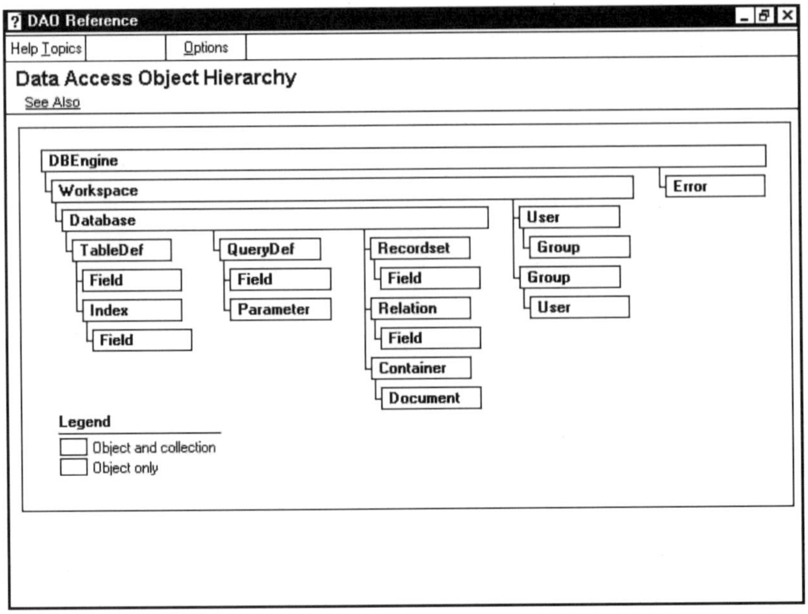


**FIG. 6.1**
The DAO Object hierarchy shown here is actually a class factory.

# The *DBEngine* Object

The first object that you will encounter is the `DBEngine` object, from which all DAO objects are derived. Although there are not many methods or properties associated with the `DBEngine` object, no DAO activity can take place without it.

By using the `DBEngine` object, you can create `Workspace` objects, encrypt and repair databases, and register new data sources. For example, consider the concurrency issues with ODBC. With DAO, if you open multiple connections or multiple tables, those tables are associated with the same transaction, and closing a single database closes them all.

To work around this issue, you can create several workspaces for a process that has multiple concurrent transactions. The code, which is not too complex, is shown in Listing 6.1.

**Listing 6.1 MWS.JAVA—Using the *DBEngine* Object to Create Multiple Workspaces**

```
Import dao350;
import dao_dbengine;
int I;
DBEngine engine = (_DBEngine) new dao_dbengine();
Workspace workspace(4);
For (I = 0; I < 3; I++)
{
workspace(I) = engine.CreateWorkspace(strName, strUser, strPassword);
}
```

**NOTE** The `DBEngine` object requires a license to use, so you need to use the `ILicenseManager` Interface to create your `DBEngine` objects, which is included in the DAOSample on the VJ++ CD-ROM.

## The *Workspace* Object

Although the `Workspace` object's use was not explained, you have seen it before in Figure 6.1. Think of the `Workspace` object as a type of work area or workbench. Everything you use will be placed in a workspace—an important point to remember. By using multiple workspaces, as in Listing 6.1, you can isolate transactions, as all transactions are global within a single workspace. Using multiple workspaces can result in performance gains as well as the capability to isolate transactions if the transactions are unrelated.

What does a `Workspace` object give us? Many things, including the capability to host up to five levels of nested transactions per `Workspace` object, which involves the `BeginTrans`, `CommitTrans`, and `Rollback` methods. You can also set security with the `Workspace` object by specifying a user and a password. ODBC transactions can also be isolated when they operate against the same database by using the `IsolateODBCTrans` property. Listing 6.2 shows how the `Workspace` object isolates an ODBC transaction.

**Listing 6.2 ISOLATE.JAVA—Isolating a Transaction with the *Workspace* Object**

```
DBEngine engine = (_DBEngine) new dao_dbengine();
Workspace workspace = engine.CreateWorkspace(strName, strUser, strPassword);

workspace.putIsolateODBCTrans(1);
```

## The *Database* Object

The `Database` object extends your reach by giving you access to queries and recordsets (think cursors) and by enabling you to refresh the schema of the database. The `Database` object will also be used in every application that you write, because you must use one to use a database. Table 6.1 details the `Database` object's methods.



**Table 6.1 DAO *Database* Object's Methods**

| Method | Description |
|---|---|
| `Close` | Closes the `Database` object and any `Recordset` objects that have been created on this database. Also rolls back any transaction affecting the `Database` object that was closed. |
| `CreateProperty` | Attaches custom properties, such as trust levels, to the `Database` object |

*continues*

**Table 6.1 Continued**

| Method | Description |
|---|---|
| `CreateQueryDef` | Creates the Query definition table, enabling you to store queries for later execution and retrieval |
| `CreateRelation` | Links two tables together and enables you to enforce referential integrity with the Relations object |
| `CreateTableDef` | Creates a `TableDef` object |
| `Execute` | Executes a `QueryDef` or SQL statement against the Database object |
| `MakeReplica` | Replicates your database if you have Microsoft Access with Briefcase Replication installed |
| `NewPassword` | Enables you to change the password for the `Database` object or a user account |
| `OpenRecordSet` | Opens a new `Recordset` object (cursor) of the type you specify |
| `Synchronize` | Enables synchronization of replicated databases, assuming that the database is replicatable |

When you create a `Database` object with the `CreateDatabase` method, you don't actually create the database until you've appended the object to the `Databases` collection. When using the `Database` object, you must also understand what happens when you open Jet databases with attached tables. These attached tables are not verified for proper access, nor are the links established until you call `OpenRecordset` or open a `TableDef` object on the attached table. If links to these tables can't be established, you recieve an error message.

Take a careful look at what happens when closing a `Database` object, as well. When the `Database` object is closed, all `Recordset` objects open against that object are also closed. This means that any transactions that you don't `Commit` are rolled back when you close the `Database` object.

A similar, if somewhat annoying, feature of the `Database` object is the lack of localized transactions. You'll recall from our discussion of the `Workspace` object that Microsoft has localized the transactions within a single `Workspace` object; this is not the case with a single `Database` object. For example, if you were to open up several tables in multiple databases and you only used a single `Workspace` object, any operations on transactions would be global in scope. Commit one transaction, and you commit them all. This also occurs when closing `Database` objects. For example, consider Listing 6.3, in which several databases are open.

**Listing 6.3 DBCLOSE—Effects of Closing the Pointer to a Single *Database* Object when Using an Array of *Database* Objects**

```
// Using the IlicenseManager COM interface to create the DBEngine object.

DBEngine engine(0)(0) = new (_DBEngine) dao_dbengine();
DBEngine engine(0)(1) = new (_DBEngine) dao_dbengine();

try
{

String name = engine(0)(0).getName();
System.out.println(name);
engine(0)(0).close();

}catch(Exception e){System.out.println(e)}

try
{

String name = engine(0)(0).getName();
System.out.println(name);
      engine(0)(1).close();

}catch(Exception e){System.out.println(e)}
```

If you close the first `Database` object, you will lose the references to the other objects in the array.

Examine Listing 6.4, which illustrates using all of the `Database` object's methods.

**Listing 6.4 DATABASE.JAVA—Using the *Database* Object**

```
ILicenseMgr mgr;
_DBEngine idbengine;
dao350.Error  m_objError;
Database m_database;
QueryDef m_query;
Recordset m_objRecordset;
Errors m_objErrors;

Parameters m_Params;
Parameter m_Parameter;
Variant m_vflExclusive = new Variant();
Variant m_vflReadOnly = new Variant();
Variant m_vRecordsetType = new Variant();
Variant m_Connect = new Variant();
Variant m_vLockType = new Variant();
```



*continues*

**Listing 6.4 Continued**

```
Variant m_vName = new Variant();
Variant m_vValue = new Variant();
Variant m_vOptions = new Variant();
Variant m_vIndex = new Variant();
Variant m_objField = new Variant();protected boolean readOnly = false;
protected String strDatabase;
protected String strRecordset;
protected int recordCount;
protected static Variant varEmpty = new Variant();

varEmpty.putEmpty();
      try{
          mgr = new LicenseMgr();
          idbengine = (_DBEngine)mgr.createWithLic
          (
              "mbmabptebkjcdlgtjmskjwtsdhjbmkmwtrak",
              "{00000010-0000-0010-8000-00AA006D2EA4}",
              null,
              ComContext.INPROC_SERVER
          );

          // Open database
      m_vflExclusive.putBoolean(false);
      m_vflReadOnly.putBoolean(readOnly);
      m_Connect.putString("");
      m_database = idbengine.OpenDatabase(strDatabase, m_vflExclusive,
      m_vflReadOnly, m_Connect);

      /* We've just opened the database SomeDatabase.mdb, taken an exclusive
      lock, and told it that we want read only access. */

      /* Create a unique application defined property */

      int default = 0;

      Variant type = new Variant();
      Type.putInt(DataTypeEnumDataTypeEnum.dbInteger);

      Property prop = engine.CreateProperty("Trust Level");

      prop.setType(type);
      prop.setValue(default);

      prop.Append();

      /* Creating a Recordset */


      m_vRecordsetType.putShort((short)RecordsetTypeEnum.dbOpenDynaset);
```

```
            m_vOptions.putShort((short)(readOnly ?
      RecordsetOptionEnum.dbReadOnly : 0));
                m_vLockType.putInt(LockTypeEnum.dbOptimistic);
                m_objRecordset = m_database.OpenRecordset(strTable,
      m_vRecordsetType, m_vOptions,m_vLockType);

                }
                catch(com.ms.com.ComFailException e)
           {m_objErrors =
➥idbengine.getErrors();System.out.println(m_objError.getDescription());}


/* Creating a TableDef */

Variant flAttributes = new Variant();
String strTableName = "SomeTable";
String Source = "";
String Connect = "";

flAttributes.putInt(TableDefAttributeEnum.dbAttachExclusive);

TableDef tdef = engine.CreateTableDef(strTableName, flAttributes, strSource,
➥strConnect);

tdef.Append();

/* Creating a QueryDef */

QueryDef query;
query = engine.CreateQueryDef("SomeQuery");

query.setSQL("SELECT * FROM SomeTable");

query.Append();

/* Execute a SQL query against the database */

String sql = "CREATE TABLE SomeTable (SiteID NUMERIC (10) CONSTRAINT PrimaryKey
➥PRIMARY KEY, SiteName TEXT(20)) ";

Variant flOptions = new Variant();
flOptions.putInt(RecordsetOptionEnum.dbFailOnError);

engine.Execute(sql, flOptions);

/* Create a Relation to another table */

Relation relate;
Variant RelationName = new Variant();
RelationName.putString("SomeRelation");
String strPrimaryTable = "SomeTable";
String strForiegnTable = "ForiegnTable";

flAttributes.putInt(RelationAttributesEnum.dbRelationUpdateCascade);
```



*continues*

**Listing 6.4 Continued**

```
relate = engine.CreateRelation(strRelationName, strPrimaryTable,
➥strForiegnTable, flAttributes);

relate.Append();

/* Close all open Recordsets and close the database */

rc.Close();
engine.Close();
```

As you can see, you can do quite a bit with the `Database` object. The `MakeReplica` and `Synchronize` methods are not covered here because you need to understand replication further, and the code to set that up is a little longer than this short example. Now that you've seen how to create `Database` objects, take a look at the rest of the DAO hierarchy. (Database replication is covered later in the section titled "Learning About Database Replication with DAO.")

## The *User* and *Group* Objects

Microsoft has built security into DAO by using `Group` and `User` objects. These objects enable you to create user accounts and group accounts specific to the objects with which you are working and are in addition to any security that a network OS might have in place. The Microsoft Jet Engine defines three default groups: Admins, Users, and Guests.

## The *TableDef* Object

The `TableDef` object enables you to set properties on the table and to perform several methods on a table that can modify its structure. You can set validation rules for transactions (enabling you to validate the data being inserted), change the connection properties, attach the table to a database, and query the structure by opening `Recordset` objects on the table definition. Table 6.2 lists the methods that you can use with a `TableDef` object.

**Table 6.2 *TableDef* Methods**

| Method | Description |
|---|---|
| `CreateField` | Enables you to create a field |
| `CreateProperty` | Creates a new property for the `TableDef` object |
| `CreateIndex` | Creates an index |
| `OpenRecordset` | Opens a `Recordset` object on the `TableDef` object and enables you to retrieve the structure |
| `RefreshLink` | Updates the connection information |

A table definition can be useful in situations in which you don't know the structure of the data or when you want to alter some part of the structure. Listing 6.5 contains operations that use each of the aforementioned methods, including setting some of the connection properties and creating a Validation rule.

**Listing 6.5 TABLEDEF.JAVA—Using a *TableDef* Object's Methods and Properties**

```
ILicenseMgr mgr;
_DBEngine idbengine;
dao350.Error  m_objError;
Database m_database;
QueryDef m_query;
Recordset m_objRecordset;
Errors m_objErrors;

Parameters m_Params;
Parameter m_Parameter;
Variant m_vflExclusive = new Variant();
Variant m_vflReadOnly = new Variant();
Variant m_vRecordsetType = new Variant();
Variant m_Connect = new Variant();
Variant m_vLockType = new Variant();
Variant m_vName = new Variant();
Variant m_vValue = new Variant();
Variant m_vOptions = new Variant();
Variant m_vIndex = new Variant();
Variant m_objField = new Variant();protected boolean readOnly = false;
protected String strDatabase;
protected String strRecordset;
protected int recordCount;
protected static Variant varEmpty = new Variant();

varEmpty.putEmpty();
      try{
          mgr = new LicenseMgr();
          idbengine = (_DBEngine)mgr.createWithLic
          (
              "mbmabptebkjcdlgtjmskjwtsdhjbmkmwtrak",
              "{00000010-0000-0010-8000-00AA006D2EA4}",
              null,
              ComContext.INPROC_SERVER
          );

          // Open database
      m_vflExclusive.putBoolean(false);
      m_vflReadOnly.putBoolean(readOnly);
      m_Connect.putString("");
      m_database = idbengine.OpenDatabase(strDatabase, m_vflExclusive,
      m_vflReadOnly, m_Connect);
```

Part II Ch 6

*continues*

**Listing 6.5 Continued**

```
      /* We've just opened the database SomeDatabase.mdb, taken an exclusive
      lock, and told it that we want read only access. */


/* Creating a TableDef */

Variant flAttributes = new Variant();
String strTableName = "SomeTable";
String Source = "";
String Connect = "";

flAttributes.putInt(TableDefAttributeEnum.dbAttachExclusive);

TableDef tdef = engine.CreateTableDef(strTableName, flAttributes, strSource,
➥strConnect);


/* Creating a Field */

String strField = "SomeField";
Variant flFieldType = new Variant();
flFieldType.putInt(Constants.dbText);

tdef.CreateField(strField, flFieldType);

/* Creating an Index */

String strIndex = "SomeIndex";
Index idx;
Field field;

idx =  tdef.CreateIndex(strIndex);
field = idx.CreateField(strField);

/* Creating a property */

int default = 0;

Variant type = new Variant();
Type.putInt(Constants.dbText);

Property prop = engine.CreateProperty("Modified by");

prop.setType(type);
prop.setValue(default);

prop.Append();


tdef.Append();
```

## The *Querydef* Object

Think of a `Querydef` object as a table of stored SQL statements. The `QueryDef` object is a temporary table that holds a collection of queries. You can manipulate the parameters, change the SQL statement, check for properties of the query, and change them if necessary.

Although the `Querydef` object is powerful, most of its complexity lies in the properties, not in the methods. The `QueryDef` object supports only three methods, all of which you have seen before (see Table 6.3).

**Table 6.3 The *QueryDef* Object's Methods**

| Method | Description |
|---|---|
| `CreateProperty` | Creates a unique property for the `QueryDef` object |
| `Execute` | Executes the `QueryDef` object |
| `OpenRecordset` | Opens a `Recordset` object to retrieve the query's results |

You will be most interested, however, in the properties of a `QueryDef` object because those properties are what make a `QueryDef` object so useful. These properties are described in Table 6.4.

**Table 6.4 The *QueryDef* Object's Properties**

| Property | Description |
|---|---|
| `Connect` | Defines the connection string to the ODBC driver |
| `DateCreated` | Holds the date that the `QueryDef` object was created |
| `KeepLocal` | Enables you to specify that this object remains local when the database is converted for replication |
| `LastUpdated` | Shows when the `QueryDef` object was last updated |
| `LogMessages` | Enables you to log return values from ODBC statements into a temporary table called ADMIN-00, ADMIN-01... |
| `Name` | Specifies the name by which you should reference an object |
| `ODBCTimeout` | Denotes the timeout value for a query run against an ODBC database |
| `RecordsAffected` | Returns the number of records affected by the last `Execute` method |
| `Replicable` | Denotes whether or not this object is capable of being replicated |
| `ReturnsRecords` | Indicates whether or not SQL passes through query returns records |

*continues*

**Table 6.4 Continued**

| Property | Description |
|---|---|
| SQL | Denotes the actual SQL statement |
| Type | Returns the type of query; for example, Select, SQLPassThrough, and Action queries |
| Updateable | Indicates whether or not you can change the QueryDef object |

Usually, the most important property is the SQL property. By using the SQL property of the QueryDef object, you can set SQL statements to execute against the database. You can use any of the SQL methods you've become familiar with, such as creating parameterized queries, which is much easier than creating the array yourself and storing the queries, as was done when using ODBC statements.

Also notice the amount of metadata that you can retrieve from the QueryDef object about the query itself. This metadata includes the number of records returned, the type of query, how many records were affected by the last execution of the query, and many other pieces of information.

## The *Recordset* Object

Think of the Recordset object as using an ODBC result set and opening a cursor on the result set. Recordset objects are the mainstay of database programming with DAO, and using them will become second nature to you as you develop applications with DAO. You can tailor many of the properties of the Recordset object, which determine how you will deal with the data. There are also several methods involved, perhaps more than any other object in the DAO hierarchy. Because the Recordset object plays a large role in your success with DAO, take a close look at what the methods are and how you can use them by examining Table 6.5.

**Table 6.5 The *Recordset* Object's Methods**

| Method | Description |
|---|---|
| AddNew | Adds a new record for the Table-type or Dynaset-type Recordset objects (does not work on Snapshots) |
| CancelUpdate | Cancels any pending updates for the Recordset object |
| Clone | Duplicates the Recordset object |
| Close | Closes the Recordset object, rolling back any pending transactions against this Recordset object |
| CopyQueryDef | Creates a copy of the QueryDef object used to create the Recordset object |
| Delete | Deletes the current record |

| Method | Description |
|---|---|
| `Edit` | Copies the current record into a buffer for editing |
| `FillCache` | Forces the cache to be filled with data from the ODBC source |
| `FindFirst` | Finds the first matching record |
| `FindLast` | Finds the last matching record |
| `FindNext` | Finds the next matching record |
| `FindPrevious` | Finds the previous matching record |
| `GetRows` | Copies one or more records into an array |
| `Move` | Moves the cursor relative to the current record a specified number of rows (you can also specify a start point from which to begin the move) |
| `MoveFirst` | Positions the cursor at the first record in the `Recordset` object |
| `MoveLast` | Positions the cursor at the last record in the `Recordset` object |
| `MoveNext` | Positions the cursor at the next record in the `Recordset` object |
| `MovePrevious` | Positions the cursor at the previous record in the `Recordset` object |
| `OpenRecordset` | Opens a `Recordset` on this `Recordset` |
| `Requery` | Refreshes the `Recordset` object by executing the `QueryDef` that was used to create the `Recordset` |
| `Seek` | Seeks a record based on the index of that record |
| `Update` | Saves the contents in the Edit buffer to the `Recordset` object |

As you can see, the `Recordset` object has many different methods, some of which seeming to perform the same function. Consider the different `Find` methods for example; these methods all have several overloaded members that enable you to do essentially the same thing but in slightly different ways. We'll take a look at the different methods for creating a `Recordset` object in a short while. Now, however, is a good time to provide an example of using the methods described in Table 6.5. Listing 6.6 illustrates opening a Dynaset-type `Recordset` object.



**Listing 6.6 RECORDSET—Creating a Dynaset-Type *Recordset* Object**

```
import dao_dbengine;
import dao350.*;
import com.ms.com.Variant;
import java.util.*;

public class records{
```

*continues*

**Listing 6.6 Continued**

```
      public records()
      {
ILicenseMgr mgr;
_DBEngine idbengine;
dao350.Error  m_objError;
Database m_database;
QueryDef m_query;
Recordset m_objRecordset;
Errors m_objErrors;

Parameters m_Params;
Parameter m_Parameter;
Variant m_vflExclusive = new Variant();
Variant m_vflReadOnly = new Variant();
Variant m_vRecordsetType = new Variant();
Variant m_Connect = new Variant();
Variant m_vLockType = new Variant();
Variant m_vName = new Variant();
Variant m_vValue = new Variant();
Variant m_vOptions = new Variant();
Variant m_vIndex = new Variant();
Variant m_objField = new Variant();
protected boolean readOnly = true;
protected String strDatabase;
protected String strRecordset;
protected int recordCount;
protected static Variant varEmpty = new Variant();

varEmpty.putEmpty();
      try{
          mgr = new LicenseMgr();
          idbengine = (_DBEngine)mgr.createWithLic
          (
              "mbmabptebkjcdlgtjmskjwtsdhjbmkmwtrak",
              "{00000010-0000-0010-8000-00AA006D2EA4}",
              null,
              ComContext.INPROC_SERVER
          );

          // Open database
      m_vflExclusive.putBoolean(false);
      m_vflReadOnly.putBoolean(readOnly);
      m_Connect.putString("");
      m_database = idbengine.OpenDatabase(strDatabase, m_vflExclusive,
      m_vflReadOnly, m_Connect);

      /* We've just opened the database SomeDatabase.mdb, taken an exclusive
      ➥lock, and told it that we want read only access. */


                  // Create Variants for Recordset parameters

              m_vRecordsetType.putShort((short)RecordsetTypeEnum.dbOpenDynaset);
              m_vOptions.putShort((short)(readOnly ?
```

```
➥RecordsetOptionEnum.dbReadOnly : 0));
            m_vLockType.putInt(LockTypeEnum.dbOptimistic);
              m_objRecordset = m_database.OpenRecordset(strTable,
➥m_vRecordsetType, m_vOptions,m_vLockType);

              }
               catch(com.ms.com.ComFailException e)
               { m_objErrors =
➥idbengine.getErrors();System.out.println(m_objError.getDescription());}
```

Now that we have a valid Dynaset-type `Recordset` object, take a look at what it takes to move through the `Recordset`. Listing 6.7 illustrates using various forms of the method `Move()` and uses `Seek()` to find key records, as well.

**Listing 6.7 RECORDSET.JAVA—Moving Through the *Recordset* with *Move()* and Searching with *Seek()***

```
            // Use the MoveFirst to scroll to the beginning of the recordset
             recordset.MoveFirst();
             recordset.MoveNext();  //Moves the cursor to the next record
             recordset.Move(5); //Moves the cursor a set number of records
➥forward
             recordset.Move(5, vBookmark); //Moves the cursor relative to the
➥record we've bookmarked
             recordset.MoveLast(0); //Moves the cursor to the last record.
             recordset.MoveFirst(); //Move the cursor back to the beginning

//Set the index for the recordset BEFORE using the SEEK methods
               recordset.putIndex("Column1");
              recordset.Seek("=", lpszSomeValue);
/*Note that using the Seek method requires an index. Indexes require having a
➥TableType recordset, so we'll assume that's what we are working with here.
➥This Seek method will return the first matching record in the Index.
*/
```

Next, you will edit a record with the `Edit()` method, which places the contents of the record into an in-memory buffer. Then you will cancel the update and toss the contents of the buffer out, never having changed the underlying record. Instead, you'll add a new record, as shown in Listing 6.8.



**Listing 6.8 RECORDSET.JAVA—Editing a Record with the *Recordset* Object**

```
// Edit this record
//Retrieve the value
            m_vName.putString("Address");
            m_vValue = m_objRecordset.getCollect(m_vName);
             String s = m_vValue.toString();
 //Now change it.
             s = "1900 Park Place";
```

*continues*

**Listing 6.8 Continued**

```
            m_vValue.putString(s);
            m_objRecordset.AddNew();
            m_objRecordset.putCollect(m_vName, m_Value);
            m_objRecordset.Update(UpdateTypeEnum.dbUpdateRegular, false);
//Change it again
            s = "1920 Park Place";
            m_vValue.putString(s);
            m_objRecordset.AddNew();
            m_objRecordset.putCollect(m_vName, m_Value);

           // Cancel the Update - using DAO 3.5 syntax
           recordset._30_CancelUpdate();

           // Add a new record the old way.
           String data;
           Field f;
           recordset.AddNew();
           Fields fields = m_objRecordset.getFields();

           // Create a Variant to get the value of each field
           Variant value = new Variant();
           Variant fldName = new Variant();
           Variant FieldName = new Variant();
           int lSiteID = 30;
           String strSiteName = "microsoft.com";

           // Get the first field
           FieldName.putString("SiteID");
           value.putInt(lSiteID);
           f = fields.getItem(FieldName);
           f.putValue(value);

           FieldName.putString("Site Name");
           value.putString(strSiteName);
           f = fields.getItem(FieldName);
           f.putValue(value);

           // Update the record
           m_objRecordset._30_Update();

           //Now for the "New" way
             m_objRecordset.AddNew();
            m_vName.putString("SiteID");
            m_vValue.putString(iSiteID);
            m_objRecordset.putCollect(m_vName, m_Value);

            m_objRecordset.AddNew();
            m_vName.putString("Site Name");
            m_vValue.putString(strSiteName);
            m_objRecordset.putCollect(m_vName, m_Value);

            m_objRecordset._30_Update();
```

Now that you know how to add new records, take a look at cloning `Recordsets`, searching with the `Find()` method, and deleting records (see Listing 6.9).

**Listing 6.9 RECORDSET.JAVA—Using the *Clone()*, *Find()*, and *Delete()* Methods on the *Recordset* Object**

```
            // Clone the recordset
           Recordset  m_objNewRecordset = m_objRecordset.Clone();

//Seek some records we're interested in with the cloned recordset
//We're assuming the SiteID is the Index here.
            long SiteID = 30;

             m_objNewRecordset.Seek(">",SiteID);

            // Delete the current record in the cloned recordset
             m_objNewRecordset.Delete();

            // Refresh the cloned set
            Variant status = new Variant();

             m_objNewRecordset.Requery(status);

// Search the first recordset for the value we deleted in the second.
            String strCriteria = ("SiteID = '30'");   // Set the criteria.

            // All Find methods have similar usages
            m_objRecordset.FindFirst( strCriteria );  // Find first matching
➥record.
            while ( ! m_objRecordset.GetNoMatch() )   // If one was found, find
➥another.
            {
                   // Delete the current record in the recordset
                    m_objNewRecordset.Delete();
                    recordset.FindNext( strCriteria );
            }
                  // Refresh the original set;
            Variant status = new Variant();
            m_objRecordset.Requery(status);

 // Open a recordset on our recordset
            String sqlQuery = "SELECT 'Site Name' FROM SomeTable WHERE 'SiteID'
➥ =>'30'";

            m_vRecordsetType.putShort((short)RecordsetTypeEnum.dbOpenDynaset);
             m_vOptions.putShort((short)(readOnly ?
➥RecordsetOptionEnum.dbReadOnly : 0));
           m_vLockType.putInt(LockTypeEnum.dbOptimistic);
            // Create the recordset
           recordset = database._30_OpenRecordset(sqlQuery, m_vRecordsetType,
➥m_vOptions, m_vLockType);
```

By examining Listing 6.9, you can clearly see the resemblance between the ODBC cursor and a `Recordset` object, a resemblance that is not accidental. Because DAO is based on data access, there has to be a way to manipulate the data returned from a query; the most obvious way is to define a cursor.

The `Recordset` object had three different types of `Recordset` objects in previous versions of DAO (3.0 and earlier), but with the new DAO 3.5, you can use five different types of `Recordset` objects. Table 6.6 lists the five `Recordset` objects and the ways in which you can expect to use them.

**Table 6.6 *Recordset* Object Types**

| Type | Description |
|---|---|
| Table | Returns the underlying structure of a table. |
| Snapshot | Holds a static image of the data that cannot be updated but can be scrolled through. |
| Dynaset | Corresponds to the ODBC Keyset-style cursor: The data is updateable, scrollable, and can be refreshed to retrieve current data. |
| Forward-only | Equivalent to a Snapshot-type `Recordset` object without the capability to scroll backward through the data. |
| Dynamic | An updateable, scrollable `Recordset` that changes to reflect updates from other users, as well as from your own updates. |

Each type has different strengths and weaknesses, some of them overlapping between the different types. The next section examines the different types of `Recordset` objects and examples of how you can use them.

**NOTE** The Dynamic and Forward-only `Recordset` objects are only available if you're using DAO version 3.5. Version 3.0 of DAO only supported Table-type, Snapshot-type, and Dynaset-type `Recordset` objects.

**The Table-Type *Recordset* Object** Table-type `Recordset` objects open a `Recordset` against a single table, so you cannot use `SQL JOINS` or multiple table queries. They have an advantage over the other types of `Recordset` objects because they are usually indexed when you retrieve the results, assuming the table has an index. Generally speaking, the performance of a Table-type `Recordset` object is better than other `Recordsets`. If you open a Table-type `Recordset` object against a database without an index, however, you won't be able to guarantee any order with the results, which means it is always a good practice to check the existing indexes for your table before opening the `Recordset`.

Another difference between this `Recordset` and the other types involves data retrieval: When you retrieve data in a Table-type `Recordset` object, you must use the `Seek` method instead of the usual `Move` method. Because the Table-type `Recordset` object doesn't have a cursor associated with it, the `Move` method doesn't have a point of reference. Because you are performing operations on the base table and no filters or sorts can be done, however, this is not a problem.

A potentially large limitation of the Table-type `Recordset` concerns the types of databases with which you can use it. The Table-type `Recordset` object is only able to access non-ODBC- type data sources. Of the data sources that you can access with a Table-type `Recordset` object, only the Jet Engine enables you to open Table-type `Recordset` objects against a query; with all other ISAM databases, you must explicitly open the table itself. Listing 6.10 illustrates using the Table-type `Recordset` object.

**Listing 6.10 TABLETYPE.JAVA—Using the Table-Type *Recordset* Object**

```
// Create Variants for Recordset parameters

_DBEngine dbengine = dao_dbengine.create();
Workspace workspace;
Database database;
String name = "SomeWorkspace";
String dbname = "Exchange";
String strUser = "Bob";
String strPassword = "";
Variant flType = new Variant();
Variant flExclusive = new Variant();
Variant flAccess = new Variant();
Variant flOptions = new Variant();

flType.putInt(WorkspaceTypeEnum.dbUseJet);
flExclusive.putBoolean(true);
workspace = dbengine.CreateWorkspace(name,strUser,strPassword, flType);
database = dbengine.OpenDatabase(dbname, flExclusive, flAccess, flOptions );

// Create Variants for Recordset parameters

Recordset recordset;

Variant flTableType = new Variant();

flTableType.putInt(RecordsetTypeEnum.dbOpenTable);
flAccess.putInt(RecordsetOptionEnum.dbReadOnly);

// Create the recordset, a read-only dynaset
recordset = database._30_OpenRecordset("SomeRecordset",flTableType,flAccess);
```

**The Snapshot-Type *Recordset* Object** Think of the Snapshot-type `Recordset` object as a static cursor—the data will never change, even if you update the table. You can scroll through the result set with the Snapshot, so it is useful for read-only queries, such as those that a search engine would return (see Listing 6.11 for an example of this object's methods). The Snapshot-type `Recordset` object also has advantages over a Table-type `Recordset` object because you have a cursor that can be opened against multiple tables and SQL statements.

**Listing 6.11 SNAPSHOT.JAVA—Creating and Using a Snapshot-type *Recordset* Object**

```
Workspace workspace;
Database database;
String name = "SomeWorkspace";
String dbname = "Exchange";
String strUser = "Bob";
String strPassword = "";
Variant flType = new Variant();
Variant flExclusive = new Variant();
Variant flAccess = new Variant();
Variant flOptions = new Variant();
ILicenseMgr mgr;
DBEngine idbengine;
dao350.Error  m_objError;
try{
               mgr = new LicenseMgr();
                    idbengine = (_DBEngine)mgr.createWithLic
                    (
                  "mbmabptebkjcdlgtjmskjwtsdhjbmkmwtrak",
                  "{00000010-0000-0010-8000-00AA006D2EA4}",
                       null,
                       ComContext.INPROC_SERVER
                    );
}
catch(com.ms.com.ComFailException e)
m_objErrors =
➥idbengine.getErrors();System.out.println(m_objError.getDescription());}

flType.putInt(WorkspaceTypeEnum.dbUseJet);
flExclusive.putBoolean(true);
workspace =i dbengine.CreateWorkspace(name,strUser,strPassword, flType);
database = idbengine.OpenDatabase(dbname, flExclusive, flAccess, flOptions );

// Create Variants for Recordset parameters
Recordset recordset;

Variant flTableType = new Variant();

flTableType.putInt(RecordsetTypeEnum.dbOpenSnapshot);
flAccess.putInt(RecordsetOptionEnum.dbReadOnly);

// Create the recordset, a read-only Snapshot
recordset = database._30_OpenRecordset("SomeRecordset",flTableType,flAccess);
```

```
//Find out the number of records in this recordset
int count = recordset.getRecordCount();

//Move the cursor to the first record
// Scroll through the recordsets in a forward fashion

            recordset.MoveFirst();

            // All Move methods work in the same manner - i.e.,
➥Recordset.MovePrevious();

            Fields fields1 = recordset.getFields();
            Field field;
            int count = fields.getCount();


            for(int I=0;I<count - 1;I++)
            {
            // Get the first field

            f = fields.getItem();

            // Get its value
                  value = f.getValue();

            // Convert the value to text for display
                  data = value.toString();

            // Add values to list boxe

            DBList1.AddNew(data);
            recordset.MoveNext();

//Scroll Backwards doing the same thing

recordset.MoveLast();

for(int I=0;count - 1=>i;count—)
{
      // Get the first field
      f = fields.getItem();

      // Get its value
      value = f.getValue();

      // Convert the value to text for display
      data = value.toString();

      // Add value to list box
DBList.AddNew(data);
      recordset.MovePrevious();

}
```

**The Dynaset-Type *Recordset* Object** This type of query is perhaps the most commonly used because it enables you to dynamically update the data as it is changed. This is what most RDBMSs (Relational Database Management Systems) would call a *view*. By combining data from several sources into a single updateable `Recordset`, you can ease the work that the application has to do to synchronize the updates (see Listing 6.12).

**Listing 6.12 DYNASET.JAVA—Using a Dynaset-Type *Recordset* Object**

```
Workspace workspace;
Database database;
String name = "SomeWorkspace";
String dbname = "Exchange";
String strUser = "Bob";
String strPassword = "";
Variant flType = new Variant();
Variant flExclusive = new Variant();
Variant flAccess = new Variant();
Variant flOptions = new Variant();
ILicenseMgr mgr;
DBEngine idbengine;
dao350.Error  m_objError;
try{
              mgr = new LicenseMgr();
                   idbengine = (_DBEngine)mgr.createWithLic
                   (
                 "mbmabptebkjcdlgtjmskjwtsdhjbmkmwtrak",
                 "{00000010-0000-0010-8000-00AA006D2EA4}",
                      null,
                      ComContext.INPROC_SERVER
                   );
}
catch(com.ms.com.ComFailException e)
m_objErrors =
➥idbengine.getErrors();System.out.println(m_objError.getDescription());}

flType.putInt(WorkspaceTypeEnum.dbUseJet);
flExclusive.putBoolean(true);

workspace = idbengine.CreateWorkspace(name,strUser,strPassword, flType);
database = idbengine.OpenDatabase(dbname, flExclusive, flAccess, flOptions );

// Create Variants for Recordset parameters

Recordset recordset;

Variant flTableType = new Variant();

flTableType.putInt(RecordsetTypeEnum.dbOpenDynaset);
flAccess.putInt(RecordsetOptionEnum.dbReadOnly);


// Create the recordset, a read-only Dynaset
```

```
recordset = database._30_OpenRecordset("SomeRecordset",flTableType,flAccess);


//Find out the number of records in this recordset
int count = recordset.getRecordCount();

//Move the cursor to the first record

recordset.MoveFirst();
 // All Move methods work in the same manner - i.e., Recordset.MovePrevious();

            Fields fields1 = recordset.getFields();
            Field field;
            int count = fields.getCount();


            for(int I=0;I<count - 1;I++)
            {
            // Get the first field

            f = fields.getItem();

            // Get its value
                  value = f.getValue();

            // Convert the value to text for display
                  data = value.toStrıng();

            // Add values to list boxe

            DBList1.AddNew(data);
            recordset.MoveNext();

//Scroll Backwards doing the same thing

recordset.MoveLast();

for(int I=0;count - 1=>i;count—)
{
      // Get the first field
      f = fields.getItem();

      // Get its value
      value = f.getValue();

      // Convert the value to text for display
      data = value.toString();

      // Add value to list box
DBList.AddNew(data);
      recordset.MovePrevious();

}
```

The code is exactly the same for the Snapshot- and Dynaset-type `Recordset` objects because they both support full cursors. In the implementation of these two, however, if you were to make a change to the database and another user were using a Snapshot, that user wouldn't see that change until a `Requery` method was invoked. On the other hand, if the user had a Dynaset-type Recordset object open, he or she could see the changes as soon as you committed them (assuming that the Jet Engine is updating the cached data frequently enough).

**The Forward-only *Recordset* Object** This `Recordset` object is simply a Snapshot-type `Recordset` without a cursor. You can only scroll forward through the `Recordset` object, as you do with the ODBC forward-only cursor. Using the Forward-only `Recordset` is beneficial in situations in which you don't want the overhead of a cursor, or you need to parse the `Recordset` object only once. Listing 6.13 shows the usage of the Forward-only `Recordset` object.

**Listing 6.13 FORWARD.JAVA—Using a Forward-only *Recordset* Object**

```
Workspace workspace;
Database database;
String name = "SomeWorkspace";
String dbname = "Exchange";
String strUser = "Bob";
String strPassword = "";
Variant flType = new Variant();
Variant flExclusive = new Variant();
Variant flAccess = new Variant();
Variant flOptions = new Variant();
flType.putInt(WorkspaceTypeEnum.dbUseODBC);
flExclusive.putBoolean(true);
ILicenseMgr mgr;
DBEngine idbengine;
dao350.Error  m_objError;
try{
               mgr = new LicenseMgr();
                    idbengine = (_DBEngine)mgr.createWithLic
                    (
                 "mbmabptebkjcdlgtjmskjwtsdhjbmkmwtrak",
                 "{00000010-0000-0010-8000-00AA006D2EA4}",
                      null,
                      ComContext.INPROC_SERVER
                    );
}
catch(com.ms.com.ComFailException e)
m_objErrors =
➥idbengine.getErrors();System.out.println(m_objError.getDescription());}
workspace = idbengine.CreateWorkspace(name,strUser,strPassword, flType);

flOptions.putInt(CursorDriverEnum.dbUseDefaultCursor);
database = idbengine.OpenDatabase(dbname, flExclusive, flAccess, flOptions );
// Create Variants for Recordset parameters
Recordset recordset;

Variant flTableType = new Variant();
```

```
flTableType.putInt(RecordsetTypeEnum.dbOpenForewardOnly);
flAccess.putInt(RecordsetOptionEnum.dbReadOnly);


// Create the recordset, a read-only Forward Only recordset
recordset = database._30_OpenRecordset("SomeRecordset",flTableType,flAccess);


// Scroll forward through the fields in a the recordset gathering data

String value;

for(int I=0;I<count - 1;I++)
{
// Get the first field
      f = fields.getItem();

// Get its value
      value = f.getValue();

// Convert the value to text for display
      data.setText(value.toString());
      value = recordset.Current().toString();

// Add value to list box

DBList.AddNew(data);
      recordset.MoveNext();

}
```

**The Dynamic *Recordset* Object** This `Recordset` object corresponds directly to the ODBC dynamic cursor. You can retrieve result sets from multiple data sources, see changes as they are committed by other users, and scroll in both directions through the data. You can use the Dynamic `Recordset` object only when using the `ODBCDirect` API in DAO. (An example of the Dynamic `Recordset` object is shown in Listing 6.14).



### Listing 6.14 Using the Dynamic *Recordset* Object

```
Workspace workspace;
Database database;
String name = "SomeWorkspace";
String dbname = "Exchange";
String strUser = "Bob";
String strPassword = "";
Variant flType = new Variant();
Variant flExclusive = new Variant();
Variant flAccess = new Variant();
Variant flOptions = new Variant();
ILicenseMgr mgr;
DBEngine idbengine;
```

*continues*

**Listing 6.14 Continued**

```
            dao350.Error  m_objError;
            try{
                     mgr = new LicenseMgr();
                    idbengine = (_DBEngine)mgr.createWithLic
                    (
                  "mbmabptebkjcdlgtjmskjwtsdhjbmkmwtrak",
                  "{00000010-0000-0010-8000-00AA006D2EA4}",
                        null,
                        ComContext.INPROC_SERVER
                    );
               }
                catch(com.ms.com.ComFailException e)
                {m_objErrors =
➥idbengine.getErrors();System.out.println(m_objError.getDescription());}
            flOptions = putInt(CursorDriverEnum.dbUseODBCCursor);
            flType.putInt(WorkspaceTypeEnum.dbUseODBC);
            flExclusive.putBoolean(true);
            workspace = idbengine.CreateWorkspace(name,strUser,strPassword,
➥flType);
            database = idbengine.OpenDatabase(dbname, flExclusive, flAccess,
➥flOptions );

            // Create Variants for Recordset parameters

            Recordset recordset;

            Variant flTableType = new Variant();

            flTableType.putInt(RecordsetTypeEnum.dbOpenDynamic);
            flAccess.putInt(RecordsetOptionEnum.dbReadOnly);


            // Create the recordset, a read-only Dynaset
            recordset =
➥database._30_OpenRecordset("SomeRecordset",flTableType,flAccess);


//Find out the number of records in this recordset
int count = recordset.getRecordCount();

//Move the cursor to the first record

recordset.MoveFirst();
// All Move methods work in the same manner - i.e., Recordset.MovePrevious();

            Fields fields1 = recordset.getFields();
            Field field;
            int count = fields.getCount();


            for(int I=0;I<count - 1;I++)
            {
```

```
            // Get the first field

            f = fields.getItem();

            // Get its value
                  value = f.getValue();

            // Convert the value to text for display
                  data = value.toString();

            // Add values to list box

            DBList1.AddNew(data);
            recordset.MoveNext();
}

//Scroll Backwards doing the same thing

recordset.MoveLast();

for(int I=0;count - 1=>i;count—)
{
      // Get the first field
      f = fields.getItem();

      // Get its value
      value = f.getValue();

      // Convert the value to text for display
      data = value.toString();

      // Add value to list box
DBList.AddNew(data);
      recordset.MovePrevious();

}
```

## The *Relation* Object



With the `Relation` object, you can get information about the current relations between tables and foreign keys and enforce business rules during changes to the base tables (but not on queries or attached tables). As soon as you create the relation, you can take advantage of features such as *cascaded* updates and deletes. Cascading defines what happens when you update one record, and the database engine automatically updates all records linked with the one that you changed.

The only method that the `Relation` object supports is the `CreateField` method, which means that most of the work is done setting the properties of the `Relation` object itself. The properties are listed in Table 6.7.

**Table 6.7 The *Relation* Object's Properties**

| Property | Description |
|---|---|
| Attributes | The properties of the relation—such as one-to-one or one-to-many |
| Foreign Table | String representing the foreign table in the relation |
| Name | Unique name for this `Relation` object |
| Table | String representing the local table in the relation |

Setting the attributes determines the nature of the relation that you create. There are several different attributes that you can set with the `Relation` object, as listed in Table 6.8.

**Table 6.8 Attributes for the *Relation* Object**

| Attributes | Description |
|---|---|
| `dbRelationDeleteCascade` | Cascade deletes. |
| `dbRelationDontEnforce` | Do not enforce referential integrity. |
| `dbRelationInherited` | This relationship is between the local table and an attached table. |
| `dbRelationUpdateCascade` | Cascade the updates. |
| `dbRelationUnique` | Relationship is one-to-one. |

An example of creating a relation is illustrated in Table 6.1, but no mention of the attributes is made. Listing 6.15 provides a simple example that sets all of the attributes for the `Relation` object. It's a slightly modified version of the Visual C++ sample in the DAO help files.

**Listing 6.15 RELATION.JAVA—Defining the Relation and Setting Its Properties**

```
ILicenseMgr mgr;
_DBEngine idbengine;
dao350.Error  m_objError; Database db;
Relation relation;
TableDef tdfReferenced, tdfReferencing;
Field fldPrimeKey;
Index idxUnique;
Relation relEnforced;
int nFld;
String strPrimary;
String strForeignName;

String name = "";
String dbname = "Master.mdb";
String strUser = "";
```

```
String strPassword = "";
Variant flType = new Variant();
Variant flExclusive = new Variant();
Variant flAccess = new Variant();
Variant flOptions = new Variant();

try{
        mgr = new LicenseMgr();
        idbengine = (_DBEngine)mgr.createWithLic
        (
                  "mbmabptebkjcdlgtjmskjwtsdhjbmkmwtrak",
                  "{00000010-0000-0010-8000-00AA006D2EA4}",
            null,
            ComContext.INPROC_SERVER
        );
}
catch(com.ms.com.ComFailException e)
{m_objErrors =
➥idbengine.getErrors();System.out.println(m_objError.getDescription());}

flType.putInt(WorkspaceTypeEnum.dbUseJet);
flExclusive.putBoolean(true);

// Open the default workspace
workspace = idbengine.CreateWorkspace(name,strUser,strPassword, flType);

database = idbengine.OpenDatabase(dbname, flExclusive, flAccess, flOptions );


// Create referenced table with primary key.
Variant tblName = new Variant();
Variant tblAttributes = new Variant();
Variant tblSource  = new Variant();
Variant tblConnect  = new Variant();

tblName.putString(strTblDefName);
tblAttributes.putInt(TableDefEnum.dbAttachExclusive);
tblSource.putString(strSource);
tblConnect.putString(strConnectInfo);


tdfReferenced = db.CreateTableDef(tblName, tblAttributes, tblSource,
➥tblConnect);

Variant fldName = new Variant();
Variant fldType= new Variant();
Variant fldSize = new Variant();

fldName.putString("PrimaryKey");
fldType.putInt(DataTypeEnum.dbLong);

fldPrimeKey = tdfReferenced.CreateField(fldName, fldType, fldSize);
➥tdfReferenced.Fields.Append(fldPrimeKey);

// Create unique index for enforced referential integrity.
```



*continues*

**Listing 6.15 Continued**

```
Variant idx = new Variant();
idx.putString("UniqueIndex");

idxUnique = tdfReferenced.CreateIndex("UniqueIndex");
idxUnique.SetPrimary(TRUE); // No Null values allowed.

fldPrimeKey = tdfReferenced.CreateField(fldName, fldType, fldSize );
idxUnique.Fields.Append(fldPrimeKey);
tdfReferenced.Indexes.Append(idxUnique);
db.TableDefs.Append(tdfReferenced);

// Create referencing table with foreign key.
tblName.putString("Referencing");
tblAttributes.putInt(TableDefEnum.dbAttachExclusive);
tblSource.putString(strSource);
tblConnect.putString(strConnectInfo);

tdfReferencing = db.CreateTableDef(tblName, tblAttributes, tblSource,
tblConnect);

fldName.putString("ForeignKey");
fldType.putInt(DataTypeEnum.dbLong);

fldPrimeKey = tdfReferencing.CreateField(fldName, fldType, fldSize);
tdfReferencing.Fields.Append(fldPrimeKey);

db.TableDefs.Append(tdfReferencing);

// Create one-to-many relationship & enforce referential integrity.
Variant relName = new Variant();
Variant relTable = new Variant();
Variant relForeignTable = new Variant();
Variant relAttributes = new Variant();

relName.putString("EnforcedOneToMany");
relTable.putString("Referenced");
relForeignTable.putString("Referencing");
relAttributes.putInt(0);

// Don't set either dbRelationUnique or dbRelationDontEnforce.

fldPrimeKey = relEnforced.CreateField(fldName, fldType, fldSize);
fldPrimeKey.putForeignTable("ForeignKey");
relEnforced.Fields.Append(fldPrimeKey);

db.Relations.Append(relEnforced);

// Enumerate relation and its fields.
String Name = relEnforced.getName();
String strTable = relEnforced.getTable();
String ForeignTable = relEnforced.getForeignTable();
String Attributes = relEnforced.getAttributes();
```

```
System.out.println("Relation: "+ Name + "\n");
System.out.println("  Primary Table: " + strTable + "\n");
System.out.println("  Foreign Table: "+ ForeignTable + "\n");
System.out.println("  Attributes: "+ Attributes +"\n");
System.out.println("Fields in Relation: Primary, Foreign");
for (nFld = 0; nFld < relEnforced.Fields.getCount(); nFld++)
      {
      fldPrimeKey = relEnforced.Fields[nFld];
strPrimary = fldPrimeKey.getName());
      System.out.println(strPrimary + "\t") ;

strForeignName = fldPrimeKey.GetForeignName());
      System.out.println(strForeignName + "\n");
      }
db.Relations.Delete("EnforcedOneToMany");
db.TableDefs.Delete("Referenced");
db.TableDefs.Delete("Referencing");
```

## The *Container* Object

`Container` objects enable you to query for information on any object stored in the `DBEngine` hierarchy. You can then get or set the owner permissions or set security information on the object.

More important than the information-gathering capabilities of the `Container` object (at least to Microsoft Access and the Jet Engine) are the contents of the `Container`—the document. Microsoft Access uses application-defined containers to store its own objects, such as forms and resources. Perhaps a future release of DAO will enable you to define your own containers and documents.

## The *Error* Object

When an error occurs, DAO returns information that is very useful to you and the user. The raw form of the information isn't very useful, however, because it is error information in a COM format. To enhance the trapping of those messages, the `Error` object, an interface through which you can discover information on the error, was created.

Like Data Access Objects, the `Error` object handles the data in a hierarchical fashion. The lowest-level error is always the first `Error` object, the next lowest is the second, and so on. In other words, when an error occurs, it is appended onto the end of the `Errors` collection.



# Learning How DAO Objects Interact

You've explored code examples and explanations of individual objects; now you will learn how to make these components work together. Because these objects can react much differently with one another depending on the methods and properties that you use, this section takes you step-by-step through the points you must consider when using the methods and properties of the DAO objects, as shown in Table 6.9.

Similar to the previous section, you will see the interactions at each level—the `DBEngine`, the `Workspace`, and the `Database` objects. First, however, you must acquaint yourself with the constants that affect the objects' behavior.

The first interaction that you will have with DAO involves the `DBEngine` object. Although much of this object's usefulness is tied to its methods, its properties are useful for determining how the `DBEngine` object behaves and what the objects that you create with it inherit.

**Table 6.9 *DBEngine* Properties**

| Property | Description |
|---|---|
| `DefaultPassword` | Sets the default user password for the Jet Engine |
| `DefaultUser` | Sets the default account used to log on to the Jet Engine |
| `IniPath` | Specifies a path in the registry to obtain configuration information |
| `LoginTimeout` | Specifies the ODBC login timeout |
| `SystemDB` | Specifies the Jet System database—must be done before creating any other objects with this `DBEngine` object |
| `Version` | Returns the version of the Jet Engine being used |

Setting the `LoginTimeout` property would have a definite impact on ODBC uses because this directly affects the amount of time you will wait for a logon request to be responded to. Setting the `IniPath` property, which stores driver configurations in the registry, can also affect the behavior of the `DBEngine` object. An example using these properties, (except for `SystemDB`, which is only for Access databases), is shown in Listing 6.16.

**Listing 6.16 DBPROPS.JAVA—Using the Properties of the *DBEngine* Object to Control Its Behavior**

```
try{
        mgr = new LicenseMgr();
        idbengine = (_DBEngine)mgr.createWithLic
        (
                  "mbmabptebkjcdlgtjmskjwtsdhjbmkmwtrak",
                  "{00000010-0000-0010-8000-00AA006D2EA4}",
            null,
            ComContext.INPROC_SERVER
        );
}
catch(com.ms.com.ComFailException e)
{m_objErrors =
➥idbengine.getErrors();System.out.println(m_objError.getDescription());}int ver;
String inipath = "HKEY_LOCAL_MACHINE\\SOFTWARE\\Microsoft\\CSVQuery\\1.0\\ODBC";
```

```
idbengine.setIniPath(inipath);
idbengine.setDefaultUser("Bob");
idbengine.setDefaultPassword("password");
idbengine.setODBCLoginTimeout(15);

ver = idbengine.getVersion();
MessageBox mb = new MessageBox("Jet Engine Version", "Version: " + ver, VJ_OK);
```

Pretty simple. By setting the default user and password, you don't have to set them for each `Workspace` object unless security is required. It is true that the `Version` property is mainly for show, unless you've built an application that designs itself around a particular version of the engine at runtime. You're already familiar with what the ODBC timeout value does. The `SystemDB` property simply specifies the path to an Access system database.

These are only some of the ways that you can influence the `DBEngine` object. Using the different constants properties when calling methods is the other way.

It makes sense when you think about it. Methods accept parameters and act according to what you pass them. In DAO, you have a standard set of parameters, which isn't really referred to in the DAO documentation, at least not in the form in which you will see them. Call the set of parameters the `Constants` collection, because this is how we use them in Visual J++. Simply create a `Variant` data type and use the `put` or `get` methods to place the value into the `Variant`, as in the following code snippet:

```
Variant flAccess = new Variant();
flAccess.putInt(RecordsetOptionEnum.dbReadOnly);
```

By using these properties, which usually are friendly names for bitmasks or integers, you can use the same method to accomplish wildly different goals. Consider the `CompactDatabase` method of the `DBEngine` object, for example. It accepts several arguments, most of which are optional, in addition to the database paths. There is a `Settings` property that defines what happens when you compact the database. Depending on the value in the `Settings` property, you could encrypt the database, set the version stamp, or change the collating order. The properties of the `CompactDatabase` method are listed in Table 6.10.

Part II Ch 6

**Table 6.10 *Settings* Properties for the *CompactDatabase* Method**

| Property value | Description |
|---|---|
| `dbLangGeneral` | English, German, French, Portuguese, Italian, and modern Spanish locales |
| `dbLangArabic` | Arabic locale |
| `dbLangCzech` | Czech locale |
| `dbLangCyrillic` | Russian locale |
| `dbLangDutch` | Dutch locale |

*continues*

**Table 6.10 Continued**

| Property value | Description |
|---|---|
| `dbLangGreek` | Greek locale |
| `dbLangHebrew` | Hebrew locale |
| `dbLangHungarian` | Hungarian locale |
| `dbLangIcelandic` | Icelandic locale |
| `dbLangNordic` | Nordic languages locale (Microsoft Jet database engine version 1.0 only) |
| `dbLangNorwdan` | Norwegian and Danish locale |
| `dbLangPolish` | Polish locale |
| `dbLangSwedfin` | Swedish and Finnish locale |
| `dbLangSpanish` | Traditional Spanish locale |
| `dbLangTurkish` | Turkish locale |
| `dbEncrypt` | Encrypts the database while compacting |
| `dbDecrypt` | Decrypts the database while compacting |
| `dbVersion10` | Creates a database that uses the Jet Engine version 1.0 data format while compacting |
| `dbVersion11` | Creates a database by using the Jet Engine version 1.1 data format while compacting |
| `dbVersion20` | Creates a database by using the Jet Engine version 2.0 data format while compacting |
| `dbVersion30` | Creates a database by using the Jet Engine version 3.0 data format while compacting |

Quite a few results could occur depending on how you use the property. You can combine properties as well, for there is no need to use just one. For example, you have a database that will be accessed internationally in several different locales. Setting the property value to `dbLangGeneral` might or might not enable different locales to access the database. The answer, then, is to sum the constants when adding them to the `Variant`, as shown in Listing 6.17.

**Listing 6.17 SUMPROPS.JAVA—Setting Multiple Properties**

```
// This program takes two command line arguments for the database paths

public static void main(String args[])
{
```

```
hr = hrParseCommandLine(args[]);


Workspace workspace;
Database db;
Variant settings = new Variant();
Variant locale = new Variant();
String ver;
String user = "Bob";
Variant password = new Variant();
Password.putString("password");
String db1 = "db1.mdb";
String db2 = "db2.mdb";
ILicenseMgr mgr;
DBEngine idbengine;
dao350.Error  m_objError;
try{
               mgr = new LicenseMgr();
                    idbengine = (_DBEngine)mgr.createWithLic
                    (
                  "mbmabptebkjcdlgtjmskjwtsdhjbmkmwtrak",
                  "{00000010-0000-0010-8000-00AA006D2EA4}",
                       null,
                       ComContext.INPROC_SERVER
                    );
}
catch(com.ms.com.ComFailException e)
m_objErrors =
➥idbengine.getErrors();System.out.println(m_objError.getDescription());}


try{
      idbengine.setDefaultUser(user);
      idbengine.setDefaultPassword(password);

ver = idbengine.getVersion();
MessageBox mb = new MessageBox("Jet Engine Version", "Version: " + ver, VJ_OK);

       locale.putInt(LanguageConstants.dbLangGeneral +
➥LanguageConstants.dbLangCyrillic);
       settings.putInt(DatabaseTypeEnum.dbEncrypt +
➥DatabaseTypeEnum.dbVersion20);
          idbengine.CompactDatabase(db1, db2, locale, settings, password );
      workspace = engine. _30_CreateWorkspace ("","","");
      db = workspace.OpenDatabase(db2);

       ver = db.getVersion();
        MessageBox mb = new MessageBox("Jet Data Format Version", "Version: " +
➥ver, VJ_OK);

}catch(Exception e){System.out.println(e);}
```

Now consider the `Workspace` object. In Listing 6.17, notice that we set the default user and password and then used those defaults to shorten the call to `CreateWorkspace`. A similar attribute can also be used with the `Workspace` object to specify the default user account for the `Database` objects that you create. The `Workspace` object has only three properties, two of which, the `Name` property and the `UserName` property, you've already seen. The third property, `IsolateODBCTrans`, informs the Jet Engine that you want to isolate the ODBC transactions that affect the same database from one another. Isolating the transactions is beneficial if you want to keep events caused by the transactions from interfering with other transactions in the same database.

The `Workspace` object has four different methods that you can use to instance other objects and to control how they act, listed as follows:

- `CreateDatabase` Saves the database to disk and returns a `Database` object
- `CreateGroup` Creates and returns a new `Group` object
- `CreateUser` Creates and returns a new `User` object
- `OpenDatabase` Opens an existing database and returns a reference to a `Database` object

Of these four methods, `OpenDatabase` is the only method that you have not fully explored. (`CreateGroup` and `CreateUser` are discussed in section "The *Group* and *User* Objects," and the `CreateDatabase` method supports the same properties as the `CompactDatabase` method.) The `OpenDatabase` method enables you to determine the lock type, sharing control, and a connection string. You can specify any string to pass through by using the same syntax you would use if setting the `Database.Connect` property, as follows:

```
Database db;
String
connect="ODBC;DATABASE=C:\CSV\Export.csv;UID=Joe;PWD=password;DSN=Exchange;LOGINTIMEOUT=
10";

Variant ConnectString = new Variant();
ConnectString.putString(connect);

db = workspace.OpenDatabase("Exchange", true, true, ConnectString);
```

**NOTE** To use the connection string argument for the `OpenDatabase` method, both the second (exclusive) and third (read-only) arguments must be set to `TRUE`.

After opening a `Database` object, you can do several things with it besides set its properties. Although you considered these methods earlier, you don't yet know the various ways that you can use them. The bulk of your coding will involve using these methods: `CreateTableDef`, `Execute`, `MakeReplica`, `OpenRecordset`, and `Synchronize`.

## The *CreateTableDef* Method

The CreateTableDef method uses the TableDef object's attribute's property to specify options for the table definition. You can use the properties listed in Table 6.11, either singly or in concert.

**Table 6.11 *TableDef* Object's Attributes**

| Attribute | Description |
|---|---|
| dbAttachExclusive | Indicates that the attached table is open for exclusive use. Valid only for local Jet databases. |
| dbAttachSavePWD | Indicates that the user ID and password for a remote attached table are saved with the connection information. This property is set for an appended TableDef object. |
| dbSystemObject | Indicates that the table is a system table provided by the Jet database engine. This property is set for an appended TableDef object. |
| dbHiddenObject | Indicates that the table is a hidden table provided by the Jet database engine. This property is set for an appended TableDef object. |
| dbAttachedTable | Indicates that the table is a non-ODBC attached table, such as FoxPro (read-only). |
| dbAttachedODBC | Indicates an attached ODBC table (read-only). |

Any of these attributes can be set after you append the TableDef object, creating the table.

## The *OpenRecordset* Method

The OpenRecordset method accepts more options than any other method of the Database object. Although changing the Recordset object type has been covered, setting the cursor options and concurrency controls has not. Table 6.12 lists the wealth of arguments that you can use for the options argument of the OpenRecordset method.



**Table 6.12 The *OpenRecordset* Options Arguments**

| Argument | Description |
|---|---|
| dbAppendOnly | You can append only new records (Dynaset-type Recordset object only). |
| dbForwardOnly | Recordset object is a forward-only scrolling Snapshot. |

*continues*

**Table 6.12 Continued**

| Argument | Description |
|---|---|
| `dbSQLPassThroughSQL` | Tells the Jet Engine to pass the SQL statement through to an ODBC database for processing without translating it. |
| `dbSeeChanges` | Generates a trappable runtime error if another user is changing data that you are editing. |
| `dbDenyWrite` | No one else can modify the table while you have it open. |
| `dbDenyRead` | No one else can view the data while you have it open (Table-type `Recordset` object only). |
| `dbReadOnly` | You can only view records. |
| `dbInconsistent` | Enables inconsistent updates (Dynaset-type `Recordset` object only). |
| `dbConsistent` | Enables only consistent updates (Dynaset-type `Recordset` object only). |

**NOTE** `Recordset` objects created with the `ForwardOnly` option set cannot be cloned and only support `MoveNext` to move through the result set.

If you open a `Recordset` object with `DenyRead` or `DenyWrite`, other users will probably experience frustration. Also, even though it improves the performance of the update, allowing inconsistent updates can get you into trouble because you could wind up violating referential integrity.

## The *Synchronize* Method

Use the `Synchronize` method when you've created a replica using the `MakeReplica` method and want to synchronize the replicas with one another. The `Synchronize` method supports three attributes to determine the replication type that takes place when you synchronize the replicas, listed as follows:

- `dbRepExportChangesSend` Exports the changes from the local table
- `dbRepImportChangesReceive` Receives the changes from the foreign table
- `dbRepImpExpChanges` (Default) Causes a bi-directional exchange of data

## The Properties of the *Database* Object

Now that you have examined the methods more fully, explore the properties of the `Database` object. You can determine a great deal of information about the current state of the database from the `Database` object's properties, as listed in Table 6.13.

**Table 6.13 Properties of the *Database* Object**

| Property | Description |
|---|---|
| `CollatingOrder` | Enables you to specify the sort order to be language specific |
| `Connect` | Enables you to specify driver-specific information |
| `Name` | Allows you to define a name for the object |
| `QueryTimeout` | Sets the ODBC timeout for a query |
| `RecordsAffected` | Holds the records affected by the last operation |
| `Transactions` | Indicates `TRUE` if the database supports transactions and `FALSE` if not |
| `Updatable` | Indicates `TRUE` if you can make changes to the database |
| `V1xNullBehavior` | Indicates whether or not zero-length strings are converted to `NULL` in a memo or text field |
| Version | Indicates the data format version |

**NOTE** You can increase the performance of your updates by removing the `V1xNullBehavior` property from the properties collection and handling the conversion of zero-length string to `NULL` values yourself.

# ODBC Programming with DAO

Now that you have learned a great deal about DAO programming, you should focus on the ODBC portion of the DAO API. Most of the code remains the same, but there are some subtle differences. For example, when you are opening a new database and you've decided to use an ODBC data source instead of a Jet database, a connection string must be supplied. Although this is still done with the `OpenDatabase` method, it is a little different.



In DAO 3.0, you have to use the `OpenRecordset` method by using an ODBC connection string, which links the ODBC to the Jet database as an attached table and enables you to execute queries, including `SQLPassThrough` queries. You could also set the ODBC options for the Jet Engine in the registry, using the new com.ms.lang package from Microsoft. This requires loading the Jet Engine, however, and running all ODBC transactions through a linked ODBC table. You can open them directly. However, the performance suffers due to the overhead of passing all of the transactions through the Jet Engine.

Enter DAO 3.5 and `ODBCDirect`. The `ODBCDirect` interface enables you to perform queries directly against the ODBC data source without loading the Jet Engine. This might not be news for VB and VC++ users, but for Java developers, it is very good news because the direct ODBC port hasn't been done (well, not exactly; the new Transaction Server has several interesting classes—ODBC classes), and a date for supporting JDBC hasn't been determined. Support to achieve greater performance hasn't been there for Java developers as it has been for C++ programmers. This has created a problem for Java programmers, because even VB users could access, load, and use ODBC32.DLL. Well, now you have two methods to use ODBC directly: DAO with `ODBCDirect` and RDO, which is covered in Chapter 7, "Remote Data Objects."

How do you use `ODBCDirect`? In DAO 3.5, Microsoft added two constants to the collection, `dbUseJet` and `dbUseODBC`, which are used as options to the `CreateWorkspace` method. You can also specify the default value if you decide not to pass the optional argument—the property to use is `DefaultType`, which defaults to `dbUseJet`. If you continue to use the `Workspace` method as usual, it will continue to function as it always has, but if you pass it the `dbUseODBC` property, you will take advantage of DAO 3.5. The way in which you use DAO to support this new capability has changed, however, including the addition of a new object.

## Changes to the *Workspace* Object

In addition to the new `Type` property, which is read-only, there are several other changes to the existing property collection of the `Workspace` object. You now have a property called `DefaultCursorDriver`—setting this property to `dbUseDefaultCursor` informs the ODBC Driver Manager that the default cursor should be used by the driver. You can also tell the driver that no cursor is needed, or to use a forward-only, read-only-type cursor, which will return a single record per fetch. To use no cursor, simply set the `DefaultCursorDriver` property to `dbNoCursor`.

## *Connection* Object and the *Database* Object

Supporting the ODBC interfaces has forced a new object type to be created, but the similarities between the `Connection` object and the `Database` object are so great that most of you probably wonder why Microsoft even added a new object. Only the `Connection` object has the capability to asynchronously execute SQL statements against the data source. The `Connection` object also can create prepared statements in the form of temporary `QueryDef` objects. In contrast, the `Database` object can't create a `QueryDef` object unless it is attached to a Jet database.

This does not mean that you will hang up the `Database` object for good: It simply makes more sense for a Java developer to use the `Connection` object. There is one cool trick Microsoft put into these objects: the capability to transform one object into another. With the addition of a `Database` property on the `Connection` object and a `Connection` property on the database object, you can change object types to suit your specific needs.

Using the `OpenConnection` and `OpenDatabase` methods of the `Workspace` object is somewhat different if the `dbUseODBC` property is set. In this case, you use the second argument to specify the driver prompting for the data source, exactly as in the ODBC `SQLConnect`, `SQLDriverConnect`, and `SQLBrowseConnect` functions. An example of opening a `Workspace` object and opening a `Connection` object is shown in Listing 6.18.

**Listing 6.18 ODBCCONN.JAVA—Creating a *Connection* Object in Java with *ODBCDirect***

```
Workspace workspace;
Database db;
Connection cn;
Variant flType = new Variant();
Variant flPrompt = new Variant();
ILicenseMgr mgr;
DBEngine idbengine;
dao350.Error  m_objError;
try{
               mgr = new LicenseMgr();
                    idbengine = (_DBEngine)mgr.createWithLic
                    (
                  "mbmabptebkjcdlgtjmskjwtsdhjbmkmwtrak",
                  "{00000010-0000-0010-8000-00AA006D2EA4}",
                       null,
                       ComContext.INPROC_SERVER
                    );
}
catch(com.ms.com.ComFailException e)
m_objErrors =
➥idbengine.getErrors();System.out.println(m_objError.getDescription());}

String
connect="ODBC;DATABASE=C:\CSV\Export.csv;UID=Joe;PWD=password;DSN=Exchange;LOGINTIMEOUT=
➥10";
flType.putInt(Constants.dbUseODBC);

workspace =idbengine.CreateWorkspace("SomeWorkspace", strUser, strPassword,
➥flType);

// Open the Database object

flPrompt.putInt(Constants.dbDriverRequired);
db = workspace.OpenDatabase("",flPrompt, true, connect);

// Open a Connection Object to the same data source
cn = workspace.OpenDatabase("",flPrompt, true, connect);
```



## Using the *QueryDef* with *ODBCDirect*

The major difference between using the `QueryDef` object with a Microsoft Jet database and using the `QueryDef` object with the new ODBCDirect interface lies in the `Connection.CreateQueryDef()`. The `Database` object still uses `QueryDef` objects in exactly the same manner as before, including the limitation of using them only against Jet databases.

The QueryDef object is created by calling to the Connection.CreateQueryDef() method. This particular implementation of the CreateQueryDef method is supported against ODBC data sources and has the added benefit of being able to run asynchronously.

The QueryDef object has several properties of a prepared statement in ODBC or RDO. Setting the SQL property generates an access plan on the data source, which is then used to actually execute the statement. By using the QueryDef object, however, you can also control the amount of records retrieved into the cache at one time with the CacheSize property. With the QueryDef object created in the ODBCDirect workspace, only the CachSize property is used. The FillCache and CacheStart properties of the QueryDef object created with the Jet type Database object cannot be used in the ODBCDirect workspace. You would use the CachSize property to determine the number of records cached by the Recordset object by using the QueryDef object. As soon as the Recordset object is created, the property becomes read-only.

You can also use DDL to create and use stored procedures with the QueryDef object. You can do this by using the DDL language to create the stored procedure, and then use the correct syntax for calling the stored procedure in your code, as shown in Listing 6.19.

**Listing 6.19 STOREDPROC.JAVA—Creating and Using a SQL Stored Procedure from Java**

```
Workspace workspace;
Database db;
Connection cn;
Variant flType = new Variant();
Variant flPrompt = new Variant();
ILicenseMgr mgr;
DBEngine idbengine;
dao350.Error  m_objError;
try{
               mgr = new LicenseMgr();
                    idbengine = (_DBEngine)mgr.createWithLic
                    (
                 "mbmabptebkjcdlgtjmskjwtsdhjbmkmwtrak",
                 "{00000010-0000-0010-8000-00AA006D2EA4}",
                       null,
                       ComContext.INPROC_SERVER
                    );
}
catch(com.ms.com.ComFailException e)
m_objErrors =
➥idbengine.getErrors();System.out.println(m_objError.getDescription());}

String
connect="ODBC;DATABASE=C:\CSV\Export.csv;UID=Joe;PWD=password;DSN=Exchange;LOGINTIMEOUT=
➥10";
flType.putInt(Constants.dbUseODBC);

workspace = idbengine.CreateWorkspace("SomeWorkspace", strUser, strPassword,
➥flType);
```

```
flPrompt.putInt(Constants.dbDriverRequired);

// Open a Connection Object to the same data source
cn = workspace.OpenDatabase("",flPrompt, true, connect);

// Create and execute the stored procedure
strSQL = "CREATE PROC storedproc AS SELECT * FROM SomeTable;"
cn.Execute(strSQL);

// Create the Query definition

QueryDef query;
query = cn.CreateQueryDef("Stored Proc Example", "{call storedproc()}");

// Set the cach size to 200 records
query.setCachSize(200);

// Open a recordset on the results
Recordset rec;
rec = query.OpenRecordset();
```

Parameterized queries are also supported by using the ODBC syntax. Microsoft also added a `Direction` property to the `QueryDef` object to better handle the return values. Listing 6.20 provides an example of using a stored procedure to return a value and retrieve it.

**Listing 6.20 STOREPROC.JAVA—Retrieving a Value from a Procedure**

```
Workspace workspace;
Database db;
Connection cn;
Variant flType = new Variant();
Variant flPrompt = new Variant();
ILicenseMgr mgr;
DBEngine idbengine;
dao350.Error  m_objError;
try{
              mgr = new LicenseMgr();
                  idbengine = (_DBEngine)mgr.createWithLic
                  (
                "mbmabptebkjcdlgtjmskjwtsdhjbmkmwtrak",
                "{00000010-0000-0010-8000-00AA006D2EA4}",
                     null,
                     ComContext.INPROC_SERVER
                  );
}
catch(com.ms.com.ComFailException e)
m_objErrors =
➥idbengine.getErrors();System.out.println(m_objError.getDescription());}

String
connect="ODBC;DATABASE=C:\CSV\Export.csv;UID=Joe;PWD=password;DSN=Exchange;
➥LOGINTIMEOUT= 10";
```

Part II

Ch 6

*continues*

**Listing 6.20 Continued**

```
flType.putInt(Constants.dbUseODBC);

workspace = idbengine.CreateWorkspace("SomeWorkspace", strUser, strPassword,
➥flType);

flPrompt.putInt(Constants.dbDriverRequired);

// Open a Connection Object to the same data source
cn = workspace.OpenDatabase("",flPrompt, true, connect);

// Create and execute the stored procedure
strSQL = "CREATE PROC storedproc AS SELECT * FROM SomeTable";
cn.Execute(strSQL);

// Create the Query definition

QueryDef query;
Parameter param1;
Parameter param2;
Variant constant;
constant.putInt(dbReturnValue);

query.Parameters(0).setDirection(constant);
query.Parameters(1).setValue(10);

query = cn.CreateQueryDef("Stored Proc Example", "{? = call storedproc(?)}");

// Set the cach size to 200 records
query.setCachSize(200);

// Open a recordset on the results
Recordset rec;
rec = query.OpenRecordset();

Variant retval =- new Variant();
retval = query.Parameters(0).Value();
```

## *Recordset* Objects with *ODBCDirect*

ODBC defines several cursors, which are now mapped directly to the `Recordsets` with which you've been dealing. Table 6.14 describes each type of cursor these `Recordsets` provide.

**Table 6.14 *Recordset* Object Types and the ODBC Cursor Equivalants**

| ***Recordset* Type** | **ODBC Cursor** |
|---|---|
| Table | None, the Table-type `Recordset` object is supported only with Jet databases |
| Snapshot | Static scrolling cursor |

| *Recordsets* Type | ODBC Cursor |
|---|---|
| Dynaset | Keyset-driven cursor |
| Forward-only | Basically no cursor, scrolls forward through the result set |
| Dynamic | Dynamic |

In addition to the recordset capabilities in `ODBCdirect`, there are now locking options that you can specify by using the `attribute's` property when opening a `Recordsets`, as shown in Table 6.15.

**Table 6.15 Locking Under *ODBCDirect***

| Property | Description |
|---|---|
| `dbOptimistic` | Same as the ODBC concur row version. |
| `dbPessimistic` | Same as the ODBC concur lock. |
| `dbOptimisticValue` | Same as the ODBC concur values. |
| `dbOptimisticBatch` | Data is not sent to the server until you call the `Update` method of the `Recordset` object with the `dbBatchUpdate` attribute set. |
| `dbReadOnly` | Read-only lock, no changes can be made. |

Thanks to the `NextRecordSet` method, you also can handle multiple returns from a single SQL statement. This method enables you to scroll forward through recordsets, as you would use `MoveNext` to move the cursor through a single recordset. You will lose the update, insert, and delete capabilities when using multiple recordsets. You also need to set them up properly. To properly set up multiple recordsets, you must use local cursors, a Forward-only `Recordset` object with the attributes set to read-only (which default for both on the `Workspace` object when using `ODBCDirect`), or use the `dbNoCursor` property when opening a recordset and set the `CacheSize` property to 1.

You also have support for batched updates, which means that all updates are cached locally until you make a call to the `Update` method of the `Recordset` object and use the `dbBatchUpdate` option. To create a batch operation:

1. Create the `ODBCDirect`-type `Workspace` object.
2. Set the `DefaultCursorDriver` property to `dbUseClientBatchCursor`. This will pass all SQL calls through to the Client cursor library.
3. Set the lock type to `dbOptimisticBatch`. If you have a dirty read or update, you can resolve the problem by using the new property of `BatchCollisions` (an array of bookmarks in which there was a failure) in concert with the `BatchCollisionCount` property, or the `Visible` and `OriginalValue` properties of the `Field` object.

As mentioned before, Asynchronous queries are now supported by the `Recordset` object's new attribute, `dbRunAsync`. When you open a recordset with this property passed to the method, your query executes while giving control back to your application. You don't have any callback functions or events to set a watch on as you do with ODBC and RDO. You can, however, check the `StillExecuting` property of the query. To cancel one of these queries, use the `Cancel` method. Be careful though, as this will only end the thread, not roll back any transactions.

Despite these enhancements, `ODBCDirect` does restrict functionality somewhat when using the `Recordset` object. For example, indexing and using the `Seek` method are not available, nor can you use the `Find` methods (although this might be a blessing, as the whole table must be cached locally for these methods).

# Working with DAO

Your assignment is to create a small application that can convert an MS-Mail import file into a Microsoft Exchange CSV import file. The administrator wants to be able to import MS-Mail users into Exchange from an MS-Mail Import-formatted file and have the option to create accounts or to create Custom Recipients (from Microsoft Exchange external addresses).

First, let's take a look at our program requirements. Using an ODBC text driver and setting the option to use the first column as a header takes care of the variable columns. By using the `getName()` method of the `Recordset` object, getting the names of the columns will be fairly easy.

Now consider the MS-Mail file. The Import format used in MS-Mail employs specific columns or tabs as delimiters. In the case of extracted addresses, the columns will be in the fixed-field format. This either requires you to set up another ODBC text driver with fixed columns and first records that are not the column headers or use a text parser (as is done in this case). The actual formats are detailed as follows.

The MS-Mail Import File comes in two forms: with fixed width fields or with columns 1–3 separated by tabs and the fourth column immediately following the third. The field widths for the fixed width version and the column names are listed as follows:

- *Column 1* (Transaction Type)—range 1
- *Column 2* (Display Name)—range 3–33 (varies)
- *Column 3* (Address Type)—range 34–37
- *Column 4* (Address)—range 38–512 (varies according to address)

The Exchange CSV file is simply a comma-delimited file with the column headers as the first record. It can be variable in length. Next, generally map out how the flow of control will run. Figure 6.2 shows a simple data flow diagram that demonstrates what the program will be doing.

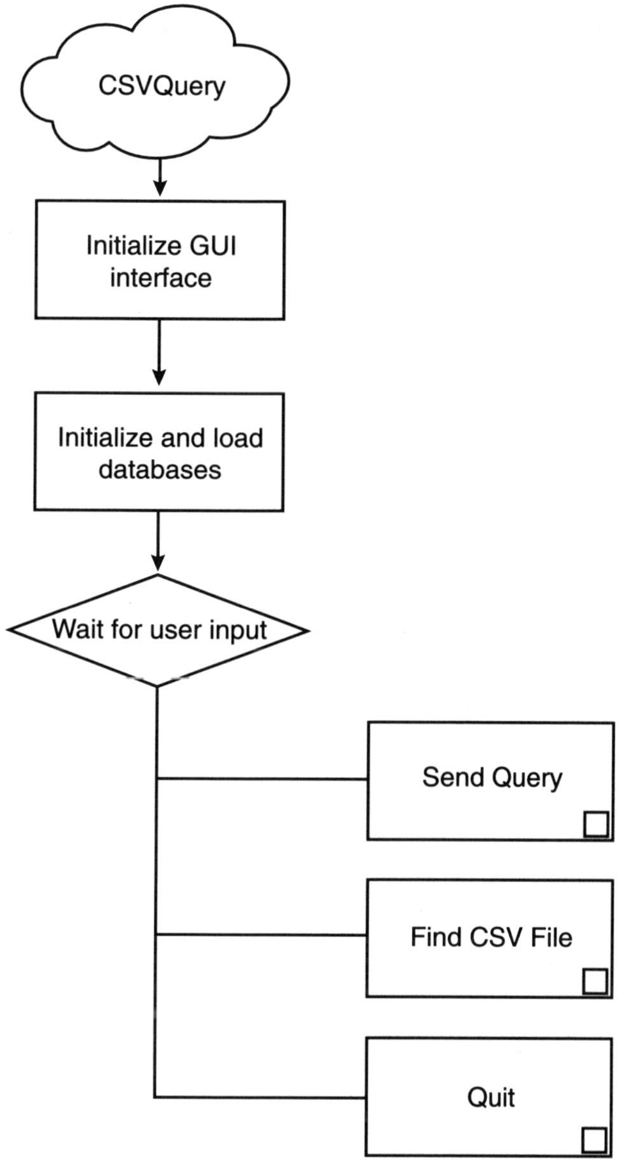


**FIG. 6.2**
This data flow diagram for the CSV program details how the data will move through the application.



Now that the data flow diagram provides a starting point for building this program, you can begin with a top-down design approach. There will be two data sources, so a class to read databases is beneficial. To that class you will add methods that append, copy sets of rows, and select and pass back columns of data. The classes and methods that you need are listed as follows:

- Methods to handle reading in the MS-Mail Import file
- Methods to deal with sets of data given a Postoffice/or Network name
- Methods dealing with spooling out the CSV file (using ODBC, of course)
- An initialization code to deal with registering data sources
- A user interface that doesn't create more confusion than it solves

This isn't too much to deal with. To begin the top-down design approach, you must build a user interface and tie the data to it, as shown in Listing 6.21.

**Listing 6.21 ICU.JAVA—Dialog Interface for the MS-Mail Import Utility**

```
//------------------------------------------------------------------------------
// IDD_CSVDialog.java:
//          Implementation for container control initialization class
IDD_CSVDialog
//
// WARNING: Do not modify this file.  This file is recreated each time its
//          associated .rct/.res file is sent through the Java Resource Wizard!
//
// This class can be use to create controls within any container, however, the
// following describes how to use this class with an Applet.  For addtional
// information on using Java Resource Wizard generated classes, refer to the
// Visual J++ 1.1 documention.
//
// 1) Import this class in the .java file for the Applet that will use it:
//
//      import IDD_CSVDialog;
//
// 2) Create an instance of this class in your Applet's 'init' member, and call
//    CreateControls() through this object:
//
//      IDD_CSVDialog ctrls = new IDD_CSVDialog (this);
//      ctrls.CreateControls();
//
// 3) To process events generated from user action on these controls, implement
//    the 'handleEvent' member for your applet:
//
//      public boolean handleEvent (Event evt)
//      {
//
//      }
//
//------------------------------------------------------------------------------
import java.awt.*;
import DialogLayout;

public class IDD_CSVDialog
{
      Container    m_Parent       = null;
      boolean      m_fInitialized = false;
      DialogLayout m_Layout;
```

```
// Control definitions
//-----------------------------------------------------------------------
TextField     m_Source;
TextField     m_Dest;
Label         m_sourceLabel;
Button        m_Convert;
Label         m_WelcomeLabel;
Label         IDC_STATIC3;
Label         IDC_STATIC4;
Label         m_destLabel;
Button        m_Browse;
Button              m_Save;


// Constructor
//-----------------------------------------------------------------------
public IDD_CSVDialog (Container parent)
{
      m_Parent = parent;
}

// Initialization.
//-----------------------------------------------------------------------
public boolean CreateControls()
{
      // Can only init controls once
      //-----------------------------------------------------------------
      if (m_fInitialized ¦¦ m_Parent == null)
            return false;

      // Parent must be a derivation of the Container class
      //-----------------------------------------------------------------
      if (!(m_Parent instanceof Container))
            return false;

      // Since there is no way to know if a given font is supported from
      // platform to platform, we only change the size of the font, and not
      // type face name.  And, we only change the font if the dialog
      // resource specified a font.
      //-----------------------------------------------------------------
      if (true)
      {
            Font OldFnt = m_Parent.getFont();
            Font NewFnt = new Font(OldFnt.getName(), OldFnt.getStyle(), 8);

            m_Parent.setFont(NewFnt);
      }

      // All position and sizes are in Dialog Units, so, we use the
      // DialogLayout manager.
```

*continues*

**Listing 6.21 Continued**

```
            //------------------------------------------------------------------
            m_Layout = new DialogLayout(m_Parent, 287, 151);
            m_Parent.setLayout(m_Layout);
            m_Parent.addNotify();

            Dimension size   = m_Layout.getDialogSize();
            Insets    insets = m_Parent.insets();

//          m_Parent.resize(insets.left + size.width  + insets.right,
//                          insets.top  + size.height + insets.bottom);

            // Control creation
            //------------------------------------------------------------------
            m_Source = new TextField ("");
            m_Parent.add(m_Source);
            m_Layout.setShape(m_Source, 95, 65, 117, 14);

            m_Dest = new TextField ("");
            m_Parent.add(m_Dest);
            m_Layout.setShape(m_Dest, 95, 85, 117, 14);


            m_sourceLabel = new Label ("Source File:");
            m_Parent.add(m_sourceLabel);
            m_Layout.setShape(m_sourceLabel, 30, 65, 60, 9);

            m_destLabel = new Label ("Destination File:");
            m_Parent.add(m_destLabel);
            m_Layout.setShape(m_destLabel, 30, 85, 60, 9);


            m_Convert = new Button ("Convert");
            m_Parent.add(m_Convert);
            m_Layout.setShape(m_Convert, 160, 130, 50, 14);

            m_Save = new Button ("Set CSV");
            m_Parent.add(m_Save);
            m_Layout.setShape(m_Save, 85,  130, 50, 14);

            m_Browse = new Button ("Browse");
            m_Parent.add(m_Browse);
            m_Layout.setShape(m_Browse, 35, 130, 50, 14);

            m_WelcomeLabel = new Label ("Welcome to the MSMail Import Conversion
➥Wizard");
            m_Parent.add(m_WelcomeLabel);
            m_Layout.setShape(m_WelcomeLabel, 30, 14, 181, 14);
```

```
            IDC_STATIC3 = new Label ("Use this wizard to convert the text files
➥created using");
            m_Parent.add(IDC_STATIC3);
            m_Layout.setShape(IDC_STATIC3, 30, 30, 181, 18);

            IDC_STATIC4 = new Label ("the Import -x command to a format suitable
➥for Exchange.");
            m_Parent.add(IDC_STATIC4);
            m_Layout.setShape(IDC_STATIC4, 30, 42, 181, 18);


            m_fInitialized = true;
            return true;
        }
}
```

We included a Register button for the data source because we expect the clients to need the data source to be installed and configured for them. This way, if the client doesn't have the Exchange data source on the machine, you can create one and all that the client has to do is browse to the file.

Now that the difficult part is finished, you must attend to the database class. Building a query engine isn't difficult: Accept whatever string is passed to you, connect to the data source, and execute. Listing 6.22 shows the `Query` method. The `Connect` method is the other part of our data class. These methods read the ODBC connection string from the registry, as well as the default data values used when creating the Exchange Data Source.

First, we'll set up our database connection in the applet's `start()` method, as shown in Listing 6.22.

**Listing 6.22 DATA.JAVA—The Implementation of the Import Conversion Wizard**

```
        public void start()
        {
                if (m_ICU == null)
                {
                        m_ICU = new Thread(this);
                        m_ICU.start();
                }
                // TODO: Place additional applet start code here
                varEmpty.putEmpty();
                try{
                mgr = new LicenseMgr();
                  idbengine = (_DBEngine)mgr.createWithLic
                (
                        "mbmabptebkjcdlgtjmskjwtsdhjbmkmwtrak",
```



*continues*

**Listing 6.22 Continued**

```
                "{00000010-0000-0010-8000-00AA006D2EA4}",
              null,
                ComContext.INPROC_SERVER
          );

          idbengine.RegisterDatabase("ICU","Microsoft Text Driver
➥ (*.txt;*.csv)","False","Mode=Import");
            // Open a connection

          }
          catch(com.ms.com.ComFailException e)
          {m_objErrors =
➥idbengine.getErrors();System.out.println(m_objError.getDescription());}


      }
```

Next, we'll have to decide how to handle the events generated for our user interface. Again, this is fairly simple, as shown in Listing 6.23, because we know what the events were when the interface was designed.

**Listing 6.23 DATA.JAVA—Using the Applet's *Action()* Method to Handle the Events Our Applet Generates**

```
      public boolean action(Event evt, Object arg)
      {
            if(evt.target instanceof Button)
            {
                  if(arg.equals("Browse"))
                  {
                        Frame f = new Frame();
                        m_fdlg = new FileDialog(f, "Choose Import File",
➥FileDialog.LOAD);
                        m_fdlg.setFile(m_ImpFile);
                        m_fdlg.show();
                        m_File = m_fdlg.getDirectory() + m_fdlg.getFile();
                        m_sourceDLG.m_Source.setText(m_File);
                  }

                  else if(arg.equals("Set CSV"))
                        {
                              Frame f = new Frame();
                              m_fdlg = new FileDialog(f, "Create CSV File",
➥FileDialog.SAVE);
                              m_fdlg.setFile(m_CSVFile);
                              m_fdlg.show();
                              m_File = m_fdlg.getDirectory() +
➥m_fdlg.getFile();
                              m_sourceDLG.m_Dest.setText(m_File);
```

```
                }
            else if (arg.equals("Convert"))
            {
                try{
                    m_sourceFile = new
➥File(m_sourceDLG.m_Source.getText());

                    if(m_sourceDLG.m_Mailbox.getState())
                         m_HS = m_sourceDLG.m_HomeServer.getText();
                    else
                        m_HS ="";

                    if(!m_sourceFile.exists())
                         this.showStatus("File Not Found");
                    else
                    {
                        this.showStatus("File OK");
                        m_destFile = new
➥File(m_sourceDLG.m_Dest.getText());
                        Convert(m_sourceFile,m_destFile);
                    }


                  }
                catch(IOException e){System.out.println(e);}
            }

            else if(arg.equals("< Back"))
            {

            }

            else if(arg.equals("Next >"))
            {

            }

            else if(arg.equals("Cancel"))
            {

                return true;
            }
            else return false;


        }
        else if(evt.target instanceof Checkbox)
        {
            if(evt.target == m_sourceDLG.m_Mailbox)
                {
                m_CreateMB = m_sourceDLG.m_Mailbox.getState();
                if(m_CreateMB)
                    m_sourceDLG.m_HomeServer.enable();
                else
                    m_sourceDLG.m_HomeServer.disable();
```

*continues*

**Listing 6.23 Continued**

```
                    }

                else if(evt.target == m_sourceDLG.m_Create)
                {
                        m_Trans = m_sourceDLG.m_Create.getState();
                        if(m_Trans)
                        m_flTransactionType = "create";
                }

                else if(evt.target == m_sourceDLG.m_Delete)
                {
                        m_Trans = m_sourceDLG.m_Delete.getState();
                        if(m_Trans)
                             m_flTransactionType = "delete";
                }
                else if(evt.target == m_sourceDLG.m_Update)
                {
                        m_Trans = m_sourceDLG.m_Update.getState();
                        if(m_Trans)
                        m_flTransactionType = "update";
                }
                else if(evt.target == m_sourceDLG.m_Modify)
                {
                        m_Trans = m_sourceDLG.m_Modify.getState();
                        if(m_Trans)
                        m_flTransactionType = "modify";
                }

            }
            return super.action(evt,arg);
    }
```

Next, we'll do the actual conversion. We opened a stream on the import file that we will be converting and parsed through it. As soon as the `readLine()` returns, we'll use DAO to add the new record to the CSV file, as shown in Listing 6.24.

**Listing 6.24 DATA.JAVA—The *Convert()* Method Responsible for the Actual Work of the Applet**

```
public void Convert(File m_source, File m_dest) throws IOException
{
   if(!m_sourceFile.exists()) this.showStatus("File Not Found - Convert");
   try{
        Workspace m_objWorkspace = idbengine.CreateWorkspace("ICU","admin",
        "password", WorkspaceTypeEnum.dbUseODBC);
        Variant flDriverPrompts = new Variant();
        flDriverPrompts.putInt(DriverPromptEnum.dbDriverCompleteRequired);
```

```
        m_vOptions.putShort((short)(readOnly ?
                        RecordsetOptionEnum.dbReadOnly : 0));
        Variant m_vConnectStr = new Variant();
        m_vConnectStr.putString("ODBC;DATABASE=;UID=admin;PWD=password;DSN=ICU");
        Connection m_objConnection = m_objWorkspace.OpenConnection("ICU",
➥flDriverPrompts, m_vOptions,m_vConnectStr);

// Create a new recordset
        m_vRecordsetType.putShort((short)RecordsetTypeEnum.dbOpenDynamic);
        m_vOptions.putShort((short)
                (readOnly ? RecordsetOptionEnum.dbReadOnly : 0));
        m_vLockType.putInt(LockTypeEnum.dbOptimistic);
        m_objRecordset = m_database.OpenRecordset(m_dest, m_vRecordsetType,
        m_vOptions,m_vLockType);

        DataInputStream in = new DataInputStream(new FileInputStream(m_source));
        String str = "";
        m_length = m_sourceFile.length();
        index = 0;

        while(!EOF)
        {
                index++;
                try{str = in.readLine();}
                catch(Exception e)
                {
                        this.m_percentDone=100;
                        showStatus("Recipients Converted");
                }
                if(str.equals(null))
                {
                        EOF = true;
                        return;
                }
                else
                {
                        m_strLength = str.length();
                        m_trans = str.substring(0,1);
                        m_Display = str.substring(2,32);
                        hrSplitDisplay(m_Display);
                        //m_proxies = hrCreateProxies();
                        m_iDelim = str.indexOf(":");
                        m_addrType = str.substring(m_iDelim-3, m_iDelim);
                        m_iLength = str.length();
                        m_addr = str.substring(m_iDelim, m_iLength);
                        s = new StringTokenizer(m_addr,"/");
                        s.nextToken();
                        s.nextToken();
                        m_alias = s.nextToken();

                        if (m_addrType.startsWith("PCM"))
                        {
                            m_ExType = "MS";
                        }
                        else if (m_addrType.startsWith("FAX"))
```



*continues*

**Listing 6.24 Continued**

```
            {
                m_ExType = "FAX";
            }
            else if (m_addrType.startsWith("MCI:"))
            {
                m_ExType = "MCI";
            }
            else if (m_addrType.startsWith("MHS"))
            {
                m_ExType = "MHS";
            }
            else if (m_addrType.startsWith("PROFS"))
            {
                m_ExType = "PROFS";
            }
            else if (m_addrType.startsWith("SMTP"))
            {
                m_ExType = "SMTP";
            }
            else if (m_addrType.startsWith("SNADS"))
            {
                m_ExType = "SNADS";
            }
            else if (m_addrType.startsWith("X.400"))
            {
                m_ExType = "X.400";
            }
            if(m_CreateMB)
                m_class = "Mailbox";
            else
                m_class = "Remote";
            add("Obj-class",m_class);
            add("mode",m_flTransactionType);
            add("Initials",m_Initial);
            add("First Name",m_FirstName);
            add("Last Name",m_LastName );
            add("Display Name",m_Display);
            add("Alias Name", m_alias);
            add("Directory Name", m_alias);
            add("E-mail address",m_ExType + m_addr);
            add("E-mail Addresses",m_proxies);
            add("Home-Server",m_HS);
            setPercentDone(m_strLength, index);
        }
}
in = null;
out = null;
}catch(Exception e)
{
```

```
                this.m_percentDone=100;
                showStatus("Recipients Converted: " + this.index);
            }
}
```

The `Add()` method abstracts the actual data access to streamline the `Convert()` method. Because we are only concerned with writing into a database, we left the database access methods in the main applet instead of implementing a generic data access class. With real projects (most of which will be much larger) you might want to move the DAO or RDO code into separate classes (see Listing 6.25).

**Listing 6.25 DATA.JAVA—Using DAO to Implement the Actual Stream Out to the CSV File**

```
public boolean add(String strCol, String strVal)
{
      Column.putString(strCol);
      Value.putString(strVal);

      try
      {
            m_objRecordset.AddNew();
            m_objRecordset.putCollect(Column, Value);
            m_objRecordset.Update(UpdateTypeEnum.dbUpdateRegular, false);
            return true;
      }
      catch(com.ms.com.ComFailException e)
      {
             m_objErrors = idbengine.getErrors();
             System.out.println(m_objError.getDescription());
             return false;
      }
}
```

## Database Replication with DAO



Database replication interests most business people, especially salesmen. For some reason, replicating a database has been the paragon to achieve of late. Just take a look at the exploding Internet markets and the e-mail and GroupWare market to see that replication is as much a buzzword as Data Warehousing is. This might be due to the growing importance of this data and the need to have redundant access to it; but it is also because replication can actually lessen the cost of ownership dramatically.

With replication, a single administrator could make changes for the entire organization that would replicate throughout the company. This is how modern operating systems and enterprise messaging systems behave. Now vendors are seeing the benefit of providing this for the Internet as a means of firewalling out the possibility of intrusion.

This interest is great if someone else writes the replication code and handles the headaches of achieving synchronicity within the data environment. Before you explore the process of implementing replication, you must consider some of the major problems that you're going to encounter.

The obvious problem concerns determining which table to update; a collision resolution mechanism needs to be implemented. The Jet Engine handles simple file time and date stamp conflicts, but what about those that go beyond that? What happens when replicating data violates the referential integrity of another table? Or you replicate a structure change that conflicts with one made from a replica? These are some of the issues that you will face in a normal environment with several database administrators; they will use your system to its limits and beyond, expecting replication to never have any problems. When problems do occur, database administrators know who to turn to though, their one programmer—you.

Does replication still sound great? Yes, it does, but you must know how to prevent a support nightmare from happening.

## Replication Topology Considerations

First, consider the replication design phase. You need to decide how best to set up your replicas and the replication topologies that you will follow. Common sense tells you most of the ways that you can set up replication—full replication, single-master replication, or multiple databases in charge of replication. Indeed, replication-topology design seems much simpler than database design, and for the most part it is.

A popular design at the moment is the Star topology, in which a single database initiates all of the replications for a particular group of databases. This solves the conflict resolution problems, as well as most of the other issues. This format is much too slow, however, if you are designing something like a groupware system such as Microsoft Exchange. As the number of replicated databases grows, you might consider a multiple master model, with several Stars linked together in a snowflake pattern, replicating with each other fully.

An alternative format, and the one used in Microsoft Exchange (which is based on a much-enhanced version of the Jet database), is the Routed topology. The basic Routed design has multiple sites where each database replicates fully within the site; the links between sites also replicate fully, based on a least-cost algorithm. Your application would determine if a route to the replica were available and would choose the route that was given the least cost. This is a good model for WANs with some slow or unreliable links due to the capability to control the replication route.

**How Does Microsoft Exchange Really Replicate?**

Microsoft Exchange doesn't use the basic replication scenarios listed in this book. Instead, replication is done via direct RPC calls between servers in the same site and via e-mail messages between sites. When replicating via e-mail, the topology takes on the Routed features by the nature of the Microsoft Exchange MTA. The MTA keeps track of seven different variables that detail the conditions of the available routes (of which the route cost is the fifth element considered) and can dynamically re-route around broken connections.

Although significantly more complex, another possible form for the Routed topology is to switch to links between the sites to replicate once to a bridgehead server for each update, setting up multiple routes to the other sites, but only replicating over a single route.

Solving the incoming replication problems could be rather ugly when a single site receives multiple replicated portions from different sites, but this can be overcome by using robust conflict resolution methods. Changing the intra-site replication could simplify problems, as well.

Make a single database the Replication Master, and then when the Replication Master is no longer up, have the rest of the site determine who has the latest replicated content and promote that database to the Replication Master.

## Programming Replication with DAO

Now that you've considered the design issues, you must actually implement the code for replication. Listing 6.26 illustrates Linked topology using the Exchange utility shown in the previous section.

**Listing 6.26 LINK.JAVA—Implementing a Linked Synchronization in Java**

```
// This will simply connect to the closest neighbor and synchronize

public static void main(String args[])
{
Database dbRouteinfo;
Database local;
int rc;
int index = 1;
ILicenseMgr mgr;
DBEngine idbengine;
dao350.Error  m_objError;
try{
              mgr = new LicenseMgr();
                   idbengine = (_DBEngine)mgr.createWithLic
                   (
                 "mbmabptebkjcdlgtjmskjwtsdhjbmkmwtrak",
                 "{00000010-0000-0010-8000-00AA006D2EA4}",
```



*continues*

**Listing 6.26 Continued**

```
                        null,
                        ComContext.INPROC_SERVER
                    );
}
catch(com.ms.com.ComFailException e)
m_objErrors =
➥idbengine.getErrors();System.out.println(m_objError.getDescription());}


// Use the defaults for now
idbengine.OpenDatabase(local);

// Code could be placed here to determine who the nearest neighbor was

Variant SyncType() = new Variant();
SyncType.putInt(SynchronizeTypeEnum.dbRepImpExpChanges);

// Test the route before trying to synchronize

rc = TestRoute(strRoute);

if (rc!=RC_SUCCESS)
            exit();

try{local.Synchronize(strRoute, SyncType);} catch(Exception
➥e){System.out.println(e)}
}


public int TestRoute(String strRoute)
{
      int rc = RC_SUCCESS;

try{Database test = idbengine.OpenDatabase(strRoute);}
catch(Exception e){rc = RC_DB_NOT_AVAILABLE;}
finally{return( rc);}
}
```

Notice that the synchronization was simply from one replica database to another. Though simple, the linked topology is very useful, its greatest drawback being the latency of the replication (see Figure 6.3).

Next take a look at how to implement the Routed Star topology synchronization. It's quite a bit more complex, but we've simplified the code in Listing 6.27 for this example.

**FIG. 6.3**
Examples of some of the replication topologies discussed here are shown only to give an idea of what is possible.

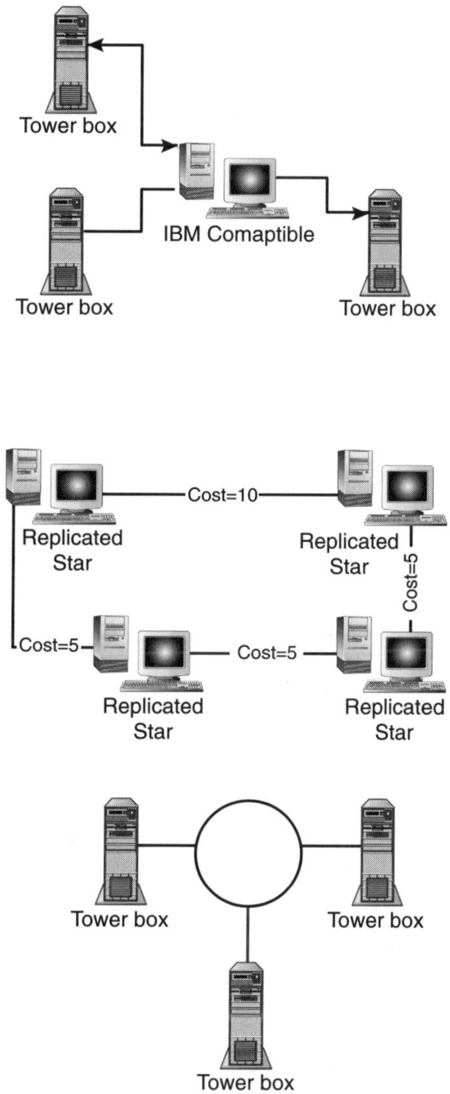




**Listing 6.27 ROUTED.JAVA—Performing a Synchronization in a Routed Star Topology Environment**

```
// Initialize routing information by reading a database holding the routing
information into an array
public static void main(String args[])
{
```

*continues*

**Listing 6.27 Continued**

```
String strRoute[];
Database dbRouteinfo;
Database local;
int rc;
int index = 1;

        ILicenseMgr mgr;
        DBEngine idbengine;
dao350.Error  m_objError;
try{
            mgr = new LicenseMgr();
                    idbengine = (_DBEngine)mgr.createWithLic
                    (
                  "mbmabptebkjcdlgtjmskjwtsdhjbmkmwtrak",
                  "{00000010-0000-0010-8000-00AA006D2EA4}",
                       null,
                       ComContext.INPROC_SERVER
                    );
}
catch(com.ms.com.ComFailException e)
m_objErrors =
➥idbengine.getErrors();System.out.println(m_objError.getDescription());}

// Use the defaults for now
idbengine.OpenDatabase(local);


rc = rcGetRoutingInfo(dbRouteInfo, strRoute[]);

if (rc = RC_NOT_FOUND)
exit();
try
{
rc = rcTestRoute(strRoute[0]);
while (rc = RC_FAILED)
{
      rcTestRoute(strRoute[index]);
            index++;
}

}catch(OutOfBoundsException e){
System.out.pritln(e);
Exit();
}

sync(strRoute[I]);

public int rcGetRouteInfo(strRouteInfo, strRoutes[])
{
      Database route;
      Recordset rec;
      String strSQL = "SELECT DBPath FROM Routes ORDER BY Cost";
```

```
        int rc = RC_DB_NOT_AVAILABLE;

Variant flTableType = new Variant();
        Variant flAccess = new Variant();

        flTableType.putInt(RecordsetTypeEnum.dbSnapshot);
        flAccess.putInt(RecordsetOptionsEnum.dbReadOnly);

        // Open the route database
try{

route = idbengine.OpenDatabase(strRouteInfo);

        // Open a recordset on the table
rec = route.OpenRecordset(strSQL,flTableType, flAccess);

int count = rec.getCount();
strRoutes[] = rec.getRows(count-1);

        }
        catch(Exception e){rc = RC_DB_NOT_AVAILABLE;}
        finally{return( rc);}
}

public void Sync(String strRoute, _DBEngine engine )
{

        Variant SyncType() = new Variant();
        SyncType.putInt(SynchronizeTypeEnum.dbRepExportChanges);

        try{local.Synchronize(strRoute, SyncType);}
catch(Exception e){System.out.println(e);}
}


public int TestRoute(String strRoute)
{
        int rc = RC_SUCCESS;

try{Database test = engine.OpenDatabase(strRoute);}
catch(Exception e){rc = RC_DB_NOT_AVAILABLE;}
finally{return( rc);}
}
```



Notice that this is a very simple example of implementing the Routing topology. We didn't check for inconsistencies or attempt to resolve conflicts. Most of the code for this type of implementation would involve error catching and resolution. Determining routes and costs is easy, as is replication.

# From Here...

You've explored SQL, ODBC, and DAO, learned the basics of building and designing a replicable data environment, and considered examples that use ODBC and text files as a data source. Sounds like a full day. Ah, but there is more. The next chapter introduces you to another interface from Microsoft called Remote Data Objects.

RDO is an ODBC wrapper, rolling up many of the ODBC functions in an attempt to make developing applications in ODBC easier. You'll notice many similarities between RDO and ODBC because much of the same syntax and processes are used with both.

- Chapter 4, "The SQL Standard: A Language for Data Access," details the intricacies of the SQL language and how to use it.
- Chapter 5, "ODBC," explores the architecture of the Open Database Connectivity standard and the APIs that lie behind DAO and RDO.
- Chapter 7, "Remote Data Objects," focuses on the fastest method currently available to Java programmers for ODBC connectivity and data access.

CHAPTER 7

# Remote Data Objects

**Installing RDO**

Installing RDO support for Visual J++ is simple with this small guide.

**Exploring RDO**

Take an in-depth journey into the objects, methods, and properties of RDO.

**Understanding RDO result sets**

RDO can bring the power of SQL to your application; learn how to deal with SQL result sets.

**Using transactions**

Learn how transactions are handled in RDO.

**Using prepared statements**

Learn how to use prepared statements with RDO.

**Creating reusable queries with parameterized queries**

Apply the ease of function style queries to your application.

**Abstracting the RDO interface for multi-tier applications**

Create an RDOQ class that enables your thin clients to harness the power of RDO.

Remote Data Objects (RDO) were introduced with Visual Basic 3.0 to ease access to remote data sources. Microsoft took the ODBC API's and wrapped most of the functionality up into a set of interfaces (a dll). Doing so gave Visual Basic users most of the power the C/C++ engineers had in dealing with remote data.

The COM implementation of RDO has also given Java developers an immediate solution to remote data access needs through Visual J++. So, until Microsoft ships a direct port of the ODBC API, RDO will be the tool of choice for dealing with ODBC data sources. ■

# Installing Remote Data Objects in Visual J++

Installing RDO is a simple task, similar to installing any other COM object. Simply use the JavaTypeLibrary Wizard and select Remote Data Objects 2.0. The JavaTypeLibraryWizard will generate a summary.txt in the <%Windir%>/Java/Trustlib/msrdo20 directory, which will contain the class reference.

Visual J++ 1.1 actually includes the installation of the database components in the setup routine, further simplifying the process.

# An Overview of RDO

Using RDO is very similar to using ODBCDirect with DAO. Both object models are almost exactly the same, with the exception of the Jet specific objects in DAO. Why should there be two interfaces that do the same thing? Well, partly because RDO has been around for a while, and DAO just entered the ODBC business, and partly because RDO still offers more features to the developer than DAO does. For example, with ODBCDirect in DAO, you have to check the `StillExecuting` property of an asynchronous query. With RDO, you can wait for events to fire. Take a look into the RDO model, explore the objects and their methods, and then go on to more theoretical pursuits.

## The RDO Object Model

At first glance, the RDO object model seems to be DAO. Well, not exactly. Although they follow a similar methodology, object-oriented design, these two are distinctly different from one another.

Remote Data Objects (RDO) got their start in ODBC wrapper functions for Visual Basic. For a long time, users of VB had to make do with DLL calls to the ODBC API or with loading the Jet Engine to access the ODBC layers. This changed with RDO 1.0. With RDO, a VB user could access the ODBC API directly, using much of the syntax that DAO does. Now those same wrapper functions are at our disposal in Visual J++ with RDO 2.0 (RDO version 1.0 is available, as well). Basically, the RDO 2.0 object hierarchy looks like this:

- `rdoEngine`
- `rdoEnvironment` and `rdoError`
- `rdoConnection`
- `rdoResultSet`, `rdoTable`, and `rdoPreparedStatement`
- `rdoColumn` and `rdoParameter`

For those of you who are more visually oriented, Figure 7.1 offers a graphical representation of the RDO object model.

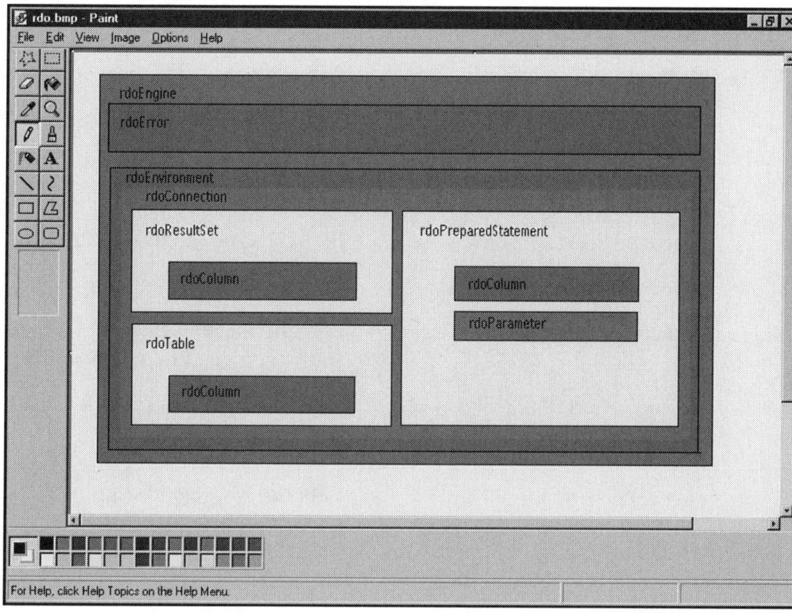


**FIG. 7.1**
RDO 2.0 object model shows the relationships of the various RDO interfaces available for the developer.

## The *rdoEngine* Object

The `rdoEngine` object is the root of the RDO hierarchy. With it, you can determine many of the defaults of the objects that you create, such as `rdoError` and `rdoEnvironment`. You can set or retrieve these properties using the methods listed in Table 7.1.

**Table 7.1 The *rdoEngine* Object**

| Method | Description |
|---|---|
| `getrdoDefaultCursorDriver` | Returns the default cursor being used by the ODBC Driver Manager |
| `getrdoDefaultErrorThreshold` | Returns the threshold at which, if an error number is less than, an exception is thrown |
| `getrdoDefaultLoginTimeout` | Returns the number of seconds that the ODBC Driver will wait while attempting to connect to a data source |
| `getrdoDefaultPassword` | Returns the default user's passwordv |
| `getrdoDefaultUser` | Returns the name of the default user |
| `getrdoEnvironments` | Returns the `rdoEnvironments` collection for the `rdoEngine` object |
| `getrdoErrors` | Returns any errors that might have occurred |

*continues*

**Table 7.1 Continued**

| Method | Description |
|---|---|
| `getrdoLocaleID` | Returns the language local |
| `getrdoVersion` | Returns the version of the RDO library associated with the object |
| `putrdoDefaultCursorDriver` | Sets the type of ODBC cursor that you can use |
| `putrdoDefaultErrorThreshold` | Sets the error threshold |
| `putrdoDefaultLoginTimeout` | Sets the number of seconds that the Driver Manager tries to connect to a data source |
| `putrdoDefaultPassword` | Sets the default password |
| `putrdoDefaultUser` | Sets the default user |
| `putrdoLocaleID` | Sets the language locale |

As you can see, most of these are related to the default connection strings and environment variables. The `rdoEngine` object also has two methods that can be used to perform tasks: the `rdoCreateEnvironment` and `rdoRegisterDataSource` methods.

The `rdoCreateEnvironment` enables you to create and control the ODBC environment, which refers to the security context and the transaction context for the connection. Unlike most methods, however, there are no optional arguments to the `rdoCreateEnvironment` method. All of the arguments must be provided by the user when making a call to this method.

The `rdoRegisterDataSource`, on the other hand, accepts many options. Although most of these options are set through the attributes argument of the method, you have the capability to specify a list of keywords to be added to the ODBC.INI (or registry).

In Listing 7.1, you'll find an example using all of the methods and properties available to the `rdoEngine`. This small application does the following:

1. Queries the `rdoEngine` object for the active workspaces.
2. If no workspace is returned (there won't be), a workspace is created after setting up the defaults for the environment.
3. Checks to see if the data source is registered.
4. If the data source is not registered, the application registers the data source.

**Listing 7.1 LITTLEENGINE.JAVA—Exploring the *rdoEngine* Object**

```
import msrdo20.*;
import java.lang.*;
import com..ms.com.*;
```

```
public class LittleEngine
{

rdoEngine engine = (rdoEngine) new rdoEngine();
rdoEnvironment environ;
rdoEnvironments environColl;
int seconds;
int threshold;
String version;
String configDSN;
rdoErrors errors;

public void LittlEngine()
{

engine.putrdoDefaultPassword("Mocha");
engine.putrdoDefaultUser("Almond");

seconds = engine.getDefaultLoginTimeout();
threshold = engine.getDefaultErrorThreshold();

if (threshold < 10)
engine.putDefaultErrorThreshold(10);

version = getrdoVersion();
locale = engine.getrdoLocaleID();

switch(locale)
{
     case 0:
     language = "System";
     break;

     case 1:
     language = "English";
     break;

     case 2:
            language = "French";
     break;

     case 3:
            language = "Italian";
     break;

     case 4:
            language = "Japanese";
     break;

     case 5:
     language = "Chinese";
     break;

     case default:
```



*continues*

**Listing 7.1 Continued**

```
        langguage="System";
    }

    // Check if we are using Server base cursors, if not, use ODBC cursors
    if(!engine.rdogetDefaultCursorDriver() = CursorDriverConstants.rdoseServer)
    {
        engine.rdoputDefaultCursorDriver(CursorDriverConstants.rdUseODBC);
    }

    environColl = engine.getrdoEnvironements();
    // Create the environment using the defaults we've supplied
    if (!environColl)
    {
        environ = engine.CreateEnvironment("Work");
    }

    configDSN = "DATABASE=\\JAKARTA\MOOSE.MDB;USER=CHRISLE;PASSWORD=;";
    engine.RegisterDataSource("Moose", "odbcjt32.dll", true, configDSN);

    errors = engine.getrdoErrors();
     }
    }
```

In Listing 7.1, notice that no check is made to ensure that your client has registered this data source. To do that, the application must

1. Attempt a connection
2. Determine whether or not the error returned was related to connecting to the DSN
3. Register the new DSN and try again

As you can see, though, RDO is somewhat easier to work in than DAO, even though the two are quite similar. This is due primarily to the fact that you can pass almost every argument as a normal data type in RDO instead of using Variants. Avoiding Variants cuts the memory footprint of your application, and enables faster response times (using atomic data types is always significantly faster than casting into a COM object).

## The *rdoEnvironment* Object

The `rdoEnvironment` is the workspace of RDO. With this object you can make connections to data sources, control transactions, find out information, and set specific environment properties, such as changing the cursor type or the security context for the environment. Table 7.2 explores this object's methods further.

**Table 7.2 Exploring the *rdoEnvironment* Object**

| Method | Description |
|---|---|
| `BeginTrans` | Begins a transaction. |
| `Close` | Closes the environment and removes it from the `rdoEnvironment` collection. |
| `CommitTrans` | Commits all open transactions for an environment. |
| `getCursorDriver` | Returns the type of cursor in use. |
| `gethEnv` | Returns the ODBC environment handle. |
| `getLoginTimeout` | Returns the login timeout value. |
| `getName` | Returns the name of the `rdoEnvironment` object. |
| `getrdoConnections` | Returns a `rdoConnections` object, enumerating all active connections. |
| `getUserName` | Returns the default user name. |
| `OpenConnection` | Opens a connection to an ODBC data source. |
| `putCursorDriver` | Specifies the type of cursor to use. |
| `putLoginTimeout` | Sets the amount of time the ODBC driver will wait for a response from the data source during a login request. |
| `putPassword` | Sets the password to be used in the environment. |
| `putUserName` | Sets the user context for the environment. |
| `RollbackTrans` | When called through the `rdoEnvironment` object, this rolls back all pending transactions for the open connections. |

With many of these methods, there are several "gotchas" to watch out for, the most notable being the scope of a transaction. RDO transactions are initiated with the `BeginTrans()` method, committed with the `Commit()` method, and rolled back with `RollbackTrans()`. The problem is that these transactions are global, just like the transactions in DAO. To isolate your transactions, you will have to create multiple environments. Rolling back one transaction in a series of transactions within a single `rdoEnvironment` rolls them all back.

In Listing 7.2, the application creates multiple environments with unique settings and opens connections in each of them. This example demonstrates the use of transactions as well as the uses of most of the methods and properties available to the `rdoEnvironment` object.

**Listing 7.2 RDOEVIRON.JAVA—Exploring the *rdoEnvironment* Object**

```
rdoEngine engine = (rdoEngine) new rdoEngine();
rdoEnvironment AdminEnviron;
rdoEnvironment ServerEnviron;
rdoEnvironment UserEnviron;
rdoEnvironments environColl;
rdoConnections AdminConnections;
rdoConnections ServerConnections;
rdoConnections UserConnections;
rdoConnection AdminConnect;
rdoConnection ServerConnect;
rdoConnection UserConnect;
rdoErrors errorColl;
rdoError error;

int seconds;
int threshold;
String version;
String configDSN;


environColl = engine.getrdoEnvironements();
// Create the environments

if(rc!=SUCCESS)
exit();


if (!environColl)
{
     ServerEnviron = engine.CreateEnvironment("WebCrawler", "WebServ", "");
     UserEnviron = engine.CreateEnvironment("WebSearch", "WebServ,"");
            AdminEnviron = engine.CreateEnvironment("WebAdmin","sa", "");

}

AdminEnviron.putCursorDriver(CursorDriverConstants.rdUseIfNeeded);
ServerEnviron.putCursorDriver(CursorDriverConstants.rdUseServer);
UserEnviron.putCursorDriver(CursorDriverConstants.rdUseServer);

AdminEnviron.putLoginTimeout(20);
ServerEnviron.putLoginTimeout(25);
UserEnviron.putLoginTimeout(10);

AdminConnections = AdminEnviron.getrdoConnections();
ServerConnectionc = ServerEnviron.getrdoConnections();
UserConnections = UserEnviron.getrdoConnections();

AdminEnviron.OpenConnection();
ServerEnviron.OpenConnection();
UserEnviron.OpenConnection();
```

## The *rdoConnection* Object

The `rdoConnection` object is to RDO what the `Connection` object is to DAO. Simply defined, it enables you to control the properties of a connection and to perform operations against data sources. You can

- Create prepared statements
- Set up asynchronous execution
- Commit or roll back transactions
- Open result sets on the data source

You can control the state and execution of those methods through the `Connection` object, and also control those same methods through any child objects created with a `Connection` object, such as an `rdoPreparedStatement` object. Table 7.3 lists the methods you can use on the `Connection` object.

**Table 7.3 Exploring the *rdoConnection* Object's Methods**

| Method | Description |
|---|---|
| `BeginTrans` | Begins a transaction. |
| `Cancel` | Cancels an executing query. This does not roll back any changes performed and could have unpredictable results unless the transactions are rolled back first. |
| `Close` | Closes a connection, rolling back all transactions for any open result sets associated with this connection. |
| `CommitTrans` | Commits the transaction. |
| `CreatePreparedStatement` | Creates a prepared statement. |
| `Execute` | Executes a prepared statement or query. |
| `getAsyncCheckInterval` | Sets the timer for checking up on asynchronous queries. |
| `getConnect` | Discovers information about the existing connection. |
| `gethDbc` | Returns the ODBC connection handle. |
| `getName` | Returns the name of the object that you called this method with. |
| `getQueryTimeout` | Returns the amount of time the Driver Manager waits for a query to execute. |
| `getrdoResultsets` | Returns the collection of result sets for this connection. |
| `getrdoTables` | Returns the collection of tables for this connection. |
| `getRowsAffected` | Returns the number of rows affected by the last `Execute`. |

*continues*

**Table 7.3 Continued**

| Method | Description |
|---|---|
| `getStillExecuting` | Returns `TRUE`, if the asynchronous query is still executing, `FALSE` otherwise. |
| `getTransactions` | Returns the transactions collection associated with this object. |
| `getUpdateable` | Returns `TRUE` if you can make changes to the data object, `FALSE` otherwise. |
| `getVersion` | Returns the version of the data source. |
| `OpenResultset` | Opens a new result set on a data source. |
| `putAsyncCheckInterval` | Sets the interval for RDO to update the status of the `StillExecuting` property. |
| `putQueryTimeout` | Sets the interval, in seconds, that the ODBC Driver Manager waits before timing out a query. |
| `RollbackTrans` | Ends all current transactions and restores the `rdoEnvironment` to its initial state before beginning the current operation. |

Obviously most of these methods concern setting the initial state of the connection or with changing it. We'll look at those methods that deal only with the `Connection` object and leave the methods for creating objects until later.

In an actual application, the order in which you call the methods really doesn't matter, except that you must call them before creating any objects in which you want to use these defaults. By using the `get` and `put` methods listed in Table 7.3, you can deal with the properties of the connections. Listing 7.3 details how to put the properties of the `Connection` object to use.

**Listing 7.3 CONNECTPROPS.JAVA—Using the Properties of the *Connection* Object**

```
rdoEngine engine = (rdoEngine) new rdoEngine();
rdoEnvironment objEnvironColl;
rdoConnections objConnectionsColl;
rdoConnection objConnect;
rdoPreparedStatements objPreparedColl;
rdoPreparedStatement objPrepared;
rdoResultsets = objResultsetColl;
rdoResultset = objResultset;
rdoTables = objTablesColl;
rdoTable = objTable;


boolean bStillExecuting;
boolean bUpdateable;
```

```
int iAsyncInterval = 0;
long hDbc = 0;
int iLoginTimeout = 10;
int iQueryTimeout = 10;
int iRowsAffected = 0;
int seconds = 0;
int iThreshold = 10;
String strVersion;
String strConfigDSN;

// init variants
Variant vflPrompt = new Variant();
Variant vflReadOnly = new Variant();
Variant vflConnectString = new Variant();


environ = engine.CreateEnvironment("WebSearch", "WebServ,"");

environ.putCursorDriver(CursorDriverConstants.rdUseServer);
environ.putLoginTimeout(iLoginTimeout);

// open the connection

vflPrompt.putInt(PromptConstants.rdDriverPrompt);
vflReadOnly.putBoolean(true);

objConnect = environ.OpenConnection("", vflPrompt, vflReadOnly,
vflConnectString);

// Get the connections current properties

iAsyncInterval = objConnect.getAsyncCheckInterval();
strConnect = objConnect.getConnect();
hDbc = objConnect.gethDbc();
strName = objConnect.getName();
iQueryTimeout = objConnect.getQueryTimeout();
iRowsAffected = objConnect.getRowsAffected();
bStillExecuting = objConnect.getStillExecuting();
objTransactions = objConnect.getTransactions();
bUpdateable = objConnect.getUpdateable();
strVersion = objConnect.getVersion();

parseConnectString(strConnect, strDatabase, strDriver, strDSN, strUserID,
strPassword);

// Display the connection parameters

ListBox lb  = new ListBox("Connection Parameters", 2);
lb.setColumns("Property",1);
lb.setColumns("Value",2);
lb.add("Async Check Interval", iAsyncCheckInterval);
lb.add("Data Source Name", strDSN);
lb.add("Database", strDatabase);
lb.add("Driver", strDriver);
lb.add("Connection Handle",lhDbc);
lb.add("Object Name", strName);
```

Part II

Ch 7

*continues*

**Listing 7.3 Continued**

```
lb.add("Password", strPassword);
lb.add("Query Timeout", iQueryTimeout);
lb.add("Row Affected", iRowsAffected);
lb.add("StillExecuting", bStillExecuting);
lb.add("User ID", strUserID);
lb.add("Version", strVersion);
lb.show();

// Change a couple of properties
InputBox("AsyncCheckInterval" iAsyncInterval)
objConnect.putAsyncIntereval(iAsyncInterval);

InputBox("Query Timeout", iQueryTimeout);
objConnect.putQueryTimeout(iQueryTimeout);

// Update the results.
lb.refresh();
```

There are three methods of the `rdoConnection` object that you will be using all of the time. Assuming that you have the `Connection` object created in Listing 7.3, you can create objects with Listing 7.4.

**Listing 7.4 RDOCONNECT.JAVA—Using *rdoConnection* to Create Other RDO Objects**

```
String strPrepared = "One";
Variant vSQL = new Variant();
Variant vLockType = new Variant();
Variant vCursorType = new Variant();
Variant vExecuteOption = new Variant();
Variant vResultsetType = new Variant();

//Set prepared statement options
vSQL.putString("SELECT Sites.Name,Webs.Name FROM Sites, Webs WHERE Site.SiteID
== Web.SiteID");

objConnect.BeginTrans();
objPrepared = objConnect.CreatePreparedStatement(strName, vSQL);

// Set the properties of the result set, including asynchronous execution.
vResultsetType.putInt(ResultsetTypeConstants.rdOpenDynamic);
vLockType.putInt(LockTypeConstants.rdConcurRowVer);
vExecuteOption.putInt(OptionConstants.rdAsyncEnable);

objResult = objConnect.OpenResultset(strName, vResultsetType, vLockType,
vExecuteOption);
```

```
// Do some stuff , but keep checking the StillUpdating property
do while(objResult.getStillExecuting()= true)
{
            // Do something else
}

// Do some stuff with the result set.

// Lets use the Execute method for an ad hoc query
objConnect.Execute(INSERT INTO Site
VALUES('00000030','00000234','microsoft.com'));
```

Only the arguments and property values for each of the methods have been overlooked. They are listed in Appendix A, Data Access Objects 3.5 API.

## The *rdoResultset* Object

You use the `rdoResultset` object to return result sets, an example of which is shown in Listing 7.4. You can specify several different options for your result set, including the cursor type (see Table 7.4), the lock type (see Table 7.5), and the type of execution that you need (see Table 7.6). Choosing the correct options can have a dramatic effect on your application's execution and performance. These options are covered in the following tables.

**Table 7.4 The *rdoCursorTypes***

| Cursor Type | Description |
|---|---|
| `rdOpenForwardOnly` | Uses a forward-only cursor with the result set |
| `rdOpenStatic` | Uses a scrollable static cursor |
| `rdOpenKeyset` | Uses a keyset-driven cursor |
| `rdOpenDynamic` | Uses a dynamic cursor |

**NOTE** When you use the `rdOpenForwardOnly` option, be sure to set the `RowsetSize` property to 1, or you'll generate an exception indicating that you've made an invalid call to `SQLSetPos`. This behavior is only seen if you have large Binary objects (BLOB'S) or IMAGE or TEXT columns. You won't see this problem with normal data types.

**Table 7.5 *rdoResultset* Lock Types**

| Lock Type | Description |
|---|---|
| `rdConcurLock` | The cursor will implement the lowest level of locking needed to enable updating of the row. |
| `rdConcurReadOnly` | No updates are enabled; the cursor is read-only. |
| `rdConcurRowVer` | The cursor uses optimistic concurrency, comparing the row versions to determine if the update is enabled. |
| `rdConcurValues` | Also uses optimistic concurrency, although this style actually compares the data instead of the version attributes. |

The executing options have only three values to set:

- `OptionsConstants.rdAsyncEnable`
- `OptionsConstants.rdExecDirect`
- `0`

The first value is self-explanatory: Using it enables asynchronous execution. The second type is the same as the ODBC function `SQLExecDirect()`; it will simply tell the Driver Manager to pass the statement directly to the Driver. Use the third value, `0`, when you don't need the other two.

The `rdoResultset` has many methods for handling data and the methods that you use to retrieve the data, most of which you will use continually in your code. Table 7.6 lists these methods.

**Table 7.6 Exploring the *rdoResultset* Object**

| Method | Description |
|---|---|
| `AddNew` | Creates a new row |
| `Cancel` | Cancels an asynchronous query |
| `CancelUpdate` | Cancels an update |
| `Close` | Closes the `rdoResultset` object |
| `Delete` | Deletes the record at the cursor position |
| `Edit` | Copies the record at the current position into an edit buffer |
| `getAbsolutePosition` | Returns the absolute row number of the cursor position |
| `getBOF` | Returns `TRUE` if this is the beginning of the file |
| `getBookmark` | Returns the bookmark value for the current row |
| `getBookmarkable` | Returns `TRUE` if the result set supports bookmarks, `FALSE` if not |

| Method | Description |
|---|---|
| getEditMode | Returns the edit state of the current row |
| getEOF | Returns TRUE if the end of file has been reached |
| gethStmt | Returns the ODBC statement handle for the result set |
| getLastModified | Returns a bookmark value of the most recently changed row |
| getLockEdits | Returns TRUE if pessimistic locking is in effect, FALSE for optimistic locking |
| getName | Returns the first 256 characters of the SQL query used to create the result set. |
| GetPercentPosition | Indicates the current row location as a percentage denoting its location in the result set |
| getrdoColumns | Returns the columns collection of the result set |
| getRestartable | Returns TRUE if the result set object supports the Requery method |
| getRowCount | Returns the number of rows accessed in the result set |
| getStillExecuting | Returns TRUE, if the asynchronous query is still executing, FALSE otherwise |
| getTransactions | Returns TRUE if the object supports transactions, FALSE otherwise |
| getType | Returns the actual cursor type |
| getUpdatable | Returns TRUE if this result set is updateable, FALSE if not |
| MoreResults | Clears the current result set and returns TRUE if there are more result sets to be processed |
| Move | Moves the cursor to a specific position in the result set |
| MoveFirst | Moves the cursor to the first record of the result set |
| MoveLast | Moves the cursor to the last record of the result set |
| MoveNext | Moves the cursor to the next record in the result set |
| MovePrevious | Moves to the previous record in the result set |
| putAbsolutePosition | Moves the cursor to a specific row, given the row number |
| putBookmark | Moves the cursor to a specific row by using the row's bookmark |
| putPercentPosition | Moves the cursor a given percentage into the result set |
| Requery | Re-executes the query that was used to create the result set |
| Update | Saves the changes made to the result set |

### Where's the Capability to Bind Columns?

If you've done any DAO or RDO development in other languages (Visual Basic or Visual C++), you have come to know and love a process known as binding. This process enables you to retrieve data several rows at a time into an array.

Well, when you look through the file that RDO 2.0 (or 1.0, for that matter) generates, you will notice the method `GetData()`. This is the method used in Visual J++ to fetch multiple rows into an array. The catch here is that `GetData` hasn't been fully implemented (due to the MIDL compiler) and is therefore unavailable in this version of Visual J++. This means that you will become very familiar with retrieving data a single column at a time.

Although you already have seen a few of the `rdoResultset`'s methods, the majority of them should be illustrated with an example. Adding records requires the `rdoColumn` object, which will be covered in the section titled "The *rdoColumn* Object." Right now, the application simply calls the methods to show the syntax in Listing 7.5.

**Listing 7.5 RDORESULT.JAVA—Using the *rdoResultset* Object**

```
rdoEngine engine = (rdoEngine) new rdoEngine();
rdoEnvironment objEnvironColl;
rdoConnection objConnect;
rdoPreparedStatement objPrepared;
rdoResultsets objResultsetColl;
rdoResultset objResultset;
rdoTransactions objTransactions;
boolean bBOF;
boolean bEOF;
boolean bRestarteable;
boolean bStillExecuting;
boolean bUpdateable;

int hStmt = 0;
int iRowsCount = 0;
int iBookmark = 0;
int iLastModified = 0;
int iLockEdits = 0;
int iEditMode = 0;
int iPos = 0;
int iThreshold = 10;

String strEditMode;
String strCursorType;

// init variants
Variant vflPrompt = new Variant();
Variant vflReadOnly = new Variant();
Variant vflConnectString = new Variant();

environ = engine.CreateEnvironment("WebSearch", "WebServ,"");

environ.putCursorDriver(CursorDriverConstants.rdUseServer);
environ.putLoginTimeout(iLoginTimeout);
```

```
// open the connection

vflPrompt.putInt(PromptConstants.rdDriverPrompt);
vflReadOnly.putBoolean(true);

objConnect = environ.OpenConnection("", vflPrompt, vflReadOnly,
vflConnectString);

// Get the connections current properties
bBOF = objResult.getBOF();
objColumns = objResult.getColumns();
iEditMode = objResult.getEditMode();
bEOF = objResult.getEOF();
hStmt = objResult.gethStmt();
iLastModified = objResult.getLastModified();
iLockEdits = objResult.getLockEdits();
strName = objResult.getName();
iPos = objResult.getPercentPosition();
bRestarteable = objResult.getRestarteable();
iRowsCount = objResult.getRowsCount();
bStillExecuting = objResult.getStillExecuting();
objTransactions = objResult.getTransactions();
iType = objResult.getType();
bUpdateable = objResult.getUpdateable();

parseType(iType, strCursorType);
parseEditMode(iEditMode, strEditMode);


// Display the result set properties

ListBox lb  = new ListBox("Connection Parameters", 2);
lb.setColumns("Property",1);
lb.setColumns("Value",2);
lb.add("Result Set Cursor Type", strCursorType);
lb.add("Absolute Postion", iPos);
lb.add("Beginning of File", bBOF);
lb.add("Bookmark", iBookmark);
lb.add("Bookmarks supported",bBookmarks);
lb.add("Edit Mode", strEditMode);
lb.add("End of File", bEOF);
lb.add("Statement handle", ihStmt);
lb.add("Last Modified Row", iLastModified);
lb.add("Lock Edits", bLockEdits);
lb.add("SQL Query ", strName);
lb.add("Percent position", iPercentPos);
lb.add("Requery Supported", bRestart);
lb.add("Rows accessed", iRowCount);
lb.add("Still Executimg", bStillExecuting);
lb.add("Supports transactions", bTransact);
lb.add("Updates allowed ", bUpdateable);
lb.show();

// Several methods for moving around in a result set
```



*continues*

**Listing 7.5 Continued**

```
objResult.putAbsolutePosition(iPos);
objResult.putBookmark(iBookmark);
objResult.putPercentPosition(iPercentPos);
objResult.Move(iRows);
objResult.MoveFirst();
objResult.MoveLast();
objResult.MoveNext();
objResult.MovePrevious();

// Perform some actions and changes
objResult.Delete();
objResult.Update();

objResult.AddNew();
objResult.CancelUpdate();

// Move off the deleted row and edit the next one.
objResult.MoveNext();
objResult.Edit();
objResult.Update();

// Update the results.
objResult.Requery();
lb.refresh();
```

There are many things to look out for when using the `rdoResultset` object. For example,

- If you delete a row, the change might or might not appear, depending on the type of cursor.
- If you want to perform any other transactions, you also must move off of a deleted row before calling the `Update` method. If you don't move the cursor, then the cursor will still be postitioned on the row marked for deletion.
- If you reposition the cursor when you are editing a row, the edits are lost without warning. Calling an `Update` method at that point would generate an exception.
- After you've begun an `AddNew` or `Edit` method, you cannot call another `AddNew` or `Edit`. This will generate an exception until you finish the operation by calling `Update`.

## The *rdoTable* Object

The `rdoTable` object enables you to perform read-only operations on the base table or on a SQL view. Unlike its DAO counterpart, the Table-type recordset, you are unable to change anything about the structure or the data in the records. Using the `OpenResultset` method on the `rdoTable` object gives you a read-only, forward-only cursor by default, although you can specify other cursor types.

To use the `rdoTable` object, you need to call the `rdoTables.Refresh()` method. This is because the `rdoTables` collection doesn't get populated with the available `rdoTable` objects until its `Refresh` method is called. The `rdoTable` object supports a few methods (see Table 7.7), and it is a very useful object when you are simply doing search and retrieve operations without updating the data. It has all of the benefits of the DAO Table-type `Recordset` without the limitation of being tied to a single Microsoft Jet database table (when opening an `rdoTable` object on SQL Views). It is limited, however, by being read-only.

**Table 7.7 Exploring the *rdoTable* Object**

| Method | Description |
|---|---|
| `getName` | Returns the name of the underlying table |
| `getrdoColumns` | Returns the columns collection of a particular result set |
| `getRowCount` | Returns the number of rows that have been accessed in a `rdoResultset` object |
| `getType` | Returns the type of table you are dealing with |
| `getUpdateable` | Returns `TRUE` if you can update this table or view |
| `OpenResultset` | Opens a result set on the `rdoTable` object |

The `rdoTable.OpenResultset()` method has an interesting limitation. When you create one, a result set is automatically returned with every row in the table or view. You cannot change this feature. In Listing 7.6, the application uses the `rdoTable` object to return all records in a database after finding out all of the information it can about the underlying table.

**Listing 7.6 TABLE.JAVA—Using the *rdoTable* Object**

```
rdoEngine engine = (rdoEngine) new rdoEngine();
rdoEnvironment objEnvironColl;
rdoConnection objConnect;
rdoTables = objTablesColl;
rdoTable = objTable;


boolean bStillExecuting;
boolean bUpdateable;

int iAsyncInterval = 0;
long hDbc = 0;
int iLoginTimeout = 10;
int iQueryTimeout = 10;
int iRowsAffected = 0;
int iRowCount = 0;
int iThreshold = 10;
String strTableType = "";
String strVersion;
String strConfigDSN;
String strTableName;
```

*continues*

**Listing 7.6 Continued**

```
// init variants
Variant vflPrompt = new Variant();
Variant vflReadOnly = new Variant();
Variant vflConnectString = new Variant();
Varaint vidxTable = new Variant();

environ = engine.CreateEnvironment("WebSearch", "WebServ,"");
environ.putCursorDriver(CursorDriverConstants.rdUseServer);
environ.putLoginTimeout(iLoginTimeout);

// open the connection

vflPrompt.putInt(PromptConstants.rdDriverPrompt);
vflReadOnly.putBoolean(false);

objConnect = environ.OpenConnection("", vflPrompt, vflReadOnly,
vflConnectString);

// Retrieve the tables collection and refresh to populate it.
objTables = objConnect.getrdoTables();
objTables.Refresh();

// Retrieve the first table
objTable = objTables.getItem(vidxTable);

// Retrieve its properties
iRowCount = objTable.getRowCount();
strTableName = objTable.getName();
strTableType = objTable.getType();
bUpdateable = objTable.getUpdateable();
objColumns = objTable.getrdoColumns();

// Open a result set on the table
vCursorType.putInt(CursorTypeConstants.rdOpenStatic);

// Use the default locking and execute options.
objTable.OpenResultset("SELECT * FROM Servers", vCursorType, vLockType,
vExecuteOptions);
```

As you can see, this application is an easy way to dump the entire table as a result set. After you have opened the table, however, you can't perform any operations on the data except for read operations. This limits the usage of the `rdoTable` object to mainly information-discovering routines, or special cases in which you would like to return all of the records for viewing.

## The *rdoPreparedStatement* Object

The `rdoPreparedStatement` is a powerful tool to add to your arsenal. When you create a SQL statement and send it to the server, an access plan is generated for each statement sent. The `rdoPreparedStatement` avoids the overhead of these multiple information transfers and processes the request significantly faster than simple SQL queries do. When you create the prepared statement:

1. It is sent across to the server via the ODBC Driver on your client machine.
2. The data source creates the action plan and returns a handle to the access plan, which is what the object that you created really represents.
3. When you use the prepared statement to open a result set, the ODBC statement handle to the access plan is passed to the server, and the server executes the access plan without processing any SQL statements from you.

As a general rule, use prepared statements everywhere unless the query is ad hoc and you can't parameterize the variable pieces of the ad hoc query. If you can parameterize the variable pieces of the query, then do so and use prepared statements. The `rdoPreparedStatement` object has several methods that are detailed in Table 7.8.

**Table 7.8 Exploring the Prepared Statement in RDO**

| Method | Description |
|---|---|
| `Cancel` | Cancels an active query running in asynchronous mode |
| `Close` | Closes the object |
| `Execute` | Executes the prepared statement or SQL statement |
| `getBindThreshold` | Returns the largest size of a column (in bytes) that can be bound without using the `AppendChunk` and `GetChunk` methods |
| `getConnect` | Returns the ODBC connection string |
| `getErrorThreshold` | Returns the error level at which a fatal error will be generated |
| `gethStmt` | Retrieves the ODBC statement handle |
| `getKeysetSize` | Retrieves the current size of the keyset buffer |
| `getLockType` | Retrieves the concurrency type that is in use |
| `getLogMessages` | Returns the path to the ODBC trace file |
| `getMaxRows` | Retrieves the maximum number of rows returned from a query |
| `getName` | Returns the name of the prepared statement object |
| `getQueryTimeout` | Retrieves the amount of time the ODBC Driver Manager waits for a query to complete execution |
| `getrdoColumns` | Returns the `rdoColumns` collection for this prepared statement |
| `getrdoParameters` | Returns the `Parameters` collection for this prepared statement |
| `getRowsAffected` | Returns the number of rows affected in the last `Execute` call |
| `getRowsetSize` | Returns the number of rows currently buffered by your application |
| `getSQL` | Returns the SQL statement for this `rdoPreparedStatement` object |

*continues*

**Table 7.8 Continued**

| Method | Description |
|---|---|
| `getStillExecuting` | Returns `TRUE` while the statement is still executing, `FALSE` otherwise |
| `getType` | Retrieves the type of prepared statement |
| `getUpdatable` | Returns `TRUE` if you can make changes |
| `OpenResultset` | Opens the result set for the prepared statement |
| `putBindThreshold` | Sets the largest amount of data (in bytes) that ODBC can bind without using `GetChunk` and `AppendChunk` |
| `putErrorThreshold` | Sets the level at which a fatal error is generated |
| `putKeysetSize` | Sets the amount of rows held in the keyset buffer (must be larger than the rowset) |
| `putLockType` | Sets the concurrency level for this prepared statement |
| `putLogMessages` | Set to `TRUE` to run an ODBC trace and log to a file |
| `putMaxRows` | Sets the maximum number of rows to be returned in a query |
| `putQueryTimeout` | Sets the query timeout (in seconds) for the prepared statement |
| `putRowsetSize` | Sets the current rowset buffer size |
| `putSQL` | Sets the SQL statement to be prepared |
| `putType` | Sets the type of prepared statement to `SELECT`, `ACTION`, or `PROCEDURE` |

This is quite a list of methods for a single object to have. Listing 7.7 illustrates building a prepared statement, using the methods in Table 7.8.

**Listing 7.7 PREPARED.JAVA—Setting Up and Executing Prepared Statements by Using the *rdoPreparedStatement* Object**

```
rdoEngine engine = (rdoEngine) new rdoEngine();
rdoEnvironment objEnvironColl;
rdoConnection objConnect;
rdoPreparedStatements objPrepStmnts;
rdoPreparedStatement objPrepared;
rdoParameters objParams;
rdoColumns objColumns;

boolean bStillExecuting;
boolean bUpdateable;

int iAsyncInterval = 0;
int iBindThreshold = 10;
```

```
int iErrorThreshold = 10;
int hStmt = 0;
int iKeyset = 0;
int iLockType = 0;
int iLoginTimeout = 10;
int iMaxRows = 0;
int iQueryTimeout = 10;
int iRowsAffected = 0;
int iRowCount = 0;
int iRowset = 0;

String strType = "";
String strVersion;
String strConfigDSN;
String strName;

// init variants
Variant vflPrompt = new Variant();
Variant vflReadOnly = new Variant();
Variant vflConnectString = new Variant();
Varaint vSQL = new Variant();

environ = engine.CreateEnvironment("WebSearch", "WebServ,"");
environ.putCursorDriver(CursorDriverConstants.rdUseServer);
environ.putLoginTimeout(iLoginTimeout);

// open the connection

vflPrompt.putInt(PromptConstants.rdDriverPrompt);
vflReadOnly.putBoolean(false);

objConnect = environ.OpenConnection("", vflPrompt, vflReadOnly,
vflConnectString);

// Set up the prepared statement
strName = "Search";

vType.putInt(QueryTypeConstants.rdQSelect);
vLockType.putInt(LockTypeConstants.rdConcurRowVer);

objPrepared = objConnect.CreatePreparedStatement(strName, vSQL)

// Return information about the prepared statement and it's environment
iBindThreshold = objPrepared.getBindThreshold();
strConnectString = objPrepared.getConnect ();
iErrorThreshold = objPrepared.getErrorThreshold();
ihStmt = objPrepared.gethStmt();
iKeysetSize = objPrepared.getKeysetSize();
iLockType = objPrepared.getLockType();
strLogPath = objPrepared.getLogMessages();
imaxRows = objPrepared.getMaxRows();
strName = objPrepared.getName();
iQueryTimeout = objPrepared.getQueryTimeout();
objColumns = objPrepared.getrdoColumns();
```

Part II Ch 7

*continues*

**Listing 7.7 Continued**

```
objParameters = objPrepared.getrdoParameters();
iRowsAffected = objPrepared.getRowsAffected();
iRowsetSize = objPrepared.getRowsetSize();
strSQL = objPrepared.getSQL();
bStillExecuting = objPrepared.getStillExecuting();
iType = objPrepared.getType();
bUpdateable = objPrepared.getUpdatable();

// Decide if these are ok, then set the ones we want to be different

objPrepared.putBindThreshold(iBindThreshold);
objPrepared.putErrorThreshold(iErrorThreshold);
objPrepared.putKeysetSize(iKeysetSize);
objPrepared.putLockType(iLockType);
objPrepared.putLogMessages(strLogPath);
objPrepared.putMaxRows(imaxRows);
objPrepared.putQueryTimeout(iQueryTimeout);
objPrepared.putRowsAffected(iRowsAffected);
objPrepared.putRowsetSize(iRowsetSize);
objPrepared.putSQL(strSQL);
objPrepared.putType(iType);

// Open a result set

vResultsetType.putInt(ResultsetTypeConstants.rdOpenDynamic);
vExecuteOption.putInt(OptionConstants.rdAsyncEnable);

objResult = objConnect.OpenResultset(strName, vResultsetType, vLockType,
vExecuteOption);
```

## The *rdoColumn* Object

The `rdoColumn` object is the lowest common denominator for operations on the data source. By using the `rdoColumn` object's methods shown in Table 7.9, you can determine a lot of detailed information about the structure and properties of the data itself.

**Table 7.9 Exploring the *rdoColumn* Object**

| Method | Description |
|---|---|
| `AppendChunk` | Inserts large chunks of data into a column |
| `ColumnSize` or `LONGVARCHAR` | Returns the number of bytes in a column of type `LONGVARBINARY` |
| `getAllowZeroLength` | Returns `TRUE` if the column allows zero-length strings |
| `getAttributes` | Indicates the type of column |
| `GetChunk` | Retrieves a specified number of bytes from a column of `LONGVARBINARY` or `LONGVARCHAR` |

| Method | Description |
|---|---|
| `getChunkRequired` | Returns `TRUE` if you need to use `GetChunk` to access the data |
| `getName` | Returns the column name |
| `getOrdinalPosition` | Returns the position of the column in the `Columns` collection |
| `getRequired` | Returns `TRUE` if a non-NULL value is required |
| `getSize` | Returns the maximum length, in bytes, of the column (unless it requires `GetChunk`, which returns 0 on those columns) |
| `getSourceColumn` | Returns the name of the original source of the data for the `rdoColumn` object |
| `getSourceTable` | Returns the name of the original table from which the column came |
| `getType` | Returns the data type of the column |
| `GetUpdatable` | Returns `TRUE` if the column is updateable, `FALSE` otherwise |
| `getValue` | Returns the contents of the current column. |
| `putValue` | Places a value into a column in the current row |

By using the `Column` object, you can easily break up individual rows and update only those columns that need to be updated. This is also the only way to retrieve BLOB's (Binary Large Objects), or CLOB's (Character Large Objects). The `Getchunk` and `AppendChunk` methods are invaluable when dealing with things like images or other multimedia formats, for they enable you to deal with the large masses in smaller chunks that conserve network bandwidth.

The metadata discovered from the `rdoColumn` object can be very useful as well. Knowing the data type is very useful when you intend to place something into a row or want to allocate the correct variable to hold the data returned by the result set. Listing 7.8 shows an example of retrieving the metadata from the `rdoColumn` object.

### Listing 7.8 COLUMN.JAVA—Creating and Using the *rdoColumn* Object

```
rdoEngine engine = (rdoEngine) new rdoEngine();
rdoConnection objConnect;
rdoPreparedStatement objPrepared;
rdoColumns objColumns;
rdoColumn objColumn;

int iChunk;
String strType;
String strName;

// init variants
```



*continues*

**Listing 7.8 Continued**

```
Variant vflPrompt = new Variant();
Variant vflReadOnly = new Variant();
Variant vflConnectString = new Variant();
Varaint vSQL = new Variant();
Variant vidxParam = new Variant();
Variant vDirection = new Varaint();

environ = engine.CreateEnvironment("WebSearch", "WebServ,"");
environ.putCursorDriver(CursorDriverConstants.rdUseServer);
environ.putLoginTimeout(iLoginTimeout);

// open the connection

vflPrompt.putInt(PromptConstants.rdDriverPrompt);
vflReadOnly.putBoolean(false);

objConnect = environ.OpenConnection("", vflPrompt, vflReadOnly,
vflConnectString);

// Open a result set

vResultsetType.putInt(ResultsetTypeConstants.rdOpenDynamic);
vExecuteOption.putInt(OptionConstants.rdAsyncEnable);

objResult = objConnect.OpenResultset(strName, vResultsetType, vLockType,
vExecuteOption);

// Retrieve the columns
objColumns = objResult.getColumns();

for(i=0;i < objColumns.count()-1;i++)
{
      vOrdinal.putInt(i);
     objColumn = objColumns.getItem(vOrdinal);

// Now we can manipulate this column
     bAllowZeroLength = objColumn.getAllowZeroLength();
     iAttributes = objColumn.getAttributes();
     bChunkRequired = objColumn.getChunkRequired();
     strName = objColumn.getName();
     iOrdinal = objColumn.getOrdinalPosition();
     bRequired =  = objColumn.getRequired();
            iSize = objColumn.getSize();
            strSourceColumn = objColumn.getSourceColumn();
            strSourceTable = objColumn.getSourceTable();
            iType = objColumn.getType();

            // Determine data type and cast the variant appropriately
            findType(iType, vValue);

            bUpdateable = objColumn.getUpdateable();

            if(!iSize = 0)
            {
```

```
                        vValue = objColumn.getValue();
        }
        else
        {
                while(true)
                {
                        read(vValue, objColumn.getChunk(iChunk);
                }
        }
}
// Append some data to the Column that we've gather from somewhere
public boolean write(vValue)
{
boolean rc = false;

        try{
                        if(!iSize = 0)
                         {
                                vValue = objColumn.putValue();

                        }
                else
                {
                     while(objColumn.Chunk(vValue))

                        }
                  rc = true;
        }catch(Exception e){System.out.println(e);}
        finally{return( rc);}
}
```

## The *rdoParameter* Object

The parameterized query has been a great help when creating reuseable queries. Without being able to parameterize the query, you couldn't change any part of the SQL statement without retrieving the SQL property of the prepared statement, changing it on-the-fly, and then using the *putSQL* method to set the `rdoPreparedStatement` object's SQL string and open a new result set on the `rdoPreparedStatement` object.

So what is a parameterized query? A parameterized query enables you to use variables inside of your query without having to build the entire statement again or having to generate new access plans on the server. These variables are referred to as parameters. In SQL statements, parameters are shown as question markS. For Java programmers, the `rdoParameter` object is used to set the values of these parameters. To create the parameterized query:



1. Create a `rdoParameters` object, which points to a collection of `Parameters`.
2. Use a SQL query with this syntax:

   ```
   SELECT ? FROM ? WHERE ? = ?
   ```

   The parameters are represented by the SQL `?` symbol.

3. After you have a SQL statement with parameters, set the direction and content of those parameters. Use input parameters for anything that you are sending to the server and the output parameters for anything you expect to be returned.

Consider the following statement, used to call a stored procedure:

```
{call some_storedproc("Bob",1234)}
```

If you wanted to set this up with parameters, you could make a few changes to it:

```
(? = call some_storedproc(?,?))
```

Then you can assign values to the two input parameters and retrieve the result of the output parameter. This enables you to place values into the `rdoParameter` object and to call the `Requery` method to run the query again. Because you can discover the data types before you allocate the buffers, this is an ideal way to improve code reuse and speed for those queries in which the structure remains static. Table 7.10 describes the methods involved in the `rdoParmeter` object, and Listing 7.9 shows an example of using these methods on the `rdoParameter` object.

**Table 7.10 Exploring the *rdoParameter* Object**

| Method | Description |
|---|---|
| `getDirection` | Returns the direction of the parameter, input or output |
| `getName` | Returns the name of the parameter |
| `getType` | Returns the data type of the parameter |
| `getValue` | Returns the value for an output parameter |
| `putDirection` | Sets the direction of the parameter |
| `putName` | Sets the name of the parameter |
| `putValue` | Sets the value for an input parameter |

**Listing 7.9 PARAMETERED.JAVA—Using Parameterized Queries and Prepared Statements with RDO**

```
rdoEngine engine = (rdoEngine) new rdoEngine();
rdoConnection objConnect;
rdoPreparedStatement objPrepared;
rdoColumns objColumns;
rdoColumn objColumn;

String strType;
String strName;

// init variants
Variant vflPrompt = new Variant();
Variant vflReadOnly = new Variant();
```

```
Variant vflConnectString = new Variant();
Varaint vSQL = new Variant();
Variant vidxParam = new Variant();
Variant vDirection = new Varaint();

environ = engine.CreateEnvironment("WebSearch", "WebServ,"");
environ.putCursorDriver(CursorDriverConstants.rdUseServer);
environ.putLoginTimeout(iLoginTimeout);

// open the connection

vflPrompt.putInt(PromptConstants.rdDriverPrompt);
vflReadOnly.putBoolean(false);

objConnect = environ.OpenConnection("", vflPrompt, vflReadOnly,
vflConnectString);

// Create the Parameterized string
vSQL.putString("(? = call sp_myproc(?,?)");


// Set up the prepared statement
strName = "Testing parameters";

vExecuteOptions.putInt(OptionsConstants.rdExecDirect);
objPrepared = objConnect.CreatePreparedStatement(strName, vSQL);

// Set the parameters and the direction
objParams  = objPrepared.getrdoParameters();

vidxParam.putInt(0);
vDirection.putInt(DirectionConstants.rdParamOutput);
objParam = objParams.getItem(vidxParam).putValue(vValue);
objParam.putDirection(vDirection);

vidxParam.putInt(1);
vValue.putString("ActiveX");
vDirection.putInt(DirectionConstants.rdParamInput);
objParam = objParams.getItem(vidxParam).putValue(vValue);
objParam.putDirection(vDirection);

vidxParam.putInt(2);
vValue.putInt(1);
vDirection.putInt(DirectionConstants.rdParamInput);
objParam = objParams.getItem(vidxParam).putValue(vValue);
objParam.putDirection(vDirection);


// Execute the statement
objPrepared.Execute(vExecuteOptions);

// Retrieve the result
vidxParam.putInt(0);
objParam = objParams.getItem(vidxParam).putValue(vValue);
strValue = objParam.getValue().toString();
```

# Understanding RDO Result Sets

Result sets are your bread and butter in RDO, retrieving the data and enabling you to perform operation on the data. Much like the `Recordset` object in DAO, result sets are quite powerful, but they have some quirks that you should be aware of before setting off into RDO programming.

There are only a couple of situations that can cause problems for you in a production environment when using RDO. The main problem is leaking memory. Although some argue over the semantics of calling it a memory leak, if you don't close the `rdoResultset` or `rdoConnection` objects explicitly, they will remain open—even if they are out of scope. (Remember, these are not really Java objects so you can't expect them to be collected as garbage when they pass out of scope. They won't be.) Use the `Close()` method to close the `rdoConnection` object when you are done. This will roll back any pending transactions and close all attached `rdoResultset` objects, even if they have gone out of scope. Otherwise they remain open, munching on your resources. When using ActiveX or COM objects, you must clean up your own garbage, and you must do the same here.

Another problem to be aware of concerns the properties of your connection and result sets—they might not be what you think they are, even if you explicitly set them. This is due to the fact that instead of returning an error when you don't have permission to use a certain type of cursor or when the data source doesn't support a feature that you've requested, RDO chooses another cursor or feature (usually the next closest match to the feature set that you've requested). As a result, you might ask for a dynamically updateable cursor, but in reality you might receive a static read-only cursor. By performing a simple check on the properties before performing any operations that change the data, you can avoid calls from clients complaining about symptoms of problems you didn't cause, but also can't handle gracefully.

## Choosing the Cursor

Choosing a cursor affects quite a few things about the way you interact with the data. With RDO you can choose from four different types of cursors.

- *Forward Only* The forward-only cursor isn't really a cursor, for you can't scroll backward through the result set. This is the default cursor that you will receive if you don't specify one on the call to `OpenResultset` or `CreatePreparedStatement`.
- *Static* The static cursor enables you to move through the result set in both directions; however, the data does not change to reflect updates. Use this cursor if you don't expect many users, or if you need to scroll in both directions through a read-only result set.
- *Keyset* The keyset-driven cursor is a hybrid of the dynamic and static cursors. You specify a default keyset size, which is fetched from the server. You also specify a rowset size, which tells your application to buffer a certain amount of the result set equal to the rowset size. When you scroll beyond the rowset, the data is fetched from the keyset buffer. Just like the static cursor, the keyset cursor retrieves data from the cache, not from the server. However, if you scroll past the keyset, the cursor becomes dynamic (for a short time) and fetches another keyset of rows from the server, which would show the updates as of the fetch. Then the process begins again.

- *Dynamic* The dynamic cursor is fairly simple in concept. You simply open a cursor that updates itself as changes are made to the underlying data.

Sound familiar? They should, for these are the same types of cursors available with the ODBC API. Of course, you need to call `rdoResultset.getType()` before making any assumptions about which cursor you have.

## Determining the Update Status

The simplest way to determine the update status of a row in the result set (assuming you aren't using a static or forward–only cursor), is to call the `LastModified` method. This provides a bookmark that you can use to move to the row that was last modified.

Another way to determine if a row has been updated is to perform an `Edit` on the row without doing anything, and then call `Update`. If the row has been changed, the `Update` method generates an exception. Not pretty, but effective.

As always, if the result set supports it, you can call `Requery` to execute the statement again, returning updated results.

# Using Transactions

It is fairly simple to use transactions with RDO. You have three methods of controlling the transaction and one method of determining if an object supports transactions, as shown in the following list. Unlike ODBC, however, RDO does not offer a choice of isolation levels for your transactions. The ODBC Driver Manager determines the default isolation level, because when you use RDO, it is assumed that you will determine concurrency through the `LockType` property. If you must have control over the isolation levels, you will need to do it in Visual C++.

- *Initiating the transaction* Call the `BeginTrans` method of the object you want to start a transaction with.
- *Committing the transaction* Call the `Commit` method to commit a transaction.
- *Cancelling the transaction* Call the `Cancel` method.
- *Rolling back a transaction* Call the `Rollback` method.

**NOTE** The `Cancel` method terminates the transaction but does not roll back any operations performed against the data source.

When using transactions, remember that all transaction operations are global in scope. If you attempt to roll back a transaction, all of your pending transactions will be rolled back for a particular environment. So if you need transaction isolation, open multiple environments, much like DAO does.

# Asynchronous Execution

Asynchronous execution enables you to return control to the application immediately following the `OpenResultset`, `MoveLast`, or `Execute` instead of waiting for the query to return. You also have more control over the transaction. For example, if the query is taking too long to return, you can offer the user a cancel option. By using the `Cancel` method, you can then reset the operation. Of course, this is not a good idea for write operations.

> **CAUTION**
>
> If you use the `Cancel` method to end an asynchronously executing operation that is updating the database in some manner, you will not be rolling the transaction back. Instead of safely returning to the state of the transaction before the change, your database will be left in an unknown state and, possibly, in a dangerous situation.

Creating an asynchronous query is simple. Pass the `OptionsConstants.rdAsyncEnable` for your execute option. Cancelling one is just as simple—use the `Cancel` method. After you've told RDO to use an asynchronous query, there are a few things you can do. Check the `StillExecuting` property to see if the query has returned, or set the `AsyncCheckInterval` to increase or decrease the time between updates.

# Using Prepared Statements

Prepared statements can be a serious tool to use with database programming. You've already seen what the code looks like and some basics about parameterized queries. Now take a look at some more theoretical ideas.

## When to use Prepared Statements

Using prepared statements all of the time would be like using the same operating system for every PC. Not all situations or environments are conducive to using prepared statements. The overhead for creating the prepared statement is much greater than a corresponding nonprepared statement. Your performance gains come from multiple executions of the same query. Ad hoc queries are not a good choice for preparing unless you can parameterize the query variables.

## Using *rdoPreparedStatement*

Using a prepared statement is very much like simply calling `OpenResultset`.

1. Set up your SQL string and give the prepared statement a name.
2. Call the Connections `CreatePreparedStatement` method to create the prepared statement.
3. Set or retrieve any of the properties you want, and then call `rdoPreparedStatement.OpenResultset` to retrieve the results, or `Execute`.

## Creating Reusable Queries with Parameters

SQL parameters enable you to create statements that can be used again even if the table or search criteria change. Although you cannot specify keywords as a parameter (what would be the point anyway?), you can use them quite effectively to decrease the amount of code you write.

Parameters are created when you create a SQL statement with a `?` for the variable parameter. The server sets up a partial access plan, and then completes it when you send across the parameters, which is done using the `setValue` method. All of this happens before you open a result set or execute the query.

How you set the query up is determined mainly by what you want to be able to do. Decide what your variables are and design the statement around them. In the Web-search examples, the queries might look ad hoc, but they are easy to parameter. For example, consider the search phrase "visual java database warehousing." This is simply fed into a `SELECT` statement, as in

```
SELECT Link, LinkName FROM Links WHERE Text  =  'visual' AND Text = 'java' AND
Text = 'database' AND Text =  'warehousing' ;
```

The parameters you want users to be able to specify are referred to as having an input direction. Those you want to return from the query or stored procedure are referred to as having an output direction. You can set the direction by setting the parameter object to a specific ordinal in the `Parameters` collection (which always starts at zero), and call the `setDirection()` method. To retrieve the value, simply call the `getValue()` method on the output parameter.

## Abstracting the RDO Interface for Multi-tier Applications

Using RDO is fine with applications that can access all of the resources of the client computer and the server. It will also work in the padded walls of the applet. If you want to increase speed, however, or have better control over the multiuser operations, you might want to consider moving to a three-tier architecture with your applications.

Abstracting the RDO interface could provide the applet with enhanced and specifically tailored functionality. You can localize the source code for the data access and not worry about people refreshing their browsers or stealing your code with a decompiler. Moving to a three-tier architecture can increase performance as well, in spite of the added layer of code.

When the applet uses the DAO, or RDO COM objects, they must be signed with a digital signature to ensure their safety. With the three-tier architecture, you remove that worry. Then you also have the overhead of instancing object variables in a browser environment. This can limit the performance of your application significantly, which you can understand if you've seen how badly the Variant data type affects performance from a Visual Basic application.



So, the benefits of *thin* client architecture are fairly clear: better performance, less code in the hands of the users, less maintenance for you, and more time to spend making the UI look good.

# A Transacted Data Class

Abstracting the data is a good idea, but should you abstract? Most database applications on the Internet today won't be using any of the more advanced features, such as replication or asynchronous execution. These features don't have much relevance for a user whose most complex task is setting the transfer mode to binary on an ftp client.

What does have relevance, and that could be used, is a class that enables the applet to send a few parameters across to a server application. The server application could then perform the processing and return an array containing the result set to the applet.

Now take a look at what we really want to have happen in this class. Assuming this is a simple Web-search tool, the users will only have what you give them. The following list defines what we'll be giving the users in the simple application in Listing 7.10.

- A field to enter keywords
- A set of radio buttons indicating the scope of the search
- The results displayed in a treeview, with the TOC being written to a file that the applet will access with an URL

This enables you to create as many asynchronous queries as you want, write the results to a file, and return the URL of the file to the applet. Then the applet can read the file and display the results in a treeview control. This enables the user to have the data organized already, and simply clicking the item in the treeview control loads it in the right frame of the browser.

# Creating the RDOQ Class

The basics of the class are fairly easy. Take the parameters from the applet and use them in a SQL parameterized query. Then, the class will take the string array and use the elements to build a SQL string, and the `dbTables` value will be mapped to a string value that designates the table to be used (see Listing 7.10).

**Listing 7.10 RDOQ.JAVA—Creating a Data Class to Deal with Multiple Parameters and Return the Result to a Stream**

```
public static final string query(String array[], int dbTables)
{

        rdoEngine engine = (rdoEngine) new rdoEngine();
        rdoConnection objConnect;
        rdoPreparedStatement objPrepared;
    rdoResultset objResult;
    rdoColumns objColumns;
    rdoColumn objColumn;

        boolean bStillExecuting;
        boolean bUpdateable;

        int iAsyncInterval = 5;
        int iBindThreshold = 10;
```

```
            int iErrorThreshold = 10;
            int iKeyset = 200;
            int iLockType;
            int iLoginTimeout = 10;
            int iMaxRows = 10000;
            int iQueryTimeout = 10;
            int iRowsAffected = 0;
            int iRowCount = 0;
            int iRowset = 25;

     String strParam[];
     String strType;
            String strName;

     URL TOC[];

            // init variants
            Variant vflPrompt = new Variant();
            Variant vflReadOnly = new Variant();
            Variant vflConnectString = new Variant();
            Varaint vSQL = new Variant();
            Variant vidxParam = new Variant();
            Variant vDirection = new Varaint();

     getTables(strTables[], dbTables);

            environ = engine.CreateEnvironment("WebSearch", "WebServ,"");
            environ.putCursorDriver(CursorDriverConstants.rdUseServer);
            environ.putLoginTimeout(iLoginTimeout);

            // open the connection
            vflConnectString.putString("");
            vflPrompt.putInt(PromptConstants.rdDriverNoPrompt);
            vflReadOnly.putBoolean(true);

            objConnect = environ.OpenConnection("", vflPrompt, vflReadOnly,
vflConnectString);

            // Create the Parameterized string
            vSQL.putString("SELECT Link, LinkText FROM ?);

            // Set up the prepared statement
            strName = "Web Query";

            vExecuteOptions.putInt(OptionsConstants.rdExecDirect);
            objPrepared = objConnect.CreatePreparedStatement(strName, vSQL);

            // Set the prepared statement attributes
            objPrepared.putBindThreshold(iBindThreshold);
            objPrepared.putErrorThreshold(iErrorThreshold);
            objPrepared.putKeysetSize(iKeysetSize);
            objPrepared.putLockType(iLockType);
            objPrepared.putLogMessages(strLogPath);
            objPrepared.putMaxRows(imaxRows);
```

Part II

Ch 7

*continues*

**Listing 7.10 Continued**

```
            objPrepared.putQueryTimeout(iQueryTimeout);
            objPrepared.putRowsAffected(iRowsAffected);
            objPrepared.putRowsetSize(iRowsetSize);
            objPrepared.putSQL(strSQL);
            objPrepared.putType(iType);

            // Set the parameters and the direction
            objParams  = objPrepared.getrdoParameters();

            vidxParam.putInt(0);
            vDirection.putInt(DirectionConstants.rdParamInput);
            objParam = objParams.getItem(vidxParam).putValue(vValue);
            objParam.putDirection(vDirection);

            // Open a result set on the parameterized query

            vResultsetType.putInt(ResultsetTypeConstants.rdOpenKeyset);
            vExecuteOption.putInt(0);

            objResult = objConnect.OpenResultset(strName, vResultsetType,
vLockType, vExecuteOption);

        objResult.MoveFirst();

        // Retrieve the columns
                objColumns = objResult.getColumns();

        do while(!objResult.getEOF()){
                for(i=0;i < objColumns.count()-1;i++)
                {
                        vOrdinal.putInt(i);
                        objColumn = objColumns.getItem(vOrdinal);

                        // Determine the type of the data and retrieve it.

                        iType = objColumn.getType();
                        findType(iType, vValue[i]);
                        vValue[i].objColumn.getValue();


        }
                        // Write the output to the file.
                        TOCStream.println(vValue[], out, TOC[]);
                        objResult.MoveNext();
        }

// Return the URL of the table of contents & index we've just created.
Return (TOC[]);
}
```

As you can see, creating the class was simple—pass some parameters and write the results to a file. Several improvements can be made to this example, however. One improvement would be to enable the client to request a sort order rather than setting it yourself. Pass an array back to the applet instead of forcing it to read from a URL to retrieve the information would be another (and possibly vast) improvement. This is due to fact that the performance degredation in reading from a URL more than outweighs the performance gains that you get by using parameters and prepared statements.

Another improvement that could be made involves multithreading. Although the class we created is running in its own thread, you could spin off worker threads to wait for the result set to return and also to write the file out. Threading is not shown in this example, so we can remove some of the complexity of thread events and notifications.

# Some Issues to Watch for

As you begin exploring RDOs feature's and expand beyond the material discussed here, avoid using the temporary tables created from some of the procedures you can call. Although they can be useful, you don't know when the server will decide to delete the temporary table, invalidating the data you are using. Also, although you can retrieve the connection and statement handles to perform ODBC API functions, do so with caution. Closing these handles externally while they are in use could result in unpredictable behavior in your application.

# From Here...

You've now been through RDO, the last of the programming interfaces you can use in Visual J++. As you can see, both DAO and RDO offer advantages, with DAO coming out slightly ahead because you can now have the functionality of both ODBCDirect and Jet database access.

Both ODBC solutions might become moot if Microsoft either ports its own ODBC API, (which we have seen with the Microsoft Transaction Server), or includes support for the JDBC API.

- Chapter 3, "Creating a Simple Database Application," explores the basics of creating a working database application.
- Chapter 4, "The SQL Standard: A Language for Data Access," offers an introduction to the world standard for database access languages and explains how to use this powerful tool.
- Chapter 5, "ODBC," is an in-depth look at Microsoft's premier data access solution, including the ODBC API and the ODBC architecture.
- Chapter 6, "Data Access Objects," covers the DAO object hierarchy and how to access the new ODBCDirect API with DAO 3.5.
- Chapter 10, "Database Development with Microsoft Visual InterDev," illustrates how easy designing and maintaining your data can be with this new tool from Microsoft.

- Chapter 12, "IIS Internet Database Connector," explores creating Web-based database applications, using simple scripting instead of a traditional programming language.
- Chapter 15, "Distributing Java Applications," offers an in-depth look at the unique problems and solutions involved in distributing Java-based applications.
- Chapter 16, "Implementing Data Warehousing with Visual J++," explains how database programming fits together with Data Design to create a cohesive unit known as the data warehouse.

PART III

# Microsoft Visual InterDev

CHAPTER 8

# Introducing Microsoft Visual InterDev

**Examining the components of Visual InterDev**

Visual InterDev has several development tools, including wizards, a Music Producer, and Image Composer, which is a full-featured graphics editor.

**Using workspaces and projects in Visual InterDev**

The Project is the principal object in Visual InterDev, and the workspace is the container.

**Exploring the important role of Active Server**

Active Server ushers in a new set of Web capabilities.

Microsoft is moving all of its developer tools into the Microsoft Visual Studio 97 environment, the successor to the Microsoft Developer Studio. One of the goals of this move is to utilize the cross-platform development possibilities that now are developing. Visual Studio 97 will include Visual Basic, Visual C++, and Visual J++, among many other tools. This will pull all of the Integrated Development Environments (IDEs) together under one umbrella container environment and make all of the documentation and reference material for the various languages available in one place. You will not only have a full suite of development tools, but also a very broad and deep development reference library. The first product in the environment is Microsoft Visual InterDev. ■

## Examining Visual InterDev

Microsoft Visual InterDev is an IDE for Internet development that concentrates on the development of the Web site. The development of components such as Java applets and ActiveX Controls is outside its realm. Visual InterDev is the first comprehensive tool kit for Web development. It does provide powerful tools—explored in later chapters—for database integration into a Web site. In this chapter, you will concentrate on getting a feel for Visual InterDev.

Table 8.1 illustrates a few of the steps involved in the creation of a Web site and the different tools that were required before Microsoft Visual InterDev. Examine the table to see how the Visual InterDev IDE simplifies and improves the process of Web site creation.

**Table 8.1 Tasks and Tools in the Visual InterDev Environmnet**

| Task | Old Tool | Visual InterDev |
|---|---|---|
| Create folder for Web | Windows Explorer File, New, Folder | Created as part of Project Creation |
| Setup Web folder in Server with alias | Server Administrator | Created as part of Project Creation |
| Create a Default .htm file for Web site | Notepad, HotDog, other editor program | Choose File, New, Files, HTML page |
| Check syntax for VBScript | Find a manual or open documentation | Check InfoView VBScript reference in Workspace |
| Check HTML tag syntax | Find a manual or open a help file | Check InfoView HTML reference in Workspace |
| Check Web page appearance in browser | Save and close HTML file and open browser | Right-click HTML page edit window and choose preview |
| Create new SQL Server database | Open SQL Server Enterprise Manager | Use Visual InterDev Database Wizard |
| Design queries for use with Web database | Find SQL manual and write SQL statements | Use Visual InterDev Query Designer |
| Add, modify, or delete data in database | Write ISQL for SQL Server or create SQL script | Open Table in DataView and add data |

When a project is created in Microsoft Visual InterDev, you have a complete set of tools at your disposal that enables you to perform the edits, additions, and deletions that are required in the creation and maintenance of your Web project. There is no longer a requirement to move from tool to tool. The following list defines the functions for some of the tools in Visual InterDev:

- *Documentation* The InfoView tab of the Workspace window provides a searchable interface to a comprehensive set of online reference material. Included are answers to questions about VBScript, HTML, Database tools, Music Generator, and other tools included with Visual InterDev.
- *Database Project Wizard* This wizard creates the files and connections necessary to add a database to a project. Databases can only be created in MS SQL Server 6.5. Connections can be created to any ODBC-compliant database.
- *Departmental Site Wizard* This wizard creates a departmental site complete with many Web pages that need only be customized to fit your organization. Many of the links needed for such a Web site are already there.
- *Sample Application Wizard* This wizard assists in the installation of sample Web applications and Web applications with an INF installation script file.
- *New Database Wizard* If you are creating a new SQL Server database, there is no need to open the SQL Server Enterprise Manager to create a Database Device, create a database, create tables, and add data to the tables. It can all be done from Visual InterDev.
- *Web Project Wizard* Use this wizard for the creation of a simple Web site.
- *Data Form Wizard* When an HTML form to add, update, and delete data from a database is required, this wizard makes the process simple.
- *Template Wizard* Use this wizard to create standard layout features and elements for your Web, such as a global.asa form, an HTML Layout Control, or a Search Page that uses the FrontPage WebBot.
- *Text File* You can create text files without opening Notepad.
- *Active Server Page* When an Active Server Page is required, a new file with the .asp extension is created with all of the standard HTML code already included.
- *HTML Page* With a few mouse clicks, create new files with the standard HTML elements and the .htm extension.
- *ODBC Script File* Use Visual InterDev to create and manage scripts for the creation or management of SQL Server objects.
- *HTML Layout* You can create, edit, and manage .alx files with HTML layout.
- *Macro File* You can record and save macros.
- *Word Document* Microsoft Word documents can be created and edited from here if you have Word installed on your system.
- *Excel Chart* Use Visual InterDev to create and edit Excel charts. All of the Excel editing features and functions that are available with your version of Excel are available.
- *Excel Worksheet* When you require an Excel worksheet, full editing and creation capability are available here.
- *PowerPoint Presentation* Create and edit PowerPoint (.ppt) files with full capability.
- *ActiveX Control Insertion* The Control Pad functionality is available from within Visual InterDev.

- *LinkView* Use LinkView to check internal and external links.
- *Preview Web Page* Right-click the HTML file in the editor and quickly preview the Web page.
- *HTML Insertion Wizard* This wizard generates HTML for the creation of conditional (True|False) logic and Data Range HTML (for example, Return and display 10 or 15 records per page).
- *Properties* You can view the properties of any file in the workspace.
- *Script Wizard* Creation of VBScript and JScript in your HTML page is simplified. Properties and events are exposed.
- *Query Designer* You can create syntactically correct SQL statements quickly.
- *Database access* Use Visual InterDev to create and manipulate SQL Server databases.
- *Media Manager* Organizing, annotating, and searching for Multimedia files that you need to use in your Web are simplified with Microsoft Media Manager.
- *Image Composer* This full-capability graphic tool assists you in the creation of graphics for your Web site.
- *Music Generator* Add royalty-free music to your site.

You can create an entire Web site with only one tool, Microsoft Visual InterDev.

# Installing Visual InterDev

You can install Visual InterDev on Windows NT 4.0 or Windows 95—there are no significant differences. When you open the Visual InterDev Setup program, you are presented with several items that can be installed. These items are divided into two groups, Server Components and Client Components, explained in the following list:

- *Personal Web Server (Windows 95 Only)* You do not need to have a Web server installed on the same system on which you are installing Visual InterDev. You must have access to a system with a Web server on a high speed connection such as a LAN. If you are installing on a Windows 95 stand-alone system, the Personal Web Server is provided. If you are installing on a Windows NT system, either IIS 2.0 or Peer Web Services is included as part of the installation set, depending on whether you are using the Server or Workstation.
- *Active Server Pages* Also called IIS 3.0, this is required for Visual InterDev. The same installation will work for IIS 2.0, Peer Web Services, and Personal Web Server.
- *FrontPage Extensions* These are the FrontPage Server Extensions only. The full FrontPage Explorer is not included. This is required for Visual InterDev.
- *Visual InterDev Client* This is the Visual InterDev IDE.
- *Image Composer* An optional component, Image Composer is a full-fledged graphic editor and creator application.

- *Media Manager* Another optional component, Media Manager provides the capability of indexing Multimedia files and displaying a thumbnail view of the files as well as additional annotation.
- *Music Producer* You can generate royalty-free music in hundreds of styles with this application. It is also an optional component.

There are Readmes on the installation CD. It is a good idea to review these, particularly if you have had a beta version of any of the software installed on your system.

## Windows 95 Personal Web Server

The setup of the Windows 95 Personal Web Server is very straightforward. If your Web Browser is not Internet Explorer 3.0 Build 1215 or later, you will be offered the option to install it. If you don't have this build, it is downloadable from **www.microsoft.com**. It is also on the installation CD-ROM in the directory Client\IE30. There are two files there. The smaller file is Internet Explorer only, and the larger includes the Microsoft Internet Mail and Internet News clients. (If you don't know the build number of your Internet Explorer, when it is open, go to Help, About. Part of the information displayed will be the version.) At this point, the setup program takes over and does the job without further input from you.

The installation process creates a directory, Webshare, on your C: Drive. After the installation is complete, you will need to restart your computer. When you have restarted, the Personal Web Server starts automatically. You will see a new icon on the lower right of the Windows 95 Task Bar by the System Time display, which is for the Personal Web Server. When you hold your mouse over the icon, a tip box appears that announces it as the Personal Web Server. When you double left-click, the Properties dialog box appears.

When you right-click the icon, a menu appears that provides three choices, one of which is the Properties dialog box. The other two menu choices are Home Page, which opens your Home Page, and Administer. Both of these can be invoked from the Properties dialog box.

The Properties dialog box has four tabs, including General, which displays information about the Personal Web Server such as the address and the URL. It also provides a More Details button to open your Home Page and to get more details about the Personal Web Server.

The Startup tab lets you start or stop the Personal Web Server and set two options. The first option determines whether or not the Personal Web Server should start automatically at system boot, while the second option determines whether or not to display the Personal Web Server on the Task Bar. Leave the one that displays the Personal Web Server in the Task Bar set to yes. It is difficult to access these properties otherwise.

The third tab is the Administration tab, which displays one button that opens the Administration pages in your Web site.

The Services tab shows that there are two services, HTTP and FTP. It also enables you to set whether the services start automatically or manually.

If the browser has difficulty finding your Web site, it might be that the TCP/IP stack is not running. An easy way to get your TCP/IP stack running is to let Internet Explorer make the usual connection to your Internet Service Provider.

## Windows NT 4.0 Internet Information Server

There are actually two Web servers for Windows NT 4.0. The Internet Information Server runs on the NT Server, and Peer Web Services runs on NT Workstation. These instructions are based on IIS 2.0 for NT Server 4.0. The Peer Web Server is so similar to the other Web servers that you will have no difficulty using these instructions.

When you install Windows NT 4.0 Server, you are offered the opportunity to install the Microsoft Internet Information Server 2.0. If you already have installed this server, you can skip this section. If you have not installed, however, and now need to, complete the following steps:

1. Place the Windows NT 4.0 Installation CD-ROM in your CD-ROM Drive.
2. If the CD-ROM starts automatically through autorun, click Browse This CD.
3. If the Installation program doesn't start automatically, open the CD-ROM in Windows NT Explorer.
4. Open the correct directory for the platform of your system, such as I386 for an Intel-based system.
5. Open the Inetsrv directory and start the program Inetstp.exe.

After the Welcome dialog box, you are presented with a dialog box from which you choose the parts of IIS that you want to install. At a minimum, you should choose the Internet Service Manager, World Wide Web Service, and the ODBC Drivers and Administration. You are then presented with directory assignment dialog boxes. After you have completed these, IIS is installed. You are then asked about the ODBC Drivers to be installed. Don't be concerned about overwriting a newer driver with an older driver—the version checking works.

To find the administration program for MS IIS, choose Start, Programs, Microsoft Internet Server (Common), Internet Service Manager. The Web site is in a directory, Inetpub, on your C drive.

## Microsoft Active Server

If the Personal Web Server is running (or for Windows NT, IIS is running), the setup program informs you that it must be stopped for the installation to continue and asks whether or not you want to stop it.

You are then presented with a dialog box with the options that you want to install. You will want all of the options that include the Active Server Core Pages, ODBC 3.0 + Access Driver, Online Documentation, and the Java VM (Virtual Machine). Next, you are presented with a directory assignment choice. Accept the default. The setup program then completes the installation and presents you with a dialog box telling you where everything was installed. Click OK.

Following installation, you are informed that a choice was added to your Microsoft Personal Web Server Group called Active Server Pages Roadmap, which is a source of much information. You are then offered the choice of restarting your system. You should restart as soon as you have closed any other programs that you might have running and have saved any work.

## FrontPage Server Extensions

The Setup program will inform you that it must stop the Personal Web Server or MS IIS before it can install the FrontPage Server Extensions.

Accept the default directory assignments. You are asked if you want Typical or Custom install. The Typical installation is a safe choice. You are then asked on which server you want to install the FrontPage Extensions. This can be any server to which you have access.

Finally, the Setup program informs you that the World Wide Web Service must be restarted to complete the installation. Say Yes. You now see information regarding User- and Share-level access control. Click OK to accept the final announcement that the task is complete, and you are finished.

## Microsoft Visual InterDev Client

When you start the installation, you can choose from a Typical, Custom, or Compact installation. The Custom option is recommended. Select all components. It does not require a great deal of additional disk space, and it adds the Books-on-line, which you will find invaluable and the sample projects, which you will use as examples.

## Microsoft Image Composer

The Image Composer is a separate and optional application from Microsoft Visual InterDev. Click the Menu item Microsoft Image Composer on the Master Setup Client Components menu to begin installation. As you go through the installation, you can choose from Typical, Custom, or Compact. In order to see what the components are, select the Custom installation. If you select Typical, the items not installed on your hard disk are the Font Samples 2 Megs, Photo Art 237 Megs, and Web Art Samples 24 Megs. If you choose not to install these components, they are still available to you on the CD-ROM. The path is \Client\ImgComp\MMFiles.

## Microsoft Media Manager

Media Manager is a separate application from Microsoft Visual InterDev. Choose the Microsoft Media Manager item from the Client Components list in the Master Setup menu and the install program starts the installation. Your first choice is to do a complete installation. Next, you are prompted to choose the Annotation database. Unless you are working as part of a Workgroup that has created a shared Annotations Database, choose the Create Default Annotations Database.

MS Media Manager then finishes the installation. When the installation is complete, you are asked to restart Windows. Before you restart, save and close work from any other programs.

After Windows restarts, you are asked whether or not you want to convert the Multimedia Files folder to a Media Manager folder. If you do convert, you can convert back. Be aware that if you decide to remove Media Manager from your system, make sure that the Multimedia Files folder is converted back to a standard folder before you remove Media Manager. If it is not converted back, the files will be unusable.

## Microsoft Music Generator

A sound card is required to use this component. Choose the Microsoft Music Generator item from the Master Setup Client Component Menu. Again, you must choose between a Typical and Custom installation. Choosing the Custom installation shows you the disk space required. You will want to install all components. After you have chosen Custom, the setup program completes installation.

# Workspaces and Projects

Central to understanding and using Visual InterDev is a familiarity with the concepts of the project workspace and the project. The short definition of a project is the set of files required to publish a single Web site; there are usually dependencies and relationships between these files, such as links from file to file.

*Workspaces* contain projects. As it is used in Visual InterDev, the term workspace has two meanings. The first meaning for workspace is a Workspace window that is displayed by Visual InterDev. This window is control central for the files that you are working with and the reference information that you might need. When you first open Visual InterDev, InfoView is the only tab in the Workspace window. This tab displays the documentation and reference material, as is shown in the Workspace window in Figure 8.1.

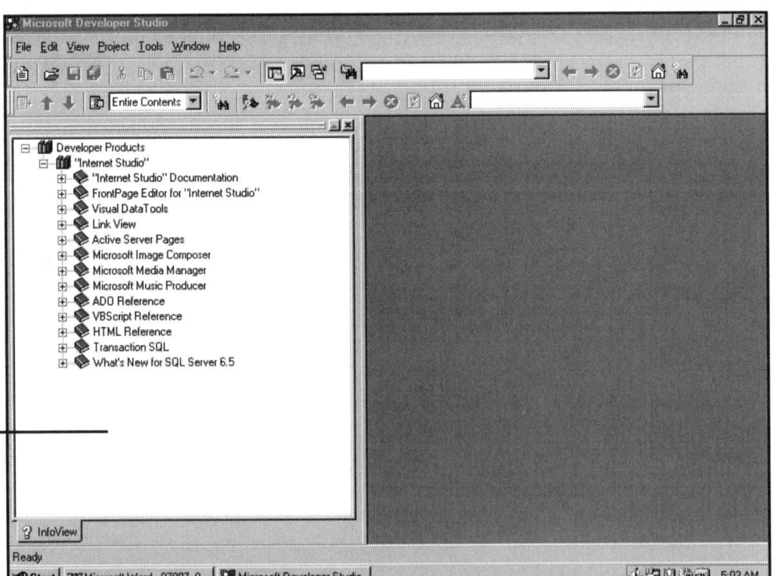


**FIG. 8.1**
Clicking the + symbols expands the list in the Workspace window.

This window is also where the workspace as described in the second meaning is displayed. The second meaning for workspace is abstract. It is the set of projects and files that you want to work on at one time. You can name a workspace, and a workspace file is created that records what you have decided to include in the workspace. If you save the workspace and then reopen it, the workspace appears exactly as saved.

When you open a workspace file, at least one (and usually two) more tabs appear: the DataView and FileView tabs. When you click the FileView tab, you see the projects and files that comprise the projects (see Figure 8.2). Double-clicking one of the file names opens it for editing.

**FIG. 8.2**
A workspace can contain more than one project. The projects also can be on different servers.

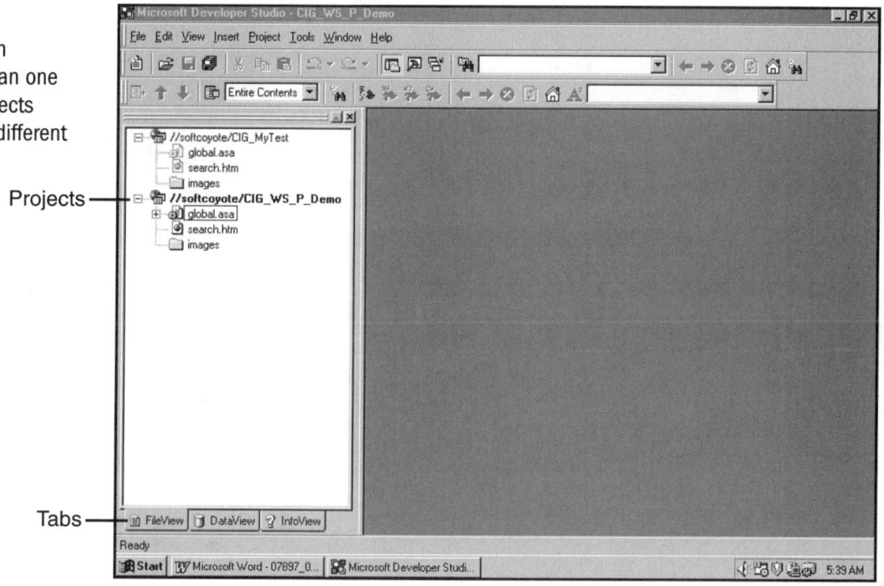


If a database connection has been included in the project, the DataView tab is also displayed. When you click this tab, the database objects appear in the Workspace window. Double-click a table name, and the contents of the table appear, as shown in Figure 8.3.

Workspaces can be created empty (with no project) or can be created in the process of creating a project. Projects can be added to existing workspaces, and files can be added to existing projects.

**FIG. 8.3**
If you have sufficient rights, data can be added and deleted from tables through the Visual InterDev workspace.

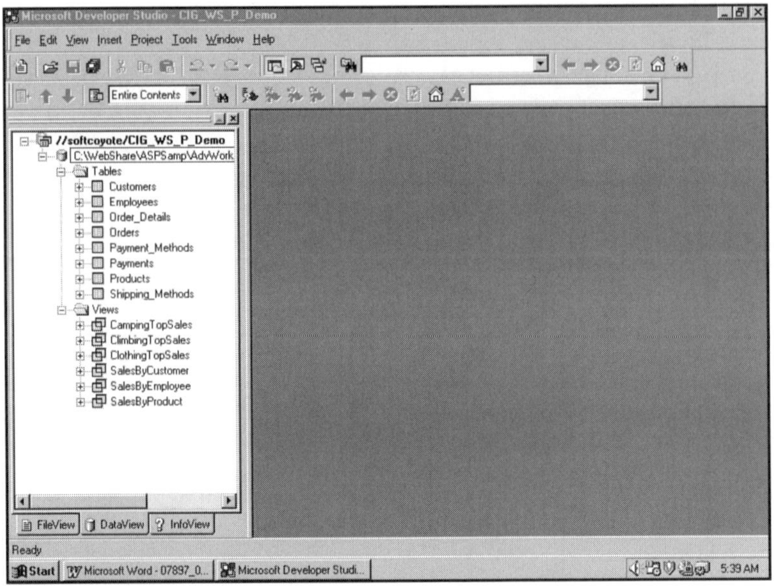


# Creating a Project

To create a project, complete the following steps:

1. With Visual InterDev open, choose File, New.
2. Click the Projects tab of the New dialog box that appears.
3. Highlight the Web Project Wizard option and enter a name for the project in the text box Project Name.

   Figure 8.4 shows the name Sample_Proj for the Project Name. The default location for the project files is shown in the Location text box: C:\Program Files\DevStudio\MyProjects. This can be changed, but it is recommended to leave it as is.
4. Because no Workspace window is open, accept the choice to Create new workspace. Click the OK button.

The Web Project Wizard displays step 1 of 2, which names the Web server upon which the project will be created. (Note that there is an option to use SSL, or Secure Sockets Layer, for the Web site that is being created.) The Web server can be on the same machine on which you are running MS Visual InterDev, or it can be on another machine. Enter the name of the Web server, as shown in Figure 8.5, and click Next.

**NOTE** Because transmission of data on the Internet is open and subject to examination by anyone with spy software and a desire to snoop, there is reluctance to send sensitive information over the Internet without encryption. Encryption usually requires that sender and receiver both have the key to the code. Secure Sockets Layer is a facility that is available in Microsoft Internet Information Server that simplifies the process of encryption and decryption of data so that sensitive data can be sent over the Internet without mutual possession of an encryption key.

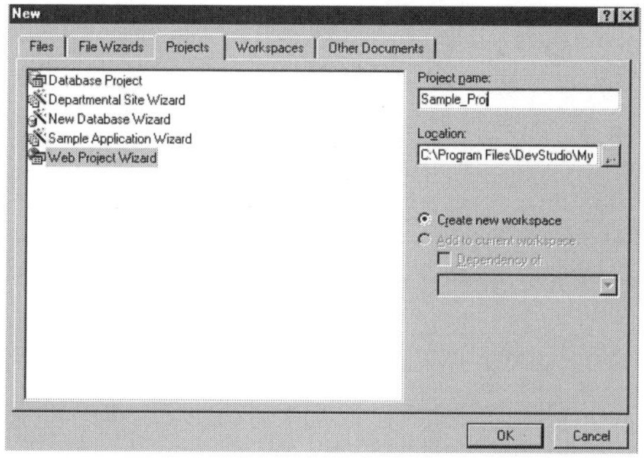


**FIG. 8.4**
Because several files are created based upon these settings, check all settings and names.

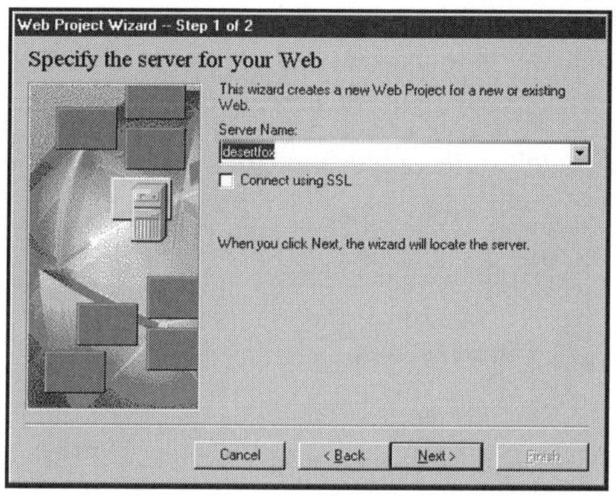


**FIG. 8.5**
If a problem is encountered contacting the server, make sure that the Web server is running.

When the Web Project Wizard moves to Step 2 of 2, you must specify whether you are creating a new Web or attaching this project to an existing Web. Figure 8.6 shows the new Web being selected.

Click Finish. The Web Project Wizard now finishes the job of creating the Project and basic Web structure and adjusting directory settings on the server (as required). You now see that the FileView tab has been added to the Workspace window.

One of the facilities now available to you is the capability to edit any file in the project. If you double-click a file name, the file is opened in a text-editing window.

**NOTE** Microsoft Visual InterDev keeps copies of the project files in two places. The Working folder copy is kept in the MyProjects directory, and the other copy is in the Web server. When changes are made to one of the files through Visual InterDev, both copies are changed. For this reason, it is extremely important to remember that the project files should always be edited through Visual InterDev.

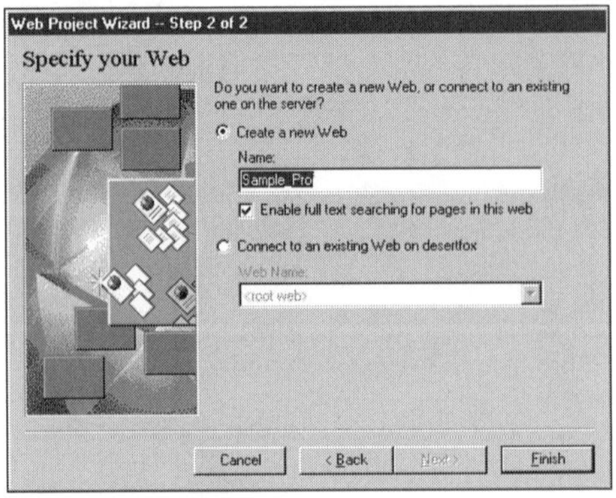


**FIG. 8.6**
The full text search is based upon the FrontPage WebBot.

When you create a project, the default location for the files is in a folder named MyProjects in the following path:

```
c:\Program files\DevStudio\MyProjects\
```

A folder is created here with the name that we assigned to the project, in the example Sample_Proj. When you examine this folder, you see that a folder and four files are present in this folder. When you create or retrieve working copies of HTML files from the Web, they will also reside in this folder. The following list describes the contents of the folder.

- The images folder contains image files that are used in the project.
- The Sample_Proj.dsp is the project file.
- The Sample_Proj.dsw file is the workspace file.
- The two files, Sample_Proj.opt and Sample_Proj.sfl, are binary files used by Visual InterDev. It is important that these files remain unaltered. If they are altered, your project might be useless.

Now examine the Web server folders to see the other copy of HTML files. The location of your Web server root file is in one of two places, depending on whether you are using the Personal Web Server for Windows 95, the MS IIS, or Peer Web Server for Windows NT:

- If you are using Windows 95 Personal Web server, you should find a directory named Webshare on the root directory of your C:\ drive. In this directory, there will be a directory named Wwwroot. This is the root directory of the Web. A file in this directory appears on the root of the Web site.
- If you are using MS IIS or Peer Web Server for windows NT.40, the directory will be InetPub, located on the root of the C:\ drive if you installed in the default location. Within this folder will be a folder named Wwwroot.

Whichever Web server you use, you will find the project folder Sample_Proj located in the Wwwroot folder. When you open this folder, you will see the HTML files in the project.

Simply creating the project folder CIG_Chap6_01 in the Wwwroot directory is not enough for it to be recognized by the Web server. For the project to be recognized as a Web by the Web server, the directory needs to be set up in the Web server administration. Visual InterDev performed this task when the project was created.

# Active Server

Microsoft has created several new technologies that are aimed at providing greater life and functionality to Web pages, among which is Microsoft Active Server. Active Server not only enlivens Web pages, but also solves a problem with Web browsers that do not support ActiveX and VBScript, which are defined as follows:

- VBScript enables interactive content in a Web page by using Visual Basic-like Script commands. This makes it possible for anyone who knows Visual Basic to use VBScript with relative ease. Even if you don't know Visual Basic, it is easy to learn.
- Microsoft created ActiveX, which makes available many existing ActiveX controls that need only be plugged into your Web page.

The limitation of VBScript and ActiveX is their requirement for support by the browser.

The fundamental function of a Web browser program is to read the HTML in the Web page that is sent by the server and to act on the HTML Tags as program instructions and display the resulting Web page. When a Web browser supports ActiveX or VBScript, it is able to understand and act on the VBScript commands and recognize the ActiveX controls. When a Web browser doesn't support ActiveX and VBScript, it ignores the VBScript commands and ActiveX control. Currently, the only Web browser that supports ActiveX and VBScript is Microsoft Internet Explorer Version 3.0 or later.

If a Web site visitor is using a Web browser such as Netscape, all of your work creating a Web page with VBScript and ActiveX controls will come to nothing. The visitor will be able to see everything on your Web page except the VBScript-driven features and ActiveX controls. As long as the Web browser program is responsible for supporting the ActiveX and VBScript, the Web developer is at the mercy of the Web browser. Fortunately, Active Server solves this problem.

Active Server supports ActiveX controls and VBScript, but it provides this support on the server rather than on the Web browser. Active Server makes it possible for you, as the Web content creator, to use ActiveX and VBScript no matter which Web browser your visitors are using. The Active Server uses ActiveX and VBScript commands to create and send an HTML page to the browser that is understood by all graphical Web browsers.

## Understanding Microsoft Active Server

Microsoft Internet Information Server 3.0 does not replace or change any of the functionality of Microsoft Internet Information Server 2.0. MS IIS 3.0 adds Active Server functionality to MS IIS 2.0. The Active Server can also be used with the MS Peer Web Server, which is available with MS Windows NT Workstation and the MS Personal Web Server for Windows 95. In all cases, the IIS 3.0 is the same installation set of software, and the functionality is identical.

Before MS IIS 3.0 can be installed, MS IIS 2.0, MS Peer Web Server, or Personal Web Server must be installed, as explained in the section, "Microsoft Active Server."

When MS Active Server Pages functioanlity is installed, an icon is added to the MS IIS, Peer Web Server, or Personal Web Server program Group, titled Active Server Pages Roadmap. When you click this icon, documentation and samples of the use of Active Server open in your Internet Explorer browser, as shown in Figure 8.7.

**FIG. 8.7**
The frame on the left contains links to the documentation on Active Server. When you choose a topic, it is displayed in the frame on the right.

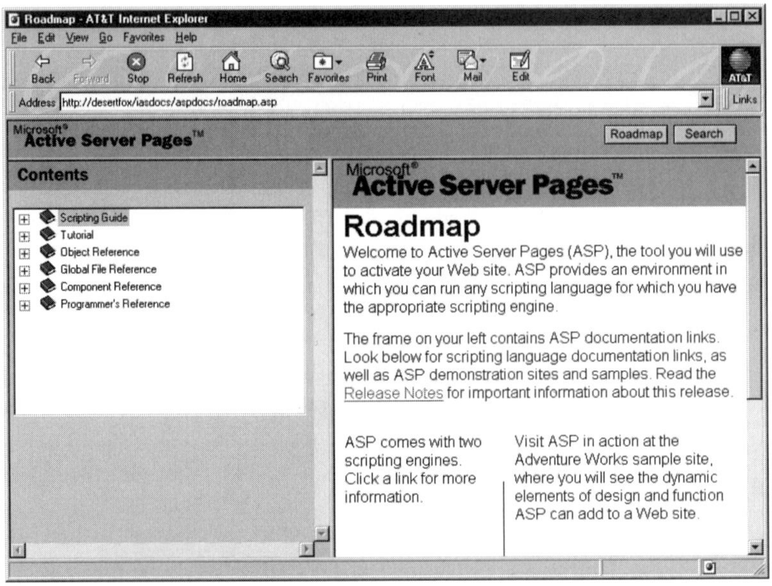


**NOTE** The TCP stack must be running for the Active Server functions to work. An easy method of starting the stack is to attach to your Internet Service Provider just as if you were going to browse Web pages. If your Internet Explorer is set to automatically connect with your Internet Service Provider when you open it, the same will happen when you click the Active Server Pages Roadmap icon. Simply allow the connection to be made, and the stack runs.

If you receive an error informing you that the pages or site can't be found or that there is no program associated with the .asp file extension, the probable cause is that the stack is not running.

## How Does the Server Know to Be Active?

When a client browser sends a request for a page to a server, the server sends the page. The server doesn't make any decisions about how to format the page; it just transmits the page. The server doesn't adjust the format of the page transmitted, based upon the Web browser making the request. The server just transmits the page. What you need is a signal that tells the server that you want it to do something in addtion to transmitting the page.

When the page requested has an .asp file extension, the Active Server reads the page, acts on the instructions, and creates a Web page of all HTML that is sent to the browser. The Web page transmitted by the Active Server does not contain any ActiveX controls or VBScript. It only contains static HTML that can be understood by almost any Web browser.

## Creating an Active Server Page

To create an Active Server Page in Visual InterDev, choose File, New. Click the Files tab and select the Active Server Page. Make sure that the Add to Project box is checked and enter the name ActSerDm.ASP in the File Name text box, as shown in Figure 8.8.

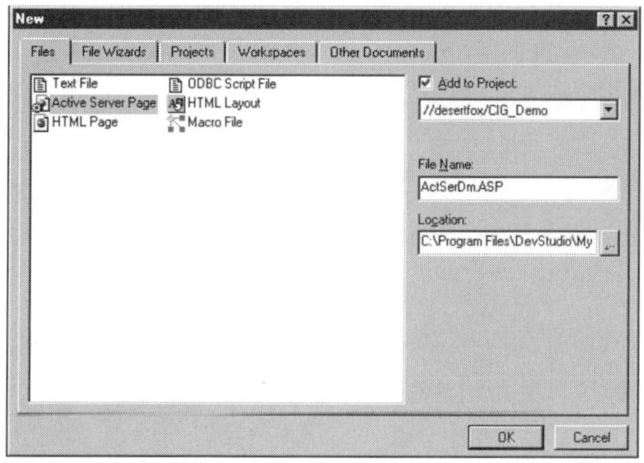


**FIG. 8.8**
You are now ready to create an Active Server Page.

Visual InterDev creates a skeleton page that is ready for the VBScript, as you can see in Figure 8.9.

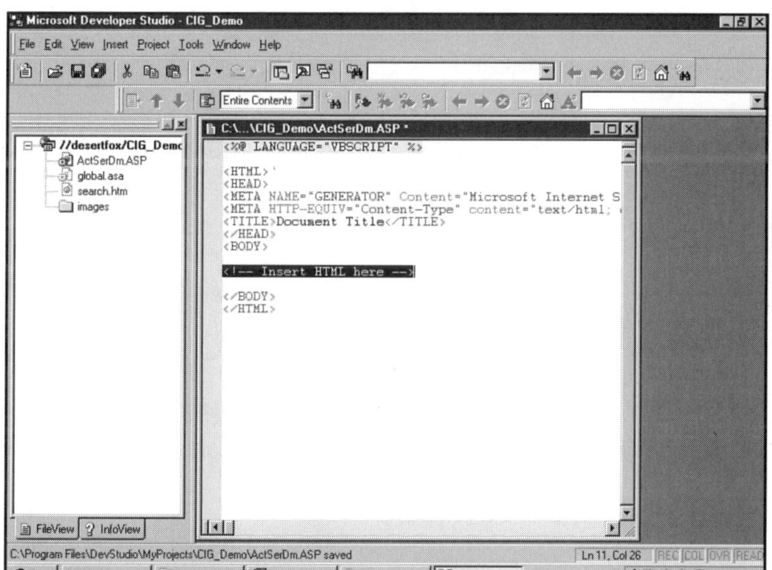


**FIG. 8.9**
Visual InterDev creates the boiler plate entries in the Active Server Page.

You are now ready to add program logic. The remarks line

```
<!-- Insert HTML Here -->
```

is highlighted. You will enter your VBScript and HTML in place of this line. Enter the following code exactly as shown in place of the remark line.

```
<% for i = 3 to 7 %>
<font size=<%=i%>>This is a test of an Active Server Page</font><BR>
<% next %>
```

Your Active Server page should now be ready for testing.

**NOTE** When your Active Server page is open in Visual InterDev, notice that the text in the file is color-coded depending on what type of code it is. For example, the VBScript is black characters on a yellow background. This strongly improves readability.

## What the Script Does

Examining VBScript line-by-line, you see:

```
<% for I = 3 to 7 %>
```

For VBScript in an Active Server page, all tags are enclosed in < > symbols. Next, all VBScript instructions are enclosed in `% %` symbols.

The second line is:

```
<font size=<%=i%>>This is a test of an Active Server Page</font><BR>
```

The first part sets the HTML font size equal to the variable `I`. The `<BR>` creates a line feed.

The third line

```
<% next %>
```

causes the loop to repeat.

If your Active Server page works properly, the page displays the line, "This is a test of an Active Server Page," five times on five separate lines, each line larger than the last.

## Testing the Active Server Page

Testing the Active Server Page that you created will help explain what happens with Active Server Pages. During the course of the test, you will see three separate versions of the Active Server Page.

**Active Server Page (ASP) Version** The first version that you will see contains the contents of the ASP file. To see this version, you can open the file ActSerDm.ASP with Notepad. Figure 8.10 shows the ASP version of the page.

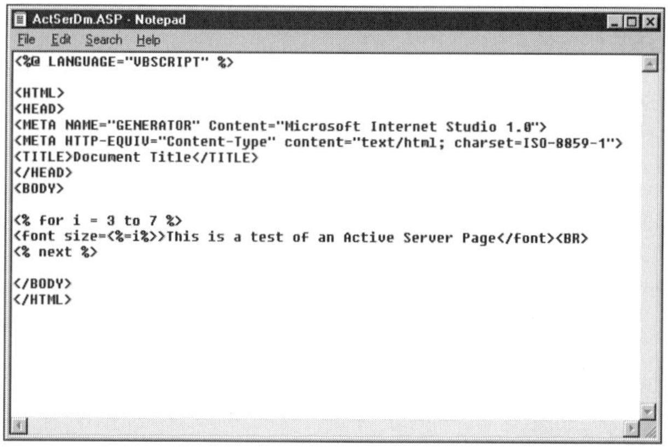


**FIG. 8.10**
Notepad can be used to edit all Web page source text files.

**The Browser Version** To view the Active Server Page with your Web browser, you must open your Web browser and set the URL to **http://servername/Sample_Proj/ActSerDm.ASP**. You should see a Web page such as Figure 8.11.

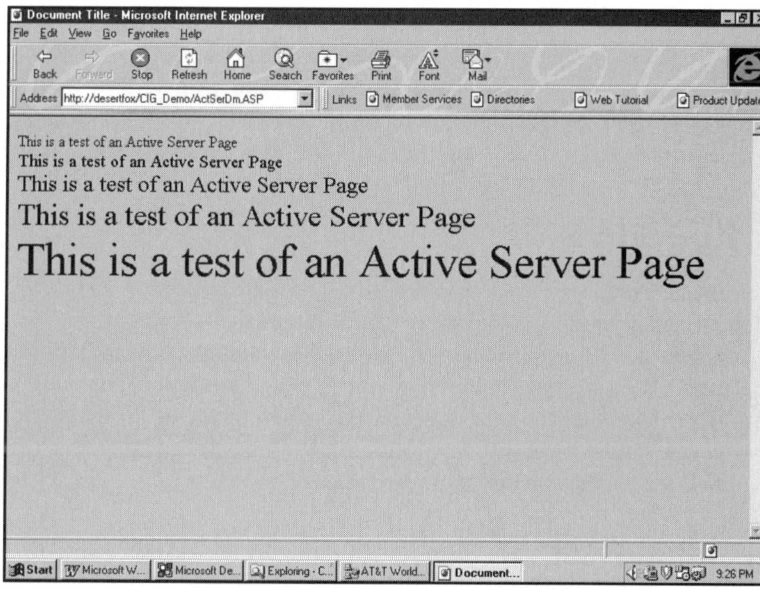


**FIG. 8.11**
The increasing size of the font is a result of the value in the variable `I`.

**The HTML Version** To see the HTML version, choose View in the Menu Bar of the Web browser and click Source. The source HTML file opens in Notepad. As you can see in Figure 8.12, the HTML actually transmitted to the Web browser by the server is different from the Active Server Page version of the file.

**FIG. 8.12**
This is standard HTML that can be displayed by any Web browser.

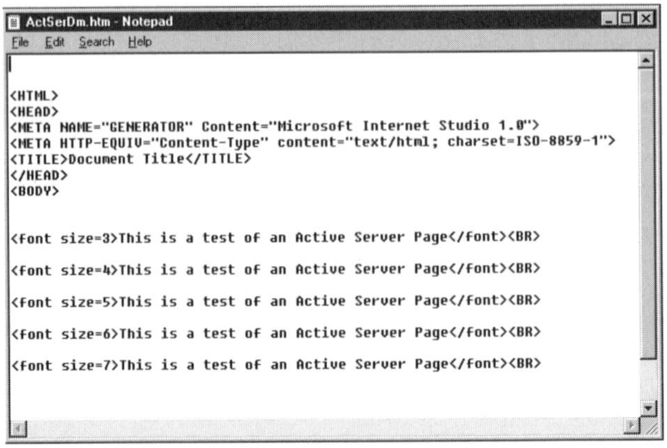


```
<HTML>
<HEAD>
<META NAME="GENERATOR" Content="Microsoft Internet Studio 1.0">
<META HTTP-EQUIV="Content-Type" content="text/html; charset=ISO-8859-1">
<TITLE>Document Title</TITLE>
</HEAD>
<BODY>

<font size=3>This is a test of an Active Server Page</font><BR>

<font size=4>This is a test of an Active Server Page</font><BR>

<font size=5>This is a test of an Active Server Page</font><BR>

<font size=6>This is a test of an Active Server Page</font><BR>

<font size=7>This is a test of an Active Server Page</font><BR>
```

The Active Server created the version that was received by the Web browser from the instructions in the Active Server Page. When you examine the HTML in the page that was transmitted, you will see that there are no elements that are not a part of standard HTML. This page can be viewed with Netscape or any of the other popular Web browsers.

# Multimedia

Image Composer and Music Producer make it possible for anyone to create art and music for their Web sites. There is one very serious consideration, however, when using art or music on a Web site. Because you are publishing the work, it is easy to infringe on someone else's copyright. The penalties for copyright infringement are serious. Image Composer and Music Producer take away that worry. All music created by Music Producer is original, and the copyright is yours. All images that come with Image Composer are provided royalty-free to eliminate all worry about any picture that you compose.

## Image Composer

Image Composer has a myriad of features and functions. You can compose images of many different separate pictures and apply effects to the pictures. In Figure 8.13, there are two pictures. The first picture appears just as it was loaded from the photos that come with Image Composer. The second picture displays the result of applying the Fresco Art Effect. The combinations are almost limitless.

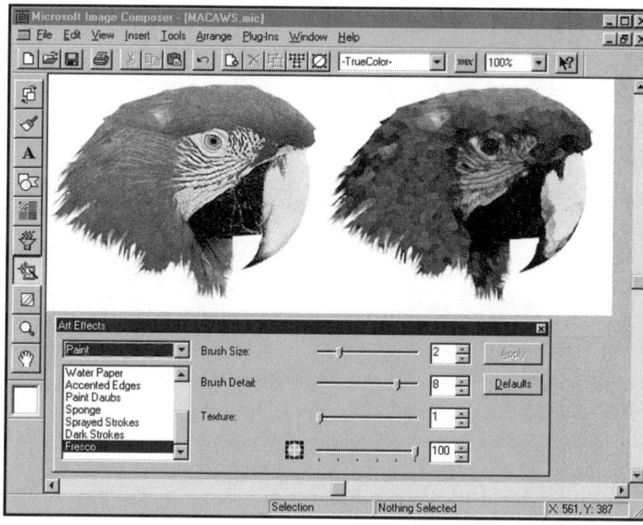


**FIG. 8.13**
The image clarity is dependent upon the capabilities of the monitor and the color settings. This monitor is set for 256 colors at 600 X 800 resolution.

**Image File Formats** There are many different image file formats. The native format for Image Composer is .mic (Microsoft Image Composer format). The two formats that are commonly used on the Internet and supported by Web browsers are .gif and .jpg. The advantage of .gif and .jpg format files is that they are reasonably compact. For example, when the same picture is saved in different formats, the size varies, as follows:

- *.bmp* (Windows Bitmap) 573K
- *.mic* (Microsoft Image Composer) 336K
- *.gif* (CompuServe GIF) 40K

It is easy to see why .gif is a good format for the Internet. Every image file in your Web page has to be transferred over a connection, which, often, is slow. At 14.4K per second, a 4K file takes 2.2 seconds. The files in the illustration would require 22 seconds for the .gif file and 5.3 minutes for the .bmp file. Be assured that after waiting less than 5 minutes, a visitor to your Web site will leave in disgust.

As you are looking for image files that you can use, it is helpful to know that Image Composer reads and writes image files in the following formats:

- *.tif* TIFF
- *.gif* CompuServe GIF
- *.tga* Targa
- *.jpg* JPEG
- *.bmp* Windows Bitmap
- *.psd* Adobe Photoshop

A discussion of the technical merits of the various formats is beyond this chapter.

**Understanding Sprites** When you are working with Image Composer files, you need to understand a *Sprite*. An Image Composer image is made up of two parts, the Sprite, which is the "picture," and the transparent background. The Sprite can be moved from the background. Multiple Sprites can be stacked one on top of another, and the order of the pile can be changed. This is similar to other graphics programs that work with layers, but Sprites are much easier to manipulate. In Figure 8.14, the Sprite has been moved from the background.

**FIG. 8.14**
There are handles around the Sprite that are used for manipulating the image.

In Figure 8.15, another Sprite has been added to the image. If this image were saved at this point, only the portion of the Sprites that are located on the white background area would form part of the image.

If the image is saved in the .mic format, the separate identity of the Sprites is preserved as separate objects. If the file is saved in .gif format, as you would do when placing the file in a Web page, the Sprites merge into one image, and you can no longer manipulate them separately.

You can use the Tools menu in Image Composer to open eight different tool palettes:

- *Arrange* Used to arrange Sprites
- *Paint* Used to color images
- *Text* Used to add text to an image
- *Shapes* Used to add geometric shapes to an image
- *Patterns and Fills* Used to fill areas with patterns and colors

- *Warps and Filters* Used to apply distortions to images
- *Art Effects* Used to make a photo look like a painting
- *Color Tuning* Used to perform color changes and filtering

In Figure 8.16, one of the Sprites has been resized using the Arrange palette.

**FIG. 8.15**
Sprites are stacked on top of one another. The order can be changed.

**FIG. 8.16**
Because the Keep Aspect Ratio check box is marked, the proportions of the Sprite remain constant during the resize operation.

Because your tour here has only scratched the surface of the capabilities of Image Composer, you should examine the Help files, which contain an excellent tutorial on the Image Composer. After you have mastered the manipulation of Sprites, you are well on your way to mastery of Image Composer. Image Composer comes with 200+MB of photo images, so you are well supplied with a starting set.

## Music Producer

Music Producer is very easy to use. There are six basic aspects of the music that you will create that you need to set. The method that you use to set these characteristics is very simple. You click the Preview button and begin changing the characteristics until they are what you want. You will see each of these characteristics in a separate control window of Figure 8.17.

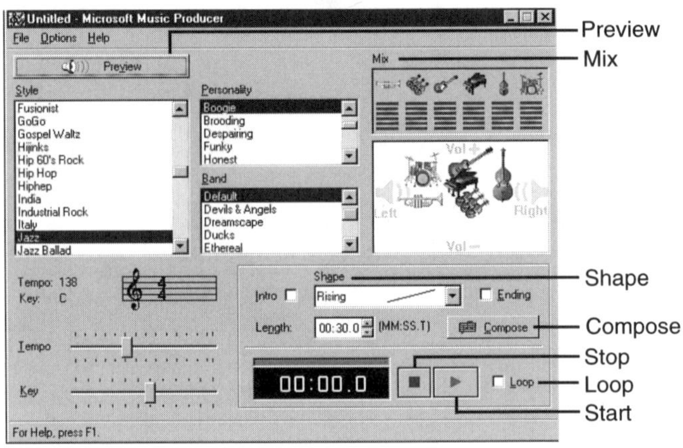


**FIG. 8.17**
Experimenting is the best method for determining the music that is correct for your Web page.

**Changing the Sound** The Style is the factor that changes the music the most. The important factor is that you can press the Preview button and while the music is playing, change any of the properties that alter the sound of the music. For example, Jazz is the default style setting the first time that you open Music Producer. To change to another Style, simply click the name. Use the same method to alter the Personality and Band. Tempo and Key are slide bars. Mix is the factor that is not immediately obvious. Clicking one of the instruments and dragging it to another area of the Mix window will increase or decrease the relative volume of the instrument. Moving the instrument right or left shifts the speaker balance. You can see an example of this in Figure 8.18.

**Composing Music** When you are ready to create a musical recording, click the Compose button, and a new unique recording is created. The settings for a composition are:

- *Intro* This creates a beginning flourish.
- *Shape* A rising shape causes the music to rise in volume and presence.

- *Ending* This creates an ending resolution.
- *Length* This sets the length of the composition in seconds.
- *Loop* If the music is to play in a continuos loop, this enables you to hear the loop transition.

After you have adjusted the settings, click the start button and sit back and listen. If you like what you hear, you can save the file.

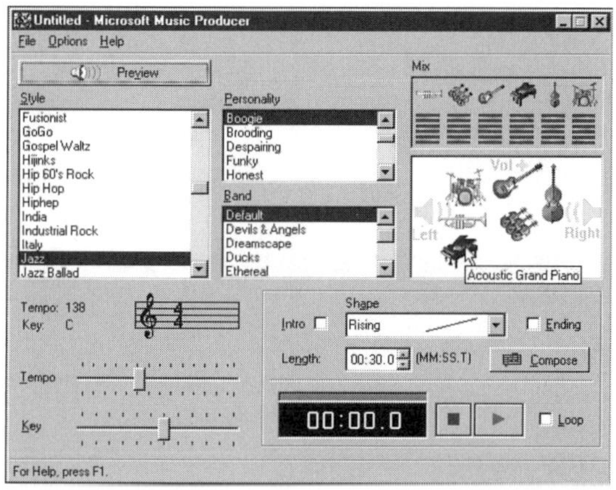


**FIG. 8.18**
The name of the instrument appears in a ToolTip box.

**Music File Formats** The native format for Music Producer is the .mmp format, which is not recognized by most Web browsers. The reason for saving music files in the .mmp format is so that they can be edited with Music Producer.

The other format supported by Music Producer that is also recognized by most Web browsers is the .mid format. The other popular format is the .wav format. The advantage of a .mid file is that it is much smaller than an equivalent .wav file. In fact, one test indicates that the .mid format is one-tenth the size of a .wav file. Whenever every byte must be transferred, size is important.

## Media Manager

Media Manager is useful when organizing multimedia files. When you first install Media Manager, the introduction window appears, as shown in Figure 8.19. There is a check box that will prevent this startup screen from appearing, but you should let this screen appear until you have become familiar with Media Manager.

When you first install Media Manager, you will be asked if you want to convert the Multimedia Files directory to a Media Manager directory. If you say yes and later change your mind, you can convert the directory back to a standard directory.

When the directory has been converted, the folder has a different icon, as shown in Figure 8.20. Also, the toolbar has an added tool for the thumbnails, which are small preview images.

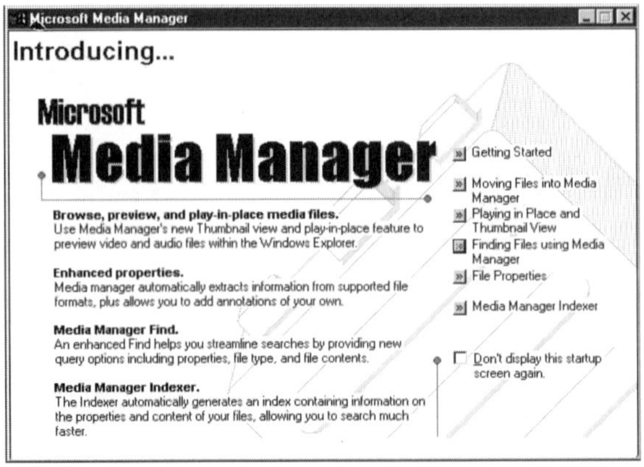


**FIG. 8.19**
The Media Manager startup screen is an easy path to the help files.

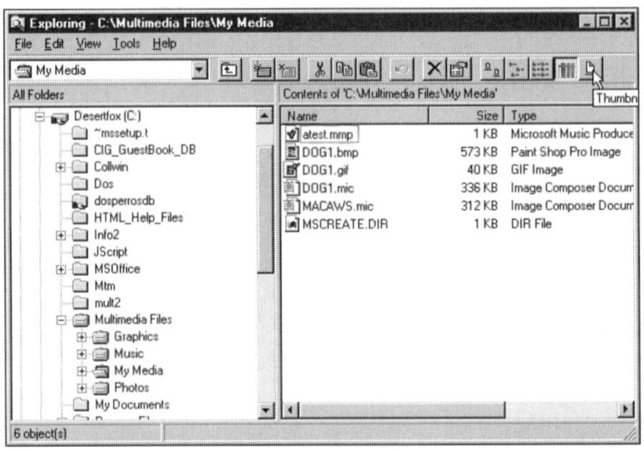


**FIG. 8.20**
The Media Manager directory functions normally in all respects.

When you click the Thumbnail tool icon, you will see thumbnail images of the picture files in the directory, as shown in Figure 8.21. This can make finding a picture much faster and easier.

In addition, annotation information on the files is available in the Media Manager directory. When you right-click a file name and choose Properties from the menu, a dialog box appears, as shown in Figure 8.22. You can add data in many categories, which can be searched to find a file. For image files, when you click the Composition tab, you will see information, as shown in Figure 8.23.

After you become familiar with Media Manager, you might turn off the startup screen. This is when you realize, however, that you can no longer find the Media Manager Help file. It is a file named MM.HLP, and it is hiding in your Windows\System directory on Windows 95 and the WINNT\System32 directory on Windows NT. When you double-click it, you will see the help for Media Manager, as shown in Figure 8.24.

**FIG. 8.21**
The thumbnail images can be of all supported image formats.

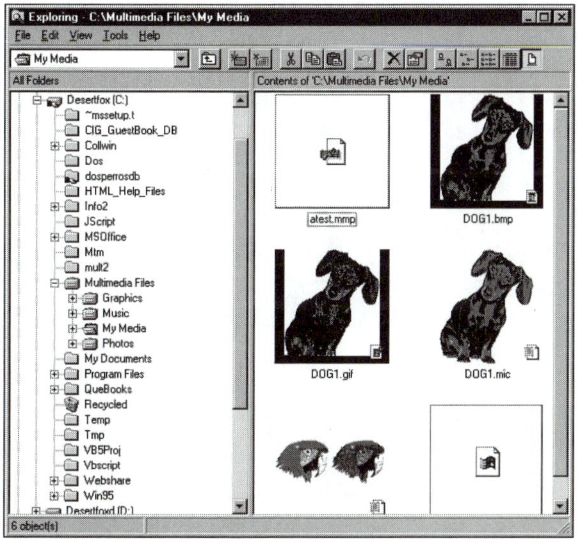


**FIG. 8.22**
Click the Modify button to change any existing values in the Annotations Database.

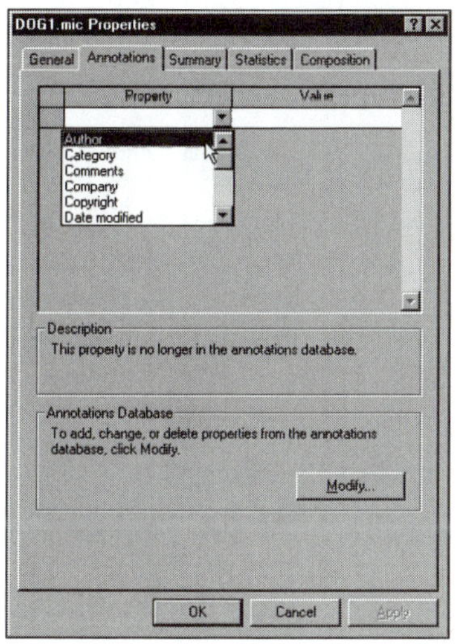


WITHDRAWN

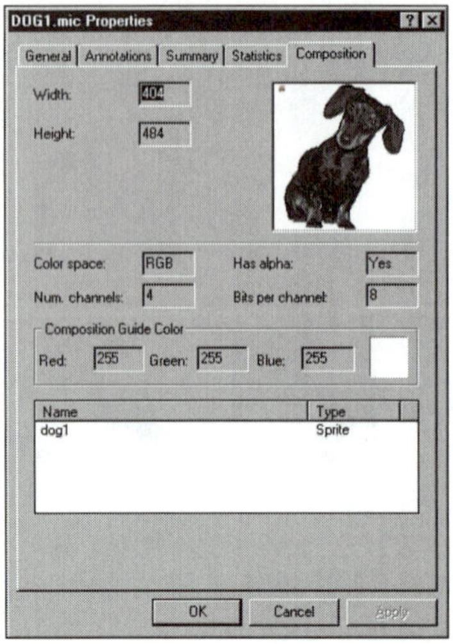


**FIG. 8.23**
The Composition tab displays useful information about the image file.

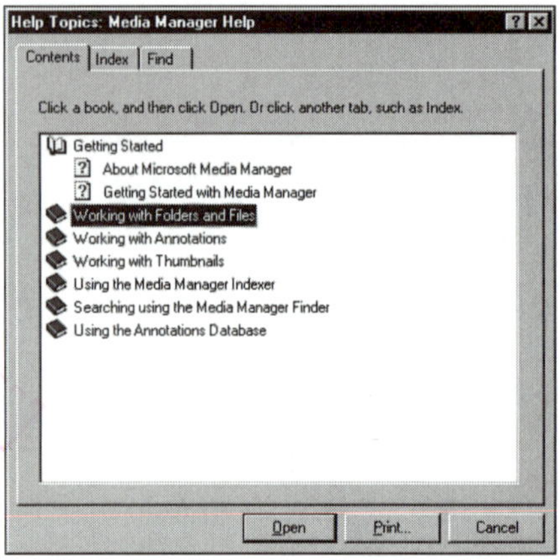


**FIG. 8.24**
The Media Manager Help files are in standard help format.

# From Here...

Visual InterDev is a powerful tool in the development of Web publishing projects for either the Internet or an intranet. The following chapters provide more information related to working with Visual InterDev.

- Chapter 9, "Microsoft Visual InterDev Web Site Design," shows you how to design Web sites with this tool.
- Chapter 10, "Database Development with Microsoft Visual InterDev," explores the use of database wizards and database tools in Visual InterDev.

CHAPTER 9

# Microsoft Visual InterDev Web Site Design

Designing a Web site is much easier and faster when you use the tools provided by Visual InterDev, due to several wizards that speed the process. For example, after you have designed the site and populated it with Web pages, the various links can be checked with Link View. Second, Scripting with VBScript or JScript adds functionality to the pages. Third, you can use FrontPage with no interference to the use of Visual InterDev. Finally, the integration of Visual SourceSafe with Visual InterDev enables seamless protection of your Web project. ■

**Using Web wizards to speed progress and attend to details**

Visual InterDev offers wizards that provide everything from basic pages to entire Web sites.

**Checking links quickly for functionality**

Broken links are identified and the error presented for repair.

**Adding ActiveX controls with the correct CLSID**

No longer will you risk the dreaded incorrect CLSID problem.

**Using VBScript and JScript to enliven your pages**

You have your choice of VBScript and JScript for use in your pages.

**Integrating FrontPage with Visual InterDev**

Visual InterDev offers the FrontPage editor for your use. Projects can be edited by both Visual InterDev and FrontPage with no problems.

**Integrating Visual SourceSafe with Visual InterDev**

Visual SourceSafe will protect the project while in development and deploy the project on completion.

# Using Web Wizards

Visual InterDev provides wizards that perform tasks as varied as creating a new database to creating a search page. Exploring the functions of several of these wizards will give you some insight into their power and utility.

**NOTE** Three wizards will not be discussed in this chapter: the Data Form Wizard, the Database Project Wizard, and the New Database Wizard. These will be covered in Chapter 10, "Database Development with Microsoft Visual InterDev."

## The Web Project Wizard

The Web Project Wizard is used to create a standard Web project and workspace. This Wizard populates the Web site with two files, a global.asa file and a search.htm file, if the options to create these files are selected. (The function of the global.asa file is discussed in the section "Template Page Wizard.") To set the options to create a global.asa file as part of the function of the Web Project Wizard, choose Tools, Options and click the Web Projects tab. Click the Create Global.asa check box for new Webs.

The search.htm file is a Web site text search page that is based on a FrontPage WebBot. The option to create this page is selected during the operation of the Wizard.

To create a new Web project employing the Web Project Wizard:

1. Choose File, New. Click the Projects tab on the New dialog box.
2. Select Web Project Wizard by highlighting it.
3. Enter a Project name, as shown in Figure 9.1, and click OK.

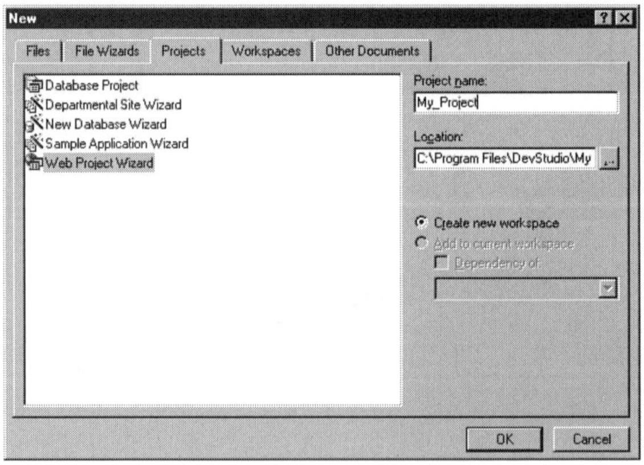


**FIG. 9.1**
Because no workspace is open, Create new workspace is the only choice available.

Step 1 of 2 of the Web Project Wizard requests the Server Name for the project and can be any server to which you have access. You are also offered the option of using SSL (Secure Sockets Layer), as shown in Figure 9.2. SSL is available only on IIS.

**FIG. 9.2**
If there is any error in the previous information, click Back to move to the previous dialog or Cancel to quit the Wizard.

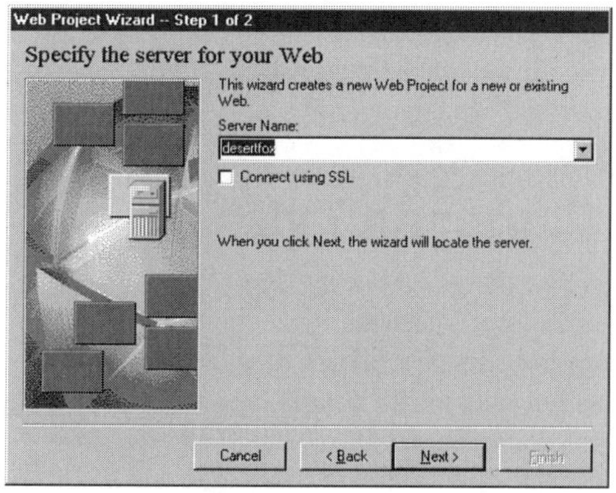




Step 2 of 2 of the Web Project Wizard enables you to select the option to create a full text search page in your project. This text search is based on a FrontPage WebBot. You are also offered the choice of creating a new Web or attaching the project to an existing Web.

Click the Finish button and the process is complete; a Web project has been established, including the creation of directories in the Web server and proper settings on the directories. There are no HTML files in the project

You can now populate the project with files. The first file that is usually created is the Default.htm file. To create this file, choose File, New and click the Files tab. Select the HTML Page and enter the file name default. Be sure to check the Add to Project check box.

Visual InterDev creates an HTML file with all of the standard HTML tags. The entry

```
<!-- Insert HTML here -->
```

is highlighted. This is where you will place the substance of the Web page.

Type the text entry `HELLO WORLD` above the `<!-- Insert HTML here -->`. Now test the Web page that has been created. Right-click the page in the editor window and choose Preview in the popup menu. The page will be displayed in an Infoviewer Topic browser window, as shown in Figure 9.3.

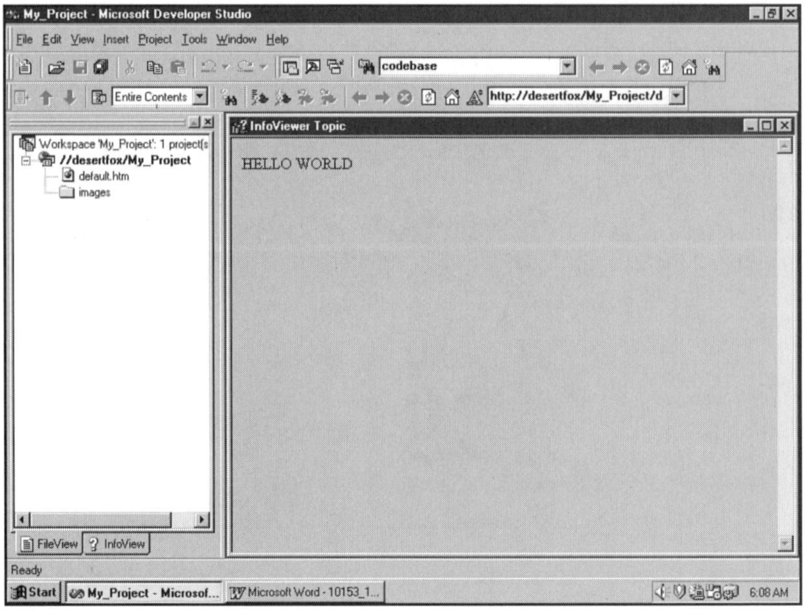


**FIG. 9.3**
This WYSIWYG view is only two clicks away at all times.

## Sample Application Wizard

The Sample Application Wizard will install one of two sample applications that come with Visual InterDev. The Sample Application Wizard is started by choosing File, New, clicking on the Project tab, and choosing the Sample Application Wizard. You will be given the choice of the two sample applications, the Dos Perros Tutorial Application and the 401k Sample Application.

The Dos Perros sample application demonstrates almost all of the concepts of Visual InterDev. It is a very large and colorful project.

## Template Page Wizard

Use the Template Page Wizard to create one of three types of HTML pages. You start it by choosing File, New and then clicking the File Wizards tab. Select the Template Page Wizard and enter a file name. The file name can be anything that is meaningful. The file extension is automatically added.

Three types of HTML pages are offered: `SEARCH`, `LAYOUT`, and `GLOBAL`. The `LAYOUT` option will create an HTML Layout page and the .ALX page that contains the parameters of the Layout Control. The Template Page Wizard now opens the HTML Layout editor, as shown in Figure 9.4.

**FIG. 9.4**
The HTML Layout control enables the precise placement of elements in a Web page.

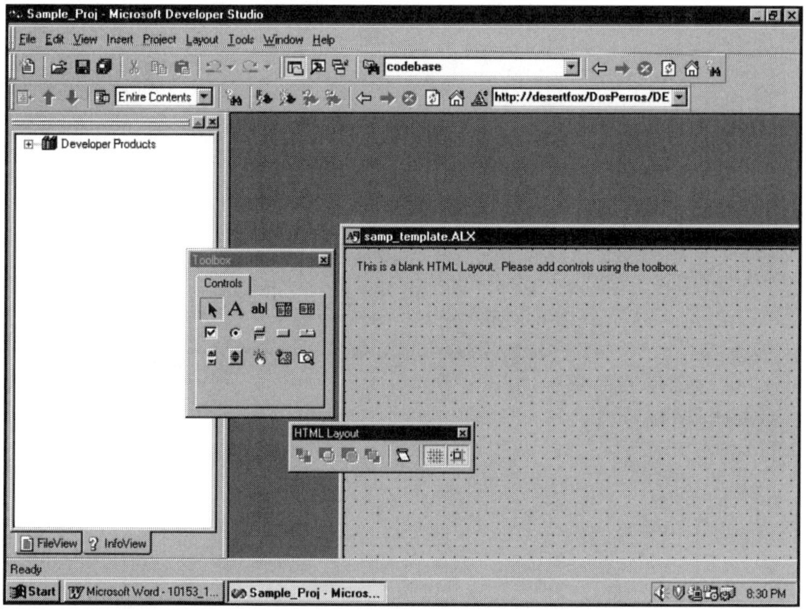




All of the wizards mentioned in this section will speed development by providing a framework for the creative efforts of the Web developer.

# Link View

Links are at the very heart of a Web site's functionality. This can be a Web site on the World Wide Web of the Internet or a Web site on an intranet. Whether the link is to another Web site, another document in the current Web site, another anchor in the current document, a sound file, or an image file, they control navigation on the Web.

A given Web site can have hundreds, even thousands, of links. Keeping track of and testing all of these links can be an impossible task. When a change is made to an HTML document, you will want to know all of the links before the change, and you will want to check to see if the change has broken any of the links.

## Links Request and Load Other Files

A link is a reference to a file, document, or page. The Web browser requests the file from the server to which the link points. Some links point to files that form part of the current page, such as image files or sound files. Other links point to other HTML documents, which will be loaded in place of the current HTML document. Still other links return you to a given Web site's home page. Whatever function it fulfills, if the link is good, your Web page functions as you want. On the other hand, if the link is broken, your Web page will not function as designed.

## Using Link View

You can use Link View to display the links for a specific object in a project, such as an HTML file or an image file. Link View also will explore the links of an entire Web site, whether that site is on the same system or elsewhere on the Web.

If the links of a specific HTML file are to be explored, Link View is opened by right-clicking the file name in the Workspace window and choosing View Links.

Using the Link View function opens a Link View window, displaying the links that are contained in the selected HTML file, as shown in Figure 9.5.

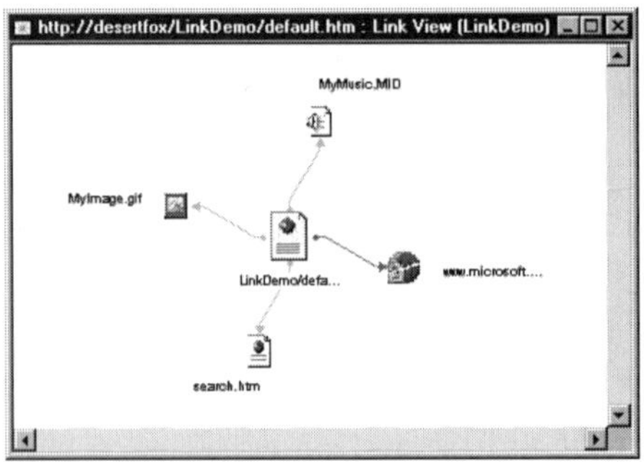


**FIG. 9.5**
You can print this Link View window by choosing File, Print. This will create a record of the condition of the links at a given point in time.

When the icon of a link is shown as broken, the link was not able to be resolved. When the mouse pointer is held over the icon, the URL and any error is displayed in a ToolTip box.

If an HTML file shown in the Link View is double-clicked, the file is opened for editing in an edit window. If the file is a multimedia file, it will be opened for viewing if it is an image or for listening if it is a sound.

## The Link View Toolbar

A look at the Link View Toolbar will help show some of the functionality of Link View. There are 12 icons and one list box. The names of the icons will be shown in a ToolTip box when the mouse pointer is held over it.

The names of the Toolbar tools explain the functions of the tools. Opening a Link View Window and clicking the various tools illustrates their function. The tools are:

- Expand Links
- Show Inbound Links
- Show Outbound Links
- Show All Objects
- Show HTML Pages
- Show Multimedia Files
- Show Documents

- Show Executable Files
- Show Other Protocols
- Show External Files
- Show Primary Links
- Show Secondary Links

The list box is used to set the display size, enabling you to expand a List View to read details or to shrink the display to see the big picture.



## Looking at a Web Site

To view a Web site, whether on your local server or elsewhere on the Internet, choose Tools, View Links on the Web and enter the URL of a Web site.

The Link View window shown in Figure 9.6 is a Web page from the Dos Perros sample project, included as part of the Visual InterDev installation set.

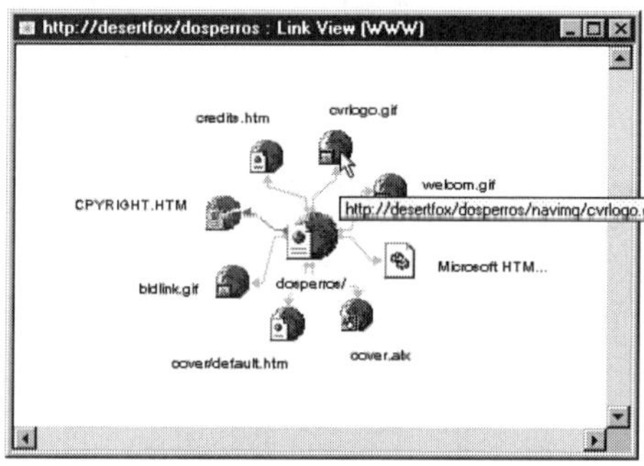


**FIG. 9.6**
Each of the links can be examined one at a time to ensure that it is as intended in the design.

# Adding ActiveX Controls

ActiveX Controls are OLE objects that have had all of the unrequired weight trimmed away. Describing them as lightweight OCXs is quite accurate. Like OCXs, they have properties, methods, and events. When an ActiveX Control is placed in a Web page, it will be loaded to the client browser, if it is not already present. For example, if the Layout Controls are not present on the client system, they will be transferred from the server. This is accomplished based on a tag, `<CODEBASE>`. The file transferred for the Layout controls is MSPERT20.CAB. When transferred to the client system, the file will be registered and used for all subsequent instances of the control.

Inserting an ActiveX Control with Visual InterDev is quite simple. With the HTML page open in the edit window, as shown in Figure 9.7, right-click the point where you wish to insert the control.

**FIG. 9.7**
The line `<!-- Insert HTML here -->` is a comment and is highlighted for you to begin typing.

A list of available ActiveX Controls is presented. When you have selected one of the controls, the Properties window and the Control window will open. The properties displayed are the design time properties.

When both of these windows are closed, the Wizard inserts the HTML for the `<OBJECT>` tag in the HTML page. In Figure 9.8, you see that all of the parameters are set and the `CLSID` has been filled in by the Wizard.

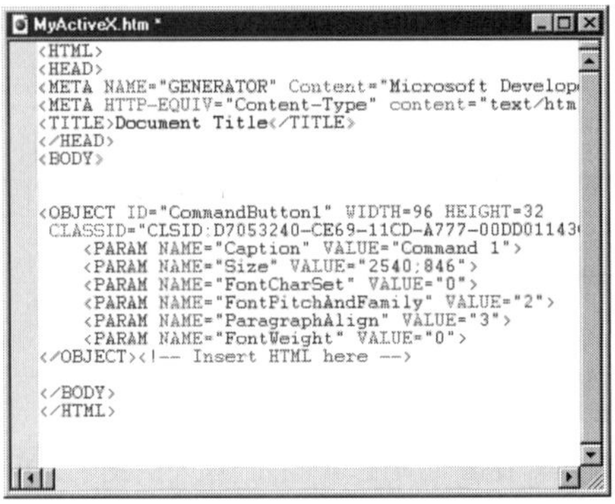


**FIG. 9.8**
Determining the `CLSID` and copying it accurately were problems before the insertion Wizard technology became available.

To view the ActiveX Control that was just inserted, right-click the edit window, and choose Preview. The HTML page is shown in an Infoviewer Topic browser window.

The HTML page can be populated with ActiveX Controls just as you would a Visual Basic form or Visual C++ dialog box.

# Scripting with the Script Wizard

You are now ready to put the control that was created to some use by employing the Script Wizard to create VBScript of JScript for the page.

To open the Script Wizard, right click the HTML page in the edit window and choose Script Wizard.

Click the expand (+) symbol next to the CommandButton1 object on the left pane of the dialog box. Click one of the events, and a Sub will begin to be built in the code pane at the bottom of the dialog box. Figure 9.9 shows that the event handler `Sub CommandButton1_Click()` is ready for the addition of code.



**FIG. 9.9**
Any of the events can be chosen for an event handler.

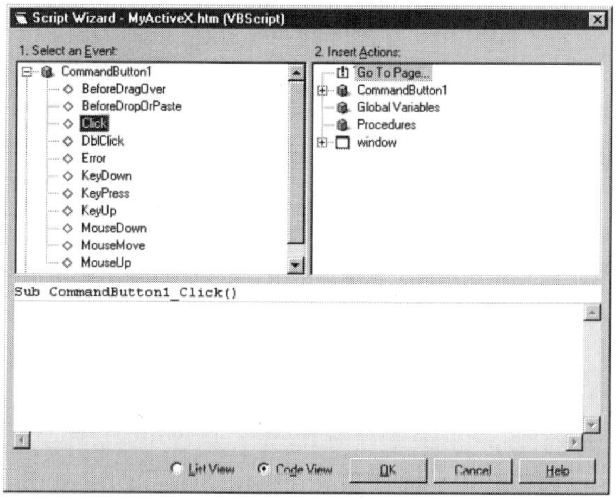


The Script Wizard saves you much time and frustration because it will expose all of the events available for a control.

# Integrating with FrontPage

One of the excellent features that Microsoft built into Visual InterDev is the interoperability with Microsoft FrontPage. FrontPage is the Web Development tool of choice for non-programmers. It is a WYSIWYG (What You See Is What You Get) Web page editor. It has many features such as Templates and Wizards for Webs and pages. The addition of the FrontPage extensions make the inclusion of the Search page in Visual InterDev possible because the search function is a FrontPage WebBot.

## FrontPage Extensions

The FrontPage Extensions add three CGI programs to each Web that provide added functionality and are as follows:

- *Author.dll* Uploads and downloads documents and updates the FrontPage ToDo List
- *Admin.dll* Sets end user, author, and administrator permissions
- *Shtml.dll (stands for Smart HTML)* Implements the browse-time WebBot components such as Search

## FrontPage Editor (Visual InterDev Version)

Visual InterDev includes a version of the FrontPage WYSIWYG Web page editor. Only files with an .htm extension can be opened with the FrontPage editor in Visual InterDev. To open a file with the FrontPage editor, right-click the file name in the Workspace window and choose Open With from the menu. Select the Microsoft FrontPage Editor (Visual InterDev Edition) by highlighting it and click the Open Button.

The page opens in the FrontPage editor in WYSIWYG mode, as shown in Figure 9.10.

**FIG. 9.10**
Notice in the lower-right corner of the window that the estimated download time at 28.8kbs is given for the page.

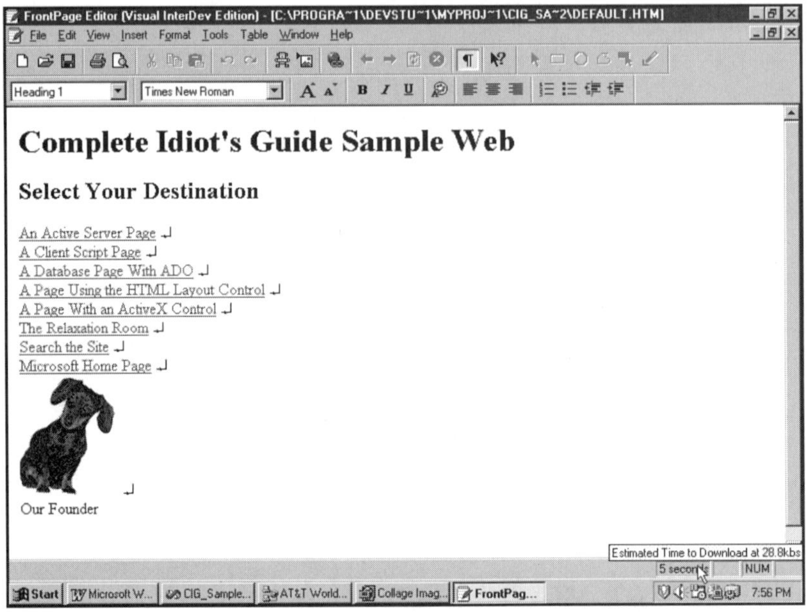


There are many useful features in the FrontPage editor. If you right-click the page, a menu appears that lets you check the Page Properties.

The Page Properties dialog box displays the relative address of the Web page, its title, and Background sound information. There are also tabs that provide additional information about the page.

If you want to see the HTML while you are editing a page in the FrontPage editor, choose View, HTML, and the HTML file will be opened in the View or Edit HTML window of the FrontPage editor.

The great advantage of having the FrontPage Editor available is that it provides an alternative view of the Web page. This can be very useful for checking details such as the Background Sound, and so forth.

## Sharing a Project Between Visual InterDev and FrontPage

The same Web can be edited by using the FrontPage Explorer and Visual InterDev. This provides great flexibility for a team of developers in which some members will be using Visual InterDev for the development of the scripting and database elements while the visual layout and design members are working with FrontPage to take advantage of its WYSIWYG features.

**NOTE** FrontPage is not part of Visual InterDev. Only the FrontPage editor is part of Visual InterDev. Also, the elements that are shown in this section are not part of Visual InterDev. Instead, they are part of the FrontPage 97 Web Development package and are sold separately.



When you open the FrontPage Explorer, you will be requested to select a server. You can select any server on your network for which you have sufficient access rights. After you have selected the server, click the List Webs button, and all of the FrontPage Webs will be listed.

Select the Web that you want to open and click the OK button. You will see the Web displayed with the links shown. In Figure 9.11, the links read from left to right, and the Default.htm file is in the center. As you can see, the same file is shown on both sides of Default.htm because there are links both ways.

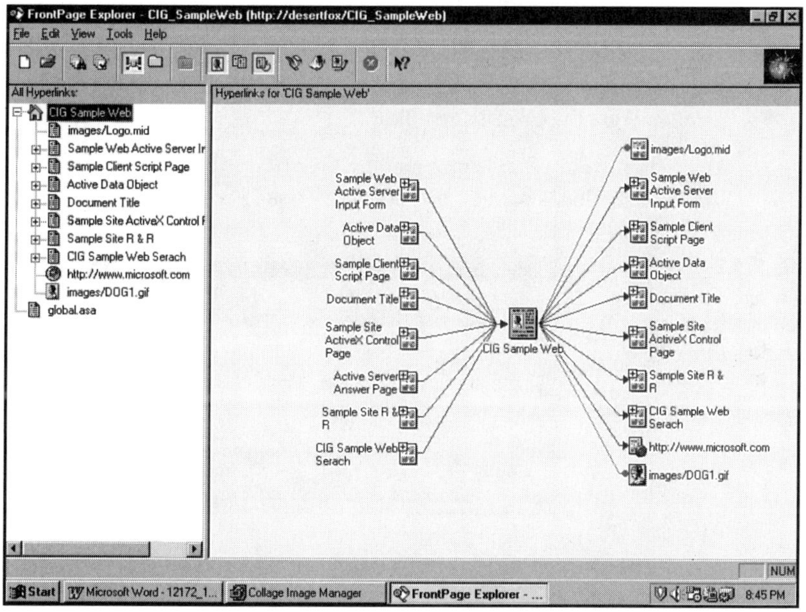


**FIG. 9.11** The links shown are not checked in order to determine whether or not they are functioning properly in this view, as in Link View in Visual InterDev.

When you click the plus (+) symbol on one of the files, the links are expanded, as shown in Figure 9.12.

**FIG. 9.12**
The CLSID is shown for any ActiveX objects.

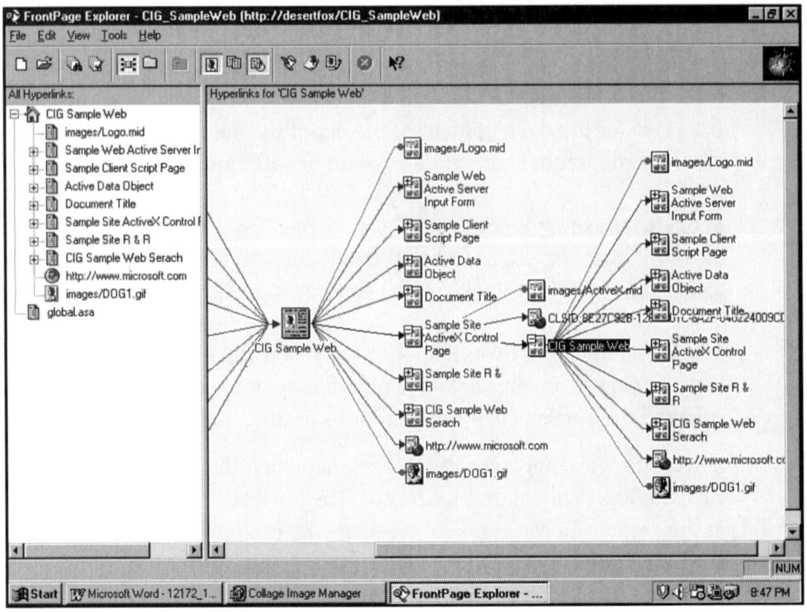


When you double-click a file icon, it is opened in WYSIWYG mode in the FrontPage editor. This is not the same program as is opened by Visual InterDev. At the present time, it is the same build of the FrontPage editor.

One other feature that is provided by FrontPage that is not supported by Visual InterDev is the To Do List. This is opened by choosing Tools, Show To Do List, as shown in Figure 9.13.

**FIG. 9.13**
Every member of the team that is using FrontPage can see the To Do List.

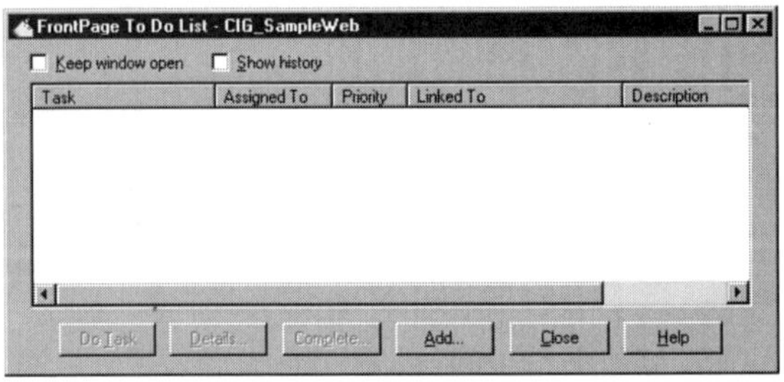


# Visual SourceSafe

One of the great frustrations of team development is discovering that the project change or addition on which you lavished time, effort, and your genius was completely lost when the change just completed by another team member was saved. Or there is the other thrilling experience of spending hours making changes to a set of files or programs that were not the latest version. And don't forget the joy that you experience when you are unable to locate or identify the latest version of a particular file.

These are the problems that source control and security applications such as Microsoft Visual SourceSafe solve.



## What Source Code Control Should Accomplish

The functional objectives of source code control systems include more than just keeping the latest version in a safe place. The objectives also include the following:

- No code can be lost.
- No changes are forgotten.
- No developer is out of the loop.
- Access to the code is controlled by the user.
- Previous versions can be re-created.
- Conflicting changes can be reconciled.
- Projects can be tested without impacting production systems.
- Finished projects can be deployed.

Microsoft Visual SourceSafe 5.0 meets all of these requirements and more. It has Web features that enhance the control and testing of Web projects. In fact, an entire book on Visual SourceSafe would be required to explain all of its capabilities. In the sections that follow, you explore some of the highlights so that you will understand the essential functions.

## Installing Visual SourceSafe

Visual SourceSafe has two elements that are installed: the server and the client. Both the server and the client can be installed on systems running either Windows NT 3.51 or later or Windows 95. There should usually be only one server installation for a team of developers and a client installation on each developer's system. When you begin the setup for Visual SourceSafe, a dialog box appears that presents you with three choices: Server, Custom, and Client. The components that you can install will be listed. The following is a list of choices for the installation:

- *Create SourceSafe Database* Creates a Visual SourceSafe database for the storage of your projects
- *Client Programs (Intel 32-bit)* Installs a Visual SourceSafe client on the same machine as the server
- *Administrative Programs (Intel 32-bit)* Controls overall configuration of the Visual SourceSafe installation such as security and user creation
- *Enable SourceSafe Integration* Integrates Visual SourceSafe into various development environments such as Visual C++ and Visual Basic

- *Help files* Of course you want the Help files
- *Conversion utilities* Provide conversion from other source control systems
- *Network Client Setup* Enables other users to install from the Server without requiring the Installation CD
- *Books Online* Installs a copy of the User's Guide in Help format.

After you install Visual SourceSafe, the first task is to open the Visual SourceSafe Administration program. Choose Start, Programs and Visual SourceSafe 5.0 Admin. The first time that you open the program, you will be presented with a Message Box informing you that there is no password set on the administrator. To set the password, after the program opens, choose Users, Change Password and change the password. After you have this, there will be a password challenge every time the Administrative program is opened.

Now users must be added. The user name can be the Windows NT domain user name, which enables automatic user login. Enter the User name and Password. The Add User dialog box is opened by choosing User, Add User.

It is now possible to install Visual SourceSafe on a client system from the server. From the client system, open the directory containing Visual SourceSafe on the server. This will be \\Servername\Program Files\DevStudio\vss for a default installation. Double-click the file Netsetup.exe.

You are now presented with the Microsoft Visual SourceSafe 5.0 Setup dialog box. Click the Network Client button and the setup will be performed.

## Project Security

The Visual SourceSafe security is turned on with the Visual SourceSafe Administrator program. Open the Visual SourceSafe Administrator and choose Tools, Options. When the SourceSafe Options dialog box appears, click the Project Security tab and mark the Enable project security check box.

There are four access levels to the Visual SourceSafe database for domain users. These rights are hierarchical and are listed as follows:

- *Read* The user can view files but not change them.
- *Check Out/Check In* The user can modify files.
- *Add/Rename/Delete* The user can add, rename, and delete files.
- *Destroy* The user can roll back and destroy a project.

Each higher level of rights includes the other lesser rights.

Using these levels of access rights, various members of a development team can be given appropriate access to the files in the project.

# Visual SourceSafe Database

The Visual SourceSafe database is the central repository under the control of Visual SourceSafe where all of the project files are stored. To connect to the Visual SourceSafe database from the client, complete the following steps:

1. From the client, connect to the Visual SourceSafe database on the server.
2. Open the Visual SourceSafe Explorer.
3. Choose File, Open SourceSafe Database. The Open SourceSafe Database dialog box appears.
4. With the Browse button, locate the directory that is the Visual SourceSafe database on the server and set it as the default database, as shown in Figure 9.14.



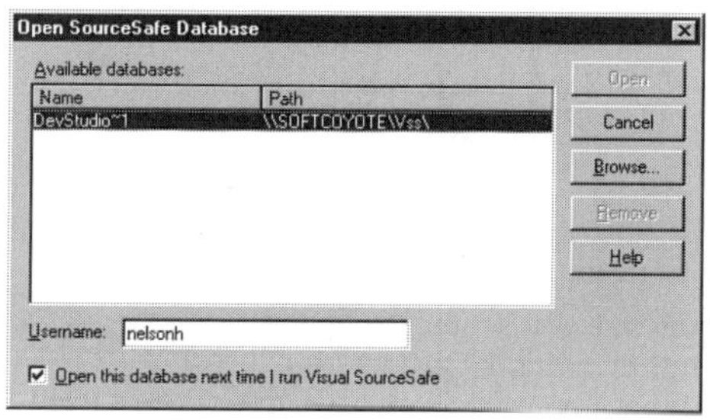


**FIG. 9.14**
The Visual SourceSafe database always contains a file srcsafe.ini. This file contains the settings for the database.

# The Working Folder

The Working Folder is the location in which you will keep files that you have checked out of the Visual SourceSafe database. To set the Working Folder, with the Visual SourceSafe Explorer open, choose File, Set Working Folder. Navigate to the folder that you will use as your working folder and click OK.

In the example that is being used here, the files that are to be added to the Visual SourceSafe database are already in the directory that has been designated as the Working Folder. These files now need to be added to the Visual SourceSafe database. This is a very easy process, shown as follows:

1. Open the Windows Explorer and navigate to the directory containing the files to be added to the database.
2. Open the Visual SourceSafe Explorer.
3. Left-click and drag the directory containing the files to be added to the File List pane of the Visual SourceSafe Explorer, as shown in Figure 9.15.

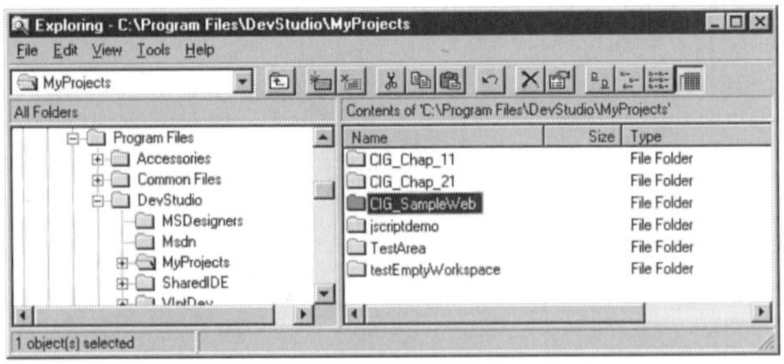


**FIG. 9.15** The files are now included in the Visual SourceSafe database.

## Web Projects

Visual SourceSafe is able to work with Visual InterDev. To fully utilize the Visual SourceSafe capabilities, a Visual SourceSafe project is designated a Web project. From the Visual SourceSafe Administrator, choose Tools, Options and click the Web Projects tab. Enter the data required, as shown in Figure 9.16 and click OK.

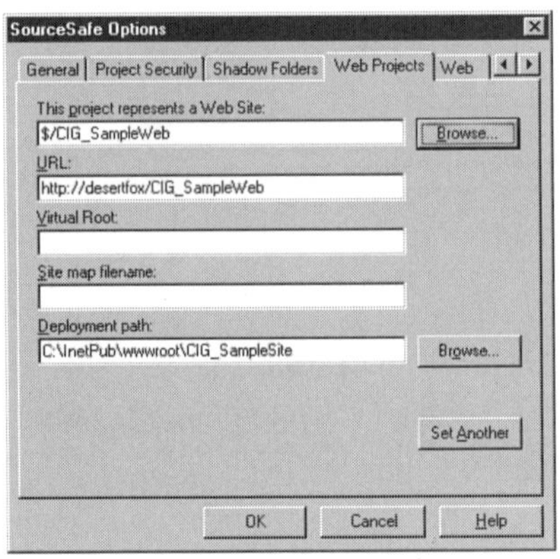


**FIG. 9.16** Designating a project as a Web project enables Hyperlink checking and Site Map creation.

The Deployment path shown in Figure 9.16 is discussed in the section "Deploying a Project."

## Shadow Folder

While a Web project is under construction or revision, you won't want to have the project as part of the operational Web. To test the project, it must be part of a Web site. The mechanism that Visual SourceSafe provides to deal with this problem is the Shadow Folder. The project is placed in a Shadow Folder, which is a functional Web site that is used for testing. When the project is finished, it is deployed to the operational Web site. To create a Shadow Folder for a project, choose Tools, Options and click the Shadow Folder tab.

# Deploying a Project

When a project is completed and ready to be added to the production Web Site, the project is deployed. To deploy a project, in the Visual SourceSafe Explorer, choose Web, Deploy. When the deployment path is correct, click OK and the project will be moved to the production Web server.

After the project is deployed, the results are shown in the Results pane of the Visual SourceSafe Explorer, as shown in Figure 9.17.



**FIG. 9.17**
The Results pane displays the effects of an action. The information is captured in a history log that can be viewed later.

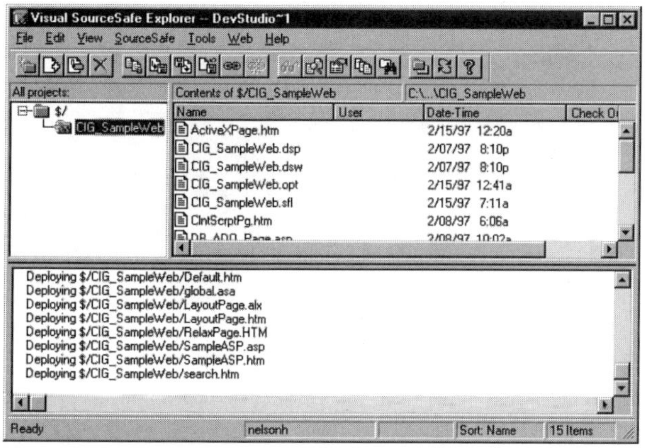


---

### Multiple Copies of Files

If you have been keeping count, we now have as many as four copies of the same file in varying conditions and versions. Each of these copies must be reconciled at some point, which is the job of Visual SourceSafe. The location of each of these copies and how Visual SourceSafe deals with them are as follows:

- *Visual SourceSafe database* This is the secure, authoritative copy of the file. If it is changed, a history of the change is available to undo the change if necessary.
- *Working Folder* The copy of the file is located here while it is checked out of the database. It is used to alter and experiment with. If this copy is deleted or completely otherwise destroyed, no real harm is done because you can get a new copy from the Visual SourceSafe database.
- *Shadow Folder* This copy is located in the test Web site and is here for test purposes. When the working copy is released in Visual InterDev, the Shadow Folder is where it goes.
- *Deployment Web* This is the production Web site. The files here are only altered by deploying new versions from the Visual SourceSafe database. This ensures that the production Web is always safe and always reproducible in the event of disaster.

This is an excellent scheme for maintaining the files and all of the past versions. If a human brain were in charge of performing this task (they are called librarians), mistakes would be made.

---

## Checking In and Checking Out

When you want to work on a file or a project, you check the necessary parts out of the Visual SourceSafe database into your working directory. You can set an option to retain or not retain a local copy of the file that is checked into the Visual SourceSafe database. To check out a file, highlight the file name or file names for multiple files.

Choose SourceSafe, Check Out, and a copy of the latest version in the Visual SourceSafe database is copied to your Working Folder. The files that are checked out are marked with the name of the user who has possession of them, as shown in Figure 9.18.

**FIG. 9.18**
Because a file cannot usually be checked out by more than one user, showing the name enables a user in need of a file to check with the current "owner."

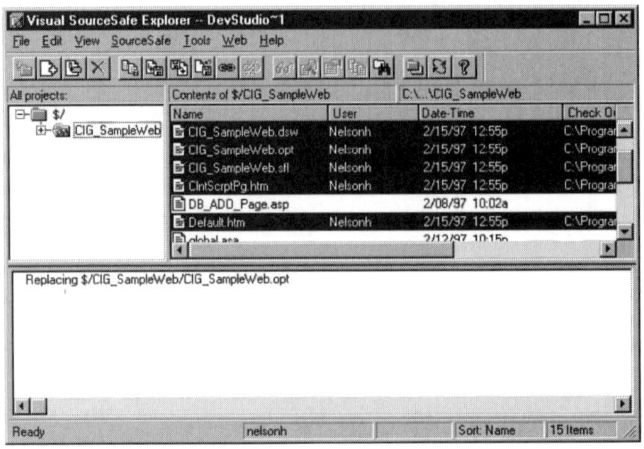


After you have completed your work with the files, you will need to check them back into Visual SourceSafe. Highlight the names of the files that you are going to check in and choose SourceSafe, Check In. The Check in Multiple dialog box appears. You are asked to enter comments at the time of checkin. These comments can be very useful, so you should always fill them in with any pertinent details such as the fact that a file is not performing properly and will be worked on again later.

## Checking Hyperlinks

To check the Hyperlinks by using the Visual SourceSafe tool, highlight the file or project to be checked. When you choose Web, Check Hyperlinks, the Check Hyperlinks dialog box appears. Click OK.

The results of the test are displayed in the Check Hyperlinks Results dialog box.

## Creating a Site Map

Visual SourceSafe will produce a Site Map of your Web site. Highlight the project for which you want to create a Site Map. Choose Web, Create Site Map. In the Create Site Map dialog box, you are asked for a location to store the Site Map. The Site Map lists the pages in the site.

The Site Map is an HTML page that is opened in a browser, as shown in Figure 9.19.

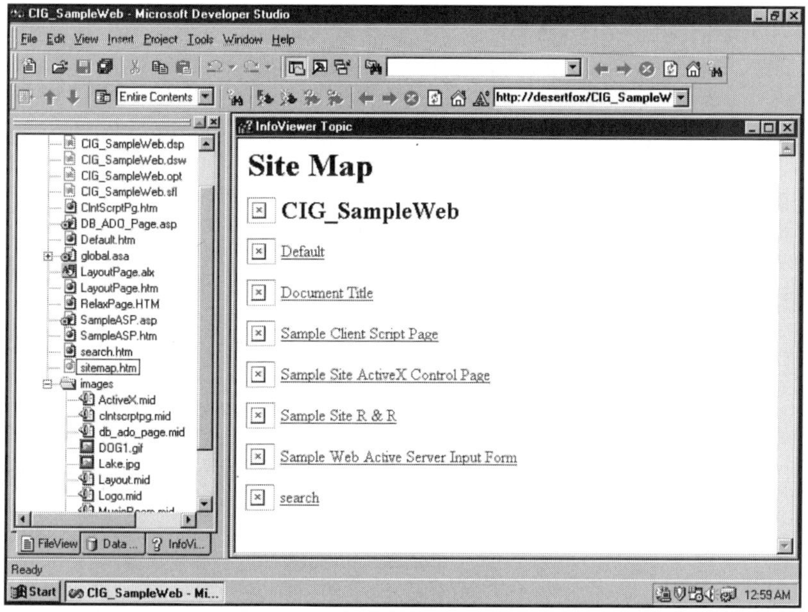


**FIG. 9.19**
The name on each item in the Site Map is the title of the document.

## Showing Project and File History

You are able to review the history of a project or file that has been controlled in Visual SourceSafe. Highlight the file or project for which you want to check the history. Choose Tools, Show History, and the History of Project dialog box opens, as shown in Figure 9.20.

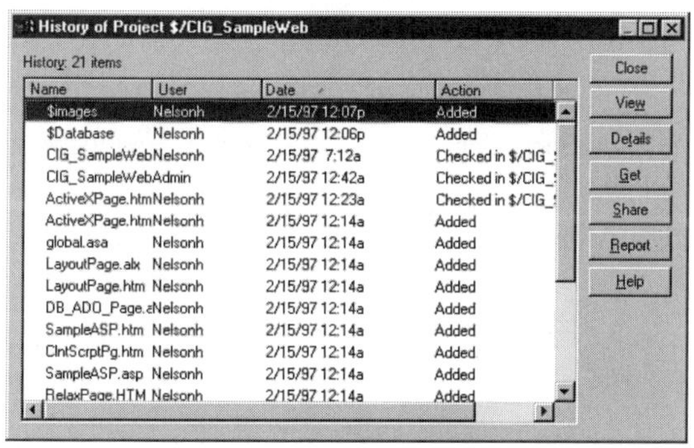


**FIG. 9.20**
The user, date and time, and action are shown in the summary list.

You can review the detailed comments by highlighting an entry and clicking the Details button. The details of the action are shown in the History Details dialog box.

## Showing Differences

Another useful tool that you have available is Show Differences. These can be the differences for an entire project or for an individual file. To show differences for a project, highlight the project name. Choose Tools, Show Differences. The Project Difference dialog box opens, as shown in Figure 9.21.

**FIG. 9.21**
The differences in a project are the files and versions of files.

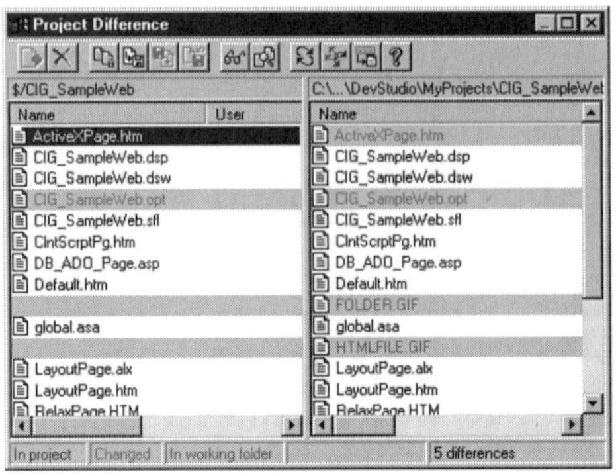


If you want to see the differences between two versions of a file, highlight the file name. Choose Tools, Show Differences. The differences are shown on a line-by-line basis.

# From Here...

Visual InterDev provides a powerful new tool for use in the development of Web sites. It will also integrate with the use of Visual J++ objects such as applets.

The following chapters will provide more information related to the use of Visual InterDev in Web Projects.

- Chapter 8, "Introducting Microsoft Visual Interdev," explores the various parts that make up Visual InterDev.
- Chapter 10, "Database Development with Microsoft Visual InterDev," examines the powerful tools that Visual InterDev provides for database development.

CHAPTER 10

# Database Development with Microsoft Visual InterDev

**The Data View**

Acquaint yourself with Microsoft Visual InterDev's new administration environment.

**Learn to use the Database Wizards**

The Database Wizards can help you automate tasks that could normally take hours of coding.

**Using the SQL Server Database Designer**

Using this database designer can greatly simplify creation of new tables, and the modification of existing ones.

**Using the Query Designer**

Visual query building has long been a hallmark of FoxPro and other ISAM databases—now you can see its power used with ODBC data sources.

**Scripting with ADO**

Microsoft has released a new API called Active Data Objects—learn to use this through scripting.

Microsoft's Visual InterDev promises to make the Webmaster's job and our jobs as database developers much easier. With a familiar development environment (at least to most of you) and decent data tools, this is a big improvement over previous attempts to integrate the Web developer's toolkit with data access tools.

Microsoft's Visual InterDev enables the developer to concentrate more on the design than the implementation. Lest you think that this isn't what real developers do, try it. You might like having your development time cut in half. ■

# The Data View

Microsoft's Visual InterDev's Data View will be a very familiar view to Visual J++ developers. As you probably know, Microsoft is integrating all of its development environments with Visual Studio (the new version of Developer Studio). Microsoft's InterDev is no exception to this. When you open Microsoft InterDev, you will see the same environment that you see when opening Visual C++, or Visual J++. Everything that makes Visual Studio a great development environment is available for you to use while working with an InterDev project, just as with the other Visual Studio products.

When you open a new InterDev project, you will first see a pane that is similar to the Class View—this is the Data View. It contains the hierarchical information on your data source, including the physical schema and any logical constraints and views defined for this data source.

The Data View works very similarly to the Class View, as well. Right-click any object in the Data View, and you will see a variety of operations that you can perform on that object.

# Using the Query Designer

The Data View works hand-in-hand with the Query Designer. By using the Query Designer, you can create queries graphically and observe the results of those queries immediately. The Query Designer is activated when you choose Insert, Database Item while in File View, or by simply right-clicking the data source that you want to query against and choosing Insert New Query. Either of these will bring up the Query Designer with the default query against the data source that you chose. You can then edit/modify or delete the query and its contents by using one of four different panes. (Yes, it does stretch the rule of no more than three or four static splitters on the same window.)

As already mentioned, you can work in four different panes within the Query Designer (five if you count the Data View). Listed in Table 10.1 are the panes of the Query Designer and what they are used for.

**Table 10.1 Components of the Query Designer**

| Component | Description |
|---|---|
| Diagram Pane | Enables you to visually interact with and build the query, much like creating relations with Microsoft Access. |
| Grid Pane | Enables you to specify sort order and type, column aliases, the columns included in the output, and search criteria. |
| SQL Pane | Enables you to specify any valid SQL statement; if the statement cannot be represented in the other panes, it is grayed out. |
| Results Pane | Enables you to see the results of the query and to edit the results; it executes asynchronously. |

As you can see, there are multiple ways of doing the same thing, depending on your preference.

## The Diagram Pane

Of the four panes, the Diagram Pane is the most popular. To include the desired tables or views into the query, simply drag them to the Diagram Pane. Use the check boxes next to the column names to determine which columns are included in the query.

You can also perform joins and grouping with the Diagram Pane. As you design the query, you will begin to notice that several icons appear to the right of the column names that you've been working on. These icons are, essentially, a roadmap to the operations that have been performed on the object. The lines between the tables (created when you create the relationship) signify the type of join that is being performed. An example of this is shown in Figure 10.1.



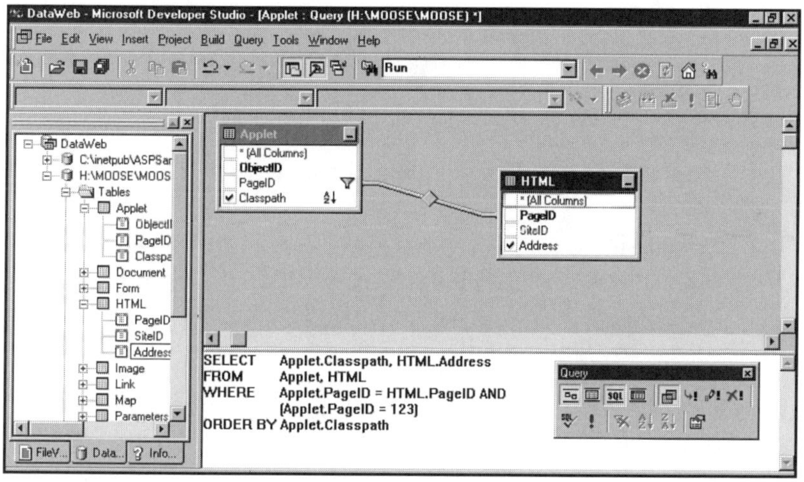


**FIG. 10.1**
Use the Diagram Pane to build your queries visually.

## The Grid Pane

The Grid Pane enables developers to set the conditions of the query. There are several columns in the Grid Pane, and each one has a different function. Table 10.2 defines the function of each column.

**Table 10.2 Functions of the Columns in the Grid Pane**

| Column | Description |
|---|---|
| Column | This contains the columns (or calculation) in which the data is included in the query. |
| Alias | The alias (if any) of the column. |

*continues*

**Table 10.2 Continued**

| Column | Description |
|---|---|
| Table | The table that the column is associated with. |
| Output | If checked, the column is included in the query output. |
| Sort Type | If specified, the column is sorted according to the value listed—ascending or descending. |
| Sort Order | The data is sorted according to the column listed as being first in the sort order, and then by the second, and so forth. |
| Group By | This specifies whether the column is included in the grouping. |
| Criteria | This specifies a search criterion, same as the SQL `Where` clause. |
| Or | This sets additional search criteria; use the tab key to add more Or columns. |
| Append | This specifies the name of the column to receive the data from the current column. It is used in an insert query when the Query Designer doesn't know which column is the query target. |
| New Value | A literal value or expression. |

As Table 10.2 shows, you can represent almost any Select or Action query by using the Grid Pane. A note about using the criteria: If you've chosen Group By from the drop-down menu in the Group By column, or chosen Group By from the Tools menu, then the criterion will be a "Having" clause. Figure 10.2 illustrates using the Query tab of the Properties dialog box.

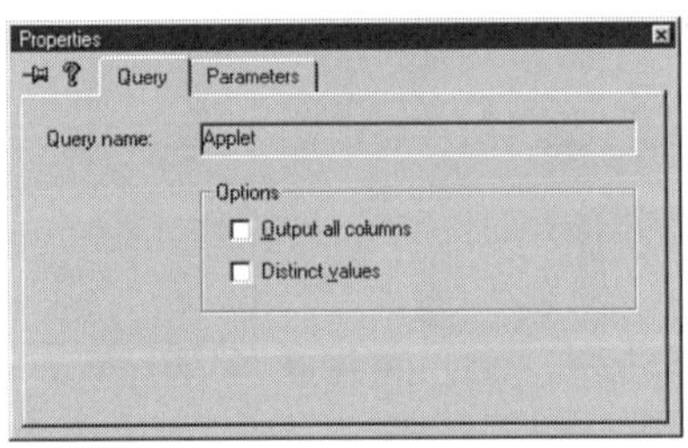


**FIG. 10.2**
This example shows the Properties dialog box of the Applet query, where you can determine the uniqueness of the output.

## The SQL Pane

The SQL Pane is where the real action begins as far as the data source is concerned. All of the work that you do in the Diagram and Grid Panes generates SQL statements that show up in the SQL Pane. You can edit or create your own statements and the other two panes will adjust to show your changes (shown in Figure 10.3) if they can. Note that things like data definition, language, and schema definitions will not show up in the other panes, and they will remain grayed out until the SQL Pane contents can be displayed.

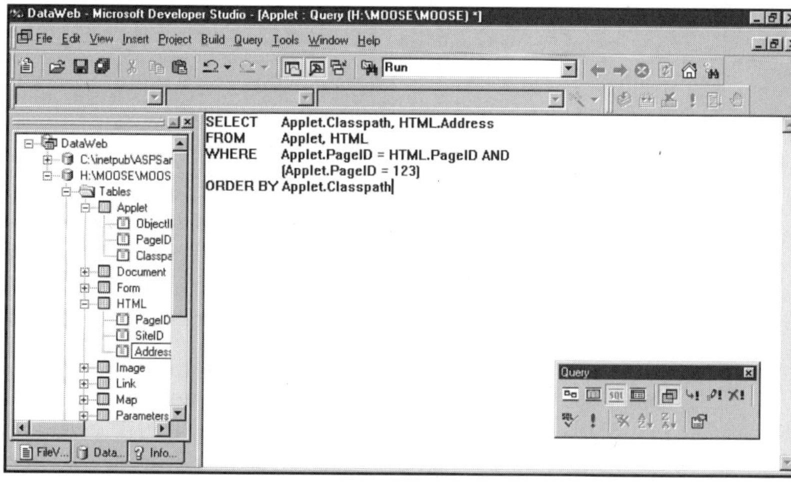


**FIG. 10.3**
Use the SQL Pane to perform data source-specific operations that cannot be shown visually.



# The Results Pane

In the Results Pane, you will be able to see the result set that is returned from any `Select` statements or stored procedures that you execute. You can also perform normal result set operations such as editing, inserting, and deleting values and rows while in the Results Pane, as shown in Figure 10.4.

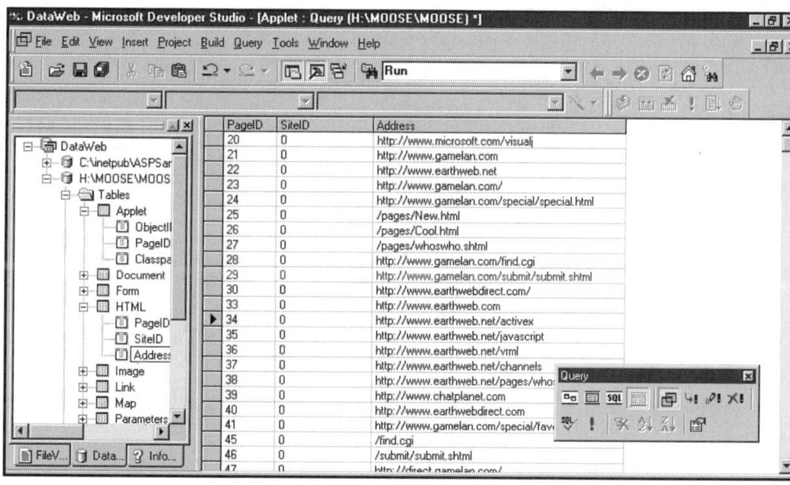


**FIG. 10.4**
Use the Results Pane to view and edit the results of the query that you've just built.

**NOTE** The columns in the Results Pane will show <NULL> if there is no value to display and <BLOB> for long binary data types. The query will also execute asynchronously so that its results begin returning immediately instead of waiting for the entire result set to return before giving control back to Visual InterDev.

# Using the SQL Server Database Designer

The Database Designer works with SQL Server 6.5 to provide a graphical interface for designing and maintaining SQL Server databases. You can even set up the schema changes and then review them before submitting them to the data source.

Database diagrams are the meat of the Database Designer because they enable you to set up a graphical representation of the tables, columns, and any relationships or constraints that you have defined for the data source. Creating a new diagram is fairly simple—instead of inserting a query, insert a database diagram. This gives you a blank diagram that you can then drag tables into. The Database Designer automatically draws the existing relations for you.

You can also create new tables in the Database Designer or copy existing tables from a different diagram. Note that copies still exist only once, and what your database receives is a reference to the table, not an actual copy of the database. This is advantageous when you divide up large diagrams to work on because changes to a single table will affect all references to it.

Specifying database owners and simple change detection are concurrency controls that are built into the database diagram. However, using these basic concurrency controls means that the person with the laziest finger gets to create the database in his or her own image. For example, let's say you are using simple change detection. If you are editing the diagram and someone saves changes that affect your unsaved changes, saving your diagram will overwrite any changes made by the other person.

One method of ensuring control in a multiuser environment is to require all changes to the database either be made by the owner or be submitted to the owner for approval. Otherwise, chaos could easily result if several people update the same database. The Database Designer enables you to save the change script to a text file for this purpose.

The objects that you can create in the Database Designer are listed in Table 10.3.

**Table 10.3 Objects Available for Use with the Database Designer**

| Object | Description |
|---|---|
| Constraints | A condition that must be met for an operation to succeed. |
| Indexes | Unique identifiers that speed the access of data in the database. These are created on certain columns enabling the database engine to know exactly where a piece of data lies when given the index. |
| Keys | A unique identifier for a single row. |
| Relationships | A reference between two rows (called relations in relational theory). |
| Tables | A collection of logically associated rows. |

Relationships are created by simply dragging a field in one table to another table. When you do so, the Create Relationship dialog box appears. You can accept the default (the Database Designer will attempt to divine your relationships) or change it. When you are satisfied, choose OK. You can also determine the type of relation and whether or not to enforce the relationship from the Create Relationships dialog box.

Creating a many-to-many (M:M) relationship is a little more difficult, simply because the relationship must be shown with a junction table. This table will look a lot like a tree, having a central table with many tables joined from this one central table (the junction table). Then create 1:M relationships between the primary keys of the other tables and the junction table.

SQL Server enables you to define auto-incremented columns, much like Microsoft Access does. You can use these columns by setting the columns' Identity Increment and Identity Seed properties within the Database Designer. The Identity Increment defines the incremental amount, and the Identity Seed defines the starting point.



You can also define the properties of the columns through the Column Properties button on the toolbar. The types of properties available to you are as follows:

- *Column Name* Denotes the name of the column in the database
- *Datatype* Sets the data type of the column
- *Length* Enables you to set the length for columns that are defined `binary`, `char`, `varbinary`, or `varchar`
- *Precision* Enables you to redefine the maximum number of digits allowed in the highlighted column
- *Scale* Sets the number of places to the right of the decimal point
- *Allow Nulls* Determines whether or not the column allows `NULL` values
- *Default Value* Assigns a default value to a column when the column is left blank

Indexing can also be accomplished from within the Database Designer. Simply get the properties of the table that you want to index by right-clicking the table and choosing the Index/Keys tab. Then choose New to create an index. The dialog box enables you to choose the columns that will be indexed.

**NOTE** You can create three types of indexes within the Database Designer—clustered, nonclustered, and unique. Clustered and nonclustered simply refer to the way that the data is stored: A clustered index stores the data sorted by the index; a nonclustered index doesn't. A unique index, however, refers to the fact that this index is unique, but is not the primary key. This is useful for guaranteeing the uniqueness of non-key data items.

Constraints are the last item on the Database Designer agenda, and most often the least understood. Indexes and relationships are an easy concept to grasp, but constraints are almost unheard of, at least with the intended audience of the Microsoft InterDev. There are several types of constraints. Although SQL-92 only defines two, SQL Server defines several, listed in Table 10.4 for reference.

**Table 10.4 Constraint Definitions Allowed with SQL Server 6.5**

| Constraint Type | Description |
|---|---|
| Check | Denotes a condition that data must meet to be entered into a column |
| Default | Supplies a value for null columns in an update |
| Foreign Key | Used in conjunction with Primary and Unique constraints to enforce referential integrity between tables |
| Primary Key | Ensures no duplicate values are entered and that the column does not contain `NULL` values |
| Unique | Ensures that no duplicates exist outside of the Primary Key |

You can also disable your constraints for replication or Inserts and Updates. You do this through the properties of the table, and then choose the constraint from the selected constraint list and choose the options that you need.

# Scripting with ADO

Microsoft has released a brand-new database API with Microsoft InterDev. Based on the OLE DB technology, ADO has been billed as the "lightweight" data access protocol. This has yet to be proven, but it does enable scripting functions to approximate the feature set of RDO or DAO, and this is no small accomplishment.

ADO is referred to as an object model or simply as an object with a set of interfaces that you can call. The model will look very familiar to you, as will the methods.

## The *Connection* Object

The `Connection` object is the highest interface that you can access in the ADO object model. This object enables you to set up and establish a connection with a data source. This is almost a direct counterpart of the DAO and RDO connection objects.

The ADO `Connection` object does allow transaction control using the `BeginTrans`, `CommitTrans`, and `RollbackTrans` methods. Direct execution is possible with the `Connection.Execute` method. Table 10.5 lists the methods and properties that make up the `Connection` object.

**Table 10.5 The ADO *Connection* Object's Methods**

| Method | Description |
|---|---|
| `BeginTrans` | Signals the beginning of a transacted sequence |
| `CommitTrans` | Signals the transaction is to be ended, committing all changes |

| Method | Description |
|---|---|
| `RollbackTrans` | Signals the transaction is to be ended, throwing away the changes made |
| `Open` | Creates the connection to a data source |
| `Close` | Closes the connection and destroys the `Connection` object |
| `Execute` | Executes a specific SQL statement or stored procedure |

These methods operate much as you would expect them to. The connection is opened with the `Open` method, closed with the `Close` method, and so forth. Listing 10.1 gives the VBScript that would actually use the `Connection` object's methods.



**Listing 10.1 HTML.ASP—Using the ADO *Connection* Object in an Active Server Script**

```
<HTML>
<TITLE>HTML</TITLE>
<BODY leftmargin = 110 background = stones.jpg>
<%
Param = Request.QueryString("Param")
Data = Request.QueryString("Data")
%>
<%
If IsObject(Session("MOOSE_conn")) Then
    Set conn = Session("MOOSE_conn")
Else
    Set conn = Server.CreateObject("ADODB.Connection")
    conn.open "MOOSE","WebServ",""
    Set Session("MOOSE_conn") = conn
End If
%>
<%
    sql = "SELECT * FROM [HTML]"
    If cstr(Param) <> "" And cstr(Data) <> "" Then
        sql = sql & " WHERE " & cstr(Param) & " = " & cstr(Data)
    End If
    Set rs = Server.CreateObject("ADODB.Recordset")
    rs.Open sql, conn, 3, 3
%>
<TABLE BORDER=1 BGCOLOR=#ffffff CELLSPACING=0><FONT FACE="Arial"
COLOR=#000000><CAPTION><B>HTML</B></CAPTION>
<THEAD>
<TR>
<TH BGCOLOR=#c0c0c0 BORDERCOLOR=#000000 ><FONT SIZE=2 FACE="Arial"
COLOR=#000000>PageID</FONT></TH>
<TH BGCOLOR=#c0c0c0 BORDERCOLOR=#000000 ><FONT SIZE=2 FACE="Arial"
COLOR=#000000>SiteID</FONT></TH>
<TH BGCOLOR=#c0c0c0 BORDERCOLOR=#000000 ><FONT SIZE=2 FACE="Arial"
COLOR=#000000>Address</FONT></TH>
```

*continues*

**Listing 10.1 Continued**

```
</TR>
</THEAD>
<TBODY>
<%
On Error Resume Next
rs.MoveFirst
do while Not rs.eof
 %>
<TR VALIGN=TOP>
<TD BORDERCOLOR=#c0c0c0  ALIGN=RIGHT>
<FONT SIZE=2 FACE="Arial" COLOR=#000000>
<%=Server.HTMLEncode(rs.Fields("PageID").Value)%>
<BR></FONT></TD>
<TD BORDERCOLOR=#c0c0c0  ALIGN=RIGHT>
<FONT SIZE=2 FACE="Arial" COLOR=#000000>
<%=Server.HTMLEncode(rs.Fields("SiteID").Value)%>
<BR></FONT></TD>
<TD BORDERCOLOR=#c0c0c0 >
<FONT SIZE=2 FACE="Arial" COLOR=#000000>
<%=Server.HTMLEncode(rs.Fields("Address").Value)%>
<BR></FONT></TD>
</TR>
<%
rs.MoveNext
loop
%>
</TBODY>
<TFOOT></TFOOT>
</TABLE>
</BODY>
<BR><BR>
<IMG SRC = "msaccess.jpg">
</HTML>
```

As you might expect, the configuration of the connection is done through the use of the object's properties. The `Connection` object has several properties that you are able to use, as listed in Table 10.6.

**Table 10.6 The ADO *Connection* Object's Properties**

| Property | Description |
|---|---|
| `ActiveConnection` | Contains the information for the active connection |
| `Attributes` | Determines whether committing or rolling back a transaction will begin a new transaction |
| `ConnectionString` | Contains the ODBC connection string |
| `ConnectionTimeout` | Denotes the timeout value to receive confirmation of a connection attempt |

| Property | Description |
|---|---|
| `DefaultDatabase` | Contains the default databases to use for the connection |
| `IsolationLevel` | Contains the isolation level for the connection |
| `Mode` | Contains the level of access that the connection is allowed |
| `Provider` | Contains the name of the provider name for this connection |

***ActiveConnection*** This property is used to return an active connection to use. If you pass a connection string along with this property (setting it), you will actually wind up creating a new `Connection` object.

**Attributes** You can set either `adXactCommitRetaining` or `adXactAbortRetaining`. Setting the `Attributes` to `adXactCommitRetaining` tells ADO that this connection will begin a new transaction as soon as the `Commit` method is called. Setting `adXactAbortRetaining` tells ADO that you want a new transaction any time that you call `RollbackTrans`. These are mainly convenience features for the developer.



***ConnectionString*** The `ConnectionString` property enables you to build the connection string in the application, set the string, and then pass it in a call to the `Open` method. This would be useful when your users could be connecting to multiple data sources depending on certain environmental variables.

***ConnectionTimeout*** This property is basically the ODBC connection timeout value. Change it if network conditions are degraded. If you set this value to zero, the `Open` method waits forever to connect.

***DefaultDatabase*** The `DefaultDatabase` property is set by the provider when you make a connection to the data source. Some providers allow you to change this value—mainly those that support multiple databases in a single connection.

***IsolationLevel*** `I`solation levels are actually expanded from those in the ODBC-based object models. You can have nine different levels of isolation, although some of the levels simply achieve the same effects through different names. In Chapter 5, "ODBC," we cover the SQL-92 isolation levels. For your convenience, a review of the events used to define these isolation levels follows.

The events that can happen to a transaction, as defined by ANSI, are as follows:

- *Dirty Reads* This event describes what happens when one transaction is able to read uncommitted data from another transaction. For example: You perform an update, but don't issue a commit. Someone else's transaction then reads from that update and you roll back the transaction instead of committing it. Now the data that someone else read doesn't exist anymore.
- *Non-Repeatable Reads* A non-repeatable read occurs when a transaction reads the same row twice but gets different data each time. This can occur when your transaction reads

a row once, and a separate transaction deletes the row and then inserts a new row at that position. When you read the row again, the data is different and a non-repeatable read occurs.

- *Phantoms* This is simply a row that matches your search criteria but for some reason doesn't show up until you refresh the query. This can happen when another transaction performs an update or an insert after you issue the query, and the information matches your transaction's search criteria.

ADO really only adds a flag to tell you that the isolation level is unknown. The other "new" isolation level constants simply perform the same function as the ones that you know. The different isolation levels available to you with ADO are listed in Table 10.7.

**Table 10.7 Isolation Levels Available Within ADO**

| Level | Description |
|---|---|
| `adXactUnspecified` | Isolation level cannot be determined. |
| `adXactChaos` | Changes pending from transactions using higher Isolation levels cannot be modified. Same as `ReadUncommitted`. |
| `adXactReadUncommitted` | Setting this means that you are not isolated from any transactions. Your transaction can see any changes in the underlying data or data structure. |
| `adXactCursorStability` | You are guaranteed no dirty reads. |
| `adXactReadCommitted` | You are guaranteed no dirty reads. |
| `adXactRepeatableRead` | The application is requesting to be isolated from dirty reads and non-repeatable reads. |
| `adXactIsolated` | The transaction is completely isolated from any dirty reads, non-repeatable reads, and phantoms. |
| `adXactSerializable` | The transaction is completely isolated from any dirty reads, non-repeatable reads, and phantoms. |

***Mode*** Setting the mode for a connection specifies what the access level for the transaction will be. You can set this property while the `Connection` object is closed, or else it will return the permission that currently is in use. The values returned could be any one of the following:

- `adModeUnknown` The permissions cannot be determined.
- `adModeRead` Read permission.
- `adModeWrite` Write permission.
- `adModeReadWrite` Read/Write permission.
- `adModeShareDenyRead` No one else can open a connection and request read permission.

- `adModeShareDenyWrite` No one else can open a connection and request write permission.
- `adModeShareExclusive` No one else can open the connection with read/write permission.
- `adModeDenyNone` No one else is allowed to open the connection.

***Provider*** The `Provider` property denotes the name of the provider for the connection. It is read only during an active connection.

# The *Command* Object

The `Command` object can be thought of as the *root* object, although a `Connection` object is instanced first. You don't have to create the `Connection` before creating a new `Command` object because the `Command` object will create its own `Connection` object if none exists. This doesn't mean, however, that you can't use the `Connection` object to set up connections for the `Command` object. It simply means that you don't have to code another line if you don't want to.



The `Command` object is where you can create prepared statements, execute direct SQL statements, or open `Recordset` objects on the result set from the operation. The methods that you can use with the `Command` object are listed in Table 10.8.

**Table 10.8 Methods of the *Command* Object**

| Method | Description |
|---|---|
| `CreateParameter` | Creates a new parameter |
| `Execute` | Executes the text specified in the `CommandText` property |

The `CreateParameter` method is used in conjunction with the `Prepared` property to set up a prepared statement. The syntax looks something like this:

```
m_param = m_command.CreateParameter(m_strName, m_nlType, m_nlDirection, m_nlSize,
m_vValue);
```

The arguments of the `CreateParameter` method are:

- *Name* Name of the parameter object to create (required).
- *Type* Specifies the data type of the parameter (optional).
- *Direction* Sets the direction of the parameter (optional). Valid values are:

  `adParamInput` for an input value

  `adParamOutput` for an output value

  `adParamInputOutput` to specify an input or output parameter

  `adParamReturnValue` to specify a Return value

- *Size* Maximum length of the parameter's data in bytes (optional).
- *Value* The value of the parameter (optional). This is a Variant.

The `Execute` method simply executes whatever statement is in the `CommandText` property.

The properties of the `Command` object are listed in Table 10.9.

**Table 10.9 The *Command* Object's Properties**

| Property | Description |
|---|---|
| `CommandText` | Sets the text to be passed to the driver |
| `CommandTimeout` | Timeout value to wait before generating an error while attempting to execute a command |
| `CommandType` | Contains the type of command that the `CommandText` property contains |
| `Prepared` | Boolean value determining if the statement that is held in the Command Text should be prepared before execution |

This is a situation in which all of the properties are actually useful most of the time. The `CommandText` property is, of course, the most commonly used property. This property holds the data that you are performing the operation on.

The `CommandType` property enables you to state the type of data that the `CommandText` property is holding. This can be any one of several values. The list that follows contains the valid settings for the `CommandType` property.

- `adCmdText` Specifies that the `CommandText` property contains text information (SQL statements)
- `adCmdTable` Specifies the `CommandText` property as containing a table name
- `adCmdStoredProc` Specifies that the `CommandText` property contains a stored procedure call
- `adCmdUnknown` Specifies that the `CommandText` property contains an unknown value (default)

The `CommandTimeout` property is useful to overcome slow links and other timing issues, and setting the `Prepared` property to true would specify the `CommandText` property to hold a prepared statement.

## The *Parameter* Object

You use the `Parameter` object when dealing with parameters. By using the methods of this object, you can set the directions, change the values, and extract information about the parameters in your parameterized query. You have one method available to you—the `AppendChunk` method, which passes a long char or long binary values in chunks.

You have several properties to use with the `Parameter` object, listed as follows:

- `Name` The name of the parameter object
- `Value` The parameter's value (you can set long binary data with this)
- `Attributes` Contains information about whether the parameter is nullable, signed, or accepts long binary data
- `Direction` Which direction the parameter is—an input direction or output direction.
- `Precision` Mathematical precision (# of digits) used to represent the value
- `NumericScale` Sets the number of decimal places to resolve the numeric values to
- `Size` Maximum size (in bytes) of the data held by the parameter
- `Type` Data type of the parameter



## The *Recordset* Object

The `Recordset` object returns data to you almost exactly as the `Recordset` object does in DAO, although the ADO `Recordset` object supports most of the syntax used in the RDO `rdoResultset` object.

Using this object will be familiar. You've been given the same choices for cursor types as in previous models (ODBC, DAO, and RDO):

- Dynamic Dynamically updates the `Recordset` object to reflect changes of the data and the state of the data as the data is scrolled through.
- Keyset Acts like both a static and a dynamic cursor. Fetches a predetermined amount of rows, called a keyset; as soon as the client scrolls beyond the keyset, another is fetched dynamically.
- Static Data is fetched only once and is not updated.
- Forward-only Same as the static cursor except that it enables forward movement only, as its name suggests.

If you don't pass any specific cursor type with the `Open` call or when creating the `Recordset` object, ADO will open a forward-only cursor by default. The normal movement methods are available to you as well:

- `Move`
- `MoveFirst`
- `MoveLast`
- `MovePrevious`
- `MoveNext`
- `AbsolutePosition`

The two new methods specific to ADO for moving through the result set are `AbsolutePage` and `Filter`.

The `Update`, `Delete`, and `AddNew` methods work exactly as they do in DAO. You also have the batch update capability via the `UpdateBatch` method and the capability for conflict resolution with the `Status` property.

The properties of the `Recordset` object are listed in Table 10.10.

**Table 10.10 Properties of the *Recordset* Object**

| Property | Description |
|---|---|
| `AbsolutePage` | The current page. |
| `AbsolutePosition` | The current position (ordinal). |
| `ActiveConnection` | The string defining a connection for this object. |
| `BOF` | Boolean value, `TRUE` if the cursor is positioned at the beginning of the result set. |
| `BookMark` | A unique value for a single record. In particular, this property pertains to the current record. |
| `EOF` | Boolean value, `TRUE` if the cursor is positioned at the end of the result set. |
| `CacheSize` | The number of records to hold in the in-memory cache. |
| `CursorType` | Contains the cursor type used in this `Recordset`. |
| `EditMode` | `TRUE` if the current record is being edited. |
| `Filter` | Enables you to determine the level of filtering done on the `Recordset` object, similar in operation to the SQL `Having` clause. |
| `LockType` | Indicates the access level on the current `Recordset` object. |
| `MaxRecords` | Indicates the maximum number of records that will be returned from the data source. |
| `PageCount` | Indicates the number of pages that a `Recordset` object contains. |
| `PageSize` | Indicates the number of records contained in a single page. |
| `RecordCount` | The number of records returned in the `Recordset` object. |
| `Source` | The source for the data returned in a `Recordset` object. |
| `Status` | A number of status flags indicating certain conditions about the `Recordset` object. |

Of the properties listed in Table 10.10, you will find the `Page`, `Filter`, and the `Status` properties to be the only ones that are completely new to the ADO object model. The concept of pages has been introduced to ease the capability to page through several records at a time in a result set, probably due to the popularity of this style of result set movement on the Internet.

The page properties, `AbsolutePage`, `PageCount`, and `PageSize`, enable you to determine (or set) the number and size of the pages, as well as which page the cursor is pointing to.

The `Filter` property provides basically the same functionality as the `Having` clause in pure SQL. It enables scalar expressions and Boolean expressions, and it is applied after the result set is returned to the client by the server.

The `Status` property gives you a wide range of questions to ask the `Recordset` object. The flags used and their values are listed in Table 10.11.

**Table 10.11 Flags for the *Status* Property**

| Flag | Its Answer, if *TRUE* |
|---|---|
| `adRecOK` | Successful udpate. |
| `adRecNew` | New record. |
| `adRecModified` | The record has been modified. |
| `adRecDeleted` | The record has been deleted. |
| `adRecUnmodified` | The record is unmodified. |
| `adRecInvalid` | The record had an invalid bookmark. |
| `adRecMulitpleChanges` | There would be multiple changes to the data if the record were saved. |
| `adRecPendingChanges` | This record refers to an insert that is in an uncommitted or pending state. |
| `adRecCanceled` | The operation was canceled. |
| `adRecCantRelease` | Locks on the record that prevented the operation from succeeding. |
| `adRecConcurrencyViolation` | Optimistic concurrency was in use, and the record was modified prior to the update attempt. |
| `adRecIntegrityViolation` | The operation would have violated integrity constraints. |
| `adRecMaxChangesExceeded` | There are too many pending changes. |
| `adRecObjectOpen` | The operation conflicts with an existing open object. |
| `adRecOutOfMemory` | The computer either has no virtual memory left, or you've read in corrupted data (either the cache or a network burp). |
| `adRecPermissionDenied` | You did not have permission to complete the operation. |
| `adRecSchemaViolation` | The operation would have resulted in structural changes to the schema that were not permitted. |
| `adRecDBDeleted` | The record from the data source has already been removed. |

You can `XOR` the properties to extract the data from the property, as the property returns the sum of these values as a 19-bit (high value 262144, 19th bit = 1) bitmask.

## The *Field* Object

This object is at the atomic level of the ADO object model, representing the single column of data within a row. Like `rdoColumn`, the `Field` object has methods to determine the data types, sizes, and attributes of the column of data. `AppendChunk` and `GetChunk` are also supported in the ADO interpretation of the `Field` object.

The methods available to you within the `Field` object are listed in Table 11.12 and its properties are listed in Table 10.13.

**Table 10.12 The ADO *Field* Object's Methods**

| Method | Description |
|---|---|
| `AppendChunk` | Used to break data blocks into smaller segments when setting a `Field` object's value. |
| `GetChunk` | Used to break the retrieval of a large data block into smaller segments. |

Table 10.13 illustrates the ADO `Field` object's properties. You will notice that for a supposed lightweight data class, ADO offers a surprising array of options for the individual fields in the database.

**Table 10.13 The ADO *Field* Object's Properties**

| Property | Description |
|---|---|
| `ActualSize` | The length of data actually stored in the field, (–1, if unknown) |
| `Attributes` | A bitmask of values describing the attributes of the `Field` object |
| `DefinedSize` | The maximum size of the `Field` object's data |
| `Name` | The name of the `Field` object |
| `NumericScale` | Number of decimal places for a numeric `Field` value |
| `OriginalValue` | The value of the `Field` object before any changes were made to it |
| `Precision` | Mathematical precision (# of digits) for a numeric `Field` value |
| `Type` | A value describing the data type stored in the `Field` object |
| `UnderlyingValue` | The value for a `Field` object as your transaction sees it: Used with `OriginalValue` to resolve conflicts |
| `Value` | Returns a variant containing the `Field` object's contents |

# From Here...

You've seen the power that Microsoft's Visual InterDev offers as well as the tools that it provides for use with your Java applications. By using the Query Designer and the Database Wizards, you can take much of the work out of scripting a database application. This is a far cry from the days of coding custom CGI scripts to deal with your data.

You've also been given another means of data access with ADO. Although the pros and cons of this new API must be measured against the existing tools and some future ones (like a direct ODBC port), this is something you'll want to add to the toolbox because the memory footprint will be slightly smaller than RDO, and it has been designed with the Internet in mind.

Several chapters in this book deal with the topics similar to those presented here.

- Chapter 4, "The SQL Standard: A Language for Data Access," explores the SQL language in depth and provides a background for many of the concepts discussed here.
- Chapter 5, "ODBC," gives a fundamental look at the underlying technology for most of Microsoft's database technologies.
- Chapter 6, "Data Access Objects," covers all aspects of the DAO 3.5 API in depth, including the new ODBCDirect features.
- Chapter 7, "Remote Data Objects," explores what is currently the fastest connection to remote data sources offered to the Java database programmer.
- Chapter 12, "IIS Internet Database Connector," covers the aspects of designing a database presence on your Web server using IIS 3.0 and the Internet Database Connector.

PART IV

# Publishing Your Data to the Web

CHAPTER 11

# Understanding SQL Server and the Internet

Corporate database systems are built on making information widely available to qualified users. The information in these situations comes from many sources, ranging from discussion groups to proprietary systems. Probably the biggest repository of "mass" information is the database. If you've ever just browsed a database without specifying meaningful criteria, you know what is meant by "mass" information. There is often so much information represented that it actually makes it less useful.

By making databases available on your site, you can help users make sense of this information and, at the same time, present your users with access to the data without the need for any special software to begin using the database effectively. In short, you have a new avenue to provide access to the information that is probably already stored on your network.

Database access with the IIS system is provided by giving you ODBC connectivity to the HTML pages that execute on the server when the user makes a request of the system. In this chapter, you see how to set up pages, what types of information you can provide, and how you can enhance the presentation of the information to make it the most meaningful to the people who request it. ■

**Database-enable your site**

Use the Internet Database Connector to add dynamic Web pages to your site.

**Use the SQL Web Page Wizard**

SQL Server's Web Page Wizard helps you create pages that can call stored procedures, run scheduled queries, and much more.

**Learn key settings to make logging access to databases work for you**

Without some key entries in your system configuration, you might have a difficult time getting valuable logging information from your system. Find out the key ingredients for successful access to your database.

**Find out how Active Server pages and new Internet components work**

There are strong efforts being made to build database access into Web sites.

**Get an early look at the Advance Data Connector**

The ADC is a new component from Microsoft that brings the DAO even closer to your Internet Explorer client-based application. It makes the use of the DAO over the Internet simple and fast.

**CAUTION**

Be aware that the database connector files are likely to contain and convey sensitive and sometimes very confidential information. For example, they'll contain query information that calls out column names, table names, and database sources that map to your ODBC configurations on the server.

In addition, when users click a link to a database connector file, they'll be able to see where you're keeping your scripts and other programs, because the location will show up in the URL that is displayed.

It is extremely important that your programs, scripts, and supporting files reside in the scripts subdirectory structure and that you provide Execute Only privileges on that directory. Be sure you do not provide Read privileges. This will open your system unnecessarily to possible trouble, because people would be able to browse and review the applications that are the core of your system.

# Setting Up the Internet Database Connector

The Internet Information Server provides access to the ODBC layer with the use of the Internet Database Connector, or IDC. The IDC acts as a go-between for your system, providing the interaction between what is seen in the viewer in terms of HTML and how the information is queried at the database level. The overall access layer map is shown in Figure 11.1.

**FIG. 11.1**
The IDC provides access to any ODBC data source.

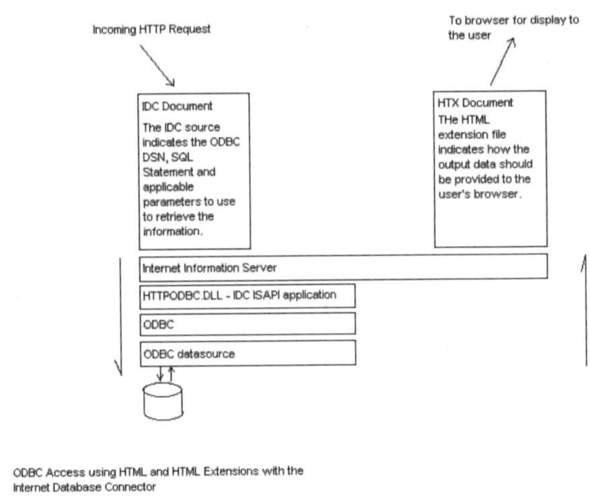


When users specify the IDC file in the URL from the browser, they are asking the IIS system to use the IDC file and its statements to query the database and return the results. The IDC is specified in the URL, but the HTX file, or HTML Extension file, is what is actually returned to the user. The HTX file, still a standard HTML file, indicates how the resulting data is displayed, what lines constitute the detail lines of information, and more.

In Figure 11.1, you can see that the engine that is doing the database work with ODBC is HTTPODBC.DLL. This DLL, included when you install the IIS system, is an Internet Server API, or ISAPI, application that runs as an extension to the server software. This extension is database aware and is able to use the two source files, the IDC and HTX files, required to give the information back to the user.

**TIP** If you did not install the ODBC component of IIS, you need to do so to use the IDC. This not only installs the ODBC portions of the environment, but also configures the server to be aware of the IDC files you will use. If you do not install the ODBC components, when users click the IDC link on their Web page, they will see a prompt to download the IDC file, rather than view the results of the query.

When you install IIS, the ODBC option must be selected. Though it might not indicate disk space requirements if you have already installed ODBC from other applications, it will still be necessary to install it to activate the IDC capabilities (see Figure 11.2).

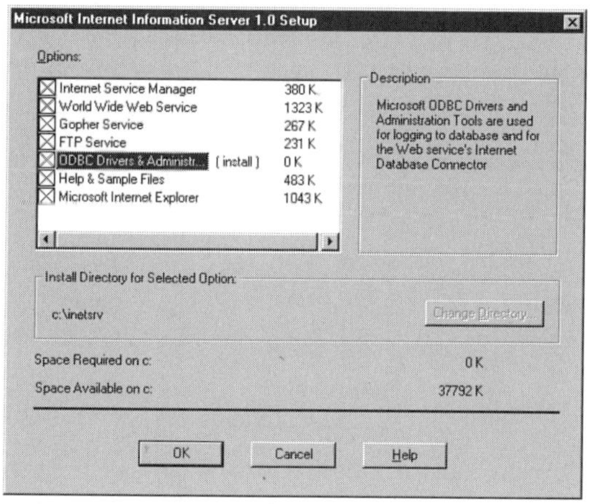


**FIG. 11.2** It's a good rule of thumb to select ODBC for all installations–the setup program also is careful not to overwrite any newer versions of the drivers you might have installed on your system.



Listing 11.1 shows a sample IDC file taken from the samples included with the server. The sample installs into the \SCRIPTS\SAMPLES subdirectory on your system in the IIS directory structure.

**Listing 11.1 A Simple IDC Source File**

```
Data source: web sql
Username: sa
Template: sample.htx
SQLStatement:
+SELECT au_lname, ytd_sales from pubs.dbo.titleview
➥where ytd_sales>5000
```

**TIP** You can indicate more than one SQL statement by using the IDC parameter more than once in the IDC file. Start each SQL statement with the `SqlStatement:` heading. You will be able to access both result sets in the HTX file.

When this file is loaded by IIS, IIS examines the extension and determines what application should be used for the source file. For certain items, including the IDC extension, the server comes pre-installed, knowing what to do with the source when it's requested. One of the very powerful capabilities and features of IIS is that it is able to use the same Windows-based extension resolution to determine what to do with a given request. Files with a .GIF extension, for example, are known to be graphic images, and files with an .IDC extension are database connector "applets." You set up custom keys in the Registry. Associations are set up in the tree location shown next.

**CAUTION**

Any time you work with the Registry you should use extreme caution. Making entries in incorrect locations or with incorrect syntax can render your system inoperable.

Use the Regedt32 application to modify the registry. When you start it, look for the following key:

```
location:HKEY_LOCAL_MACHINE
      SYSTEM
            CurrentControlSet
                  Services
                        W3SVC
                             Parameters
                                   ScriptMap
```

If you add a new entry, make it of the type `REG_SZ` and indicate the extension to associate. You need to include the period before the extension—.IDC, for example—to correctly map the association. For the value, indicate the path and file name that should be executed when the specified extension is loaded. Remember to provide the path from the root and start the path with a backslash, because this will ensure that IIS will be able to locate the application, regardless of the current working directory.

If you are indicating parameters to the call, you can use `%s` on the key value where you indicate the application to run. For example, suppose that you have a DLL that you want to run whenever a request is received to open a file with a .FUN extension. Your entry would be as follows:

```
.fun = c:\inetsrv\scripts\test\fundll.dll %s %s
```

When you use this option, the first time you use `%s`, you'll receive the application to run that was passed to the URL. For example, if your FUNDLL is an application that processes a text file and searches it for a given value, you would expect the user to be passing in the text file and the value to search for. When you provide the URL at the browser level, you first indicate the location of the file you want to run. A question mark is next, followed by any applicable parameters to the call.

For the examples here, the URL that would be used would be something like the following:

```
http://holodeck3/scripts/search.fun?text+to+find
```

The resulting command line would be

```
c:\inetsrv\scripts\test\fundll.dll search.fun text+to+find
```

where each of the two items specified, the source file and search text, is passed as a parameter.

**NOTE** Because parameters are passed as a single string to your application, as in the previous example with the `text+to+find` string, your application must be able to parse out the plus signs and rebuild the string, most likely in a buffer that can be used by your application to search the database or text file, as needed.

The results-formatting file, or HTX file, is where things can get a little tricky. As you see throughout this chapter, the real power and capability of your system is exposed with the HTX file. Until the information is provided to the template, it's of no use to the requester, as he or she will not yet have seen the information. You can have one of the best, most comprehensive databases around, but if the presentation of the data is not what your audience needs, the information might as well be under lock and key.



Listing 11.2 shows a simple HTX template, provided in the samples with the IIS product, that displays the results of a query.

**Listing 11.2 HTX Source Files Provide Template Information for the Display of Results from Database Queries**

```
<HTML>
<HEAD><TITLE>Authors and YTD Sales</TITLE></HEAD>
<BODY BACKGROUND="/samples/images/backgrnd.gif">
<BODY BGCOLOR="FFFFFF">
<TABLE>
<TR>
<TD><IMG SRC="/samples/images/SPACE.gif" ALIGN="top" ALT=" "></TD>
<TD><A HREF="/samples/IMAGES/db_mh.map"><IMG SRC="/SAMPLES/images/db_mh.gif"
➥ismap BORDER=0 ALIGN="top" ALT=" "></A></TD>
</TR>
<tr>
<TD></TD>
<TD>
<hr>
<font size=2>
<CENTER>
<%if idc.sales eq ""%>
<H2>Authors with sales greater than <I>5000</I></H2>
<%else%>
```

*continues*

**Listing 11.2 Continued**

```
<H2>Authors with sales greater than <I><%idc.sales%></I></H2>
<%endif%>
<P>
<TABLE BORDER>
<%begindetail%>
<%if CurrentRecord EQ 0 %>
<caption>Query results:</caption>
<TR>
<TH><B>Author</B></TH><TH><B>YTD Sales<BR>(in dollars)</B></TH>
</TR>
<%endif%>
<TR><TD><%au_lname%></TD><TD align="right">$<%ytd_sales%></TD></TR>
<%enddetail%>
<P>
</TABLE>
</center>
<P>
<%if CurrentRecord EQ 0 %>
<I><B>Sorry, no authors had YTD sales greater than </I><%idc.sales%>.</B>
<P>
<%else%>
<HR>
<I>
The web page you see here was created by merging the results
of the SQL query with the template file SAMPLE.HTX.
<P>
The merge was done by the Microsoft Internet Database Connector and the results
 were returned to this web browser by the Microsoft Internet Information Server.
</I>
<%endif%>
</font>
</td>
</tr>
</table>
</BODY>
</HTML>
```

You'll probably notice several different things right away with this file. First, it's a standard HTML document. There is no strange formatting to speak of, and certainly many of the tags will be familiar if you've developed HTML before. Some of the real fun begins in the new capabilities offered by the HTX file. These new functions, above and beyond standard HTML, enable you to have the resulting Web page react to and change depending on the information that is, or is not, returned from the query. For example, in the section of code noted in the following, you'll see the introduction of conditional testing, examining for an empty set:

```
<%if idc.sales eq ""%>
      <H2>Authors with sales greater than <I>5000</I></H2>
<%else%>
      <H2>Authors with sales greater than <I><%idc.sales%></I></H2>
<%endif%>
```

Several operators are available when you design your pages. Throughout this chapter, you learn more about how to use these new database-oriented features.

As mentioned earlier, the IDC source file indicates the ODBC data source that is used to access the database on your system. From the IDC file listing, notice the `Data source` item. This item indicates that the `web sql` data source will be used. Before this sample will work on your system, you must have installed and configured the data source for that name using the ODBC control panel applet.

In the next couple of sections, you see how to set up the ODBC data sources for both SQL Server and Microsoft Access. You can use any 32-bit ODBC data source with your IIS application, and changes between setting up other data sources should be minimal; therefore, if you use the information presented here, you'll find that the IDC can work with nearly any database installation you might need to use.

## Building ODBC Data Sources for SQL Server Databases



One of the most common reasons for problems with the database connector is the setup of the ODBC data source. This is true across database sources not specific to SQL Server, so it's important to understand the details of setting up the driver for access by IIS.

You might recall that IIS is running as a service. This means that while it's running, it's not logged in as you, the administrator; instead, it's running in the background, logging in when needed as either the anonymous user you've set up or as the validated user who has been authenticated by the NT security subsystem. Because you want to give this service access to a database, and because you don't know whom the service will be logging in as, you need to set up the database source a bit differently than you might be accustomed to do.

Microsoft has added a new option to the ODBC configurations to support a System DSN. These special data sources give you a way to set up a globally available data source. Because users who log on might be set up to have different access to your system and resources, you need to use the System DSN to make sure they have access to the right databases, regardless of where they log on or who they log on as. Figure 11.3 shows the Data Sources setup dialog box, started from the Control Panel.

**TIP** If you find that you receive errors trying to access an ODBC data source from your Web pages, one of the first things you should check is that the data source you're referencing is set up as a system data source.

When you start the ODBC manager utility, if the data source is listed in the initial dialog box, it's defined as a user-based data source, not a System DSN. Remove the user-based DSN and redefine it as a System DSN, and you'll be able to see the database.

Remember that the only data sources that the Database Connector can use are the System-level data sources.

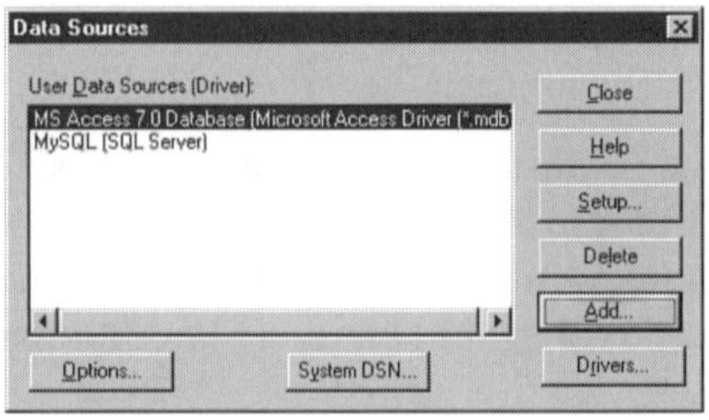


**FIG. 11.3**
ODBC setup for IIS requires that you select the System DSN to configure the driver.

After you select System DSN, you can use essentially the same options to set up the drivers. Note, too, that you can have more than one driver set up at the system level. This enables you to set up drivers for the different applications you'll be running on the Web. Figure 11.4 shows the System Data Sources setup dialog box.

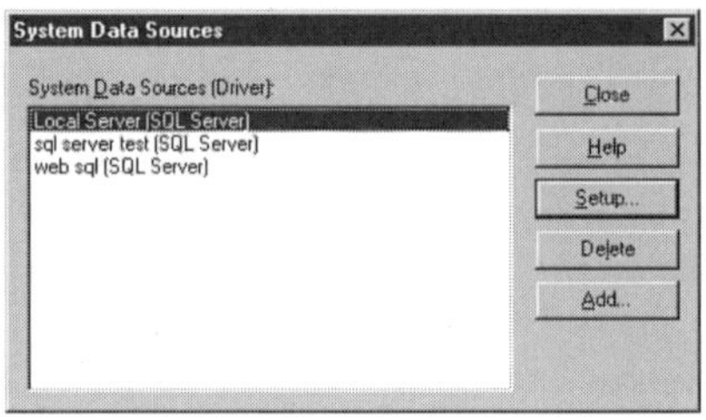


**FIG. 11.4**
Setting up a system-level ODBC driver configuration is much the same as establishing a new ODBC configuration. You need to indicate the driver, database, and other information required to connect to your database engine.

The Data Source Name that you provide in the Data Source Name Text box is what you'll be using in the IDC file as the data source, so be sure to make note of the database configuration names you set up.

In most cases, you'll want the configuration to be as specific as possible. If it's possible to indicate a default database or table, be sure to do so. It will take some of the variables out of the Web page design you'll be doing. By specifying as much information as possible, you'll help ensure that the information is accessible.

# Building ODBC Database Sources for Microsoft Access Databases

Microsoft Access database data sources are established the same way as they are for SQL Server. You must set up each data source as a System DSN, making it available to the IDC as it logs into NT's security subsystem.

Of course, there will likely be changes in the `SQLStatement` options you indicate in the IDC file. These differences relate to how Access interprets the SQL language elements. However, the statements should be nearly identical, especially in those cases where you're issuing SQL statements that are basically SELECT statements, rather than calling stored procedures, which are not supported by Access.

When you create the DSN, you'll be prompted to select the database with which ODBC should connect. Be sure to provide this information because, even though you can indicate it in code, you can make the connection to the database far more bulletproof with this option turned on. The system won't have to guess where to go to get the information.

## User Rights and Security Concerns

Database access using the IDC provides a wide open query system to your database. You should not allow users to have system administrator level access to your databases just because it provides a way for someone to gain unwanted administrative access to your system. Instead, consider one of two options. First, if you're allowing anonymous connections to your site, be sure the user you have indicated as the anonymous user (usually `IUSR_<machine name>`) has appropriate rights to the databases that will be needed.



The way the logon process works is to first validate the user using the anonymous logon if it's enabled. If enabled and the user indicated as the anonymous user does not have sufficient rights, he'll receive an error message that indicates the fact that he might not have rights to the object(s) requested.

If anonymous logon is disabled, the IDC will use the current user's name and password to log on to the database. If this logon fails to gain access, the request is denied, and the user is prevented from accessing the database requested.

In short, if you want anonymous users to gain access to your system, you'll need to create the user account you want to access the information. Next, assign the user to the database and objects, allowing access to the systems needed.

The second option you have is to use NT's integrated security with SQL Server. Using this method, the currently logged on user will be logged on to SQL Server, and the same rights will be in force.

## Building Dynamic Web Pages

Dynamic Web pages, those that build themselves on-the-fly to provide up-to-date information, are going to quickly become the mainstay of the intranet and Internet. This is because with a dynamic Web page, you always can count on getting the latest and greatest information. With the IDC, you can create these dynamic Web pages and have them work against a database to retrieve the information you need to let the user review.

There are three components to this type of page:

- Initial source HTML document often containing form fields or other options

- The IDC file for making and carrying out the database commands and data acquisition
- The HTX file for presenting the information returned

Although it's not the intent of this book to teach all aspects of HTML, it's important to keep in mind that the samples provided are just that—samples. You'll need to take these samples and adapt them to your organization's way of doing business on the Internet. In short, the HTML code that might be required consists of the field, list box, and check box options provided by HTML. By using these options and the ODBC connectivity, you enable the user to search the possibilities for making a meaningful interface for the user.

When you create a form that you'll be using to prompt the user for information, you create fields and other controls much as you do when creating an application. You name the fields and then pass the name and its value to the IDC to be used in your database query, if you desire. In the next sections, you see how to create these files and what makes them derive the output pages with the information from the database.

## Building Initial Forms to Prompt for Values

Generally speaking, you start the process of working with a database by presenting the users with a form, allowing them to select what information they need. As will often be the case, you have the capability to create forms that allow input that can be used to form the SQL statements you'll be passing to the data source. In the cases where you're creating a form, you see two basic HTML tags: the `<INPUT>` and `<FORM>` tags that allow you to designate actions to take and information to accept on behalf of the user. Listing 11.3 shows a simple form that prompts for an author name to be searched for in the author's table.

**Listing 11.3 Simple HTML Form to Initiate a Database Query—(queform.htm)**

```
<HTML>
<HEAD>
<TITLE>
Que Publishing's Very Simple Demonstration Form
</TITLE>
</HEAD>
<h1>Sample Form for Database Access</h1>
<FORM METHOD="POST" ACTION="/scripts/que/QueForm1.idc">
Enter Name to Find in the Pubs Database: <INPUT NAME="au_lname">
<p>
<INPUT TYPE="SUBMIT" VALUE="Run Query">
</FORM>
</BODY>
</HTML>
```

The key elements are the `"POST"` instructions and the text box presented to the user. The `<FORM>` tag indicates what should happen when the form is executed. In this case, the form will send information to the server, hence the `POST` method. The `<ACTION>` tag calls out the program or procedure that is run on the server to work with the information sent in. In the example, the QUEFORM1.IDC is called and passed the parameters.

**NOTE** The letter case is not significant when you're specifying HTML tags. "INPUT" is the same as indicating "input" and will not cause any different results when it's processed by IIS.

It's not immediately apparent what those parameters might be, but if you examine the one or more INPUT fields, you can see that they are named. The following syntax is the basic, required element if you need to pass information back to the host in a forms-based environment:

```
<INPUT NAME="<variable name>">
```

The <variable name> is the name you'll use to reference the value provided by the user. Much as you define a variable in Visual Basic by dimensioning it, you must define and declare the different variables and other controls that are used by your HTML. There are other tags that can be used with the <INPUT NAME> tag, including <VALUE>, which allows you to set the initial value of the item you're declaring. For example, the following line declares a new variable, MyName, and assigns an initial value of "Wynkoop" to it:

```
<INPUT NAME="MyName" VALUE="Wynkoop">
```



For the preceding example, the intention is to create a very simple form that enables the user to type in a name, or portion of the name, that can be used to search the Authors table in the Pubs database. When the HTML is loaded, as shown in the preceding, Figure 11.5 is the result.

**FIG. 11.5**
Allowing the user to indicate values to pass to the database engine adds polished, functional benefits to your application.

As you can see, the text box size is automatically determined for you as a default. There are <MAXLENGTH> and <SIZE> tags you can place in the INPUT NAME directive if you need to increase the size of the text box. You'll also notice that if you press Enter while you're using this form, the form will automatically be submitted to the server just as if you'd pressed the Submit button. Because there is only a single button on this form, the browser interprets this as a type of "There is only one thing for me to do, so I'll just do it automatically" situation.

What happens in this example from Listing 11.3 is that the browser opens a new URL on the server with the specification

```
http://holodeck3/scripts/que/QueForm1.idc?au_lname=<name>
```

**NOTE** If you watch your Web browser, it might indicate only that it's loading the URL that is included up to the `?` in these examples. The protocol is still passing the parameters to the host; they are simply not shown during the transfer by some browsers.

The `<NAME>` is the name you indicate in the text box prior to pressing Enter or clicking the Submit button. The next step in the process is to run the query against the database engine and see what results are returned.

## Building Server Query Source Files

The query source files reside in files in your `SCRIPTS` area and have a file-name extension of .IDC by convention. When the URL is accessed, the server will run the indicated IDC file. As mentioned earlier in this chapter, the IDC file contains the SQL statements and directives necessary to carry out the commands as needed. For this example, Listing 11.4 shows the source for querying the database.

**CAUTION**

To reiterate the note earlier about security, be sure you place your IDC files in directories that have been set up with Execute, but not Read, privileges. This is important because if users can review your source files, they can see column names, table names, SQL logon names and passwords, and so on. This is information you want to make sure is private.

**Listing 11.4 The IDC File Called by QUEForm.HTM—(queform1.idc)**

```
Datasource: web sql
Username: sa
Template: queform1.htx
SQLStatement:
+SELECT au_lname, phone, address, city, state, zip
+ from authors
+ where au_lname like '%au_lname%%'
```

The output from this specific file is really nothing. The user will never directly see this file or output from it. This seems a bit strange, but the entire intent of the IDC is to define and perform the query against the data source indicated. After the information is retrieved, the IDC calls the Template indicated and passes in the results to be returned as a Web page.

**NOTE** In the example in Listing 11.4, notice that the `Where` clause specifies `like` and that there is an extra percent sign in the comparison field. This is standard SQL syntax that enables you to search for wild-carded strings. You specify the part you know, and the IDC will append an extra `%` character at the end. Because the percent sign is the wild card for SQL Server, you'll be able to return all items that start with `B`, for example.

Before working down through it, some basics about this source file are important to understand for you to know how it works. First, to reference a variable, place it between percentages, as is the case with `'%au_lname%'` in Listing 11.4. Note that the single quotes are required because the field is a text-based type.

You can reference variables anywhere in the script. This means that even for the items that are seemingly hard-coded, like parameters, you can enable the user to specify them and then call them dynamically from the IDC file.

Second, in cases where your line length is shorter than your actual line, you can call out the item you want to work on, begin specifying the values, and continue indicating the expanding values as long as you place the + in the first column of the file. The plus sign acts as a line-continuation character for these source files.

The data source indicated in the IDC relates to the ODBC data source you establish with the ODBC manager in the control panel. Remember that the data source you use with the IDC must be a system DSN. If it's not, the call to the database will fail.

The `Username`, and optionally the `Password`, will override any settings you might have established in ODBC, and they'll override the current user name, as well as how it relates to the execution of the query. Other parameters that might be of interest or use in your integration of the IDC file into your installation are shown in Table 11.1.



**Table 11.1 IDC Optional Parameters**

| Parameter | Description |
|---|---|
| `RequiredParameters` | By naming the parameters that you must have represented from the form filled out by the user, you can make sure the user didn't just press Enter or otherwise ignore a field. Name the fields you want to assure information from, and IIS will kick back a message if the field is left blank for any reason. When you specify the fields, do not use percent signs but simply name the field. To indicate more than one field, separate each field in the list with a comma. |
| `DefaultParameters` | You can set up defaults for the fields you are expecting to receive from the user. Name each field, followed by an equal sign and the value you want it to have. When the field is retrieved from the form, if it's a blank or nonspecified field, the value you indicate will be filled in. Note that `DefaultParameters` are applied prior to `RequiredParameters` being checked, effectively making the use of `RequiredParameters` unnecessary if you can indicate an acceptable default. Keep in mind that your page should indicate what the default will be, because the user will not see the substitution that is made in the IDC file when it's processed. |

*continues*

**Table 11.1 Continued**

| Parameter | Description |
|---|---|
| `Expires` | If you submit a query over and over again, you might find that you're retrieving a cached copy of the information rather than an updated database query. This can be especially problematic when developing applications, because you'll be continually testing the system, resubmitting queries, and so on. By setting the `<EXPIRES>` tag, established in seconds, to a value that represents a timeframe that should have passed before the query is retried, you will avoid this problem. In other words, how long will it be before the information should be considered "stale" or in need of being refreshed for viewing? |
| `MaxRecords` | If you are connected over a slower speed connection, there are few things more frustrating than receiving a huge data file, then realizing that you needed only certain bits of information. For example, you might need to return only the first 100 rows of a table because they will provide the most current, meaningful data to your sales effort. By limiting the `MaxRecords`, you can indicate this in the IDC file, limiting traffic and database interaction with the new option. |

**TIP** You can call SQL Server's stored procedures from an IDC file if you want to specify it in the SQL statement portion of the file. To do so, use the following syntax:

```
EXEC MySP_Name Param1[, Param2...]
```

Include the name of your stored procedure in place of `MySP_Name`.

In the stored procedure, be sure you're returning result sets, even if they represent only a status value indicating success or failure of the operation. Remember, as with other ODBC data sources, the stored procedure will be passed to the server, and the client will await the response. If your stored procedure does not return a value to the calling routine, you might give the user the impression that you've caused the browser to become frozen.

From here, after you've retrieved the values you want to display, you can move on to the results set source files. These files do the work of formatting and displaying information to the user and are explained next.

## Building Results Source Files

The results files are where the fun begins in working with the data that comes back from the query. The HTML extension files, with file-name extensions of .HTX, are referenced in the Template entry in the IDC. These files dictate how the information is presented, what the user will see, whether items that are returned actually represent links to other items, and so on.

Listing 11.5 shows the sample HTX file for the example you've been reviewing throughout this chapter. You can see that it has a few extra, not-yet-standard items that make the display of information from the database possible.

**Listing 11.5 A Sample HTX File—(QueForm1.htx)**

```
<!-- Section 1>
<HTML>
<HEAD>
<TITLE>Authors Details</TITLE>
</HEAD>
<TABLE>
<tr>
<TD>
<hr>
<P>
<TABLE BORDER>
 <caption>Query results:</caption>
 <TR>
 <TH><B>Author</B></TH>
 <TH><B>Phone</B></TH>
 <TH><B>Address</B></TH>
 <TH><B>City</B></TH>
 <TH><B>State</B></TH>
 <TH><B>Zip</B></TH>
 </TR>

<!-- Section 2>
<%begindetail%>
 <TR>
 <TH><B><%au_lname%></B></TH>
 <TH><B><%phone%></B></TH>
 <TH><B><%address%></B></TH>
 <TH><B><%city%></B></TH>
 <TH><B><%state%></B></TH>
 <TH><B><%zip%></B></TH>
 </TR>
<%enddetail%>

<!-- Section 3>
<P>
</TABLE>
<%if CurrentRecord EQ 0%>
  <H2>Sorry, no authors match your search criteria (<%idc.au_lname%>).</H2>
<%else%>
  <H2>Authors with names like "<I><%idc.au_lname%></I>"</H2>
<%endif%>
</center>
</td>
</tr>
</table>
</BODY>
</HTML>
```

When the URL is accessed, the server is going to run the indicated IDC file. As mentioned earlier in this chapter, the IDC file contains the SQL statements and directives necessary to carry out the commands as needed. For this example, Listing 11.4 shows the source for querying the database.

**NOTE** The lines starting with "<!--" are comments and are not interpreted by the HTML client.

When you design data-oriented pages, you'll want to make sure you take advantage of HTML's start- and end-tag metaphor. To put it simply, for many of the different items in HTML, when you establish a tag, for instance `<HEAD>`, until the reciprocal argument, `</HEAD>`, is encountered, the feature you enabled with the first instance of the keyword is in force.

As you can see in Figure 11.6, the sample file turns on the `H1` heading style and then doesn't turn it off, resulting in the entire page using oversized fonts.

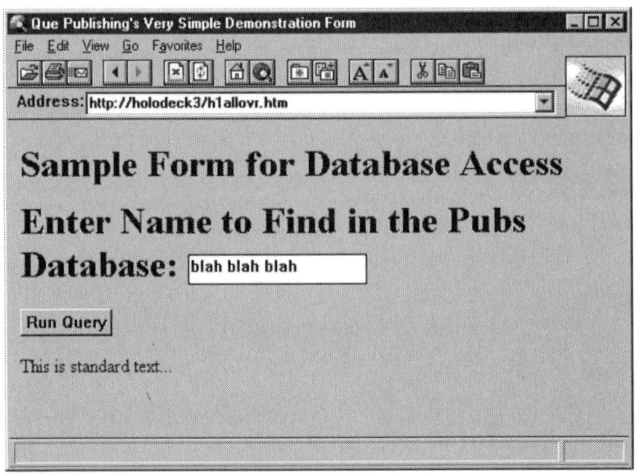


**FIG. 11.6**
Because HTML tags are evaluated in pairs, missing the closing tag can make a style run through the balance of your HTML document.

In the sample HTML in Listing 11.5, notice that there are three sections called out. These sections are inserted only to make reading and explaining the HTML a bit easier. They aren't necessary for the functioning of the document.

In Section 1, the entire purpose is to set up the page. You need to establish fonts, set up background images, do any initial formatting, and so on. You also need to start any tables that you want to use. Because you initiate a table, add the rows to it, and then turn off the table, tables represent an excellent way to present data that will include an unknown number of rows.

For example, as in Figure 11.7, though two rows are shown, there could just as easily have been 20. The other advantage of using tables to display your database information is that the table will size to the user's visible browser area automatically. You won't need to worry about column widths and other formatting issues.

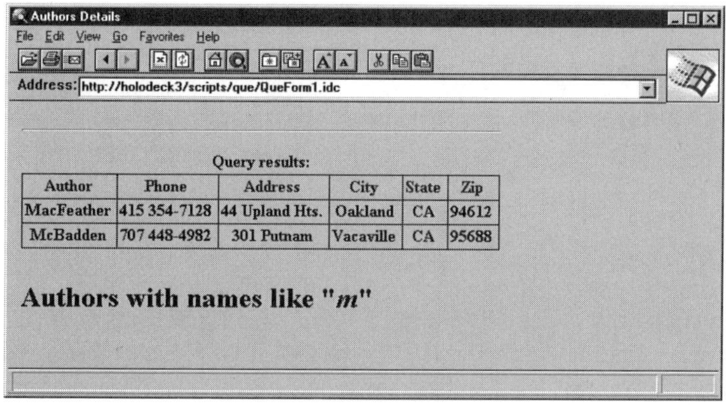


**FIG. 11.7**
If you can use tables to display data to the user, you'll be keeping with an already familiar metaphor for the presentation. People are used to table-based data represented in a columnar fashion.

Section 2 is where you'll work with the detail lines that are returned as part of the data set. Notice that this section is bracketed with `<%begindetail%>` and `<%enddetail%>` tags. Everything between these two tags will repeat once for every row returned in the data set. In the preceding example, section 2 consists largely of building the table that will display the information that was returned.



```
<! Section 2>
<%begindetail%>
 <TR>
 <TH><B><%au_lname%></B></TH>
 <TH><B><%phone%></B></TH>
 <TH><B><%address%></B></TH>
 <TH><B><%city%></B></TH>
 <TH><B><%state%></B></TH>
 <TH><B><%zip%></B></TH>
 </TR>
<%enddetail%>
```

When you indicate the data to include, you refer directly to the column names that are in the table or view that is referenced by the IDC file. Place a `"<%"` before and a `"%>"` after each column name. In English, the preceding code snippet is reserving a row to put new data into with the `<TR>` tag, placing the information into the row with the `<TH>` tags, and ending the row with the closing `</TR>` tag.

You can do comparisons in your file, as well. For example, if you want to check to make sure that the State was returned as `AZ`, you could do so in one of two ways. Obviously, the preferred method would be to change your `Where` clause in the IDC to reflect the fact that you want to filter out non-Arizona states.

Alternatively, you could indicate here what you want to test. Consider the following code sample:

```
<! Section 2>
<%begindetail%>
```

```
<%if <%state%> eq "AZ"%>
     <TR>
     <TH><B><%au_lname%></B></TH>
     <TH><B><%phone%></B></TH>
     <TH><B><%address%></B></TH>
     <TH><B><%city%></B></TH>
     <TH><B><%state%></B></TH>
     <TH><B><%zip%></B></TH>
     </TR>
<%endif%>
<%enddetail%>
```

By using the `If` construct, you can test values and conditions in the data set. You can reference variables that come from the IDC file, as well. To reference these, simply prefix the variable name with `IDC`. So, if you want to reference the incoming variable from the original `HTML` form, you can do so by a statement similar to the following:

```
<%if <%idc.au_lname%> eq "Wynkoop">
     <TH><B>Building series...</B></TH>
<%endif%>
```

In this case, the query would go back to the IDC and pull the value for the `au_lname` variable, make the comparison, and either execute or ignore the statements in the loop following the test. There are three different tests that you can perform. Each is described in Table 11.2.

**NOTE** You can also use `<%else%>` in your `If...else...endif` loop.

**Table 11.2 Comparison Operators for Use in HTX Files**

| Operators | Description |
|---|---|
| EQ | Indicates an equivalent test. "Is item A equal to item B?" |
| GT | Tests for a condition where one item is greater than the other. |
| LT | Tests for the condition where one item is less than the other. |

In addition, there are two different data set-related variables. `CurrentRecord` enables you to reference the number of times the Detail section has executed. If, after the detail loop has run, you want to determine whether there are records in the data set, you can test this variable to see if it's 0. If it is, no information was returned, and you should display a meaningful message to that effect:

```
<%if CurrentRecord EQ 0>
  <H2>Sorry, no authors match your search crit...
<%else%>
  <H2>Authors with names like "<I><%idc.au_lname%>...
<%endif%>
```

The other tag that corresponds directly to database-oriented actions is the MaxRecords option. MaxRecords relates to the MaxRecords IDC variable. Using this value, you can determine the total number of records that the IDC file will enable.

You use both CurrentRecord and MaxRecords in conjunction with <%if%> statements. They are implemented as controlling variables that help in your structuring of the logical flow of the HTX file. Just keep in mind that, after the processing of the detail section has completed, if CurrentRecord EQ 0, there were no results returned from the call.

The final section of the HTX file is used largely to close different HTML tags that were used to set up the display of information on the resulting page. Remember, HTML expects most tags in pairs, so it's a good idea to close each item properly.

```
<!-- Section 3>
<P>
</TABLE>
<%if CurrentRecord EQ 0%>
  <H2>Sorry, no authors match your search criteria (<%idc.au_lname%>).</H2>
<%else%>
  <H2>Authors with names like "<I><%idc.au_lname%></I>"</H2>
<%endif%>
</center>
</td>
</tr>
</table>
</BODY>
</HTML>
```



Notice, too, that the CurrentRecord variable is used to determine the message that is displayed to the user. There either will be a message indicating no matches, or one explaining what was searched for is shown. You also can see that by referencing the "<%idc.au_lname%>" variable, you can pull the user-specified value from the form.

The results of a successful search are shown in Figure 11.8.

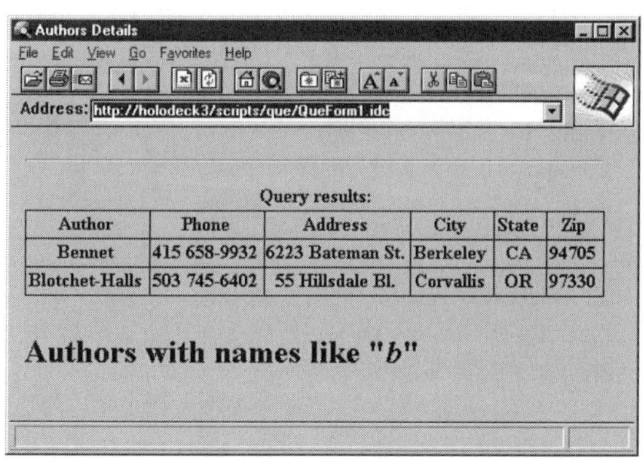


**FIG. 11.8**
A successful match will show the hits on the PUBS database table, and then will show the message indicating what was searched for.

If the search of the database tables is not fruitful, the HTX will display a different message indicating the failure of the process. Figure 11.9 shows this dialog box.

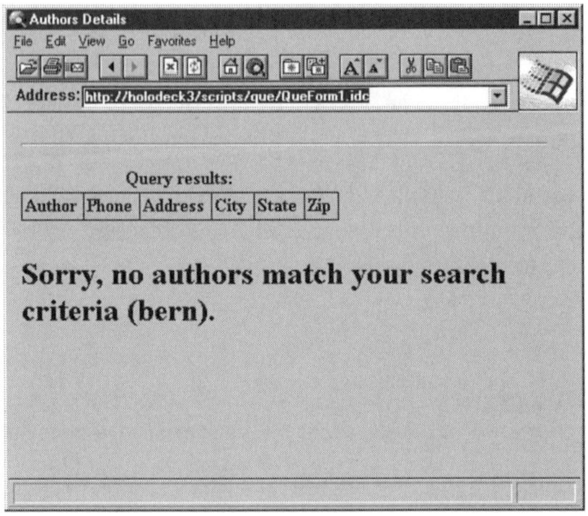


**FIG. 11.9**
If matches for information are not found, you should code a branch of logic to indicate the problem to the user.

# Internet Database Connector: A Summary and Example

To recap how the IDC works overall, first you will code a form or other HTML document that calls the IDC file on the server. The IDC file is located in the protected /SCRIPTS directory and contains the information necessary to open the ODBC connection and submit a query to the database engine. As the results are returned, they are merged into another document, the HTX or HTML extension document. This HTX file includes the information needed to work with both the detail records and the header/footer information for the page.

The result to the user is the display of the requested information in an HTML document style. Of course, the resulting document, based on the HTX file, can include further links to queries or drill-down information if needed. By using this technique, you can enable a user to select high-level values and then narrow the scope, but increase the detail level provided, for the information, because the user is able to narrow the parameters for the operation.

An excellent example of the drill-down technique is provided in Microsoft's samples in the GuestBook application. As you query the guestbook, you are returned high-level detail about the names found. Here's a look at the HTX file's Detail section to see what exactly is done to display the information from the database.

```
<%begindetail%>
Name: <a href="/scripts/samples/details.idc?FName=<%FirstName%>&
➥LName=<%LastName%>"><b><%FirstName%> <%LastName%></b></a>
<p>
<%enddetail%>
```

So, for each name returned by the original query, the result will be to show the first and last names. This HTML sets up the names as links to their own details. The code indicates the `<A HREF>` tag and references the IDC that retrieves the detail information, `DETAILS.IDC`. As a result, when the users click this in their browsers, they'll immediately be executing the IDC file and retrieving the next level of detail. Figure 11.10 shows what this initial screen of details looks like when the items are first retrieved.

**FIG. 11.10**
The initial display of the guestbook contents enables the user to select a name and drill down into the details for that name.

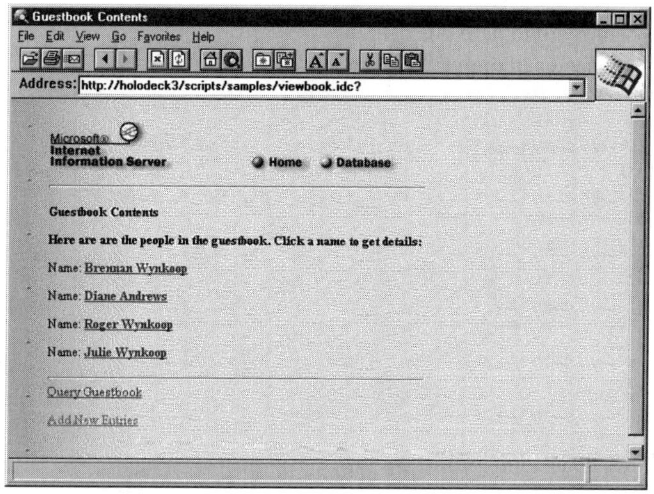




When you click a name to get the details, the IDC is called that retrieves the details from the Guests table on your system. If you take a look at the IDC, you'll see that it's quite simple, returning only a few columns of information based on the name selected from the previous query:

```
Datasource: Web SQL
Username: sa
Template: details.htx
SQLStatement:
+SELECT FirstName, LastName, Email, Homepage, Comment, WebUse
+FROM Guests
+WHERE FirstName = '%FName%' and LastName = '%LName%'
```

The final step is to show the information to the requester. The `DETAILS.HTX` template is called out in the IDC file, and it shows the detail information for the user as requested. The detail section simply displays the user information that has been provided. The HTX file makes heavy use of the `<%if%>` operator and the comparison of the contents of a given field to ensure that the only information provided to the user are those fields that are non-blank (see Listing 11.6).

**Listing 11.6 The Detail Section from the DETAILS.HTX File**

```
<%begindetail%>
<h2>Here are details for <%FirstName%> <%LastName%>:</h2>
<p>
<b><%FirstName%> <%LastName%></b><br>
<p>

<%if Email EQ " "%>
<%else%>
Email Address: <%Email%> <br>
<%endif%>
<%if Homepage EQ " "%>
<%else%>
Homepage: <%Homepage%>
<%endif%>
<p>
Primary Web Role: <%WebUse%>
<p>
<%if Comment EQ " "%>
<%else%>
Comments: <%Comment%>
<%endif%>
<p>
<%enddetail%>
```

Providing this type of increasing detail based on a user's selection is good for all parties concerned. It's good for your system because it can provide only the information needed to determine the direction to go to for the next level of detail. In addition, it's good for the users because it can mean less content to shuffle through to get to the information they really need. Because they will be determining what information is delved into, they'll be able to control how deep they want to go into a given item.

This technique is really great for supplying company information. You can provide overview type items at the highest level on everything from marketing materials to personnel manuals. Letting people select their research path also relieves you of the responsibility of second-guessing exactly what the user is expecting of the system.

# Using SQL Server's Web Page Wizard

As you're sure to have noticed, the race to bring content to your Internet site and make all different types of information available to the user base has been fast and furious. One of the recent advances is the capability to have the database engine automatically generate Web pages for you based on content in the database.

With SQL Server 6.5, you have the capability to schedule a task in the system to automatically create these HTML documents at time intervals ranging from a one-time run to many times per day. You can use this capability for a number of things, including reporting on your server's activity levels to you as an administrator.

In this section, you see how to set up these automatically generating pages and what the results of the process are. It's not possible to go into great detail on how to use SQL Server, form good database table design, and other administrative issues regarding SQL Server, because they warrant a much more comprehensive discussion than the single group of sections here.

## Prerequisites for SQL Server

Before you can successfully use the Web Page Wizard and the processes that it will create, you'll have to have set up your server to allow for this type of access. Specifically, the Web Page Wizard relies on the task manager and `SQLExecutive` service. You must have the `SQLExecutive` service set up to automatically begin the startup of your server.

To confirm that the service is set to start automatically, select Services from the Control Panel. Scroll down the list of services installed until you see the `SQLExecutive` service (see Figure 11.11).

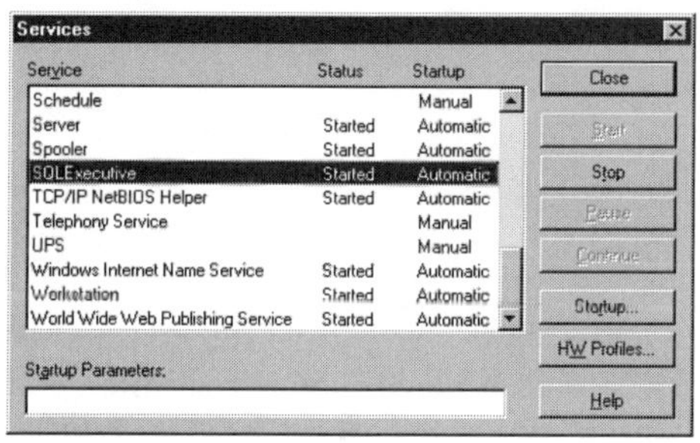


**FIG. 11.11**
Make sure the `SQLExecutive` service is listed with a Status of Started and that Startup is listed as Automatic.



If the service is not already started, click the service and select Startup. You can set the options that govern when the service is active and, most importantly, when it will be started by the operating system. Make sure you indicate a valid user account that will be used to log on to SQL Server. This account must exist in both SQL Server and the User database for your domain if you are not using Integrated security, and the user name and password must be the same in both SQL Server and the domain.

If you're using integrated security, selecting a user from the domain user's list also will provide the name to be logged on to the SQL Server.

**NOTE** It's a requirement that the information you provide as it relates to the user and password is valid in SQL Server. You also will need to ensure that the account you indicate has access to the database that you're reporting against and the MSDB database, because these are key to the creation of the page (see Figure 11.12).

*continues*

*continued*

If you do not set up the `SQLExecutive` to automatically start, the services required to generate the Web content you are setting up will not be available, and the page will not be generated.

If this is the first time you're setting these options, and the `SQLExecutive` was not previously started, when you select OK to save the user ID and startup option changes, you need to reselect the `SQLExecutive` service and then select Start.

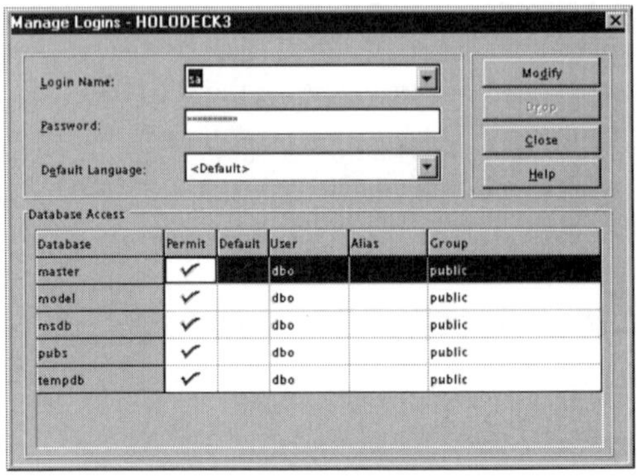


**FIG. 11.12**
The account that you indicate for logon for the service must have access to the different objects in your database(s).

## Using the Wizard

The SQL Web Page Wizard is located in the SQL Server program group on your system. You can run the Wizard from a workstation or the server. In either case, it will generate the pages for you in a directory you'll specify later in the process.

Figure 11.13 shows the initial SQL Server login dialog box you're presented with from the wizard. From this dialog box, you'll need to provide an appropriate login that will enable you access to all tables and databases you want to use in providing content for your page.

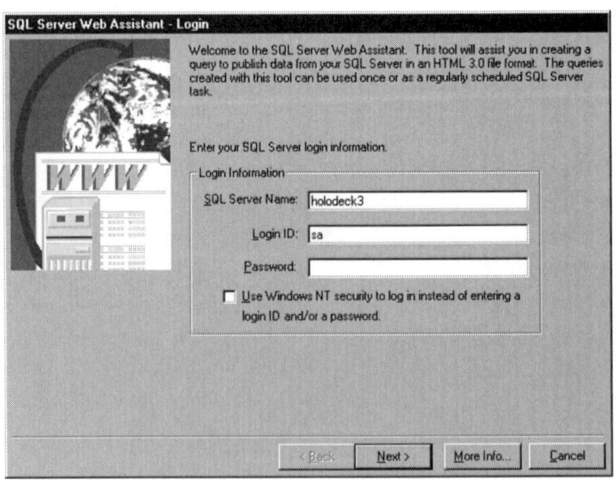


**FIG. 11.13**
Login to SQL Server is the first step to using the Web Page Wizard.

The option to use Windows NT Security to log on assumes you're using integrated security. If you are, selecting this item means that you don't have to provide separate logon account and password information prompted for earlier in the dialog box and that the users will be logged on with their own security rights intact for SQL Server. Their NT logon name is used as their SQL Server logon name.

**Selecting the Content for the Page** When you select `Next >`, you have three initial options. The first option, Build a query from a database hierarchy, allows you to use the point-and-click interface and indicate the tables and other items you want to include in your query that will be used to generate the page. Figure 11.14 shows an example of what the tree-based architecture will look like if you select this option.

**FIG. 11.14**
The easiest interface is the Database Hierarchy option, because it enables you to select from the listing of objects on your server when deciding which items to provide for a report.

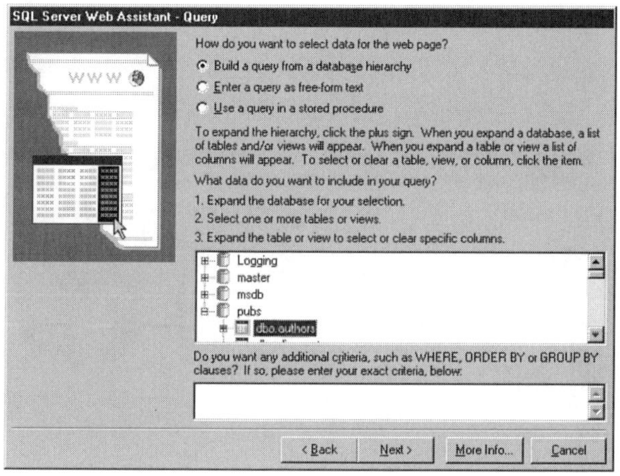




If you select the Free Form query option, you'll be able to create any SQL statement you need to fulfill the requirements for your software. Be sure to select the database you need to work against from the "Which database do you want to query?" list box, or you might end up querying the wrong table, and you'll need to come back and rewrite the query or queries on which you based the page.

Using this option also means that you're taking all responsibility for the formation of SQL Server specific calls. The query you enter will be passed along and executed by the server. Figure 11.15 shows an example of how the dialog options work when working with the Wizard in this scenario.

The final option you have in setting up the source of information for your page is to call a stored procedure. When you select the Use a query in a stored procedure button, you'll be able to provide information on the database and stored procedure you want to use. Also notice that the text of the stored procedure is shown in the dialog box. You can use this information to verify that you have selected the correct stored procedure (see Figure 11.16).

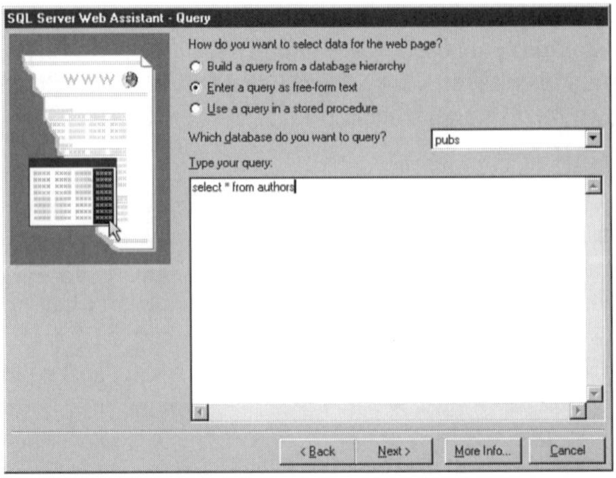


**FIG. 11.15**
Entering the query manually can be powerful and painful all at once. If you're not sure of the syntax, use the more automated features of the Wizard for a few instances of information you want to publish.

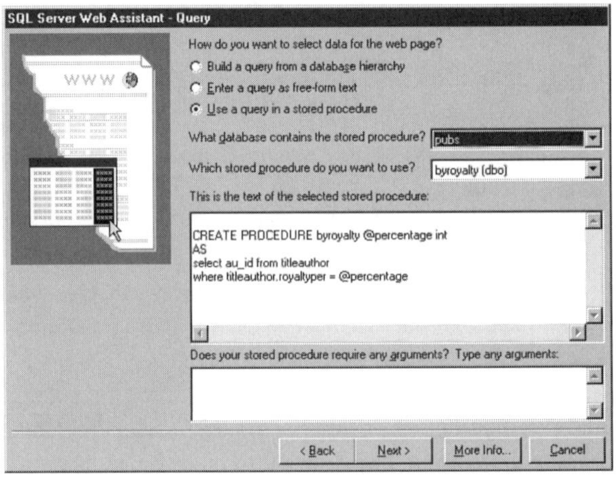


**FIG. 11.16**
Calling a stored procedure can be a good way to share coding that you've done for an application and put it to use on your Internet server.

Stored procedures are a powerful mechanism for optimizing your server and providing good database query tuning. You also can take advantage of the fact that if you have another system based on SQL Server, and you're using a stored procedure to produce the results for a printed report, you might be able to reference the same stored procedure in the dialog box and create the report in HTML, making it available at any time.

The text box showing your stored procedure is provided as reference only; you cannot make changes to the code here. If you need to make changes to the code, do so by updating the stored procedure in SQL Server. This can be done with ISQL/W, the SQL Enterprise Manager, or any other utility you might be using to manage your stored procedures.

**Setting the Update Interval** The next dialog box will prompt you for the frequency at which you'd like to have the page rebuilt. Because the database is the source of information for the page, this item can take some work. The reason is that you'll need to talk with all of the users of the application that creates the data in the database and determine how frequently it is changed.

A frequency set to be too small will cause additional overhead on the server as it handles the request. The impact on performance should be minimal, but if there are many, many requests for data pages such as this, it might begin to show on the access times to the server. For an example, look at Figure 11.17.

Your time-frame options and their associated parameters are

- Now, no parameters.
- Later, specify date and time that the page should be created (once only).
- When data changes, select data tables and indicate anticipated change that should be monitored as a trigger to update the HTML code.
- On certain days of the week, indicate day of week and time of day.
- On a regular basis, specify number of hours, days, or weeks that should pass before the item is regenerated.



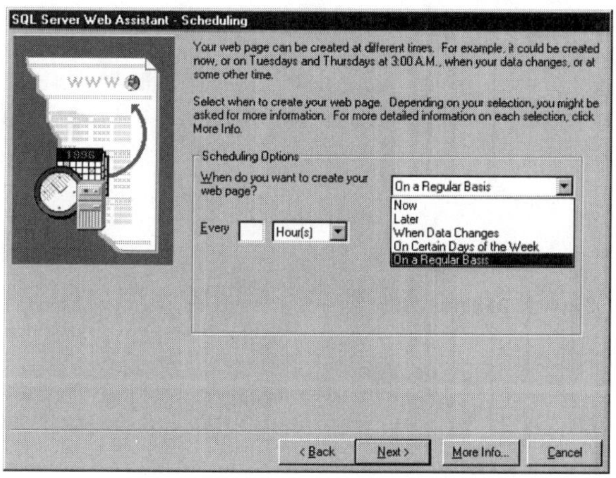


**FIG. 11.17**
Be sure to select a useful time interval: Too frequent will force the server to rebuild the page without reason; too infrequent an update process makes the information a bit less useful because it might go out of date for the users of the information.

**Setting Page Options** There are two different dialog boxes with information about final formatting. Formatting options include headings for the page, column names on the resulting document, or changing the title or output location of the resulting HTML code. These are the steps you'll be using to create the database-related HTML that you set up. See Figures 11.18 and 11.19 for examples.

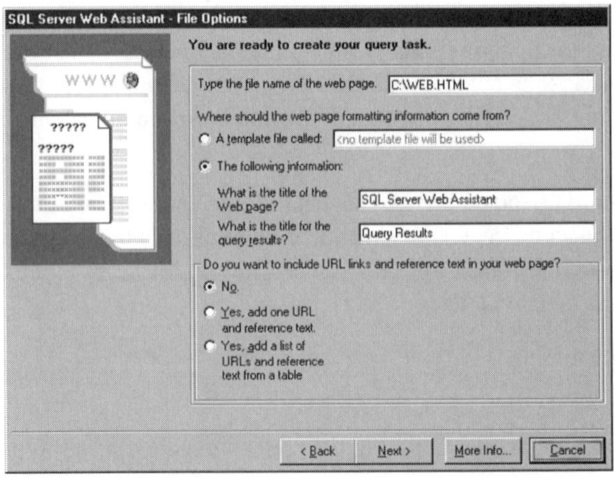


**FIG. 11.18**
Review the formatting options carefully. These are the items that will be used to manage the content, appearance, and other facets of your HTML's presentation.

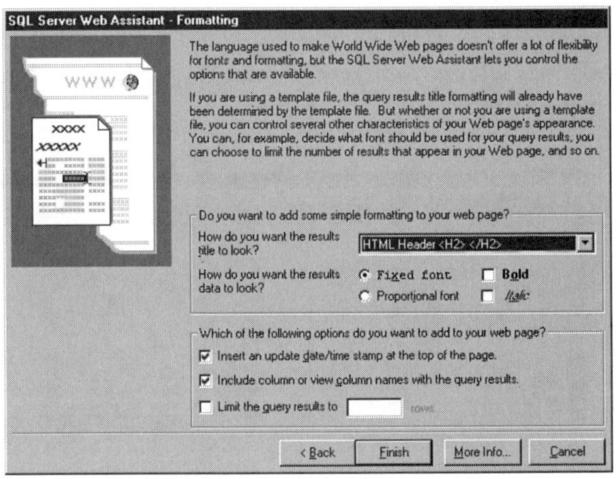


**FIG. 11.19**
If you are relying on the engine to do formatting for your tables of data, be sure to select the "Include column or view column names with the query results" when you set up the Wizard's Web page.

**TIP** One thing you should consider including on every page you generate is a link to another page on your site. For example, you might want to always include a link with the following attributes:

Description: Return to Home Page

*URL*: `http://www.<your site>.com/default.htm`

It's a good idea to come up with a set of links that you include on each page on your site. These can be back to the home page, a search page, and a copyright page, for example. Consistency across your site will make it much easier for users to navigate and understand.

After you've made any changes you need, you can select Finish to generate the code that will be used to execute the different operations that manage the Wizard and its pages. Now, whenever the page is referenced by a browser, the HTML generated by the Wizard will be the result. The user will be able to see the new view you've constructed and will be assured of up-to-date information.

## Seeing the Results in SQL Server

It's helpful to review your SQL Server installation to understand what's happening when you implement a wizard-generated Web page. There are a couple of things that happen when you create a page in this manner.

- A master stored procedure is inserted into your database.
- A page-specific stored procedure is inserted into your database.
- A new task is created to be run by the SQL Executive at the intervals you requested.

The master stored procedure, `sp_makewebpage`, is created in the database you're setting up. This is used by the Wizard to create the code necessary to generate the page. You won't be making changes to this or the other stored procedures, and if you ever want to re-create it, you can run the Wizard again and create another page in the same database. This will create the stored procedure for you.



The page-specific stored procedure is created with a name that begins with `Web_` and includes a unique numeric name that states the date it was created. In the example shown in Figure 11.20, you can see that the stored procedures created to support the demonstration pages are named `Web_96042622390211` and `Web_96042700554612`. If you review the stored procedures, you'll see that they're encrypted, so you won't be able to make any changes to them directly. Of course, the easiest way to make any changes you need is to remove the stored procedures and their associated tasks from SQL Server and then re-create them using the Web Page Wizard.

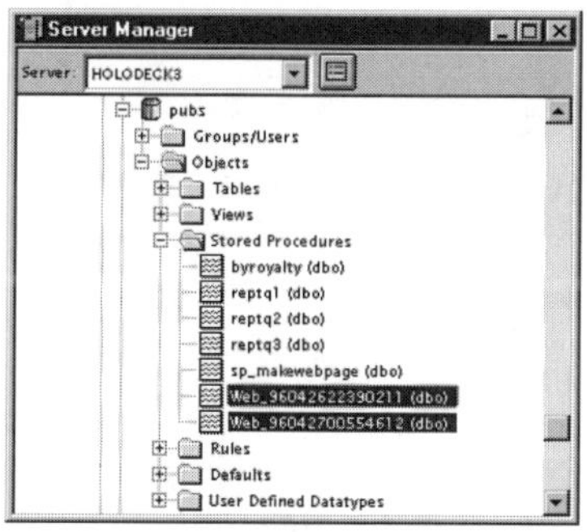


**FIG. 11.20**
Be sure not to remove the stored procedures from the database unless you also remove the corresponding task entries from the task scheduler.

By selecting Server, Tasks... from the menus, you can review the tasks that have been created to run the page at the intervals you set up. Figure 11.21 shows what you'll see. You can quickly determine that the Web pages are queued up and ready to go.

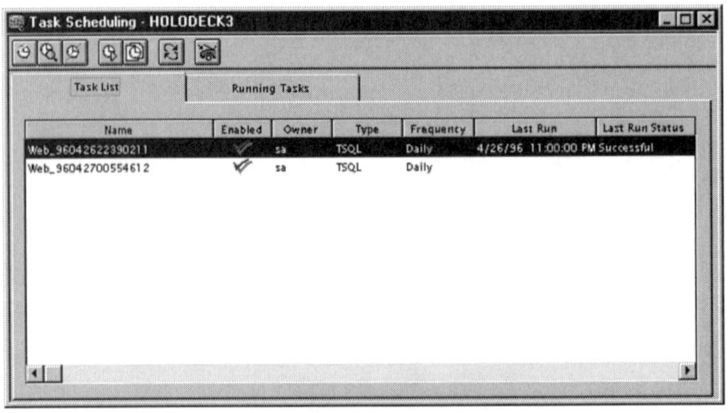


**FIG. 11.21** After the Wizard has finished, the task is entered into SQL Server for processing as you established.

You also can check to make sure a Web page generation process is occurring as you'd expect by clicking the History button from the Task Scheduling dialog box. When you do, you'll see the dialog box shown in Figure 11.22, which indicates the times the procedure has run and whether it was successful. It's a good idea to start with the history review process in any diagnostics you need to run in the future should you encounter problems. In most cases, you can quickly determine exactly what's wrong by just doing some quick investigation with the Task Scheduler.

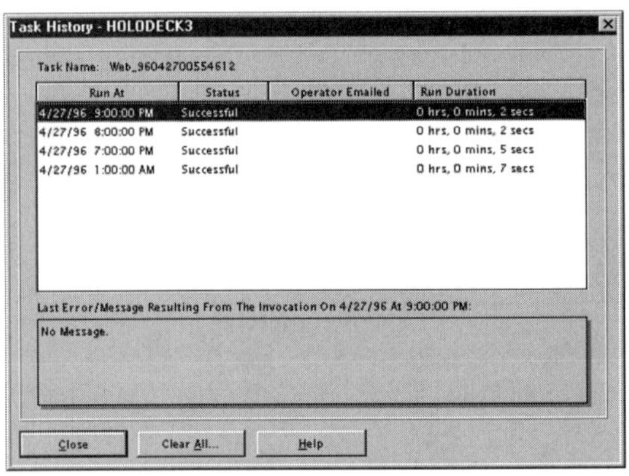


**FIG. 11.22** You can verify that the pages are being generated successfully by reviewing the History logs.

Keep in mind that you also can change the frequency at which your page is generated by modifying the task scheduling options. If you double-click the page you want to modify, you can set all the different options that control how often the page is generated. This might be helpful if you find that, after installing several pages and your site traffic picks up, you need to lessen server load a bit to provide better throughput at peak times. Simply change the times at which the pages are generated, and you'll be set.

## Seeing the Results on Your Web Site

Implementing the page(s) you create on your site is a simple matter. You need to create a link to the pages or publish the URL to your user base. After the page is created by the SQL engine, it appears just as any other HTML document. Listing 11.7 shows the sample page created by the Web Page Wizard.

**Listing 11.7 A Sample Page Created by the Web Page Wizard—(Web.html)**

```
<HTML>
<HEAD>
<TITLE>SQL Server Web Page Wizard</TITLE>
<BODY>
<A HREF = /default.htm>Back to top of site</A>.<P>
<HR>
<H1>Query Results</H1>
<HR>
<PRE><TT>Last updated: Apr 26 1996 10:43PM</TT></PRE>
<P>
<P><TABLE BORDER>
<TR><TH ALIGN=LEFT>au_id</TH><TH ALIGN=LEFT>au_lname</TH><TH Align=Left>au_fname
➥</TH><TH ALIGN=LEFT>phone</TH><TH ALIGN=LEFT>address</TH><TH ALIGN=LEFT>city</
➥TH><TH ALIGN=LEFT>state</TH>
➥<TH ALIGN=LEFT>zip</TH><TH ALIGN=LEFT>contract</TH></TR>
<TR><TD NOWRAP>172-32-1176</TD><TD NOWRAP>White</TD><TD NOWRAP>Johnson</TD><TD
NOWRAP>408 496-7223</TD><TD><NOWRAP>10932 Bigge Rd.</TD><TD NOWRAP>Menlo
Park</TD><TD NOWRAP>CA</TD><TD NOWRAP>94025</TD><TD NOWRAP>1</TD></TR>
<TR><TD NOWRAP>213-46-8915</TD><TD NOWRAP>Green</TD><TD NOWRAP>Marjorie</TD><TD
NOWRAP>415 986-7020</TD>
➥<TD NOWRAP>309 63rd St. #411</TD><TD NOWRAP>Oakland</TD><TD NOWRAP>CA</TD><TD
NOWRAP>94618</TD><TD NOWRAP>1</TD></TR>

...
<Edited for brevity see disk file for full listing>
...

<TR><TD NOWRAP>899-46-2035</TD><TD NOWRAP>Ringer</TD><TD NOWRAP>Anne</TD><TD
➥NOWRAP>801 826-0752</TD>
➥<TD NOWRAP>67 Seventh Av.</TD><TD NOWRAP>Salt Lake City</TD><TD
NOWRAP>UT</TD><TD NOWRAP>84152</TD><TD NOWRAP>1</TD></TR>
<TR><TD NOWRAP>998-72-3567</TD><TD NOWRAP>Ringer</TD><TD NOWRAP>Albert</TD><TD
NOWRAP>801 826-0752</TD>
➥<TD NOWRAP>67 Seventh Av.</TD><TD NOWRAP>Salt Lake City</TD><TD
NOWRAP>UT</TD><TD NOWRAP>84152</TD><TD NOWRAP>1</TD></TR>
</TABLE>
</BODY>
</HTML>
```

When you view the page, all of your SQL table data will be placed into an HTML table. The links you specified will be shown at the top of the page prior to the data from the site. Figure 11.23 shows what the top portion of this sample page looks like when presented in the browser.

**FIG. 11.23**
The sample Web page includes information from the Pubs database and a link back to the site home page.

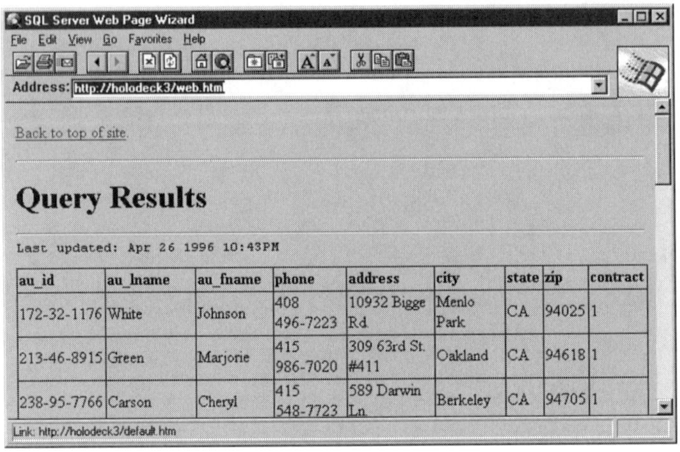


A great use of the Web Page Creation is to query the IIS logs that can be placed into SQL Server. For more information, see the next section, which shows how this can be used to remotely monitor your site.

# Examining Additional Emerging Options

**ON THE WEB**

Internet development tools are evolving so quickly that it's nearly impossible to keep up. Be sure to check in at the Reality Check site frequently to see what's new. The URL for the site is

**www.pobox.com/~swynk**

It contains information on all sorts of technologies, including those briefly mentioned here.

Database access is one of the most hotly developed areas on the Internet. This is due to the obvious fact that if you are to use your existing systems to their fullest potential, you'll almost certainly be referencing existing or new databases. This chapter has focused on the IDC and HTX combination as a good way of accessing this information. There are additional means of getting to this information, including your choice of scripting languages.

Microsoft has been pushing hard into the Active Server components and technologies. This approach moves the processing to the server for some or all of the content customization, including database access, for your pages. This brings back the whole approach that has been emphasized so heavily with SQL Server, that of providing client/server applications as an efficient way to use both your server and the client systems.

## Choosing the Right Approach

There is a lot of debate right now about the "right" approach to providing database access to users. The choices fall into two distinct areas: providing client-side access to server-based databases and providing server-resolved access to server-based databases.

This might seem strange, but the issues really come down to how well defined and controlled your audience is. The choice is how the connection to the database will be handled. Because Microsoft is providing the software, and because it has a Web browser, if you can ascertain that all users of your systems will have a Microsoft product, you can pretty much pick and choose between the approaches.

If, on the other hand, you can't absolutely promise what browser will be used, you need to consider using a server-based approach. A big benefit of the IDC approach is that it's server-based and completely browser-independent. When it was first released, it was the *only* way of getting to databases; now it's become what amounts to the lowest common denominator.

When you move to very recent browsers, like Internet Explorer 3.0x (and greater) and upcoming promised versions of Netscape's product, you get some additional options, outlined next.

## Active Server Pages, Advanced Data Control, and ActiveX Data Objects



Most of the options that you have available to you are moving to using DAO-like statements in VBScript or other scripting languages. These statements are getting added functionality that lets them reference server-based objects that are handling the server-side connection to the database. For example, consider Listing 11.8, taken from one of the sample files provided with IIS.

**Listing 11.8 ADO1.ASP—Sample VBScript for Database Access**

```
<HTML>
<HEAD><TITLE>ActiveX Data Object (ADO)</TITLE><HEAD>
<BODY>
<H3>ActiveX Data Object (ADO)</H3>
<%
  Set Conn = Server.CreateObject("ADODB.Connection")
  Conn.Open "ADOSamples"
  Set RS = Conn.Execute("SELECT * FROM Orders")
%>
<P>
<TABLE BORDER=1>
<TR>
  <% For i = 0 to RS.Fields.Count - 1 %>
     <TD><B><%= RS(i).Name %></B></TD>
  <% Next %>
</TR>
<% Do While Not RS.EOF %>
  <TR>
```

*continues*

**Listing 11.8 Continued**

```
    <% For i = 0 to RS.Fields.Count - 1 %>
      <TD VALIGN=TOP><%= RS(i) %></TD>
    <% Next %>
    </TR>
<%
    RS.MoveNext
    Loop
    RS.Close
    Conn.Close
%>
</TABLE>
</BODY>
</HTML>
```

The first thing you'll notice is the `CreateObject` method referenced as a server object. The ADOBB object, based on the server, provides the information needed to connect to the server based on the connection information provided in the `Conn.Open` call. After the connection is opened, the server is ready to receive statements. You might recall from the chapters on developing with SQL Server that you initiate a recordset by setting up the SQL statement that is used to define the recordset.

This is accomplished with the `EXECUTE` method, establishing the results to work on. You then can reference the results set exactly as you do with standard DAO calls. You'll recognize the balance of the logic as being identical to how you work with the DAO in Visual Basic or other languages you use with the objects and collections.

As soon as you're working with the information in your database in this manner, it's a simple thing to populate the page and get the data formatted the way you need.

# Sneaking a Peek at the Advanced Data Connector

As of this writing, a new technology has started to arrive from Microsoft, the Advanced Data Connector. The ADC, available from the Web at **www.microsoft.com/adc**, is a new client/server development model for Web-based database development.

Traditionally, the challenge facing the Web-based application developer is that of data handling at the client and server sides of the application. It was not possible to keep an active, open session on the server because of the inherent limitations built into the HTTP protocol. HTTP was designed to let you make a request, have the request fulfilled, and then have no further communication until you make another request.

With the IDC, you gained the capability to query and use an ODBC data source. This is a very good way to query a database independent of the browser. It's also a low-overhead approach to working with the database. Of course, the downside to this is how limited you are in terms of what you can do with the information because the results are static and you're forced to manage the logic to perform any updates.

In the ideal world, you'd be able to manipulate the database as you do others, using the DAO. The DAO objects and methods give you full access to the database, tables, and queries or views. This is where the ADC comes in. The ADC gives you access to these types of methods.

The ADC gives you an interface to the remote data sources in ways similar to the traditional Visual Basic approach. Specifically, you have a control that is responsible for the connection to the server, and you can manipulate either that control, or others dependent on it, to retrieve and work with the database information. The ADC is based on the OLEDB specification for working with databases and business objects. You can find more about OLEDB at **www.microsoft.com/oledb**.

## Understanding the Core ADC Components

The ADC includes several core components, shown in Table 11.4.

**Table 11.4 ADC Core Components**

| ADC | Core Components |
|---|---|
| Virtual Table Manager (VTM) | You can think of the VTM as "faking out" the data objects, giving them a logical table to work with that represents the data returned from the server. |
| `AdvancedDataControl` object | This control and the `AdvancedDataSpace` object let you set up forms that are bound to the database columns or fields. This is like the data control in VB. |
| `AdvancedDataSpace` object | As with the `AdvancedDataControl` object, this control helps set up the environment to support the use of bound controls over the Internet. |
| `AdvancedDataFactory` object | The data factory is responsible for communicating over HTTP and working with the VTM to create the locally cached virtual tables, making them accessible to your application. This is the query and update interface to your database. |
| ADISAPI | ADISAPI (Advanced Data Internet Server API) is the API used by IIS to work with ODBC and the server-side data factory objects. |
| Advanced TableGram Streaming Protocol (ADTG) | The ADTG is the internet-shortcomings-aware protocol that is used to shuttle the information between the client and server systems. |



With all of these objects, you might wonder how this will affect the code you write for these Web-based applications. The good news is that the code is much like Visual Basic and you will be able to leverage much of your education, testing, and experience to date with VB in your development of these applications. The bad news is that the HTML is getting longer, but you probably have expected that by now.

## Reviewing an Example HTML Page

In the following listing snippets, you can see an abbreviated listing from the sample application provided by Microsoft with the ADC documentation. It gives you a good look at building a form that not only uses these concepts, but also a grid from Sheridan that helps display the information from the server.

**NOTE** In the following section of code, portions of the code that have been removed are represented by an ellipsis, "..."

```
...
<PRE> First Name     <INPUT NAME=SFirst SIZE=30> </PRE>
<PRE> Last Name      <INPUT NAME=SLast  SIZE=30> </PRE>
<PRE> Title          <INPUT NAME=STitle SIZE=30> </PRE>
<PRE> E-mail Alias   <INPUT NAME=SEmail SIZE=30> </PRE>

<INPUT TYPE=BUTTON NAME="Find"                VALUE="Find">
<INPUT TYPE=BUTTON NAME="Clear"         VALUE="Clear">
<INPUT TYPE=BUTTON NAME="Update"         VALUE="Update Profile">
<INPUT TYPE=BUTTON NAME="Cancel"        VALUE="Cancel Changes">
```

Standard form definition tags are used to set up the form. In these opening HTML statements, the input forms are implemented and named. They can be referenced later for database updates and queries as needed.

The next section, outlined by the `<Object>` tags, initiates the Sheridan grid control. Note that this control is assumed to be at the location specified on the server. The reference to `Request.ServerVariables("SERVER_NAME")` lets you find out the server name that is currently working with the Internet Explorer client.

The balance of the properties, for example `AllowAddNew`, are specific to the control and let you configure the control to suit your needs.

```
<OBJECT CLASSID="clsid:BC496AE0-9B4E-11CE-A6D5-0000C0BE9395"
      ID=Grid1
      CODEBASE="HTTP://<%=Request.ServerVariables("SERVER_NAME")%>/MSADC/
      ➥Samples/Sheridan.cab"
      HEIGHT= 125
      Width = 495>
      <PARAM NAME="AllowAddNew"   VALUE="TRUE">
      <PARAM NAME="AllowDelete"   VALUE="TRUE">
      <PARAM NAME="AllowUpdate"   VALUE="TRUE">
      <PARAM NAME="BackColor"     VALUE="-2147483643">
      <PARAM NAME="BackColorOdd"  VALUE="-2147483643">
      <PARAM NAME="ForeColorEven" VALUE="0">
</OBJECT>
```

Next, you must set up the `AdvancedDataControl` object so that it provides the connectivity to the backend database. This object is linked to the `Grid` control with the `BINDINGS` property. The properties for this object include the connect string that will be used to gain access to the remote database. As with the grid control, this object will be downloaded from the server, so you need to make sure you have it installed at the location indicated in the `CODEBASE` parameter.

**TIP** Note the `ID` property in particular, as this is what you'll use to refer to the control later when you move around the virtual dataset.

One thing to keep in mind is that the ODBC data source you indicate for the `CONNECT` property is a data source located and defined on the server, not on your workstation. This data source must be defined as a system data source and must be available in order for you to connect to the database.

This is one control measure that helps to make sure you're aware of all connections to your database and what their intent is. With this in mind, you want to make sure your ODBC configurations are as specific as possible. If you're providing SA-level access to data on your server, you're asking for problems as these approaches to working with the database become more prevalent.



```
...
<!-- Non-visual controls - AdvancedDataControl -->
<OBJECT CLASSID="clsid:9381D8F2-0288-11d0-9501-00AA00B911A5"
      ID="SControl"
      CODEBASE="HTTP://<%=Request.ServerVariables("SERVER_NAME")%>/MSADC/
      ➥msadc10.cab"
      WIDTH=1 HEIGHT=1>
      <PARAM NAME="BINDINGS" VALUE="Grid1;">
      <PARAM NAME="Connect" VALUE="DSN=ADCDEMO;UID=guest;PWD=guest;">
      <PARAM NAME="Server" VALUE="http://<%=Request.ServerVariables
      ➥("SERVER_NAME")%>">
</OBJECT>
```

Finally, now that the objects are initiated, you can work with the objects and the results set and perform the operations that you need to complete your application. The first subroutine, the `LOAD` routine, will run immediately on loading of the form. This routine populates the grid control with the initial results from the database. The `.Refresh` method is used to accomplish this, just as it is when the control is based in Visual Basic.

```
...
<!-- VBS scripting for composing queries, updating profiles, and retrieving
➥search results. -->

<SCRIPT LANGUAGE="VBScript">

Dim myQuery
```

```
SUB Load
      Grid1.CAPTION = "Arcadia Bay Corporate Phone Directory"
      'Initialize data grid with column names only.
      SControl.SQL = "Select FirstName, LastName, Title, Email, Building, Room,
      ➥Phone from Employee where 2 < 1 for browse"
      SControl.Refresh
END SUB
```

If the user clicks the FIND button, you can see a great example of how a query is issued against the database and how it is used to return the results of the query. The query is built in the variable `myQuery`. This string variable will contain the select statement that will be submitted against the grid control.

If you work down through this listing, you'll see that the query is driven by using the `.Value` properties for the fields defined on the HTML form. These properties are inserted into the string if they are non-blank, and then a percent-sign, "`%`," is appended, making the entry a wild card.

Finally, the `.SQL` property of the grid control is set to the value of the `myQuery` variable, and the grid is refreshed to show the results of the query.

```
...
'Implement "Find" button - composes a dynamic SQL query to be processed by the
➥database and returns matching records to be bound to the SGrid object.

SUB Find_OnClick
      myQuery = "Select FirstName, LastName, Title, Email, Building, Room, Phone
      ➥from Employee"
      'Check QBE fields and compose a dynamic SQL query.
      IF (SFirst.Value <> "") THEN
            myQuery = myQuery + " where FirstName like '" + SFirst.Value + "%'"
      END IF
      IF (SLast.Value <> "") THEN
            myQuery = myQuery + " where LastName like '" + SLast.Value + "%'"
      END IF
      IF (STitle.Value <> "") THEN
            myQuery = myQuery + " where Title like '" + STitle.Value + "%'"
      END IF
      IF (SEmail.Value <> "") THEN
            myQuery = myQuery + " where Email like '" + SEmail.Value + "%'"
      END IF
      myQuery = myQuery + " for browse"  'Mark recordset for editing.
      'Set the new query and then refresh the SControl so that the new results
      ➥are displayed.
      SControl.SQL = myQuery
      SControl.Refresh

END SUB
```

If you're familiar with the DAO approach to database objects and methods, the navigation routines will look very obvious to you. You'll notice the following statements in the next few subroutines:

```
SControl.MoveFirst
SControl.MoveNext
SControl.MovePrevious
SControl.MoveLast
```

Each performs as it does with the DAO, moving the logical record pointer around the dataset. The `SubmitChanges` method sends all updates to the server. When you call this method, the virtual tables are not updated, though they will likely reflect your changes as the control is bound to the data source.

**NOTE** One thing to keep in mind as a difference between this and Visual Basic data-bound controls is that the information is not updated until you call the `SubmitChanges` method. To restore your dataset to its original state, use the `CancelUpdate` method. This will drop all changes you've made to the dataset.

```
'Submits edits made and pull a clean copy of the new data.
SUB Update_OnClick
      SControl.SubmitChanges
      SControl.Refresh
END SUB

'Cancel edits and restores original values.
SUB Cancel_OnClick
      SControl.CancelUpdate
END SUB
```



There's an interesting trend here that you've either noticed or will notice soon after you implement these types of pages on your Web site. There's a fair amount of code, ActiveX controls, and logic running behind this type of application. This is a far cry from the typically light-interaction-based systems that HTML is currently sporting on the Internet.

Be careful in your use of this technology. Only use the active connection and dataset pooling capabilities in those cases where another approach simply won't cut it. It's recommended that you consider the IDC approach first, if only for its smaller footprint at both the client and the server.

Because you can mix and match your approach to different portions of a given application, be sure you keep in mind that each page you design and develop should be considered alone relative to the best approach to the data management.

The ADC is the technologically and functionally superior model to use for developing applications. The downside is that it requires the use of Internet Explorer for the Visual Basic scripting, as of this writing, and it's heavy on the initial downloads of the various ActiveX controls. It might be better suited for intranet application development in cases where an application usage is casual.

In cases where you are building an application that will be used quite a lot, the initial download of the components is not much more than a typical installation of other software and might play out to be less of an issue in the design considerations.

Finally, be sure to review the DAO appendix for details regarding different methods that are supported. Also, check the Microsoft site frequently as more methods are added and additional controls become available. This is a technology that can bring some solid tools to the mainstream, frequently used Web-based application development arena.

# From Here...

As you can see, the IDC is a very powerful extension to the IIS environment. Chances are good that after your initial installation of IIS to provide access to static HTML content, you'll quickly find that database-driven information is even more popular with the users you are serving.

This chapter touches on a number of different things. More information is provided about these topics in the following areas:

- See Que's *Special Edition Using SQL Server 6.5,* Second Edition, for more information on using SQL Server on the Internet, as well as administering SQL Server.
- See Que's *Publishing's BackOffice Intranet Kit* for more information about setting up and configuring IIS's Web, FTP, and other services.
- See **www.swynk.com** for updates to this material, and review the Microsoft site at **www.microsoft.com** frequently for new releases and additional references.
- The Que site, **www.quecorp.com**, contains many of its books in online, fully searchable format. You can use these tools to determine which books best answer your questions. Visit frequently to see the new titles that become available.
- For ADC-specific information, see **www.microsoft.com/adc**.

CHAPTER 12

# IIS Internet Database Connector

Microsoft has been moving onto the Internet with amazing speed, and one of the first and most direct results of this has been the Internet Information Server. Built with the intent of being the fastest Web server, IIS also has the capability to use ISAPI DLLs instead of CGI scripts. These DLLs are much faster than their CGI counterpart because they are able to run in the same address space as the server components. This is where the Internet Database Connector (IDC) comes in. The IDC is an ISAPI extension DLL that wraps the ODBC library functions to connect to a data source and to directly execute SQL statements against that data source (this includes data definition statements). This has had a significant impact on the burgeoning Webmasters, as they have been given tools for creating IDC-based Web applications, such as the classified ads example in the section on "Creating a Classified Ads Example" later in this chapter.

The real power of the IDC is its potential for playing an active part in a data warehousing scheme. This is one of the reasons that the Database Wizards were developed for Microsoft InterDev: You can take advantage of a GUI development environment and have wizards script the files for you. Still, understanding how something actually works is very beneficial, which is the purpose of this chapter.

- **Exploring the purpose of the IDC**

  Microsoft has several database solutions already, why IIS?

- **Learning how the IDC works**

  Explore the architecture of the Internet Database Connector and see what is really going on.

- **Building .idc files**

  The Internet Database Connector uses script files to query the database. Find out how to design them.

- **Formatting your results**

  The Internet Database Connector dynamically generates HTML pages to send back the results. Find out how to use the HTX templates.

- **Creating a classified ads example**

  Create a working classified ads Web site with the Internet Database Connector.

# Exploring the Purpose of the IDC

The IDC was created to provide a tool for data access using less complicated programming techniques. This product was aimed squarely at the people who, for whatever reason, can deal with scripting languages better than they can deal with programming languages. This is key to the popularity of JavaScript and VBScript. "Normal" computer people finally have something that they can use and understand.

Essentially, the IDC enables you to script a database connection that could take far more effort in a language like C, and about an equal amount of effort in Java. Anything allowed in a SQL statement is allowed in an .idc file, as long as the data source supports it. There isn't much error handling, so you must be careful, or the server will awaken the user rather rudely to the fact that something is wrong.

The IDC is a powerful tool because it, not only executes SQL statements, but also returns the result set in an automatically generated HTML form. This form is drawn from templates called HTX files, which basically allow you to format the return data in a manner in which you would like it to appear. So, instead of having to develop a client interface, you can use several tools together, from JavaScript and VBScript to ActiveX controls and plain HTML forms as your front-end.

# Learning How the IDC Works

The IDC is basically an ISAPI DLL, an extension of the Internet Information Server that sits in and filters the stream of data, looking for the certain "magic" phrases that tell the IDC that it is time to act. In this case, that means making a query on an .idc file. Those queries look like normal URL-type queries:

**http://webfind.home.msn.com/ISAPI/fts.dll?db=mssite&gr=msdn&qu=iis idc htx**

Except that instead of a DLL or CGI application, you will reference the .idc file. The IDC then knows to insert the parameters following the `?` into the .idc file's SQL statements. So an IDC query looks like this:

**http://www.domain.com/scripts/idcfile.idc?param1=value&param2=value2**

The only difference between the two examples is that the first requires only the DLL or CGI executable, whereas in the second, the IDC expects the script file.

In fact, if you want to, you could extend the IDC's capabilities by developing your own ISAPI DLL to access your data source. To implement an ISAPI DLL, first you need to export the following functions in your DLLs:

- `GetExtensionVersion` Basically, this is your initial entry point into the DLL for IIS. It is used to provide the version and description information about the extension.
- `HttpExtensionProc` This is equivalent to `main()`. It is used as the main entry point for most of the DLL's functions. Multiple concurrent threads can call this particular function, so it must be a threadsafe implementation.

In addition to exporting and implementing these functions, an ISAPI DLL must use the `EXTENSION_CONTROL_BLOCK` data structure, which contains data about the client request. You can use four callback functions with this data structure:

- `ReadClient` Obtains data from an incoming HTTP stream
- `WriteClient` Writes to the outgoing HTTP stream
- `GetServerVariable` Returns information about the server, the connection, or the client
- `ServerSupportFunction` Provides a set of basic worker functions: client URL redirection, return of another URL's data, and return of detailed header information

As mentioned before, you can combine your extension DLL with the IDC, which enables you to create custom data access and retrieval. With an ISAPI extension DLL you can capture the stream of HTML and preprocess it, redirect requests, and perform operations on the responses to HTML requests.

This is exactly what the IDC is doing. When your client clicks the Search button, the client sends an `HTTP GET` request for the URL:

```
&query=this that who
```

After the request is sent to IIS:

1. The IIS "wakes up" the IDC Httpodbc.dll and passes the IDC the request through one of the exported entry points.
2. The DLL then passes the parameters through to the Driver Manager.
3. The Driver Manager looks at the parameters and verifies the data source, the login, and the validity of the SQL statement. The Driver Manager then passes the SQL query through to the ODBC driver.
4. The driver maps the SQL query to the native SQL dialects and connects to the data source.
5. After the result set is returned, the IDC parses the HTX file for the formatting information and copies the results in the HTML file as text and returns this information to the user.

Figure 12.1 shows a graphical representation of the process.

**NOTE** HTML streams are similar in form to sending SMTP mail, unless it is encrypted (although unless the data is PGP-encrypted, you can break DES encryption using statistical differential analysis methods and analyzing the occurrences of common characters). Users could sit on the net and read your database traffic all day with Network Monitor or another sniffer. So before you put the company on the Web, think about whether or not you want someone to see the queries and results of those queries.

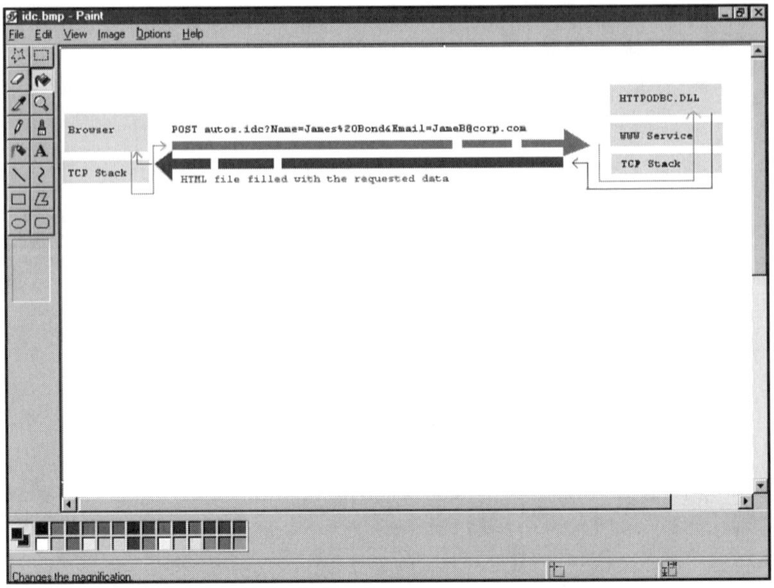


**FIG. 12.1**
The IDC in action: Watch the life cycle of an HTTP request made to the IDC.

# Exploring Security and the Internet Database Connector

IIS has two different methods for actually logging a user in and for granting access: anonymous authentication and Basic/NT Challenge Response authentication. Using anonymous authentication simply means that the Web service is going to impersonate the client by using the credentials supplied by the IIS itself with the anonymous login account.

Using Basic/NT Challenge Response authentication essentially means that the user will be asked for credentials. If the credentials are incorrect, on IIS 3.0 (and 2.0) the user will have three chances to enter the correct information; in contrast, on IIS 1.0, the client immediately receives an `Access Forbidden` message if the incorrect username or password is specified.

When the user enters a password and user account, these are used in the impersonation process that the IIS goes through.

In addition to passing NT accounts and their passwords across the wire, you have another means of controlling security. You can set up groups and users on the data source itself, either through the data sources administration program or through the ODBC API. This has the added benefit of enabling access across the network for the ODBC data source (although the data source must be defined locally, your driver accesses the actual database behind the data source, which is usually on a different PC). In contrast, the NT account impersonation only works on the local PC. Trying to launch DLLs on remote servers will use the Web services logon account, although we assume this will change when our security model changes to conform to the X500 directory tree.

# Building .idc Files

Now that you are familiar with the background and concepts of the IDC, you can begin to learn the language to interact with it. The IDC uses scripts called, appropriately, .idc files. These files contain the ODBC environment settings, any parameters for the connection, and the SQL statement, among other things. Listed in Table 12.1 are the items required in an .idc file.

**Table 12.1 Required Items in an .idc File**

| Item | Description |
|---|---|
| `Datasource` | This is the ODBC data source name that the operation will run against. |
| `Username` | The username to log onto the server with. This can be set to the IUSR account for anonymous logons. |
| `Template` | The name of the HTX template file to use when returning the results. |
| `SQLStatement` | If your statement runs more than a single line in length, use the + sign to indicate that the query is continued. |

**NOTE** When using SQL Servers integrated security, the username is actually optional, for the username is ignored. Without integrated security the username is a required field.

Optionally, you can include several other items listed in Table 12.2 in the .idc files.



**Table 12.2 Optional Items Allowed in the .idc File**

| Item | Description |
|---|---|
| `DefaultParameters` | Used as defaults in case the clients don't specify a parameter value. |
| `Expires` | The number of seconds that the IDC will wait to refresh a cached output page. This is useful because, unless the query is different, the same cached page will be accessed each time. If this field is not specified, the pages are not cached. |
| `MaxFieldSize` | The maximum buffer space allocated by httpodbc.dll per record. Any characters beyond this buffer space will be truncated. Only applies for fields in the database that exceed 8,192 bytes. The default value is 8,192 bytes. |
| `MaxRecords` | Because the default is not to specify a maximum number of records in the result set, and that result set can be up to 4 billion records, you might want to limit the number returned. |
| `Password` | The password. This is ignored if you are using SQL Server's integrated security. |

*continues*

**Table 12.2 Continued**

| Item | Description |
|---|---|
| RequiredParameters | Tells the httpodbc.dll that these parameters are required or that an error is to be returned to the client. |

The .idc file can also contain several variables passed to it in the HTTP stream. These are included in the .idc file by specifying <%*variablename*%> in the .idc or HTX file. You can use the parameters shown in Table 12.3 to return information.

**Table 12.3 HTTP Header Information Allowed in the .idc File**

| IDC Variable | Description |
|---|---|
| <%ALL_HTTP%> | HTTP headers that haven't been parsed yet. They look like HTTP_<%TYPE%>, where type is something like EXTENSION or ACCEPT. |
| <%AUTH_PASS%> | Retrieves the password of the REMOTE_USER. |
| <%AUTH_TYPE%> | Retrieves the authorization type currently in use, either BASIC or not present. |
| <%CONTENT_LENGTH%> | Returns the size in bytes of the information that will be received from the client. |
| <%CONTENT_TYPE%> | Returns the content type of the POST request. |
| <%GATEWAY_INTERFACE%> | Returns the version number of the CGI interface. |
| <%HTTP_ACCEPT%> | Returns a comma-delimited string of the ACCEPT fields in the HTTP header. |
| <%PATH_INFO%> | Returns the subpath between the /scripts/ and the /httpodbc.dll. |
| <%PATH_TRANSLATED%> | Returns the value of PATH_INFO with the virtual paths expanded into directories. |
| <%QUERY_STRING%> | Returns all information following the ?. |
| <%REMOTE_ADDR%> | Returns the IP address of the client. |
| <%REMOTE_HOST%> | Returns the client's hostname. |
| <%REMOTE_USER%> | Returns the username of the client. |
| <%REQUEST_METHOD%> | Returns the HTTP request method. |
| <%SCRIPT_NAME%> | Returns the name of the script currently executing. |
| <%SERVER_NAME%> | Returns the host or IP address of the server. |

| IDC Variable | Description |
|---|---|
| <%SERVER_PORT%> | Returns the port that the request came through on. |
| <%SERVER_PROTOCOL%> | Returns the name and version of the protocol making the request. |
| <%SERVER_SOFTWARE%> | Returns the name and version of the Web server. |

The first step in creating your .idc file is to create the data source. You can do this either programmatically or by pushing buttons. Either way, create the data source, and then decide on the authentication methods. You can use the username and password variables, go with anonymous access by specifying a username, or use integrated security with SQL Server. In this instance, use anonymous access:

```
Username: IUSR_computername
```

Next, you need a template file. In this case, the SQL statement creates a table, so we'll specify an HTML file that tells you that the `CREATE TABLE` statement worked:

```
Template: CreateDone.htm
```

The last required item in your file is the actual SQL statement. Because we'll need a table anyway, create one now called Autos for use in this experiment. The SQL Statement is:

```
+CREATE TABLE Autos (Make VARCHAR(15)),(Line VARCHAR(15)),(Model VARCHAR(15)),
➥(StickerShock INTEGER(6))
```

This completes the simple form of the .idc file. For this example, assume that the data source `DealerNet` exists on this machine and that `IUSRcomputername` has `CREATE DATABASE` rights for the database that you are connecting to. The complete file thus far is given in Listing 12.1.



**Listing 12.1 SAMPLE.IDC—The Required Fields for a Simple .idc File when Using Normal Security**

```
Datasource: DealerNet
Username: IUSR_computername
Template: CreateDone.htm
SQLStatement:
+CREATE TABLE Autos (Make VARCHAR(15)),(Line VARCHAR(15)),(Model VARCHAR(15)),
(VIN INTEGER(20))
```

As it stands right now, you could use Listing 12.1 to create a table called Autos in the data source DealerNet. But what about doing a `SELECT` statement or multiple `SELECT` statements? First, we need another table for referencing which car belongs to which dealer and what the prices are. So now create a `CONSTRAINT` for the data source (assume that the data source driver is at least ODBC core level SQL conformance), add that `CONSTRAINT` to the Autos table, and create another table all in the same file. No need to have more work if you don't need it. The .idc file that accomplishes this is shown in Listing 12.2.

**Listing 12.2 CREATECONST.JAVA—Creating the Second Table and Setting Up Referential Integrity**

```
Datasource: AutoNet
Username: IUSR_computername
Template: CreateDone.htm
SQLStatement:
+ CREATE TABLE Intersect (DealerID VARCHAR(15)),(VIN INTEGER(20)), (Price
➥INTEGER(6)), (CONSTRAINT Dealer_Const FOREIGN KEY (DealerID) REFERENCES
Dealers(DealerID)),(CONSTRAINT Auto_Const FOREIGN KEY (VIN) REFERENCES
➥Autos(VIN)
+ CREATE TABLE Dealers (DealerID INTEGER(10) CONSTRAINT Dealer_Const PRIMARY
(DealerID)),(Name VARCHAR(15)),(Dealership VARCHAR(15)), (Address VARCHAR(20)),
➥(City VARCHAR(15)), (State CHAR(2)),(ZipCode CHAR(5))
+ ALTER TABLE Autos ADD(DealerID CONSTRAINT PRIMARY (DealerID))
```

Listing 12.2 creates the two tables, as well as a one-to-many relationship between Dealers and Intersect and a one-to-many relationship between Autos and Intersect. The constraints on the columns will enforce the referential integrity so that when a dealer submits an entry that would violate these constraints, the transaction is rolled back.

Next, a query must be built for the database. We'll use three parameters for the query: the price, the make, and the model. The `Autos.Line` column will be used to group the results. This query is shown in Listing 12.3.

**Listing 12.3 INITIALQ.IDC—Creating the Initial Query for the User**

```
Datasource: AutoNet
Username: IUSR_computername
DefaultParameters: Make=*, Model=*
MaxRecords: 100
RequiredParameters: Low, High
Template: Show.htx
SQLStatement:
+ SELECT Autos.Make, Autos.Model, Intersect.Price, Dealer.Name, COUNT(*) AS
➥Count
+ FROM Dealer, Autos, Intersect
+ WHERE (Autose.Make='%Make%' )AND (Autos.Model='%Model%') AND (Intersect.Price
➥BETWEEN '%Low%' AND '%High')
```

This query requires the user to at least enter the price range for the car. The script will supply the default information for the other parameters. `MaxRecords` was also specified to prevent the user from dumping the database and creating bandwidth problems for both the developer and the user.

Next, the dealers need a way to place ads in the database, so you must create an IDC script for them. Use the `DealerID` for a login and a password to prevent unauthorized people from creating ads. The dealer provides five variables:

- VIN number of the car
- Price
- Make
- Model
- Line

For the information needed in the `DealerID` column of the Intersect table, we'll pull from the login name using a server variable. This action is shown in Listing 12.4.

**Listing 12.4 DEALERADD.IDC—Using the Server Variable to Update the Intersect Database**

```
Datasource: DealerNet
RequiredParameters: VIN, Make, Mode, Line, Price
Template: InsertAd.htx
SQLStatement:
+ INSERT INTO Autos, Intersect VALUES('%Make%', '%Line%', '%Model%', '%VIN%'),
➥('%REMOTE_USER%', '%VIN%', '%Price%')
```

This listing provides a complete database capable of holding the simple transactions of users searching for particular makes, models, and price ranges.

# Formatting Your Results

Now that you've built the rudimentary database application by using IDC scripts, you need to format the results. This can be an arduous task for a normal application (in Java). With HTX files, however, the data is already formatted when your client receives it, so you have no work to do to determine how to handle the data except to create the HTX file. An HTX file can contain any normal HTML syntax, as well as six keywords controlling how the data is formatted in the result set. Those keywords are defined in Table 12.4.



**Table 12.4 Keywords in an HTX File**

| Keyword | Description |
|---|---|
| `<%begindetail%>` | Signals the beginning of the data section. |
| `<%enddetail%>` | Signals the end of the data section. |
| `<%`*column*`%>` | Denotes the column name. This determines where the columns will be placed. This does not have to occur between the `<%begindetail%>` and `<%enddetail%>`. |
| `<%if condition %>` | Signals the beginning of an `IF...ELSE` statement. The condition can be `EQ`, `LT`, `GT`, or `CONTAINS`. |

*continues*

**Table 12.4 Continued**

| Keyword | Description |
| --- | --- |
| `[<%else%> HTML text]` | If the condition of an `IF` statement is unsatisfied, this HTML code will be returned instead. |
| `<%endif%>` | Signals the end of an `IF...ELSE` block. |
| `EQ` | Operator, means `Value1 = Value2` |
| `LT` | Operator, means `Value1 < Value2` |
| `GT` | Operator, means `Value1 > Value2` |
| `CONTAINS` | Operator, means `Value1 CONTAINS Value2`. Used to find a substring matching `Value2` in `Value1`. |

An example of using these types of constructs would be to base content on a per browser basis, or per user basis. This could create a feeling of customization on the front-end. Listing 12.5 is an example of an HTX file, showing the basics by simply returning the data to the user.

**Listing 12.5 SHOW.HTX—Returning the Data to the User with the Bare Minimum of Required Fields**

```
<%if HTTP_USER_AGENT CONTAINS "Mozilla"%>
<html>

<head><title>Automobiles for Sale</title></head>

<body bgcolor=white link=maroon alink=maroon vlink=maroon>
<BASEFONT FACE="Times New Roman" SIZE=2>
<table border=0 cellpadding=0 cellspacing=0 width=100% bgcolor=white>
<tr><td width=70% bgcolor=white valign=top>
<br><img src="images/title.gif" alt="Welcome to AutoSearch, the Ulitmate source
➥of Automotive information" border=0>
</td><td width=30% valign=top>
<br><a href="http://www.nada.com"><img src="images/Nada.gif" alt="Check it out
➥with NADA" border=0>
</center></td></tr>
</table>


<h1>Your Search returned <%idc.Count%> items</h1>

<body bgcolor=white link=blue alink=maroon vlink=maroon>

<BASEFONT FACE="Times New Roman" SIZE=2>

<table border=1 cellpadding=0 cellspacing=0 width=100% bgcolor=white>
<tr><td width=70% bgcolor=white valign=top>
```

```
<!--The Autos table has four columns in the return>

<%if idc.table EQ "Autos"%>
<tr><th>Make</th><th>Model</th><th>Price</th><th>Dealer</th></tr>
<%endif%>


<%begindetail%>

<%if idc.table EQ "Autos"%>

<tr> <td><%Make%></td><td><%Model%></td> <td><%Price%></td><td><%Dealer%></td></
➥tr>
<%endif%>
<%enddetail%>
</table>

<font face="Arial, Helvetica" size="1">
<b>
Best experienced with
<br>
<A HREF="/ie_setup/msie30.exe"><img src="graphics/ie_animated.gif" width="88"
height="31" border="0" alt="Microsoft Internet Explorer"></a><br>
Click here to download.
</b>
</font>

<%else%>

//Do something else depending on the browser type (User Agent)

<%endif%>
```



In this HTX file, the ISAPI DLL is making a decision based on the `USER_AGENT` value. This is another name for the browser. In this case, if the browser doesn't return Mozilla as its tag, we set the background to be the Internet Explorer's logo. It's a nice trick, and you can actually do useful things with it, such as use the advanced features of each browser, or formatt pages according to who is logged in. Also, if you look inside the `IF...THEN` statement, the variables don't have to be surrounded with `<%` ***variable name*** `%>`.

The only tag not covered in Listing 12.5 is the new `%z` escape character. The `%z` character is mainly for links, in which returning a name with spaces or other formatting would be truncated. The `%z` character escapes out of that behavior, enabling links such as `Error! Bookmark not defined` to actually work without the `%20%`. This allows you to forget about specifying the `%20%` for a space in your HTX files. An escaped entry looks like this: `<%"%z", DisplayName%>`, where the actual data returned would be `Last, First MI`.

# Understanding How the HTX File Is Processed

The ISAPI DLL httpodbc.dll file loads the HTX file based on the template information in the .idc file. The file will be opened either with a specific path name, or in reference to the path of the .idc file it was called from. The account used to access the file must have access to the directory in which it is located, including read permission. This means that your scripts directory probably isn't a good place for these files, unless you don't mind people reading the scripts used to create your site.

The IDC uses the account specified in the .idc file or the anonymous user account specifically created for IIS. Then the IDC attempts to send an HTTP 200 OK signal to the client; if that fails, you will see error messages on the client.

The last step is to copy in the data and flush the data to the cache. This is where the `Expires` field comes into play. The settings for that parameter determine how long this page of cached data remains in the cache. Then the completed page is returned to the client.

# The Classified Ads Example

Now that you've gone over most of the concepts behind the IDC and have seen how the scripting files look, consider a real example. To do this, we'll simply expand on the Autos example used previously. This time, though, our goal is to make it work and to look good at the same time.

The client interface is going to be using the latest gadgets from IE3.0, including floating frames, Java applets, and ActiveX components. This will keep the users sufficiently dazzled so that they won't get tired of our UI and go elsewhere. An example of how this interface might look is in Figure 12.2.

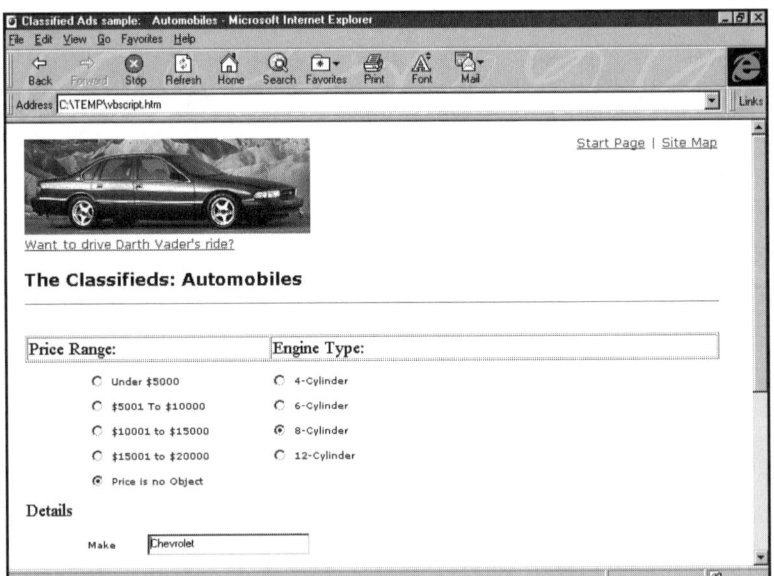


**FIG. 12.2**
This is the Classified Ads user interface.

Extending the sophistication of the earlier examples to allow for grouping and drill-downs is an excellent goal. Integrating drill-down and grouping with enhanced tables from IE3.0 would allow for some good-looking client interfaces.

## Creating the Tables

The .idc files for creating the basic tables are already in place. The only thing left to do is to modify them to include a means for the user to get in touch with a dealer and for users to post and hold "auctions" for their own automobiles. To enable that, another database needs to be created and a few new fields need to be added to the existing tables.

First, the existing databases. The Autos database is fine as it is, except for one thing. The `DealerID` field needs to be renamed to the `ContactID`. This enables normal people to participate in the sales process without becoming dealers.

A much more significant change is also needed for the Dealers table. In fact, the Dealers table needs to be scrapped and a new table called *Contacts* needs to be built. The existing Dealers table has lots of information that should not be given out, and most user's reactions would be adverse to giving this kind of information. A safe bet is to make a mandatory e-mail address the extent of the information required for placing an ad. Making the address and phone number optional allows people to disclose just the amount of information that they want—obviously a Dealer wants you to have his address, but other users might not want that information to be available. After all of thc changes are made to the existing tables, the result is shown in Figure 12.3.

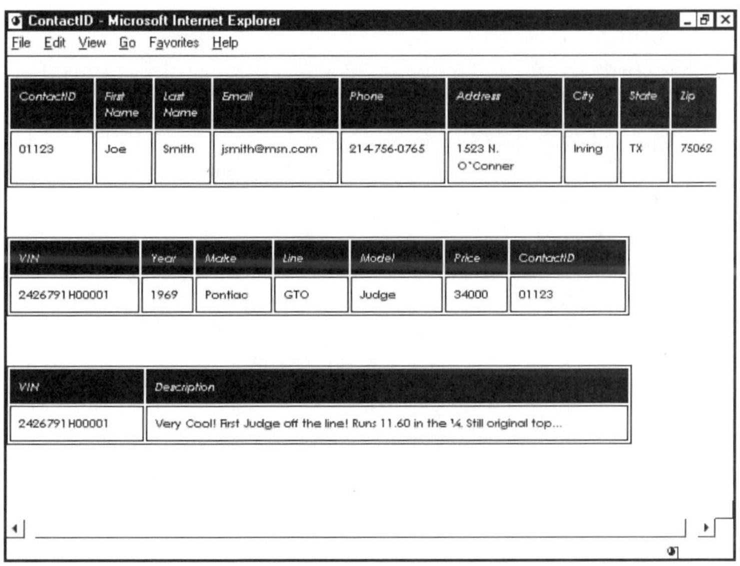


**FIG. 12.3**
This is the new table structure for the Autos database.

What happened to the intersection table? A decision was made to drop it. Intersection tables do make for quicker lookups, especially for large records. However, in this case there is no clear reason to add several bytes of storage per record simply to return queries to a Web client who wouldn't see the time savings anyway. The added table enables lookups to proceed on the data items normally returned to the client. The description field will only be accessed in a drill-down, so returning it every time by default would waste bandwidth. You can give clients the option to decide whether or not they want to use extended information and see the description with every record.

Now, the .idc files need to be built. This requires anticipating what people will want to do in terms of queries. Are you going to allow for specific regions, cities, or any other filters for the data? Ranged queries for the price are already included, as are parameters for the model, line, and make. Geographical queries could be included by requiring the sellers to enter a city and state information or by requiring them to enter the phone number—the city and state could then be determined from the prefix and area code. Because the shortest path is often the best one when dealing with application design, make the city and state a requirement.

Assume, then, that the client will allow for price ranges, geographical limitations, and of course, the year, make, model, and line of the automobile. The .idc files will look like Listing 12.6.

**Listing 12.6 AUTOS.IDC—Creating the .idc File Neccessary to Support the Optional Values that the Clients Can Use**

```
Datasource: AutoNet
Username: IUSR_computername
DefaultParameters: oldest =*, newest =*, make =*, line =*, model =*, high =*,
low =*, city =*, state =*
MaxRecords: 100
RequiredParameters:
Template: drilldown.htx
SQLStatement:
+ SELECT Autos.year, Autos.Make, Autos.Model, Autos.Price, Contact.Name,
➥COUNT(*) AS Count
+ FROM Contact, Autos
+ WHERE (Year BETWEEN '%oldest%' AND '%newest%') AND (Autose.Make='%Make%' ) AND
➥(Autos.Line='%line%') AND (Autos.Model='%Model%') AND (Autos.Price BETWEEN
➥'%Low%' AND '%High') AND (Contact.City='%city%') AND (Contact.state='%state%')
```

After you have this .idc file, the only other files that you need are the HTX files and the detail.idc and drilldown.idc files. These files enable the user to simply send a single value to a `SELECT` query, either drilling down and narrowing the original query or displaying a single record's detail information (see Listing 12.7).

**Listing 12.7 DETAIL.IDC—Implementing the Details Feature with a Simple IDC Query**

```
Datasource: AutoNet
Username: IUSR_computername
```

```
DefaultParameters: oldest =*, newest =*, make =*, line =*, model =*, high =*,
low =*, city =*, state =*
MaxRecords: 100
RequiredParameters:
Template: details.htx
SQLStatement:
+ SELECT DISTINCT Autos.year, Autos.Make, Autos.Model, Autos.Price,
➥Contact.Name, Desc.Desctiption COUNT(*) AS Count
+ FROM Contact, Autos, Desc
+ WHERE (VIN = '%VIN%')
```

The file that enables users to narrow their searches by selecting a column value and then uses that value in the original query is shown in Listing 12.8.

**Listing 12.8 DRILLDOWN.IDC—Allowing Users to Narrow Their Searches**

```
Datasource: AutoNet
Username: IUSR_computername
DefaultParameters: oldest=<%idc.oldest%>, newest = <%idc.newest%>,
make=<%idc.make%>, line= <%idc.line%>, model=<%idc.model%>,
high=<%idc.high%>,low=<%idc.low%>, contact=<%idc.contact%>, city=<%idc.city%>,
state=<%idc.state%>
MaxRecords: 100
RequiredParameters:
Template: drilldown.htx
SQLStatement:
+ SELECT Autos.year, Autos.Make, Autos.Model, Autos.Price, Contact.Name,
➥COUNT(*) AS Count
+ FROM Contact, Autos
+ WHERE ((Year BETWEEN '%oldest%' AND '%newest%')OR(Year = '%year%')) AND
➥(Autose.Make='%Make%' ) AND (Autos.Line='%line%') AND (Autos.Model='%Model%')
➥AND (Autos.Price BETWEEN '%Low%' AND '%High') AND (Contact.City='%city%') AND
➥(Contact.state='%state%')
```



# Designing the Result

Drill-down support in the HTX file is the first thing that you need to tackle. This is somewhat tricky because you are setting up the queries beforehand. Listing 12.9 shows how this will be accomplished.

**Listing 12.9 DRILLDOWN.HTX—Using the HTX Formatting Capabilities to Provide Drill-Down into the Database**

```
<%begindetail%>

<%if idc.table EQ "Autos"%>
<table>
```

*continues*

**Listing 12.9 Continued**

```
<tr>
<td><A HREF="scripts/drilldown.idc?VIN=<%VIN%>
<IMG SRC=images/spyglass.gif" alt="View details about this car">
<td><A HREF="scripts/narrow.idc?year=<%Year%>"><%Year%></td>
<td><A HREF="scripts/narrow.idc?make=<%Make%>"><%Make%></td>
<td><A HREF="scripts/narrow.idc?model=<%Model%>"><%Model%></td>
<td><A HREF="scripts/narrow.idc?price=<%Price%>"><%Price%></td>
<td><A HREF="scripts/narrow.idc?contact=<%contact%>"><%Name%></td>

</tr>
<%endif%>
<%enddetail%>
</table>
```

Listing 12.9 sets up a table with links to an IDC query, which enables drill-down on the actual automobile. This can also be used in conjunction with narrowing query parameters, to return only those records matching the original query and the new parameter. In the code example, the GIF is used to indicate more detail about a particular car, and the other links will query an IDC with the particular parameters associated with the link passed to the new .idc file. This enables users to browse, and if they decide that they like a particular model, they can click a link that will take them to a page devoted to only that model.

The only thing left to implement regarding HTX is an individual record detail page, which simply needs to display the individual records in a vertical format. The file in Lisitng 12.10 should work fine.

The first scripting we'll do is to account for the differences in browsers by checking the HTTP_USER_`AGENT environment variable.`

```
<%if HTTP_USER_AGENT CONTAINS "Mozilla"%>

...html code and detail work

<%else%>

...html code and detail work

<%endif%>
```

The next step, as shown in Listing 12.10, is to format the table and tell the user what the `VIN #` and detail data are for the particular car. We'll do this through the use of IDC variables.

**Listing 12.10 DETAIL.HTX—Displaying the Individual Records**

```
<html>

<head><title>Automobiles for Sale</title></head>

<body bgcolor=white link=maroon alink=maroon vlink=maroon>
```

```
<BASEFONT FACE="Times New Roman" SIZE=2>
<table border=0 cellpadding=0 cellspacing=0 width=100% bgcolor=white>
<tr><td width=70% bgcolor=white valign=top>
<br><img src="images/title.gif" alt="Welcome to AutoSearch, the Ulitmate source
➥of Automotive information" border=0>
</td><td width=30% valign=top>
<br><a href="http://www.nada.com"><img src="images/Nada.gif" alt="Check it out
➥with NADA" border=0>
</center></td></tr>
</table>


<h1>Details on <%idc.VIN%></h1>

<body bgcolor=white link=blue alink=maroon vlink=maroon>

<BASEFONT FACE="Times New Roman" SIZE=10>
<%begindetail%>

Year:          <A HREF="scripts/narrow.idc?year=<%Year%>"><%Year%>
Make:          <A HREF="scripts/narrow.idc?make=<%Make%>"><%Make%>
Model:         <A HREF="scripts/narrow.idc?model=<%Model%>"><%Model%>
Price:         <A HREF="scripts/narrow.idc?price=<%Price%>"><%Price%>
Seller:        <A HREF="scripts/narrow.idc?contact=<%ContactID%>"><%Contact%>
Email:         <%Email%>
Phone:         <%Phone%>
Address:       <%Address%>
City:          <%City%>
State:         <%State%>

Description:  <%Description%>
<font face="Arial, Helvetica" size="1">
<b>
Best experienced with
<br>
<A HREF="/ie_setup/msie30.exe"><img src="graphics/ie_animated.gif" width="88"
height="31" border="0" alt="Microsoft Internet Explorer"></a><br>
Click here to download.
</b>
</font>
```

This HTX file includes HREFs with the data, allowing for the query to be re-executed in a drill-down fashion from this page as well. This way, if a user wants to localize the search, there is no need to hit the back button, which can lose the query information if caching is disabled by the user.

Now that you have a way to perform searches, you might consider enhancing the concept somewhat to create an online auction, enabling people to submit bids online in a related portion of your Web site. Some of the newsgroups dealing with collectors hold something similar, if not quite as popular, to a normal auction. Holding auctions at your Web site could attract people. Especially because these are non-binding auctions, users don't have to worry about how to escape after accidentally raising their hands and buying something.

# From Here...

The IIS Internet Database Connector is a powerful tool to add to your arsenal, and basically it is free. Creating multiuser database applications doesn't get much easier, unless you count Microsoft InterDev, which uses the wizards to make designing complex IDC applications simple. The next few chapters will be building up to Chapter 16, "Implementing Data Warehousing with Visual J++," where we'll cover Data Warehousing in depth, learn what all of the terminology is, and design a simple tool for creating Data Marts from the Data Warehouse.

- Chapter 13, "Security Issues," discusses the Internet and why security has become a large issue. Millions of dollars are pouring into databases and technologies that anyone with a connection to the Internet can access. This chapter discusses some strategies for protecting your investments.
- Chapter 14, "Dealing With Disaster Before It Happens," looks at some of the steps that you can take to prevent problems, and how to deal with them more effectively.
- Chapter 15, "Distributing Java Applications," explains how to get your design out the door and into users' hands without an installation manual.
- Chapter 16, "Implementing Data Warehousing with Visual J++," teaches the concepts behind data warehousing and OLAP technology, and examines ways to use your skills in this environment.

PART V

# Advanced Issues with Visual J++

CHAPTER 13

# Security Issues

**Understanding encryption**

Familiarize yourself with current encryption schemes and how they can affect the implementation of security.

**Learning about authentication**

Discover some of the ways passwords are authenticated.

**Investigating Visual J++ and encryption**

Learn how Java applications can make use of current encryption techniques.

**Explore new and existing security protocols**

Discover what security protocols are currently available.

Today's Internet is like the Wild West of a century ago—a large frontier with lots of potential for fun and profit with very few regulations. Just as the Wild West had sheriffs providing security for each town, today's Internet has many different protocols designed to provide security for electronic transactions and commerce.

This chapter takes you on a tour of some of the new security protocols designed to protect your electronic data against the bandits on the I-way. You will also examine some methods for implementing security in your Java/J++ applications.

# Understanding Encryption

Essentially, encryption is the process of disguising a message to hide its contents from eavesdroppers. An encryption system consists of the following parts:

- The message to be encrypted.
- The encryption algorithm—a mathematical function that is used to provide the encryption for the message.
- The encrypted message.
- The key—a number, letter, or any combination thereof. The encrypted data cannot be read until it has been decrypted with the proper key.

The process of encryption and decryption is illustrated in Figure 13.1.

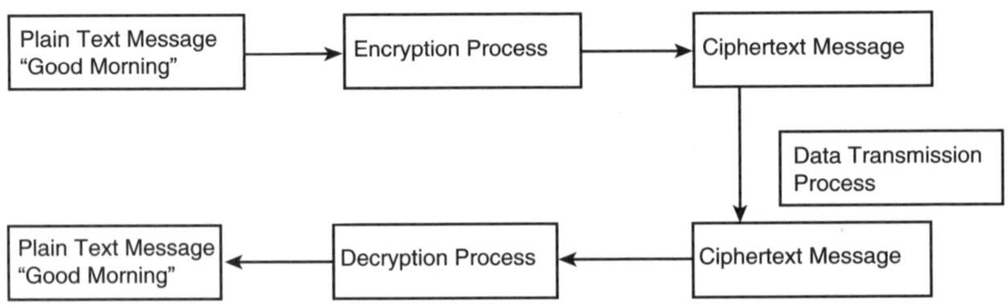


**FIG. 13.1**
The process of encryption and decryption enables the secure transmission of electronic information.

The sections that follow introduce you to the strengths and weaknesses of current encryption schemes, the differences between Public and Private Keys, and the government's regulations over encryption.

## Current Encryption Schemes

There are many different encryption schemes on the market today, making the choice of one scheme confusing. The following highlights some of the more popular schemes available.

**RSA** The RSA algorithm was invented in 1977 by Ron Rivest, Adi Shamir, and Leonard Adleman. RSA gets its name from the first letter of each of the inventors' names. These three MIT professors later formed RSA Data Security, Inc., which holds the patent for the RSA algorithm and sells encryption software based upon it. Some of the key features of the RSA algorithm are:

- The RSA algorithm became the first Public-Key algorithm that works for encryption and digital signatures.
- The RSA algorithm is easy to understand and implement.
- RSA is the most widely used Public-Key cryptosystem today and has often been called a de facto standard.
- RSA is a Public-Key cryptosystem designed to provide both encryption and authentication.

RSA is found in Internet standards and proposed protocols including PEM (Privacy Enhanced Mail), S/MIME, PEM-MIME, S-HTTP, and SSL, as well as the PKCS standard for the software industry.

If you intend to use the algorithm in any product that you make or sell, RSA requires a commercial license. However, RSA Data Security usually enables free, noncommercial use of RSA, with written permission, for academic or university research purposes. In addition, RSA Data Systems has made available (in the U.S. and Canada) a collection of cryptographic routines in source code, including the RSA algorithm at no charge; it can be used, improved, and redistributed noncommercially.

### ON THE WEB

**http://www.rsa.com** Parties interested in the RSA algorithm should contact RSA Data Systems.

**DSA and DSS** The *Digital Signature Algorithm* (DSA) was published by the National Institute of Standards and Technology (NIST) in the *Digital Signature Standard* (DSS).

Based on the discrete logarithm problem and derived from cryptosystems proposed by Schnorr and ElGamal, DSA is for authentication purposes only. The algorithm is generally considered secure when the key size is sufficiently large. Although DSS originally had a 512-bit key size, after much anxiety concerning security was voiced, NIST revised DSS to enable key sizes up to 1,024 bits.

**DES** Data Encryption Standard (DES) is the default data encryption algorithm used for protecting financial information. It was originally published in 1977 by IBM for use by the U.S. Government to protect valuable and sensitive, but unclassified data. DES was subsequently adopted by the American National Standards Institute (ANSI) as the Data Encryption Algorithm (DEA).

DES can trace its lineage back to the early days of computers. During the late 1960s, Dr. Horst Feistel led a research project at IBM that developed the Lucifer cipher. This cipher, which later became DES, was adopted as the federal standard late in 1976. The terms of the standard required a review of DES every five years. Although the National Institute of Standards and Technology (NIST) has recertified DES as an official U.S. Government encryption standard every five years, NIST has indicated that it might not recertify DES again because it is not as strong as the Clipper Chip projects under consideration.



### What Is a Clipper Chip?

The Capstone project and its twin, the Clipper Chip project, are designed to incorporate security protocols into electronic circuit chips. Recently, these projects have gained public exposure through the government's attempts to hold the keys to the security codes contained within the chips. The Clipper Chip has received a lot of publicity since its official announcement by the White House on April 16, 1993.

The Clipper Chip is designed to be used with a regular telephone. It is an electronic circuit designed to encrypt the outgoing message with a special key. A person on the receiving end of the

*continues*

*continued*

conversation can decrypt the message if he has the proper key. On the surface, this looks like a great way to enjoy a private conversation without the fear of eavesdroppers. The Clipper Chip is such a hot topic, however, because the U.S. Government wants the capability to hold all of the keys for all of the Clipper Chips that are produced. This means that the government would have the capability to listen to our private conversations without breaking any laws.

The U.S. Government's response has been that it needs strong encryption devices such as the Clipper Chip to prevent criminals from hiding their activities.

DES is a block-cipher, which means that it encrypts the plaintext in blocks of data rather than as a stream of bits. DES has a 64-bit block size and uses a 56-bit key during encryption. Originally designed for hardware, DES operates on the text 16 times by these two techniques, as dictated by the key. In communication implementations, both the sender and the receiver must know the same secret key, which is used both to encrypt and decrypt the message. DES can also be used for single-user encryption, such as storing files on a hard disk in encrypted form. Secure key distribution in a multiuser environment can cause security problems—DES provides an ideal solution to this.

## Private-Key Encryption

Private-Key encryption systems are also known as secret-key cryptography, symmetric cryptography, or conventional cryptography. Private-Key encryption systems use a single key or a Private Key for both encryption and decryption. This key must be shared by both the sender and the recipient. In other words, if Bob sends a message to Julie, it is encrypted using one key. When Julie receives the message sent by Bob, she will use the same key to decrypt the message.

This encryption method has some rather important disadvantages. For instance, in the preceding example, Julie must have the same key as Bob to read the encrypted message; as a result, there must be a secure way to send the key to Julie. Second, if an urgent encrypted message needs to be sent to Joe, who might not have the Private Key, the encrypted message cannot be done easily. Third, a separate Private Key is needed for each party that you want to communicate with, if you want to keep all of your messages to each party private. To overcome these weaknesses of Private-Key encryption systems, the Public-Key encryption system was introduced (see Figure 13.2).

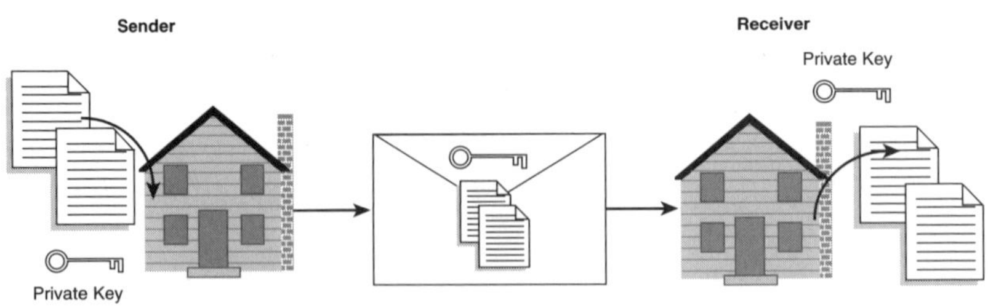


**FIG. 13.2**
A typical use of Private-Key Cryptography is shown here.

In general, there are two types of Private-Key algorithms:

- *Stream Algorithms/Stream Ciphers* These operate on the plaintext a single bit at a time.
- *Block Algorithms/Block Ciphers* These operate on the plaintext in groups of bits called blocks. A typical block size is 64 bits.

Some well known examples of Private-Key Algorithms are as follows:

- *Data Encryption Standard (DES)* Adopted as a U.S. Government standard in 1977 and as an ANSI standard in 1981. Uses a key length of 56 bits. DES is used by financial institutions to encrypt Personal Information Numbers (PINs). This type of security is also found in some implementations of smart card products.
- *Triple-DES* A method that makes the DES twice as secure by using the DES encryption algorithm three times with two different keys.
- *CRYPT* A DES variant found on UNIX systems. Used as a one-way function for passwords, it sometimes can be used for encryption purposes.
- *RC2, RC4* Rivest's Code #2 and #4 are named after MIT Professor Ronald Rivest, the coinventor of the RSA Public-Key algorithms distributed by RSA Data Security. RC2 is a block cipher like DES. RC4 is a stream cipher. They can both be used with keys up to 1,024 bits in length.
- *Skipjack* A secret algorithm developed by the National Security Agency (NSA) for civilian use, it uses an 80-bit key and forms the basis of the NSA's Clipper and Capstone chips.

Private-Key encryption techniques have to protect the key used to encrypt and decrypt the message, resulting in greater compromise of either key. Even though Private-Key encryption techniques provide excellent security for the plaintext message, they do not provide any security for the key to unlock the plaintext.

## Public-Key Encryption

Public-Key, or Asymmetric, encryption is a relatively recent technology. Public-Key encryption does not require the sender and the receiver of a message to know each other's key to access an encrypted file.



With the Public-Key encryption system, a mathematical process generates two keys to encrypt and decrypt messages. These keys are sometimes referred to as a key pair. The following describes the keys used in Public-Key encryption systems:

- *The Public Key* This key can be made known without imposing a security risk. A message is encrypted using the receiving party's Public Key, which means that only the person receiving the message can decrypt the message.
- *The secret key* This key should not be made known. A message that has been encrypted with a Public Key can only be decrypted with the proper secret key. With Public-Key encryption systems, public and secret keys are also used to make and verify digital signatures.

- *The session key* The session key is created randomly for every Public-Key message. It is a one-shot Private Key, used to encrypt a message. The session key is itself encrypted by the Public Key and packaged with the encrypted message. To decrypt the message, the receiving party needs to decrypt the session key. The receiving party then uses the decrypted session key to decrypt the message. The session key was added to help speed up the overall process of key verification, encryption, and decryption.

Figure 13.3 depicts a typical use of a Public Key.

**FIG. 13.3**
This is a diagram of a Public-Key system. One of the keys is made public while the other is kept private.

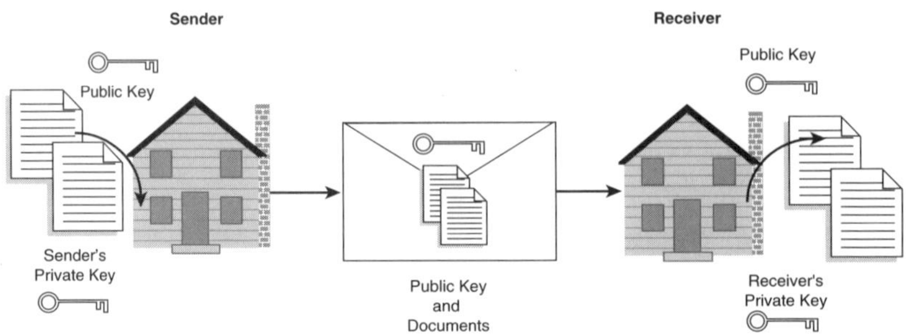


The following are some of the more commonly used Public-Key algorithms in practical applications:

- *Diffie-Hellman Key-Exchange Algorithm* One of the first Public-Key algorithms invented, this algorithm can be used for key distribution but not for encryption and decryption of messages.
- *RSA* One of the more common uses of this algorithm is to create privacy-enhanced mail (PEM) Internet applications.
- *Digital Signature Algorithm (DSA)* Cannot be used for encryption but only for digital signatures.

## Government Regulations

The current regulations regarding the export of encryption tools can be traced back to the early '60s at the height of the Cold War. At that time, the U.S. Government passed laws that affected encryption algorithms and products containing those algorithms. This attitude was fostered by the belief that a foreign power could endanger our national security after learning our encryption algorithms.

Even 30 years after the height of the Cold War, the export of cryptographic technology outside the United States is severely restricted. U.S. export policy prohibits citizens from disclosing or transferring the encrypted products outside of U.S. control, for encryption algorithms are classified as munitions. Any product, whether it be a software application or an electronic circuit that contains encryption algorithms, is subject to the export policy.

The current restrictions are on products with keys greater than 40 bits in length, a restriction that is very outdated. Encryption products with less than 40 keys are no match for even the most novice hacker with a few encryption tools. DES, currently the standard against which all other encryption products are measured, uses 56-bit encryption, which by international standards is nowhere near enough. There are literally hundreds of products overseas that use encryption algorithms greater than 128 bits in length. Why is a country that is technologically inferior to no other using security measures that are weaker than those of neighboring countries?

The real reason probably originates not from foreign soil, but rather from American soil. What our government really fears is that someone will create an encryption system that the U.S. Government can't crack. As a testament to this, the Clipper Chip's failure to become reality was due to the government wanting to have total access to the keys that were to be used to provide the encryption. A statement made by the director of the FBI suggests that without knowledge of the keys, effective surveillance against wiretapping and drug trafficking would be severely hampered.

The current U.S. export controls are designed to prevent the acquisition of cryptographic systems that are difficult to crack. The Export Administration Regulations (EAR) and the International Traffic in Arms Regulations (ITAR) govern the export of encryption software. Of the two regulations, ITAR is the more stringent. The ITAR regulations deny export of all cryptographic software that is as strong or stronger than DES. Only those products that lack the capability of being adapted for encryption or are designed for the banking industry are given export rights.

Even with the severe limitations placed on cryptographic software by the ITAR, software with strong encryption is routinely shipped overseas, primarily through the use of e-mail.

**ON THE WEB**

**http://www.bsa.org** See the Business Software Alliance's home page for more information.

Software developers in the U.S. should be aware that under existing export law, products that derive security from third-party providers (such as RSA) or implement encryption on their own are export-controlled. Developers must file a Commodity Jurisdiction Request (CJR) with the State Department to obtain export approval.



# Using Digital Signing

Digital signing verifies the software publisher and the software, guaranteeing that the software code has not been tampered with in any way. Users can then be confident that the code will not harm their systems.

## Digital Signatures

A digital signature is a fixed-length binary data stream that is attached to the data to be signed. It can be used with all types of digital data, the most common type at this time being software. Digital signatures are not limited to code, however. They can be used on passwords, e-mail, or electronic documents. Functions of digital signatures include:

- Preventing your original documents from being tampered with or altered
- Preventing people from distributing fraudulent messages in your name
- Providing proof that you are the original author of a document

Digital signatures make use of Public-Key algorithms designed to work with a key pair.

Because of the one-to-one relationship that exists between the Public and Private Keys, data encrypted with the Private Key can be decrypted only with the Public Key. This enables the sender of a message to encrypt it by using the sender's Private Key. Any recipient can determine that the message came from the sender by decrypting the message using the sender's Public Key.

For example, Alice can encrypt a message with her Private Key and transmit it to Bob. When Bob decrypts the message using Alice's Public Key, he can be sure that the message could only have been encrypted by using Alice's Private Key.

The digest is a one-way encryption of the document. The encrypted document is signed instead of the document itself. The encryption algorithm is smart enough to determine if any changes have been made to the original data. This can be determined by applying the encryption routine again to determine if the digest has changed. If the signed encryption matches the recipient's encryption, the recipient can be sure that the message was not changed after the message digest was generated.

For example, Alice creates the digest of a financial statement and encrypts it with her Private Key, obtaining a digital signature for the message. She transmits both the message and the digital signature to Bob. When Bob receives the message, he computes the message digest of the financial statement and decrypts the digital signature with Alice's Public Key. If the two values match, Bob knows that the message was signed using Alice's Private Key and that it has not changed since it was signed.

## Digital Signing with Java

One of the new security enhancements available in JDK1.1 is javakey. Javakey is provided by Sun as a command-line tool to generate digital signatures for archive files. An additional benefit of javakey is its capability to manage a database of keys and certificates that are deemed to be "trustworthy." Certificates are digital signatures that verify the integrity of your code. These digital signatures are provided by organizations that have, through public acceptance, become trustworthy. We will take a look at certificates in greater detail in the section "Examining Other Security Technologies." The syntax for javakey is:

```
Javakey [options]
```

To create a certificate, you first need to supply a directive file that contains the following information:

- *Information about the issuer* Who's signing the certificate
- *Information about the subject* The Public Key being referred to in the certificate

- *Information about the certificate* Includes the issuer and the length of time the certificate is valid
- *Name of the file to store a copy of the certificate* Optional

To create a certificate, you will need to use the -gc option and give it a name of a directive file such as:

```
javakey -gc mydirectivefile
```

**NOTE** A directive file is a text file that contains various information about you and the certificate. You can find a sample directive file on the Java security site at **http:/www.microsoft.com/workshop/java/cab-f.htm/**.

At this point, you will create a certificate using information provided by the directive file.

# Password Authentication Methods

Before we look at some of the methods for password authentication, we must first define what authentication means with respect to the transfer of information over networks and the Internet.

Authentication enables the recipient of a digital signal to have confidence in the integrity of the sender and the message. Authentication protocols can be based on either conventional Private-Key encryption systems such as DES or on Public-Key systems like RSA. Authentication in Public-Key systems uses digital signatures.

## Clear Text

Clear text, sometimes known as plaintext, is the original data of an encrypted message. After the message has been encrypted, it is then referred to as a ciphertext. Ciphertext is the encrypted data that is the primary target of any attacks.



## Kerberos

*Kerberos* is a third-party authentication protocol designed for UNIX TCP/IP networks. A Kerberos service, sitting on the network, acts as a trusted arbitrator. Kerberos provides secure network authentication, giving a user access to different machines on the network. Kerberos is based on symmetric cryptography. It shares a different secret key with every entity on the network, and knowledge of the secret key is proof of identity.

Kerberos works on a principle of *tickets*. A ticket is essentially a unique string of data that is used to identify a user to other users for the purpose of establishing secure communications. It is possible to embed these tickets into any network protocol.

In real world use, Kerberos is used primarily for TELNET or FTP communications to provide host-based security. It has also been used in less frequent installations in which authentication of a data stream is required.

The Kerberos authentication service was originally developed at MIT for Project Athena. Since then, the UNIX software has been put in the public domain and can be used by anyone. The Kerberos model is based in part on Needham and Schroeder's third-party protocol and on modifications by Denning and Sacco.

**ON THE WEB**

**ftp://athena-dist.mit.edu/pub/kerberos** Kerberos is free for download from the Kerberos site.

## Challenge and Response

On every Windows NT-based network, there is a NETlogon service, the primary job of which is to facilitate communication among systems. Part of that communication process is *passthrough authentication*. Passthrough authentication requires that there be a secure communications channel between each of the NETlogon services. After this is confirmed and before the systems give any information to one another, they perform a handshake called Challenge and Response, which validates the authenticity of the originating systems and determines whether or not the existing communication channels are secure.

## Microsoft's NT Domain Authentication

As soon as the connection to a remote site is determined to be secure by the NETlogon process, NT performs domain-name validation. This validation is performed in one of the following ways:

- Storage of passwords in the SAM Database
- User Authentication by the MSV1_0 Authentication package

**SAM Database** When first logging on to an NT server, you need to specify a username and password and then fill in the domain name field. The domain name and your user profile are stored in the *security accounts manager database (SAM)*. The SAM database contains two records for each user: the LAN manager password and the Windows NT password. Both passwords are stored with two forms of encryption in the SAM database. The first form of encryption is a one-way hash of the clear text that is considered to be non-decryptable. The second form of encryption is performed on the user's ID. Anyone who has access to the password and the algorithm can decrypt this ID.

**NT's Authentication Package** The *local security administrator (LSA)* is the manager of all of NT's authentication services. The LSA is actually an API that invokes the native MSV1_0.dll authentication package. The MSV1_0.dll package, located in the system32 directory of the system, is actually split into two portions. The top portion executes on the system that you are connected to (the local system). The bottom portion executes on the system containing the desired domain SAM database (the remote system). In the case of a local logon, both halves operate on the same system. The top half will encrypt the plaintext password and pass it on to the lower half. Upon receipt of the password, the lower half checks the SAM database to verify the existence of the password. If a match is found at this point, the logon request is granted.

If for some reason a match is not found, an error message will be displayed requesting that you confirm your password and user logon.

Upon acceptance of the password, the SAM database returns an identifier containing the rights associated with the logon ID to the lower half of MSV1_0. At that point, the lower half passes the ID on to the LSA. Upon receipt of the identifier, the LSA creates a token containing all rights that then is attached to the process initiated on the workstation.

# Using Encryption with Visual J++

One of the most enticing features of Java is its capability to automatically download and run platform-independent code without so much as a second thought.

With the exciting benefits of Java, however, come some dangers. It is critical that Java performs these tasks in a secure fashion—something that its designers tried to ensure.

It has become increasingly difficult to find a Java article or posting that does not address the issues of Java and security. Early in 1996, several reports surfaced that a security hole in Java had been uncovered. Sun Microsystems quickly released an update to Java that has quelled those fears for now. In this section, we will look at the issues concerning Java and security.

## Dangers of Not Encrypting

Nothing in life is completely secure, and Java is no exception. The risks associated with unsecured data transmission include:

- *Eavesdropping on sensitive electronic messages* This can include e-mail, Private Keys, passwords, and normal data such as financial information.
- *The capability to reroute the transmission of data* This occurs when a Private Key is compromised. A hacker with a Private Key could intercept a private message and send it to another location.
- *The distribution of viruses* Viruses can be distributed fairly easily on unsecured electronic transmissions.
- *The compromise of passwords* Attackers can easily intercept unencoded password information.



As the popularity of the Web increases, the probability of these dangers occurring increases. Possibly the greatest danger to unencrypted electronic data is the opportunity for eavesdropping. All unencrypted data, whether it be e-mail or credit card information, has the potential to be rerouted into the wrong hands.

In the not so distant past, the thought of encrypting data was reserved for governments and the Mission Impossible team. Today, with a growing population of Internet users, the need to encrypt is becoming a reality. Add to this the growing number of private networks that are currently attached to the Internet, and you begin to see the real potential for harm.

## Java Security Manager

One way that Java prevents attacks is through the use of the *Security Manager*. The Security Manager is an application-wide object, the main role of which is to prevent potentially damaging attacks. The Security Manager acts very much like a store security guard for each Java application.

The Security Manager is an abstract class in the java.lang package. The Java runtime does not automatically create a Security Manager for every Java application. As a result, an application using the default settings will not hinder those operations that might be prevented by including the Security Manager. To change this default setting, an application must create and install its own security manager.

**NOTE** On startup, existing applet viewers such as Netscape do create their own Security Managers. You are limited, however, to whatever security restrictions have been set by the existing Security Manager.

You can return the current Security Manager object for an application using the `getSecurityManager()` method:

```
SecurityManager appsm = System.getSecurityManager();
```

At this point, you have the capability to select the options that will be active, illustrated by the following code. The `System.exit()` method uses the Security Manager's `checkexit()` method to approve the exit operation:

```
SecurityManager security= system.getSecurityManager();
if (security !=null)
  security.checkexit(status);
}
...
// balance of code if checkedExit() returns
```

If the Security Manager approves the exit operation, the `checkexit()` returns normally; otherwise, the `checkexit()` performs a `SecurityException`. In this way, the Security Manager can control a potentially damaging operation before it is completed.

## Public Domain Utilities

There are several public domain utilities on the Web that perform any number of encryption routines for Java, one of which is *Systemics*. Systemics has recently released version 2.01 of their *Cryptix library*. The Cryptix library is a library of cryptographic classes for Java, one of the key features of which is support for Pretty Good Privacy (PGP). At the time of this writing, the library was still undergoing improvements. Systemics recommends that you use the earlier 1.1 version if you need to have a stable environment. Some of the key features of their Cryptix 1.1 library are:

- A class for all block ciphers
- A DES block cipher
- A class encapsulating MD5 hashes

- A class encapsulating SHA hashes
- An RSA Public Key
- A class for generating RSA public/secret key pairs

**ON THE WEB**

**http://www.systemics.com** Systemics can be reached on their Web site. They also maintain a Cryptix mailing list at **majordomo@systemics.com**.

# Examining Other Security Technologies

You can implement security for your Java/J++ applications in other ways as well. In this section, you will examine some new and updated protocols to secure your Java applications, some of which are still in the early stages of development.

## Certificates

A certificate is a collection of data that uniquely identifies an entity, such as a person or a company. The certificate, issued by the *Certification Authority (CA)* only after the verification process is complete, includes the Public Key of the certificate owner.

**Certification Authorities(CA)** are persons or organizations that have gained a general public trust and approval. Some organizations that currently qualify as CAs are VeriSign, GE, and Microsoft. The main duties of a Certification Authority are to:

- Publish the criteria for granting certificates
- Grant certificates if an applicant meets the published criteria

Applicants for a commercial software publishing certificate must meet the criteria described in Table 13.1.

**Table 13.1 Criteria for a Corporate Certificate**

| Criteria | Description |
|---|---|
| Identification | Applicants must submit proof of identity. This could be either a personal presence or registered credentials. |
| The Contract | Applicants must sign a contract stating that they will not distribute software that contains or might contain viruses or has the potential to cause harm to a user's computer or code. |
| Dun & Bradstreet approval | Applicants must maintain a certain level of financial stability. This stability is identified as a D-U-N-S number. This rating indicates that the corporation is a business in good standing. A provision is made for those corporations that do not have a rating. |
| Security of Private Keys | Applicants must agree to generate and store their Private Keys by using a dedicated hardware solution, such as a smart card. |

Applicants for an individual software publishing certificate need to meet only the identification and the contract portions of the requirements for issuance of a certificate. In all cases, there is a fee ranging from a few dollars for individuals to several hundred dollars for corporations.

The value of the certificate is not the certificate itself, but what it represents. The certificate enables a software vendor to provide a level of security to the users about the code in question. Users value the assurance that the code has not been tampered with and that the publisher stands behind it.

**X.509 Certificate** After successfully completing either one of the two types of the application processes, you will be issued the X.509 certificate. The information contained within the certificate is described in Figure 13.4.

**FIG. 13.4**
The X.509 certificate contains information about the person or company holding the certificate.

| | |
|---|---|
| Version: | 0 (0x0) |
| Serial Number: | 0 (0x0) |
| Signature Algorithm: | md5withRSAencryption |
| Issuer: | |
| Valid from: | Jan 01 14:00:00 1997 GMT |
| Valid to: | Jan 01 14:00:00 2001 GMT |
| Commercial usage: | Yes |
| Individual usage: | No |
| Subject: | |
| Subject Public Key info | |
| Subject Public Key Algorithm: | rsaEncryption |
| Signature Algorithm: | |

The most visible applications of the X.509 certificate are in Web browsers that support the SSL protocol. In addition, several e-mail standards such as PEM and S/MIME use the X.509 certificates. Figure 13.5 shows what an actual certificate looks like as viewed from a Web browser.

## PCT

Today, regular users of the Internet are inundated with products and services that can be purchased over the Web. We also have numerous ways to use the Internet for electronic commerce, some of which include:

- *Home Banking* The capability to conduct personal bank transactions from the comfort of home. This includes the capability to make electronic fund transfers and to view account balances for your personal account.

- *Consumer Purchasing via the Internet* The Internet enables users to buy a wide range of good and services over the Internet. These services range from picture processing to the purchasing of automobiles.
- *Electronic funds transfer* This includes the capability to purchase shares of stock with money transferred from users' virtual checking accounts in their virtual bank accounts.

**FIG. 13.5**
This is an actual X.509 certificate as viewed in a Web browser.

With all of these methods for sending money over the Internet, transaction security is vital. One protocol that promises to provide this security is *Private Communications Technology.*

Private Communications Technology (PCT) is a specification that Microsoft created in the fall of 1995, the goal of which was to provide secure communications between client and server applications. A major part of the specification provides for authentication of the server and, optionally, for the client. The PCT specification is based on the assumption that there is a stable and reliable transport protocol (TCP/IP) for transmitting and receiving data on networks and on the Internet.



The protocol is a security protocol designed to provide secure transmissions of data over the Internet. This protocol provides some of the same basic functionality as Server-Side Includes (SSIs)—it prevents users from snooping through data involved in the following:

- *Communications security* The capability to encrypt communications will provide protection against anyone eavesdropping on the network.
- *Financial transaction privacy* Only those sites or individuals authorized to receive data will be able to read it.
- *Authentication* This can be thought of as ensuring that all communications appearing to be from a single person have actually originated from that person and have not been altered in the transmission process.

Although in the early stages of development, the specification has already gained support from such companies as CyLink Corp., FTP Software, Netmanage, and RSA Data Security, among many others. The specification attempts to solve several of the issues in Secure Sockets Layer (SSL) by using technology developed for Secure Transaction Technology (STT).

The PCT specification is significantly stronger than the current key limitations imposed by the U.S. Government. This increased resistance to attacks is derived through the separation of authentication from encryption. Even with this new feature, the new PCT specification is still backward-compatible with SSL. This is good news for all of those application developers who have created applications designed to use SSL as their security protocol.

Essentially, PCT 1.0 is a Dynamic Link Library (DLL) for MS Information Server running under Windows NT 4.0. Microsoft offers no support for the use of the specification. According to Microsoft, you will also need RSAref and RC4 available from RSA Data Security, Inc., at **http://www.rsa.com**.

## Licensing Issues for PCT

Unlike other software that is marketed over the Internet, three very important conditions apply when obtaining a license for PCT.

- Any person who fills out the form must be a citizen of the United States or Canada.
- An application form must be completed.
- Microsoft will send the software to you via courier. All this is done because PCT 1.0 is classified as "munitions" under the International Traffic in Arms Regulations (ITAR,22CFR 120-130). As a result, if you want to export this software outside of the United States, especially in machine-readable form, you will need to obtain a special permit from the U.S. State Department, Office of Defense Trade Controls.

**ON THE WEB**

The version currently available in source code is the version of PCT 1.0 (Beta), which can be downloaded free from:

**http://sectest.microsoft.com/pct10/pct10regf.htm**

This link will take you to the Distribution Request Form page, which Microsoft requires you to complete before downloading the source code. This software is provided free of charge.

## PFX

*Personal Information Exchange* (PFX) is a recent protocol introduced by Microsoft that attempts to provide secure storage and transport of personal information. Although currently only the specification is available, this protocol is promised to be in a future release of Internet Explorer.

The basic premise behind the protocol is that a user has a right to his personal information, such as Private Keys, certificates, password, and so on. The user also should have the freedom to transfer this information to any computer system desired. Finally, the user should not be concerned that the information will be compromised as a result of this transfer.

For example, Bob wants to take out a personal loan from his bank. His bank is closed, however, so he proceeds to use the bank's loan kiosk to complete the transaction. During the process, Bob needs to supply several pieces of private information, such as his SSN and bank account number. Upon approval of the loan, Bob is given a Private Key that enables his savings account to receive the amount of the loan he was approved for.

In this example, PFX will provide protection from eavesdropping on the Private-Key exchange and any certificate information that Bob or the bank uses. PFX also provides protection services while the information entered by Bob on the kiosk is transferred to his bank's computer system.

The ultimate goal for PFX is to provide multiple platforms and applications with the capability to enable a user to import, export, and use a single set of personal identity information at any time and in any place.

The PFX protocol is actually two separate protocols working together. The first of the protocols supports the direct transfer of personal information under several privacy and integrity levels. The highest level requires per-platform, trusted Public Keys dedicated to PFX. The base level supports lower security, password-based privacy, and integrity modes for those cases in which trusted PFX Public Keys are not available. In the case of password-based protection, the standard also supports such devices as smart cards for the transport of passwords.

The second of the protocols supports implicit transport of keys by regenerating them on any machine in which they are needed. This standard permits generation of asymmetric Private Keys without revealing information to servers or eavesdroppers. This protocol supports key recovery and advanced logon protocols. This standard could find its way into security systems for computers. Sensitive data could be stored in smart cards, or security could be implemented via PCMCIA (Personal Computer Memory Card International Association) devices.

At this time, the PFX standard enables test and pilot implementations only. The PFX standard is currently awaiting inclusion in PKCS #12 by RSA Data Security, Incorporated. It has also been proposed to the World Wide Web Consortium (W3C).

## Secure Sockets Layer



Secure Sockets Layer was developed by Netscape Communications. The current version (3.0) was jointly developed by Netscape Communications and Consensus Development.

Some of the basic functions that SSL protocol was designed to accomplish are:

- Server authentication
- Privacy through encryption
- Data integrity

The SSL protocol is essentially a layer on top of the typical protocol such as HTTP, Telnet, FTP, Gopher, and NNTP. The SSL protocol is positioned above the TCP/IP connection protocol.

This placement enables SSL to operate independently of other Internet protocols. With an SSL implementation residing on both the client and the server, electronic commerce can be easily transmitted in an encrypted form, thereby protecting the data from eavesdroppers.

Secure Sockets first gained widespread public exposure with SSL version 2.0. This version answered a lot of issues about security on the Internet. As the protocol began to receive exposure and competition, some of the cracks in the SSL dike started to leak. In response to the public need for increased security for credit card transactions and increased competition, version 3.0 of the protocol was released in the summer of 1996. Currently, there are well over 100 different servers and clients that support the various implementations of SSL. The newest release of SSL answers a lot of the issues that were plaguing the release of the previous version.

One of the primary security holes in version 2.0 that has been changed in version 3.0 involves encryption. The issue centered around the capability for an attacker to edit lists of cybersuite preferences in certain messages. This type of activity forced both the client and the server to use a less secure form of encryption. In version 3.0, this type of attack will now be ineffectual due to modifications made to handshake messaging.

Some of the improvements that have been made to the newest version include the following:

- A handshake routine can be initiated at any time, even in an open session, enabling the change of keys at any time.
- The client and server can now send chains of certificates, enabling the use of certificates that are more than two levels deep.
- SSL version 3.0 now supports the capability to use a number of different protocols for key exchange.
- Support for record compression and decompression now exist.

A significant feature in version 3.0 is backward-compatibility. An SSL 3.0 server now has the capability to recognize a version 2.0 client. When this happens, the version 3.0 server will use version 2.0 handshaking. This same type of backward-compatibility exists when a version 3.0 client recognizes a version 2.0 server.

As is true with most security protocols, SSL is virtually impossible to detect as it performs its duties of authentication and encryption of data. There are, however, a few ways to determine its presence, especially if you use Netscape Naviagator version 3.0. Netscape Navigator will replace **http://** with **https://** in the URL field if you are receiving secure documents. Another way to determine whether or not the document has security is to examine the doorkey located on the bottom left of the navigator window. If the doorkey is solid, security is in place. If the doorkey is broken, the document is insecure. In addition, color on the key and banner will change from blue to gray when security is in effect. This change is so slight, however, that you might not notice it.

Although SSL was designed to provide security on the Internet, it is not necessarily the perfect solution for every situation. Some of the perceived flaws of the SSL protocol include:

- Authentication is needed at the application layer in the long term.
- SSL requires a new proxy protocol.
- There is no way to obtain a vendor-signed receipt.

- Certificate handling is more easily accomplished with S-HTTP.
- The cost of a commercial license is high.
- Certificates must be used.

These perceptions have fueled continued expansion in Internet security, with a growing number of companies trying to build the perfect security protocol. Although SSL might not be perfect, it has done something not many other protocols have: SSL has created a benchmark that other protocols must either emulate or improve upon to be accepted by consumers.

## Licensing Issues for SSL

SSL is available as a reference implementation called SSLRef. SSLRef contains a library in ANSI C that can be compiled and linked into an application program. The code can be compiled for a Windows or UNIX platform and linked into TCP/IP application programs.

**ON THE WEB**

The SSLRef can be downloaded from

**http://http://wwwus.netscape.com/eng/us-current/**

The SSLRef 3.0 distribution is licensed for noncommercial use. If you plan to use the SSLRef in a commercial implementation, the one-time license fee is approximately $30,000.

Anyone who wants to use the reference implementation of SSL must meet the following qualifications:

- Any person who fills out the form must be a citizen of the United States or Canada.
- An application form must be completed.
- SSLRef 3.0 cannot be exported, nor can any applications using SSLRef be exported because SSLRef 3.0 is classified as "munitions" under the International Traffic in Arms Regulations (ITAR,22CFR 120-130). As a result, if you want to export this software outside of the United States, especially in machine-readable form, you will need to obtain a special permit from the U.S. State Department, Office of Defense Trade Controls.



**ON THE WEB**

The SSLRef does not include the RSA license needed to perform cryptographic functions. If you need this license, you can obtain it from RSA at:

**http://www.rsa.com**

You might also want to contact Consensus Development at

**http://www.consensus.com/rsaref/**

for information about their BSAFE license.

# SET

*Secure Electronic Transactions* (*SET*) is a technical specification that describes the process of protecting the security of credit card transactions over the Internet. SET was jointly developed by Microsoft and Visa with support from IBM, Netscape, GTE, VeriSign, and other technology companies. The SET specification incorporates specially developed encryption technology from RSA Data Security Systems.

In addition to providing a high level of security for credit card transactions over the Internet, the SET specification also provides a method for positively identifying merchants to the purchaser. This authentication procedure will help reduce fraud and chargebacks.

The SET specification is actually the combined result of two separate specifications that were developed independently of each other. SET started life as Secure Transaction Technology (STT) and Secure Electronic Payment Process (SEPP). Thanks to the efforts of Microsoft, a combined specification (SET) was finalized in 1996. This combined specification was later submitted to more than 76 countries for a 30-day comment period. As a result of this comment period, the SET specification is evolving even further.

The SET specification is currently undergoing several tests designed to answer concerns and questions raised during the comment period. Upon completion of the testing, the specification will be available to the general development community in 1997. The SET specification has been broken into three distinct components:

- A business description
- A protocol description
- A programmer's guide

**ON THE WEB**

**http://www.set.com** These three components are available for download from the SET Web page.

SET uses Public Keys that are distributed via certificates signed by well known certification authorities (CAs). Provisions are made so that cardholders, merchants, and payment gateways can verify the certification authorities and root keys recognized by their software. The following encryption algorithms are used in SET:

- RSA asymmetric (Public Key) is an encryption algorithm for digital signatures and digital envelopes. Signatures are based on the PKCS#7 RSA with SHA-1 algorithm.
- Data Encryption Standard (DES) is the default symmetric key algorithm used in SET to protect sensitive financial data.
- Commercial Data Masking Facility (CDMF) is another symmetric-key algorithm used for protecting the acquirer-to-cardholder messages.

## From Here...

In this chapter, you explored some ways to provide security for your Java/J++ applications and looked at some exciting new security protocols and what their impact could be on your applications. You concluded your tour of security issues with a look at some of the protocols that promise to raise the bar for security on Java-based applications.

If you would like to continue your tour of the topics and technologies discussed in this chapter, you might want to visit the following Web sites.

For Java security, try:

- **http://ww.javasoft.com**
- **http://www.javasoft.com/products/jdk**
- **http://java.sun.com/sfaq**
- **http://www.microsoft.com/workshop/java/cab-f.htm/**

For Personal Information Exchange (PFX), try:

- **http://www.microsoft.com/intdev/security/pfx**

For Secure Electronic Transactions (SET), try:

- **http://www.visa.com**

For Secure Sockets Layer (SSL), try:

- **http://www.microsoft.com/intdev/security/**
- **http://www.consensus.com/security/ssl-talk-faq.html**
- **http://microsoft.com/InfoServ/Samples/Tour/ssl.htm**
- **http://home.netscape.com/eng/ssl3/ssl-toc.html**

For Personal Communications Technology (PCT), try:

- **http://www.microsoft.com/intdev/security/**

For Kerberos, try:

- **ftp://athena-dist.mit.edu/pub/kerberos**
- **http://www.ov.com/misc/krb-faq.html**
- **http://pscinfo.psc.edu/~studarus/Kerberos**

For General Security Information, try:

- **http://www.rsa.com**
- **http://www.verisign.com**
- **http://tsunami.tig.com/tig/html/standard.html**
- **http://webcompare.iworld.com/compare/security.shtml**

CHAPTER 14

# Dealing with Disaster Before It Happens

**Discover how to use transactions to ensure that your operations all succeed**

Transactions are key to making sure that all or none of your work applies against key database tables. Find out how to use transactions and how they help ensure that your database is updated correctly, even in times of hardware failures.

**See how to use Replication**

Replication gives you the tools to make sure your information is up-to-date at different locations, all without your intervention. Find out how to set up publications and subscriptions to dispense information from one SQL Server to other ODBC data sources.

**Learn how to implement a backup strategy that works**

Backups are a requirement for any important application. The information presented in this chapter will explain how to do both automated and manual backups of your SQL Server, as well as show you how to apply those backups in times of need.

Building database-based applications adds a new level of responsibility to your applications—a responsibility to the user. This is due to the fact that you're maintaining the information that users enter and update. You have the responsibility for making sure that information posted to the system is complete and that it hits the database tables that it needs to impact, preferably with as little client-side intervention as possible.

That's where this chapter comes in. Two key features make it possible for you to add functionality to the processing of database information and give your users that added level of assurance in their applications. These features are transaction processing and database replication. ■

**NOTE** You should also make sure that you're familiar with database backup and restore procedures. These are key in making your system as fault-tolerant as possible. For information on SQL Server administration issues, see Que's *Special Edition Using SQL Server 6.5, Second Edition.*

# Understanding Transactions and Rollbacks

A good understanding of transactions and locking is essential if you want to write database applications for more than one user. Even single-user applications require some understanding of locking, although the impact of locking your own system is not nearly as drastic as that of locking an enterprise network of hundreds of users.

SQL Server offers the programmer several different styles of locking. This chapter provides you with the information that you need to accurately assess what your application requires in terms of transaction control and locking.

As a programmer, you should always concentrate on minimizing the amount of locking that occurs so that you decrease the chances of users interfering with one another. Table 14.1 outlines the basics of a transaction, whether imposed implicitly by SQL Server or explicitly by your application.

**Table 14.1 The ACID Requirements for Transactions**

| Requirement | Description |
|---|---|
| Atomicity | A transaction is assumed to be complete or incomplete. Although this requirement seems obvious, it's important to understand that either all or none of the transaction becomes final. For example, if you're posting a transfer of funds from one account to another, the funds are deposited into the target account and they are removed from the original account, as in a commit, or nothing happens at all, as in an abort. |
| Consistency | A transaction should "leave things as it found them." In other words, when a transaction starts, the system is in a known state. When a transaction commits, the system must once again be in a known, consistent state. You cannot leave anything hanging from a transaction; it must be a full and complete operation. Of course, by definition, an aborted transaction also fulfills these requirements because it reverts to the state of the system prior to opening the transaction. |
| Isolation | Transactions must stand alone and have no effect or dependence on other transactions. Dependence on another transaction causes deadlocks, resulting in rollback operations. This attribute is also known as *serializability.* |
| Durability | As soon as it is completed, the transaction's objective has been met and there is no further reason for the operation to be undone. In other words, as soon as a transaction is completed, it remains completed even if |

| Requirement | Description |
|---|---|
| | something happens to the system. Typically, this is the reason for wrapping an important operation in one large transaction, ensuring that all or nothing applies to the database tables. |

A transaction does not enforce these rules in and of itself. Instead, you must keep these requirements in mind. You should strive to meet each of these objectives for each transaction that you create, without exception. If an operation doesn't measure up to the ACID test, don't continue coding until the operation meets the requirements. You won't be sorry later.

# Defining Transactions

A *transaction* is a logical unit of work that you want the SQL Server to perform for you. That unit of work can include one or many SQL statements, if you appropriately define the unit of work to the server by delineating which statements within a batch are part of a transaction.

In ISQL (Interactive SQL), you can execute single-statement transactions by entering their text and typing **go**. Single-statement transactions are ideal if the required results are simple and self-contained. For example, the following statement returns a list of tables from the database currently being used:

```
Select      *
From  SYSOBJECTS
Where TYPE = 'U'  /* user-defined tables */
Order By NAME
```

In some instances, however, you must do more than one thing in a transaction and conditionally undo it if something goes wrong. In such cases, multistatement transactions come into play. Such transactions enable you to combine two or more SQL statements and send them to the server for processing. You can also define an event that undoes any work submitted. Listing 14.1 shows an example of a multistatement transaction.

**Listing 14.1 An Example of a Multistatement Transaction**

```
Create Table TABLE_A(
      X     smallint null,
      Y     smallint null)
Go
Create Table TABLE_B(
      Z     smallint null)
Go

Begin Tran
      Update      TABLE_A
      Set   X = X + 1
      Where       Y = 100

      Update TABLE_B
      Set   Z = Z + 1
```

continues

Part V Ch 14

**Listing 14.1 Continued**

```
        If @@rowcount = 0 or @@error !=0 /* no rows where hit by our update */
        Begin
              Rollback Tran
              Print 'Error occurred, no rows were updated'
              Return
        End
Commit Tran
```

**TIP** To make your scripts and stored procedures easier to read, format them with indented sections within transaction blocks.

**CAUTION**

You can also set up SQL Server to start transactions automatically when certain operations are performed. You shouldn't use this technique in a production environment, because in such environments it is better to have your application declare explicit transactions. However, the IMPLICIT_TRANSACTIONS option can be helpful in a development or testing environment because you can let the system attempt to manage the transactions for you. You set this option with the SET statement as follows:

```
set IMPLICIT_TRANSACTIONS ON ¦ OFF
```

If you set IMPLICIT, you still must issue corresponding COMMIT statements. Otherwise, the transactions remain open and can bog down, if not lock up, your system. You should not use this option in a production environment. Instead, set your transactions explicitly in your routines.

After you set up SQL Server, the following operations automatically begin transactions:

- ALTER TABLE
- CREATE
- DELETE
- DROP
- FETCH
- GRANT
- INSERT
- OPEN
- REVOKE
- SELECT
- TRUNCATE TABLE
- UPDATE

## Limitations on Transactions

Within a transaction, you cannot perform certain actions. These are general actions that you cannot undo, at least not without significant repercussions to major components of the system. Keep in mind that transactions are meant to protect groups of processing statements, not so much to back up the management of your system. If you want to protect yourself from a potential system-damaging change, consider dumping the database and transaction log prior to the operation that you want to perform.

The following actions are not allowed within a transaction:

- Altering a database
- Creating a database
- Creating an index
- Creating a procedure
- Creating a table
- Creating a view
- Initializing a disk
- Dropping
- Dumping a transaction
- Granting
- Loading a database
- Loading a transaction
- Reconfiguring
- Revoking
- SELECTing into
- Truncating a table
- Updating statistics
- Performing `sp_dboption` or other procedures that modify the master database

**NOTE** A new type of transaction enables you to distribute transactions. The Distributed Transaction Coordinator controls such transactions. This type of transaction is quite useful for transactions that occur at remote locations but that affect centralized inventory levels.



## Optimistic versus Pessimistic Locking

When you write multiuser database applications, you can take one of two approaches to transaction control: *optimistic* or *pessimistic* locking. Optimistic locking assumes that your application code does nothing to explicitly enforce locks on records while you work on them. Instead, you rely on the database to manage this enforcement on its own while you concentrate on application logic. Pessimistic locking assumes that the application code attempts to enforce some type of locking mechanism.

To implement optimistic locking in your application without having it grind to a halt under excessive locks on the server, you must carefully observe some simple rules:

- Minimize the amount of time that a transaction is held open by limiting the amount of SQL code that occurs within a `BEGIN TRAN...COMMIT TRAN` section.
- Rely on application code to guarantee that updates are hitting the right record instead of holding locks while a user browses data.
- Ensure that all application codes update and select from tables in the same order. This prevents any deadlocks from occurring.

If you assume that SQL Server will manage locking and that you have nothing to worry about, you are taking a *very* optimistic locking approach. Unfortunately, such an approach isn't very pragmatic because it assumes that a programmer or user can do nothing to explicitly cause locking. In fact, many situations can cause a large amount of locking to occur on a server, potentially disabling it for the enterprise that it supports.

## Creating and Working with Transactions

In the "Defining Transactions" section earlier in this chapter, you saw how to delineate a transaction using `BEGIN`, `COMMIT`, and `ROLLBACK`. This section describes SQL Server's keywords or Transact-SQL statements that are required for transaction control.

**CAUTION**

At some point in your code, you must follow each `BEGIN TRAN` with a matching `COMMIT TRAN` or `ROLLBACK TRAN`. Transactions *must* begin and end in pairs; otherwise, the server continues holding locks until the client is disconnected.

**The *BEGIN TRAN* Keyword** When you issue a `BEGIN TRAN` to the database, SQL Server marks the point to return to in the database's transaction logs in the event of a `ROLLBACK TRAN`. `BEGIN TRAN` explicitly tells SQL Server to treat all of the following work, until a `COMMIT` or `ROLLBACK` is encountered, as one logical unit. The work can contain many operations.

You can issue operations that affect a database without a `BEGIN TRAN` statement. You cannot, however, conditionally undo work that you send to the server without indicating the start of the transaction. You call out the start of the transaction with the `BEGIN TRAN` statement so that SQL Server knows the state to which it must return the database.

**NOTE** SQL Server's transaction logs monitor transactions contained within `BEGIN` and `COMMIT` statements. If a media failure occurs before data physically changes on the database, SQL Server recovers or ensures that it applies those changes by "rolling forward" those unapplied transactions to the database the next time that the server is brought back online.

**The *COMMIT TRAN* Keyword** Issuing a `COMMIT TRAN` to the database signals SQL Server that the work succeeded and that you no longer want to group any additional work inside the transaction. By definition, a `COMMIT TRAN` also implies that you've fulfilled the requirements of the ACID test, as presented in Table 14.1.

**The *ROLLBACK TRAN* Keyword** `ROLLBACK TRAN` is SQL Server's equivalent of your favorite word processor's Edit, Undo menu option. Sending a `ROLLBACK` to the database server causes it to undo all the work to the most recent `BEGIN TRAN` statement. Typically, a `ROLLBACK TRAN` is issued during a long transaction if any particular part of it encounters any SQL error.

**CAUTION**

SQL Server enables you to call *remote* stored procedures within a transaction. Because of the nature of the *Remote Procedure Call* (RPC) interface with the other server on which the RPC executed, however, SQL Server cannot roll back any such calls. When writing applications that require RPCs, make sure that you include additional RPCs to undo your previous work programmatically.

## Understanding DDL and Database Statements

As a new feature to SQL Server 6.5, *DDL* (Data Definition Language) and database modification statements are now allowed inside a transaction. The following statements can appear in transactions:

| | | |
|---|---|---|
| `ALTER TABLE` | `CREATE TRIGGER` | `DROP TABLE` |
| `CREATE DEFAULT` | `CREATE VIEW` | `DROP TRIGGER` |
| `CREATE INDEX` | `DROP DEFAULT` | `DROP VIEW` |
| `CREATE PROCEDURE` | `DROP INDEX` | `GRANT & REVOKE` |
| `CREATE RULE` | `DROP PROCEDURE` | `SELECT INTO` |
| `CREATE TABLE` | `DROP RULE` | `TRUNCATE TABLE` |

These statements are important because they enable SQL Server 6.5's new database schema management features to function. Many of these statements modify the table structures on the system or create new ways to access the information.

**TIP** SQL Server does not provide a direct way to drop a table column, but you can work around this omission. Create a new table with the required schema, minus the column, and use the `SELECT INTO` Transact-SQL command to copy the data.



## Using Named Transactions and SavePoints

When you examine large, stored procedures and applications with large bodies of SQL code, the code is inevitably quite unreadable. Such code is text-based and relies heavily on the premise that all programmers work with the same style of format and layout. For this reason, when transactional programming is involved, it becomes even more important to use good indenting to mark blocks of code clearly.

However, even the most careful programmer will find it a nightmare to remember how many indents to roll back out of in the event of an error condition or some programmatic constraint. Named transactions and SavePoints are used for just this purpose—they provide a way to roll back work to a given *named* or *saved* portion of the code that has been executing, even if the portion of code is at a higher nesting level.

**Using Named Transactions** Named transactions provide a convenient way to attach an identifier to a whole body of work. Use named transactions to make it easier to undo large portions of code. To create a named transaction, add the name of the transaction to the `BEGIN TRAN` statement, as shown in Listing 14.2.

**Listing 14.2 Demonstrating How to Add the Transaction's Name to a *BEGIN TRAN* Statement**

```
/* Open outer transaction */
Begin Tran UPDATE_AUTHORS
      Update AUTHORS
      Set    CONTRACT = 1
      Where  AU_ID = '341-22-1782'

      /* Open inner transaction */
      Begin Tran UPDATE_TITLEAUTHOR
            Update TITLEAUTHOR
            Set   ROYALTYPER = ROYALTYPER + 25
            Where AU_ID = '341-22-1782'
            If @@error != 0
            Begin
                  Rollback Tran UPDATE_TITLEAUTHOR
                  Print 'Failed to update Royalties'
                  Return
            End
      Commit Tran UPDATE_TITLEAUTHOR
Commit Tran UPDATE_AUTHORS
```

**NOTE** If you omit the transaction's identifier or name when committing or rolling back a transaction, SQL Server simply undoes the work to the most recent `BEGIN TRAN`, regardless of the transaction's name. When using named transactions, be careful to code all your work consistently, either using names or not, throughout your work. If you do not use a consistent style, programmers might step on each other's transactions inadvertently.

**Using SavePoints** SavePoints are simply another way to perform a named transaction by marking a place in the code at which you can use a ROLLBACK to undo work. To create a SavePoint, issue the following SQL command:

```
SAVE TRANSACTION <TRAN_NAME>
```

You then use only the identifier, *<TRAN_NAME>*, when performing your ROLLBACK, as shown in Listing 14.3.

**Listing 14.3 Performing a *ROLLBACK* with a SavePoint**

```
Begin Tran
      Update AUTHORS
      Set    CONTRACT = 1
      Where  AU_ID = '341-22-1782'

      /* save our work to this point */
      Save Transaction AuthorDone

      Update TITLEAUTHOR
            Set    ROYALTYPER = ROYALTYPER + 25
            Where  AU_ID = '341-22-1782'
      If @@error != 0 Or @@RowCount > 1
      Begin
            /* rollback and exit */
            Rollback Tran AcctDataDone
            Print 'Error occurred when updating TitleAuthor'
            Return
      End
Commit Tran
Print 'Transaction Committed'
```

**CAUTION**

Although the transaction in Listing 14.3 rolls back the UPDATE on TITLEAUTHOR, SQL Server holds locks on the TITLEAUTHOR table until either COMMIT or ROLLBACK completes the entire transaction. This side effect of using a SavePoint can cause an application to lock unexpectedly.

**TIP** If your application seems to hold locks continuously after the first transaction executes, you probably have issued more BEGIN TRANs than you have corresponding COMMIT TRANS or ROLLBACK TRANS.

Remember that you must enclose transactions in pairs of BEGIN and COMMIT or ROLLBACK. If you fail to do so, you tell SQL Server that you want to keep the transaction open longer.

To help identify your code problems, walk through your application and monitor error conditions carefully. Probably an error condition is occurring and some code is returning control before closing an open transaction. Also, check the value of the system variable @@trancount, which indicates how deeply nested in transactions you are.



## Using Serialized Columns Without *IDENTITY*

SQL Server 6.0 introduced a *serial* datatype called the IDENTITY. In this datatype, SQL Server automatically assigns the next sequential value to a column in a table. IDENTITYs are valuable in applications that have a high transaction volume and must identify each record uniquely.

For some applications that must support multiple database back ends and for those applications that require SQL Server 4.x compatibility, you can implement the same kind of feature as an `IDENTITY` column by performing the following steps:

1. Create a table with columns in it to store a table name and the current value.

```
/* create the table */
Create Table Record_IDs(
      Table_Name  varchar(30),
      Current_ID  int)
Go

/* add a primary clustered index */
Create      Unique Clustered Index PK_Record_IDs
      on Record_IDs( Table_Name ) with FILLFACTOR = 1
Go
```

2. Insert into the table some records that correspond to tables in the target database:

```
Insert Record_IDs
      Select   Name,     1
      From   Sysobjects
      Where  Type = 'U' /* user-defined tables */
```

3. Create a stored procedure that has a consistent access interface to the table and locks the table so that no other users can modify the data while a given process is accessing it:

```
Create Procedure up_GetID                   /* up = user procedure */
      @psTableName      varchar(30),              /* p = parameter */
      @rnNewID    int OUTPUT          /* r = receive or output parameter */
As
Declare
      @nSQLError int,
      @nRowCount int

Begin Tran
      /* First update the record to acquire the exclusive lock on the page
*/
      Update Record_IDs
      Set    Current_ID = Current_ID + 1
      Where  Table_Name = @psTableName

      /* Check for errors */
      Select    @nSQLError = @@error,
            @nRowCount = @@rowcount
      If @nSQLError != 0 OR @nRowCount != 1
      Begin
            Rollback Tran
            Return -999 /* failed to update the record correctly */
      End

      /* Select back the value from the table that we've already locked */
      Select      @rnNewID = Current_ID
      From   Record_IDs
      Where  Table_Name = @psTableName

      /* Check for errors */
```

```
        Select      @nSQLError = @@error,
              @nRowCount = @@rowcount
        If @nSQLError != 0 OR @nRowCount != 1
        Begin
              Rollback Tran
              Return -998 /* failed to select record correctly */
        End
Commit Tran
Return 0
Go
```

4. Test the new procedure, as shown next:

```
Declare
      @nRecordID  int,
      @nRC        int,
      @sMsg       varchar(255)

/* Fetch a record ID for use in inserting the new record */
Exec @nRC = up_GetID 'table_A', @nRecordID OUTPUT

If @nRC != 0
      Print 'An error occurred fetching new Record ID'
Else
Begin
      Select @sMsg = 'New Record value is ' + Convert( varchar(4),
@nRecordID )
      Print @sMsg
End
Go
```

**TIP** To create identifying columns, always use the new `IDENTITY` column rather than the `TIMESTAMP` datatype. The `IDENTITY` column is much easier to reference and use in application code and can impose less data overhead if you use a small datatype for it, such as `TINYINT` or `SMALLINT`.

# Using Database Replication

Replication with SQL Server gives you the capability to duplicate information between servers and synchronize information sources for multiple domains, even in cases in which they are physically separated by distance and possibly poor communication links. Replication, at its most fundamental level, recognizes changes made to information in a database and sends these changes to the remote system or systems for their use.

**NOTE** Replication to non-SQL Server databases, other ODBC data sources, is just a matter of setting up the ODBC data source to point to the right destination system. In these cases, where non-SQL Server systems are involved, information can be pushed out to those remote systems, but the remote system cannot serve as a publication server. In other words, they can *receive* information but cannot be the source of replicated information.

For information about testing the ODBC connection, see "Before You Start–Test the Connection" later in this chapter.

Microsoft has employed what is called *loose integration* in its replication model. You might have heard the phrase ***real-enough time*** in systems implementation. Loose integration follows the real-enough time model. This means that information will flow across the system of servers not in real-time and not necessarily in batch mode, but *as quickly as it can.* The phrase real-enough time was first introduced when information was being distributed by e-mail to remote locations. It was certainly not real-time, as no live connection was maintained between sites.

Using e-mail didn't implement a batch approach, as transactions were often still addressed on a transaction-by-transaction basis. With the e-mail system, you're certain that your transactions are going to make it to the destination when a connection is completed between the remote system and yours.

SQL Server synchronizes the database tables, almost immediately in many cases, but not concurrently with the transaction that made the original change that is to be replicated.

Certainly there are pros and cons to this approach. On the positive side, the user of the system will not be waiting for a remote server to respond before the application can continue. This alone can be a big time saver. Another benefit is that the system can manage some fault-tolerance in the queue of things to be done.

If you have a transaction that is going to a remote server and the remote system is down, the transaction can be queued for later processing. The server engine on the local side, the distribution engine, can retry the connection to and the update of, the remote server at regular intervals and make sure the transaction occurs as soon as possible.

A positive side effect of this approach is to consider that, in reality, wide area networks might need to be connected over slow links. Transactions can be handled as quickly as the connection allows, without bogging down applications that might be using the database tables that are to be replicated.

On the negative side, it's possible to have information in two databases using this schema that is out-of-date or different on different sides of the replication equation. With true replication as implemented in SQL Server at this time, out-of date schemas is a situation you cannot control, but might have to address if this presents a problem. Remember, there are limited situations where this might occur, such as if a scheduled connection is unavailable or a server goes down. In either case, as soon as the connection is available, the databases are re-synchronized at the next communication with one other.

**NOTE** If you have multiple databases, tables, or other entities that must be absolutely in sync, you need to work with the two-phase commit capabilities of SQL Server. This entails custom development on your part by using the C API and working with DB-Library. Be sure to review Chapter 11, "Understanding SQL Server and the Internet," for more information about developing applications for use with SQL Server.

There are three different key physical layer components to the SQL replication model: subscriber, publisher, and distributor. Each of these components must be in place to have a functioning replication model.

# Understanding the Difference Between Distributed and Replicated Information

There is a distinct implementation difference between *distributing* your information and *replicating* it. In many installations, you'll probably find that you have both scenarios. When you decide to implement a system based on multiple SQL Servers, you need to be very careful to define what information will reside on which SQL Servers. This sounds obvious, but you need to take it to the next step, which is beyond just determining functional requirements.

In many systems that are disbursed, the requirement to implement replication comes from the desire to have information available at a central location. This requirement, combined with a remote starting location available for the information to be centralized, provides the foundation for a replication scenario.

This is certainly a system that can be automated using the replication capabilities of SQL Server. The primary requirement is that you put a SQL Server at each location and initiate the replication from the remote locations to the central location. Another alternative might be available if you reverse the flow of information shown in Figure 14.1.

**FIG. 14.1**
The basic replication model shows information flowing between different points in your system.

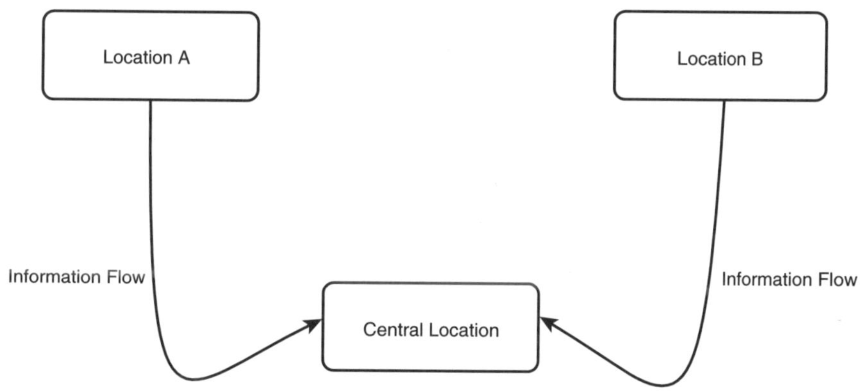


Adding a distributed approach to this scenario might be helpful to enhance your application's performance. Distributed systems, or components of systems, lend themselves to situations that include some or all of the following attributes:

- The information required at each individual location is different and distinct.
- The information from one location does not need to be available, in its most up-to-date form, at other locations. Somewhat aged information, if it's needed at all, must suffice at the alternate locations.
- There is an intelligent agent running at the remote locations, and that agent must be able to respond to basic data request and manipulation requirements, such as copying working sets to a temporary database, and so on.

A good example of a distributed system is a point-of-sale (POS) system. In a POS system, you often have sales information at each individual location, but other locations do not have to have that sales information until it has been posted to a central location, if at all (see Figure 14.2).

**FIG. 14.2**
A typical wide area network point-of-sale system lends itself to a mixed distribution- and replication-based system.

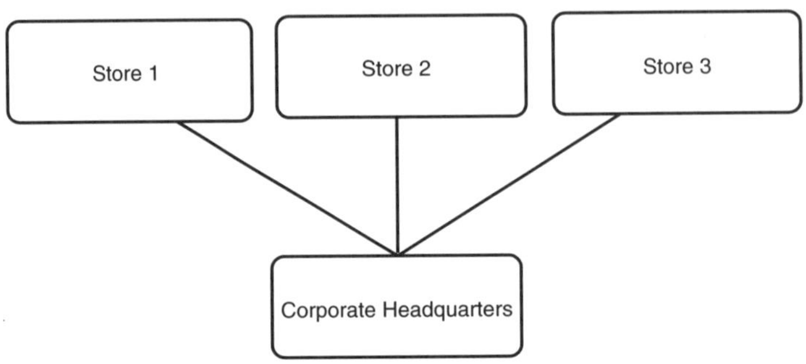


In this configuration, you can see that information flow between the store locations is minimal, and, when it does occur, it's likely to come from the corporate headquarters. Systems such as these lend themselves to both a distributed information approach and a replicated scenario. Keep in mind that replicated information is read-only at the recipient location. You can use the fact that things are read-only to your advantage.

**TIP** SQL Server's replicated tables are read-only on the subscribing system. If replicated tables are needed, you have to either create triggers on the incoming table that insert the replicated information into a working table, or you need to modify your system to use the tables differently, allowing for the read-only nature of the replicated tables.

In our POS example, you can use replication to send all inventory information, including pricing, store inventory levels, and other stores' sales information, to the different remote locations. Because this information is reasonably static, you can use a scheduled exchange of this information rather than a continuous update. You might want to keep this in mind as the process of setting up replication is discussed in the coming sections.

Distributed information can be maintained at the stores. This information includes sales information, customer update information about purchases, credit payments, and so on. You can refer to this as distributed because the stores operate on this information separately from the corporate headquarters. They can create, update, delete, and otherwise manage this information on their own.

**TIP** Using SQL Server to manage distributed information at the remote locations is not a requirement. You can consider using less expensive options if needed. Other databases that use ODBC are key candidates for the remote locations, as they are able to connect most easily to SQL Server later to update the main database systems.

In short, you should use a distributed environment to provide a fault-tolerant, independent system. The information produced under these routines and the routines designed to create the distributed information might or might not be required at the central location. Replicated systems are ideal for information that doesn't change very frequently at the recipients' locations. Keep this in mind as you review the different replication and installation options throughout this chapter.

**NOTE** The processes that make up the replication model are all managed by the SQL Executive service. If you experience problems with replication, you might want to check whether or not the `USERID` and `PASSWORD` used by the SQL Executive are still available and unchanged. You specified these values during the installation process.

# SQL Server Replication Fundamentals

SQL Server's replication features follow a magazine-type analogy to relate the different roles that are parts of the equation. The model follows an *I'll Publish—You Subscribe* approach that's easy to follow and implement. In the next sections, setting up the different options for replication on both sides of the equation is covered.

**NOTE** SQL Server 6.5 has added the capability to replicate to ODBC subscribers, such as Access and Oracle. As stated in the SQL Server documentation, the ODBC subscriber must meet the following criteria:

- Must be ODBC Level 1-compliant
- Must be 32-bit, thread safe, and for the processor architecture—for example, Intel, PPC, MIPS, Alpha—that the distribution process runs on
- Must be transaction-capable
- Must support the Data Definition Language (DDL)
- Cannot be read-only

One last consideration that you might want to be aware of concerns the replication between a SQL Server version 6.5 environment and one running version 6.0 of SQL Server. If you'll be working in a mixed environment such as this, you might want to make sure that the publisher and distributor components are running on the 6.5 server.



In addition, you have to treat the 6.0 server as if it were a standard ODBC data source, which means that you need to set up an ODBC configuration in the control panel. The positive side is that you'll be working around the limitations of the 6.0 replication, and you can use all of the features outlined in this chapter against the downlevel server. This is the same approach you use if you want to replicate to any other non-SQL Server database.

The final step in preparing the downlevel server is installing the sqlole65.sql script. This script makes the replication possible, and it makes it possible to use Enterprise Manager from 6.5 against the 6.0 server.

## Before You Start—Test the Connection

Before you go much further, you need to test your connection to remote servers to make sure that you can connect to them appropriately. Microsoft provides a utility, located in your `BINN` subdirectory on the server, that helps you test the ODBC connection between your server and the remote system.

**TIP** Even if you're not using an ODBC connection directly to work with the other server, as would be the case with a remote SQL Server 6.5 system, it's still a good idea to check your connection with this fast test. It removes a variable should you encounter any problems later.

As you can test a TCP/IP connection with the `PING` utility, you can test an ODBC connection with the `ODBCPING` utility. `ODBCPING` has the following syntax:

```
odbcping [-s servername] [-d dsn] [-u username] [-p password]
```

Although the utility is a command-line, DOS window utility, it provides a solid test of the connection between your servers.

When you run the utility, you can check a direct login by specifying the server name or test a DSN that you've set up by indicating the Datasource (or data set) Name, or DSN. Either way, provide the *username* and *password* for the connection.

When the utility runs, you should receive a message similar to the following:

```
CONNECTED TO SQL SERVER
ODBC SQL Server Driver Version: 02.65.0213
SQL Server Version: Microsoft SQL Server  6.50 - 6.50.201 (Intel X86)
        Apr  3 1996 02:55:53
        Copyright (c) 1988-1996 Microsoft Corporation
```

If you cannot connect successfully, you receive an error message that resembles the following:

```
COULD NOT CONNECT TO SQL SERVER
SQLState: 08001  Native Error: 6
Info. Message: [Microsoft][ODBC SQL Server Driver][dbnmpntw]Specified SQL server
not found.
SQLState: 01000  Native Error: 53
Info. Message: [Microsoft][ODBC SQL Server Driver][dbnmpntw]ConnectionOpen
(CreateFile()).
```

If you cannot connect successfully, check the following:

- Confirm that the remote server is available.

- Make sure that the DSN you've defined for the ODBC connection is a *System DSN*. This means that you should not be able to see it when you first start up the ODBC manager from the control panel.
- Make sure that you've indicated the right server name on the command line for the `ODBCPING` command.
- Make sure the user name you provided exists on the remote server, not just the local server, and that it has permission to log on to the server.

If all else fails, consider re-creating the connection in ODBC and try connecting to the server by using standard network drive mapping conventions. Chances are good that the server is unavailable or the SQL Server process on the remote server has not yet been started.

## Publishing: Providing Information to Other Systems

When you decide to use replication to provide information to other systems, you, in effect, become a publisher. You publish your information for other systems to receive. At the highest level, the information that you provide to other systems is called a ***publication***. Publications consist of ***articles,*** which are the items that are provided to the other systems. Articles are discrete pieces of information that range from the entire contents of a database to a single row or the result of a query. As you'll see later in the chapter, there are several different ways to dissect the information that you'll provide via replication, as follows:

- Entire databases
- Entire tables
- Horizontal partitions of information
- Vertical partitions of information
- Custom views of information

Each of these has its advantages and disadvantages. Which you use depends entirely on what types of information you're replicating and how that information will be used by the remote system.

**NOTE** Any table that you want to replicate must have a unique index defined for it. If you don't have one defined, it will not show up in the list of available tables when you define the publication.

If, after you've installed and configured the necessary components of replication, you have problems, consider the following troubleshooting tips:

- Replication might have been established on a scheduled basis. It might be that you set up the replication to occur, at least for synchronization tasks, during the night or some other off-peak time. Check the publication setup options on the publication server to verify when you expect table synchronization tasks to be performed.
- It's possible that sufficient time has not elapsed since the publication and subscription were set up. By default, synchronization occurs every five minutes. If your table is large,

it can take some time to physically transfer the information to the subscription system, or it might be that the initial five minutes has not yet passed.

- Finally, the connection between the two servers might be down. Check to see that you can otherwise connect to the servers and make sure that they are up, running, and allowing logons. You should also check utilization on the servers. Microsoft recommends 32M of RAM on the publication system. With less RAM, it's possible that you're running into memory constraint issues and that the server is swapping more information than it should have to while performing the operations demanded of it with replication.

**Entire Databases** When you provide entire database articles to the remote system, you are asking SQL Server to monitor all activity for that database and update the users of the information with any changes that occur. This is probably the simplest form of replication to administer, as you're telling SQL Server to send everything.

Keep in mind the basic covenant of replicated tables, though, is that the information is read-only at the recipient. It might be that this would be too restrictive on your system to implement this type of full-blown replication.

**NOTE** If you're creating a *data warehousing* application—one in which you simply provide Snapshot-type information to other locations—this just might be the ticket. In these types of applications, you want to provide a picture of the information at a given time. You can create a database of queriable information, provide it to these remote users, and need not worry about the information being changed. You also can be assured of the most recent and updated information at these locations, as SQL Server will monitor it for you and initiate updates on the schedule that you designate.

The replication of tables and specific partitions of tables is often the way to go when you have a modifiable production environment that you're exporting information to.

**Entire Tables** When you replicate entire tables, you specify a table that is monitored and sent out by the replication engine whenever changes are made. This table is kept up-to-date based on the export timing and criteria that you establish in setting up the publication article.

**NOTE** You can establish more than one article for a given table. This might be helpful if you want to provide all information to a production, administrative server, but only limited information to a reports-only server that is used by non-administrative personnel. Be aware, though, that each publication that you establish requires resources on the server to process the replication event. If possible, consider publishing the table once. After this, you can create a view or other protected viewing mechanism on the receiving server as it works with the client-side software.

**Horizontal and Vertical Partitions of Information** When you publish horizontal partitions, you're using a SELECT statement that provides all columns of information but that is selective on the rows of information that will be considered. For example, consider the following simple SELECT statement:

```
Select * from Authors where au_lname like "W%"
```

This selects only those authors whose last names start with a *W.* These are the authors that are included in published information.

On the other hand, you might want to only publish certain columns of information to the remote system. For example, the Authors table in the Pubs database installed by default with SQL Server includes a Contract field indicating whether or not the author is under contract. If you're replicating a list of authors to a remote location, the users might not need to know whether or not you've established a contract with the author. In that case, you can include all fields except the Contract field in the replication article.

You also can export a combination of a vertical and horizontal partition, or you can replicate the results of a view. The selective replication capabilities of SQL Server are the power behind the tool that really begins to broaden the appeal of replication.

## Subscribing: the Recipients of Information

After you've established what information you'll be publishing with the articles and other information covered earlier, you need to move to the subscription system and let it know where to find the information of which it will be the recipient. The recipient is called the *subscriber* in the replication scenario. The subscriber sets up a connection to the distribution server and receives the information at the intervals that you established when you created the article to be replicated.

Subscriptions include the capability to designate where the information will go, which enables you to control who has access to it by using the standard NT and SQL security capabilities.

## The Log Reader Process

There are two silent partners in the replication process that are always running and performing their tasks, but are much less visible when compared to the subscriber and publisher roles. These are the log reader process and the distribution database.

Replication in SQL Server is transaction log-based. As changes are made to articles that are declared for replication, they show up in the transaction log. The log reader process, an automatic background task on the server, detects these changes and logs them to the distribution server's distribution database.

After a transaction has been processed for replication and placed in the distribution database, the replication engine publishes it and makes it available to the other servers that need it. You can see the log reader process if you look at the running processes in SQL Server. You can see the process in the list of active connections.



**NOTE** If there are any synchronization jobs pending, you also can see those jobs listed in the pending tasks area of the running tasks list.

## Distribution Server: the Source of Information

The distribution server and database serve as the go-between for the publication server and the subscription server. When you set up the system, as you'll see when you go through the installation process, you have the option to set up a local distribution server or a remote system.

Although the distribution database is separate from the other databases in your SQL Server system, it can still be on the same physical server. When you set up a local distribution database on the publication server, SQL Server uses this new database as the mechanism to keep track of the different items that need to be provided to the subscription servers on the network.

The distribution database is also the storage location for the different stored procedures that make up the replication engine. These stored procedures are automatically called when you use replication and are used to automate the different processes that happen under the covers when replication is running.

If you choose to use a remote system as your distribution database, the database is created or referenced on a different server from the publication server. This can be beneficial on a system in which you might have high transaction volumes or might otherwise have a server that is bogged down just in the normal processing of transactions or network requests. In these situations, it can be beneficial to have this other system, the distribution database hosting system, manage the replication of information to the subscription servers.

**CAUTION**

You must have 32M of RAM on the server that will be the distribution system if you combine the distribution and publication operations on a single server. Furthermore, you might have to install additional memory if a given distribution server is to be used by more than one publication server. It might also be beneficial to implement a multi-processor server in cases in which workload on the server is substantial.

You generally won't work directly with the log reader processes or the distribution database, but it's important to understand their functions to correctly set up your system.

# Installing the SQL Server Replication Services

The first step in installing replication is registering the remote server in the Enterprise Manager. There is nothing unique that you need to do to accomplish this, but you must have the server predefined prior to beginning the installation of the replication and subscription services.

**NOTE** When you define servers in the Enterprise Manager, it's important that you select the correct type of security to be installed at each server. Selecting the Trusted Connection indicates that Integrated Security is in use. If you select the standard logon connection, you must specify a user who is a valid user on the remote system and one who has sufficient rights to work with the database tables that you are replicating. If you do not, you'll receive errors when the replication service tries to connect to the remote server.

When you start the replication installation process, one of the first things SQL Server does is verify that you've declared enough memory for SQL Server processes. The minimum required memory allocated to SQL Server is 8196K, or 8M. You set this option in the Server Configuration dialog box, selected from the Server menu's Configurations option, as shown in Figure 14.3.

**FIG. 14.3**
You must have a minimum of 8M allocated to the SQL Server replication features of your system.

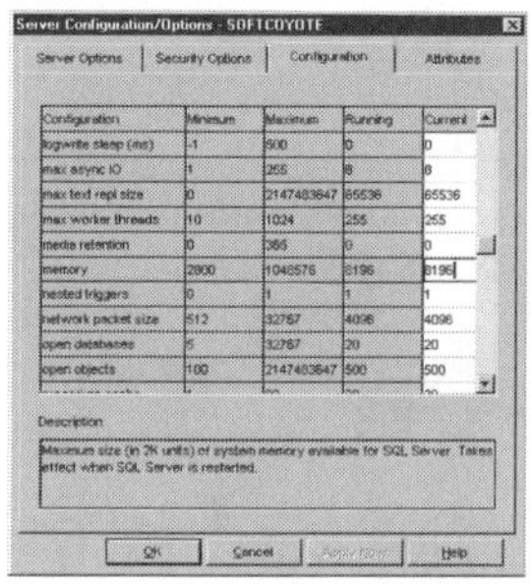

**TIP** It's generally recommended that you allocate as much RAM as possible to SQL Server. Allocating all but approximately 24M of RAM to the SQL Server process is a good guideline to follow. For example, in a 64M system, you should allocate approximately 40M to SQL Server. The 24M handles the network operating system and other base operating requirements of the system.

**NOTE** After you establish the memory configuration, you need to restart SQL Server. You can do this from the Enterprise Manager by selecting the server and then right-clicking it. Select Stop from the menu. After the server has been stopped, as indicated by the red traffic light, restart it. This institutes the changes to the memory configuration that you just made.

The next step starts the process of installing replication as a publishing server on your system. Prior to setting up the distribution database, you need to have established both database and log devices. These must have sufficient disk space allocated to support the database that you'll be replicating. These are the devices onto which you'll place the distribution database and logs. The recommended minimum size for these items is 30M, but your size depends significantly on several different factors, as follows:

- What are the sizes of the databases that you'll be replicating? Remember, for each subscriber, there is an initial synchronization that must take place. This means that your distribution database should be at least as large as the combined maximum table size for each table that will be replicated. This size represents the size to support a single article. If you will be publishing multiple articles, you need to figure out a total size based on all articles combined.

- What will the traffic on your system be? More transactions mean more staging of information as it's passed along to the subscribing servers. This affects the database size requirements, and, therefore, the device size requirements.
- How many different articles will you be publishing? Try to avoid using several different articles against a single information source. If you have a table that you need to provide to multiple subscribers, it's worth the effort to try to use only one publication/article combination to fulfill their needs. This is better utilization of disk resources, processing resources, and general processing bandwidth at the server.

Choose Replication Configuration from the Server menu, and then choose Install Publishing from the submenu. This begins the process of setting up the distribution database and other options that govern the server's operation for replication. Figure 14.4 shows the dialog box that you use to set up replication options.

**FIG. 14.4**
Set the options for the distribution database and processes for replication, including device sizes and naming.

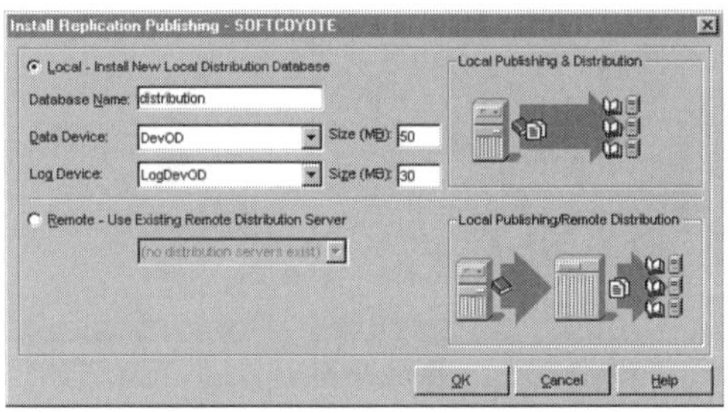


This dialog box enables you to define whether the distribution process will be local or located on a remote system. If you select local, you need to indicate where the distribution database will be installed. If you indicate a remote server, you need to know the server name, and the SQL Server process already must be running on that system.

When you click OK, the new database is added to the system, and you are ready to start setting up specific options to enable publishing on your system. If all goes well, you receive a prompt, as shown in Figure 14.5, that enables you to go directly to where you can set up publications on your system.

**FIG. 14.5**
After the distribution database is created, you can go directly to the definition of your publications and subscriptions.

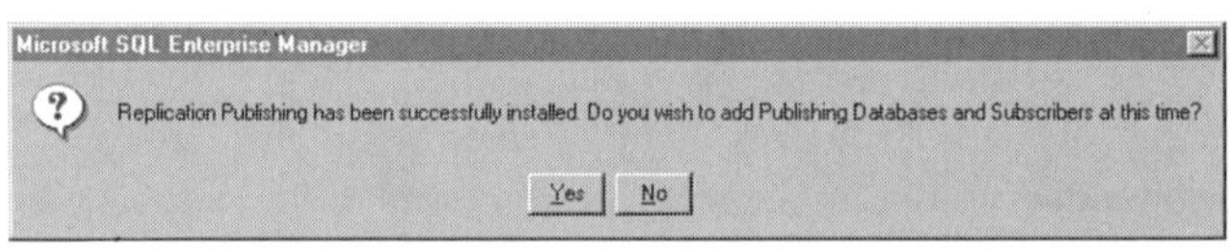


**NOTE** If the installation of the distribution database fails for any reason, you need to address the problem before you can continue. A possible reason for experiencing a problem here is if you've registered a server with a user that is nonexistent or has insufficient rights on the remote system. If you experience this problem, make sure to create an appropriate user prior to continuing.

After you address any system problems, you might need to completely uninstall replication before you can continue. For more information, see the "Uninstalling Replication" section at the end of this chapter.

# Enabling Publishing

The first step in creating your own publications is to, in essence, turn on publication services, designate a frequency for the services, and indicate which databases are candidates for replication. You can get to the configuration options, shown in Figure 14.6, from the Yes/No dialog box after defining the distribution database, or you can choose the Publishing option from the Server, Replication Configuration menu.

**FIG. 14.6**
You can indicate the frequency of updates and the databases that are available for replication.

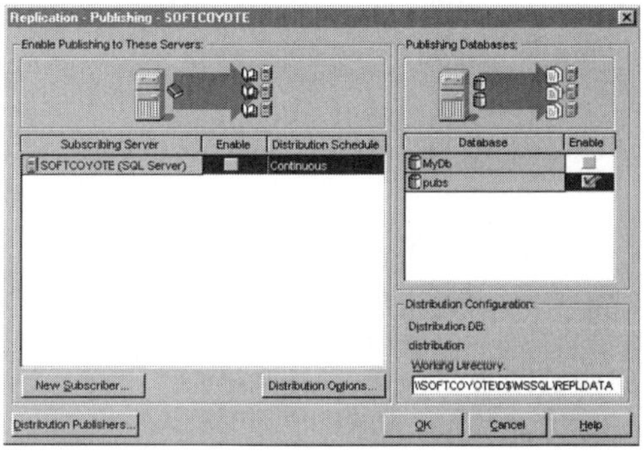

For each server you have registered to the Enterprise Manager, you can indicate whether or not it is allowed to subscribe to this server by selecting or deselecting the Enable option from the Enable Publishing grid. For each server you allow to subscribe, you can indicate at what frequency you'll be replicating information to the server. The default is to replicate information continuously starting at 12:00 AM and continuing throughout the day.

If you are using a remote link or are only providing snapshot information to the subscription servers, you might want to change this value to a time when the system is generally under less load. This can help decrease the impact on network traffic that will be incurred when the replication process kicks off. Of course, this places your data into a batch-type mode and might not be acceptable at the end user's application.

Selecting or deselecting databases controls which databases you will have to select from when you define publications. If you have a secure database that you want to control, this is the ultimate protection. By not making the database available to the replication process, you can be assured that it will not be included in publications.

You might notice the working directory option shown in the dialog box just below the designation of the distribution database in Figure 14.6. This directory is where information is kept and staged as it is sent out to the subscription servers. You can change this directory if needed. When SQL replicates a database, it is using a method somewhat like a BCP to copy the data from one system to another. This directory is where the data files are built.

**NOTE** It might be desirable to indicate a secured location for this directory if you have concerns about other users modifying or reviewing this information when it's staged. The information is not readily discernible but should be protected nonetheless.

If you want to create a custom distribution schedule or control how often information is sent based on transaction volume, you can click the Distribution Options button. As shown in Figure 14.7, this option also enables you to indicate how long information is maintained at the distribution server after it has been sent to the remote system.

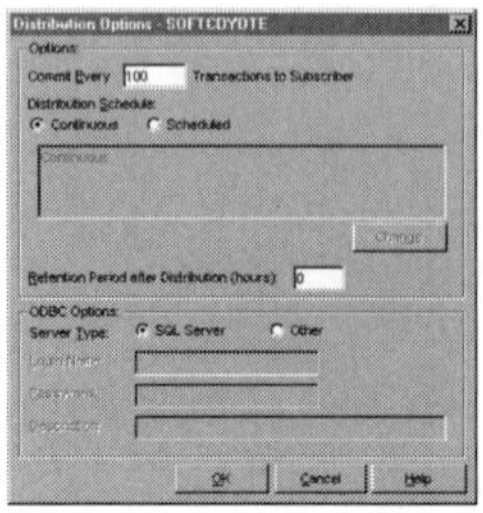

**FIG. 14.7**
You can create custom distribution schedules on a server-by-server basis. This can be helpful when dealing with time zone changes and other loading factors.

If you do opt to establish a custom distribution schedule, a separate dialog box enables you to change a number of options. As shown in Figure 14.8, you can set up how often, on a macro level, the replication takes place. This option allows values that range from daily to monthly. As you select this highest level interval, the balance of the options change to reflect values that enable you to define how you would like the replication to be carried out.

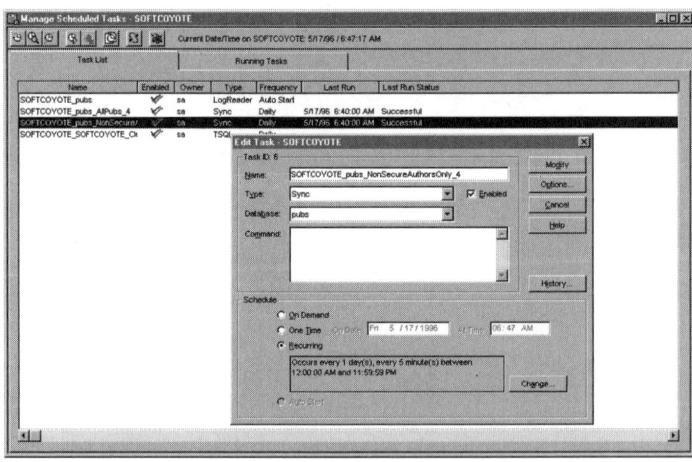

**FIG. 14.8**
You can define custom timing for replication for a number of time intervals.

At this point, you're ready to set up the specific publications and articles that you'll make available to other systems. You've defined the servers that have access to the information, the frequency at which it will be provided, and where the information will come from in your system. The next step is to create the publications that will be replicated.

**TIP** If have trouble getting information to the subscribing systems, make sure the replication users, `repl_publisher` and `repl_subscriber`, are still defined on the systems that are taking part in the replication.

## Publishing Databases: How to Replicate Entire Databases

You might recall that you have two different options when it comes to replicating information on your system. You can either publish the entire database or you can select specific information in the database to replicate. In this section, setting up replication for an entire database is covered. In the coming sections, setting up targeted articles is discussed. To begin, examine the Replication management options (see Figure 14.9).

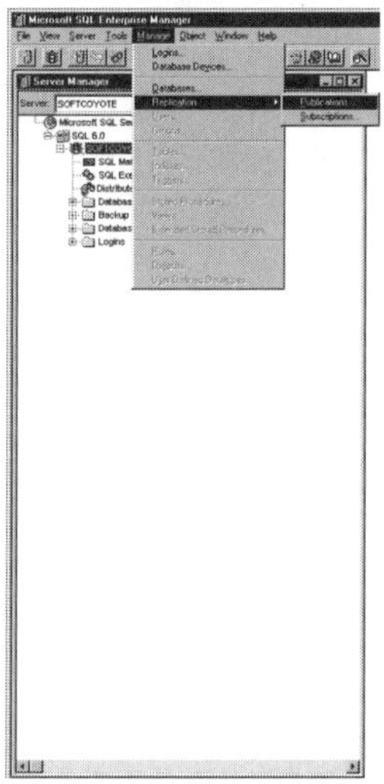

**FIG. 14.9**
Use the Manage menu to control all aspects of the replication process after you complete the initial setup.

**NOTE** Remembering which option to use from the menus or the topology dialog box can be confusing. It helps to keep in mind that you don't generally use the options on the Server menu after you've installed and set up the basic configuration for replication on your system. All aspects that deal with the specific publications and subscriptions are controlled from the Manage menu.

Select Manage, Replication, Publications from the menus to begin working with the different publications that are on your system (see Figure 14.10). This takes you to the dialog boxes that enable you to define and configure the publications and articles that you will be offering.

The dialog box shows each database for which you've enabled replication during the setup phase. Of course, there are no publications listed initially because you've not defined them yet. You use the New, Change, and Remove buttons to manage the different replications in your system. The tree display expands under each database, showing the different publications that are available after they are defined. Under each publication, you can see the articles that have been created. From this display, you can manage all active publications.

**FIG. 14.10**
The initial Manage Publications dialog box shows the databases that you've selected to enable replication.

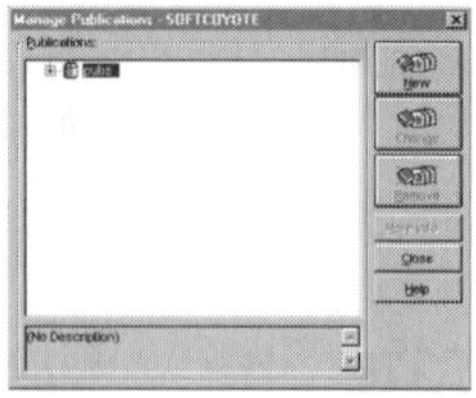

**Selecting the Tables to Be Published** In the first example, an AllPubs publication is set up to replicate all eligible tables in the PUBS database. Remember, you must define a primary key for each table that you need to replicate. You can use the Alter Table command to institute a primary key if needed.

When you select New, you're presented with the dialog box that enables you to set up the publication and indicate the information that should be replicated. Figure 14.11 shows the dialog box that lists the different tables that are available and enables you to set up the specifics of the article.

**FIG. 14.11**
Setting up the article to publish an entire database only entails selecting <all tables> for the article definition.

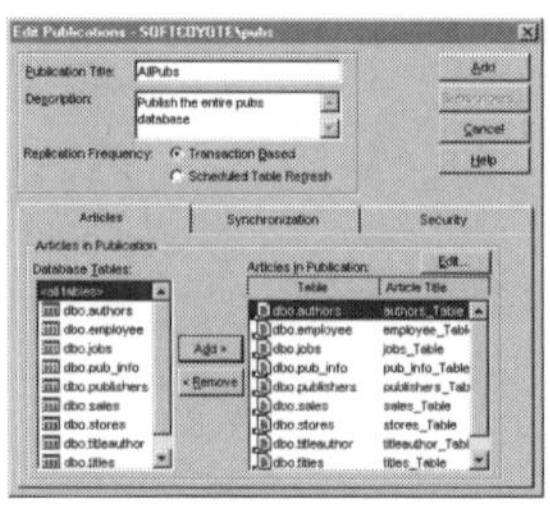

First, you need to name the article that you're defining. When you do, make sure you do not include spaces or wild-card characters, such as an asterisk, in the name. If you do, when you click Add to save the publication, you are prompted to change the name.

**NOTE** You might want to create a naming convention for your publications that indicates what kind of information they provide. This is completely optional, but if you're publishing numerous articles, this information helps the subscription systems determine which publications they need to be working with.

As this article publishes all eligible tables from the PUBS database, simply selecting the <all tables> option will suffice for the definition. Each table is copied to the Articles in Publication pane, and you can tell that they're included by the shared icon that you're familiar with in Explorer and File Manager.

**Establishing Table Synchronization** When you establish a publication, you are guaranteed that the subscribing system's tables will be initialized to contain the same information as the replicated table. To do this, an initial synchronization step is completed. You can control how and when this step occurs by selecting the Synchronization tab from the Edit Publications dialog box shown in Figure 14.12.

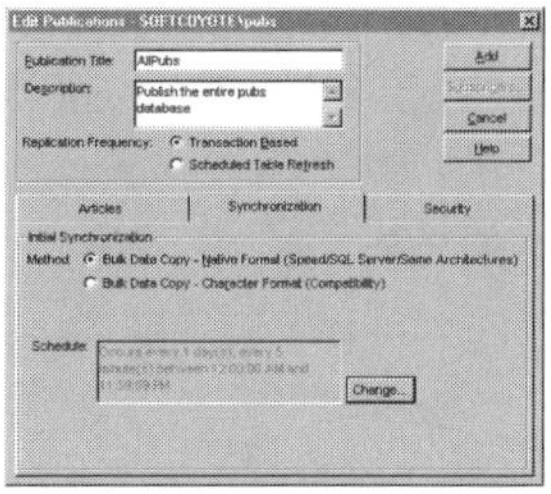


**FIG. 14.12**
You can defer synchronization to a time that suits your system requirements better, possibly saving money if remote connections are used.

If you are replicating information between SQL Servers, make sure to leave the default copy method, using Native Format data files, selected. This enables SQL Server to save the information in as optimized a format as possible when it creates the export file used to initialize the subscriber's database tables. The other option, Character format, saves the exported information in a format that you can use if you are importing to the receiving database using other utilities or if you're using the information produced by the initial synchronization in a third-party system.

**TIP** If the transaction log fills up and you're forced to dump and truncate it, you should first unsubscribe any replication servers. After you have done this, dump and truncate the log, and then re-subscribe the servers. When you do, the servers automatically re-synchronize with the publishing server.

You can also set up the schedule of times that controls when the synchronization occurs by clicking the Change button. Establishing these times is very similar to the time frames you set up during the initial configuration of the replication services.

**Controlling the Recipients of Subscriptions** A key feature and concern regarding replication of databases is security. When you set up your system for replication, you've seen that you can determine what subscribing systems will have overall access to your replication services. This presents a possible challenge, though, when you need to provide access to some, but not all, publications that reside on your replication server.

SQL Server enables you to indicate, on a case-by-case basis, what servers have access to any given publication. By default, when you set up a new subscription, SQL Server makes it available to any server with overall access to the replication system of your server. To change this, select the Security tab of the Edit Publications dialog box, as indicated in Figure 14.13.

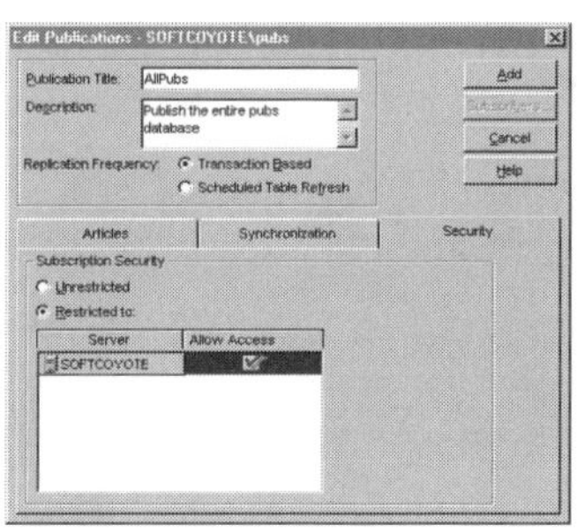


**FIG. 14.13**
You can easily prevent access to specific publications, depending on which servers are requesting the information.

If a server's system has not been authorized to use a given publication and the server looks to your system to select available publications, the publication does not show up in the list of available items. You can change this option later to allow or disallow access to a publication by selecting Security from the initial Publications dialog box.

**Making Changes to Publications** After you've set up publications, you can review them from the Manage Publications window. In Figure 14.14, you can see that each database shows its related publications and articles as they've been defined on the server.

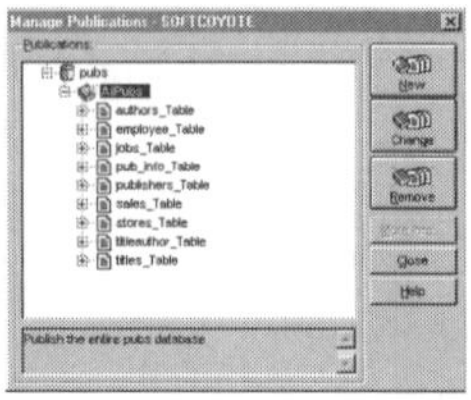


**FIG. 14.14**
You can use the tree view of the replication system to select a publication or article to review or modify.

If you want to make a change to a publication, simply highlight it and select Change. You are presented with the same dialog box that enabled you to define the publication in the first place. You can modify the tables that are included, how the information is synchronized, and the security aspects of the publication.

## Publishing Partial Databases and Tables

Now that you understand how to publish entire databases, this section reviews how to selectively publish information from your replication server. As you might imagine, publishing select information can be quite complicated, although it depends a great deal on how you're trying to limit the information being replicated and how you define that information.

**Limiting Publications to a Single Table** The first, and most basic, selective publication is limiting the publication to a single table. You might have noticed that each table available for replication is listed when you define a given publication. In the first example, the entire database was published by selecting the <all tables> option at the top of the list of tables. The alternative to this is to select the individual tables that you want to include in the subscription from the Database Tables list. After you've highlighted the different tables that you want to include, click the Add button, and they are copied to the Articles list (see Figure 14.15).

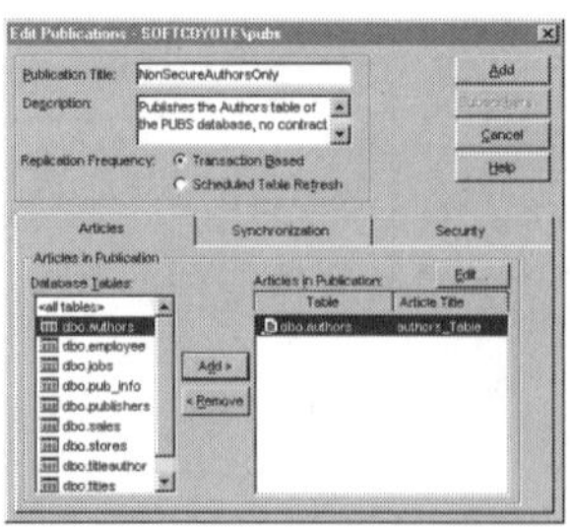


**FIG. 14.15**
You can select one or more individual tables to be included in the publication.

If you do nothing more for this publication, the entire table will be monitored and replicated as part of this publication. You have the same options for managing how the publication will be synchronized and what servers will have access to it as you do when setting up a full-database replication.

The alternative to publishing the entire database table is to partition it. You might recall that you can partition a table in one of two ways: horizontally or vertically.

**Partitioning Information to Be Included in a Publication** The two partitioning options, horizontal and vertical, correspond to looking at views of your information based on selectively retrieving rows (horizontal) or columns (vertical) from your database tables. Of course, you can combine these two techniques to provide a concise view of the information in the table if needed.

To establish a partition of information to be used in the article, click the Edit button on the Edit Publications dialog box's Articles tab. This calls up the Manage Article dialog box that shows two new tabs, Filters and Scripts (see Figure 14.16).

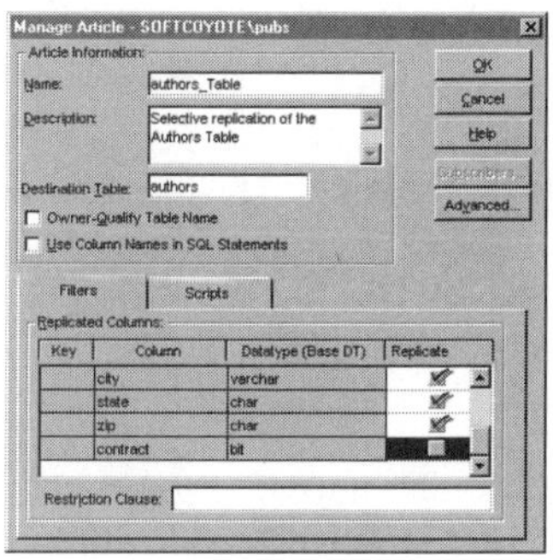


**FIG. 14.16**
You can select the columns that you want to be included in the replication process.

In the example, as discussed earlier in this section, the Contract column information shouldn't be included in the replicated information that is provided to other sites with this publication. By scrolling down the list of columns, you can select and deselect the different columns that you want to include. When you've completed the selection, you will have vertically partitioned the database if you've deselected any columns because the publication will include only those fields that you allowed.

Normally, the SQL Server replication process manages insert, delete, and update operations automatically. This can be a problem, for example, if you're inserting information and need to have another process kicked off by the action of inserting a new row. In this case, you can click the Advanced button and specify the Insert, Update, and Delete scripts that you'd like to run when records are modified with these operations.

In addition, if you need to do so, you can provide a table-creation script that you want to use in initializing tables. This script is run instead of the standard table script generated by SQL Server based on the source table's definition. This can be helpful if you're defining tables that will receive replicated data, but perhaps not all columns that need to be in a table.

By default, when the table is created, it is created with columns to match the article's definition. This means that, in the example of not copying the Contract column, the column would not exist at all in the recipients' databases. You can modify the creation script here and make sure that all appropriate information and columns are included. Figure 14.17 shows how you can modify these values.

**FIG. 14.17**
You can override SQL's default methods that are used to implement changes to the underlying database tables.

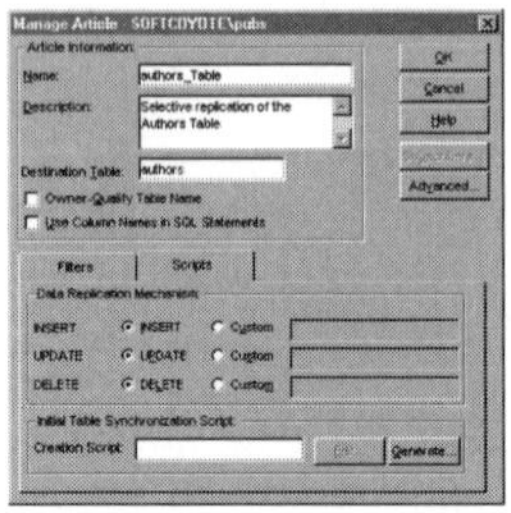

> **CAUTION**
>
> Unless you are very comfortable with modifying these types of SQL scripts, you should consider alternative ways to make the changes you need. For example, perhaps you could create a series of triggers on the subscriber that would institute changes needed in the storage of the information so that only certain columns were reused in the end user's system. Remember that changes made here will affect all subscribing systems, and you should ensure that this will not cause unforeseen problems on systems that might vary in their implementation of database structures and table layouts.

You also have the option of controlling the synchronization scripts that SQL Server will run. Clicking the Advanced button enables you to edit what actions will be taken on synchronization of tables between the publication and subscription systems. The dialog box is shown in Figure 14.18.

**FIG. 14.18**
You have full control over how indexes and existing tables will be managed during the synchronization process.

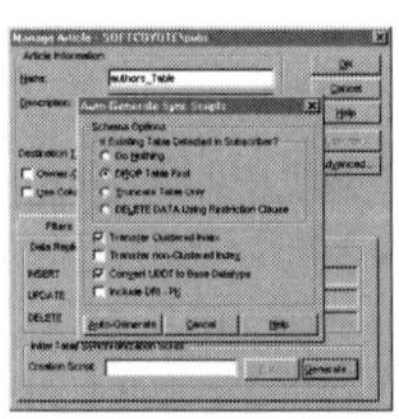

> **TIP** If there is a chance that the table might already exist on the user's system, be sure to check the DROP Table First option. If you don't, you might have a database table in an unknown state.

If you want to see or edit the actual script that will be created when the table is synchronized, you can click the Auto-Generate button. You are presented with the listing that will be used to create the table when it's initialized.

After you've completed your changes, click OK from the Manage Article dialog box and then Add from the Manage Publications dialog box. The publication is added to the list of available publications, and you're ready to allow other users to start accessing the publications on your system.

You might notice in Figure 14.19 that the AllPubs publication shows a secure publication, which is one with additional limits on who can see and use the information. The key that is showing over the book icon next to the publication name indicates this. On the NonSecureAuthorsOnly publication, there is no key, indicating that the publication is open to subscription by any subscription server with access and overall replication authority on your server.

**FIG. 14.19**
The new publication and articles are added to the list of active publications, ready for a subscriber to begin receiving the replicated information.

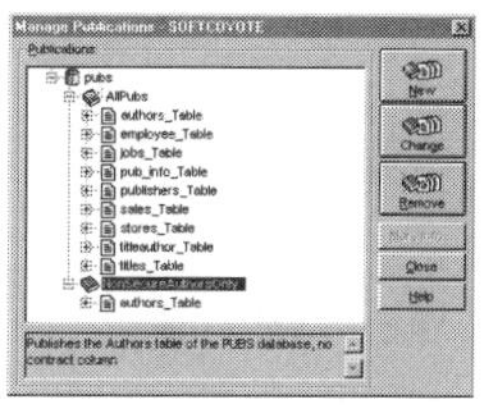


Now that you've set up the publications, it's a straightforward process to indicate which publications any given subscription server needs to begin receiving replication updates for.

# Enabling Subscribing

After the publications have been set up on the publication server, it's a simple task to set up the subscription server to begin receiving the information. Before you can subscribe to a given article, you must follow the same installation steps outlined earlier in this chapter. These steps set up the distribution database and prepare your system to begin working with the replicated information. The only difference is that, when it comes to specifying which databases are visible to the replication process, you'll specify which ones can be the *recipients* of information rather than the sources of the information.

When you're ready to initiate subscriptions, select Manage, Replication, Subscriptions from the menu in Enterprise Manager. As shown in Figure 14.20, this brings up a dialog box very similar to the Manage Publications dialog box used to define and create publications.



**FIG. 14.20**
Select the publication to which you want to subscribe from the list of available items for the server and database in which you are interested.

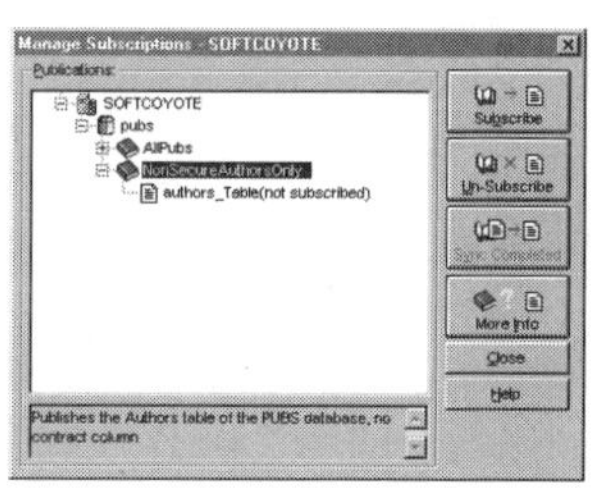

You can drill down into any given publication to see what articles are available and whether you're already subscribed to them or not. After you've found the publication to which you want to subscribe, highlight it and select Subscribe. You can specify where you want the information to go on your local system after it begins arriving from the replication server (see Figure 14.21).

**FIG. 14.21**
When you select a publication, you need to indicate where you want to store the incoming information on your server.

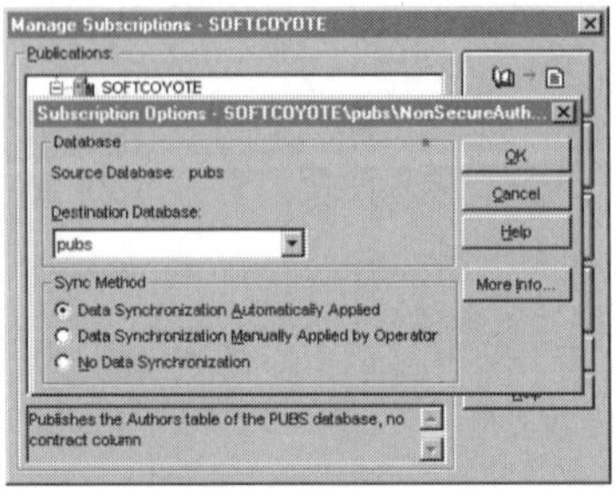


You might notice that there are three different options available to you for synchronization of the database. The last option is to turn off the synchronization altogether. This means that you know for a fact that the database and the concerned tables are in sync with the master system by some other means.

**CAUTION**

If you are unsure at all about the validity of the information in the database, it's best to allow the system to perform an initial synchronization on the database.

The first option enables you to let the system do the work for you and do the synchronization of information over the standard network connection between this system and the publication server. If you're on a locally attached LAN or a fast connection that is reliable, this is the best option to select and is the default.

If you're on a slower link, it might be that you've opted to bring the update to the system by another means. This includes copying the initial synchronization files from the publication server to tape or disk and then physically bringing them to the subscription system. If you have a slow link and initially populated tables, this might be a good option, as it avoids the initial rush of information across an already slow connection between the two systems.

**TIP** Remember, you can schedule the time at which synchronization takes place. Moving it to off-hours can ease network loading significantly.

After you've set up the subscription to the publication server, you might notice that the display of subscriptions is updated to show the active subscription. You can see in Figure 14.22 that, although the subscription is active, it has not yet been synchronized with the publication server.

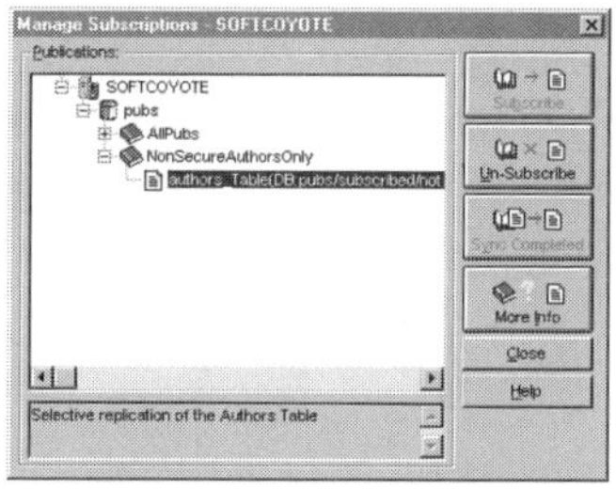


**FIG. 14.22**
The list of subscriptions changes to indicate that you're now subscribed to the publication. It also indicates the destination database.

# Uninstalling Replication

There might be times when you need to uninstall replication, either on a server-specific basis or on an overall basis. Examples include a server changing physical locations and no longer needing access to sensitive information, or when you've installed several test scenarios and simply want to start over.

The next two sections show how you can cover both of these types of situations using facilities within SQL Server.

## Disallowing Specific Servers

If you find that you need to remove a server from the list of servers that are eligible to receive information from your publication server, you need to determine whether you need to restrict only individual publications or if you need to revoke access altogether. If your intent is to remove access completely, you simply remove the server from the list of eligible candidates that can see the publications on this server.

From the Server menu, select Replication, Publishing. You can indicate which servers are able to subscribe to your server. Figure 14.23 shows the server selection dialog box that appears.

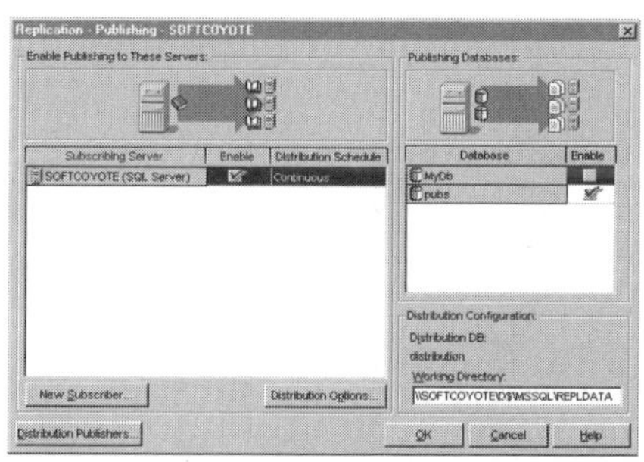


**FIG. 14.23**
Deselect any servers that you no longer want to make publications available to.

A list of subscriptions that are about to be removed appears and you must confirm that you want to remove the server from the list of eligible systems. After you confirm, the server still shows up on the list, but the server will not be able to select publications on the publication server.

## Uninstalling Replication Completely

Carefully consider all options before you opt to remove replication entirely from the system. This operation shuts down *all* replication to *all* subscribing servers, and it does so in a somewhat brute force manner by removing the replication option from the server and deleting the distribution database.

There are three steps for uninstalling replication in SQL Server, as follows:

1. Discontinue all replication services, all publication and subscription services, between this system and other servers with which it is working.
2. Turn off the replication option at the server engine level.
3. Drop the distribution database.

You need to follow these steps to restore your system to its state prior to installing replication. Removing connections to other servers is covered in the section immediately preceding this one, "Disallowing Specific Servers." If you're removing replication from a subscription server, choose Server, Replication, Subscriptions instead of Publications, but the operations of removing references to foreign servers are the same.

The next step requires issuing an interactive SQL command, so you need to use ISQL/W or another utility to enter the command. Enter the following stored procedure call to turn off the replication option on your system:

```
sp_ServerOption "<servername>", "dist", false
```

**NOTE** You must be logged in as SA to complete this option.

Replace `<servername>` with the name of your server. Because our server name is PLUTO in this example, the command would be:

```
sp_ServerOption "pluto", "dist", false
```

**NOTE** No results are returned from the call.

This removes the distribution option from your system, disabling replication. The distribution database you established when you first installed replication still remains in the system. Dropping this database is the final step in removing replication from your system.

From the Enterprise Manger, right-click the table that you specified.

**CAUTION**

Be sure that you select the *distribution* database you specified, *not* your databases that contain active, important production information. If you have any doubt about which database to select, you can review the stored procedures for the database, and you can see the replication stored procedures there. If you select an incorrect database, you permanently drop production information, and your only recourse is to restore it from a backup.

From the menu, select Drop Database and confirm that you want to drop the database. If all has gone well, you can make a quick check by choosing Server, Replication from the menus. You should have the Install Replication option available once again.

# Backing Up Your SQL Server Databases and Logs

One of the most dreaded questions when you call for help with your application is, "When was your last backup?" Getting caught without a backup can be quite painful.

With SQL Server, backing up is often much more important than it is on a stand-alone system. If you support a database with many users, keeping those users' confidence in the system's information is very important. Data loss might incur costs across departments and might require significant data reentry.

SQL Server provides a couple of different ways to protect from data loss, or at least minimize it, should the worst happen. These techniques range from physical duplication of the information to backing up the databases and transaction logs at specific intervals during the course of business.

## Determining How Often to Back Up

One of the first questions that a new SQL Server customer ponders is how often he or she needs to back up. The answer is simple, but seems sarcastic when first given: Quite simply, how much data can you afford to lose?

The initial answer is usually "none." This answer is fine, but then you must determine what the effect will be on the system plan to incur no loss of data if a catastrophic system failure occurs. Typically, such a plan involves mirroring databases, which costs money to implement. For more information on mirroring a database on your system, see the section "Understanding and Using Mirroring" later in this chapter.

Because the cost of mirroring a system can be quite steep, the next step is to determine the amount of data that can truly be at risk at any given time. To determine this amount, you must first understand that you have to back up two different components to the system. As you've seen throughout this book, the database contains the different tables and all other objects associated with the database. The transaction log contains an incremental log of the things that happen to a database and change it. Essentially, the transaction log contains a "before and after" picture of the data that changes with each block of work that the server performs.

Keep in mind that the database backup is a snapshot in time, and the transaction logs contain all the changes since you took that snapshot. At a minimum, you'll want to back up the database weekly and the transaction log daily.

The best plan is a system of rotating backups. Such a system is the safest way to ensure that you have the correct fault tolerance for any system failures that you might experience. All computer professionals agree on one thing: Any system will fail; it's only a question of when. You should have complete, concise, and accurate backups. They are the only lifeline you have in times of hardware failure.

Table 14.2 illustrates a suggested backup schedule. If you're backing up to tape, this approach requires 29 tapes over the course of a year. The weekly backup of your system requires 14 tapes, and maintaining the monthly archives requires 13. You use the remaining two tapes as working transaction log backups, and as an initial, baseline backup of the database. Remember, this schedule is to maintain backups, not to retain historical data on the system. You should not count on backups for retention and research on historical information. For those purposes, you must rely on alternative backups. Number the tapes sequentially on a permanent label on each tape cassette.

**NOTE** If your database is large, you might need more than one tape per day, week, or month. In such cases, consider the tape-numbering scheme to be a *tape set* numbering approach.

**Table 14.2 Suggested Backup Approach**

| Tape Number | Used for | Comments |
|---|---|---|
| 1 | Monday backup | Backup for the first Monday of a two-week cycle |
| 2 | Tuesday backup | |
| 3 | Wednesday backup | |
| 4 | Thursday backup | |
| 5 | Friday backup | |
| 6 | Saturday backup | |
| 7 | Sunday backup* | |
| 8 | Monday backup | Backup for the second Monday of the cycle |
| 9 | Tuesday backup | |
| 10 | Wednesday backup | |
| 11 | Thursday backup | |
| 12 | Friday backup | |
| 13 | Saturday backup | |
| 14 | Sunday backup* | |
| 12 tapes | Monthly backups | |
| 1 tape | Yearly backup | |

**You should remove these tapes from the physical site and place them in a separate location to assure their safety.*

This backup schedule gives you a full two-week backup to fall back on if a problem arises. You should implement a two-week backup cycle because you might not immediately recognize when a problem has arisen. For example, a program change or other system event might cause a problem that isn't detected for a few days. By keeping the two weeks of backups, the odds are good that you will have a clean copy of the information in the recent archives.

## Backing Up and Restoring Databases

When you back up your databases and transaction logs, you do so by dumping the information in your system to a *dump device,* which SQL Server recognizes as a repository for information and can be either a disk file or a tape device. If you dump information to a disk-based device, for example, the file that SQL Server creates can be backed up to tape, another server, or some other location at which you will manage the backup files.

The best way to manage the backup of information is with the SQL Enterprise Manager. Choose Tools, Database Backup/Restore to start working with the backup subsystem. The main Database Backup/Restore dialog box then appears (see Figure 14.24).

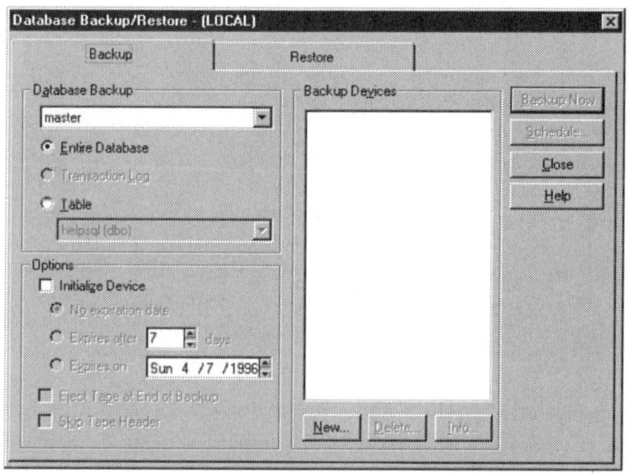


**FIG. 14.24** The main control panel for backup and restore operations enables you to select and create devices and set scheduling options.

**Setting Up Backup Devices** First you must establish the backup devices to use as the destination for information dumped from the working databases and tables. The Database Backup/Restore dialog box's Backup Devices window lists the devices already known to the system. You can accept one of these devices or create your own device.

To create a device, choose the New button below the Backup Devices window. The SQL Enterprise Manager then displays the New Backup Device dialog box, shown in Figure 14.25, and prompts you to name the device.

Notice that as you type the name for the device, the location is updated to include the name that you use.

You can specify a path that points to another physical system when you indicate the backup devices that you want to use. By doing so, you can provide good backup coverage without the need for additional storage media.

**FIG. 14.25**
You can create new devices that identify a tape or disk destination for backups.

Consider creating a new device for each day in the 14-day cycle mentioned previously. Then, when you create a scheduled backup, you don't necessarily have to use a tape to store the information if you point to the device on the remote system and use it as a backup destination. If you set up the system to back up to the devices without the append flag, each of the devices that you create will be only as big as needed for a single copy of the database that you're backing up.

Also, because both your core SQL Server system and the remote system are very unlikely to experience downtimes simultaneously, you have the assurance of solid backups for your system.

This approach also has the following disadvantages:

- The remote system must always be accessible to the backup and restore process.
- The remote system must have enough disk space to support the dump devices.
- If both systems are in the same building and that building suffers catastrophic damage such as a fire, you'll lose your backup system. This is a major reason for using offsite tape or other media backups.

Keeping these rules in mind, you can see that a solution that offers the best of both worlds combines remote system backups and offsite storage for tape backups made slightly less frequently.

**NOTE** Be sure to note the file name if you're backing up to a file on disk rather than on tape. When you copy the backup file from the system for storage, you need to use this file name to back up to tape or elsewhere on the system.

After indicating the name of the device that you want to create, simply choose Create. SQL Server then creates the new device and lists it in the Backup Devices window of the Database Backup/Restore dialog box. You're all set to start creating the backups that you'll need to support your SQL Server. Figure 14.26 shows a database with 14 backup devices, one for each day of a two-week backup cycle.

**TIP** The Master database does not have an explicit transaction log because it always has the Truncate Log on Checkpoint option set. For this reason, when you back up this database, you cannot do a transaction log backup. You must do a database dump and backup.

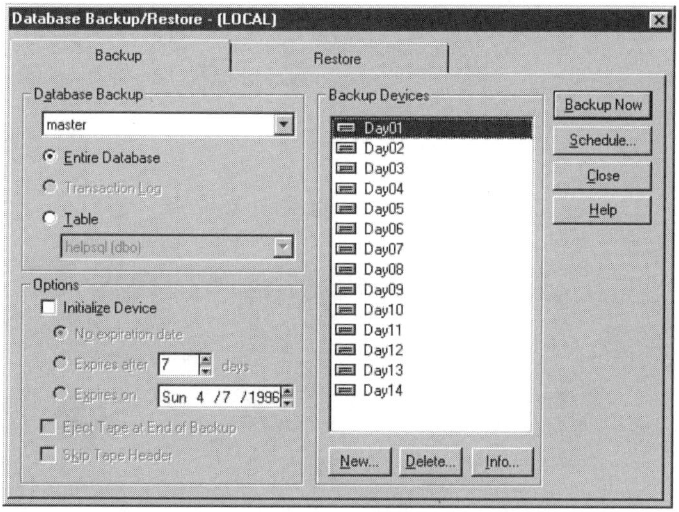


**FIG. 14.26**
The Master database now has a backup device for each day of a two-week backup cycle.

The next sections describe in detail what's involved in setting up the backups on the system.

**Running the Backup** After creating the devices that you need to support the backups, you must perform the actual backup. You have two options available. The first option is to run backups on demand. Although this option works fine, it requires manual intervention each time that you want to back up the system. This approach is more prone than an automated solution to forgetfulness, unexpected meetings, and similar mishaps. The second option is to implement a scheduled backup series and have the system complete the database dumps for you automatically.

The following are some general points to keep in mind as you determine your backup strategy:

- Be sure to back up the transaction logs between backups of the databases. Backing up the transaction log is no different than backing up a database. It's simply an option that you select while defining the backup.
- Make sure that you back up each database that you need to protect. No command backs up the entire system, so you must create backup processes for all databases that you are concerned with.
- Be sure to back up the Master database. Because this database includes all information about the other database objects in the system, having this information is very important in case you have to restore the entire system and rebuild from scratch.

You must select the type of backup, either manual or scheduled/automatic, that best fits the systems that you are supporting.

**Completing Manual Backups** Manual backups are quite straightforward and are a good way to get a feel for how the system works, the time that it takes to back up, and how much impact a database backup will have on your system if other users are on the system when a backup starts.

**NOTE** When you first back up, you must initialize the device. To do so, select the Initialize Device check box in the Options panel of the Database Backup/Restore dialog box's Backup page. If you attempt a backup without initializing the device, the SQL Enterprise Manager displays a warning that the device is either offline or uninitialized.

To complete the backup, select the device that you want to back up to and choose Backup Now. The Backup Volume Labels dialog box appears (see Figure 14.27).

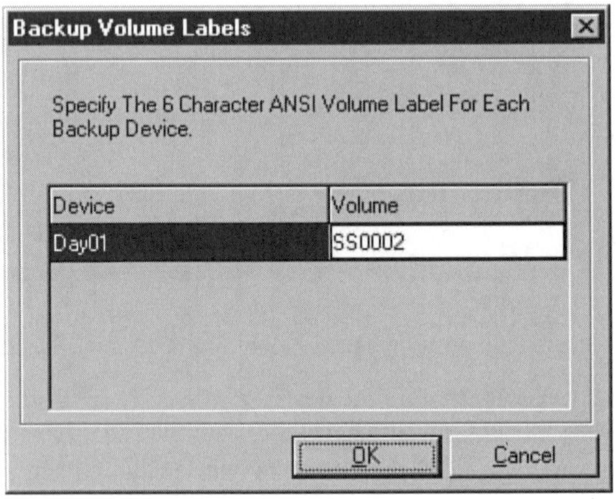


**FIG. 14.27** If you select a device that already has had a backup completed, the Backup Volume Labels dialog box prompts you to pick the label to which to append information.

After you select the device and choose OK, the SQL Enterprise Manager completes the backup. A status indicator shows the backup's progress. Finally, a dialog box confirms that the backup succeeded.

Here are a couple of items to keep in mind as you run your backups of the system:

- If you experience difficulty completing a backup, examine the free space on the dump device that you've created. Make sure that you have enough free space for the device to grow to accommodate the information that you're saving. Remember also that if you have selected the Append option, the information that you save is added to the prior information each time that you back up. This option will eventually lead to some very sizable dump devices. By using the rotating tapes as noted previously, you can safely back up to separate dump devices each time that you back up because you'll have the prior backup's information stored safely away.
- If you set the Truncate Log on Checkpoint option, you cannot back up the transaction log. From the earlier section "Understanding and Performing Checkpoints," you might recall that one way to help manage transaction log size is to turn on the Truncate Log on Checkpoint option. Another way to manage the size of the log is to dump the transaction log to a backup device. By default, SQL Server also truncates the log after a successful backup. Because both operations take control over truncating the log, they are mutually exclusive. You must turn off the Truncate Log on Checkpoint option before you can successfully back up the transaction log.

# From Here...

In this chapter, you've seen how you can put the many different recovery mechanisms for SQL Server into use for your system. From using transactions to running backups and implementing replication, there are a number of different ways you can approach maximizing your uptime and disaster recovery planning.

For additional information on these topics, consider the following sources:

- Que's *Special Edition Using SQL Server 6.5,* Second Edition, is a complete guide to administering and working with SQL Server. This guide includes Internet-related development, administration, and more.

CHAPTER 15

# Distributing Java Applications

**Examining Microsoft's CAB technology**

Learn how to use this technology to distribute your applets.

**Packaging your application**

Learn how to shrink your applet download time.

**Exploring the support issues**

Learn how to provide documentation for your applet.

The previous chapters have discussed everything from what an applet is to how to connect your applet to a database. Now that you have that killer applet, what's next? Even the coolest Java applet in the world is utterly useless until it can be used. Therefore, the next most logical step is to actually place your applet in the hands of those who can benefit from it—the users. In this chapter, then, you learn how to prepare your applet for distribution to as many users as possible. ■

# Examining Microsoft's CAB Technology

Today's Java applets are becoming larger with the inclusion of multiple .class, .audio, and .visual files. Typically, each file required for the applet is downloaded one at a time to the awaiting computer system. The problem is, as the files increase in number and size, the download time increases proportionately. This download process is further increased as the .audio, .visual, and .class files have to download in uncompressed format. Feature-rich applets can create an extremely long wait. Fortunately for Java users, Microsoft has recently introduced a solution to this problem—*Cabinets*.

## Cabinet Files

Cabinet Files (CAB) reduce download time by compressing the actual files that make up the applet into a single CAB file. The CAB file becomes a single file that actually houses all of the .class, .audio, and .visual files required by the applet. Because only the CAB file must be downloaded, the download time is determined by the CAB file size. Upon completion of the download, the receiving system extracts the various files contained within the CAB files and performs any installation routines. Some key features of CAB files are:

- Enable automatic file updates and version control
- Can be digitally signed
- Make use of efficient compression technology
- Make use of proven technology that is used on Windows 95 and Office 95

## Using CAB with Visual J++

The Visual J++ CD-ROM contains everything that you need to make CAB files for your applications. The self-installing file, cabdevki.exe, is located in the Cab&sign directory on the CD-ROM. These tools are not installed as part of the normal installation process. You can either copy the cabdevki.exe file to a separate directory or launch the installation process directly from the CD-ROM. Table 15.1 describes the files that are created after running cabdevki.exe.

**Table 15.1 Cabinet Files Copied to Hard Disk**

| Name | Description |
|---|---|
| diamond.exe | The compression tool to make CAB files |
| cabarc.exe | A complementary tool to diamond.exe that makes constructing CAB files easier |
| classpck.ddf | Files you will update to make this CAB file |
| master.ddf | Files used to make the CAB file |
| master.inf | Setup information file for use with diamond.exe |
| readme.txt | Release documentation and last-minute updates to the executables |

| Name | Description |
|---|---|
| overview.htm | Document explaining the basics of cab |
| diamond.doc | An overview of the compression technology |

**NOTE** Full support for cabinets is available only in Internet Explorer 3. However, for users with an earlier version of Internet Explorer or other Java-enabled browsers, you can design the `APPLET` tag so that the applet will still be downloaded in the regular fashion.

Table 15.2 describes the commands that can be passed to cabarc.exe, and the syntax for cabarc.exe is as follows:

```
cabarc [<options>] <command> <cabfile> [<filelist...>] [dest_dir]
```

**Table 15.2 cabarc.exe—Commands**

| Command | Description |
|---|---|
| `L` | List contents of cabinet |
| `N` | Create new cabinet |
| `X` | Extract file(s) from cabinet |

Table 15.3 describes the option flags that can be set for the carbarc.exe utility.

**Table 15.3 cabarc.exe—Flags**

| Flag | Description |
|---|---|
| `-c` | Confirm files to be operated on |
| `-o` | When extracting, overwrite without asking for confirmation |
| `-m` | Set compression type `[MSZIP ¦ NONE]`, (default is `MSZIP`) |
| `-p` | Preserve path names (absolute paths not allowed) |
| `-P` | Strip specified prefix from files when added |
| `-r` | Recurse into subdirectories when adding files (see `-p`) |
| `-s` | Reserve space in cabinet for signing (in other words, `-s` 6144 reserves 6K bytes) |
| `-I` | Set cabinet ID when creating cabinets (default is 0) |
| `--` | Stop option parsing |

The following are some helpful notes on the proper uses of the cabarc.exe utility:

- When creating a cabinet, the plus sign (+) can be used as a file name to force a folder boundary; in other words:

  ```
  cabarc n test.cab *.c test.h + *.bmp
  ```

- When extracting files to disk, the `<dest_dir>`, if provided, must end in a backslash; in other words:

  ```
  cabarc x test.cab bar*.cpp *.h d:\test\
  ```

- The `-P` (strip prefix) option can be used to strip out path information; in other words:

  ```
  cabarc -r -p -P myproj\ a test.cab myproj\balloon\*.*
  ```

- The `-P` option can be used multiple times to strip out multiple paths.

These flags and notes are also visible by typing cabarc.exe on the command line with no parameters given.

**NOTE** The cabarc.exe and diamond.exe utilities are both command-line driven. In other words, at the `C:>` prompt when in DOS mode, you would type the following: **cabarc.exe**.

A typical example of using cabarc is:

```
c:>cabarc -s 6144 n master.cab myprogram.cab master.inf
```

(The number 6144 represents 6K that is reserved for a digital signature.)

The final phase is to sign your code, which is covered in the section "Using Digital Signing." This is an important step, for users must know if they can trust your code before downloading it to their machines. The default settings in Internet Explorer will reject any unsigned code.

## CAB Files and Your Web Pages

The following APIs are used to support the loading of audio and visual images from CABs.

java.lang.Applet.getImage(URL)

java.lang.Applet.getAudioClip(URL)

If an applet uses these methods to load its images or audio clips, then those files can be stored in the CAB along with the class files.

Applet developers will want to use the `APPLET` tag. This should be done as follows:

```
<applet code="myapplet.class" width=m height=n>
<param name="cabbase" value="myapplet.cab">
</applet>
```

For browsers that do not yet support the `cabbase` parameter, you can use the `codebase` parameter instead:

```
<applet code="myapplet.class" codebase="/java/classes/" width=m height=n>
<param name="cabbase" value="myapplet.cab">
</applet>
```

This code creates an applet that will transparently work with or without the CAB and also enables the applet to work on browsers that do not yet support CABs without any modification to the code. These APIs are the most popular ones used for video and audio clips, resulting in very few if any changes to the code.

## Using Digital Signing

As mentioned earlier, you must sign your code for the default implementation of Internet Explorer to accept it. The Visual J++ CD-ROM contains the utilities that you need to sign your application. The self-installing file, codesign.exe, is located in the Cab&sign directory. These tools are not installed as part of the normal installation process. You can either copy the codesign.exe file to a separate directory or launch the installation process directly from the CD-ROM. Table 15.4 describes the files that are created after running codesign.exe.

**Table 15.4 Programs Installed to the Hard Drive**

| Name | Description |
|---|---|
| makecert.exe | Creates a certificate for testing purposes only |
| cert2spc.exe | Creates a Software Publisher Certificate |
| signcode.exe | Uses a Software Publisher Certificate to sign code |
| pesigmgr.exe | Inspects the certificate in a signed file |
| chktrust.exe | Checks the validity of a signed file |

All of the utilities included for code signing are command-line driven with the exception of signcode.exe.

**NOTE** You cannot create a valid signed certificate using the makecert.exe and cert2spc.exe. These utilites are provided only for testing purposes until you receive your real certificate from an authorized Certification Authority.

**Using *MakeCert*** The `MakeCert` utility enables you to create a test certificate. This utility enables you to create an X.509 certificate that binds your name to a Public Key.

▶ **See** "Using Digital Signing" and "Public-Key Encryption" for more information about digital signing and Public Keys, **p. 371** and **p. 369**

The command-line syntax for the makecert.exe utility is:

```
MakeCert [options] outputCertificateFile
```

Table 15.5 shows what options can be set for the makecert.exe utility:

**Table 15.5 Command-Line Options for *MakeCert***

| Option | Description |
|---|---|
| `-u:subjectKey` | Specifies the publisher key pair name. If none is found, it will be created. |
| `-U:subjectCertFile` | Denotes the certificate with existing subject Public Key to use. Indicates the file name to use. |

*continues*

**Table 15.5 Continued**

| Option | Description |
|---|---|
| `-k:subjectKeyFile` | Designates the location of the subject's Private-Key (.pvk) file. |
| `-n:name` | Designates the certificate's X.509 name (in other words, `"CN=Fred Dews"`). |
| `-d:displayname` | Designates name of the publisher displayed. |
| `-s:issuerKey(File)` | Indicates the location of issuer's key. The default to root key is provided for testing purposes. |
| `-i:issuerCertFile` | Indicates the location of the issuer's certificate. |
| `-#:serialNumber` | Indicates the serial number of the certificate. This is an optional value. The maximum value is two to the 31 power ($2^{31}$). The default value generated is guaranteed to be unique. |
| `-l:policyLink` | Indicates a hyperlink to SPC Agency policy information (this could be an URL). |
| `-I` | Explicitly specifies that individual software publishers can use the certificate. |
| `-C` | Explicitly specifies that commercial software publishers can use the certificate. |
| `-C:f` | Indicates that the publisher has met the minimal financial criteria. |
| `-S:session` | Indicates the session name for the enrollment session. |
| `-P:purpose` | Indicates why the certificate is to be generated: `CodeSigning` (default) or `Clientauth`. |
| `-x:providerName` | Indicates which `CryptoAPI` provider to use. |
| `-y:nProviderType` | Indicates which `CryptoAPI` provider type to use. |
| `-K:keyspec` | Designates the key. Possible values are: `S` signature key (default), `E` key-exchange key. |
| `-B:dateStart` | Specifies the start date of the validity period. The default is the certificate generation date. |
| `-D:nMonths` | Indicates the duration of the validity period. |
| `-E:dateEnd` | Indicates the end of validity period; defaults to the year 2039. |
| `-h:numChildren` | Indicates the maximum of certificates on the tree following this certificate. |
| `-t:types` | Indicates the certificate type: either/both of End-entity; Certification authority. |
| `-r` | Creates a self-signed certificate. |

| Option | Description |
|---|---|
| `-m` | Uses MD5 hash algorithm (default). |
| `-a` | Uses SHA1 hash algorithm. |
| `-N` | Includes the Netscape client authentication extension. |

The flags and notes mentioned in Table 15.5 are also visible by typing **makecert.exe** on the command line with no parameters given.

For the `-u` and `-k` options, if the indicated subject's key (key pair) cannot be found, then it is created. For `-u`, it is created in the `CryptoAPI` keyset; for `-k`, it is created in a file.

Alternatively, the subject Public Key can be obtained from an already existing certificate by using the `-U` option. `-U` makes the default subject name the same as that of the indicated certificate. A typical use of MakeCert is:

```
c:>MakeCert -u:myKey -k: myKeyfile -n:CN=mySoftwareCompanyName myCert.cer
```

This generates a certificate file called `myCert.cer`. The public part of the key pair, called `myKey`, is bound to the publisher `mySoftwareCompanyName`. If the key pair `myKey` does not already exist, it is generated along with `myKeyfile`.

**NOTE** The certificate that you just created using MakeCert is NOT a valid certificate. This certificate is designed for test purposes only until you receive a valid X.509 certificate from a valid Certification Authority (CA). One such valid Certification Authority is VeriSign located at **http://WWW.verisign.com/**.

Upon receipt of a valid X.509 certificate, use of the makecert.exe utility will no longer be needed.

**Using Cert2spc** The next step to digitally sign code is to create a Software Publisher Certificate (SPC) with the Cert2spc program. This program combines the X.509 certificate and the root certificate into a PKCS#7 signed-data object. PKCS#7 objects enable the inclusion of several certificates in a single object. The syntax for Cert2SPC is:

```
Cert2SPC cert1.cer cert2.cer...certN.cer output.spc
```

The following lists the Cert2spc command-line options:

| Option | Description |
|---|---|
| `cert1...certN` | The names of the X.509 certificates to be included |
| `output.spc` | A PKCS#7 object containing the X.509 certificate and the root certificate |

The following represents a typical invocation of Cert2spc:

```
C:>Cert2Spc root.cer mycert.cer ... mycert.spc
```

This combines `mycert.cer` and `root.cer` to make an SPC called `mycert.spc`.

**NOTE** The SPC `mycert.spc` that you just created is NOT a valid SPC. You need to obtain a valid SPC from a Certification Authority whose certificate you used to sign your code.

**Using *SignCode*** The last step needed to digitally sign code is to use the SPC to actually sign a file. This is accomplished with the `SignCode` program, which does the following:

- Creates a cryptographic digest of the file
- Signs the digest with your Private Key
- Extracts the X.509 certificates from the SPC
- Creates a new PKCS#7 signed-data object that contains the serial numbers of the certificates and the signed digest information
- Embeds the object into the file

If you have a valid SPC, then you can use this program to actually sign your code. The `SignCode` program has a wizard to help you do this. To sign code using the wizard, simply type **SignCode** without any options. If you want to sign your code manually, the syntax is:

```
SignCode [-prog filename -spc credentials -pvk privateKeyFile ] [options]
```

Table 15.6 lists the `SignCode` command-line parameters. You can include as many options as needed.

**Table 15.6 *SignCode* Command-Line Parameters**

| Option | Description |
|---|---|
| `-prog` | The name of the file to sign |
| `-spc` | The file that contains the credentials—usually an .spc file |
| `-pvk` | The file containing the Private Key of the publisher: a .pvk file |

Table 15.7 lists the `SignCode` command-line options. You can include as many options as needed.

**Table 15.7 *SignCode* Command-Line Options**

| Name | Description |
|---|---|
| `-name` | This is the name of your program. |
| `-info` | This is a location for obtaining more information about your program, such as an URL. |
| `-gui` | This will invoke the Code Signing Wizard. |
| `-nocerts` | You do not want any X.509 certificates embedded in the PKCS#7 signed-data object. In this case, the relevant certificates must already be stored on the client computer. |

| Name | Description |
|---|---|
| `-provider` | This is the name of the Cryptographic service provider to use. |
| `-provider` | This is the Cryptographic provider type to use. |
| `-commercial` | This indicates that the code was signed by a commercial software publisher. |
| `-individual` | This indicates that the code is from an individual software publisher. |
| `-sha` | This indicates that you want to use the SHA hashing algorithm. |
| `-md5` | This indicates that you want to use the MD5 hashing algorithm. This is the default hashing algorithm. |
| `-?` | This will display all of the options mentioned in this table. |

The following line provides an example for signing a file:

```
c:>SignCode -prog MyProgram.exe -spc Cert.spc -pvk MyKey
```

This embeds a PKCS#7 object, `Cert.spc`, into the digest of file, `MyProgram`. The digest is signed with the Private Key of the `MyKey` key pair.

After this is done—assuming you have a valid certificate—the file can be distributed to your customers.

The `SignCode` utility also allows for the use of a wizard to guide you through the process of digitally signing a file. To invoke the Code Signing Wizard, type **SignCode** on the command line without any parameters. The main screen of the Code Signing Wizard as shown in Figure 15.1 is then displayed.

**FIG. 15.1**
The Code Signing Wizard greeting screen informs users of what wizard they are using.

By pressing the Next button, you will then see the Code Signing Wizard setup screen, as shown in Figure 15.2

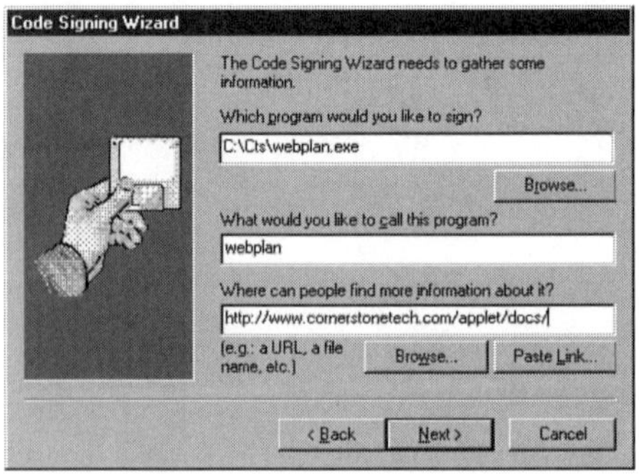


**FIG. 15.2**
The Code Signing Wizard setup screen prompts you for a Web site where additional information is available about your control.

This screen asks for some background information on the program that you want to sign, such as the name and location of the program you are about to sign. You will also be prompted to enter where users can find additional information about the program. After you have entered this information, press the Next button. The next screen displayed is shown in Figure 15.3.

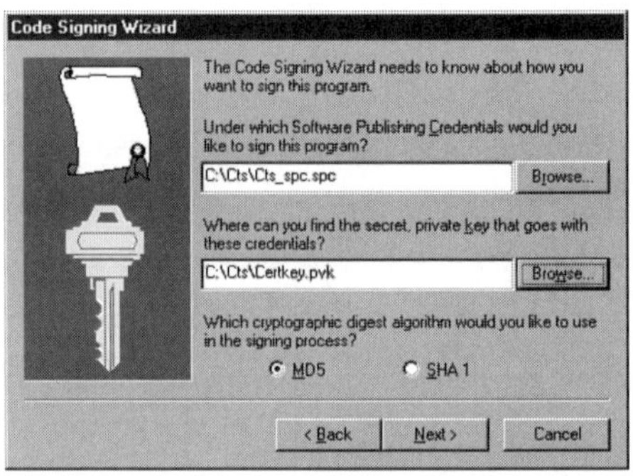


**FIG. 15.3**
The Code Signing Wizard credentials information screen prompts you for specifics about your Private Key.

At this point, you need to fill in the credential information. You will also be prompted for the location of the Private Key with which to sign the program and the hashing algorithm you want to use to create the digest from your program.

Pressing the Next button will display a review of the information that you have supplied, as seen in Figure 15.4. The information shown in Figure 15.4 is actually a compilation of all the information that you have supplied in the previous steps. If you need to make any changes to any of the information presented, now is a good time. You can do so by clicking the Back button to return to the previous screen.

After verifying that the appropriate information is displayed, press the Next button to view the final phase of the code signing process, as shown in Figure 15.5.

**FIG. 15.4**
The Code Signing Wizard overview screen enables you to view the information that you entered into the Wizard.

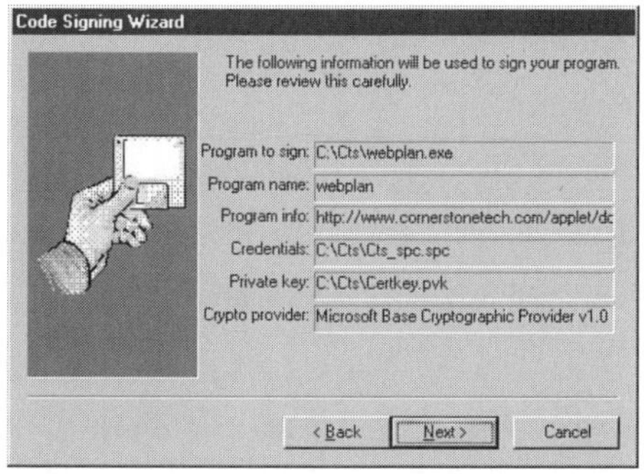


**FIG. 15.5**
The Code Signing Wizard confirmation screen enables you to start the code signing process.

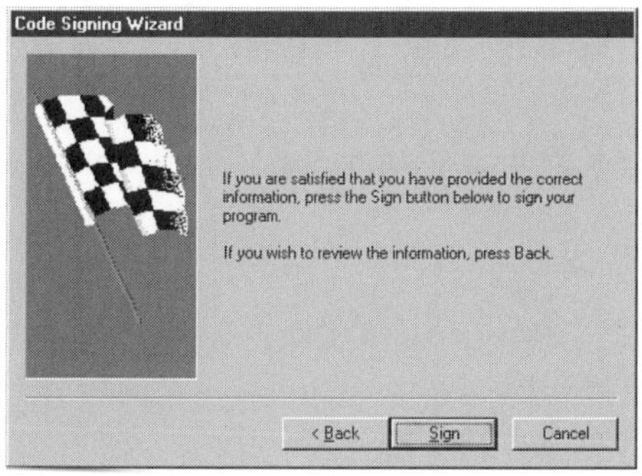


Pressing the Sign button actually starts the signing process. Upon successful completion, the Code Signing Wizard will display the screen, as shown in Figure 15.6.

**FIG. 15.6**
The Code Signing Wizard success screen is displayed after you have successfully signed your code.

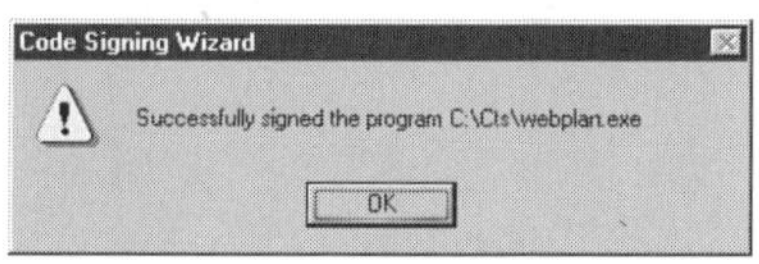


Congratulations, you have successfully signed your code. All that is left is to actually verify that the program was signed correctly.

***Using PeSigMgr*** The `PeSigMgr` program checks to see if `SignCode` was successful. This means that the file should have a PKCS#7 object embedded in it. The syntax is as follows:

```
PESIGMGR [options] signedfile
```

Table 15.8 lists the PeSigMgr command-line parameters.

**Table 15.8 *PeSigMgr* Command-Line Parameters**

| Parameters | Description |
|---|---|
| -l | This will list all of the certificates in an image. |
| -a:<-filename -> | This will add a certificate file to an image. |
| -r:<-index -> | This will remove a certificate <-index -> from an image. |
| -s:<-filename -> | This is used with -r to save the removed certificate. |
| -t:<-CertType -> | This is used with -a to specify the type of certificate, where CertType can be X509 or PKCS7. The default is PKCS7. |
| -? | This displays all of the options. |
| Signedfile | This is the name of the signed file that you want to check. |

To check for the existence of signed code within the MyProgram.exe file, you would execute the following statement:

```
c:>PeSigMgr -l MyProgram.exe
```

If a certificate is found in MyProgram.exe, PeSigMgr returns the number, revision, and type of the certificate. A sample response is:

```
>Certificate 0 Revision 256 Type PKCS#7
```

**NOTE** PeSigMgr does not provide for signature verification. Its sole purpose is to verify that SignCode actually did its job.

**Using *Chktrust*** The purpose of the ChkTrust program is to check the validity of the signed file. The syntax is:

```
CHKTRUST [switches] signedfile
```

Table 15.9 lists the ChkTrust command-line parameters.

**Table 15.9 *ChkTrust* Command-Line Parameters**

| Parameters | Description |
|---|---|
| -c | Designates a cabinet file |
| -i | Designates a Portable Executable (PE) image file |
| -j | Designates a Java class file |

ChkTrust performs the following actions when invoked:

1. Extracts the PKCS#7 signed-data object.
2. Extracts the X.509 certificates from the PKCS#7 signed-data object.

3. Computes a new hash of the file and compares it to the signed hash in the PKCS#7 object.
4. `ChkTrust` then verifies that the signer's X.509 certificate points back to the root certificate and that the correct root key was used.
5. `ChkTrust` then verifies that the code has not been modified or tampered with and that the root authority authorized the vendor to publish the file. After the proper verification is made, `ChkTrust` returns a `0`.

To perform validity checking on a file, execute the following line:

```
ChkTrust MyProgram.exe
```

Upon completion of the validity check, `ChkTrust` will return a

```
Result: 0
```

# Packaging Your Application

Cabinet files work well for deploying Java applets over the Web, but what about distributing a Java applet on a disk or CD-ROM? The size of today's applets and support files can make the process expensive when you consider all of the disks and CD-ROMs used.

Microsoft has recently introduced a new disk compression tool named Diamond, which is designed to handle the special needs of cabinet files. Diamond is a lossless disk compression tool that can trace its roots to early setup programs used by Microsoft. In addition to much of the same technology offered by cabinets, Diamond provides greater flexibility.

Diamond has the following key features:

- The capability to store multiple files in a single cabinet file
- The capability to perform compression across file boundaries
- The capability to span cabinets
- The capability to create self-extracting archives

Diamond offers some distinct advantages over traditional compression tools by offering all four of the above features in a single tool.

Diamond offers great flexibility in the creation of cabinet files through the use of folders, which are a collection of one or more files that are compressed together as a single object. Diamond uses a script to build the disk images for a particular application. This script, commonly called a Diamond Directive File (DDF), lists all of the files in a product and any special considerations such as directory paths.

In operation, Diamond will read the DDF to determine the files to be used. After completing this phase, Diamond creates cabinets of data that can contain one of more folders of data. A folder can contain a complete file or a portion of a file—this determination is made by the cabinet size and the DDF. Typically, a larger folder will produce greater compression due to the amount of data to find patterns in. The disadvantage is that large folders need to be completely uncompressed before the desired data can be extracted.

Figure 15.7 depicts what a typical Java application might look like after Diamond has been used. For purposes of this example, we will assume that the total number of disks needed after compression is three.

**FIG. 15.7**
The Java application to be distributed has been compressed to fit on three disks.

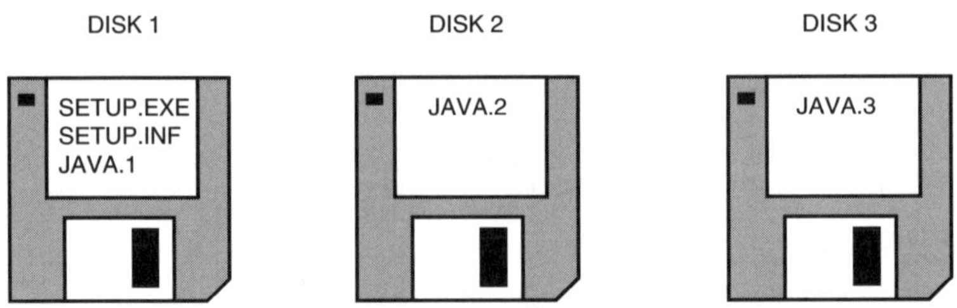


By using the example in Figure 15.7, you see a couple of files on the first disk, SETUP.EXE, SETUP.INF, and JAVA.1. SETUP.EXE is the actual setup program that reads the data stored in SETUP.INF to determine what setup parameters are active. The second and third disks contain the balance of the data stored in JAVA.2 and JAVA.3. In actual practice, the number of disks needed will vary from the example in Figure 15.7. Diamond can easily distribute the data over as many disks as are needed.

## Using Diamond with J++

The Visual J++ CD-ROM contains everything that you need to use Diamond. The self-installing file, cabdevki.exe, contains the diamond.exe and its support files. The cabdevki.exe is located in the Cab&sign directory on the J++ CD-ROM.

These tools are not installed as part of the normal installation process. You can either copy the cabdevki.exe file to a separate directory or launch the installation process directly from the CD-ROM. Table 15.10 shows what files are created after running cabdevki.exe.

**Table 15.10 Diamond Files**

| File | Description |
|---|---|
| diamond.exe | Command-line tool to perform disk layout (uses FCI.LIB) |
| fdi.lib | File Decompression Interface library (uses MDI.LIB) |
| extract.Exe | Command-line tool to expand files (uses FDI.LIB) |
| ddump.Exe | Tool to dump internal format of a Diamond cabinet file |
| fci.Lib | File Compression Interface library (uses MCI.LIB) |
| mci.Lib | MSZIP Memory Compression Interface library |
| mdi.Lib | MSZIP Memory Decompression Interface library |

The parameters syntax for diamond.exe is described in Table 15.11, and its syntax is as follows:

```
DIAMOND  [/Vn] [/D variable=value ...] [/L directory] source [destination]
DIAMOND  [/Vn] [/D variable=value ] /F directives_file [...]
```

**Table 15.11 Parameters for DDF**

| Parameter | Description |
|---|---|
| source | The name of the file to be compressed. |
| destination | The name of the file to receive the compressed version of the source file. If not supplied, a default destination name is constructed from the source file name. |
| /L directory | Specifies an output directory in which the compressed file will be placed. Equivalent to using the `SET` command in the directive file. |
| /F directives_file | A file containing commands for diamond.exe to execute. If more than one directive file is specified (/F `file1` /F `file2`...), they are processed in the order (left to right) specified on the command line. |
| /Vn | Set debugging verbosity level (0 = none...3=full). |
| /D | Defines variable with a specified value. |

# Creating a DDF

A DDF contains a listing of all the files for the JAVA application. The DDF will also contain parameters that control various aspects of the compression process, as follows:

- The capacity of the disks
- The cabinet file names
- The labels for each disk
- The amount of random access of files allowed within each cabinet

An example of a Diamond directive file can be found in the documentation that is supplied with Diamond. This documentation is located in the folder that was created when you installed Diamond from the J++ CD-ROM.

You can create a Diamond directive file using a standard text editor such as the Windows notepad or the DOS editor. After you have a DDF, you are now able to execute the following command to create the disk layout:

```
Diamond /f JAVA.DDF
```

Diamond now creates directories to hold the data for each disk. Diamond will also copy uncompressed files or create cabinet files in each directory. The setup.rpt will contain a summary of what actions were taken by diamond. The setup.inf will contain details on every disk and cabinet created for the disk set.

A complete listing of the commands available for the Diamond Directive Files (DDF) is included in the documentation that ships with Diamond, located in diamond.doc.

# Java Packages

The Java programming environment provides a unique method of collecting like classes together in one unit called a *package*. A package is a collection of related classes and methods (interfaces). Classes that are placed in packages can share common resources or one another's class information.

A package enables the effective management of classes and methods used within an application and the elimination of naming conflicts.

## Creating a Package

A package can be created from existing classes by including the following line:

```
package identifier/packagename;
```

at the beginning of each source file to be packaged before any other declarations. Packages can be nested within each other, as well; however, Java expects the class hierarchy to match that of the package. Upon compilation of the source files, a package will be created with the name specified. For example:

```
Package mypackage.pk
```

The above example will create the `mypackage.pk` package that contains all of the classes and interfaces specified.

The advantage of creating a package is that all of the classes and methods needed for your application are contained in one file. This provides the user with an efficient method of distribution.

## Existing Java Packages

Java contains several prebuilt packages that are installed in the \windows\java\classes directory. The packages contain a number of classes that you can borrow from as needed. The packages that come with Java are listed as follows:

- *java.applet* Provides the basic set of classes used to create a Java applet
- *com.ms* Contains subpackages that can be used to create COM applications
- *java.awt* Provides the classes that make up the Java Abstract Windowing Toolkit (AWT), which provides the core GUI classes.

- *java.io* Contains the classes needed for input/output control in Java, enabling Java developers to read and write from streams to standard input/output files.
- *java.lang* Contains the classes for the data types supported by Java
- *java.net* Contains the classes for the programming of winsockets
- *java.util* Contains the utility classes such as hashtable, dictionary, stack, and vector

# Exploring the Support Issues

If your organization is typical, then the documentation phase is usually the last phase undertaken. Documentation has been the bane of programmers from the time of the first computer program. In the early days of programming, documentation usually consisted of some cryptic notations made by scientists after the application was completed, and even today documentation takes a back seat to the actual development process. For example, you might hear the question, "How can we document something until after we know it works?" in project planning meetings. Although one of the junior members usually makes this statement, the underlying mindset is still prevalent.

Fortunately for our users, we are using Java to create our applications. Java actually encourages the process of creating documentation. This not only enables user documentation, but system documentation as well.

## Creating Decent Help Files

In the early days of Java, it was not uncommon to take part in discussions concerning the development of help files. These discussions very often left Java developers with no hope of designing a decent help file that did not require a specialized tool. Worse yet would be having to create the help file using an unwieldy text format. As you will see, the creation of Java help files can be both inexpensive and painless. Java is a tool that creates applications primarily for the Web. The main interface to the user is represented as the Browser.

The relationship that exists between a Java applet and the Browser makes HTML the most logical choice for the creation of Web-based Java applications. The use of HTML as a help file creation tool offers several distinct advantages over traditional means of file creation:

- *Capability to include graphics* Graphics files are easy to include in standard HTML format and offer a new dimension as compared to traditional help files.
- *Capability to include multimedia files* HTML 3.2 offers the help file creator to include such things as AVI files and Virtual Reality files in a standard help format.
- *Capability to incorporate complete hypertext linking* HTML offers unparalleled linking to other documents. This linking can enable a single document to be completely cross-linked, enabling simple changes to be made to the existing documentation.
- *Portability to other platforms* Portability across multiple platforms was one of the main goals for Java. HTML is equally at home on UNIX as it is on Windows 95. This portability means that version control of help files is no longer an issue.

Java includes a nifty utility called javadoc. This command-line utility can be used to create both documentation and help files. In the next section we will take a brief look at javadoc.

## Being User Friendly

One of the key components to any application, in addition to the help files, is the included documentation. In this section we will examine some of the key issues regarding the creation of documentation for Java-based applications.

### ON THE WEB

**http://www.javasoft.com** A good example of HTML documentation is on the SUN Java site, created exclusively with the Javadoc utility.

Figure 15.8 shows the first screen of the Java *API Users Guide*.

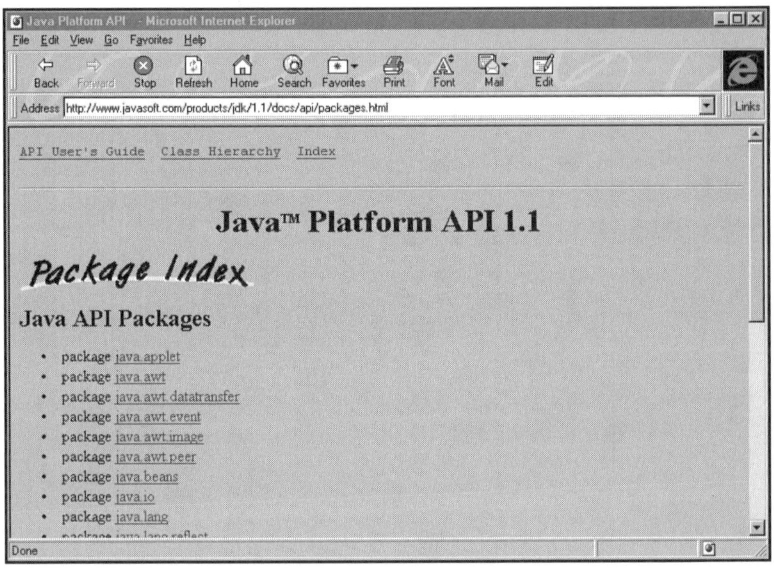


**FIG. 15.8**
Java *API Users Guide* was created using Javadoc.

Remember that online help files as well as documentation can be created using javadoc. Javadoc enables you to create documentation for the following:

- Packages
- Classes
- Interfaces
- Exceptions
- Methods
- Variables

The following syntax applies to javadoc:

```
javadoc [options] {package name/file type}
```

Table 15.12 lists the command-line options that Javadoc can take.

**Table 15.12 Javadoc Command-Line Options**

| Parameter | Description |
|---|---|
| `-d <directory>` | This causes javadoc to redirect output to the specified directory. |
| `-classpath` | This enables a classpath to be specified. |
| `-verbose` | This causes javadoc to print a list of files loaded during execution. |

# From Here...

In this chapter, you looked at methods for distributing your programs and some ways of adding value to your code. You explored Microsoft's Cabinet and Diamond technologies and how you can use them to distribute your applets. You also considered what is involved in the process of digitally signing your applications.

If you would like to find out more information about these topics, visit the following Web sites:

For more information about Microsoft's Cabinet/Diamond Technology, try:

**http://www.microsoft.com/workshop/java/cab.htm**

For more information about Java API Information, try:

**http://www.javasoft.com/products/**

CHAPTER 16

# Implementing Data Warehousing with Visual J++

**Understanding the concept of data warehousing**

The term data warehousing is thrown around often these days; find out what it really means.

**Exploring the benefits of data warehousing**

Data warehousing has been hailed as the miracle cure for nearly everything, and companies are dying to have one; find out what the real benefits are.

Although it has existed in its current form for more than a decade, only recently has the term data warehousing become a buzzword in the industry. The advent of the Internet, which brings lifetimes of information within a person's reach, and the recognition by companies that information is a strategic resource has driven the push for data warehousing. Most companies that have tried to implement data warehousing, however, have seen the process fail, for one reason or another.

One problem is that the data warehouse might take a very long time before the data in it becomes strategically useful. This is partly due to the simple fact that it will take time before your data has a statistically significant time dimension. In the mean time, you are left answering questions from fellow employees such as "Is it done yet?" and "Why can't I pull up this report?"

Another obstacle to overcome is the lack of a clear reason for building a data warehouse. RDBMS vendors are comparing data warehousing to a miracle elixir—drink and grow healthy. In reality, however, you must have a business reason for creating a data warehouse. Think about it: You put massive amounts of data into the warehouse and then hope that people find it useful. This isn't a good idea, but it is what most managers have been led to believe.

Some environments don't even have a need for data warehousing because warehousing your data won't help you design the next generation processor or build a better Windows. In creative markets, the emphasis is not on historical data but on market conditions and technological breakthroughs. On the other hand, a product support department might find data warehousing to be very beneficial. ■

# Understanding the Concept of Data Warehousing

Data warehousing has been associated with data marts, data mining, extraction tools, metadata tools, and anything that can deal with large amounts of data. A data warehouse can be difficult to describe due to its sheer scope. Indeed, a data warehouse isn't just a large database. In fact, it contains several things.

## The Data Source for the Data Warehouse

The data source for the data warehouse is normally thought of as an OLTP system, or online transaction processing. Although this is certainly true for most of the data flowing into the data warehouse, data can come from anywhere. You can also extract data from the queries performed, the history concerning how results were used, the effects of the business environment, and so forth.

The components of the data warehouse are described in the following list.

- OLTP systems are involved as a source for the data coming into a warehouse.
- Transformers and extraction tools are needed to move the data from the source into the data warehouse target database.
- Maintenance and administration utilities are needed to monitor and modify schema changes in the data warehouse, as well as to maintain the metadata.
- The OLAP applications come into play as the interface to the summarized data—the front end.

A data warehouse is really a data system—a defined set of events and procedures that take data in at one end and change it into useful, strategic information at the other. This process is more difficult than it sounds, but by no means is it impossible to accomplish.

**OLTP Systems** Of all the sources of data for your warehouse, OLTP is the most likely source and the easiest to get to. Extracting heuristic data about the queries or tracking the use of such queries is much more complicated, and probably not something that you will do if you are under time constraints.



OLTP systems are put into place to deal with large amounts of data that are generally repetitive in nature and extremely detailed. An example is a financial institution. Tracking and recording the activities of the accounts would be an OLTP process. Nearly all of the OLTP systems built and being considered are based on relational technology and use SQL to access and manipulate the data and the schemas of the system.

**Transformation and Extraction Tools** Between the OLTP and the data source are the data transformation and extraction tools. These act as a sort of gateway between the detail-level data stored in an OLTP system and the summarized data lying in the data warehouse by transforming data from one form to the other. For developers, this is probably the largest area of growth (along with administration) in data warehousing.

Developing these types of tools is difficult because you must decide which types of metadata are needed, as well as transform and aggregate the data into the data warehouse. It is fairly easy to pull data out of a SQL database, but summarizing that data is somewhat difficult, depending on the summaries needed. Deciding what metadata to keep is also a difficult decision that can affect the administration of the data warehouse. Metadata also has a direct impact on how valuable the information is, and without metadata, the user has no way to decide the value of the source for the information.

Transformation and extraction tools are also in charge of integrating all of the data sources into a single general form when placing the data into the data warehouse. You could be extracting data from twelve different types of databases and decisions on data types, data names, and attributes will be based on the metadata extracted from each of the OLTP systems. Open Database Connectivity (ODBC) alleviates this problem by enabling a single API to access and retrieve the data in addition to specifying common data types and structures. Another approach could be the use of DBMS Gateways, which transform one DBMS call to the native DBMS type.

However you decide to access these databases, using SQL views can aggregate the data from multiple data sources. With the new features in SQL-92, such as schema manipulation and administration, your application could make intelligent choices about transforming the data and converting it into summarized form.

## Metadata Administration

An ongoing process that takes place with data warehousing is the collation and maintenance of the metadata. This is done for the entire system, using metadata gathered in the OLTP systems, from the data extraction and transformation tools and in the target databases themselves. This data is used for expansion plans, new tool development, data mining, and data mart operations. The biggest advantage to using metadata is the capability to make informed decisions based on the value of the information to you. If you can determine how the data is gathered, where it came from, and how it is being used, not only can you make better decisions, but you have an opportunity to see where the data could be improved. The quality of the data in the warehouse is often determined by how much metadata exists about it. When the data appears to pop out of a "black box," it is much more difficult to determine its value to the company.

This area is where some of the most important tools exist. Several products offer the capability to visually design and manipulate your schemas. Visual manipulation of the abstract data such as SQL query decomposition and extraction and transformation rules can also be done. Microsoft's Visual InterDev is an example of such a tool. With it, you can administer the entire site and change anything that you need to. This is also an area where Java developers will be best able to fit into the data warehousing picture.

## The Target Database

The target database is an area of some debate in the database community. Relational technology tends to process serial data very well, but when faced with data that cannot be indexed properly, the performance degrades dramatically.

Because of these obstacles, a new breed of database engines is coming into play, called *multidimensional databases*. Rather than store indexes into the records, multidimensional databases store the data on the disk in small clusters of data that are related to one another. These small clusters are stored internally as arrays, eliminating the need for indexing because the arrays are already indexed by their very nature. Then the multidimensional database engine indexes the clustered arrays. When you send a query to the multidimensional database, it simply finds the clusters most closely matching your request and returns them rather than looking up the record in an index. Sorting or transforming the dimensions of the data is easily done due to the array-like structure of the data.

Gains in performance come mainly from the multidimensional database's capability to exponentially narrow the amount of data to retrieve. It accomplishes this by reading only through the individual columns of data that make up the query. Whereas a relational database must contend with millions or billions of records, multidimensional databases narrow the search down to thousands or even hundreds of records. A relational database vendor, however, is capable of doing the same thing, which makes the philosophical "war" between the multidimensional database vendors and the relational database vendors rather amusing.

SQL is simply an interface for data access, which doesn't deter the relational database from using the same principles internally for its storage mechanisms. In fact, the relational database might actually be a better choice because of its good performance with large loads. Whether a relational database or a multidimensional database is better is a decision for other language's developers to make, because multidimensional databases usually have proprietary APIs and do most of the functions people call on us to do internally. Throughout the remainder of this chapter, we will use relational databases because the tools that we have been given in Visual J++ and Visual InterDev will work only with ODBC.

The issues to address when converting the relational database to use a dimensional data model are complicated. Most relational databases don't handle summarized data that cannot be indexed very well because all of the operations on a relational database assume that you have keys that relate different tables together and primary keys that are used to index records within those tables. Take those primary keys away and suddenly your database is very unstable.



This is where you must either become very creative with database schemas or design an application that takes care of deciding where the summarized data lies. Most likely, you will have a burst of creativity and use a dimensional model for your relational database. Although adding dimensions will be troublesome, at least with relational databases you can summarize data while still being able to determine what order it is in.

The dimensional model was briefly discussed in Chapter 2, "Database Design Concepts," on database design. Basically you are storing the indexed data into a *fact* table, which contains enough information to reliably locate the actual summary data stored in several "dimensions" or leaf tables. The fact table contains a composite primary key consisting of multiple foreign keys, which are then used along with level IDs and generations to locate the data. Basically, the design of the dimensional model is that of a binary tree. The fact tables are located at the intersection point of the tree, containing what is essentially a union of the domains of the nodes below them. They also include data indicating their level IDs and generation, as well as any parents that they might have.

There are probably fifteen or twenty different ways to implement the dimensional model. The end result is usually a table that results in 0NF, a process that is referred to as denormalization. Of course, placing a database back into 0NF precludes the fact that you won't be modifying it. In reality, however, you must allow the data to change (see Figure 16.1).

## Data Marts

Data marts are often confused with data warehouses because, in a sense, that is what they are. However, data marts are more completely summarized than the corporate data warehouse. In fact, they might not even be attached to a data warehouse. More often than not, though, they are. Because of the constraints of an entire organization accessing a single data warehouse, data marts were created from the summarized data in a data warehouse. Most members of a company don't need or care about the majority of the data in the data warehouse, but they need access to smaller portions of the data. At first, the data was extracted when needed and calculations were performed on it manually. Then someone set up an extraction agent to summarize and perform transformations on a subset of the data in a data warehouse—the data mart was the result.

**FIG. 16.1**
The database shown is in a denormalized form.

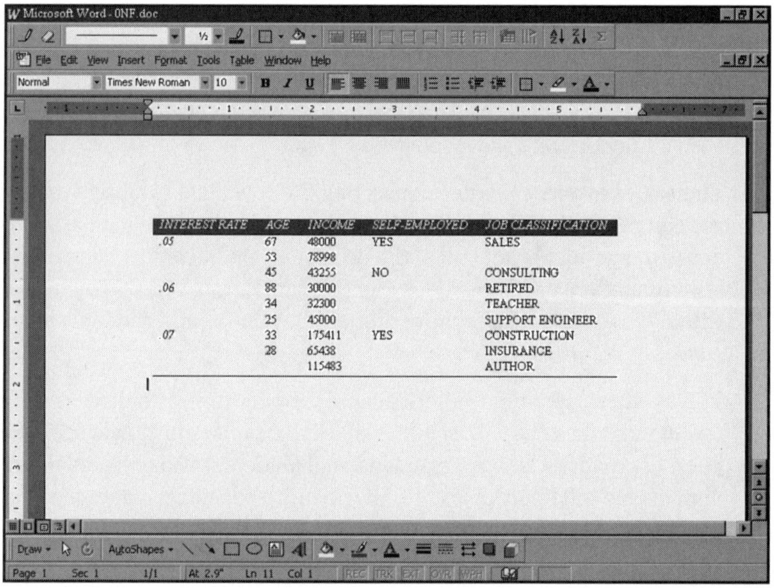

| INTEREST RATE | AGE | INCOME | SELF-EMPLOYED | JOB CLASSIFICATION |
|---|---|---|---|---|
| .05 | 67 | 48000 | YES | SALES |
| | 53 | 78998 | | |
| | 45 | 43255 | NO | CONSULTING |
| .06 | 88 | 30000 | | RETIRED |
| | 34 | 32300 | | TEACHER |
| | 25 | 45000 | | SUPPORT ENGINEER |
| .07 | 33 | 175411 | YES | CONSTRUCTION |
| | 28 | 65438 | | INSURANCE |
| | | 115483 | | AUTHOR |

These smaller versions of the data warehouse are generally fed by extractors and transformers just as the data warehouse is, except that the data comes from the data warehouse rather than from the OLTP systems. The SQL decompositions and calculations required to transform the data from the data warehouse to the data mart are stored as metadata to make adjusting them an easy task should changes be needed.

# Data Mining

Data mining enables you to drill through tons of data in a data warehouse. This is your front-end, or the client application. Because the server must be optimized to support data mining, a "fuzzification" of the existing relational models has been suggested to deal with the huge sets of data resulting from entities such as a data warehouse.

---

**What Is Fuzzification?**

Fuzzification refers to using certain techniques to extract data that was previously unknown or only inferred from the data itself. Some means of "fuzzification" might be table algebra, viewing keys as statistical dependencies, or using techniques such as nearest neighbor selects and clustering of data according to similarity.

---

Associating data mining with clients, as has been done in several cases, can lead to dismal response times. Data mining is actually a server process, sometimes referred to as OLAP, and the engine behind the OLAP front-ends to a data warehouse.

## The Front-End Tools

The portion of your application that most people will actually see is the front-end, consisting of everything from HTML pages to sophisticated query tools. The focus of the front-end is singular, however, presenting a view of the data and enabling the user to perform analytical queries on the summarized information in the data warehouse. This is not as easy as it is with relational queries, for you are providing a method for examining the data in any dimension: time, geographic, statistical distributions, and others. SQL doesn't have this kind of mathematical processing functionality, so your application must convert the request to SQL, retrieve the results, and perform complex algorithmic transformations on the data. If your user is looking for simple calculations such as set functions, SQL can handle those. If your user is expecting to receive a statistical variance between data of different sets, however, you have to provide the code.



When designing front-end tools, you must present the data needed in a form familiar to the user. Cross tabulation is a great tool that Visual J++ will support through Microsoft Jet's concept of pivot tables. Using pivot tables can present the data in an easily recognizable format.

Another method, of course, is to use a multidimensional database engine that can perform such complex permutations on the data internally and return the results much more quickly than an equivalent relational OLAP (Online Analytical Processing) application. This is not an option when using standardized interfaces such as ODBC or SQL, however. Coding to one of these is similar to interfacing with IBM—proprietary all the way.

Creating an application that supports these features against a database that enables their use is usually just as proprietary, however. The highly de-normalized structure of the dimensional models used with the relational OLAP architecture force the application in need of access to the metadata to make sense of the data. Although this data is accessible through normal means, (ODBC, SQL, and so forth), it is rarely intelligible without referring to the metadata.

In general, you work with SQL databases, so a lot of work must go into the schema definitions and the OLAP front-end to make the data warehousing work with relational architectures. For example, the application often is responsible for implementing security on the dimensional tables simply because relational models have no concept of dimensions. Another problem arises when you have pre-calculated the queries, which is almost a requirement to achieve adequate performance with any database engine. There is no relevance for the SQL database between the pre-calculated data and the actual data that the calculations were drawn from. So if those become out of line with the actual data, no one will know unless you keep checks on the calculations.

Perhaps as object-oriented databases become more mainstream (as multidimensional databases are still in their infancy), we'll see some of these issues addressed. Until then, designing the engines behind the front-ends will challenge you.

# Recognizing the Benefits of Data Warehousing

Now that you've read about the horror of data warehousing, you're probably wondering why any sane person wants to build and maintain one. It's simple really: If implemented correctly, data warehouses do wonders for your organization. Data warehousing is not a magic wand you wave to make problems disappear, but they can be advantageous.

The greatest benefit of a data warehouse is for managers, who can use it to make better informed decisions. Trend analysis, statistical deviance, and comparison of different product entries and their effects can be determined with a properly implemented data warehouse. You won't have the capability to see into the future, but you won't be blind to the past.

# Examining Issues in Program Design

Now that you are familiar with how a data warehouse works and the difficulties involved, you will help a fictional company develop one. After taking a look at the following scenario and a systems analysis of the situation, you will also help design one of the company's server processes and a schema development tool.

## A Look at a Fictional Company

RDO Inc. is a fictional financial brokerage located in Dallas. They want to design a data-warehousing environment to compensate for the lack of abstract data being generated by the current OLTP system. The competitive environment is fierce, and the need for accurate forecasting is essential, something that the current system fails to provide.

The management supports the project but believes that it is necessary only because the information system (IS) is not using its current resources efficiently. As a result, you have creative control, but the purse strings are tight. No additional hardware will be implemented, and you are expected to create the data warehouse by using the current site license for SQL Server.

The current IS department is also being phased out for outsourcing, so you can't expect much help there. In fact, because you are the enemy, the outsourcing firm, expect resistance. Upper management ordered several of the backup domain controllers released to you for use with the data warehouse, so you do have the minimum hardware necessary. This is the current situation.

## Problem Definition

There are in-place systems to gather massive amounts of data and place it into a normalized database. The metadata for these systems is non-existent, however, and will have to be built from reverse engineering the database.

More specifically, the company has an OLTP system that is processing several hundred thousand transactions per day, pulling in everything from market conditions to customer transactions. The current state of the environment is good, so we'll assume that there were no normalization problems with a hastily implemented OLTP system. The main reason for embarking on this path is to take advantage of the huge amount of data that the company has collected from its OLTP system and translate that into a strategic resource. Several competitors have done so and are now eating away at RDO's market share and clientele.

The problems identified by management are as follows:

- Lack of statistical forecasting
- Lack of trend analysis in the current front-end
- Inability to accurately simulate business conditions with the current forecasting models
- A need to view the data in several different dimensions, not just a single one



This sounds like a custom-made problem list for data warehousing, and they are for this scenario. In other scenarios you might also see the current sales force showing reluctance to use new tools or even existing ones that might be able to solve some of the problems facing them.

## Requirements Definition

In this instance, a data warehouse might not be the only alternative. Discussing alternatives might cut down the work that we currently have to do.

The first problem is not really a data collection problem, for the data is currently in the company's databases; instead, the problem involves retrieval. The tools that they have in place will work, but little thought was given to the interface, and the tools are rarely used.

We can solve the first problem by simply using an ISAPI DLL that management can access from their browser. This will be a server process that accesses the pre-calculated data in the database and returns the requested data to management. The forecasting will also be a server process that will enable adjustments to be made to the calculations so that you can see the effect of different forecasting methodologies.

The second problem lies in SQL's inability to correlate data between columns or rows. The current tools do not support trend analysis—this is currently done by hand-using Microsoft Excel. You will have to address trend analysis by allowing for pre-determined calculations and ad-hoc calculations performed by the client. This will require a tool to extract and transform the data and to store the results for re-use.

The third problem is one of volume. The sheer amount of data that the OLTP processes every day has prevented attempts to collate the data into accurate reflections of the business environment. No attempts were made to determine exactly what data was relevant to the business environment. Summarizing the data will definitely help with this problem, although the success of a simulation is somewhat subjective.

The fourth problem is one that only a multidimensional architecture can solve. Viewing the data in multiple logical dimensions cannot be accomplished with normal relational queries. This requires designing an OLAP application and the subsequent dimensional model database—the data warehouse.

Although we could solve a majority of these problems with individual solutions, a data warehouse makes sense in this environment because it would solve the problems more completely. This involves writing a completely new schema, designing the dimensional model architecture, creating the extraction and transformation tools, and designing front-ends. Here is what you could devise to present to management:

- Data exists that meets the needs of the company, so no new collection mechanisms need to be implemented.
- Tools can be developed within the current system to solve most, but not all, of the issues listed by management.
- Summarizing the data into a data warehouse solves the problem of having the data in a readily useable form but does not solve the issue of putting the data to use.
- To handle the perceived lack of sophistication in many of the existing front-end tools, we will move the client to the Web browser. This will reduce resource utilization and centralize administration of client changes.

## Design Considerations

In designing a data warehouse, you need to consider several factors. These factors range from environmental to common sense issues. In this section we'll cover some of the major issues you might face when designing a data warehouse. Keep in mind, however, that each of these topics can span an entire book.

**Security** Security is implemented in several ways. If you are using a decent NOS such as NT, you can set permissions on objects and use integrated security so that the user doesn't have to be authenticated more than once. You can also use ODBC security and the individual database's authentication methods.

Preventing people from seeing your data across the Internet is a little bit more difficult, but not much more. Most Web servers accept basic plain-text authentication in addition to a challenge-response mode of authentication (which is covered in Chapter 13, "Security Issues"). As soon as the generic authentication is done, you can use the database's internal security to log the user into the system. If you are designing replication using the Internet as a backbone (some people do this—especially with mail servers), you might think of using point-to-point tunneling protocol or secure sockets to set up secure, encrypted sessions across the Internet.

**Reliability** Reliability is something that everyone wants and most assume. If you're talking about the reliability of the data, using integrity constraints is the answer, especially with summarized data in the data warehouse. Unless these constraints are enforced in the warehouse, it will be almost impossible to guarantee repeatable queries.

Usually when using relational databases with the dimensional model, you will have to implement the integrity constraints yourself because the database doesn't understand the relations between the dimensions and levels, generations and parents. Another alternative is to construct SQL views that approximate the dimensional model, work from those, and then use the relational databases built-in integrity constraints and references.

To most people, reliability concerns the hardware, the network connection, and the client staying up. Because most of these components are beyond your control, the best you can hope for is a good network and a RAID array (NT does software raid level 5). Putting replication strategies and backups into place also helps.

**NOTE** RAID is an acronym for Redundant Array of Inexpensive Drives. The term RAID Level 5, denotes that at least three drives are being used. One writes parity information, and the other two drives are written with stripes of data in alternate writes (or reads). This enhances redundancy because a single drive loss does not affect the data (although losing a drive does significantly affect performance). Performance for an unbroken RAID Level 5 array is also faster than normal access due to the capability to read from several drives at once. Windows NT offers three levels of RAID, Levels 1,2, and 5, and can regenerate information from a failed disk by using the parity information with RAID Level 5.



**Performance** Performance is a big factor when designing the database schema. The advantage of storing the summary data and performing calculations at runtime must be weighed against the massive network traffic and the option of using pre-calculated data that you have to keep track of.

As usual, the solution lies somewhere in between: Using the Web-based client almost guarantees a two-tier architecture. Taking that to a three-tier client/server architecture could have benefits in allowing the calculations to be performed on the same server as the database for smaller calculations, and using predefined, calculated data for the larger analysis.

The more involved decisions concern the actual layout of the schema and the summary information. To obtain adequate performance from the SQL tables on a scale of several hundred gigabytes means optimizing the way in which the drill-downs and data retrieval is done. By using a vertical dimensional model, you could increase performance if you don't have a lot of pre-calculated data. You could drill down to any depth with a single join. Determining what data is needed and how it is to be delivered will help to analyze the schema. For example, RDO Inc. is looking for summarized statistical data, as well as the capability to correlate sets of data with one other. Say that they track market fluctuations, interest rates, customer income level, and purchasing habits. The resulting dimensional model might look like Table 16.1.

**Table 16.1 Placing the Data into a Correlated Table Showing Some of the Dimensions Available**

| Money | Age | Interest Rate |
|---|---|---|
| < $20,000 | < 21 | +0% |
| | 21–35 | +5% |
| | 36–55 | +0% |
| | 56+ | +10% |

*continues*

**Table 16.1 Continued**

| Money | Age | Interest Rate |
|---|---|---|
| $20,000–35,000 | < 21 | +3% |
| | 21–35 | +5% |
| | 36–55 | +7% |
| | 56+ | +10% |
| $35,000–$45,000 | < 21 | +0% |
| | 21–35 | +12% |
| | 36–55 | +17% |
| | 56+ | +20% |

The information in Table 16.1 could be used to show correlation's between interest rates and the amount of investment by people of different age and income groups. This query would be very difficult to construct using normal relational models, but if the data is stored dimensionally with categories like those in Table 16.1, the data is almost in the form that you need it. Informational dimensions would be nice to have as well, but the relational model doesn't enable you to relate columns within the relation. As you can see, if you plan out your structure and data models well, performance will be much better.

## Using Metadata

Metadata collection has been stressed throughout this book and is one of the more important topics in data warehousing. This metadata can be either summaries of the actual data or information about the database itself. In this section, we'll deal with the structural information, which is most relevant to our project.

The database schema represents an interesting opportunity to explore what we can do with Java because Visual J++ can access the schema through direct SQL statements if the database supports it.

This metadata is used mainly to aid integration and to make schema definition much easier when integrating new systems into the organization. Data warehousing is certainly one of the areas in which metadata definition is of paramount importance, due to the many different sources of data and the uses that the data will be put to once it is summarized and placed into the target database.

In a larger sense, data warehouses can be thought of as a collection of views that summarize the data from which they are drawn. From this, you can conclude that information about how these views came to be leads to a greater understanding of how to use the data warehouse. Storing the definitions concerning how the summarized data is being generated and placed in the warehouse is also needed.

Data dictionaries are generally thought of as the "metadata" databases, but these dictionaries do not store semantic information such as correspondence of the semantic data, (does employee.id in one table correspond to worker.id in another?). Nor are assumptions and derivation formulas stored in a traditional data dictionary. The SQL schema object limits you to identifying the traditional data dictionary, so this must be extracted and merged with the more semantic and heuristic data. This data can then be accessed by the front-end systems that need to make sense of the underlying table structures.



Still, the majority of information in the schema will relate directly to the data itself: what views are defined, the domains, what procedures and modules are available for use and how they can be used. The multiple types of metadata that can be extracted from the schema was covered in Chapter 4,"The SQL Standard: A Language for Data Access."

## Determining the Data to Be Summarized

The most difficult aspect about designing a summarized data model is deciding which data to summarize and how. This is as complicated as the English language because everyone can have a different view of the same summarized data even if it were extracted in the exact same manner each time. For this reason, actually deciding how the summaries are rolled up and which data attributes to include in those rollups can keep you awake at night.

A good idea is to set the schema aside for a second and decide what really matters to the business that this is being developed for. Identify the strategic factors that drive the industry and then the specific region of the industry this company belongs to. As soon as you've determined the strategic information, you can summarize the data with those goals in mind. Most of the time, you will use almost all of the data in the OLTP databases to pull the summaries from, and the strategic goals of the company will simply drive how those summaries are calculated.

## Placing the data into the Dimensional model

After you have decided on the summary methods and calculations, you can then begin placing the data into an abstracted data model. The model used throughout this book, and the most popular analytical model, is the dimensional model. The dimensional model enables the use of fact tables and leaf nodes. No matter what the dialect is for the dimensional model you choose, the underlying components will remain the same, as shown in the following list.

- *Fact tables* These contain what is essentially a composite primary key consisting of the foreign keys of each of the leaf nodes plus any additional numeric data that is accessed often.
- *Dimensions* A group of attributes that are similar in type in the user's perspective, such as years, months, weeks, and days for the time dimension.

This organization results in a very efficient and intuitive model. On paper, the actual model looks like a binary tree, or conceptually like a cube. The best way to conceptualize how dimensions are used is to think of the cube as being the data that is referenced in the fact table. Viewing this by the time dimension would rotate the cube so that all rows were ordered and summarized through the time dimension, as shown in Figure 16.2.

**FIG. 16.2**
This is the dimensional model as it really looks and acts. The actual dimensions are implied; only the attributes are included in the data model.

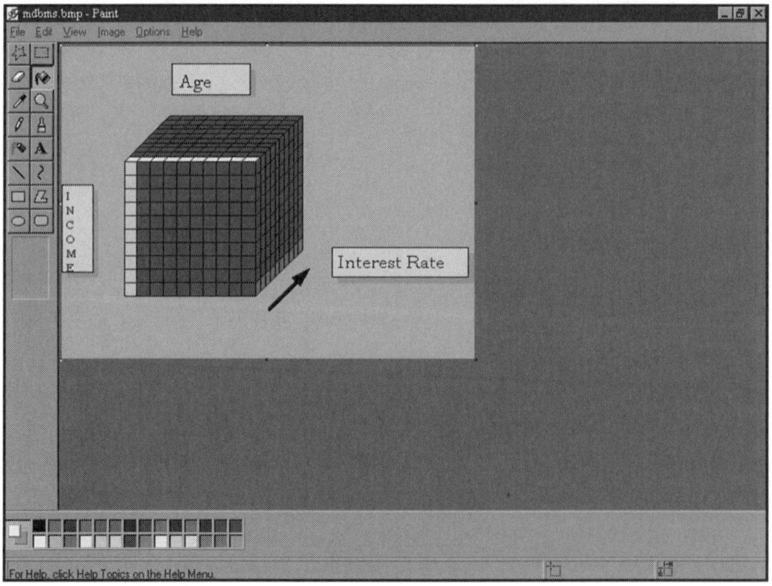


For now, though, the concept is easier to visualize in a linear fashion. Basically, the simplest dimensional model would look much like Figure 16.3.

**FIG. 16.3**
This shows the linear representation of the Dimensional data model, with the relationship between the fact table and the leaf nodes (dimensions).

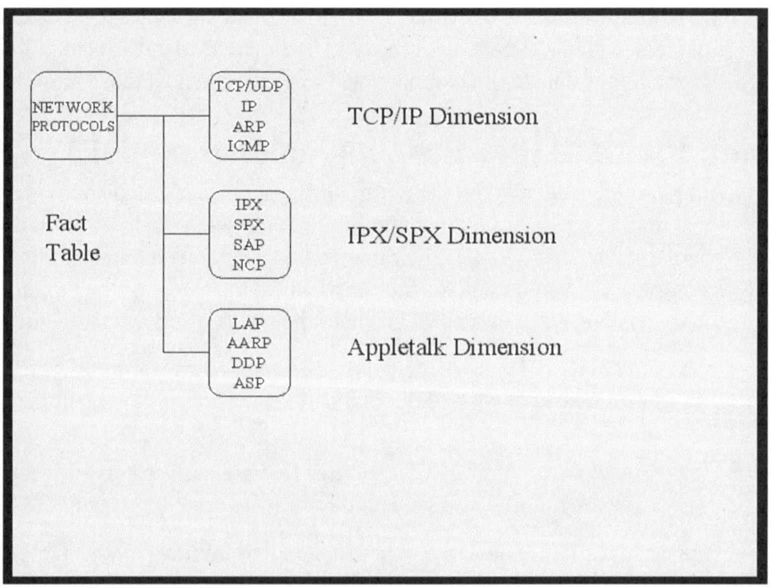

There are several distinct versions of the dimensional model that deal with the depth of the tree structure and how the nodes and leafs are referenced. The simplest dimensional schema simply calls for four columns of data to be included with each dimension. They are:

- *Dimension Key* This contains all possible values for the dimension. For example, if General Motors were the dimension, the key would contain Oldsmobile, Pontiac, Chevrolet, and so on.
- *Parent* This holds the key of the parent node. (Optional for performance.)
- *Level* This describes at what level the dimension member is located.
- *Generation* Describes at which generation the dimension member lies.



The difference between the level and generation can be explained this way. The level identifies all dimensional members having the same number of descendants in any single path below them. A generation describes how many parents a member has, how many hops to the top so to speak.

The differences between the differing dialects of the dimensional models basically have to do with how they are structured—by depth or by width. This affects the performance of certain queries, of course, making some faster than others. For example, on a horizontal model, only a single join is required to drill to any depth.

However you decide to structure the model, this will be the form taken by the data warehouse because the intent in a data warehouse is to enable analytical processing, not transactions.

## De-Normalizing the Data

The data in a data warehouse is actually de-normalized when the developer places it into the dimensional structure. You can retain some form of normalization by using a star or snowflake schema, but the data is still being de-normalized. This isn't a big concern because you are not intending this to be used for transaction processing. Most updates will occur in scheduled batches.

The performance degradation associated with a database in normalized form simply cannot be tolerated, hence the development of multidimensional data models. Some of the extensions proposed for SQL3 enable object-oriented data to be stored, so there might be more help on the way for using relational databases in a multidimensional environment.

## Designing the OLAP Front-End

By their very nature, OLAP applications are difficult to implement at times because of the feature sets required by their users. The next section discusses some of the problems and issues in developing these tools.

## Design Considerations

Designing a front-end application has the same requirements as designing any other application, with the added complexity of being multiuser. The database engine can handle most of the difficulties with multiuser programming. To implement thin clients, however, you need to deal with the issue directly. This means taking on the sticky security and performance-under-heavy-load conditions, as well as thread synchronization and notification. The next few topics deal directly with some of the issues that you might face when developing these types of applications.

**Security** Security in the client application can also be implemented in several ways, the most obvious of which are identical to the data warehouse itself. Another way, however, is through the use of an encryption algorithm such as PGP (Pretty Good Privacy), which would prevent anyone from determining the data being transmitted.

Most OLAP applications are not based externally on the Internet, however. Most are internal to the corporation, so the people who are accessing the data already have been logged into the corporate network. In this case, the best security would still be the NOS security, combined with the database's capability to place permissions on certain objects inside the tables.

**Consistency** Consistency is a holy grail to users. When they see something familiar, they cling to it as if it were their favorite toy. If you keep your interfaces consistent with one other, the user will feel re-assured. This is the main reason for the OS wars—not because one is inherently better but because everyone likes to think that his toy is the best.

It is easy with Java to design a user interface that is consistently bad, however. Eliminating the quirks that separate your application from the others on the users' systems will constitute the majority of your workload—simple things like handling the tab functionality to customizing toolbars so that your application will look "normal." Microsoft provides some help in this area, as have a multitude of developers. By using the built-in resource editor in Visual J++, you can design decent applets (with only basic controls, however). I recommend learning to use the GridBagLayout and also developing custom layout managers to handle things like toolbars and tree controls. There are hundreds of examples of these on the Internet, and most are free.

Users expect a certain level of functionality in their applications, however, which is the major reason for going with Web-based clients. You have much more creative control over the user interface than using pure Java, and you can still call on Java's power to do the types of things that it was written for.

**Performance** Performance is the second holy grail, right next to consistency. Performance is accomplished mainly by moving most of the calculations and data manipulation out of the client and into the server. The thin client architecture has a definite advantage here, because, by definition, your server application is doing the work. All the client needs to do is display the data and store it locally for later use, if necessary.

Multithreading the application will improve performance in some instances, especially in cases of dual processor boards or single processors that have parallel instruction pipelines. These are becoming a reality for the average user.

**CAUTION**

Don't overdo multithreading, though. Creating too many threads could be as bad or worse than using a single thread. Each thread uses system resources, and synchronization of threads can become difficult.

This is probably as good a place as any to deal with the issue of thread synchronization. When coding multithreaded applications, there are two standard issues that will arise if you are not careful: the race condition and the deadly embrace.

In the race condition two or more threads access an object, producing chaotic results. For example, consider an investment account. Your application calls a function that moves the money into the account. This seems simple, but there are problems. Money keeps disappearing or appearing, seemingly, out of thin air. If you take a look at how the money moves into the account, you will notice that on an atomic level, the value moves into a register (or two depending on the value) and then into the memory address of the variable. This is where the problem lies: If one thread is interrupted before it has a chance to move the data into the memory address of the account, the data is lost because the other thread will move the money into a register when it attempts to credit or debit the account.



A deadly embrace is a situation in which there are two threads and each is waiting for the other to release an object before completing its own operation. Because neither can complete its operation, a deadly embrace results, and both will remain blocked indefinitely. There is no way to exit this condition except by killing one of the threads.

Using thread synchronization and building your own synchronized methods can eliminate the first problem. Eliminating the second simply requires careful planning.

The second way to achieve better performance is to implement separate classes for your data access functions to be downloaded to the client. Most of the time, the overhead is small (less than 5 or 6 K in most instances) for simple applications. This can allow you to depend on the database engine for your synchronization and multiuser capabilities. However, for more intensive calculations or when dealing with massive data sets, consider the performance tradeoffs of going over a 28.8 line or doing the processing locally on the server.

**Friendliness** As noted in the section on the fictional company, sometimes the existing clients would have served to deliver some of the functions that management expects. However, the interface was poorly implemented or the performance wasn't good, so the products were not taken seriously as real information retrieval tools. Instead, people will intentionally abuse and exaggerate the problems facing the existing software. This means that you will need to listen to their real needs, not always the complaints. Use the old programming maxim: Make it simple and make it work. Don't try to add features just because they would be cool. If you can design a decent-looking application with a minimum of effort that does what users want, then you'll have a winner.

This isn't an impossible goal to attain, for Web-based applications are fairly easy to build and inherently easy to use. Because you can implement an ISAPI DLL for the functionality required by the application, Web-based solutions can be ideal.

# From Here...

You now have enough information to formulate your own opinions about data warehousing and how to use it. We haven't shown any specific examples because the scope of this topic requires you to build custom solutions for each data warehouse that you design. Every environment will be different and most of what you do at one site will not work for another. Basically, all you will be able to take with you from one environment to another is the experience that you gain.

- Chapter 2, "Database Design Concepts," introduces many of the design topics discussed in this chapter.
- Chapter 4, "The SQL Standard: A Language for Data Access," explores the SQL-92 grammar and the concepts behind the language.
- Chapter 5, "ODBC," covers Microsoft's interface to the SQL Call Level Interfaces and the foundation for Microsoft's data access technologies.
- Chapter 17, "Building a Web Crawler with DAO," looks at developing a somewhat simple database application based on the MOOSE Web Crawler discussed in Chapter 2, "Database Design Concepts." You'll see how easy it is to wrap up DAO (or any other data access class) into a reusable class.
- Chapter 18, "The Client/Server Quandary," discusses many of the basic issues when developing database applications.

CHAPTER 17

# Building a Web Crawler with DAO

**Adding the parser**

With this type of program, perhaps the most difficult part is implementing the HTML parsing routines.

**Building the data access classes**

Discover how easy it is to drop RDO or DAO modules into the design.

In Chapter 2, "Database Design Concepts," we developed a data design for a Web crawler. We explored normalizing and breaking out the relations, but never really discussed how this would be implemented. Well, the actual program has been saved until you had a firm grounding in database programming.

This chapter covers the development of the back end, the applet that connects to and categorizes everything it comes across. You will be taken from the main routine, through the development of an HTML parser, and then the data access class. The most interesting code is the data access class, simply because you can take any data access method—be it JDBC, ODBC, RDO, or DAO—and the applet will perform exactly the same way.

# Adding the Parser

Designing the parser is always the most difficult part of any search engine or Web crawler. Because of this difficulty, we have left room for extensions and implemented only the basic functionality. The following is a list of several basic items in an HTML page that were included in the parsing routines.

- Applets
- Forms
- Images
- Links
- Imagemaps
- Tables
- Tags

Deciding the best implementation for this parser is somewhat difficult. There are several ways to do this, most of which are more sophisticated than the method chosen here for expedience. For instance, the parsing routines in this application simply accept a stream for input and use the `getUntil()` and `skipUntil()` to scan for characters in which we are interested. Perhaps a better implementation would be to implement the parser by overloading `FilterInputStream` or `PushedBackInputStream()` to gain some efficiency.

Take a look at Listing 17.1, which provides the code for implementing the parser. Notice that our constructor accepts the `InputStream`, and we've implemented the parser through the `Next()` method.

**Listing 17.1 PARSER.JAVA—Implementing the Main HTML Parsing Method**

```
public String next(MOOSE app)
{
     m_app = app;
     while (true)
     {
          boolean ok = skipUntil((char)'<');
                    if (!ok) return null;
          String s = getUntil((char)'>');
                    m_app.showStatus("String Found: " + s);
          if (s.length() == 0) return null;
                    if (s.toLowerCase().startsWith("img src"))
               nextIMG(s);
          else if (s.toLowerCase().startsWith("a href"))
              nextURL(s);
          else if(s.toLowerCase().startsWith("applet"))
               nextApplet(s);
          else if(s.toLowerCase().startsWith("script"))
               nextScript();
          else if(s.toLowerCase().startsWith("form"))
               nextForm();
```

```
            else if(s.toLowerCase().startsWith("table"))
                 nextTable();
            else if(s.toLowerCase().startsWith("map"))
                 nextMap();
            else if(s.toLowerCase().startsWith("—"));
            else
                 nextTag(s);
        return s;
      }
}
```

After you've implemented the main method (which is simply a comparison structure), the methods called need to be implemented. The easiest to implement are those that have limited or no parsing to do and simply set the type and return a value. These are shown in Listing 17.2.



**Listing 17.2 PARSER.JAVA—Handling the Calls from Our Main Parsing Loop**

```
void nextApplet(String s)
{
     m_Type = "APPLET";
     m_app.addApplet(s);
}

String nextForm()
{
     m_Type = "FORM";
     String s = getForm();
     return s;
}

void nextMap()
{
     m_Type = "FORM";
     getMap();
}

void nextScript()
{
     m_Type = "SCRIPT";
     getScript();
}

void nextTable()
{
     m_Type = "TABLE";
     getTable();
}

public void nextTag(String s)
{
     m_Type = "TAG";
     m_app.addTag(s);
}
```

*continues*

**Listing 17.2 Continued**

```
public String getType()
{
     return m_Type;
}
```

The next pieces of the puzzle are the character scanning methods, `getUntil()` and `skipUntil()`. These methods simply test for a certain character pattern and return a Boolean value. Listing 17.3 details these two methods.

**Listing 17.3 PARSER.JAVA—The *getUntil()* and *skipUntil()* Methods**

```
private boolean skipUntil(char ch)
{  try
   {  while (true)
      {  int nextch = is.read();
         if (nextch == -1) return false;
         if ((char)nextch == ch) return true;
      }
   } catch(IOException e)
   {  return false;
   }
}

private String getUntil(char ch)
{  String s = "";
   try
   {  while (true)
      {  int nextch = is.read();
         if (nextch == -1 ¦¦ (char)nextch == ch) return s;
         else s = s + (char)nextch;
      }

   } catch(IOException e)
   {  return s;
   }
}
```

Next, we'll need routines that break apart the streams of information once we've determined what type of information is contained in the line. Perhaps the hardest implementation will be those for tables and imagemaps, as these can contain any number of items. (For those of you who have done MAPI programming, this is much the same as recursively enumerating a hierarchy of folders using MAPI tables.) Listing 17.4 shows the `getTable()` method.

**Listing 17.4 PARSER.JAVA—Implementing the *getTable()* Method to Parse Through the HTML Tables**

```
private String getTable()
{
     boolean m_parsingTable = true;
     int index = 0;
     m_Table = new Table();

     while(m_parsingTable)
     {
        boolean ok = skipUntil((char)'<');

        if (!ok) return null;
        String s = getUntil((char)'>');
        m_app.showStatus("Parsing Table: " + s);

        if (s.length() == 0) return null;
        if(s.toLowerCase().startsWith("a href")) nextURL(s);
        else if(s.toLowerCase().startsWith("img")) nextIMG(s);
        else if(s.toLowerCase().startsWith("tb")) m_app.addTableElement(s);
        else if(s.toLowerCase().startsWith("td")) m_app.addTableElement(s);
        else if(s.toLowerCase().startsWith("tr")) m_app.addTableElement(s);
        if(s.toLowerCase().startsWith("/table"))
        {
               m_app.addTableElement(s);
               m_parsingTable = false;
        }
        else
               m_app.addTableElement(s);
               m_Table.add(s);
        index++;

       }
   return m_Table.getTitle();
}
```

Imagemaps also present a challenge since they can contain many different elements. This method is somewhat similar to the `getTable()` method in that we recursively search the construct for map elements. Now for parsing the imagemaps a similar construct is needed, this is listed in Listing 17.5.

**Listing 17.5 PARSER.JAVA—Implementing the *getTable()* Method to Parse Through the HTML Imagemaps**

```
private void getMap()
{
     boolean m_parsingMap = true;
     int index = 0;
     m_Map = new Map();
```

*continues*

**Listing 17.5 Continued**

```
     while(m_parsingMap)
     {
          boolean ok = skipUntil((char)'<');
          if (!ok) return;
          String s = getUntil((char)'>');
          m_app.showStatus("Parsing Map: " + s);
                if (s.length() == 0) return;
          if(s.toLowerCase().startsWith("map"))
          {
               m_ifDelim = s.indexOf("\"");
               m_str = s.substring(m_ifDelim, s.lastIndexOf("\"")-1);
               m_app.addMapElement(m_str);
          }
          if(s.toLowerCase().startsWith("area"))
          {
               nextURL(s);
               m_app.addMapElement(s);
          }
          if(s.toLowerCase().startsWith("/map"))
          {
               m_app.addMapElement(s);
               m_parsingMap = false;
          }
          else
               m_Map.add(s);
      index++;

}
}
```

Next, we'll create a script parsing method in case we run into any VBScript or JScript tidbits we want to keep. This is shown in Listing 17.6.

**Listing 17.6 PARSER.JAVA—Implementing the *getScript()* Method to Parse Through the HTML Scripts**

```
private void getScript()
{
     boolean m_parsingScript = true;
     int index = 0;
     m_Script = new Script();

     while(m_parsingScript)
     {
          boolean ok = skipUntil((char)'<');

          if (!ok) return;
          String s = getUntil((char)'>');
          m_app.showStatus("Parsing Script: " + s);
```

```
            if (s.length() == 0) return
            if(s.toLowerCase().startsWith("script"))
                 m_app.addScriptElement(getScriptType(s));
            if(s.toLowerCase().startsWith("/script"))
            {
                 m_app.addScriptElement(s);
                m_parsingScript = false;
            }
            else
                 m_app.addScriptElement(s);
                 m_Script.add(s);
            index++;

      }
}

// Helper method for parsing script type.

String getScriptType(String s)
{
      int from = s.indexOf("\"");
      if (from >= 0)
      {  int to = s.indexOf("\"", from + 1);
            if (to > 0)
            {  s = s.substring(from + 1, to);}
      }
      return s;
}
```

The next method parses through a form and breaks out the form's elements for addition to our database, as shown in Listing 17.7.

**Listing 17.7 PARSER.JAVA—Implementing the *getForm()* Method to Parse Through HTML Forms**

```
private String getForm()
{
      boolean m_parsingform = true;
      int index = 0;
      m_form = new Form();

      while(m_parsingform = true)
      {
           boolean ok = skipUntil((char)'<');
           if (!ok) return null;
           String s = getUntil((char)'>');
           m_app.showStatus("Parsing Form: " + s);

           if (s.length() == 0) return null;
           if(s.toLowerCase().startsWith("a href")) nextURL(s);
           else if(s.toLowerCase().startsWith("img")) nextIMG(s);
```

*continues*

**Listing 17.7 Continued**

```
            if(s.toLowerCase().startsWith("/form")) m_parsingform = false;
            else
                 m_app.addForm(s);
                 m_form.add(s);
            index++;
       }
       return m_form.getHeader();
}
```

We only have a few things left that we need to look out for, one of those being the most obvious—URLs. Listing 17.8 shows the method used to filter out the URLs from the input stream.

**Listing 17.8 PARSER.JAVA—Implementing the *nextURL()* Method to Parse Through the HTML for URL Tags**

```
public String nextURL(String s)
{
   int from = s.indexOf("\"");
   if (from >= 0)
   {  int to = s.indexOf("\"", from + 1);
     if (to > from + 1)
     {  s = s.substring(from + 1, to);
            if(s.startsWith("http://") || s.startsWith("/"))
            {
                  m_Type = "HTTP";
                  m_app.addLink(s);
            }
            else if(s.startsWith("mailto:"))
              m_Type = "MAILTO";
            else if(s.startsWith("file://"))
              m_Type = "FILE";
            else if(s.startsWith("ftp://"))
              m_Type = "FTP";
            else if(s.startsWith("gopher://"))
              m_Type = "GOPHER";
            else if(s.startsWith("wais://"))
              m_Type = "WAIS";
     }
   }
return s;
}
```

Another important part of the HTML world is its images, so we need a method for capturing the HTML image tags. This is shown in Listing 17.9.

**Listing 17.9 PARSER.JAVA—Implementing the *nextIMG()* Method to Parse Through the HTML for IMG Tags**

```
String nextIMG(String s)
{
    int from = s.indexOf("\"");
       if (from >= 0)
       {  int to = s.indexOf("\"", from + 1);
          if (to > 0)
          {  s = s.substring(from + 1, to);
             m_Type = "IMAGE";
                 m_app.addImage(s);
          }
       }
          return s;
}
```



# Building the Data Access Classes

Using data access is the center of this entire exercise, so database support is definitely needed here. In designing the database portion of this application, we wanted to minimize the effects of changing the actual database code.

This design sets all of the code dealing directly with the database (or ODBC data source) into a single small file. If you are interested in adding delete support, you simply add a method for DB.delete (Variant m_vColumn) or even have multiple interfaces to support positioned deletes or updates when links change. This is much like designing an API around the APIs. Abstracting in this manner enables you to free your application from any ties to a particular data access method.

Listing 17.10 implements a simple way to add data to any database, accepting arguments for the database, table, column, and the value. Two different versions are implemented, one in DAO and the other in RDO. Both have the same functionality.

**Listing 17.10 DB.JAVA—Encapsulating the DAO Code in an Easily Replaceable Module**

```
import dao350.*;
import com.ms.com.*;
/0/
//
// DB
//
//
public class DB
{
```

*continues*

**Listing 17.10 Continued**

```
_DBEngine idbengine;
      dao350.Error  m_objError;
     Database m_database;
     QueryDef m_query;
     Recordset m_objRecordset;
     Errors m_objErrors;

     Parameters m_Params;
     Parameter m_Parameter;
     Variant m_vflExclusive = new Variant();
     Variant m_vflReadOnly = new Variant();
     Variant m_vRecordsetType = new Variant();
     Variant m_Connect = new Variant();
     Variant m_vLockType = new Variant();
     Variant m_vName = new Variant();
     Variant m_vOptions = new Variant();
     Variant m_vIndex = new Variant();
     Variant m_objField = new Variant();

     protected boolean readOnly = false;
      protected String strDatabase;
      protected String strRecordset;
         protected int recordCount;
     protected static Variant varEmpty = new Variant();

     public DB()
     {
     }

     public boolean send(String strDatabase, String strTable, Variant Column,
➥Variant Value)
     {
          varEmpty.putEmpty();
           try{
              ILicenseMgr mgr = new LicenseMgr();
                  idbengine = (_DBEngine)mgr.createWithLic(
                  "mbmabptebkjcdlgtjmskjwtsdhjbmkmwtrak",
               "{00000010-0000-0010-8000-00AA006D2EA4}",
            null,
            ComContext.INPROC_SERVER
        );

        // Open database
        m_vflExclusive.putBoolean(false);
        m_vflReadOnly.putBoolean(readOnly);
        m_Connect.putString("");
        m_database = idbengine.OpenDatabase(strDatabase, m_vflExclusive,
➥m_vflReadOnly, m_Connect);


        // Create a new recordset
        m_vRecordsetType.putShort((short)RecordsetTypeEnum.dbOpenDynaset);
        m_vOptions.putShort((short)(readOnly ? RecordsetOptionEnum.dbReadOnly :
```

```
➥0));
      m_vLockType.putInt(LockTypeEnum.dbOptimistic);

      m_objRecordset = m_database.OpenRecordset(strTable, m_vRecordsetType,
m_vOptions,m_vLockType);
      m_objRecordset.AddNew();
      m_objRecordset.putCollect(Column, Value);
      m_objRecordset.Update(UpdateTypeEnum.dbUpdateRegular, false);
      m_objRecordset.Close();
      m_database.Close();
      idbengine=null;
      return true;
}
catch(com.ms.com.ComFailException e)
{m_objErrors =
idbengine.getErrors();System.out.println(m_objError.getDescription());return
➥false;}
      }

}
```



Listing 17.11 provides the RDO code. It looks and performs in almost exactly the same way as the DAO code, with the exception of a little additional work to set up RDO to add a new record.

**Listing 17.11 RDB.JAVA—Designing an RDO Data Access Class**

```
import msrdo20.*;
import com.ms.com.*;
//
//
// RDB
//
//
public class RDB
{
      // RDO Interfaces
      protected static _rdoEngine m_objEngine;
      protected static _rdoEnvironment m_objEnvironment;
      protected static _rdoConnection m_objConnection;
      protected static rdoPreparedStatement m_objPreparedStatement;
      protected static _rdoResultset m_objResultset;

      protected      Variant m_vflExclusive = new Variant();
      protected      Variant m_vflReadOnly = new Variant();
      protected      Variant m_vPromptType = new Variant();
      protected      Variant m_Connect = new Variant();
      protected      Variant m_vLockType = new Variant();
      protected      Variant m_vName = new Variant();
      protected     Variant m_vOptions = new Variant();
      protected      Variant m_vIndex = new Variant();
      protected static Variant varEmpty = new Variant();
```

*continues*

**Listing 17.11 Continued**

```
     protected boolean readOnly = false;

      protected String m_strConnect;
         protected String strRecordset;
     protected String m_strDummyQueryName = "Query";
     protected int recordCount;

     public RDB()
     {
     }

     public boolean send(String strDatabase, String strTable, Variant Column,
➥Variant Value)
     {
          try
          {
          varEmpty.putEmpty();
          String m_Column = Column.toString();
          ILicenseMgr mgr = new LicenseMgr();
          m_objEngine = (_rdoEngine)mgr.createWithLic(
               "B1692F60-23B0-11D0-8E95-00A0C90F26F8",
               "{5E71F04C-551F-11CF-8152-00AA00A40C25}",
               null,
               ComContext.INPROC_SERVER);

          m_objEnvironment = m_objEngine.rdoCreateEnvironment("", "", "");

          // Set the OpenConnection parameters
          m_vPromptType .putInt(PromptConstants.rdDriverComplete);
          m_vflReadOnly.putBoolean(readOnly);
          m_Connect.putString(m_strConnect);

          // Open a connection
          m_objConnection = m_objEnvironment.OpenConnection("", m_vPromptType ,
               m_vflReadOnly, m_Connect, m_vOptions);

          // Set the SQL
          String strSQL = "SELECT " + m_Column + " FROM " + strTable;
          Variant m_vSQL = new Variant();
          m_vSQL.putString(strSQL);

          // Set the prepared statement
          m_objPreparedStatement =
➥m_objConnection.CreatePreparedStatement(m_strDummyQueryName, m_vSQL);

          // Get a resultset, setting cursor type and concurrency
          Variant m_vType = new Variant();
          Variant m_vConcurrency = new Variant();
          m_vOptions = varEmpty;
          m_vType.putInt(ResultsetTypeConstants.rdOpenKeyset);
          m_vConcurrency.putInt(LockTypeConstants.rdConcurRowVer);
          m_objResultset = m_objConnection.OpenResultset(m_strDummyQueryName,
               m_vType , m_vConcurrency, m_vOptions);
```

```
            m_objResultset.AddNew();
            m_objResultset.putCollect(Column, Value);
            m_objResultset.Update();
            m_objResultset.Close();
            m_objPreparedStatement.Close();
            m_objConnection.Close();
            m_objEnvironment.Close();
            m_objEngine = null;

            return true;
        }
        catch(com.ms.com.ComFailException e)
        {
                  m_objErrors = idbengine.getErrors();
                   System.out.println(m_objError.getDescription());
                   return false;
        }
    }
}
```



# From Here...

Using DAO or RDO is a natural means of creating an indexed table for search engines. Due to the speed and the fact that your server is where a Web crawler will reside, perhaps DAO would be a better choice, with the possibility for upsizing the database at a later date.

This chapter is not intended to give exact instructions but to give a general idea of what you can do with database programming. For another much more complex example, take a look at Microsoft Exchange or SQL Mail. Mail systems are basically large (usually complex) databases that utilize the cutting edge in technology for our industry, such as replication, directory services, and many other database technologies.

- Chapter 18, "The Client/Server Quandary," introduces you to the concept of client/server and how this concept affects the way you design and develop applications.

CHAPTER 18

# The Client/Server Quandary

**Exploring client/server architecture**

Learn about client/server architecture and the key advantages and disadvantages of a client/server environment.

**Applying client/server architecture to database design**

Discover how to apply client/server concepts when designing a database application. Learn about logical and physical application architectures, including a comparison of single-tier to multi-tier architectures. Explore "thin" client architectures and the ramifications of this approach.

The last two decades have witnessed tumultuous change in the computer industry. The advent of the mini-computer started a trickle of enterprising developers moving away from the massive mainframes of the day. The introduction of the early personal computers hastened this flow into a raging river. A torrent of products claiming to pull all of the diverse pieces together now swirl through the marketplace. This chapter discusses client/server application development and some of the challenges it presents. It covers the key advantages and disadvantages of using this approach, as well as many of the problems that you will face when creating a client/server application and how to avoid or overcome them. You will learn how to apply the concepts when designing a database application by using an object-oriented language such as Java. ■

# Understanding Client/Server

As you probably know, client/server is a method of building a software solution by dividing the solution into two or more applications that cooperate to provide a total solution, instead of using a single monolithic application that provides all of the functionality. Servers are stand-alone external applications that provide a dedicated, specialized functionality. Server applications implement tasks that are complex, time consuming, redundant, and repetitive. Any application that makes use of the services provided by the server is referred to as a client of that server. The client application communicates with the server application by sending a request via a predefined protocol. The server performs the requested task(s) and returns results as appropriate.

One of the most common implementations of client/server architecture is the separation of the data management functionality from the business logic of the application. Dedicated database management systems function as stand-alone server applications and provide data storage and retrieval to the business applications. The arrival of the personal computer propelled the concept of client/server technology. It provided the capability of using the smart personal workstation to provide a user-friendly graphical user interface as a *front-end* to the business logic application on the *back-end*.

---

**Comparison of Modularized Application to a Client/Server Application**

Developers have practiced structured programming for years, focusing on modularizing their application code into modules that provide a certain type of functionality, such as file input/output and printing. Isn't this really the same thing as client/server? Yes and No. It is similar to client/server in that it separates out the tasks into modules that are reusable by many applications. The important distinction is that modularized code is compiled into your application. Every line of code in that module will be compiled into your executable. Recall that the definition of client/server states that the server application is external to the client application. Modularized code is internal to your application.

For example, Sol and Mark are developing software for their company ACME Widgets. Sol is developing an application for 25 users in the operations department, and Mark is developing an application for 25 users in the marketing department. Sol has developed a file management utility module to store data on his PC. Mark has also developed a file management utility, but it is a stand-alone application, not a module. Both decide to use linked lists to internally store the data. Both applications are deployed to the 25 users in each department.

After months of work, both applications are performing poorly. Sol and Mark discuss using a binary tree data structure for the file management utility, which will improve performance. Both Sol and Mark decide to implement the binary tree within their file management utilities.

Both Sol and Mark make the changes so that their file systems use binary trees instead of linked lists. This is when the difference between modular and client/server becomes apparent. Sol must recompile his application, and then he must redeploy it to all 25 users. Not only is this not a trivial task, but each of his users will experience downtime until Sol can load the new application on his or her PC. Mark, on the other hand, replaces the old file management application with the new file management application, and none of his 25 users ever know that anything has changed.

---

# Advantages Provided by Client/Server Technology

Client/server architecture has revolutionized the way that applications are designed and built. It has impacted almost every business and developer in the world. Client/server has stormed onto the scene because it offers several tremendous advantages. These advantages include the following.

## Reuse

By separating your tasks into a stand-alone application, you have created a server application that can serve other applications, as well as your own. Now the server application can start paying for itself with each incremental reuse. Each client application that leverages the functionality of your server can now be spared the time of developing and debugging the same functionality.

## Client Applications are Less Complex and More Intuitive

If you have ever developed a large application, you have probably noticed that you spent more time developing code that dealt with infrastructure types of tasks such as storing and retrieving data than you did actually writing the business logic of the application. This problem is averted by using a client/server architecture.

Developing the client application is simpler and more intuitive. You no longer have to write hundreds and thousands of lines of code to perform the complex and time consuming tasks for which you have elected to use a server application. The complexity of performing those tasks has been shifted to the server application.

The client application is also more intuitive because it focuses on doing what it is meant to do. For example, writing an accounts receivable application focuses on the logic of generating invoices and receiving payments, not on writing code to store and receive data.

## Quicker Application Development

As noted previously, you no longer have to devote your time and energy with developing the server functionality. Instead, you can focus on the true scope of your application. The end result is that your application will be done more cleanly and quickly than ever.

## Higher Quality

Client/server design can lead to a higher quality application. Quality is improved within both the client application and the server application. The client application will be of higher quality because it is more intuitive, has fewer lines of code, and has shifted complexity to the server application. The server application will be of higher quality because its code is highly focused on implementing specific functionality. It remains pure and uncluttered. This greatly improves the design, development, and debugging of the server application. In addition, as other applications reuse your server, the application becomes exercised to a much higher degree than if you would have embedded the code within you own application.

Additionally, it is common to purchase off-the-shelf packages to function as your server—relational database management systems, for example. These packages can often provide high quality because they are developed by experts in that given subject area and the code is highly focused toward best implementing the desired functionality. It is often preferable and cost effective to leverage the expertise of software vendors as opposed to attempting to grow such an application in-house. If you are searching for very specialized server functionality, however, you might have no choice but to implement the server yourself.

## Easier to Maintain

Because the server is written once and only once, it is logical that it is easier to maintain than if it were implemented repeatedly for every application you have developed that needs that functionality. Regarding the maintainability of the client application, you need only to refer back to the earlier sidebar with Sol and Mark to see that the client applications are easier to maintain with client/server architecture. The client application has been shielded from the server due to the public interface of the server. Changes to the server need not impact the client applications so long as the public interface is not changed.

# Potential Pitfalls of Client/Server Technology

As is true with any good thing, there are definitely some items to be concerned about. You will see that most of the issues that you need to be wary of, however, are not showstoppers by any means. Instead, they are natural side effects to be expected and managed.

## Application Performance Might Be Poor

This is probably the granddaddy of all the problems that you will see with client/server architecture. If you don't take caution up front when you design your solution, this can be a major problem. There are several factors that impact the overall performance. In fact, this topic is too large to address here. Instead, the remaining sections are devoted to discussing the pertinent issues. For now, let it be said that if you don't take the time to devise a solution that works in your environment, then performance will most likely be poor.

## New protocols to Be Set Up and Learned

After you decide to use client/server architecture, you need to determine how to enable your client/server applications to talk to one other. This might involve simple process-to-process communications, or it might entail more complex communications over a local area network or even over the Internet. Most server applications that you purchase will provide an Application Programming Interface (APIs) for the client application to use to send requests to the server and to receive the returned data. The major adjustment is simply to make certain that the environment is set up to accommodate the communications between the client and server. For a developer to implement a client/server architecture, he needs to learn the protocols that enable the client to make a request of the server.

### Client Application Is Dependent upon the Server Application

It goes without saying that your client application is dependent upon the server application to be up, running, and available for requests. This can become a larger issue if you run the client application on a different physical machine than the server. The section, "Single-Tier versus Multi-Tier Architectures" examines this in greater detail. What you should keep in mind while designing your application is what it should be able to do if the server application is unavailable. You might be able to design the application to be very useful and functional in a standalone mode. As soon as the server becomes available, the client can then take the necessary steps to update and synchronize with the server. It's up to you, however, to proactively design for this situation.

## Applying Client/Server Design to Database Development

Now that you've seen some of the pros and cons of client/server architecture, you are ready to move on to the nitty gritty of applying client/server design to database development.



Although there are several data management architectures available for your use, this book focuses on the use of relational database management systems (RDBMS). Relational databases have become almost synonymous with client/server programming. Relational databases have become prevalent in client/server programming because they

- Store and retrieve data in a very intuitive fashion
- Are very flexible because their structure can be altered fairly easily
- Are standardized
- Offer excellent multi-user environments

Client/server development is so heavily hinged upon the concept of relational database management systems that a brief look at these systems will prove valuable.

### Relational Database Primer

The key strength of relational databases is that they are extremely flexible and intuitive in the way in which they store data. Their flexibility has made it easier for application developers to build solutions upon their framework. They have also made the data more readily accessible to the owners of the data, even if they aren't technical.

Relational databases use tables to store related pieces of data. Each piece of data is referred to as a column. A row of data is the collection of all of the related columns in a table. The concept of tables, rows, and columns seems to be how people intuitively think about and use the data.

**Why Are They Called "Relational" Databases?**

Relational databases are said to be relational because they are designed around the concept of sets and the relationships between sets. You probably recall working with sets when you were in school. A set contains zero or more elements. Two sets can be compared by using set operations, like performing the union or intersection of the two sets. These set operations are the *relationships* between the sets, and they can be applied to gain a unique result set based upon the chosen operation.

Relational databases store data in tables, like sets, and enable you to perform operations, like a join, to bring the data from two or more tables together based on some common element to form a new result set. Tables can be joined by relating columns from separate tables via a logical operator. In addition, relational databases enable you to formally define the relationships between tables, and these relationships will be used to guide the operations upon the data.

This formal relationship is referred to as a *foreign-key* relationship because you can set a relationship between columns in one table to the existence of a row in a foreign table. The foreign-key that you define must directly correspond to the primary key of the foreign table. For example, you can create a Department table and an Employee table. You would probably set up a foreign-key relationship within the Employee table to the primary key of the Department table, in this case `Department_Number`. Creating this foreign-key relationship between these tables would guarantee that no employee record can be added without a department number that is already defined in the Department table.

## Working with a Relational Database

You must design and implement a database to store the data for your application. You will use SQL Data Definition Language (DDL) commands to create tables and indexes. You will then use SQL Data Manipulation Commands such as Insert, Update, Delete, and Select to put the data into those tables. Chapter 3, "Creating a Simple Database Application," and Chapter 4, "The SQL Standard: A Language for Data Access," cover in detail the steps that you take to create and manipulate your database.

## Problems to Watch Out For

There are a few areas of concern that are worth noting. You can save yourself many a headache by heeding the following sections on "Lazy Selects" and "Managing Transactions."

**Lazy Selects** This `SQL` command enables you to read or retrieve data from within the database management system. Select has two nuances that you need to be aware of. First of all, it enables you to specify which data columns you want to select from a table. If you want to, you might specify `Select *`, which is a shorthand way of requesting all of the columns in the table. If you are anything like me—always looking for the easiest way to do something—this sounds quite tempting. This can save you a lot of typing when creating your query; however, it can also lead to a lot of unnecessary data flowing between your application and the database server. You might not want to select every column when selecting data. For example, you might only want to look up a `Department_Name` where for `Department_Number = 100`. If you notice performance problems with your application, look over your select queries to ensure that they are only getting the data that they need.

The second nuance is that the `Select` command is capable of manipulating multiple rows of multiple tables simultaneously. Bringing multiple table sets together into a single result set is known as performing a join. Joins are covered in detail in Chapter 5, "ODBC."

For purposes of applying client/server design principles, just let it be said that care must be taken when performing joins because they can lead to unexpected results. For example, if an employee were accidentally inserted with no `Department_Number`, your Employee list would not contain this employee. When working with large volumes of data, it is very difficult to notice things that aren't there that should be. Special types of joins can be performed to avoid this problem. An inner join can be used to provide all Employees, even if they don't successfully match a value in the Department table. Conversely, an outer join could be used to force the report to list departments that have no employees. It will be up to you as a developer to understand the relationships between tables and the types of joins that are available for your use and then to use the appropriate operation. Even worse, if you join two tables without specifying which columns need to match between the two tables, the database will return the "Cartesian product" of the two tables. This basically returns a result of every possible row combination between the two tables. This is a gigantic result set that you definitely do not want flowing between your applications.

**Managing Transactions** The last relational database concept that needs to be covered is that of a transaction. A transaction is a "unit of work" that is performed by the application and applied to the database. A transaction is an all-or-nothing proposition. Either all of the operations are performed, or none of the operations are performed. It is not possible to have a partial transaction applied.



The classic example of a transaction involves a banking system in which a deposit is made and then a withdrawal is made from the deposited funds. For example, you have a balance of $0, and you step up to the Automated Teller Machine to deposit your $1000 paycheck. Immediately following this, you make a $500 withdrawal. Consider what would happen if the application didn't use a transaction to unite these two operations together as they occurred. If only the deposit of $1000 dollars were successfully applied to the database, it would be good for you but bad for the bank. On the other hand, if only the $500 withdrawal operation were recorded, it would be bad for you! The data is only valid if both operations are successfully recorded.

You create a transaction within your application by sandwiching your SQL operations between a SQL "`Begin Transaction`" and a SQL "`Commit Transaction`"—the exact syntax might vary depending upon the RDBMS that you are using. By doing this, you ensure that all of your SQL operations between the `Begin Transaction` and the `Commit Transaction` are treated as a single unit of work. Should your application encounter an error condition, it can execute a `Rollback Transaction` command, which undoes all of the SQL operations performed back to the last Begin Transaction.

To successfully develop client/server applications, it is critical that you understand the concept of transactions and unit of work. Because your application might be physically removed from the data server and connected via a LAN, you run an increased risk of an unexpected interruption to communications between your applications. You can increase the quality and reliability of your application data by using transactions to ensure that outside forces don't compromise the integrity of your data.

**TIP** The definition of client/server cites the use of personal workstations to develop user-friendly graphical user interfaces to separate the front-end presentation from the back-end data storage. One additional step that you might want to take is using Open Database Connectivity, ODBC, which is an open format for connecting and working with relational databases. By doing this, you decouple your application from using a specific relational database in the back-end storage of the data. As long as you use a database and driver that provide ODBC connectivity within your application, you will have flexibility to use any database management system as the back-end. ODBC is covered in greater detail in Chapter 5, "ODBC."

# Understanding the Quandary of Client/Server

You've reviewed client/server and some of its advantages and disadvantages, but might be wondering what the quandary is. Fundamentally, the quandary is determining how to use this architecture appropriately to provide a well designed solution. In other words, how do you use these principals to devise a solution?

There are actually many dimensions of this quandary to worry about. The use of client/server architecture requires that you architect both a logical design and a physical design. Your overall solution must successfully join the logical architecture with the physical to provide the necessary functionality. If you do either incorrectly, your application will fail. You might have the perfect logical design for your application, but if the physical architecture isn't suitable for the task, your application will meet a quick and untimely death. The reverse is also true. If you construct a wonderful physical architecture but the logical application architecture was done poorly, your application will soon be history.

## The Logical Architecture

Designing the logical architecture focuses on separating the application into logical components. One of the most common implementations of client/server architecture is to separate the business logic layer from the data storage and retrieval logic layer.

A further refinement of this architecture is to separate the application into three logical layers: Presentation and User Interface, Business Logic, and Data Logic. Layering your application in this manner enables you to isolate the logic so that these layers operate independently of one another. Designing and implementing good public interfaces for each layer will make your application much easier to maintain and understand. Changes to one of the layers should only impact the other layers if the change impacts the public interface.

Determining the logical components of your application might also be based upon leveraging server applications that you might already have in use. Other client/server applications might have been developed, and you know that you want to take advantage of the existing server functionality. However, there might be additional functional areas within your application that could benefit from the use of a server application. You are not limited to using only one server, and database servers aren't the only server applications that add value.

## The Physical Architecture

A physical architecture is a map of where and how you plan to implement each logical component of your application. Obviously, some of this might be predetermined by your existing environment. For example, you might know that your users will be using Macintosh computers as their workstation, so that is the target environment for your application. Furthermore, you might know that you will be using a Unix-based workstation as a relational database server. However, before you leap to a physical architecture, you should understand the concept of tiered architectures and the ramifications of single- versus multi-tiered architectures. As stated in the definition of client/server, the tasks are divided into those that will be implemented within your application and those tasks that will be implemented by a server external to your application. A tier can be viewed as the physical platform upon which the logical components of your application are placed.

**Single-Tiered Architecture** The single-tiered architecture places the client application and the server application on the same physical machine. Many people envision two or more machines when they think of client/server architectures, but that doesn't need to be. Recall that according to the definition, the server application is external, not on a separate machine. It is a perfectly valid approach to plan for a single-tiered architecture.

**Multi-tiered Architecture** With a multi-tiered architecture, the client is on one machine, and the server can be one or more other physical machines. The client and server machines might even be different hardware platforms and run completely different operating system software.

**Single-Tier versus Multi-Tier Architecture** One of the most critical decisions that you must make about your physical design is how to physically distribute your application and data components within your target environment. As you will see there are direct ramifications to either architecture that you choose. The following items provide a checklist regarding when it might be beneficial to consider using a single-tiered architecture. Remember that you need to evaluate your total environment. It is not uncommon that some requirements make you lean toward a single-tiered architecture, while other factors point you to a multi-tiered architecture.

***Application Availability Is Critical*** Recall that one of the pitfalls of client/server architecture was that the client depended upon the server to be running and available for processing requests. Obviously, the more complex your environment is, the higher the risk. In a multi-tiered environment, your server machine or your LAN can crash and leave you dead in the water. Using the single-tiered architecture removes the server machine and LAN from the picture and increases the likelihood of functional uptime.

**CAUTION**

Note that you aren't guaranteed that something won't happen to your system. If your application is really mission critical, then use fault tolerant machines for both your client and server machines or have multiple backup machines that are available for use if one conks out on you.

***Application Response Time Is Critical*** It is rare to develop an application in which response time isn't critical. If it is critical, and you are developing an application that deals with large volumes of data or it executes a large number of database transactions, then it might be expeditious to put the database server and the client on the same machine. Your local area network might not be effective at moving large chunks of data around. When working with data, especially on select queries, only deal with the columns that you need. This sounds simple, but it is not uncommon for a developer to simply code the `select *`, instead of itemizing exactly what columns are needed.

Regarding the number of transactions in your application, think about the overhead that is added when you are using a different server machine. For each transaction, time is required for:

- Generating the transaction
- Transmitting over the LAN to the server
- Waiting for the server to receive and process (possibly even competing with other clients attempting the same types of transactions)
- Waiting for the LAN to transmit the data back to the client machine
- Waiting for the client application to receive the data

Prudent design should minimize the number of transactions needed. You might have to do some benchmark testing when designing your application. It might prove quicker to do one query and bring back all of the data you need (but only the data you need), or it might be quicker to do multiple transactions. If you do attempt to do benchmarks, remember to try to simulate the production environment as accurately as possible—this includes simulating LAN traffic and other client interactions appropriately.

**TIP** If your relational database management system enables the use of stored procedures, then use them! Stored procedures are independent modules of code that are stored within the database. These stored procedures are precompiled by the database system–this might even include optimizing the code when it is stored. This saves your application the compilation time of each of your queries. Tremendous performance improvement can be attained with this approach. Stored procedures provide an excellent centralized repository to store and implement your business logic.

***Existing Servers on Client Machine Can Be Leveraged*** If your end user(s) already have an application that makes use of a local relational database management system, then you should take advantage of this. This doesn't automatically mean that you design the solution with a single-tiered architecture. What it does mean is that if you plan to use a local database on the client machine, then you should strongly consider using the same database that the client has. Your users don't want to stack numerous applications that do the same thing on their PCs.

***Shared Data Is Relatively Static*** If you are building an application for multiple end users, you need to evaluate the data that is shared commonly between all users. If this data is relatively static, meaning it doesn't change frequently, then you might want to consider putting the data locally. This would be useful if the amount of data is large and the performance of the application seems to be hampered due to the remote data access. If you only have a small volume of data, however, the performance improvement might only be nominal.

**Appropriate Use of a Multi-tiered Architecture** The following items are factors to consider when designing your physical architecture. The presence of any one of these items should make you consider multi-tiered architecture.

***Target Hardware Can't Support Application and Server*** One obvious clue that you need a multi-tiered architecture might be that the client machines just don't have the resources to support the additional load of a server. It is easy for us to lose sight of this as developers. Hardware is cheap, right? We often have the latest greatest beasts on our desks just waiting to chomp off any application without effort. However, not everyone is so fortunate. Consider your target environment carefully. There are still many low-end machines out there. If your intent is to upgrade all of the users to high-end machines, make sure that is in the budget and estimated out. The last thing you want to do is drop a big dollar surprise at the last minute.

***Cost Prohibitive*** The previous section looked at the fact that the client machine might not have the horsepower to run the server application and that upgrading all of the end users' machines might be too cost prohibitive. Even if the end users' machines can handle it, there is still one more cost to consider—the server application software. If you plan on having a fully functional copy of the server on each of your end user's machines, then you should plan on buying a license for every machine. There might be some vendors that don't require this or some vendors might offer package deals. Just don't let this one surprise you. Be proactive when you are planning your physical architecture. If you think that you will need the server software on each user's machine, then determine the cost and make an informed decision.



***Shared Data Changes Frequently*** Even if you can afford to put the server on each machine, you need to consider the data that needs to be shared among your end users. If the users do a lot of data modification, inserts, updates, and deletes, you might be forced to use a central database repository. By using a single data repository, you can leverage the locking capabilities within your database to ensure that no two users are changing the same record at the same time. Contrast that with each user having a local copy of the data on his machine. He is the only user within his copy of the database, just as you are the only user within your local database. There is nothing to prevent the two of you from changing the same record in a conflicting manner. Furthermore, if each of the local databases is being changed, how will they be merged back into a single cohesive database with no conflicts?

Some databases include utilities for data replication and synchronization. Read up on the capabilities of your relational database management system to see if it supports data replication or synchronization, and make sure that you understand what it can and cannot do. Data synchronization can end up being a nightmare to maintain and manage. Thoroughly evaluating your options up front will lead you to the design that is right for your application.

**What if Neither Architecture Fits?** Unfortunately, it is not an uncommon dilemma to find that neither architecture meets the needs of your users. Your users need lightning-fast response time, your LAN doesn't have a lot more bandwidth to give, and your users' data is volatile. It seems as if no solution will work. If you find yourself in this position, you might have no alternative but to consider combining both architectures. This becomes a true balancing act because it entails having the database server on both the end users' machines and on a central server machine. This scenario might work if you find that you can migrate some of the data locally to each user. By doing this, the client application can use the local data whenever possible and use the user interface to speed the application along while the remote data can be queried and received from the remote server. It is hoped that the local data won't be too volatile.

Bear in mind that mixing the two architectures creates the most complex and expensive environment possible. You might get the best of both worlds when it comes to performance, but you might also get an environment far more difficult to maintain and far more expensive.

These architectures can be mixed successfully. It requires a great deal of planning and foresight. It requires you to evaluate the finest minutia of your application environment so that each component can be placed appropriately. It can be done.

## Using the Thin Client

Many applications have taken an architectural approach of putting as much functionality on the server as possible and minimizing the size of the client. When the client application is stripped down to the minimum possible size, this is known as the *thin* client.

After all of the previous discussion about architectures, you are probably wondering why someone would choose this approach. The main reason is that it enables the client machines to be minimal configuration machines. The client machines might have less powerful CPUs, less disk, and possibly even less memory. If you are dealing with a large number of end users, the dollar savings can be tremendous.

There are some obvious drawbacks to this approach. First of all, a thin client places higher demand and dependence upon the network. The client application will not be designed to offer much in a stand-alone mode. More important, the client application might perform slowly. Performance will hinge on how quickly data can be received from the server. Typically, a thin client will include a high performance modem or LAN connection to minimize this delay.

Java development over the Internet is a perfect candidate for thin client architecture. For that matter, Java itself was designed to develop small, portable applications. When you design a Java-based application over the net, you should keep your client applications as small as possible. Obviously, you can't design toward each user having a database server, so you must design the application to make use of your own server. The end result is that the Java application is built for a thin client environment.

One of the most recent trends within the thin client architecture is the use of ***network computers***, the ultimate thin client. They are designed with no local disk storage, and they run all applications from a local area network or from the Internet. The advent of network computers will put the thin client architecture to the maximal test.

This is advantageous because client computers should be cheaper and provide large savings. Additionally, this architecture is viewed as being easier to maintain because application software only needs to be installed once in a central area instead of on each client machine, saving time on configuration, deployment, maintenance, and debugging after problems are found.

The other side of the coin views this as a reversion to the old days: The network computers are analogized to dumb terminals hanging off a mainframe-centric type of server. From a software developers standpoint, the network computer architecture will offer challenges to design small, portable applications with executables small enough to flow over the network inundating it. Additionally, you must consider the application design from a new standpoint. If a single copy of the software is run by all users, then will any customization be allowed on an individual basis? How will these custom settings be stored and retrieved? It is your responsibility as a designer to analyze the environment, to understand the ramifications and limitations of the environment, and to design a solution that maximizes the environment to satisfy the user.

The success of this architecture is yet to be determined. Will end users be satisfied with no local storage? Will a single copy of a software application provide enough flexibility to each individual user? Can LAN performance in the typical environment provide sufficient performance? Network computers might offer compelling benefits, but they will offer new challenges for application developers to conquer.



## From Here...

Building a client/server solution requires the design and implementation of both a good logical and a good physical architecture. The logical architecture should attempt to separate the application into a Presentation layer, a Business Logic layer and a Data layer. Designing clean public interfaces for each layer will increase maintainability by isolating each layer from changes within the other layers. The physical architecture will leverage the use of a single- or multi-tiered environment. Selecting single-tiered or multi-tiered is a balancing act based upon several factors.

Relational databases are highly integrated with client/server application development. Proper use of SQL commands for manipulating the data can improve the performance of your application and protect the integrity of your data.

The following chapters will provide greater detail on accessing relational databases using Microsoft J++:

- Chapter 3, "Creating a Simple Database Application," will introduce you to the steps you need to take to create a database for your application.
- Chapter 4, "The SQL Standard: A Language for Data Access," provides additional information about SQL commands.
- Chapter 5, "ODBC," discusses using the Open Database Connectivity method for accessing databases and the benefits of doing so.

PART VI

# Appendixes

APPENDIX A

# Data Access Objects 3.5 API

The DAO 3.5 API provides a set of Component Object Model interfaces that expose several ODBC and Microsoft Jet APIs. DAO was designed to provide direct access to the Microsoft Jet Engine and only in the last two versions has ODBC become a significant feature in DAO. Having been designed for native ISAM access, DAO is a very fast ISAM database API and the natural choice for such databases. The ODBC access is still in its infancy under DAO, however, and is much faster through RDO (or direct ODBC C++ APs) than with DAO—even with the new ODBCDirect interfaces. With this in mind, RDO might be a better choice for Internet-centric SQL databases. The option exists, however, to use DAO for all database connectivity, especially for those of you who have a knowledge of and skills investment in DAO.

# DAO 3.5

The DAO object model has grown a new member with the addition of the `ODBCDirect` Connection object. The rest of the API has been tweaked, and some parameters for asynchronous execution of certain operations have been added. Those of you familiar with the 3.0 specification, however, will not find many surprises here. The new object model (or `vtable` in the COM language) is listed in Figure A.1.

**FIG. A.1**
This is the DAO 3.5 object model.

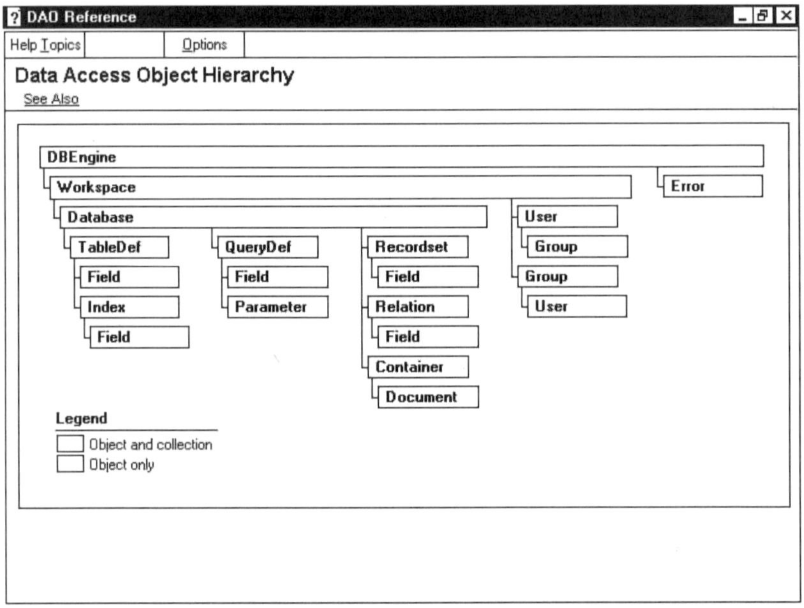


# The *DBEngine* Object

This object must be created to perform any operations that use DAO, except for the new ODBC Direct functions. You also need to cast the `DBEngine` object to its interface when constructing a new instance of this object.

## Constructor

The DBEngine object has the following constructor:

```
ILicenseMgr mgr;
DBEngine idbengine;
dao350.Error  m_objError;
try{
        mgr = new LicenseMgr();
        idbengine = (_DBEngine)mgr.createWithLic
            (
                   "mbmabptebkjcdlgtjmskjwtsdhjbmkmwtrak",
```

```
                    "{00000010-0000-0010-8000-00AA006D2EA4}",
                    null,
                    ComContext.INPROC_SERVER
          );
          idbengine.RegisterDatabase("ICU","Microsoft Text Driver
(*.txt;*.csv)",false,"Mode=Import");
         // Open a connection
}
catch(com.ms.com.ComFailException e)
{m_objErrors = idbengine.getErrors();System.out.println(m_objError.
➥getDescription());}
```

You need to use the ILicenseManager interface to create the instances (unlike RDO), because DAO requires a license to use.

# Methods

The `DBEngine` object has the following methods:

`dbEngine._30_CreateWorkspace(String m_Name, String m_User, String m_Password);`

Returns a `Workspace` Object.

| Argument | Data Type | Description |
|---|---|---|
| `m_Name` | String | Sets the name for the `Workspace` object |
| `m_User` | String | Sets the default user account for the `Workspace` object |
| `m_Password` | String | Sets the default password for the `Workspace` object |

`dbEngine.BeginTrans();`

Begins a new transaction.

`dbEngine.CommitTrans(CommitTransOptionsEnum.dbForceOSFlush);`

Ends all transactions for a single `Workspace` object by saving the changes to the data source.

| Argument | Data Type | Description |
|---|---|---|
| `dbForceOSFlush` | int | Forces the OS to write the data to disk immediately on a `Commit` (Optional) |

```
dbEngine.CompactDatabase(String m_OldDB, String m_NewDB, Variant m_Locale,
➥Variant m_Options, Variant m_Password);
```

Copies and compacts a Jet database.

| Argument | Data Type | Description |
|---|---|---|
| `m_OldDB` | String | The full path to the database. |
| `m_NewDB` | String | A different path to the (new) database. |

| | | |
|---|---|---|
| m_Locale | Variant String | CollatingOrderEnum constant. The password can also be changed by specifying dbSortPDXIntl & ";pwd=password". |
| m_Options | Variant int | DatabaseTypeEnum constant. |
| m_Password | Variant String | Specifies the password to use if the password is not set in the locale argument. |

```
dbEngine.CreateDatabase(String m_Name, String m_Locale, Variant m_Options );
```

Creates a new (physical) Jet database.

Return Type: A `Database` object

| **Argument** | **Data Type** | **Description** |
|---|---|---|
| m_Name | String | The absolute path and name of the database |
| m_Locale | String | Specifies the collating order for creating the database; can also be used to specify the password: dbLangSpanish & ";pwd=NewPassword" |
| m_Options | Variant | DatabaseTypeEnum constant |

```
dbEngine.CreateWorkspace(String m_Name, String m_User, String m_Password, Variant
➥m_Type);
```

Creates a new `Workspace` object.

Return Type: A `Workspace` object

| **Argument** | **Data Type** | **Description** |
|---|---|---|
| m_Name | String | Sets the name for the Workspace object |
| m_User | String | Sets the default user account for the Workspace object |
| m_Password | String | Sets the default password for the Workspace object |
| m_Type | Variant | A variant containing a WorkspaceTypeEnum constant |

```
dbEngine.getDefaultType();
```

Returns a value of `WorkspaceTypeEnum` corresponding to the default `Workspace` Type that any new `Workspace` objects will be created with.

Return Type: int

```
dbEngine.getErrors();
```

Returns an `Errors` collection for this object.

Return Type: An `Errors` object

```
dbEngine.getIniPath();
```

Returns the path to the INI file.

Return Type: String

```
dbEngine.getLoginTimeout();
```

Returns the default login timeout.

Return Type: short

```
dbEngine.getProperties();
```

Returns the `Properties` collection for this object.

Return Type: A `Properties` object

```
dbEngine.getSystemDB();
```

Returns the path to the System Database—useful only on Microsoft Jet databases.

Return Type: String

```
dbEngine.getVersion();
```

Returns the version of the Jet Engine.

Return Type: String

```
dbEngine.getWorkspaces();
```

Returns the `Workspaces` collection for this object.

Return Type: A `Workspaces` Object

```
dbEngine.Idle();
```

Enables the Jet Engine to perform background processing immediately—similar to `thread.sleep()`.

```
dbEngine.OpenConnection(String m_Name, Variant m_Prompt, Variant m_ReadOnly,
➥Variant m_Connect);
```

Opens a connection to an ODBC data source.

Return Type: A `Connection` object

| Argument | Data Type | Description |
|---|---|---|
| m_Name | String | Sets the name for the connection |
| m_Prompt | Variant int | A DriverPromptEnum constant (Optional) |
| m_ReadOnly | Variant Boolean | TRUE if the connection is to be opened for read-only access (Optional) |
| m_Connect | Variant String | An ODBC connect string (Optional) |

```
dbEngine.OpenDatabase(String m_strDatabase, Variant m_Prompt, Variant m_ReadOnly,
➥Variant m_Connect);
```

Opens a database.

Return Type: A `Database` object

| Argument | Data Type | Description |
|---|---|---|
| m_strDatabase | String | The name of the Jet database or ODBC DSN |
| m_Prompt | Variant int | A DriverPromptEnum constant (Optional) |
| m_ReadOnly | Variant Boolean | TRUE if the connection is to be opened for read-only access (Optional) |
| m_Connect | Variant String | An ODBC connect string (Optional) |

```
dbEngine.putDefaultPassword(String m_Password);
```

Sets the default password.

| Argument | Data Type | Description |
|---|---|---|
| m_Password | String | A password |

```
dbEngine.putDefaultType(int m_DefaultType);
```

Sets the default type for the `Workspace` object that will be created next.

| Argument | Data Type | Description |
|---|---|---|
| m_DefaultType | int | A constant matching a value in WorkspaceTypeEnum |

```
dbEngine.putDefaultUser(String m_UserName);
```

Sets the default user account for new `Workspace` objects created with this `dbEngine` object.

| Argument | Data Type | Description |
|---|---|---|
| m_UserName | String | The user account to use by default for new Workspace objects |

```
dbEngine.putIniPath(String m_IniPath);
```

Sets the Registry key from which to read settings. For example:

```
dbEngine.putIniPath("HKEY_LOCAL_MACHINE\SOFTWARE\Microsoft\Jet\3.5\ ISAM
➥Formats\FoxPro 3.0")
```

| Argument | Data Type | Description |
|---|---|---|
| `m_IniPath` | String | A registry key or path to an INI file |

```
dbEngine.putLoginTimeout(short m_defaultTimeout);
```

Sets the default login timeout.

| Argument | Data Type | Description |
|---|---|---|
| `m_defaultTimeout` | short | The timeout value, specified in seconds |

```
dbEngine.putSystemDB(String m_SysDB);
```

Sets the Microsoft Jet Workgroup access file.

| Argument | Data Type | Description |
|---|---|---|
| `m_SysDB` | String | Path to the System database |

```
dbEngine.RegisterDatabase(String m_DSN,  String m_Driver, boolean m_Silent,
➥String m_Attributes);
```

Registers a new ODBC data source.

| Argument | Data Type | Description |
|---|---|---|
| `m_DSN` | String | Data Source Name |
| `m_Driver` | String | Friendly name of the driver as shown in the ODBC Administrator. (Not the file name.) |
| `m_Silent` | Boolean | Set to `TRUE` if you don't want to show the ODBC Register Data Source dialog box. (This will be ignored if you don't provide complete information.) |
| `m_Attributes` | String | A list of keywords to be added to the Windows Registry. |

```
dbEngine.RepairDatabase(String m_DBName);
```

Attempts to repair a Jet database.

| Argument | Data Type | Description |
|---|---|---|
| `m_DBName` | String | Absolute path to the Jet database file |

```
dbEngine.Rollback();
```

Ends all transactions created by this `DBEngine` object by throwing away the buffered changes.

```
SetOption(int m_Parameter, Variant m_NewValue);
```

Overrides the registry settings.

| Argument | Data Type | Description |
|---|---|---|
| `m_Parameter` | int | A `SetOptionEnum` constant |
| `m_NewValue` | Variant | The new value of the paramter |

# The *Error* Object

The `Error` object is the only object in DAO without a true constructor. This interface is always available through the methods of the `Errors` collection. It was created to pass back the COM errors encountered in their proper context so that the application developer could have more useful debugging and the user could have better information available concerning what went wrong.

## Constructor

No Constructor provided, use the Errors.getNextError() method

## Methods

The Error object has the following methods:

```
Error.getNumber;
```

Returns the error number.

Return Type: int

```
Error.getDescription();
```

Returns: A description of the error.

Return Type: String

```
Error.getHelpFile();
```

Returns the path to the help file associated with the source of the error.

Return Type: String

```
Error.getHelpContext();
```

Returns the help context ID.

Return Type: int

```
Error.getSource();
```

Returns the source of the error.

Return Type: String

# The *Workspace* Object

The `Workspace` object controls the state of the transactions created within it as well as the connection information about the open data sources or databases. The `Workspace` object is also responsible for setting the default properties of the objects created with it.

## Constructor

The Workspace object has the following constructor:

```
Workspace m_objWorkpsace  = dbEngine.CreateWorkspace(String Name,
➥String User, String Password, Variant Type;
```

## Methods

The Workspace object has the following methods:

```
Workspace.put_30_UserName(String m_strUser);
```

Sets the default user account for this `Database` object.

| Argument | Data Type | Description |
|---|---|---|
| `m_strUser` | String | Name of the default user |

```
Workspace.getDatabases();
```

Returns the `Database` collection.

Return Type: A `Database` object

```
Workspace.CreateDatabase(String m_Name, String m_Locale, Variant m_Options);
```

Creates a new (physical) Jet database.

| Argument | Data Type | Description |
|---|---|---|
| `m_Name` | String | The absolute path and name of the database |
| `m_Locale` | String | Specifies the collating order for creating the database; can also be used to specify the password: `dbLangSpanish & ";pwd=NewPassword"` |
| `m_Options` | Variant | `DatabaseTypeEnum` constant |

```
Workspace.getLoginTimeout();
```

Returns the default login timeout for this `Database` object.

Return Type: int

```
Workspace.putLoginTimeout(int m_iLoginTimeout);
```

Sets the default login timeout for this `Database` object.

```
Workspace.getUsers();
```

Returns the `User` collection for this object.

Return Type: A `User` object

```
Workspace.put_30_Password(String m_Password);
```

Sets the default password for objects created through this object using DAO 3.0 syntax.

| Argument | Data Type | Description |
|---|---|---|
| `m_Password` | Variant (String) | Sets the password for the new user account |

```
Workspace.CreateUser(Variant m_Name, Variant m_PID, Variant m_Password);
```

Returns a new `User` object.

Return Type: A `User` object.

| Argument | Data Type | Description |
|---|---|---|
| `m_Name` | Variant (String) | Sets the name for the user (Optional) |
| `m_PID` | Variant (String) | A unique identifier, 4–20 characters in length—alphanumeric |
| `m_Password` | Variant (String) | Sets the password for the new user account (Optional) |

```
Workspace.BeginTrans();
```

Begins a new transaction for this `Workspace` object.

```
Workspace.CommitTrans(CommitTransOptionsEnum.dbForceOSFlush );
```

Ends all transactions for this `Workspace` object by saving the changes to the data source.

| Argument | Data Type | Description |
|---|---|---|
| `dbForceOSFlush` | int | Forces the OS to write the data to disk immediately on a `Commit` (Optional) |

```
Workspace.OpenConnection(String m_DSN, Variant m_VOptions, Variant m_vReadOnly,
➥Variant m_vConnect);
```

Returns a new `Connection` object.

Return Type: A `Connection` object

| Argument | Data Type | Description |
|---|---|---|
| `m_DSN` | String | The data source name |
| `m_vOptions` | Variant (int) | Any combination of `DriverPromptEnum` constants and/or `RecordsdetOptionEnum.dbAsyncEnable` |
| `m_vReadOnly` | Variant (Boolean) | Sets the access to read-only if `TRUE` |
| `m_vConnect` | Variant (String) | A variant containing an ODBC connection string |

`Workspace.getDefaultCursorDriver();`

Returns the default cursor for `Recordset` objects opened on this `Database` object.

Return Type: int

`Workspace.putDefaultCursorDriver(int m_CursorDriver);`

Sets the default cursor for `Recordset` objects opened on this `Database` object.

| Argument | Data Type | Description |
|---|---|---|
| `m_CursorDriver` | int | A constant of `CursorDriverEnum` type |

`Workspace.getIsolateODBCTrans();`

Returns the isolation Level for this `Database` object.

`Workspace.getName();`

Returns the name for this `Database` object.

Return Type: String

`Workspace.putName(String m_Name);`

Sets the name for the `Workspace` object.

| Argument | Data Type | Description |
|---|---|---|
| `m_Name` | String | The name of the `Workspace` connection string |

`Workspace.putIsolateODBCTrans(short m_dbIsolationLevel);`

Sets whether or not the transactions are isolated.

| Argument | Data Type | Description |
|---|---|---|
| `m_dbIsoaltionLevel` | short | A value of 0 or 1 |

`Workspace.Close();`

Closes the open `Database` object.

```
Workspace.OpenDatabase(String m_dbName, Variant m_vOptions, Variant m_vReadOnly,
➥Variant m_vConnect);
```

Returns a new `Database` object.

| Argument | Data Type | Description |
|---|---|---|
| `m_dbName` | String | The name of the actual database file or DSN |
| `m_vOptions` | Variant (Boolean) | `TRUE` for exclusive access, `FALSE` for shared access |
| `m_vReadOnly` | Variant (Boolean) | Sets the access to read-only if `TRUE` |
| `m_vConnect` | Variant (String) | A variant containing a connection string |

```
Workspace.Rollback();
```

Rolls back any transactions pending for the current `Workspace` or `Connection` objects.

```
Workspace.CreateGroup(Variant m_Name, Variant m_PID);
```

Creates a new group.

| Argument | Data Type | Description |
|---|---|---|
| `m_Name` | Variant (String) | Name of the new group (Optional) |
| `m_PID` | Variant (String) | PID of the new group (4–20 alphanumeric characters; Optional) |

```
Workspace.getType();
```

Returns a `DatabaseTypeEnum` constant.

Return Type: int

```
Workspace.gethEnv();
```

Returns the ODBC Environment handle.

Return Type: int

```
Workspace.getConnections();
```

Returns the `Connections` collection for this `Database` object.

Return Type: A `Connections` object

```
Workspace.getProperties();
```

Returns the `Properties` collection for this `Database` object.

Return Type: A `Properties` object

```
Workspace.getGroups();
```

Returns the `Groups` collection for this `Database` object.

Return Type: A `Groups` object

```
Workspace.getUserName();
```

Returns the user account with which this `Database` object was accessed.

Return Type: String

# The *Database* Object

The `Database` object is the interface that is optimized for ISAM database access (such as Microsoft Jet databases, Oracle, Paradox). This object controls the connection to a single, physical database and maintains state information about that connection.

## Constructors

The Database object has the following constructors:

```
Database = dbEngine.CreateDatabase(String m_Name, String m_Locale, Variant
➥m_Options);
```

```
Database = Workspace.CreateDatabase(String m_Name, String m_Locale, Variant
➥m_Options);
```

```
Database = dbEngine.OpenDatabase(String m_strDatabase, Variant m_Prompt, Variant
➥m_ReadOnly, Variant m_Connect);
```

```
Database = Workspace.OpenDatabase(String m_strDatabase, Variant m_Prompt, Variant
➥m_ReadOnly, Variant m_Connect);
```

```
Database = Recordset.getParent();
```

## Methods

The `Database` object has the following methods:

```
Database.Close();
```

Closes an open `Database` object.

```
Variant m_vDDL);
```

Creates a new `Property` object.

Return Type: A `Property` object

| Argument | Data Type | Description |
|---|---|---|
| m_PropName | Variant (String) | The name of the new property |
| m_vType | Variant (int) | A member of the DataTypeEnum constants |
| m_vDataType | Variant | The initial property value |
| m_vDDL | Variant (Boolean) | TRUE if this property is a Data Definition Language property |

```
Database.CreateRelation(Variant m_RelationName, Variant m_vPrimary, Variant
➥m_vForeign, Variant m_vAttributes);
```

Creates a new `Relation object` (Jet Workspaces only).

Return Type: A `Relation` object

| Argument | Data Type | Description |
|---|---|---|
| m_RelationName | Variant (String) | The name of the relation to be created |
| m_vPrimary | Variant (String) | Name of the primary table in the relation |
| m_vForeign | Variant (String) | Name of the foreign table in the relation |
| m_vAttributes | Variant (String) | A member of the RelationAttributeEnum constants |

```
Database.CreateQueryDef(Variant m_Name, Variant m_vSQL);
```

Returns a new `QueryDef` object.

| Argument | Data Type | Description |
|---|---|---|
| m_Name | String | The name of the new QueryDef object |
| m_vSQL | Variant (String) | A variant containing a SQL statement |

```
Database.CreateTableDef(Variant m_dbName, Variant m_vAttributes, Variant
➥m_vSource, Variant m_vConnect);
```

Returns a new `TableDef` object.

Return Type: A `TableDef` object

| Argument | Data Type | Description |
|---|---|---|
| m_dbName | String | The name of the actual database file or DSN |
| m_vAttributes | Variant (int) | A member of the TableDefAttributeEnum constants |
| m_vSource | Variant (String) | Sets the source table name for the TableDef |
| m_vConnect | Variant (String) | A variant containing a connection string |

```
Database.Execute(String m_Source, Variant m_vOptions);
```

Executes a SQL statement or a `QueryDef` object.

| Argument | Data Type | Description |
|---|---|---|
| `m_Source` | String | The SQL statement or name of a `QueryDef` object |
| `m_vOptions` | Variant (int) | A member of the `RecordsetOptionEnum` constants |

```
Database.getCollatingOrder();
```

Returns the collating order for this `Database` object.

Return Type: An int matching a value in `LanguageConstants`

```
Database.getConnect();
```

Returns the connection string used to create this `Database` object.

Return Type: String

```
Database.getConnection();
```

Returns the corresponding `Connection` object for this `Database` object.

Return Type: A `Connection` object

```
Database.getContainers();
```

Returns the `Containers` collection for this `Database` object.

Return Type: A `Containers` object

```
Database.getRecordsAffected();
```

Returns the number of records affected in the last `Execute` method.

Return Type: int

```
Database.getName();
```

Returns the name for this `Database` object.

Return Type: String

```
Database.getDesignMasterID();
```

Returns the GUID for the master replica `Database` object.

Return Type: String

```
Database.getRecordsets();
```

Returns the `Recordsets` collection for this `Database` object.

Return Type: A `Recordsets` object

```
Database.getReplicaID();
```

Returns the `Connections` collection for this `Database` object.

Return Type: String

```
Database.getTableDefs();
```

Returns the `TableDefs` collection for this Database object.

Return Type: A `TableDefs` object

```
Database.getQueryDefs();
```

Returns the `QueryDefs` collection for this `Database` object.

Return Type: A `QueryDefs` object

```
Database.getQueryTimeout();
```

Returns the query timeout for this `Database` object.

Return Type: int

```
Database.getRelations();
```

Returns the `Relations` collection for this `Database` object.

Return Type: A `Relations` object

```
Database.getTransactions();
```

Returns whether or not this object supports transactions.

Return Type: Boolean

```
Database.getConnection();
```

Returns the `Connection` object for this `Database` object.

Return Type: A `Connection` object

```
Database.getProperties();
```

Returns the `PropertiesCollection` for this `Database` object.

Return Type: A `Properties` object

```
Database.getUpdatable();
```

Returns whether or not this object allows changes.

Return Type: Boolean

```
Database.getVersion();
```

Returns the version of the Jet Engine used to create this `Database` object.

Return Type: String

```
Database.MakeReplica(String m_ReplicaName, String m_Description, Variant
➥m_vOption);
```

Creates a replica of the database.

| Argument | Data Type | Description |
|---|---|---|
| `m_ReplicaName` | String | The path and file name to the replica |
| `m_Description` | String | Description of the replica |
| `m_vOption` | Variant (int) | A member of the `ReplicaTypeEnum` constants |

```
Database.NewPassword(String m_OldPassword, String m_NewPassword);
```

Changes the password of the database.

| Argument | Data Type | Description |
|---|---|---|
| `m_OldPassword` | String | The old password |
| `m_NewPassword` | String | An alphanumeric string representing the new password |

```
Database.OpenQueryDef(String m_Name);
```

Returns an existing `QueryDef` object.

| Argument | Data Type | Description |
|---|---|---|
| `m_Name` | String | The name of the `QueryDef` object stored in the database |

```
Database._30_OpenRecordset(String m_Source, Variant m_vType, Variant m_vOption);
```

Returns a new `Recordset` object (using DAO 3.0 syntax).

| Argument | Data Type | Description |
|---|---|---|
| `m_Source` | String | The name of the actual database file or DSN |
| `m_vType` | Variant (int) | A member of the `RecordsetTypeEnum` constants |
| `m_vOption` | Variant (int) | A member of the `RecordsetOptionsEnum` constants |

```
Database.OpenRecordset(String m_Source, Variant m_vType, Variant m_vOption,
➥Variant m_vLockType);
```

Returns a new `Recordset` object.

| Argument | Data Type | Description |
|---|---|---|
| `m_Source` | String | The name of the actual database file or DSN |
| `m_vType` | Variant (int) | A member of the `RecordsetTypeEnum` constants |
| `m_vOption` | Variant (int) | A member of the `RecordsetOptionsEnum` constants |
| `m_vLockType` | Variant (int) | A member of the `LockTypeEnum` constants |

```
Database.putConnect(String m_ConnectString);
```

Sets the connection information for this object.

| Argument | Data Type | Description |
|---|---|---|
| `m_ConnectString` | String | A string of `Connection` parameters separated by semicolons |

```
Database.PopulatePartial(String m_Target);
```

Repopulates a partial replica with fresh information.

| Argument | Data Type | Description |
|---|---|---|
| `m_Target` | String | The name of the target database with which to replicate |

```
Database.putDesignMasterID(String m_GUID);
```

Sets the GUID for the Design Master in a replication environment.

| Argument | Data Type | Description |
|---|---|---|
| `m_GUID` | String | The GUID of the master design database |

```
Database.Synchronize(String m_Target, Variant m_Direction);
```

Sets the target and the direction of synchronization between two database replicas

| Argument | Data Type | Description |
|---|---|---|
| `m_Target` | String | The absolute path to the replica database file |
| `m_Direction` | Variant | A member of `SynchronizeTypeEnum` constants |

```
Database.putQueryTimeout(short m_Timeout);
```

Sets the default query timeout for this database.

| Argument | Data Type | Description |
|---|---|---|
| m_Timeout | Short | The number of seconds to wait before timing out a query |

# The *Connection* Object

The `Connection` object is used to control the connection to ODBC data sources, including maintaining state information about the current connections.

## Constructors

The `Connection` object has the following constructors:

```
Connection = Workspace.OpenConnection(String m_DSN, Variant m_VOptions, Variant
➥m_vReadOnly, Variant m_vConnect);
```

```
Connection = Recordset.getConnection();
```

```
Conection = Database.getConnection();
```

## Methods

The `Connection` object has the following methods:

```
Connection.Cancel();
```

Cancels a pending update.

```
Connection.Close();
```

Closes an open `Database` object.

```
Connection.CreateQueryDef(Variant m_Name, Variant m_vSQL);
```

Returns a new `QueryDef` object.

| Argument | Data Type | Description |
|---|---|---|
| m_Name | String | The name of the new `QueryDef` object |
| m_vSQL | Variant (String) | A variant containing a SQL statement |

```
Connection.Execute(String m_Source, Variant m_vConnect);
```

Executes a SQL statement or `QueryDef` object.

| Argument | Data Type | Description |
|---|---|---|
| m_Source | String | The SQL statement or name of a QueryDef object |
| m_vConnect | Variant (int) | A member of the RecordsetOptionEnum constants |

`Connection.getConnect();`

Returns the connection string used to create this Database object.

Return Type: String

`Connection.getRecordsAffected();`

Returns the number of records affected in the last Execute method.

Return Type: int

`Connection.getDatabase();`

Returns the Database object for this connection.

Return Type: A Database object

`Connection.gethDbc();`

Returns the ODBC connection handle for this Connection object.

Return Type: int

`Connection.getName();`

Returns the name for this Connection object.

Return Type: String

`Connection.getRecordsets();`

Returns the Recordsets collection for this Database object.

Return Type: A Recordsets object

`Connection.getQueryDefs();`

Returns the QueryDefs collection for this Database object.

Return Type: A QueryDefs object

`Connection.getQueryTimeout();`

Returns the default query timeout for this Connection object.

Return Type: short

```
Connection.getStillExecuting();
```

Returns `TRUE` if the asynchronous query is still executing.

Return Type: Boolean

```
Connection.getTransactions();
```

Returns whether or not this object supports transactions.

Return Type: Boolean

```
Connection.getUpdatable();
```

Returns whether or not this object allows changes.

Return Type: Boolean

```
Connection.OpenRecordset(String m_Source, Variant m_vType, Variant m_vOption,
➥Variant m_vLockType);
```

Returns a new `Recordset` object.

Return Type: A `Recordset` object.

| Argument | Data Type | Description |
|---|---|---|
| `m_Source` | String | The name of the actual database file or DSN |
| `m_vType` | Variant (int) | A member of the `RecordsetTypeEnum` constants |
| `m_vOption` | Variant (int) | A member of the `RecordsetOptionsEnum` constants |
| `m_vLockType` | Variant (int) | A member of the `LockTypeEnum` constants |

```
Connection.putConnect(String m_ConnectString);
```

Sets the connection information for this object.

| Argument | Data Type | Description |
|---|---|---|
| `m_ConnectString` | String | A string of `Connection` parameters separated by semicolons |

```
Connection.putQueryTimeout(short m_Timeout);
```

Sets the default query timeout for this database.

| Argument | Data Type | Description |
|---|---|---|
| `m_Timeout` | Short | The number of seconds to wait before timing out a query |

# The *Recordset* Object

The `Recordset` object does most of the work for you. It is used for operations on the data itself, such as data retrieval or updates and deletes.

## Constructors

The `Recordset` object has the following constructors:

```
recordset = Recordset.Clone();
```

```
recordset = Recordset.OpenRecordset(Variant m_vOptions, Variant
➥m_vLockType);recordset = tabledef.OpenRecordset();
```

```
recordset = QueryDef._30_OpenRecordset(String m_Source, Variant m_vType);
```

```
recordset = QueryDef.OpenRecordset(String m_Source, Variant m_vType, Variant
➥m_vOption, Variant m_vLockType);
```

```
recordset = Connection.OpenRecordset(String m_Source, Variant m_vType, Variant
➥m_vOption, Variant m_vLockType);
```

```
recordset = Database.OpenRecordset(String m_Source, Variant m_vType, Variant
➥m_vOption, Variant m_vLockType);
```

```
recordset = Database._30_OpenRecordset(String m_Source, Variant m_vType, Variant
➥m_vOption);
```

## Methods

The `Recordset` object has the following methods:

```
Recordset. _30_CancelUpdate();
```

Cancels any pending updates.

```
Recordset._30_MoveLast();
```

Moves the cursor to the last record in the `Recordset`. (No option to run asynchronously.)

```
Recordset._30_Update();
```

Saves the changes made to a `Recordset` object.

```
Recordset.AddNew();
```

Adds a new record to the `Recordset` object.

```
Recordset.Cancel();
```

Cancels a `MoveLast` or `OpenRecordset` method call.

```
Recordset.CancelUpdate(int m_Type);
```

Cancels pending updates. Enables you to specify the type of updates.

| Argument | Data Type | Description |
|---|---|---|
| `m_Type` | int | A member of the `UpdateTypeEnum` |

`Recordset.Clone();`

Clones the current `Recordset` Object (except for the indexes).

`Recordset.Close();`

Closes the `Recordset` object.

`Recordset.CopyQueryDef();`

Returns a new `QueryDef` object that is a copy of the query used to create the `Recordset` object.

Return Type: A `QueryDef` object

`Recordset.Delete();`

Deletes the current record from the `Recordset` object.

`Recordset.Edit();`

Copies the current record to an Edit Buffer, and saves the changes made. Uses the `Update` method to save the changes permanently.

`Recordset.FillCache(Variant m_iRows, Variant m_vBookmark);`

| Argument | Data Type | Description |
|---|---|---|
| `m_viRows` | Variant (integer) | The number of rows to hold in the cache (Optional) |
| `m_vBookmark` | Variant (String) | The bookmark from which to begin filling the cache (Optional) |

`Recordset.FindFirst(String m_SearchCriteria);`

Moves the cursor to the first occurrence of the specified string.

| Argument | Data Type | Description |
|---|---|---|
| `m_SearchCriteria` | String | A string value |

`Recordset.FindLast(String m_SearchCriteria);`

Finds the last record that matches the string value specified and positions the cursor on that record.

| Argument | Data Type | Description |
|---|---|---|
| `m_SearchCriteria` | String | A string value |

`Recordset.FindNext(String m_SearchCriteria);`

Returns the next record matching the specified search string and sets the cursor to the record's position.

| Argument | Data Type | Description |
|---|---|---|
| `m_strSearch` | String | The search string |

`Recordset.FindPrevious(String m_SearchCriteria);`

Finds the record previous to the current record that matches the string value specified and positions the cursor on that record.

| Argument | Data Type | Description |
|---|---|---|
| `m_SearchCriteria` | String | A string value |

`Recordset.getAbsolutePosition();`

Returns the ordinal position of the current record.

Return Type: int:

`Recordset.getBatchCollisions();`

Returns an array of bookmarks indicating the records where the collisions took place.

Return Type: Variant

`Recordset.getBatchCollisionCount();`

Returns the number of collisions encountered in the last Batch Update.

Return Type: int

`Recordset.getBatchSize();`

Returns the number of statements that can be sent to the server at one time.

Return Type: int

`Recordset.getBOF();`

Returns whether or not the current record is the beginning of the `Recordset` object.

Return Type: Boolean

`Recordset.getBookmarkable();`

Returns whether or not the `Recordset` supports bookmarks.

Return Type: Boolean

`Recordset.getBookmark();`

Returns the bookmark of the current record.

Return Type: `SafeArray`

`Recordset.getCacheStart();`

Returns the bookmark of the first record in a Dynaset-type `Recordset` object to be locally cached from the ODBC data source (Jet Workspaces only).

Return Type: `SafeArray`

`Recordset.getCacheSize();`

Returns the number of rows that can be held in the cache.

Return Type: int

`Recordset.getCollect(Variant m_vFieldName);`

Returns the value contained in a `Field` object.

Return Type: Variant

| Argument | Data Type | Description |
|---|---|---|
| `m_vFieldName` | Variant (String) | The name of a field in the `Recordset` object |

`Recordset.getConnection();`

Returns the `Connection` object associated with this `Recordset` object.

Return Type: A `Connection` object

`Recordset.getDateCreated();`

Returns the date that the base table was created.

Return Type: Variant

`Recordset.getEditMode();`

Returns `EditModeEnum` constants value.

Return Type: short

`Recordset.getEOF();`

Returns `TRUE` if the current position of the cursor is at the end of the `Recordset` object.

Return Type: Boolean

`Recordset.getFields();`

Returns the `Fields` collection for this `Recordset` object.

Return Type: A `Fields` object

`Recordset.getFilter();`

The setting or return value is a String data type that contains the `WHERE` clause of an SQL statement without the reserved word `WHERE`.

`Recordset.getIndex();`

Returns the index being used by this `Recordset` object.

Return Type: String

`Recordset.getIndexes();`

Returns the `Indexes` collection for the current `Recordset` object.

Return Type: An `Indexes` Object

`Recordset.gethStmt();`

Returns the ODBC statement handle.

Return Type: int

`Recordset.getLastUpdated();`

Returns the last record updated

Return Type: Variant

`Recordset.getLastModified();`

Returns a bookmark of the last modified record.

Return Type: `SafeArray`

`Recordset.getLockEdits();`

Returns the locking in effect, `TRUE` for pessimistic and `FALSE` for optimistic.

`Recordset.getName();`

Returns the first 256 characters of the SQL statement used to create this `Recordset` object.

Return Type: String

`Recordset.getNoMatch();`

Specifies whether or not the last search or seek operation returned a match.

Return Type: Boolean (`False` if a match is found)

`Recordset.getODBCFetchCount();`

Returns the number of records fetched at one time from the server.

Return Type: int

`Recordset.getODBCFetchDelay();`

Returns the estimated latency of the last ODBC fetch.

Return Type: int

`Recordset.getParent();`

Returns the parent `Database` object of this `Recordset` object.

Return Type: Database

`Recordset.getPercentPosition();`

Returns the position of the cursor as being a percentage relative to the entire `Recordset` object.

Return Type: float

`Recordset.getProperties();`

Returns the `Properties` collection for this `Recordset` object.

Return Type: A `Properties` object

`Recordset.getRecordCount();`

Returns the number of records in the `Recordset` object.

Return Type: int

`Recordset.getRecordStatus();`

Returns a value matching a `RecordStatusEnum` constant.

Return Type: short

`Recordset.getRestartable();`

Returns whether or not the `Recordset` object supports the `Requery` method.

Return Type: Boolean

`Recordset.GetRows(Variant m_vNumrows);`

Returns an array of records.

Return Type: Variant array

| Argument | Data Type | Description |
|---|---|---|
| `m_vNumrows` | Variant (int) | The number of rows to return with this method |

`Recordset.getStillExecuting();`

Returns whether or not an asynchronous operation is still executing.

Return Type: Boolean

`Recordset.getSort();`

Returns the parameters of the `ORDER BY` clause in the SQL statement that created this `Recordset` object.

Return Type: String

`Recordset.getTransactions();`

Returns whether or not transactions are supported for this `Recordset` object.

Return Type: Boolean

`Recordset.getType();`

Returns a constant of `RecordsetTypeEnum` constants.

Return Type: short

`Recordset.getUpdateOptions();`

Returns the type of `Update` options being used with a Batch update.

Return Type: int (of type `UpdateCriteriaEnum`)

`Recordset.getUpdatable();`

Returns whether or not the `Recordset` object supports changes.

Return Type: Boolean

`Recordset.getValidationText();`

Returns the text of the message that your application displays if the value of a `Field` object doesn't satisfy the validation rule (Jet Workspaces only).

Return Type: String

`Recordset.getValidationRule();`

Returns the update, insert, or delete constraints on the object.

Return Type: String

```
Recordset.Move(int m_iRows, Variant m_vBookmark);
```

Moves the cursor a specified number of rows from this bookmark, or from a specific bookmark.

| Argument | Data Type | Description |
|---|---|---|
| `m_iRows` | int | The number of rows to move; can be positive or negative |
| `m_vBookmark` | Variant | A bookmark from which to begin the move |

```
Recordset.MoveFirst();
```

Moves the cursor to the first record in the `Recordset`.

```
Recordset.MoveLast(RecordsetOptionEnum.dbRunAsync);
```

Moves the cursor to the last record in the `Recordset`.

| Argument | Data Type | Description |
|---|---|---|
| `dbRunAsync` | int | Use to enable asynchronous execution of this method (Optional) |

```
Recordset.MoveNext();
```

Moves the cursor to the next position.

```
Recordset.MovePrevious();
```

Moves the cursor to the previous record.

```
Recordset.NextRecordset();
```

Loads the next batch of records (from a different query) into the `Recordset` object.

Return Type: Boolean (`TRUE` if more `Recordset` objects are available)

```
Recordset.OpenRecordset(Variant m_vOptions, Variant m_vLockType);
```

Opens a `Recordset` object on this `Recordset` of the same type, except for Table-type `Recordset` objects (which return a Dynaset-type).

| Argument | Data Type | Description |
|---|---|---|
| `m_vOptions` | Variant (int) | A member of the `RecordsetOptionsEnum` constants |
| `m_vLockType` | Variant (int) | A member of the `LockTypeEnum` constants |

`Recordset.putAbsolutePosition(int m_Ordinal);`

Sets the position of the cursor to a specific record by using the ordinal value of its place in the `Recordset`.

| Argument | Data Type | Description |
|---|---|---|
| `m_Ordinal` | int | The row number to set the cursor to |

`Recordset.putBatchSize(int m_BatchSize);`

Sets the number of statements sent to the server in each Batch.

| Argument | Data Type | Description |
|---|---|---|
| `m_BatchSize` | int | The number of statements in each batch sent, using batch updates. |

`Recordset.putBookmark(SafeArray m_Bookmark);`

Sets the bookmark for the current record.

| Argument | Data Type | Description |
|---|---|---|
| `m_BookMark` | SafeArray | A string of bytes representing a unique ID—a bookmark |

`Recordset.putCacheSize(int m_nRows);`

Sets the cache to a specified number of rows.

| Argument | Data Type | Description |
|---|---|---|
| `m_nRows` | int | The number of rows to hold in the cache |

`Recordset.putCacheStart(SafeArray m_Bookmark);`

Sets the bookmark of the first record in a dynaset-type `Recordset` object to be locally cached from the ODBC data source (Jet Workspaces only).

| Argument | Data Type | Description |
|---|---|---|
| `m_Bookmark` | SafeArray | A bookmark |

`Recordset.putCacheSize(int m_nRows);`

Sets the cache to a specified number of rows.

| Argument | Data Type | Description |
|---|---|---|
| `m_nRows` | int | The number of rows to hold in the cache |

`Recordset.putCollect(Variant m_vFieldName, Variant m_vValue);`

Sets the value contained by a `Field` object.

| Argument | Data Type | Description |
|---|---|---|
| `m_vFieldName` | Variant (String) | The field name to populate |
| `m_vValue` | Variant | The field value |

`Recordset.putConnection(Connection m_objConnection);`

Sets the `Connection` object for this `Recordset` object.

| Argument | Data Type | Description |
|---|---|---|
| `m_objConnection` | Connection | The `Connection` object to associate this recordset with |

`Recordset.putFilter(String m_strFilter);`

The setting or return value is a String data type that contains the `WHERE` clause of an SQL statement without the reserved word `WHERE`.

| Argument | Data Type | Description |
|---|---|---|
| `m_strFilter` | String | Filter criteria in the SQL `WHERE` clause |

`Recordset.putIndex(String m_Index);`

Sets the index for the `Recordset` object.

| Argument | Data Type | Description |
|---|---|---|
| `m_Index` | String | The name of an `Index` object in the indexes collection |

`Recordset.putLockEdits(boolean m_LockEdit);`

Sets the locking for the `Recordset`, `TRUE` for pessimistic and `FALSE` for optimistic.

| Argument | Data Type | Description |
|---|---|---|
| `m_LockEdit` | Boolean | Set to `TRUE` to lock the record while editing and updating the record, `FALSE` to hold lock only to update the record. |

`Recordset.putPercentPosition(float m_Position);`

Moves the cursor a specified percentage of the way through the `Recordset`.

| Argument | Data Type | Description |
|---|---|---|
| `m_Position` | float | The percentage (of the whole) to move through the Recordset |

`Recordset.putSort(String m_SortString);`

Sets the sort order for a Dynaset- or Snapshot-type `Recordset` object.

| Argument | Data Type | Description |
|---|---|---|
| `m_SortString` | String | A string representing the parameters of the `SQL ORDER BY` clause |

```
Recordset.putUpdateOptions(int m_UpdateOptions);
```

Sets the `Update` options for a Batch update.

| Argument | Data Type | Description |
|---|---|---|
| `m_UpdateOptions` | int | A constant of the `UpdateCriteriaEnum` |

```
Recordset.Requery(Variant m_QueryName);
```

Refreshes the `Recordset` object's data. If the argument is left out, the data is refreshed using the `QueryDef` that created the `Recordset` object.

| Argument | Data Type | Description |
|---|---|---|
| `m_QueryName` | Variant (String) | A Variant containing the name of a `QueryDef` (Optional) |

```
Recordset.Seek(String m_Operand, Variant m_Key);
```

Locates the next record matching the values in the key fields and positions the cursor on the new record.

| Argument | Data Type | Description |
|---|---|---|
| `m_Operand` | String | A logical operand |
| `m_Key` | Variant | Up to 13 values corresponding to fields in the `Recordset` object's current index, as specified by its `Index` property setting |

```
Recordset.Update(int m_UpdateType, boolean m_forceUpdate);
```

Saves the changes made to a `Recordset`.

| Argument | Data Type | Description |
|---|---|---|
| `m_UpdateType` | int | A value matching a member of `UpdateTypeEnum` constants |
| `m_forceUpdate` | Boolean | Set to `TRUE` to overwrite any changes made since the `Recordset` was fetched |

# The *TableDef* Object

The `TableDef` object can be thought of as the raw data of a database. Its methods and properties allow information discovery operations and read-only access, using indexes to the data that it contains.

## Constructor

The `TableDef` object has the following constructor:

```
TableDef = Database.CreateTableDef(Variant m_dbName, Variant m_vAttributes,
➥Variant m_vSource, Variant m_vConnect);
```

## Methods

The `TableDef` object has the following methods:

```
TableDef.CreateField(Variant m_vName, Variant m_vDataType, Variant m_vSize);
```

Creates a new `Field` object (and a new field in the underlying database).

| Argument | Data Type | Description |
|---|---|---|
| `m_vName` | Variant (String) | The name of the `Field` object to be created (Optional) |
| `m_vDataType` | Variant (int) | A member of the `DataTypeEnum` constants (Optional) |
| `m_vSize` | Variant (int) | The size of the `Field` (read/write only for a Text field, up to 255) |

```
TableDef.CreateIndex(Variant m_vName);
```

Creates an index for the `TableDef` object.

| Argument | Data Type | Description |
|---|---|---|
| `m_vName` | Variant (String) | The name of the index |

```
TableDef.getAttributes();
```

Returns the attributes for this `TableDef` object.

Return Type: int (of type `TableAttributesEnum`)

```
TableDef.getConflictTable();
```

Returns the path to the conflict table, if one exists.

Return Type: String

```
TableDef.getConnect();
```

Returns the connection string used to create this `Database` object.

Return Type: String

`TableDef.getDateCreated();`

Returns the date that the table was created.

Return Type: Variant

`TableDef.getFields();`

Returns the `Fields` collection for this `TableDef` object.

Return Type: A `Fields` object

`TableDef.getIndexes();`

Returns the `Indexes` collection for this `TableDef` object.

Return Type: An `Indexes` object

`TableDef.getLastUpdated();`

Returns the last time that this table was updated.

Return Type: Variant

`TableDef.getName();`

Returns the name of the `TableDef` object.

Return Type: String

`TableDef.getReplicaFilter();`

Returns the SQL WHERE clause (or Boolean value) used to filter the data that is replicated.

Return Type: Variant

`TableDef.getRecordCount();`

Returns the number of records in the `TableDef` object.

Return Type: int

`TableDef.getValidationRule();`

Returns the update, insert, or delete constraints on the object.

Return Type: String

`TableDef.getValidationText();`

Returns the text of the message that your application displays if the value of a `Field` object doesn't satisfy the validation rule (Jet Workspaces only).

Return Type: String

```
TableDef.getProperties();
```

Returns the `Properties` collection for this `TableDef` object.

Return Type: A `Properties` object

```
TableDef.getSourceTableName();
```

Returns the source table of this `TableDef` object.

Return Type: String

```
TableDef.putAttributes(int m_Attribute);
```

Sets the attributes for this `TableDef` object.

| Argument | Data Type | Description |
|---|---|---|
| `m_Attribute` | int | A member of the `TableDefAttributeEnum` constants |

```
TableDef.putConnect(String m_ConnectString);
```

Sets the connection information for this object.

| Argument | Data Type | Description |
|---|---|---|
| `m_ConnectString` | String | A string of `Connection` parameters separated by semicolons |

```
TableDef.putName(String m_strName);
```

Sets the name for this `TableDef` object.

| Argument | Data Type | Description |
|---|---|---|
| `m_strName` | String | The name of the `TableDef` object |

```
TableDef.putReplicaFilter(Variant m_vFilter);
```

Sets the filter (A SQL `WHERE` clause) or sets the replication to all records or none.

| Argument | Data Type | Description |
|---|---|---|
| `m_vFilter` | Variant | A Boolean or String value |

```
TableDef.putSourceTableName(String m_strSource);
```

Sets the source of the `TableDef` object.

| Argument | Data Type | Description |
|---|---|---|
| `m_strSource` | String | The name of a linked table or base table |

```
TableDef.putValidationRule(String m_Rule);
```

| Argument | Data Type | Description |
|---|---|---|
| m_Rule | String | A SQL Where clause without the "WHERE" keyword. |

```
TableDef.OpenRecordset(Variant m_vOptions, Variant m_vLockType);
```

Opens a Recordset object on this Recordset of the same type, except for Table-type Recordsets, which return a Dynaset-type.

| Argument | Data Type | Description |
|---|---|---|
| m_vOptions | Variant (int) | A member of the RecordsetOptionsEnum constants |
| m_vLockType | Variant (int) | A member of the LockTypeEnum constants |

```
TableDef.RefreshLink();
```

Refreshes the connection information for a linked table. (Used to update the connection string after changing it with the putConnect method).

# The *QueryDef* Object

The QueryDef object is to DAO what the SQL statement is to ODBC. The QueryDef object can also determine the properties of the statement being sent to the data source and supports prepared statements through the use of the Parameters object.

## Constructors

The QueryDef Object has the following constructors:

```
QueryDef = Database.CreateQueryDef(Variant m_Name, Variant m_vSQL);
```

```
QueryDef = Connection.CreateQueryDef(Variant m_Name, Variant m_vSQL);
```

```
QueryDef = Recordset.CopyQueryDef();
```

## Methods

The QueryDef object has the following methods:

```
QueryDef._Copy();
```

Creates a copy of the QueryDef object.

Return Type: A Querydef object

```
QueryDef.Cancel();
```

Cancels a `MoveLast` or `OpenRecordset` method call.

```
QueryDef.Close ();
```

Closes the open `QueryDef` object.

```
QueryDef.CreateProperty(Variant m_PropName, Variant m_vType, Variant m_vDataType,
➥Variant m_vDDL);
```

Creates a new Property.

Return Type: A `Property` object

| Argument | Data Type | Description |
|---|---|---|
| `m_PropName` | Variant (String) | The name of the new property |
| `m_vType` | Variant (int) | A member of the `DataTypeEnum` constants |
| `m_vDataType` | Variant | The initial property value |
| `m_vDDL` | Variant (Boolean) | `TRUE` if this property is a Data Definition Language property |

```
QueryDef.Execute(String m_Source, Variant m_vConnect);
```

Executes a SQL statement or `QueryDef` object.

| Argument | Data Type | Description |
|---|---|---|
| `m_Source` | String | The SQL statement or name of a `QueryDef` |
| `m_vConnect` | Variant (int) | A member of the `RecordsetOptionEnum` constants |

```
QueryDef.getCacheSize();
```

Returns the number of rows that can be held in the cache.

Return Type: int

```
QueryDef.getConnect();
```

Returns the connection string used to create this `Database` object.

Return Type: String

```
QueryDef.getDateCreated();
```

Returns the date that the table was created.

Return Type: Variant

```
QueryDef.getFields();
```

Returns the `Fields` collection for this `TableDef` object.

Return Type: A `Fields` object

`QueryDef.gethStmt();`

Returns the ODBC statement handle.

Return Type: int

`QueryDef.getLastUpdated();`

Returns the last time this `QueryDef` object was updated.

Return Type: Variant

`QueryDef.getMaxRecords();`

Returns the maximum number of records that can be retrieved from the server in a single fetch.

Return Type: int

`QueryDef.getName();`

Returns the name of the `QueryDef` object.

Return Type: String

`QueryDef.getODBCTimeout();`

Returns the ODBC timeout in seconds.

Return Type: short

`QueryDef.getParameters();`

Returns the `Parameters` collection.

Return Type: A `Parameters` object

`QueryDef.getProperties();`

Returns the `Properties` collection for this `QueryDef` object.

Return Type: A `Properties` object

`QueryDef.getRecordsAffected();`

Returns the number of records affected by the last `Execute` method call.

Return Type: int

`QueryDef.getReturnsRecords();`

Returns whether or not this `QueryDef` object returns a `Recordset`.

Return Type: Boolean

```
QueryDef.getSQL();
```

Returns the SQL property of the `QueryDef` object.

Return Type: String

```
QueryDef.getStillExecuting();
```

Returns whether or not an asynchronous operation is still executing.

Return Type: Boolean

```
QueryDef.getType();
```

Returns a constant of `RecordsetTypeEnum` constants.

Return Type: short

```
QueryDef._30_OpenRecordset(String m_Source, Variant m_vType);
```

Returns a new `Recordset` object.

Return Type: A `Recordset` object

| Argument | Data Type | Description |
|---|---|---|
| `m_Source` | String | The name of the actual database file or DSN |
| `m_vType` | Variant (int) | A member of the `RecordsetTypeEnum` constants |

```
QueryDef.OpenRecordset(String m_Source, Variant m_vType, Variant m_vOption,
➥Variant m_vLockType);
```

Returns a new `Recordset` object.

Return Type: A `Recordset` object

| Argument | Data Type | Description |
|---|---|---|
| `m_Source` | String | The name of the actual database file or DSN |
| `m_vType` | Variant (int) | A member of the `RecordsetTypeEnum` constants |
| `m_vOption` | Variant (int) | A member of the `RecordsetOptionsEnum` constants |
| `m_vLockType` | Variant (int) | A member of the `LockTypeEnum` constants (Optional) |

`QueryDef.putCacheSize(int m_nRows);`

Sets the cache to a specified number of rows.

| Argument | Data Type | Description |
|---|---|---|
| `m_nRows` | int | The number of rows to hold in the cache |

`QueryDef.putConnect(String m_ConnectString);`

Sets the connection information for this object.

| Argument | Data Type | Description |
|---|---|---|
| `m_ConnectString` | String | A string of `Connection` parameters separated by semicolons |

`QueryDef.putMaxRecords(int m_nMaxRecords);`

Sets the maximum number of records to return in a single `Recordset`.

| Argument | Data Type | Description |
|---|---|---|
| `m_nMaxRecords` | int | The number of records to return |

`QueryDef.putName(String m_Name);`

Set the name of the `QueryDef` object.

| Argument | Data Type | Description |
|---|---|---|
| `m_Name` | String | Sets the name of the `QueryDef` object |

`QueryDef.putPrepare(Variant m_vPrepared);`

Sets the `QueryDef` object to call either `SQLPrepare` or `SQLExecDirect` on execution.

| Argument | Data Type | Description |
|---|---|---|
| `m_vPrepared` | Variant (int) | A member value of `QueryDefStateEnum` |

`QueryDef.putODBCTimeout(short m_sTimeout);`

Sets the period of time (in seconds) that the `QueryDef` object will wait for a return of the result set from the ODBC data source.

| Argument | Data Type | Description |
|---|---|---|
| `m_sTimeout` | short | ODBC Timeout (in seconds) |

`QueryDef.putReturnsRecords(boolean m_HasRecords);`

Sets the value that determines whether or not the `QueryDef` object returns a `Recordset`.

(*Note: Setting this value to true and then using DDL won't cause a `Recordset` to be returned.)

| Argument | Data Type | Description |
|---|---|---|
| `m_HasRecords` | Boolean | Value denoting whether or not the `QueryDef` object returns a `Recordset` object |

```
QueryDef.putSQL(String m_SQL);
```

Sets the SQL text string to be used as the query.

| Argument | Data Type | Description |
|---|---|---|
| `m_SQL` | String | SQL statement |

# The *Parameters* Object

The `Parameters` object enables you to use prepared statements in DAO. The properties of the `Parameters` object enable control of the parameters sent to the SQL database and enable you to determine information about the statement.

## Constructors

The `Parameters` object has the following constructors:

```
Parameter = Parameters.getItem(Name);
```

```
Parameter = Parameters.getItem(Index);
```

## Methods

The `Parameters` object has the following methods:

```
Parameters.getDirection();
```

Returns the direction of the parameter; matches a value in the `ParameterDirectionEnum` constants.

Return Type: short

```
Parameters.getName();
```

Returns the name of the `Parameter`.

Return Type: String

```
Parameters.getProperties();
```

Returns the `Properties` collection.

Return Type: A `Properties` object

```
Parameters.getType();
```

Returns a member of the `DataTypeEnum` constants.

Return Type: short

```
Parameters.getValue();
```

Returns the value of the `Parameters` object.

Return Type: A variant containing the value of the `Parameters` object

```
Parameters.putDirection(short m_Direction);
```

Sets the direction of the `Parameters` object.

| Argument | Data Type | Description |
|---|---|---|
| `m_Direction` | Short | A member of the `ParameterDirectionEnum` constants |

```
Parameters.putType(short m_DataType);
```

Sets the data type of the `Parameters` object.

| Argument | Data Type | Description |
|---|---|---|
| `m_DataType` | Short | A member of the `DataTypeEnum` constants |

```
Parameters.putValue(Variant m_vValue);
```

Sets the value of the `Parameters` object.

| Argument | Data Type | Description |
|---|---|---|
| `m_vValue` | Variant | The parameter value |

# The *Relation* Object

The `Relation` object is used in DAO to set referential integrity through the creation and maintainance of relations (even through database replication).

## Constructors

The `Relation` object has the following constructors:

```
Relation = Database.CreateRelation(Variant m_RelationName, Variant m_vPrimary,
➥Variant m_vForeign, Variant m_vAttributes);
```

```
Relation = Database.CreateRelation(Variant m_RelationName, Variant m_vPrimary,
➥Variant m_vForeign, Variant m_vAttributes);
```

## Methods

The `Relation` object has the following methods:

```
Relation.CreateField(Variant m_vName,  Variant m_vDataType, Variant m_vSize);
```

| Argument | Data Type | Description |
|---|---|---|
| `m_vName` | Variant (String) | The name of the `Field` to be created (Optional) |
| `m_vDataType` | Variant (int) | A member of the `DataTypeEnum` constants (Optional) |
| `m_vSize` | Variant (int) | The size of the `Field` (read/write only for a Text field, up to 255; Optional) |

`Relation.getAttributes();`

Returns the attributes for this `TableDef` object.

Return Type: int (of type `TableAttributesEnum`)

`Relation.getFields();`

Returns the `Fields` collection for this `Relation` object.

Return Type: A `Fields` object

`Relation.getForeignTable();`

Returns the name of the foreign table in the relation.

Rcturn Type: String

`Relation.getName();`

Returns the name for this `Connection` object.

Return Type: String

`Relation.getPartialReplica();`

Returns whether or not the `relation` is enforced during synchronization.

Return Type: Boolean

`Relation.getProperties();`

Returns the `Properties` collection.

Return Type: A `Properties` object

`Relation.getTable();`

Returns the name of the primary `Table` object, a `QueryDef` or `TableDef` object.

Return Type: String

`Relation.putAttributes(int m_Option);`

Sets the attributes for this `Relation` object.

| Argument | Data Type | Description |
|---|---|---|
| `m_Option` | int | A member of the `RelationAttributeEnum` constants |

`Relation.putForeignTable(String m_ForeignTable);`

Sets the name of the `TableDef` or `QueryDef` object that will be the foreign table in the `Relation` object.

| Argument | Data Type | Description |
|---|---|---|
| `m_ForeignTable` | String | The name of a `QueryDef` object or `TableDef` object |

`Relation.putName(String m_Name);`

Sets the name for this Relation.

| Argument | Data Type | Description |
|---|---|---|
| `m_Name` | String | A name |

`Relation.putPartialReplica(boolean m_Enforce);`

Determines whether or not the relation is enforced during synchronization.

| Argument | Data Type | Description |
|---|---|---|
| `m_Enforce` | Boolean | `TRUE` if the relation is to be enforced |

`Relation.putTable(String m_Table);`

Sets the name of the `TableDef` or `QueryDef` object that you are using.

| Argument | Data Type | Description |
|---|---|---|
| `m_Table` | String | The name of a `TableDef` object or `QueryDef` object |

# The *Field* Object

The `Field` object is the smallest common denominator in the DAO heirarchy. The `Field` object is used to set properties and manipulate the data in the database fields.

## Constructors

The `Field` object has the following constructors:

```
Field = Fields.getItem(Variant name);
```

```
Field = Fields.getItem(Variant index);
```

```
Field = TableDef.CreateField(Variant m_vName, Variant m_vDataType, Variant
m_vSize);
```

```
Field = Index.CreateField(Variant m_vName, Variant m_vDataType, Variant m_vSize);
```

## Methods

The `Field` object has the following methods:

```
Field._30_FieldSize();
```

Returns the size of the field (in bytes)

Return Type: int

```
Field.AppendChunk(Variant m_vChunk);
```

Used to break up large data types during submission to the data source. Improves performance and decreases load on the network.

| Argument | Data Type | Description |
|---|---|---|
| `m_vChunk` | Variant | The piece of data that you want to send |

```
Field.CreateProperty(Variant m_PropName, Variant m_vType, Variant m_vDataType,
➥Variant m_vDDL);
```

Creates a new `Property` object.

Return Type: A `Property` object

| Argument | Data Type | Description |
|---|---|---|
| `m_PropName` | Variant (String) | The name of the new property |
| `m_vType` | Variant (int) | A member of the `DataTypeEnum` constants |
| `m_vDataType` | Variant | The initial property value |
| `m_vDDL` | Variant (Boolean) | `TRUE` if this property is a Data Definition Language property |

```
Field.getAllowZeroLength();
```

Returns whether or not the `Field` object allows zero-length strings.

Return Type: Boolean

```
Field.getAttributes();
```

Returns the attributes for this `Field` object.

Return Type: int (of type `FieldAttributesEnum`)

```
Field.getCollectionIndex();
```

Returns a short value equal to the index of this `Field` object in the collection.

Return Type: short

```
Field.getCollatingOrder();
```

Returns the collating order for this `Database` object.

Return Type: An int matching a value in `LanguageConstants`

```
Field.getDataUpdatable();
```

Returns `TRUE` if the data in the `Field` object is updatable.

Return Type: Boolean

```
Field.getDefaultValue();
```

Returns the default value of the `Field` object.

Return Type: Variant

```
Field.getFieldSize();
```

Returns the size of the `Field` object.

Return Type: int

```
Field.getForeignName();
```

Returns the name of the `Field` in a foreign table that is the foreign key in the `Relation` object.

Return Type: String

```
Field.GetChunk(int m_Offset, int m_Bytes);
```

Used to break up large data types during retrieval to improve performance and decrease load on the network.

| **Argument** | **Data Type** | **Description** |
|---|---|---|
| `m_Offset` | int | The byte offset at which to begin retrieval |
| `m_Bytes` | int | The number of bytes to retrieve each time |

```
Field.getName();
```

Returns the name of this `Field` object.

Return Type: String

```
Field.getOrdinalPosition();
```

Returns the ordinal position of this `Field` object in the `Fields` collection.

Return Type: short

`Field.getOriginalValue();`

Returns the original value in the case of a collision during a Batch Update.

Return Type: Variant

`Field.getProperties();`

Returns the `Properties` collection for this object.

Return Type: A `Properties` object

`Field.getRequired();`

Returns whether or not this `Field` object requires non-null values.

Return Type: Boolean

`Field.getSourceTable();`

Returns the name of the source table for this `Field` object.

Return Type: String

`Field.getSize();`

Returns the size of the `Field` object.

Return Type: int

`Field.getType();`

Returns a constant of `RecordsetTypeEnum` constants.

Return Type: short

`Field.getValue();`

Returns the value of the `Field` object.

Return Type: Variant

`Field.getValidateOnSet();`

Returns `TRUE` if the Field Validation Rule is checked when the `Field` object's value is set.

Return Type: Boolean

`Field.getValidationText();`

Returns the text of the message your application displays if the value of a `Field` object doesn't satisfy the Field Validation Rule (Jet Workspaces only).

Return Type: String

`Field.getValidationRule();`

Returns the update, insert, or delete constraints on the object.

Return Type: String

`Field.getVisibleValue();`

Returns the newest value in the case of a collision.

Return Type: Variant

`Field.putAllowZeroLength(boolean m_AllowZeros);`

Sets the value that determines whether or not this field allows zero-length strings.

| Argument | Data Type | Description |
|---|---|---|
| `m_AllowZeros` | Boolean | `TRUE` if zeros are an allowed value in this field |

`Field.putAttributes(int m_Attribute);`

Sets the attributes for this `Field` object.

| Argument | Data Type | Description |
|---|---|---|
| `m_Attribute` | int | A member of the `FieldAttributeEnum` constants |

`Field.putForeignName(String m_Name);`

Sets the name of the foreign table in a `Field` constraint.

| Argument | Data Type | Description |
|---|---|---|
| `m_Name` | String | The name of a `QueryDef` object or `TableDef` object |

`Field.putName(String m_Name);`

Sets the name of this `Field` object.

| Argument | Data Type | Description |
|---|---|---|
| `m_Name` | String | The name of the `Field` object |

`Field.putOrdinalPosition(short m_Ordinal);`

Sets the position of the `Field` object in the `Fields` collection before it is appended.

| Argument | Data Type | Description |
|---|---|---|
| `m_Ordinal` | short | Sets the position of the `Field` object |

`Field.putRequired(boolean m_ValRequired);`

| Argument | Data Type | Description |
|---|---|---|
| `m_ValRequired` | Boolean | Set to `TRUE` if a value is required of this `Field` object |

```
Field.putSize(int m_Size);
```

Sets the size of the `Field` object before it is appended.

| Argument | Data Type | Description |
|---|---|---|
| `m_Size` | int | The size (in characters) of a text field |

```
Field.putType(short m_DataType);
```

Sets the data type of the Field object before it is appended.

| Argument | Data Type | Description |
|---|---|---|
| `m_DataType` | short | A member of the `DataTypeEnum` constants |

```
Field.putValidationRule(String m_Rule);
```

Sets the expression that is checked when data is updated.

| Argument | Data Type | Description |
|---|---|---|
| `m_Rule` | String | The expression, in the form of a valid SQL `WHERE` clause expression. |

```
Field.putValidationText(String m_ValidText);
```

Sets the message to use when a client activates a Validation Rule.

| Argument | Data Type | Description |
|---|---|---|
| `m_ValidText` | String | The message seen when a Validation Rule is activated |

```
Field.putValue(Variant m_vValue);
```

Sets the `Field` value.

| Argument | Data Type | Description |
|---|---|---|
| `m_vValue` | Variant | The value of the `Field` object |

```
Field.putDefaultValue(Variant m_DefaultValue);
```

| Argument | Data Type | Description |
|---|---|---|
| `m_DefaultValue` | Variant (String) | Default Value for the `Field` object if not specified in the SQL statement |

```
Field.putValidateOnSet(boolean m_ValidateNow);
```

Enables you to set whether or not the field is validated when the value is set or when the update takes place.

| Argument | Data Type | Description |
|---|---|---|
| m_ValidateNow | Boolean | TRUE, if you want to validate the fields as they are set |

# The *Index* Object

The Index object is only available when working with TableDef objects. It represents the index consisting of one or more columns and is searchable. This is a quick way to sift through large data sets when read access is all that is required.

## Constructors

The Index object has the following constructors:

```
Index = Indexes.getItem(Variant name)
```

```
Index = Indexes.getItem(Variant index)
```

```
Index = TableDef.CreateIndex(Variant fieldname)
```

## Methods

The Index object has the following methods:

```
Index.CreateField(Variant m_vName, Variant m_vDataType, Variant m_vSize);
```

Creates a new field to be used for the Index object.

Return Type: A Field object

| Argument | Data Type | Description |
|---|---|---|
| m_vName | Variant (String) | The name of the Field object to be created (Optional) |
| m_vDataType | Variant (int) | A member of the DataTypeEnum constants (Optional) |
| m_vSize | Variant (int) | The size of the Field object (read/write only for a Text field, up to 255; Optional) |

```
Index.CreateProperty(Variant m_PropName, Variant m_vType, Variant m_vDataType,
➥Variant m_vDDL);
```

Creates a new Property object.

Return Type: A Property object

| Argument | Data Type | Description |
|---|---|---|
| `m_PropName` | Variant (String) | The name of the new `property` |
| `m_vType` | Variant (int) | A member of the `DataTypeEnum` constants |
| `m_vDataType` | Variant | The initial property value |
| `m_vDDL` | Variant (boolean) | `TRUE` if this property is a Data Definition Language property |

`Index.getClustered();`

Returns `TRUE` if the `Index` is clustered.

Return Type: Boolean

`Index.getDistinctCount();`

Returns the number of unique keys in the `Index`.

Return Type: int

`Index.getFields();`

Returns the `Fields` collection for this `Index`.

Return Type: A `Fields` object

`Index.getForeign();`

Returns `TRUE` if the object is a foreign key.

Return Type: Boolean

`Index.getIgnoreNulls();`

Returns `TRUE` if null values do not have an entry in the `Index`.

Return Type: Boolean

`Index.getName();`

Returns the name of the `Index`.

Return Type: String

`Index.getProperties();`

Returns the `Properties` collection for this object.

Return Type: A `Properties` object

`Index.getRequired();`

Returns `TRUE` if the `Field` cannot contain null values.

Return Type: Boolean

`Index.getPrimary();`

Returns `TRUE` if this is the primary `Index`.

Return Type: Boolean

`Index.getUnique();`

Returns `TRUE` if this is a unique Index.

Return Type: Boolean

`Index.putClustered(boolean m_Clustered);`

Sets this `Index` to be clustered.

| Argument | Data Type | Description |
|---|---|---|
| `m_Clustered` | Boolean | Set to `TRUE` to indicate this index is clustered |

`Index.putFields(Variant m_vFields);`

Sets the `Field` objects in the `Index`.

| Argument | Data Type | Description |
|---|---|---|
| `m_vFields` | Variant (String) | Sets the `Field` objects in an `Index` |

`Index.putIgnoreNulls(boolean m_Ignore);`

Sets the property that determines whether the `Index object` ignores null values.

| Argument | Data Type | Description |
|---|---|---|
| `m_Ignore` | Boolean | Set to `TRUE` to ignore `NULL` values in the `Index` object |

`Index.putName(String m_Name);`

Sets the name of this `Index`.

| Argument | Data Type | Description |
|---|---|---|
| `m_Name` | String | The name of the `Index` object |

`Index.putPrimary(boolean m_Primary);`

Sets the primary `Index`.

| Argument | Data Type | Description |
|---|---|---|
| `m_Primary` | Boolean | Set to `TRUE` to make this the primary index |

```
Index.putRequired(boolean m_Required);
```

Set to `TRUE` to require `Fields` to be non-null.

| Argument | Data Type | Description |
|---|---|---|
| `m_Required` | Boolean | Determines whether or not null values are allowed |

```
Index.putUnique(boolean m_Unique);
```

Sets this `Index` to be unique.

| Argument | Data Type | Description |
|---|---|---|
| `m_Unique` | Boolean | `TRUE` if the `Index` is unique, `FALSE` otherwise. |

# The *Group* Object

The `Group` object allows Microsoft Jet workspaces to set security permissions based on group membership.

## Constructors

The `Group` object has the following construtors:

```
Group = Workspace.CreateGroup(Variant m_Name, Variant m_PID);

Group = User.CreateGroup(Variant m_GroupName, Variant m_PID);
```

## Methods

The `Group` object has the following methods:

```
Group.CreateUser(Variant m_vUserName, Variant m_vPID, Variant m_vPassword);
```

Creates a new user.

| Argument | Data Type | Description |
|---|---|---|
| `m_UserName` | Variant (String) | The name of the new user (optional) |
| `m_vPID` | Variant (String) | A unique identifier for this user (optional) |
| m_vPassword | Variant (String) | A password up to 14 characters in length (optional) |

```
Group.getUsers();
```

Returns the `Users` collection for this group.

Return Type: A `Users` object

```
Group.getProperties();
```

Returns the `Properties` collection for this object.

Return Type: A `Properties` object

```
Group.getName();
```

Returns the name of the group.

Return Type: String

```
Group.putName(String m_GroupName);
```

Sets the name of the group.

| Argument | Data Type | Description |
|---|---|---|
| `m_GroupName` | String | The name of a group |

```
Group.putPID(String m_PID);
```

Sets the PID of the group.

| Argument | Data Type | Description |
|---|---|---|
| `m_PID` | String | A 4–20 character long sequence of alphanumeric characters |

# The *User* Object

The `User` object represents a single entity accessing the database. This object allows permissions to be granular to the user level.

## Constructors

The `User` object has the following constructors:

```
User = Users.getItem(Variant name);

User = Users.getItem(Variant index);

User = Group.CreateUser(Variant m_vUserName, Variant m_vPID, Variant m_vPassword);

User = Workspace.CreateUser(Variant m_Name, Variant m_PID, Variant m_Password);
```

## Methods

The `User` object has the following methods:

```
User.CreateGroup(Variant m_GroupName, Variant m_PID);
```

Creates a new `Group`.

Return Type: A `Group` object

| Argument | Data Type | Description |
|---|---|---|
| `m_GroupName` | Variant (String) | The name for the new Group object |
| `m_PID` | Variant (String) | The unique ID for the Group object |

`User.NewPassword(String m_OldPassword, String m_NewPassword);`

Creates a new password for the `User` object.

| Argument | Data Type | Description |
|---|---|---|
| `m_OldPassword` | String | The old password |
| `m_NewPassword` | String | The new password |

`User.getProperties();`

Returns the `Properties` collection for this object.

Return Type: A `Properties` object

`User.getName();`

Returns the name of the `User` object.

Return Type: String

`User.putName(String m_UserName);`

Sets the name for a `User` object.

| Argument | Data Type | Description |
|---|---|---|
| `m_UserName` | String | The user name |

`User.putPassword(String m_Password);`

Sets the password for the `User`.

| Argument | Data Type | Description |
|---|---|---|
| `m_Password` | String | An alphanumeric string up to 14 characters long |

`User.putPID(String m_PID);`

Sets the PID of the `User` object.

| Argument | Data Type | Description |
|---|---|---|
| `m_PID` | String | A 4–20 character long sequence of alphanumeric characters |

# The *Container* Object

The `Container` object is used to store application-specific information called documents. The Microsoft Jet Containers collection defines three of these to store information: the Databases (saved databases), the Tables (saved tables and queries), and the Relations (saved relationships).

## Constructors

The `Container` object has the following constructors:

`Container = Containers.getItem(Variant name);`

`Container = Containers.getItem(Variant index);`

## Methods

The `Container` object has the following methods:

`Container.getAllPermissions();`

Returns the sum of the permissions on the `Container` object (matching members of the `PermissionsEnum` constants) including the inherited permissions.

Return Type: int

`Container.getDocuments();`

Returns the `Documents` collection for this `Container` object.

Return Type: String

`Container.getInherit();`

Returns `TRUE` if the `Documents` placed into this `Container` object will inherit permissions from this `Container` object.

Return Type: Boolean

`Container.getName();`

Returns the name of the `Container` object.

Return Type: String

`Container.getOwner();`

Returns the name of a `User` object that is set as the owner of this `Container` object.

Return Type: String

`Container.getPermissions();`

Returns the sum of the permissions on the `Container` object (matching members of the `PermissionsEnum` constants) excluding inherited permissions.

Return Type: int

`Container.getProperties();`

Returns the `Properties` collection for this object.

Return Type: A `Properties` object

`Container.getUserName();`

Returns the user account with permissions on this object.

Return Type: String

`Container.putInherit(boolean m_Inherit);`

If `TRUE`, causes all `Documents` created in this `Container` object to inherit its permissions.

| Argument | Data Type | Description |
|---|---|---|
| `m_Inherit` | Boolean | If `TRUE`, inherit permissions, if `FALSE`, do not |

`Container.putOwner(String m_UserName);`

Sets the user account who has ownership of this object.

| Argument | Data Type | Description |
|---|---|---|
| `m_UserName` | String | The name of a `User` object |

`Container.putPermissions(int m_Permissions);`

Sets the permissions for this `Container` object.

| Argument | Data Type | Description |
|---|---|---|
| `m_Permissions` | int | A member of the `PermissionEnum` constants |

`Container.putUserName(String m_User);`

Sets the user account for this `Container` object.

| Argument | Data Type | Description |
|---|---|---|
| `m_User` | String | A user account |

# The *Property* Object

The `Property` object is used to create and store application-defined properties.

## Constructors

The `Property` object has the following constructors:

```
Property = Database.CreateProperty(Variant m_PropName, Variant m_vType, Variant
➥m_vDataType, Variant m_vDDL);
```

```
Property = Document.CreateProperty(Variant m_PropName, Variant m_vType, Variant
➥m_vDataType, Variant m_vDDL);
```

```
Property = Field.CreateProperty(Variant m_PropName, Variant m_vType, Variant
➥m_vDataType, Variant m_vDDL);
```

```
Property = Index.CreateProperty(Variant m_PropName, Variant m_vType, Variant
➥m_vDataType, Variant m_vDDL);
```

```
Property = QueryDef.CreateProperty(Variant m_PropName, Variant m_vType, Variant
➥m_vDataType, Variant m_vDDL);
```

```
Property = Properties.getItem(name);
```

```
Property = Properties.getItem(index);
```

## Methods

The `Property` object has the following methods:

```
Property.getInherited();
```

Returns whether or not this property is inherited.

Return Type: Boolean

```
Property.getName();
```

Returns the name of the property.

Return Type: String

```
Property.getProperties();
```

Returns the `Properties` collection.

Return Type: String

```
Property.getType();
```

Returns a `PropertTypeEnum` value.

Return Type: int

```
Property.getValue();
```

Returns the value of a property.

Return Type: Variant

```
Property.putName(String m_Name);
```

Sets the name for the `Property`.

| Argument | Data Type | Description |
|---|---|---|
| `m_Name` | String | A name |

```
Property.putType(short m_DataType);
```

Sets the data type of the `Property`.

| Argument | Data Type | Description |
|---|---|---|
| `m_DataType` | short | A member of the `DataTypeEnum` constants |

```
Property.putValue(Variant m_vValue);
```

Sets the `Property` value.

| Argument | Data Type | Description |
|---|---|---|
| `m_vValue` | Variant | The value of the property |

# The *Document* Object

The `Document` object is an application-specified storage type.

## Constructors

The `Document` object has the following constructors:

```
Document = Documents.getItem(name);
```

```
Document = Documents.getItem(index);
```

## Methods

The `Document` object has the following methods:

```
Document.CreateProperty(Variant m_PropName, Variant m_vType, Variant m_vDataType,
➥Variant m_vDDL);
```

Creates a new `Property`.

Return Type: A `Property` object

| Argument | Data Type | Description |
|---|---|---|
| m_PropName | Variant (String) | The name of the new property |
| m_vType | Variant (int) | A member of the DataTypeEnum constants |
| m_vDataType | Variant | The initial property value |
| m_vDDL | Variant (Boolean) | TRUE if this property is a Data Definition Language property |

`Document.getAllPermissions();`

Returns an int that is the sum of all of the PermissionsEnum constants representing the permissions on this object.

Return Type: int

`Document.getContainer();`

Returns the string with the name of the Container object associated with this Document.

Return Type: String

`Document.getDateCreated();`

Returns the date that this Document was created.

Return Type: Variant

`Document.getLastUpdated();`

Returns the last date that the Document was updated.

Return Type: Variant

`Document.getName();`

Returns the name of the Document.

Return Type: String

`Document.getOwner();`

Returns a string with the name of the user who is the owner of this object.

Return Type: String

`Document.getPermissions();`

Returns the sum of the permissions on the Container object (matching members of the PermissionsEnum constants) excluding inherited permissions.

Return Type: int

`Document.getProperties();`

Returns the `Properties` collection for this object.

Return Type: A `Properties` object

```
Document.getUserName();
```

Returns the user name of the `User` object associated with this `Document` object.

Return Type: String

```
Document.putPermissions(int m_Permissions);
```

Sets the permissions for an object.

| Argument | Data Type | Description |
|---|---|---|
| `m_Permissions` | int | A member (or sum) of the `PermissionsEnum` constants |

```
Document.putOwner(String m_Owner);
```

Sets the user account that has ownership of this object.

| Argument | Data Type | Description |
|---|---|---|
| `m_Owner` | String | A user account |

# Collections in DAO

The objects in DAO are automatically added to a default set of collections. These collections provide a convenient method of accessing multiple objects of the same type. In fact, some objects, such as the `Error` object, can only be accessed through its collection.

The default collections defined for DAO are listed as follows. They are self explanatory (in other words, `Field` objects are added to the `Fields` collection; those `Fields` that are `Indexes` are in the `IndexFields` collection).

- `Fields`
- `Groups`
- `Indexes`
- `IndexFields`
- `Properties`
- `QueryDefs`
- `Relations`
- `TableDefs`
- `Users`
- `Workspaces`

These collections support the following methods:

| Method | Argument List | Description |
|---|---|---|
| `Delete` | None | Deletes the collection member |
| `Append` | (Object) | Appends the object to the collection |
| `getItem` | (Variant) | Returns the collection member at the specified index |
| `getCount` | None | Returns the number of members in the collection |
| `_NewEnum` | None | |
| `Refresh` | None | Enumerates the members of the collection |

The collections in the following table support far fewer methods than the ones in the previous table. These collections are listed in the table, followed by the methods that they support.

- `Connections`
- `Containers`
- `Databases`
- `Documents`
- `Errors`
- `Parameters`
- `Recordsets`

| Method | Argument List | Description |
|---|---|---|
| `getItem` | (Variant) | Returns the collection member at the specified index |
| `getCount` | None | Returns the number of members in the collection |
| _NewEnum | None | Returns a type `com.ms.com.IUnknown` |
| `Refresh` | None | Enumerates the members of the collection |

# Constants

Constants are a means of making sense of numerical arrays (similar to using #DEFINE'S in C/C++). Java makes liberal use of these through the class structure. Microsoft has migrated the following constants for use with DAO to the com.ms.com Package.

## The *_DAOSuppHelp* Constant

- `int LogMessages;`
- `int KeepLocal;`

- int Replicable;
- int ReplicableBool;
- int V1xNullBehavior;

## The *CollatingOrderEnum* Constant

- int dbSortNeutral;
- int dbSortArabic;
- int dbSortCyrillic;
- int dbSortCzech;
- int dbSortDutch;
- int dbSortGeneral;
- int dbSortGreek;
- int dbSortHebrew;
- int dbSortHungarian;
- int dbSortIcelandic;
- int dbSortNorwdan;
- int dbSortPDXIntl;
- int dbSortPDXNor;
- int dbSortPDXSwe;
- int dbSortPolish;
- int dbSortSpanish;
- int dbSortSwedFin;
- int dbSortTurkish;
- int dbSortJapanese;
- int dbSortChineseSimplified;
- int dbSortChineseTraditional;
- int dbSortKorean;
- int dbSortThai;
- int dbSortSlovenian;
- int dbSortUndefined;

## The *CursorDriverEnum* Constant

- int dbUseDefaultCursor;
- int dbUseODBCCursor;
- int dbUseServerCursor;

- int dbUseClientBatchCursor;
- int dbUseNoCursor;

## The *DatabaseTypeEnum* Constant

- int dbVersion10;
- int dbEncrypt;
- int dbDecrypt;
- int dbVersion11;
- int dbVersion20;
- int dbVersion30;

## The *DataTypeEnum* Constant

- int dbBoolean;
- int dbByte;
- int dbInteger;
- int dbLong;
- int dbCurrency;
- int dbSingle;
- int dbDouble;
- int dbDate;
- int dbBinary;
- int dbText;
- int dbLongBinary;
- int dbMemo;
- int dbGUID;
- int dbBigInt;
- int dbVarBinary;
- int dbChar;
- int dbNumeric;
- int dbDecimal;
- int dbFloat;
- int dbTime;
- int dbTimeStamp;

## The *DriverPromptEnum* Constant

- int dbDriverPrompt;
- int dbDriverNoPrompt;
- int dbDriverComplete;
- int dbDriverCompleteRequired;

## The *EditModeEnum* Constant

- int dbEditNone;
- int dbEditInProgress;
- int dbEditAdd;
- int dbEditChanged;
- int dbEditDeleted;
- int dbEditNew;

## The *FieldAttributeEnum* Constant

- int dbFixedField;
- int dbVariableField;
- int dbAutoIncrField;
- int dbUpdatableField;
- int dbSystemField;
- int dbHyperlinkField;
- int dbDescending;

## The *IdleEnum* Constant

- int dbFreeLocks;
- int dbRefreshCache;

## The *LanguageConstants* Constants

- Generic dbLangArabic;
- Generic dbLangCzech;
- Generic dbLangDutch;
- Generic dbLangGeneral;
- Generic dbLangGreek;
- Generic dbLangHebrew;
- Generic dbLangHungarian;
- Generic dbLangIcelandic;

- `Generic dbLangNordic;`
- `Generic dbLangNorwDan;`
- `Generic dbLangPolish;`
- `Generic dbLangCyrillic;`
- `Generic dbLangSpanish;`
- `Generic dbLangSwedFin;`
- `Generic dbLangTurkish;`
- `Generic dbLangJapanese;`
- `Generic dbLangChineseSimplified;`
- `Generic dbLangChineseTraditional;`
- `Generic dbLangKorean;`
- `Generic dbLangThai;`
- `Generic dbLangSlovenian;`

## The *LockTypeEnum* Constant

- `int dbPessimistic;`
- `int dbOptimistic;`
- `int dbOptimisticValue;`
- `int dbOptimisticBatch;`

## The *ParameterDirectionEnum* Constant

- `int dbParamInput;`
- `int dbParamOutput;`
- `int dbParamInputOutput;`
- `int dbParamReturnValue;`

## The *PermissionEnum* Constant

- `int dbSecNoAccess;`
- `int dbSecFullAccess;`
- `int dbSecDelete;`
- `int dbSecReadSec;`
- `int dbSecWriteSec;`
- `int dbSecWriteOwner;`
- `int dbSecDBCreate;`
- `int dbSecDBOpen;`
- `int dbSecDBExclusive;`

- int dbSecDBAdmin;
- int dbSecCreate;
- int dbSecReadDef;
- int dbSecWriteDef;
- int dbSecRetrieveData;
- int dbSecInsertData;
- int dbSecReplaceData;
- int dbSecDeleteData;

## The *QueryDefStateEnum* Constant

- int dbQPrepare;
- int dbQUnprepare;

## The *QueryDefTypeEnum* Constant

- int dbQSelect;
- int dbQProcedure;
- int dbQAction;
- int dbQCrosstab;
- int dbQDelete;
- int dbQUpdate;
- int dbQAppend;
- int dbQMakeTable;
- int dbQDDL;
- int dbQSQLPassThrough;
- int dbQSetOperation;
- int dbQSPTBulk;
- int dbQCompound;

## The *RecordsetOptionEnum* Constant

- int dbDenyWrite;
- int dbDenyRead;
- int dbReadOnly;
- int dbAppendOnly;
- int dbInconsistent;
- int dbConsistent;
- int dbSQLPassThrough;
- int dbFailOnError;

- `int dbForwardOnly;`
- `int dbSeeChanges;`
- `int dbRunAsync;`
- `int dbExecDirect;`

## The *RecordsetTypeEnum* Constant

- `int dbOpenTable;`
- `int dbOpenDynaset;`
- `int dbOpenSnapshot;`
- `int dbOpenForwardOnly;`
- `int dbOpenDynamic;`

## The *RecordStatusEnum* Constant

- `int dbRecordUnmodified;`
- `int dbRecordModified;`
- `int dbRecordNew;`
- `int dbRecordDeleted;`
- `int dbRecordDBDeleted;`

## The *RelationAttributeEnum* Constant

- `int dbRelationUnique;`
- `int dbRelationDontEnforce;`
- `int dbRelationInherited;`
- `int dbRelationUpdateCascade;`
- `int dbRelationDeleteCascade;`
- `int dbRelationLeft;`
- `int dbRelationRight;`

## The *ReplicaTypeEnum* Constant

- `int dbRepMakeReadOnly;`
- `int dbRepMakePartial;`

## The *SetOptionEnum* Constant

- `int dbPageTimeout;`
- `int dbLockRetry;`
- `int dbMaxBufferSize;`

- int dbUserCommitSync;
- int dbImplicitCommitSync;
- int dbExclusiveAsyncDelay;
- int dbSharedAsyncDelay;
- int dbMaxLocksPerFile;
- int dbLockDelay;
- int dbRecycleLVs;
- int dbFlushTransactionTimeout;

## The *SynchronizeTypeEnum* Constant

- int dbRepExportChanges;
- int dbRepImportChanges;
- int dbRepImpExpChanges;
- int dbRepSyncInternet;

## The *TableDefAttributeEnum* Constant

- int dbAttachExclusive;
- int dbAttachSavePWD;
- int dbSystemObject;
- int dbAttachedTable;
- int dbAttachedODBC;
- int dbHiddenObject;

## The *UpdateCriteriaEnum* Constant

- int dbCriteriaKey;
- int dbCriteriaModValues;
- int dbCriteriaAllCols;
- int dbCriteriaTimestamp;
- int dbCriteriaDeleteInsert;
- int dbCriteriaUpdate;

## The *UpdateTypeEnum* Constant

- int dbUpdateBatch;
- int dbUpdateRegular;
- int dbUpdateCurrentRecord;

## The *WorkspaceTypeEnum* Constant

- `int dbUseODBC;`
- `int dbUseJet;`

# Obsolete Features Still Supported

The following features are left over from the previous version of DAO but are being phased out and might not be included in the next version update.

- All `CreateDynaset` methods
- All `CreateSnapshot` methods
- All `ListFields` methods
- All `ListIndexes` methods
- `CompactDatabase` statement
- `CreateDatabase` statement
- `DBEngine.FreeLocks`
- `DBEngine.SetDefaultWorkspace`
- `DBEngine.Password`
- `DBEngine.SetDataAccessOption`
- `Database.BeginTrans`
- `Database.CommitTrans`
- `Database.Rollback`
- `Database.DeleteQuerydef`
- `Database.ExecuteSQL`
- `Database.ListTables`
- `Database.OpenQuerydef`
- `Database.OpenTable`
- `FieldSize`
- `Index.Fields`
- `OpenDatabase` statement
- `Querydef.ListParameters`

APPENDIX B

# RDO 2.0 API

The Remote Data objects were created to give Visual Basic users a more robust API for accessing ODBC data sources than DAO provided. The ODBC API was abstracted into a set of COM interfaces so that applications can take advantage of the COM architecture to manipulate data they might not otherwise have access to. (The ODBC APIs are only translated into C/C++ and SQL CLI interfaces, and embedded SQL has not yet been defined for interpreted languages like Visual Basic and Java.)

RDO 2.0 is the latest set of Remote Data interfaces from Microsoft. They work within the Win32 environments and show considerable performance advantages over DAO when accessing ODBC data sources. ■

# The *rdoEngine* Object

The `rdoEngine` object is the root interface from which you gain access to RDO. It allows you to set certain global state information and access into the other RDO interfaces (objects).

## Constructor

The `_rdoEngine` object has the following constructors:

```
_rdoEngine = (_rdoEngine) new rdoEngine();
```

```
_rdoEngine = (_rdoEngine) new rdoEngine();
```

## Methods

The `_rdoEngine` object has the following methods to control its properties and manipulate its object:

```
_rdoEngine.rdoCreateEnvironment(String m_Name, String m_User, String m_Password);
```

Creates a new `_rdoEnvironment`.

Return Type: An `_rdoEnvironment` object

| Argument | Data Type | Description |
|---|---|---|
| `m_Name` | String | A name for the new environment |
| `m_User` | String | A user account |
| `m_Password` | String | A password |

```
_rdoEngine.getrdoDefaultCursorDriver();
```

Returns the default cursor drivers in use.

Return Type: A member of the `CursorDriverConstants` (int)

```
_rdoEngine.getrdoDefaultErrorThreshold();
```

Returns the fatal error level.

Return Type: int

```
_rdoEngine.getrdoDefaultLoginTimeout();
```

Returns the default ODBC login timeout.

Return Type: int

`_rdoEngine.getrdoDefaultPassword();`

Returns the default password.

Return Type: String

`_rdoEngine.getrdoDefaultUser();`

Returns the default user account.

Return Type: String



`_rdoEngine.getrdoEnvironments();`

Returns the `rdoEnvironments` collection.

Return Type: An `rdoEnvironments` object

`_rdoEngine.getrdoErrors();`

Returns the `rdoErrors` collection.

Return Type: An `rdoErrors` object

`_rdoEngine.getrdoLocaleID();`

Returns the locale.

Return Type: A member of the `LocaleIDConstants` (int)

`_rdoEngine.getrdoVersion();`

Returns the RDO version.

Return Type: String

`_rdoEngine.IsGlobalDebugMode();`

Returns `TRUE` if Global Debug mode is set.

Return Type: Boolean

`_rdoEngine.putrdoDefaultCursorDriver(int m_CursorDriver);`

Sets the default cursor driver for all environments created with this object.

| Argument | Data Type | Description |
|---|---|---|
| m_CursorDriver | int | A member of CursorDriverConstants |

```
_rdoEngine.putrdoDefaultErrorThreshold(int m_Fatal);
```

Sets the default fatal error threshold.

| Argument | Data Type | Description |
|---|---|---|
| m_Fatal | int | An error level to begin throwing fatal errors |

```
_rdoEngine.putDefaultLoginTimeout(int m_LoginTimeout);
```

Sets the number of seconds the ODBC Driver Manager will wait before timing out a login attempt.

| Argument | Data Type | Description |
|---|---|---|
| m_ LoginTimeout | int | The number of seconds before timing out. |

```
_rdoEngine.putDefaultPassword(String m_Password);
```

Sets the default password.

| Argument | Data Type | Description |
|---|---|---|
| m_Password | String | A password |

```
_rdoEngine.putDefaultUser(String m_UserName);
```

Sets the default user name that will be used when logging into ODBC data sources.

| Argument | Data Type | Description |
|---|---|---|
| m_ UserName | String | A user account |

```
_rdoEngine.putrdoLocaleID(int m_Locale);
```

Sets the locale to use.

| Argument | Data Type | Description |
|---|---|---|
| m_Locale | int | A member of LocaleIDConstants |

```
_rdoEngine.rdoRegisterDataSource(String m_DSN, String m_DriverName, boolean
➥ m_Silent, String m_Attributes);
```

| Argument | Data Type | Description |
|---|---|---|
| m_DSN | String | A data source name |
| m_DriverName | String | The friendly name of the ODBC driver |
| m_Silent | Boolean | Set to TRUE if you don't want to be prompted for missing information |
| m_Attributes | String | A semicolon-delimited set of data source-specific attributes |



# The *rdoError* Object

The rdoError object is used to wrap the errors returned by COM in an understandable context.

## Constructor

The rdoError object has the following constructor:

```
rdoError = rdoErrors.getItem(errorindex);
```

## Methods

The rdoError object has the following methods to control its properties and manipulate its object:

```
rdoError.getDescription();
```

Returns the error description.

Return Type: String

```
rdoError.getHelpContext();
```

Returns the help context ID.

Return Type: int

```
rdoError.getHelpFile();
```

Returns the path to the help file associated with the source of the error.

Return Type: String

```
rdoError.getNumber();
```

Returns the error number.

Return Type: int

```
rdoError.getSource();
```

Returns the source of the error.

Return Type: String

```
rdoError.getSQLRetcode();
```

Returns the SQL Return code.

Return Type: A member of the `SQLRetCodeConstants` (int)

```
rdoError.getSQLState();
```

Returns a value describing the SQL state.

Return Type: String

# The *_rdoEnvironment* Object

The `_rdoEnvironment` object maintains the connection and state information about RDO objects created in its namespace. It is the root interface for most of the data source level operations.

## Methods of Instantiating the *_rdoEnvironment* object

To "create" an _rdoEnvironment object, use the constructor:

```
_rdoEnvironment = _rdoEngine.CreateEnvironment(m_Name, m_User, m_Password);
_rdoEnvironment = rdoEnvironments.getItem(name);
_rdoEnvironment = rdoEnvironments.getItem(index);
```

## Methods

The `_rdoEnvironment` object has the following methods to control its properties and to manipulate the object:

```
_rdoEnvironment.BeginTrans();
```

Begins a new transaction.

```
_rdoEnvironment.Close();
```

Closes an open `Connection` object.

`_rdoEnvironment.CommitTrans();`

Ends a transaction by sending the updates to the server.

`_rdoEnvironment.getCursorDriver();`

Returns the default cursor driver.

Return Type: A member of `CursorDriverConstants` (int)

`_rdoEnvironment.gethEnv();`

Returns the ODBC environment handle.

Return Type: int

`_rdoEnvironment.getLoginTimeout();`

Returns the ODBC login timeout in seconds.

Return Type: int

`_rdoEnvironment.getName();`

Returns the name of the `_rdoEnvironment` object.

Return Type: String

`_rdoEnvironment.GetOwner();`

Returns the object that created this `Environment` object.

Return Type: `_rdoEngine`

`_rdoEnvironment.getrdoConnections();`

Returns the `rdoConnections` collection.

Return Type: An `rdoConnections` object

`_rdoEnvironment.getUserName();`

Returns the default user name for this connection.

Return Type: String

```
_rdoEnvironment.OpenConnection(String m_DSN, Variant m_vPrompt, Variant
➥ m_vReadOnly, Variant m_vConnect, Variant m_vOptions);
```

Opens a new connection to a data source.

Return Type: An `rdoConnection` object

| Argument | Data Type | Description |
|---|---|---|
| m_DSN | String | A data source name |
| m_vPrompt | Variant (int) | A member of the DriverPromptConstants |
| m_vReadOnly | Variant (boolean) | Set to TRUE for this connection to be read-only |
| m_vConnect | Variant (String) | An ODBC connection string |
| m_vOptions | Varaint (int) | A member of the rdDriverPrompt constants |

```
_rdoEnvironment.putCursorDriver(int m_CursorDriver);
```

Sets the default cursor usage for objects created with this `_rdoEnvironment` object.

| Argument | Data Type | Description |
|---|---|---|
| m_CursorDriver | int | A member of the CursorDriverConstants |

```
_rdoEnvironment.putLoginTimeout(int m_LoginTimeout);
```

Sets the number of seconds that the ODBC Driver Manager will wait before timing out a login attempt.

| Argument | Data Type | Description |
|---|---|---|
| m_ LoginTimeout | int | The number of seconds to wait before timing out |

```
_rdoEnvironment.putPassword(String m_Password);
```

Sets the default password for this `Environment` object.

| Argument | Data Type | Description |
|---|---|---|
| m_Password | String | A password |

```
_rdoEnvironment.putUserName(String m_UserName);
```

Sets the default user name that will be used when logging into ODBC data sources.

| Argument | Data Type | Description |
|---|---|---|
| m_ UserName | String | A user account |

```
_rdoEnvironment.RollbackTrans();
```

Ends all transactions for this environment by throwing away the changes and restoring the data source to the original values.

# The _rdoConnection Object



The `_rdoConnection` object is used to control the connection to the data source and to hold state information about a single connection.

## Constructors

There are two methods to "create" an `_rdoConnection` object. The first is the constructor:

```
_rdoConnection = rdoEnvironment.OpenConnection();
```

The second is the collection methods to retrieve existing (or default) `rdoEnvironment` objects.

```
_rdoConnection = rdoConnections.getItem(name);
```

```
_rdoConnection = rdoConnection.getItem(index);
```

## Methods

The `_rdoConnection` object has the following methods to control its properties and manipulate the object:

```
rdoConnection.BeginTrans();
```

Begins a new transaction.

```
_rdoConnection.Cancel();
```

Cancels an asynchronous operation.

```
_rdoConnection.Close();
```

Closes an open `Connection` object.

```
_rdoConnection.CommitTrans();
```

Ends a transaction by sending the updates to the server.

```
_rdoConnection.CreateQuery(String m_Name, Variant m_vSQL);
```

Creates a new `rdoQuery` object.

| Argument | Data Type | Description |
|---|---|---|
| m_Name | String | The name of the prepared statement |
| m_vSQL | Variant (String) | A SQL expression |

```
_rdoConnection.CreatePreparedStatement(String m_Name, Variant m_vSQL);
```

Creates a prepared statement.

| Argument | Data Type | Description |
|---|---|---|
| m_Name | String | The name of the prepared statement |
| m_vSQL | Variant (String) | A SQL expression |

```
_rdoConnection.Execute(String m_Query, Variant m_vOption);
```

Executes a query.

| Argument | Data Type | Description |
|---|---|---|
| m_Query | String | The name of a prepared Statement or SQL expression. |
| m_vOption | Variant (OptionsConstants) | Sets the execution method for this statement (optional) |

```
_rdoConnection.getAsyncCheckInterval();
```

Returns the number of seconds between updates for the `StillExecuting` property.

Return Type: int

```
_rdoConnection.getConnect();
```

Returns the ODBC connection string.

Return Type: String

```
_rdoConnection.getCursorDriver();
```

Returns the default cursor driver.

Return Type: A member of `CursorDriverConstants` (int)

`_rdoConnection.gethDbc();`

Returns the ODBC connection handle.

Return Type: int

`_rdoConnection.getLastQueryResults();`

Returns a result set with the results of the last `rdoQuery`.

Return Type: `_rdoResultset`



`_rdoConnection.getLoginTimeout();`

Returns the ODBC login timeout in seconds.

Return Type: int

`_rdoConnection.getLogMessages();`

Returns the path to the ODBC trace file.

Return Type: String

`_rdoConnection.getName();`

Returns the DSN for this connection.

Return Type: String

`_rdoConnection.GetOwner();`

Returns the object that created this.

Return Type: An `_rdoEnvironment` object

`_rdoConnection.getQueryTimeout();`

Returns the number of seconds the query has to return the results before being timed out.

Return Type: int

`_rdoConnection.getrdoQueries();`

Returns the `rdoQueries` collection.

Return Type: An `rdoQueries` object

`_rdoConnection.getrdoPreparedStatements();`

Returns the `rdoPreparedStatements` collection.

Return Type: An `rdoPreparedStatements` object

`_rdoConnection.getrdoResultsets();`

Returns the `rdoResultsets` collection.

Return Type: An `rdoResultsets` object

`_rdoConnection.getRowsAffected();`

Returns the number of rows affected by the last `Execute` method.

Return Type: int

`_rdoConnection.getStillConnecting();`

Returns `TRUE` if the ODBC Driver Manager is still attempting to connect to the data source.

Return Type: Boolean

`_rdoConnection.getStillExecuting();`

Returns `TRUE` if the asynchronous method is still executing.

Return Type: Boolean

`_rdoConnection.getrdoTables();`

Returns the `rdoTables` collection.

Return Type: An `rdoTables` object

`_rdoConnection.getTransactions();`

Returns `TRUE` if the data source supports transactions.

Return Type: Boolean

`_rdoConnection.getUpdatable();`

Returns `TRUE` if the data source is updatable.

Return Type: Boolean

```
_rdoConnection.getVersion();
```

Returns the version of the data source.

Return Type: String

```
_rdoConnection.OpenResultset(String m_Name, Variant m_vCursorType, Variant
➥ m_vLockType, Variant m_vOptions);
```

Opens a result set on the data returned by a SQL statement.

| Argument | Data Type | Description |
|---|---|---|
| m_Name | String | The name of the Resultset |
| m_vCursorType | Variant (ResultsetTypeConstants) | Indicates the type of cursor to use with this result set |
| m_vLockType | Variant (LockTypeConstants) | Indicates the type of lock to use |
| m_vOptions | Variant (OptionsConstants) | Indicates the method used for returning the data |

```
_rdoConnection.putAsyncCheckInterval(int m_Seconds);
```

Sets the interval to update the StillExecuting property.

| Argument | Data Type | Description |
|---|---|---|
| m_ Seconds | int | A number of seconds |

```
_rdoConnection.putConnect(String m_ConnectString);
```

Sets the ODBC Connection string for this rdoConnection.

| Argument | Data Type | Description |
|---|---|---|
| m_ ConnectString | String | An ODBC connection string |

```
_rdoConnection.putCursorDriver(int m_CursorDriver);
```

Sets the default cursor usage for objects created with this rdoConnection object.

| Argument | Data Type | Description |
|---|---|---|
| m_CursorDriver | int | A member of the CursorDriverConstants |

```
_rdoConnection.putLoginTimeout(int m_LoginTimeout);
```

Sets the number of seconds that the ODBC Driver Manager will wait before timing out a login attempt.

| Argument | Data Type | Description |
|---|---|---|
| `m_ LoginTimeout` | int | The number of seconds |

```
_rdoConnection.putLogMessages(String m_TraceFile);
```

Sets the ODBC trace file location.

| Argument | Data Type | Description |
|---|---|---|
| `m_TraceFile` | String | Path to a file |

```
_rdoConnection.putName(String m_Name);
```

Sets the DSN to use for this `rdoConnection` object.

| Argument | Data Type | Description |
|---|---|---|
| `m_Name` | String | An ODBC DSN |

```
_rdoConnection.putQueryTimeout(int m_Timeout);
```

Sets the default query timeout.

| Argument | Data Type | Description |
|---|---|---|
| `m_Timeout` | int | A specified number of seconds before timing out |

```
_rdoConnection.RollbackTrans();
```

Rolls back all transactions active for this `rdoConnection` object.

# The *rdoParameter* Object

The `rdoParameter` object is used to construct prepared statements to represent the SQL parameters sent across to the data source.

## Constructor

There is no `rdoPreparedStatment.CreateParam();` method to instance this object. Instead, to gain access to the `rdoParamter` object, you must use the collection methods to retrieve existing `rdoParameter` objects (which exist when you indicate parameters in the SQL syntax of the `rdoPrepared` statement.

```
rdoParameter = rdoParameters.getItem(ParamName);
```

```
rdoParameter = rdoParameters.getItem(ParamIndex);
```

## Methods

The `rdoParameter` object has the following methods to control its properties and to manipulate the object:



```
rdoParameter.AppendChunk(Variant m_Chunk);
```

Appends a specified amount of data into the column.

| Argument | Data Type | Description |
|---|---|---|
| `m_Chunk` | Variant | The data that you want to append |

```
rdoParameter.getDirection();
```

Returns the `Parameter` object's direction.

Return Type: A member of the `DirectionConstants` (int)

```
rdoParameter.getName();
```

Returns the name of the `Parameter` object.

Return Type: String

```
rdoParameter.getType();
```

Returns the data type of the `Parameter` object.

Return Type: A member of the `DataTypeConstants` (int)

```
rdoParameter.getValue();
```

Returns the data stored in a `Parameter` object.

Return Type: Variant

```
rdoParameter.putDirection(int m_Direction);
```

Sets the `Parameter` object's direction.

| Argument | Data Type | Description |
|---|---|---|
| `m_Direction` | int | A member of the `DirectionConstants` |

```
rdoParameter.putName(String m_Name);
```

Sets the name of the `Parameter` object.

| Argument | Data Type | Description |
|---|---|---|
| `m_ Name` | String | A name for the `rdoParameter` object. |

```
rdoParameter.putType(int m_DataType);
```

Sets the data type for the `Parameter` object.

| Argument | Data Type | Description |
|---|---|---|
| `m_ DataType` | int | A member of `DataTypeConstants` |

```
rdoParameter.putValue(Variant m_vValue);
```

Sets the value of a `Parameter` object.

| Argument | Data Type | Description |
|---|---|---|
| `m_vValue` | Variant | The data to pass to the parameter |

# The *rdoPreparedStatement* Object

The `rdoPreparedStatement` object is used for the obvious purpose—creating prepared statements. It controls both the syntax of the statement and takes care of creating the buffers and maintaining the state information (including the tracking of parameters in parameterized queries).

## Constructors

There are two methods to "create" an `rdoPreparedStatement` object. The first is the constructor:

```
rdoPreparedStatement =
_rdoConnection.CreatePreparedStatement(String m_Name, Variant m_vSQL);
```

The second is the collection methods to retrieve existing (or default) `rdoEnvironment` objects:

```
rdoPreparedStatement = _rdoConnection.getrdoPreparedStatements();

rdoPreparedStatement = _rdoPreparedStatements.getItem(name);

rdoPreparedStatement = _rdoPreparedStatements.getItem(index);
```

## Methods

The `rdoPreparedStatement` object has the following methods to control its properties and manipulate the object:

```
rdoPreparedStatement.Cancel();
```

Cancels a pending action.

```
rdoPreparedStatement.Close();
```

Closes the open prepared statement.

```
rdoPreparedStatement.Execute(Variant m_vOption);
```

Executes a prepared statement.

| Argument | Data Type | Description |
|---|---|---|
| `m_vOption` | Variant (`OptionsConstants`) | Sets the execution method for this statement |

```
rdoPreparedStatement.getActiveConnection();
```

Returns the active `Connection` object.

Return Type: A `Connection` object

```
rdoPreparedStatement.getBindThreshold();
```

Returns the largest column (in bytes) that will be automatically bound to a string.

Return Type: int

```
rdoPreparedStatement.getConnect();
```

Returns the connection string.

Return Type: String

```
rdoPreparedStatement.getErrorThreshold();
```

Returns the fatal error level.

Return Type: int

```
rdoPreparedStatement.gethStmt();
```

Returns the ODBC statement handle.

Return Type: int

```
rdoPreparedStatement.getLockType();
```

Returns the lock type as a member of `LockTypeConstants`.

Return Type: int

```
rdoPreparedStatement.getKeysetSize();
```

Returns the number of rows buffered (the keyset).

Return Type: int

```
rdoPreparedStatement.getLogMessages();
```

Returns the path to the ODBC trace file.

Return Type: String

```
rdoPreparedStatement.getMaxRows();
```

Returns the maximum number of rows to be fetched from the server in a single query.

Return Type: int

```
rdoPreparedStatement.getName();
```

Returns the name of the prepared statement.

Return Type: String

```
rdoPreparedStatement.GetOwner();
```

Returns the `rdoConnection` object that created this prepared statement.

Return Type: An `_rdoConnection` object

```
rdoPreparedStatement.getrdoParameters();
```

Returns the `Parameters` collection.

Return Type: A `Parameters` object

`rdoPreparedStatement.getQueryTimeout();`

Returns the default `QueryTimeout`.

Return Type: int

`rdoPreparedStatement.getrdoColumns();`

Returns the `rdoColumns` collection.

Return Type: An `rdoColumns` object

`rdoPreparedStatement.getRowsAffected();`

Returns the number of rows affected by the last `Execute` statement.

Return Type: int

`rdoPreparedStatement.getRowsetSize();`

Returns the number of rows returned to the application's buffers.

Return Type: int

`rdoPreparedStatement.getSQL();`

Returns the SQL statement used in this prepared statement.

Return Type: String

`rdoPreparedStatement.getStillExecuting();`

Returns `TRUE` if this is still executing asynchronously.

Return Type: Boolean

`rdoPreparedStatement.getType();`

Returns the SQL statement type of the prepared statement.

Return Type: A member of the `QueryTypeConstants` (int)

`rdoPreparedStatement.getUpdatable();`

Returns `TRUE` if the data in the result set returned by this prepared statement is updatable.

Return Type: Boolean

```
rdoPreparedStatement.OpenResultset(Variant m_vType, Variant m_vLockType, Variant
m_vOption);
```

Opens a result set on the data returned by the prepared statement.

| Argument | Data Type | Description |
|---|---|---|
| m_vCursorType | Variant (ResultsetTypeConstants) | Indicates the type of cursor to use with this result set |
| m_vLockType | Variant (LockTypeConstants) | Indicates the type of lock to use |
| m_vOptions | Variant (OptionsConstants) | Indicates the method used for returning the data |

```
rdoPreparedStatement.putActiveConnection(msrdo20._rdoConnection m_objConnection);
```

Sets the active connection for this prepared statement.

| Argument | Data Type | Description |
|---|---|---|
| m_objConnection | _rdoConnection | A Connection object |

```
rdoPreparedStatement.putBindThreshold(int m_Threshold);
```

Sets the limit (in bytes) for binding columns to strings without using AppendChunk and GetChunk.

| Argument | Data Type | Description |
|---|---|---|
| m_Threshold | int | The total number of bytes in the largest bound column |

```
rdoPreparedStatement.putCursorType(int m_CursorType);
```

Sets the cursor type to use on the result set.

| Argument | Data Type | Description |
|---|---|---|
| m_CursorType | int | A member of ResultsetTypeConstants |

```
rdoPreparedStatement.putErrorThreshold(int m_errThreshold);
```

Sets the maximum level for non-fatal errors.

| Argument | Data Type | Description |
|---|---|---|
| m_errThreshold | int | A value representing the desired fatal error level |

`rdoPreparedStatement.putKeysetSize(int m_Keyset);`

Sets the size for the keyset, the number of rows buffered by the system.

| Argument | Data Type | Description |
|---|---|---|
| `m_Keyset` | int | A number representing the amount of rows to buffer |



`rdoPreparedStatement.putLockType(int m_LockType);`

Sets the locking control for the result sets created from this object.

| Argument | Data Type | Description |
|---|---|---|
| `m_LockType` | int | A member of the `LockTypeConstants` |

`rdoPreparedStatement.putLogMessages(String m_TraceFile);`

Sets the path to the ODBC trace file.

| Argument | Data Type | Description |
|---|---|---|
| `m_TraceFile` | String | Path to a file |

`rdoPreparedStatement.putMaxRows(int m_MaxRows);`

Sets the maximum number of rows returned in a single query.

| Argument | Data Type | Description |
|---|---|---|
| `m_MaxRows` | int | A value representing the desired number of rows |

`rdoPreparedStatement.putQueryTimeout(int m_QueryTimeout);`

Sets the timeout (in seconds) for the query.

| Argument | Data Type | Description |
|---|---|---|
| `m_QueryTimeout` | int | The default query timeout in seconds |

`rdoPreparedStatement.putRowsetSize(int m_Rowset);`

Sets the size of the application buffer (in rows).

| Argument | Data Type | Description |
|---|---|---|
| `m_Rowset` | int | The size of the buffer in number of rows |

```
rdoPreparedStatement.putSQL(String m_SQL);
```

Sets the SQL statement for the prepared statement.

| Argument | Data Type | Description |
|---|---|---|
| m_SQL | String | A valid SQL statement |

# The *rdoQuery* Object

The rdoQuery object represents a SQL query to the data source. It is somewhat interesting because this object is abstract, having no methods of its own. The interface exists, however, to create these objects and to retrieve them for execution.

## Constructors

There are two methods to "create" an _rdoQuery object. The first is the constructor:

```
rdoQuery = _rdoConnection.CreateQuery(String m_Name, Variant m_vSQL);
```

The second consists of the collection methods to retrieve existing (or default) rdoEnvironment objects:

```
rdoQuery = rdoQueries.getItem(name);

rdoQuery = rdoQueries.getItem(index);
```

# The *rdoResultset* Object

The rdoResultset object is the workhorse of the RDO object family. It is used to retrieve the data and to deal with it after retrieval.

## Constructors

There are two methods to "create" an _rdoResultset object. The first is the constructor:

```
_rdoResultset = _rdoConnection.OpenResultset(String m_Name, Variant m_vCursorType,
Variant m_vLockType, Variant m_vOptions);

_rdoResultset = rdoPreparedStatement.OpenResultset(Variant m_vType, Variant
m_vLockType, Variant m_vOption);

_rdoResultset = rdoTable.OpenResultset(Variant m_vCursorType, Variant m_vLockType,
Variant m_vOption);
```

The second consists of the collection methods to retrieve existing (or default) rdoEnvironment objects.

```
_rdoResultset = _rdoConnection.getrdoResultsets();

_rdoResultset = rdoResultsets.getItem(name);

_rdoResultset = rdoResultsets.getItem(index);
```

## Methods

The `_rdoResultset` object has the following methods to control its properties and manipulate the object:

`_rdoResultset.AddNew();`

Adds a new record to the result set.



`_rdoResultset.Cancel();`

Cancels a current asynchronous method.

`_rdoResultset.CancelUpdate();`

Cancels any pending updates.

`_rdoResultset.Close();`

Closes the result set.

`_rdoResultset.Delete();`

Deletes the record at the current position of the cursor.

`_rdoResultset.Edit();`

Begins copying changes for the current record into a copy buffer.

`_rdoResultset.getAbsolutePosition();`

Returns the position of the current record as an ordinal value.

Return Type: int

`_rdoResultset.getActiveConnection();`

Returns the active connection for this result set.

Return Type: An `_rdoConnection` object

`_rdoResultset.getBatchCollisionCount();`

Returns the number of collisions occurring in a batch update.

Return Type: int

```
_rdoResultset.getBatchCollisionRows();
```

Returns an array of bookmarks for the rows involved in the collisions.

Return Type: Variant

```
_rdoResultset.getBatchSize();
```

Returns the size of the last batch.

Return Type: int

```
_rdoResultset.getBOF();
```

Returns `TRUE` if the current row is the beginning of the result set.

Return Type: Boolean

```
_rdoResultset.getBookmark();
```

Returns the bookmark of the current row.

Return Type: Variant

```
_rdoResultset.getBookmarkable();
```

Returns `TRUE` if the bookmarks are available.

Return Type: Boolean

```
_rdoResultset.getCollect(Variant m_vColumn);
```

Returns the value of the column specified.

Return Type: Variant

| Argument | Data Type | Description |
|---|---|---|
| m_vColumn | Variant (String) | A column name |

```
_rdoResultset.getEditMode();
```

Returns the edit state of the current row.

Return Type: A member of the `EditModeConstants` (int)

```
_rdoResultset.getEOF();
```

Returns true if the current row is the end of the Resultset.

Return Type: Boolean

```
_rdoResultset.gethStmt();
```

Returns the ODBC statement handle.

Return Type: int

```
_rdoResultset.getLastModified();
```

Returns a bookmark of the most recently modified rows.

Return Type: Variant

```
_rdoResultset.getLockEdits();
```

Returns `TRUE` if pessimistic locking is being used.

Return Type: Boolean

```
_rdoResultset.getLockType();
```

Returns the concurrency control in use.

Return Type: A member of `LockTypeConstants` (int)

```
_rdoResultset.getName();
```

Returns the first 256 characters of the SQL statement used to create this result set object.

Return Type: String

```
_rdoResultset.getPercentPosition();
```

Returns the current position of the cursor as a percentage of the result set.

Return Type: float

```
_rdoResultset.getrdoColumns();
```

Returns the `rdoColumns` collection.

Return Type: An `rdoColumns` object

`_rdoResultset.GetOwner();`

Returns the object that created this.

Return Type: An `_rdoQuery` object

`_rdoResultset.getRestartable();`

Returns `TRUE` if the `Requery` method is available to use.

Return Type: Boolean

`_rdoResultset.getRowCount();`

Returns the number of rows accessed in the result set.

Return Type: int

`_rdoResultset.getStatus();`

Returns the status of the current row.

Return Type: A member of the `RowStatusConstants`

`_rdoResultset.getStillExecuting();`

Returns `TRUE` if the asynchronous operation is still executing.

Return Type: Boolean

`_rdoResultset.getTransactions();`

Returns whether or not the result set supports transactions.

Return Type: Boolean

`_rdoResultset.getType();`

Returns the type of the result set.

Return Type: A member of `ResultsetTypeConstants` (int)

`_rdoResultset.getUpdatable();`

Returns whether or not the result set is updatable.

Return Type: Boolean

```
_rdoResultset.getUpdateCriteria();
```

Returns the criteria specified in the update.

Return Type: A member of the `UpdateCriteriaConstants` (int)

```
_rdoResultset.getUpdateOperation();
```

Returns the type of `Update` operation this is, `Update`, `Insert`, or `Delete`.

Return Type: A member of the `UpdateOperationsConstants` (int)

```
_rdoResultset.MoreResults();
```

Returns `TRUE` if there are more result sets to be processed. If you call this method and there are more results to be processed, RDO flushes the current results, replacing them with the next result set.

Return Type: Boolean

```
_rdoResultset.Move(int m_NumRows, Variant m_vBookmark);
```

Moves a specified number of rows beginning at the bookmark.

| Argument | Data Type | Description |
|---|---|---|
| `m_NumRows` | int | The number of rows to move |
| `m_vBookmark` | Variant | A bookmark of the starting row from which to begin the move |

```
_rdoResultset.MoveFirst();
```

Positions the cursor to the first record in the result set.

```
_rdoResultset.MoveLast(Variant m_Async);
```

Moves the cursor to the last row of the result set.

| Argument | Data Type | Description |
|---|---|---|
| `m_Async` | int | A member of `OptionsConstants` |

```
_rdoResultset.MoveNext();
```

Moves the cursor to the next record in the result set.

```
_rdoResultset.MovePrevious();
```

Moves the cursor to the previous record.

```
_rdoResultset.putAbsolutePosition(in m_Ordinal);
```

Moves the cursor to a specific position.

| Argument | Data Type | Description |
|---|---|---|
| m_Ordinal | int | A row number |

```
_rdoResultset.putActiveConnection(__rdoConnection m_objConnection);
```

Sets the active connection.

| Argument | Data Type | Description |
|---|---|---|
| m_objConnection | _rdoConnection | An _rdoConnection object |

```
_rdoResultset.putBatchSize(int m_Size);
```

Sets the size (in rows) to send to the server at once.

| Argument | Data Type | Description |
|---|---|---|
| m_Size | int | Number of rows in the batch |

```
_rdoResultset.putBookmark(Variant m_Bookmark);
```

Sets the bookmark for the current record.

| Argument | Data Type | Description |
|---|---|---|
| m_Bookmark | Variant (String) | A bookmark |

```
_rdoResultset.putCollect(Variant m_Field, Variant m_vValue);
```

Sets the value for a column, given its name.

| Argument | Data Type | Description |
|---|---|---|
| m_Field | Variant (String) | A column name |
| m_vValue | Variant | The data to set into the column |

```
_rdoResultset.putLockType(int m_LockType);
```

Sets the locking for the current result set.

| Argument | Data Type | Description |
|---|---|---|
| `m_ LockType` | int | A member of the `LockTypeConstants` |

```
_rdoResultset.putName(String m_Name);
```

Sets the name for this object.

| Argument | Data Type | Description |
|---|---|---|
| `m_Name` | String | A name |

```
_rdoResultset.putPercentPosition(float m_Percent);
```

Sets the cursor to a position that is a percentage of the way into the result set.

| Argument | Data Type | Description |
|---|---|---|
| `m_ Percent` | float | A percent value |

```
_rdoResultset.putStatus(int m_Status);
```

Sets the status of the current row.

| Argument | Data Type | Description |
|---|---|---|
| `m_Status` | int | A member of the `RowStatusConstants` |

```
_rdoResultset.putUpdateCriteria(short m_Criteria);
```

Sets the criteria for a batch update.

| Argument | Data Type | Description |
|---|---|---|
| `m_ Criteria` | short | A member of the `UpdateCriteriaConstants` |

```
void putUpdateOperation(short m_Operation);
```

Sets the type of update being done.

| Argument | Data Type | Description |
|---|---|---|
| `m_Operation` | short | A member of the `UpdateOperationsConstants` |

```
_rdoResultset.Requery(Variant m_Async);
```

Refreshes the result set by executing the query that created this result set again.

| Argument | Data Type | Description |
|---|---|---|
| m_ Async | Variant(boolean) | A flag stating whether or not this will be an asynchronous operation |

```
_rdoResultset.Update();
```

Saves the pending changes to the data source.

# The *rdoColumn* Object

The `rdoColumn` is the atomic portion of RDO. It is essentially a view into a single cell of data at the column/row intersection. It can be used to set properties, determine information about the column, or manipulate the data contained within.

## Constructor

There is no `rdoResultSet.CreateColumn();` method to instance the `rdoColumn` object. Instead, to gain access to the `rdoColumn` object, you must use the collection methods to retrieve existing `rdoColumn` objects, which exist with every `rdoResultSet.OpenResultSet()` returned to the application.

```
rdoColumn = rdoColumns.getItem(ColumnName);
```

```
rdoColumn = rdoColumns.getItem(ColumnIndex);
```

## Methods

The `rdoColumn` object has the following methods to control its properties and to manipulate the object:

```
rdoColumn.AppendChunk(Variant m_Chunk);
```

Appends a specified amount of data into the column.

| Argument | Data Type | Description |
|---|---|---|
| m_Chunk | Variant | The data that you want to append |

```
rdoColumn.ColumnSize();
```

Returns the number of bytes in a column of type `LONGVARBINARY` or `LONGVARCHAR`.

Return Type: int

`rdoColumn.getAllowZeroLength();`

Returns whether or not this column will allow null values.

Return Type: Boolean

`rdoColumn.getAttributes();`

Returns the attributes of the column.

Return Type: A member (or sum of) the `AttributesConstants` (int)

`rdoColumn.getCSize();`

Returns the length of a column in characters.

Return Type: int

`rdoColumn.GetChunk(int m_NumBytes);`

Returns a specified number of bytes of data from the column.

Return Type: Variant

| Argument | Data Type | Description |
|---|---|---|
| `m_NumBytes` | int | The number of bytes to return |

`rdoColumn.getChunkRequired();`

Returns `TRUE` if the `GetChunk` or `AppendChunk` methods are required to extract the data from this column.

Return Type: Boolean

`rdoColumn.getName();`

Returns the name of the column.

Return Type: String

`rdoColumn.getOrdinalPosition();`

Returns the position of the `rdoColumn` object within the `rdoColumns` collection.

Return Type: short

`rdoColumn.getOriginalValue();`

Returns the original value of the column before the batch update.

Return Type: Variant

`rdoColumn.getRequired();`

Returns whether or not non-null values are required.

Return Type: Boolean

`rdoColumn.getSize();`

Returns the size of the column in bytes.

Return Type: int

`rdoColumn.getSourceColumn();`

Returns the source column for this column.

Return Type: String

`rdoColumn.getSourceTable();`

Returns the source table for this column.

Return Type: String

`rdoColumn.getStatus();`

Returns the column's status.

Return Type: A member of `ColumnStatusConstants` (int)

`rdoColumn.getType();`

Returns the data type of the column.

Return Type: A member of `DataTypeConstants` (int)

`rdoColumn.getUpdatable();`

Returns whether or not updates are allowed on this column.

Return Type: Boolean

```
rdoColumn.getValue();
```

Returns the value of the column.

Return Type: Variant

```
rdoColumn.getVariantType();
```

Returns the sub-type of Variant used to store the column's data.

Return Type: int

```
rdoColumn.putAllowZeroLength(boolean m_AllowZero);
```

Determines whether or not the column will accept zero-length strings.

| Argument | Data Type | Description |
|---|---|---|
| `m_AllowZero` | boolean | Set to `TRUE` to allow zero-length strings |

```
rdoColumn.putName(String m_Name);
```

Sets the name of the `rdoColumn` object.

| Argument | Data Type | Description |
|---|---|---|
| `m_Name` | String | A name |

```
rdoColumn.putSize(int m_Size);
```

Sets the size of a column for text fields.

| Argument | Data Type | Description |
|---|---|---|
| `m_Size` | int | A number between 1 and 255 |

```
rdoColumn.putSourceColumn(String m_Column);
```

Sets the source for a column.

| Argument | Data Type | Description |
|---|---|---|
| `m_Column` | String | The name of a `Column` object |

```
rdoColumn.putSourceTable(String m_Table);
```

Sets the source table for a column.

| Argument | Data Type | Description |
|---|---|---|
| m_Table | String | The name of an rdoTable object |

```
rdoColumn.putStatus(int m_ColStatus);
```

Sets the status of the column.

| Argument | Data Type | Description |
|---|---|---|
| m_ColStatus | int | A member of the ColumnStatusConstants |

```
rdoColumn.putUpdatable(boolean m_UpdateAllowed);
```

Sets whether or not you can change the data in this column.

| Argument | Data Type | Description |
|---|---|---|
| m_ UpdateAllowed | Boolean | Set to TRUE to enable updates |

```
rdoColumn.putValue(Variant m_vValue);
```

Sets the value for a column.

| Argument | Data Type | Description |
|---|---|---|
| m_vValue | Variant | The column's value |

# The *rdoTable* Object

The rdoTable object is used to represent the base table (or view) that the data source is based upon. This is analogous to the TableDef object from DAO.

## Constructor

To create an rdoTable object, use the collection methods to retrieve existing (or default) rdoEnvironment objects.

```
rdoTable = rdoTables.getItem( tablename);
```

## Methods

The rdoTable object has the following methods to control its properties and to manipulate the object:

```
rdoTable.getName();
```

Returns the name of the rdoTable object.

Return Type: String

```
rdoTable.getRowCount();
```

Returns the number of rows in the `rdoTable` object.

Return Type: int

```
rdoTable.getType();
```

Returns the type of `rdoTable` object, like `TABLE` or `VIEW`.

Return Type: String

```
rdoTable.getrdoColumns();
```

Returns the `Columns` collection for this `rdoTable` object.

Return Type: An `rdoColumns` object

```
rdoTable.getUpdatable();
```

Returns true if the data in the `rdoTable` is changeable.

Return Type: Boolean

```
rdoTable.OpenResultset(Variant m_vCursorType, Variant m_vLockType, Variant
➥ m_vOption);
```

Opens a result set on the data returned by the prepared statement.

| Argument | Data Type | Description |
|---|---|---|
| `m_vCursorType` | Variant (`ResultsetTypeConstants`) | Indicates the type of cursor to use with this result set |
| `m_vLockType` | Variant (`LockTypeConstants`) | Indicates the type of lock to use |
| `m_vOptions` | Variant (`OptionsConstants`) | Indicates the method used for returning the data |

# RDO Constants

As in every API, there exist certain parameters that are better remembered by their names than an 8-or 16-digit hex number. These are the defined constants for RDO 2.0.

## The *AttributeConstants* Interface

The following constants are used to set the attributes with which certain objects are created:

- `rdFixedColumn;`
- `rdVariableColumn;`
- `rdAutoIncrColumn;`
- `rdUpdatableColumn;`
- `rdTimestampColumn;`

## The *ColumnStatusConstants* Interface

The following constants are used to ascertain the status of the column with which you are working:

- `rdColUnmodified;`
- `rdColModified;`

## The *CursorDriverConstants* Interface

The following constants are used to set the cursor set that will be used for the duration of the workspace:

- `rdUseIfNeeded;`
- `rdUseOdbc;`
- `rdUseServer;`
- `rdUseClientBatch;`
- `rdUseNone;`

## The *DataTypeConstants* Interface

The following constants are used to set the data type of a column (or to determine the data type):

- `rdTypeBIGINT;`
- `rdTypeBINARY;`
- `rdTypeBIT;`
- `rdTypeCHAR;`
- `rdTypeDATE;`
- `rdTypeDECIMAL;`
- `rdTypeDOUBLE;`
- `rdTypeFLOAT;`
- `rdTypeINTEGER;`
- `rdTypeLONGVARBINARY;`
- `rdTypeLONGVARCHAR;`
- `rdTypeNUMERIC;`
- `rdTypeREAL;`

- rdTypeSMALLINT;
- rdTypeTIME;
- rdTypeTIMESTAMP;
- rdTypeVARCHAR;
- rdTypeVARBINARY;
- rdTypeTINYINT;



## The *DirectionConstants* Interface

The following constants are used to set the direction of the SQL parameters created with the `rdoParameter` object:

- rdParamInput;
- rdParamInputOutput;
- rdParamOutput;
- rdParamReturnValue;

## The *EditModeConstants* Interface

The following constants are used to determine the edit mode:

- rdEditAdd;
- rdEditInProgress;
- rdEditNone;

## The *LockTypeConstants* Interface

The following constants are used to set the lock type to be used on the connection:

- rdConcurReadOnly;
- rdConcurLock;
- rdConcurRowVer;
- rdConcurValues;
- rdConcurBatch;

## The *PromptConstants* Interface

The following constants are used to determine how the ODBC Driver Manager will attempt to locate the proper data source:

- rdDriverComplete;
- dDriverCompleteRequired;
- rdDriverNoPrompt;
- rdDriverPrompt;

## The *OptionConstants* Interface

The following constants are used to set the execution options on various methods:

- `rdAsyncEnable;`
- `rdExecDirect;`
- `rdFetchLongColumns;`

## The *rdoLocaleIDConstants* Interface

The following constants are used to set the locale of the connection:

- `rdLocaleChinese;`
- `rdLocaleEnglish;`
- `rdLocaleFrench;`
- `rdLocaleGerman;`
- `rdLocaleItalian;`
- `rdLocaleJapanese;`
- `rdLocaleKorean;`
- `rdLocaleSpanish;`
- `rdLocaleSimplifiedChinese;`
- `rdLocaleSystem;`

## The *QueryTypeConstants* Interface

The following constants are used to determine the type of query created with the `CreateQuery` method:

- `rdQAction;`
- `rdQCompound;`
- `rdQProcedures;`
- `rdQSelect;`

## The *ResultsetTypeConstants* Interface

The following constants are used to determine the type of result set to create on a call to the `OpenResultset` method:

- `rdOpenForwardOnly;`
- `rdOpenKeyset;`
- `rdOpenDynamic;`
- `rdOpenStatic;`

## The *RowStatusConstants* Interface

The following constants are used to determine the state of a row:

- `rdRowDBDeleted;`
- `rdRowDeleted;`
- `rdRowModified;`
- `rdRowNew;`
- `rdRowUnmodified;`



## The *SQLRetcodeConstants* Interface

The following constants are used to determine the actual SQL error returned by the driver:

- `rdSQLError;`
- `rdSQLInvalidHandle;`
- `rdSQLNoDataFound;`
- `rdSQLSuccess;`
- `rdSQLSuccessWithInfo;`

## The *UpdateCriteriaConstants* Interface

The following constants are used to set the criteria to match before an update will be performed on a record:

- `rdCriteriaAllCols;`
- `rdCriteriaKey;`
- `rdCriteriaUpdCols;`
- `rdCriteriaTimeStamp;`

## The *UpdateOperationConstants* Interface

The following constants are used to set the type of update operation being performed:

- `rdOperationDelIns;`
- `rdOperationUpdate;`

## The *UpdateReturnCodeConstants* Interface

The following constants are used to determine the status of an update:

- `rdUpdateFailed;`
- `rdUpdateNotHandled;`
- `rdUpdateSuccessful;`
- `rdUpdateWithCollisions;`

# Collections in RDO

Collections in RDO are used in exactly the same manner as in DAO. As an object is created, it is added to the default collection, which you can use to enumerate the objects and get references to those that you need.

- `rdoColumns`
- `rdoConnections`
- `rdoEnvironments`
- `rdoErrors`
- `rdoParameters`
- `rdoPreparedStatements`
- `rdoQueries`
- `rdoResultsets`
- `rdoTables`

These collections support the following methods.

| Method | Argument List | Return Type | Description |
|---|---|---|---|
| `Add` | (Object) | Void | Deletes the collection member |
| `Clear` | (Object) | Void | Appends the object to the collection |
| `getCount` | None | int | Returns the number of members in the collection |
| `getEditable` | None | Boolean | Returns whether or not the object's data is editable |
| `getItem` | (Variant) | Object | Returns an object from the collection |
| `_NewEnum` | None | Void | |
| `putEditable` | (Boolean) | Void | Sets the edit property of the collection |
| `Remove` | (Variant) | Void | Removes an item from the collection |
| `Refresh` | None | Void | Enumerates the members of the collection |

APPENDIX C

# SQL-92 Grammar Specification

This appendix offers the complete SQL-92 grammar specification. The specification is diagrammed using what is referred to as Bakus Naur Form. This style of layout allows for successive levels of detail while retaining the capability to find information quickly. ■

# The Format of Bakus Naur Form

The format of this style is as follows:

- `< >` Angle brackets delimit character strings that are the names of syntactic elements, the non-terminal symbols of the SQL language.
- `::=` This symbol denotes that the element on the left is assigned the value of the expression on the right.
- `[ ]` Square brackets denote optional elements in the expression.
- `{ }` These group the elements within the braces.
- `¦` This specifies the element(s) on the left and right of the operator as a list of exclusive choices for the expression.
- `...` The ellipsis indicates that the element to which it applies in a formula can be repeated any number of times.
- `!!` These denote English text.

The following example details the use of Bakus Naur Form on the concept of a processor.

```
<processor>::=
      <CISC>¦<RISC>
<CISC>::=
      <8Bit>¦<16Bit>¦<32Bit>¦<64Bit>¦<128Bit>
<8Bit>::=!!Obsolete
<16Bit>::=
      <8086>¦<80286>¦<80386>
<32Bit>::=
      <80486>¦<P5>¦<K5>¦<M5>
```

# SQL-92 Syntax Rules

The fifteen SQL-92 syntax rules are:

1. An <identifier start> is one of:

   A <simple Latin letter> or character

   A character in the <module character set specification>

   A character in the <character set specification>

2. A syllable in the character repertoire is identified by the <module character set specification> or by the <character set specification>.
3. A character that is identified as an ideograph in the character repertoire identified by the <module character set specification> or by the <character set specification>.
4. With the exception of the <space> character explicitly contained in <timestamp string> and <interval string> and the permitted <separator>s in <bit string literal>s and <hex string literal>s, a <token>, other than a <character string literal>, a <national character string literal>, or a <delimited identifier>, shall not include a <space> character or other <separator>.

5. A <nondoublequote character> is any character other than a double quote.
6. The two <doublequote>s contained in a <doublequote symbol> shall not be separated by any <separator>.
7. Any <token> can be followed by a <separator>.
8. There shall be no <space> nor <newline> separating the <minus sign>s of a <comment introducer>.
9. SQL text containing one or more instances of <comment> is equivalent to the same SQL text with the <comment> replaced with <newline>.
10. The sum of the number of <identifier start>s and the number of <identifier part>s in a <regular identifier> shall not be greater than 128.
11. The <delimited identifier body> of a <delimited identifier> shall not comprise more than 128 <delimited identifier part>s.
12. The <identifier body> of a <regular identifier>.
13. If an <identifier> is the same as a <reserved word> and the <character set specification> is set to SQL_TEXT, they will not be equal when tested in a <comparison predicate>.
14. If two <identifier>s have the same <identifier body>s and the <character set specification> is set to SQL_TEXT, they will be equal when tested in a <comparison predicate>.
15. For the purposes of identifying <key word>s, any <simple Latin lower case letter> contained in a candidate <key word> shall be effectively treated as the corresponding <simple Latin uppercase letter>.



# SQL-92 Grammar

```
<SQL terminal character> ::=
      <SQL language character>
    | <SQL embedded language character>

<SQL language character> ::=
      <simple Latin letter>
    | <digit>
    | <SQL special character>

<simple Latin letter> ::=
      <simple Latin upper case letter>
    | <simple Latin lower case letter>

<simple Latin upper case letter> ::=
          A | B | C | D | E | F | G | H | I | J | K | L | M | N | O
    | P | Q | R | S | T | U | V | W | X | Y | Z

<simple Latin lower case letter> ::=
          a | b | c | d | e | f | g | h | i | j | k | l | m | n | o
    | p | q | r | s | t | u | v | w | x | y | z

<digit> ::=
    0 | 1 | 2 | 3 | 4 | 5 | 6 | 7 | 8 | 9
```

```
<SQL special character> ::=
        <space>
      | <double quote>
      | <percent>
      | <ampersand>
      | <quote>
      | <left paren>
      | <right paren>
      | <asterisk>
      | <plus sign>
      | <comma>
      | <minus sign>
      | <period>
      | <solidus>
      | <colon>
      | <semicolon>
      | <less than operator>
      | <equals operator>
      | <greater than operator>
      | <question mark>
      | <underscore>
      | <vertical bar>

<space> ::= !! <EMPHASIS>(space character in character set in use)

<double quote> ::= "

<percent> ::= %

<ampersand> ::= &

<quote> ::= '

<left paren> ::= (

<right paren> ::= )

<asterisk> ::= *

<plus sign> ::= +

<comma> ::= ,

<minus sign> ::= -

<period> ::= .

<solidus> ::= /

<colon> ::= :

<semicolon> ::= ;

<less than operator> ::= <
```

```
<equals operator> ::= =

<greater than operator> ::= >

<question mark> ::= ?

<underscore> ::= _

<vertical bar> ::= ¦

<SQL embedded language character> ::=
      <left bracket>
    ¦ <right bracket>

<left bracket> ::= [

<right bracket> ::= ]

<token> ::=
      <nondelimiter token>
    ¦ <delimiter token>

<nondelimiter token> ::=
      <regular identifier>
    ¦ <key word>
    ¦ <unsigned numeric literal>
    ¦ <national character string literal>
    ¦ <bit string literal>
    ¦ <hex string literal>

<regular identifier> ::= <identifier body>

<identifier body> ::=
    <identifier start> [ { <underscore> ¦ <identifier part> }... ]

<identifier start> ::= <EMPHASIS>(!! See the Syntax Rules)

<identifier part> ::=
      <identifier start>
    ¦ <digit>

<key word> ::=
      <reserved word>
    ¦ <non-reserved word>

<reserved word> ::=
      ABSOLUTE ¦ ACTION ¦ ADD ¦ ALL
    ¦ ALLOCATE ¦ ALTER ¦ AND
    ¦ ANY ¦ ARE
    ¦ AS ¦ ASC
    ¦ ASSERTION ¦ AT
    ¦ AUTHORIZATION ¦ AVG
    ¦ BEGIN ¦ BETWEEN ¦ BIT ¦ BIT_LENGTH
    ¦ BOTH ¦ BY
    ¦ CASCADE ¦ CASCADED ¦ CASE ¦ CAST
```

```
| CATALOG
| CHAR | CHARACTER | CHAR_LENGTH
| CHARACTER_LENGTH | CHECK | CLOSE | COALESCE
| COLLATE | COLLATION
| COLUMN | COMMIT
| CONNECT
| CONNECTION | CONSTRAINT
| CONSTRAINTS | CONTINUE
| CONVERT | CORRESPONDING | COUNT | CREATE | CROSS
| CURRENT
| CURRENT_DATE | CURRENT_TIME
| CURRENT_TIMESTAMP | CURRENT_USER | CURSOR
| DATE | DAY | DEALLOCATE | DEC
| DECIMAL | DECLARE | DEFAULT | DEFERRABLE
| DEFERRED | DELETE | DESC | DESCRIBE | DESCRIPTOR
| DIAGNOSTICS
| DISCONNECT | DISTINCT | DOMAIN | DOUBLE | DROP
| ELSE | END | END-EXEC | ESCAPE
| EXCEPT | EXCEPTION
| EXEC | EXECUTE | EXISTS
| EXTERNAL | EXTRACT
| FALSE | FETCH | FIRST | FLOAT | FOR
| FOREIGN | FOUND | FROM | FULL
| GET | GLOBAL | GO | GOTO
| GRANT | GROUP
| HAVING | HOUR
| IDENTITY | IMMEDIATE | IN | INDICATOR
| INITIALLY | INNER | INPUT
| INSENSITIVE | INSERT | INT | INTEGER | INTERSECT
| INTERVAL | INTO | IS
| ISOLATION
| JOIN
| KEY
| LANGUAGE | LAST | LEADING | LEFT
| LEVEL | LIKE | LOCAL | LOWER
| MATCH | MAX | MIN | MINUTE | MODULE
| MONTH
| NAMES | NATIONAL | NATURAL | NCHAR | NEXT | NO
| NOT | NULL
| NULLIF | NUMERIC
| OCTET_LENGTH | OF
| ON | ONLY | OPEN | OPTION | OR
| ORDER | OUTER
| OUTPUT | OVERLAPS
| PAD | PARTIAL | POSITION | PRECISION | PREPARE
| PRESERVE | PRIMARY
| PRIOR | PRIVILEGES | PROCEDURE | PUBLIC
| READ | REAL | REFERENCES | RELATIVE | RESTRICT
| REVOKE | RIGHT
| ROLLBACK | ROWS
| SCHEMA | SCROLL | SECOND | SECTION
| SELECT
| SESSION | SESSION_USER | SET
| SIZE | SMALLINT | SOME | SPACE | SQL | SQLCODE
| SQLERROR | SQLSTATE
```

```
    ¦ SUBSTRING ¦ SUM ¦ SYSTEM_USER
    ¦ TABLE ¦ TEMPORARY
    ¦ THEN ¦ TIME ¦ TIMESTAMP
    ¦ TIMEZONE_HOUR ¦ TIMEZONE_MINUTE
    ¦ TO ¦ TRAILING ¦ TRANSACTION
    ¦ TRANSLATE ¦ TRANSLATION ¦ TRIM ¦ TRUE
    ¦ UNION ¦ UNIQUE ¦ UNKNOWN ¦ UPDATE ¦ UPPER ¦ USAGE
    ¦ USER ¦ USING
    ¦ VALUE ¦ VALUES ¦ VARCHAR ¦ VARYING ¦ VIEW
    ¦ WHEN ¦ WHENEVER ¦ WHERE ¦ WITH ¦ WORK ¦ WRITE
    ¦ YEAR
    ¦ ZONE

<non-reserved word> ::=

      ADA
    ¦ C ¦ CATALOG_NAME
    ¦ CHARACTER_SET_CATALOG ¦ CHARACTER_SET_NAME
    ¦ CHARACTER_SET_SCHEMA ¦ CLASS_ORIGIN ¦ COBOL ¦ COLLATION_CATALOG
    ¦ COLLATION_NAME ¦ COLLATION_SCHEMA ¦ COLUMN_NAME ¦ COMMAND_FUNCTION
    ¦ COMMITTED
    ¦ CONDITION_NUMBER ¦ CONNECTION_NAME ¦ CONSTRAINT_CATALOG ¦ CONSTRAINT_NAME
    ¦ CONSTRAINT_SCHEMA ¦ CURSOR_NAME
    ¦ DATA ¦ DATETIME_INTERVAL_CODE
    ¦ DATETIME_INTERVAL_PRECISION ¦ DYNAMIC_FUNCTION
    ¦ FORTRAN
    ¦ LENGTH
    ¦ MESSAGE_LENGTH ¦ MESSAGE_OCTET_LENGTH ¦ MESSAGE_TEXT ¦ MORE ¦ MUMPS
    ¦ NAME ¦ NULLABLE ¦ NUMBER
    ¦ PASCAL ¦ PLI
    ¦ REPEATABLE ¦ RETURNED_LENGTH ¦ RETURNED_OCTET_LENGTH ¦ RETURNED_SQLSTATE
    ¦ ROW_COUNT
    ¦ SCALE ¦ SCHEMA_NAME ¦ SERIALIZABLE ¦ SERVER_NAME ¦ SUBCLASS_ORIGIN
    ¦ TABLE_NAME ¦ TYPE
    ¦ UNCOMMITTED ¦ UNNAMED

<unsigned numeric literal> ::=
      <exact numeric literal>
    ¦ <approximate numeric literal>

<exact numeric literal> ::=
      <unsigned integer> [ <period> [ <unsigned integer> ] ]
    ¦ <period> <unsigned integer>

<unsigned integer> ::= <digit>...

<approximate numeric literal> ::= <mantissa> E <exponent>

<mantissa> ::= <exact numeric literal>

<exponent> ::= <signed integer>

<signed integer> ::= [ <sign> ] <unsigned integer>

<sign> ::= <plus sign> ¦ <minus sign>
```

```
<national character string literal> ::=
    N <quote> [ <character representation>... ] <quote>
      [ { <separator>... <quote> [ <character representation>... ] <quote> }... ]

<character representation> ::=
      <nonquote character>
    ¦ <quote symbol>

<nonquote character> ::= !! <EMPHASIS>(See the Syntax Rules.)

<quote symbol> ::= <quote><quote>

<separator> ::= { <comment> ¦ <space> ¦ <newline> }...

<comment> ::=
    <comment introducer> [ <comment character>... ] <newline>

<comment introducer> ::= <minus sign><minus sign>[<minus sign>...]

<comment character> ::=
      <nonquote character>
    ¦ <quote>

<newline> ::= !! <EMPHASIS>(implementation-defined end-of-line indicator)

<bit string literal> ::=
    B <quote> [ <bit>... ] <quote>
      [ { <separator>... <quote> [ <bit>... ] <quote> }... ]

<bit> ::= 0 ¦ 1

<hex string literal> ::=
    X <quote> [ <hexit>... ] <quote>
      [ { <separator>... <quote> [ <hexit>... ] <quote> }... ]

<hexit> ::= <digit> ¦ A ¦ B ¦ C ¦ D ¦ E ¦ F ¦ a ¦ b ¦ c ¦ d ¦ e ¦ f

<delimiter token> ::=
      <character string literal>
    ¦ <date string>
    ¦ <time string>
    ¦ <timestamp string>
    ¦ <interval string>
    ¦ <delimited identifier>
    ¦ <SQL special character>
    ¦ <not equals operator>
    ¦ <greater than or equals operator>
    ¦ <less than or equals operator>
    ¦ <concatenation operator>
    ¦ <double period>
    ¦ <left bracket>
    ¦ <right bracket>

<character string literal> ::=
    [ <introducer><character set specification> ]
```

```
    <quote> [ <character representation>... ] <quote>
      [ { <separator>... <quote> [ <character representation>... ] <quote> }... ]

<introducer> ::= <underscore>

<character set specification> ::=
      <standard character repertoire name>
    | <implementation-defined character repertoire name>
    | <user-defined character repertoire name>
    | <standard universal character form-of-use name>
    | <implementation-defined universal character form-of-use name>

<standard character repertoire name> ::= <character set name>

<character set name> ::= [ <schema name> <period> ]
      <SQL language identifier>

<schema name> ::=
    [ <catalog name> <period> ] <unqualified schema name>

<catalog name> ::= <identifier>

<identifier> ::=
    [ <introducer><character set specification> ] <actual identifier>

<actual identifier> ::=
      <regular identifier>
    | <delimited identifier>

<delimited identifier> ::=
    <double quote> <delimited identifier body> <double quote>

<delimited identifier body> ::= <delimited identifier part>...

<delimited identifier part> ::=
      <nondoublequote character>
    | <doublequote symbol>

<nondoublequote character> ::= <EMPHASIS>(!! See the Syntax Rules)

<doublequote symbol> ::= <double quote><double quote>

<unqualified schema name> ::= <identifier>

<SQL language identifier> ::=
    <SQL language identifier start>
       [ { <underscore> | <SQL language identifier part> }... ]

<SQL language identifier start> ::= <simple Latin letter>

<SQL language identifier part> ::=
      <simple Latin letter>
    | <digit>

<implementation-defined character repertoire name> ::=
    <character set name>
```

```
<user-defined character repertoire name> ::= <character set name>

<standard universal character form-of-use name> ::=
    <character set name>

<implementation-defined universal character form-of-use name> ::=
    <character set name>

<date string> ::=
    <quote> <date value> <quote>

<date value> ::=
    <years value> <minus sign> <months value>
        <minus sign> <days value>

<years value> ::= <datetime value>

<datetime value> ::= <unsigned integer>

<months value> ::= <datetime value>

<days value> ::= <datetime value>

<time string> ::=
    <quote> <time value> [ <time zone interval> ] <quote>

<time value> ::=
    <hours value> <colon> <minutes value> <colon> <seconds value>

<hours value> ::= <datetime value>

<minutes value> ::= <datetime value>

<seconds value> ::=
      <seconds integer value> [ <period> [ <seconds fraction> ] ]

<seconds integer value> ::= <unsigned integer>

<seconds fraction> ::= <unsigned integer>

<time zone interval> ::=
    <sign> <hours value> <colon> <minutes value>

<timestamp string> ::=
    <quote> <date value> <space> <time value>
        [ <time zone interval> ] <quote>

<interval string> ::=
    <quote> { <year-month literal> ¦ <day-time literal> } <quote>

<year-month literal> ::=
      <years value>
    ¦ [ <years value> <minus sign> ] <months value>
```

```
<day-time literal> ::=
      <day-time interval>
    ¦ <time interval>

<day-time interval> ::=
    <days value>
      [ <space> <hours value> [ <colon> <minutes value>
        [ <colon> <seconds value> ] ] ]

<time interval> ::=
      <hours value> [ <colon> <minutes value> [ <colon> <seconds value> ] ]
    ¦ <minutes value> [ <colon> <seconds value> ]
    ¦ <seconds value>

<not equals operator> ::= <>

<greater than or equals operator> ::= >=

<less than or equals operator> ::= <=

<concatenation operator> ::= ¦¦

<double period> ::= ..

<module> ::=
    <module name clause>
    <language clause>
    <module authorization clause>
    [ <temporary table declaration>... ]
    <module contents>...

<module name clause> ::=
    MODULE [ <module name> ]
      [ <module character set specification> ]

<module name> ::= <identifier>

<module character set specification> ::=
    NAMES ARE <character set specification>

<language clause> ::=
    LANGUAGE <language name>

<language name> ::=
    ADA ¦ C ¦ COBOL ¦ FORTRAN ¦ MUMPS ¦ PASCAL ¦ PLI

<module authorization clause> ::=
      SCHEMA <schema name>
    ¦ AUTHORIZATION <module authorization identifier>
    ¦ SCHEMA <schema name>
          AUTHORIZATION <module authorization identifier>

<module authorization identifier> ::=
    <authorization identifier>

<authorization identifier> ::= <identifier>
```

Part VI
App C

```
<temporary table declaration> ::=
    DECLARE LOCAL TEMPORARY TABLE
        <qualified local table name>
      <table element list>
      [ ON COMMIT { PRESERVE ¦ DELETE } ROWS ]

<qualified local table name> ::=
    MODULE <period> <local table name>

<local table name> ::= <qualified identifier>

<qualified identifier> ::= <identifier>

<table element list> ::=
      <left paren> <table element> [ { <comma> <table element> }... ] <right
      ➥paren>

<table element> ::=
      <column definition>
    ¦ <table constraint definition>

<column definition> ::=
    <column name> { <data type> ¦ <domain name> }
    [ <default clause> ]
    [ <column constraint definition>... ]
    [ <collate clause> ]

<column name> ::= <identifier>

<data type> ::=
      <character string type>
           [ CHARACTER SET <character set specification> ]
    ¦ <national character string type>
    ¦ <bit string type>
    ¦ <numeric type>
    ¦ <datetime type>
    ¦ <interval type>

<character string type> ::=
      CHARACTER [ <left paren> <length> <right paren> ]
    ¦ CHAR [ <left paren> <length> <right paren> ]
    ¦ CHARACTER VARYING <left paren> <length> <right paren>
    ¦ CHAR VARYING <left paren> <length> <right paren>
    ¦ VARCHAR <left paren> <length> <right paren>

<length> ::= <unsigned integer>

<national character string type> ::=
      NATIONAL CHARACTER [ <left paren> <length> <right paren> ]
    ¦ NATIONAL CHAR [ <left paren> <length> <right paren> ]
    ¦ NCHAR [ <left paren> <length> <right paren> ]
    ¦ NATIONAL CHARACTER VARYING <left paren> <length> <right paren>
    ¦ NATIONAL CHAR VARYING <left paren> <length> <right paren>
    ¦ NCHAR VARYING <left paren> <length> <right paren>
```

```
<bit string type> ::=
      BIT [ <left paren> <length> <right paren> ]
    ¦ BIT VARYING <left paren> <length> <right paren>

<numeric type> ::=
      <exact numeric type>
    ¦ <approximate numeric type>

<exact numeric type> ::=
      NUMERIC [ <left paren> <precision> [ <comma> <scale> ] <right paren> ]
    ¦ DECIMAL [ <left paren> <precision> [ <comma> <scale> ] <right paren> ]
    ¦ DEC [ <left paren> <precision> [ <comma> <scale> ] <right paren> ]
    ¦ INTEGER
    ¦ INT
    ¦ SMALLINT

<precision> ::= <unsigned integer>

<scale> ::= <unsigned integer>

<approximate numeric type> ::=
      FLOAT [ <left paren> <precision> <right paren> ]
    ¦ REAL
    ¦ DOUBLE PRECISION

<datetime type> ::=
      DATE
    ¦ TIME [ <left paren> <time precision> <right paren> ]
          [ WITH TIME ZONE ]
    ¦ TIMESTAMP [ <left paren> <timestamp precision> <right paren> ]
          [ WITH TIME ZONE ]

<time precision> ::= <time fractional seconds precision>

<time fractional seconds precision> ::= <unsigned integer>

<timestamp precision> ::= <time fractional seconds precision>

<interval type> ::= INTERVAL <interval qualifier>

<interval qualifier> ::=
      <start field> TO <end field>
    ¦ <single datetime field>

<start field> ::=
    <non-second datetime field>
        [ <left paren> <interval leading field precision> <right paren> ]

<non-second datetime field> ::= YEAR ¦ MONTH ¦ DAY ¦ HOUR
    ¦ MINUTE

<interval leading field precision> ::= <unsigned integer>

<end field> ::=
      <non-second datetime field>
    ¦ SECOND [ <left paren> <interval fractional seconds precision> <right paren>]
```

```
<interval fractional seconds precision> ::= <unsigned integer>

<single datetime field> ::=
      <non-second datetime field>
          [ <left paren> <interval leading field precision> <right paren> ]
    ¦ SECOND [ <left paren> <interval leading field precision>
          [ <comma> <interval fractional seconds precision> ] <right paren> ]

<domain name> ::= <qualified name>

<qualified name> ::=
    [ <schema name> <period> ] <qualified identifier>

<default clause> ::=
      DEFAULT <default option>

<default option> ::=
      <literal>
    ¦ <datetime value function>
    ¦ USER
    ¦ CURRENT_USER
    ¦ SESSION_USER
    ¦ SYSTEM_USER
    ¦ NULL

<literal> ::=
      <signed numeric literal>
    ¦ <general literal>

<signed numeric literal> ::=
    [ <sign> ] <unsigned numeric literal>

<general literal> ::=
      <character string literal>
    ¦ <national character string literal>
    ¦ <bit string literal>
    ¦ <hex string literal>
    ¦ <datetime literal>
    ¦ <interval literal>

<datetime literal> ::=
      <date literal>
    ¦ <time literal>
    ¦ <timestamp literal>

<date literal> ::=
    DATE <date string>

<time literal> ::=
    TIME <time string>

<timestamp literal> ::=
    TIMESTAMP <timestamp string>
```

```
<interval literal> ::=
    INTERVAL [ <sign> ] <interval string> <interval qualifier>

<datetime value function> ::=
      <current date value function>
    ¦ <current time value function>
    ¦ <current timestamp value function>

<current date value function> ::= CURRENT_DATE

<current time value function> ::=
      CURRENT_TIME [ <left paren> <time precision> <right paren> ]

<current timestamp value function> ::=
      CURRENT_TIMESTAMP [ <left paren> <timestamp precision> <right paren> ]

<column constraint definition> ::=
    [ <constraint name definition> ]
    <column constraint>
      [ <constraint attributes> ]

<constraint name definition> ::= CONSTRAINT <constraint name>

<constraint name> ::= <qualified name>

<column constraint> ::=
      NOT NULL
    ¦ <unique specification>
    ¦ <references specification>
    ¦ <check constraint definition>

<unique specification> ::=
    UNIQUE ¦ PRIMARY KEY

<references specification> ::=
    REFERENCES <referenced table and columns>
      [ MATCH <match type> ]
      [ <referential triggered action> ]

<referenced table and columns> ::=
     <table name> [ <left paren> <reference column list> <right paren> ]

<table name> ::=
      <qualified name>
    ¦ <qualified local table name>

<reference column list> ::= <column name list>

<column name list> ::=
    <column name> [ { <comma> <column name> }... ]

<match type> ::=
      FULL
    ¦ PARTIAL

<referential triggered action> ::=
      <update rule> [ <delete rule> ]
    ¦ <delete rule> [ <update rule> ]
```

```
<update rule> ::= ON UPDATE <referential action>

<referential action> ::=
      CASCADE
    ¦ SET NULL
    ¦ SET DEFAULT
    ¦ NO ACTION

<delete rule> ::= ON DELETE <referential action>

<check constraint definition> ::=
    CHECK
        <left paren> <search condition> <right paren>

<search condition> ::=
      <boolean term>
    ¦ <search condition> OR <boolean term>

<boolean term> ::=
      <boolean factor>
    ¦ <boolean term> AND <boolean factor>

<boolean factor> ::=
    [ NOT ] <boolean test>

<boolean test> ::=
    <boolean primary> [ IS [ NOT ]
          <truth value> ]

<boolean primary> ::=
      <predicate>
    ¦ <left paren> <search condition> <right paren>

<predicate> ::=
      <comparison predicate>
    ¦ <between predicate>
    ¦ <in predicate>
    ¦ <like predicate>
    ¦ <null predicate>
    ¦ <quantified comparison predicate>
    ¦ <exists predicate>
    ¦ <unique predicate>
    ¦ <match predicate>
    ¦ <overlaps predicate>

<comparison predicate> ::=
    <row value constructor> <comp op>
        <row value constructor>

<row value constructor> ::=
       <row value constructor element>
    ¦ <left paren> <row value constructor list> <right paren>
    ¦ <row subquery>
```

```
<row value constructor element> ::=
      <value expression>
    | <null specification>
    | <default specification>

<value expression> ::=
      <numeric value expression>
    | <string value expression>
    | <datetime value expression>
    | <interval value expression>

<numeric value expression> ::=
      <term>
    | <numeric value expression> <plus sign> <term>
    | <numeric value expression> <minus sign> <term>

<term> ::=
      <factor>
    | <term> <asterisk> <factor>
    | <term> <solidus> <factor>

<factor> ::=
    [ <sign> ] <numeric primary>

<numeric primary> ::=
      <value expression primary>
    | <numeric value function>

<value expression primary> ::=
      <unsigned value specification>
    | <column reference>
    | <set function specification>
    | <scalar subquery>
    | <case expression>
    | <left paren> <value expression> <right paren>
    | <cast specification>

<unsigned value specification> ::=
      <unsigned literal>
    | <general value specification>

<unsigned literal> ::=
      <unsigned numeric literal>
    | <general literal>

<general value specification> ::=
      <parameter specification>
    | <dynamic parameter specification>
    | <variable specification>
    | USER
    | CURRENT_USER
    | SESSION_USER
    | SYSTEM_USER
    | VALUE

<parameter specification> ::=
    <parameter name> [ <indicator parameter> ]
```

```
<parameter name> ::= <colon> <identifier>

<indicator parameter> ::=
    [ INDICATOR ] <parameter name>

<dynamic parameter specification> ::= <question mark>

<variable specification> ::=
    <embedded variable name> [ <indicator variable> ]

<embedded variable name> ::=
    <colon><host identifier>

<host identifier> ::=
      <Ada host identifier>
    ¦ <C host identifier>
    ¦ <COBOL host identifier>
    ¦ <Fortran host identifier>
    ¦ <MUMPS host identifier>
    ¦ <Pascal host identifier>
    ¦ <PL/I host identifier>

<Ada host identifier> ::= !! <EMPHASIS>(See the Syntax Rules.)

<C host identifier> ::=
    !! <EMPHASIS>(See the Syntax Rules.)

<COBOL host identifier> ::= !! <EMPHASIS>(See the Syntax Rules.)

<Fortran host identifier> ::= !! <EMPHASIS>(See the Syntax Rules.)

<MUMPS host identifier> ::= !! <EMPHASIS>(See the Syntax Rules.)

<Pascal host identifier> ::= !! <EMPHASIS>(See the Syntax Rules.)

<PL/I host identifier> ::= !! <EMPHASIS>(See the Syntax Rules.)

<indicator variable> ::=
    [ INDICATOR ] <embedded variable name>

<column reference> ::= [ <qualifier> <period> ] <column name>

<qualifier> ::=
      <table name>
    ¦ <correlation name>

<correlation name> ::= <identifier>

<set function specification> ::=
      COUNT <left paren> <asterisk> <right paren>
    ¦ <general set function>

<general set function> ::=
      <set function type>
          <left paren> [ <set quantifier> ] <value expression> <right paren>
```

```
<set function type> ::=
    AVG ¦ MAX ¦ MIN ¦ SUM ¦ COUNT

<set quantifier> ::= DISTINCT ¦ ALL

<scalar subquery> ::= <subquery>

<subquery> ::= <left paren> <query expression> <right paren>

<query expression> ::=
      <non-join query expression>
    ¦ <joined table>

<non-join query expression> ::=
      <non-join query term>
    ¦ <query expression> UNION  [ ALL ]
          [ <corresponding spec> ] <query term>
    ¦ <query expression> EXCEPT [ ALL ]
          [ <corresponding spec> ] <query term>

<non-join query term> ::=
      <non-join query primary>
    ¦ <query term> INTERSECT [ ALL ]
          [ <corresponding spec> ] <query primary>

<non-join query primary> ::=
      <simple table>
    ¦ <left paren> <non-join query expression> <right paren>

<simple table> ::=
      <query specification>
    ¦ <table value constructor>
    ¦ <explicit table>

<query specification> ::=
    SELECT [ <set quantifier> ] <select list> <table expression>

<select list> ::=
      <asterisk>
    ¦ <select sublist> [ { <comma> <select sublist> }... ]

<select sublist> ::=
      <derived column>
    ¦ <qualifier> <period> <asterisk>

<derived column> ::= <value expression> [ <as clause> ]

<as clause> ::= [ AS ] <column name>

<table expression> ::=
    <from clause>
    [ <where clause> ]
    [ <group by clause> ]
    [ <having clause> ]
```

```
<from clause> ::= FROM <table reference>
    [ { <comma> <table reference> }... ]

<table reference> ::=
      <table name> [ [ AS ] <correlation name>
          [ <left paren> <derived column list> <right paren> ] ]
    ¦ <derived table> [ AS ] <correlation name>
          [ <left paren> <derived column list> <right paren> ]
    ¦ <joined table>

<derived column list> ::= <column name list>

<derived table> ::= <table subquery>

<table subquery> ::= <subquery>

<joined table> ::=
      <cross join>
    ¦ <qualified join>
    ¦ <left paren> <joined table> <right paren>

<cross join> ::=
    <table reference> CROSS JOIN <table reference>

<qualified join> ::=
    <table reference> [ NATURAL ] [ <join type> ] JOIN
      <table reference> [ <join specification> ]

<join type> ::=
      INNER
    ¦ <outer join type> [ OUTER ]
    ¦ UNION

<outer join type> ::=
      LEFT
    ¦ RIGHT
    ¦ FULL

<join specification> ::=
      <join condition>
    ¦ <named columns join>

<join condition> ::= ON <search condition>

<named columns join> ::=
    USING <left paren> <join column list> <right paren>

<join column list> ::= <column name list>

<where clause> ::= WHERE <search condition>

<group by clause> ::=
    GROUP BY <grouping column reference list>
```

```
<grouping column reference list> ::=
    <grouping column reference>
        [ { <comma> <grouping column reference> }... ]

<grouping column reference> ::=
    <column reference> [ <collate clause> ]

<collate clause> ::= COLLATE <collation name>

<collation name> ::= <qualified name>

<having clause> ::= HAVING <search condition>

<table value constructor> ::=
    VALUES <table value constructor list>

<table value constructor list> ::=
    <row value constructor> [ { <comma> <row value constructor> }... ]

<explicit table> ::= TABLE <table name>

<query term> ::=
      <non-join query term>
    ¦ <joined table>

<corresponding spec> ::=
    CORRESPONDING [ BY <left paren> <corresponding column list> <right paren> ]

<corresponding column list> ::= <column name list>

<query primary> ::=
      <non-join query primary>
    ¦ <joined table>

<case expression> ::=
      <case abbreviation>
    ¦ <case specification>

<case abbreviation> ::=
      NULLIF <left paren> <value expression> <comma>
            <value expression> <right paren>
    ¦ COALESCE <left paren> <value expression>
            { <comma> <value expression> }... <right paren>

<case specification> ::=
      <simple case>
    ¦ <searched case>

<simple case> ::=
    CASE <case operand>
      <simple when clause>...
      [ <else clause> ]
    END
```

Part VI
App C

```
<case operand> ::= <value expression>

<simple when clause> ::= WHEN <when operand> THEN <result>

<when operand> ::= <value expression>

<result> ::= <result expression> ¦ NULL

<result expression> ::= <value expression>

<else clause> ::= ELSE <result>

<searched case> ::=
    CASE
      <searched when clause>...
      [ <else clause> ]
    END

<searched when clause> ::= WHEN <search condition> THEN <result>

<cast specification> ::=
    CAST <left paren> <cast operand> AS
        <cast target> <right paren>

<cast operand> ::=
      <value expression>
    ¦ NULL

<cast target> ::=
      <domain name>
    ¦ <data type>

<numeric value function> ::=
      <position expression>
    ¦ <extract expression>
    ¦ <length expression>

<position expression> ::=
    POSITION <left paren> <character value expression>
        IN <character value expression> <right paren>

<character value expression> ::=
      <concatenation>
    ¦ <character factor>

<concatenation> ::=
    <character value expression> <concatenation operator>
        <character factor>

<character factor> ::=
    <character primary> [ <collate clause> ]

<character primary> ::=
      <value expression primary>
    ¦ <string value function>
```

```
<string value function> ::=
      <character value function>
    ¦ <bit value function>

<character value function> ::=
      <character substring function>
    ¦ <fold>
    ¦ <form-of-use conversion>
    ¦ <character translation>
    ¦ <trim function>

<character substring function> ::=
    SUBSTRING <left paren> <character value expression> FROM <start position>
                [ FOR <string length> ] <right paren>

<start position> ::= <numeric value expression>

<string length> ::= <numeric value expression>

<fold> ::= { UPPER ¦ LOWER }
     <left paren> <character value expression> <right paren>

<form-of-use conversion> ::=
    CONVERT <left paren> <character value expression>
        USING <form-of-use conversion name> <right paren>

<form-of-use conversion name> ::= <qualified name>

<character translation> ::=
    TRANSLATE <left paren> <character value expression>
        USING <translation name> <right paren>

<translation name> ::= <qualified name>

<trim function> ::=
    TRIM <left paren> <trim operands> <right paren>

<trim operands> ::=
    [ [ <trim specification> ] [ <trim character> ] FROM ] <trim source>

<trim specification> ::=
      LEADING
    ¦ TRAILING
    ¦ BOTH

<trim character> ::= <character value expression>

<trim source> ::= <character value expression>

<bit value function> ::=
    <bit substring function>

<bit substring function> ::=
    SUBSTRING <left paren> <bit value expression> FROM <start position>
        [ FOR <string length> ] <right paren>
```

```
<bit value expression> ::=
      <bit concatenation>
    ¦ <bit factor>

<bit concatenation> ::=
    <bit value expression> <concatenation operator> <bit factor>

<bit factor> ::= <bit primary>

<bit primary> ::=
      <value expression primary>
    ¦ <string value function>

<extract expression> ::=
    EXTRACT <left paren> <extract field>
        FROM <extract source> <right paren>

<extract field> ::=
      <datetime field>
    ¦ <time zone field>

<datetime field> ::=
      <non-second datetime field>
    ¦ SECOND

<time zone field> ::=
      TIMEZONE_HOUR
    ¦ TIMEZONE_MINUTE

<extract source> ::=
      <datetime value expression>
    ¦ <interval value expression>

<datetime value expression> ::=
      <datetime term>
    ¦ <interval value expression> <plus sign> <datetime term>
    ¦ <datetime value expression> <plus sign> <interval term>
    ¦ <datetime value expression> <minus sign> <interval term>

<interval term> ::=
      <interval factor>
    ¦ <interval term 2> <asterisk> <factor>
    ¦ <interval term 2> <solidus> <factor>
    ¦ <term> <asterisk> <interval factor>

<interval factor> ::=
    [ <sign> ] <interval primary>

<interval primary> ::=
      <value expression primary> [ <interval qualifier> ]

<interval term 2> ::= <interval term>
```

```
<interval value expression> ::=
      <interval term>
    ¦ <interval value expression 1> <plus sign> <interval term 1>
    ¦ <interval value expression 1> <minus sign> <interval term 1>
    ¦ <left paren> <datetime value expression> <minus sign>
          <datetime term> <right paren> <interval qualifier>

<interval value expression 1> ::= <interval value expression>

<interval term 1> ::= <interval term>

<datetime term> ::=
      <datetime factor>

<datetime factor> ::=
      <datetime primary> [ <time zone> ]

<datetime primary> ::=
      <value expression primary>
    ¦ <datetime value function>

<time zone> ::=
    AT <time zone specifier>

<time zone specifier> ::=
      LOCAL
    ¦ TIME ZONE <interval value expression>

<length expression> ::=
      <char length expression>
    ¦ <octet length expression>
    ¦ <bit length expression>

<char length expression> ::=
    { CHAR_LENGTH ¦ CHARACTER_LENGTH }
        <left paren> <string value expression> <right paren>

<string value expression> ::=
      <character value expression>
    ¦ <bit value expression>

<octet length expression> ::=
    OCTET_LENGTH <left paren> <string value expression> <right paren>

<bit length expression> ::=
    BIT_LENGTH <left paren> <string value expression> <right paren>

<null specification> ::=
    NULL

<default specification> ::=
    DEFAULT

<row value constructor list> ::=
    <row value constructor element>
        [ { <comma> <row value constructor element> }... ]
```

```
<row subquery> ::= <subquery>

<comp op> ::=
      <equals operator>
    | <not equals operator>
    | <less than operator>
    | <greater than operator>
    | <less than or equals operator>
    | <greater than or equals operator>

<between predicate> ::=
    <row value constructor> [ NOT ] BETWEEN
      <row value constructor> AND <row value constructor>

<in predicate> ::=
    <row value constructor>
      [ NOT ] IN <in predicate value>

<in predicate value> ::=
      <table subquery>
    | <left paren> <in value list> <right paren>

<in value list> ::=
    <value expression> { <comma> <value expression> }...

<like predicate> ::=
    <match value> [ NOT ] LIKE <pattern>
      [ ESCAPE <escape character> ]

<match value> ::= <character value expression>

<pattern> ::= <character value expression>

<escape character> ::= <character value expression>

<null predicate> ::= <row value constructor>
    IS [ NOT ] NULL

<quantified comparison predicate> ::=
    <row value constructor> <comp op> <quantifier> <table subquery>

<quantifier> ::= <all> | <some>

<all> ::= ALL

<some> ::= SOME | ANY

<exists predicate> ::= EXISTS <table subquery>

<unique predicate> ::= UNIQUE <table subquery>

<match predicate> ::=
    <row value constructor> MATCH [ UNIQUE ]
        [ PARTIAL | FULL ] <table subquery>
```

```
<overlaps predicate> ::=
    <row value constructor 1> OVERLAPS <row value constructor 2>

<row value constructor 1> ::= <row value constructor>

<row value constructor 2> ::= <row value constructor>

<truth value> ::=
      TRUE
    | FALSE
    | UNKNOWN

<constraint attributes> ::=
      <constraint check time> [ [ NOT ] DEFERRABLE ]
    | [ NOT ] DEFERRABLE [ <constraint check time> ]

<constraint check time> ::=
      INITIALLY DEFERRED
    | INITIALLY IMMEDIATE

<table constraint definition> ::=
    [ <constraint name definition> ]
    <table constraint> [ <constraint attributes> ]

<table constraint> ::=
      <unique constraint definition>
    | <referential constraint definition>
    | <check constraint definition>

<unique constraint definition> ::=
            <unique specification>
    <unique specification><left paren> <unique column list> <right paren>

<unique column list> ::= <column name list>

<referential constraint definition> ::=
    FOREIGN KEY
        <left paren> <referencing columns> <right paren>
      <references specification>

<referencing columns> ::=
    <reference column list>

<module contents> ::=
      <declare cursor>
    | <dynamic declare cursor>
    | <procedure>

<declare cursor> ::=
    DECLARE <cursor name> [ INSENSITIVE ] [ SCROLL ] CURSOR
      FOR <cursor specification>

<cursor name> ::= <identifier>
```

```
<cursor specification> ::=
    <query expression> [ <order by clause> ]
      [ <updatability clause> ]

<order by clause> ::=
    ORDER BY <sort specification list>

<sort specification list> ::=
    <sort specification> [ { <comma> <sort specification> }... ]

<sort specification> ::=
    <sort key> [ <collate clause> ] [ <ordering specification> ]

<sort key> ::=
      <column name>
    ¦ <unsigned integer>

<ordering specification> ::= ASC ¦ DESC

<updatability clause> ::=
    FOR
        { READ ONLY ¦
          UPDATE [ OF <column name list> ] }

<dynamic declare cursor> ::=
    DECLARE <cursor name> [ INSENSITIVE ] [ SCROLL ] CURSOR
        FOR <statement name>

<statement name> ::= <identifier>

<procedure> ::=
    PROCEDURE <procedure name>
        <parameter declaration list> <semicolon>
      <SQL procedure statement> <semicolon>

<procedure name> ::= <identifier>

<parameter declaration list> ::=
      <left paren> <parameter declaration>
          [ { <comma> <parameter declaration> }... ] <right paren>
    ¦ <parameter declaration>...

<parameter declaration> ::=
      <parameter name> <data type>
    ¦ <status parameter>

<status parameter> ::=
    SQLCODE ¦ SQLSTATE

<SQL procedure statement> ::=
      <SQL schema statement>
    ¦ <SQL data statement>
    ¦ <SQL transaction statement>
    ¦ <SQL connection statement>
    ¦ <SQL session statement>
```

```
    | <SQL dynamic statement>
    | <SQL diagnostics statement>

<SQL schema statement> ::=
      <SQL schema definition statement>
    | <SQL schema manipulation statement>

<SQL schema definition statement> ::=
      <schema definition>
    | <table definition>
    | <view definition>
    | <grant statement>
    | <domain definition>
    | <character set definition>
    | <collation definition>
    | <translation definition>
    | <assertion definition>

<schema definition> ::=
    CREATE SCHEMA <schema name clause>
      [ <schema character set specification> ]
      [ <schema element>... ]

<schema name clause> ::=
      <schema name>
    | AUTHORIZATION <schema authorization identifier>
    | <schema name> AUTHORIZATION
          <schema authorization identifier>

<schema authorization identifier> ::=
    <authorization identifier>

<schema character set specification> ::=
    DEFAULT CHARACTER
        SET <character set specification>

<schema element> ::=
      <domain definition>
    | <table definition>
    | <view definition>
    | <grant statement>
    | <assertion definition>
    | <character set definition>
    | <collation definition>
    | <translation definition>

<domain definition> ::=
    CREATE DOMAIN <domain name>
        [ AS ] <data type>
      [ <default clause> ]
      [ <domain constraint>... ]
      [ <collate clause> ]

<domain constraint> ::=
    [ <constraint name definition> ]
    <check constraint definition> [ <constraint attributes> ]
```

```
<table definition> ::=
    CREATE [ { GLOBAL ¦ LOCAL } TEMPORARY ] TABLE
        <table name>
      <table element list>
      [ ON COMMIT { DELETE ¦ PRESERVE } ROWS ]

<view definition> ::=
    CREATE VIEW <table name> [ <left paren> <view column list>
                                  <right paren> ]
      AS <query expression>
      [ WITH [ <levels clause> ] CHECK OPTION ]

<view column list> ::= <column name list>

<levels clause> ::=
    CASCADED ¦ LOCAL

<grant statement> ::=
   GRANT <privileges> ON <object name>
     TO <grantee> [ { <comma> <grantee> }... ]
       [ WITH GRANT OPTION ]

<privileges> ::=
      ALL PRIVILEGES
    ¦ <action list>

<action list> ::= <action> [ { <comma> <action> }... ]

<action> ::=
      SELECT
    ¦ DELETE
    ¦ INSERT [ <left paren> <privilege column list> <right paren> ]
    ¦ UPDATE [ <left paren> <privilege column list> <right paren> ]
    ¦ REFERENCES [ <left paren> <privilege column list> <right paren> ]
    ¦ USAGE

<privilege column list> ::= <column name list>

<object name> ::=
      [ TABLE ] <table name>
    ¦ DOMAIN <domain name>
    ¦ COLLATION <collation name>
    ¦ CHARACTER SET <character set name>
    ¦ TRANSLATION <translation name>

<grantee> ::=
      PUBLIC
    ¦ <authorization identifier>

<assertion definition> ::=
    CREATE ASSERTION <constraint name> <assertion check>
      [ <constraint attributes> ]

<assertion check> ::=
    CHECK
        <left paren> <search condition> <right paren>
```

```
<character set definition> ::=
    CREATE CHARACTER SET <character set name>
        [ AS ]
      <character set source>
      [ <collate clause> ¦ <limited collation definition> ]

<character set source> ::=
      GET <existing character set name>

<existing character set name> ::=
      <standard character repertoire name>
    ¦ <implementation-defined character repertoire name>
    ¦ <schema character set name>

<schema character set name> ::= <character set name>

<limited collation definition> ::=
    COLLATION FROM <collation source>

<collation source> ::=
      <collating sequence definition>
    ¦ <translation collation>

<collating sequence definition> ::=
      <external collation>
    ¦ <schema collation name>
    ¦ DESC <left paren> <collation name> <right paren>
    ¦ DEFAULT

<external collation> ::=
    EXTERNAL <left paren> <quote> <external collation name> <quote> <right paren>

<external collation name> ::=
      <standard collation name>
    ¦ <implementation-defined collation name>

<standard collation name> ::= <collation name>

<implementation-defined collation name> ::= <collation name>

<schema collation name> ::= <collation name>

<translation collation> ::=
    TRANSLATION <translation name>
        [ THEN COLLATION <collation name> ]

<collation definition> ::=
    CREATE COLLATION <collation name> FOR
        <character set specification>
      FROM <collation source>
        [ <pad attribute> ]

<pad attribute> ::=
      NO PAD
    ¦ PAD SPACE
```

```
<translation definition> ::=
    CREATE TRANSLATION <translation name>
      FOR <source character set specification>
        TO <target character set specification>
      FROM <translation source>

<source character set specification> ::= <character set specification>

<target character set specification> ::= <character set specification>

<translation source> ::=
      <translation specification>

<translation specification> ::=
      <external translation>
    ¦ IDENTITY
    ¦ <schema translation name>

<external translation> ::=
    EXTERNAL <left paren> <quote> <external translation name> <quote> <right
    ➥paren>

<external translation name> ::=
      <standard translation name>
    ¦ <implementation-defined translation name>

<standard translation name> ::= <translation name>

<implementation-defined translation name> ::= <translation name>

<schema translation name> ::= <translation name>

<SQL schema manipulation statement> ::=
      <drop schema statement>
    ¦ <alter table statement>
    ¦ <drop table statement>
    ¦ <drop view statement>
    ¦ <revoke statement>
    ¦ <alter domain statement>
    ¦ <drop domain statement>
    ¦ <drop character set statement>
    ¦ <drop collation statement>
    ¦ <drop translation statement>
    ¦ <drop assertion statement>

<drop schema statement> ::=
    DROP SCHEMA <schema name> <drop behavior>

<drop behavior> ::= CASCADE ¦ RESTRICT

<alter table statement> ::=
    ALTER TABLE <table name> <alter table action>

<alter table action> ::=
      <add column definition>
```

```
    | <alter column definition>
    | <drop column definition>
    | <add table constraint definition>
    | <drop table constraint definition>

<add column definition> ::=
    ADD [ COLUMN ] <column definition>

<alter column definition> ::=
    ALTER [ COLUMN ] <column name> <alter column action>

<alter column action> ::=
      <set column default clause>
    | <drop column default clause>

<set column default clause> ::=
    SET <default clause>

<drop column default clause> ::=
    DROP DEFAULT

<drop column definition> ::=
    DROP [ COLUMN ] <column name> <drop behavior>

<add table constraint definition> ::=
    ADD <table constraint definition>

<drop table constraint definition> ::=
    DROP CONSTRAINT <constraint name> <drop behavior>

<drop table statement> ::=
    DROP TABLE <table name> <drop behavior>

<drop view statement> ::=
    DROP VIEW <table name> <drop behavior>

<revoke statement> ::=
    REVOKE [ GRANT OPTION FOR ]
        <privileges>
        ON <object name>
      FROM <grantee> [ { <comma> <grantee> }... ] <drop behavior>

<alter domain statement> ::=
    ALTER DOMAIN <domain name> <alter domain action>

<alter domain action> ::=
      <set domain default clause>
    | <drop domain default clause>
    | <add domain constraint definition>
    | <drop domain constraint definition>

<set domain default clause> ::= SET <default clause>

<drop domain default clause> ::= DROP DEFAULT
```

```
<add domain constraint definition> ::=
    ADD <domain constraint>

<drop domain constraint definition> ::=
    DROP CONSTRAINT <constraint name>

<drop domain statement> ::=
    DROP DOMAIN <domain name> <drop behavior>

<drop character set statement> ::=
    DROP CHARACTER SET <character set name>

<drop collation statement> ::=
    DROP COLLATION <collation name>

<drop translation statement> ::=
    DROP TRANSLATION <translation name>

<drop assertion statement> ::=
    DROP ASSERTION <constraint name>

<SQL data statement> ::=
      <open statement>
    ¦ <fetch statement>
    ¦ <close statement>
    ¦ <select statement: single row>
    ¦ <SQL data change statement>

<open statement> ::=
    OPEN <cursor name>

<fetch statement> ::=
    FETCH [ [ <fetch orientation> ] FROM ]
      <cursor name> INTO <fetch target list>

<fetch orientation> ::=
      NEXT
    ¦ PRIOR
    ¦ FIRST
    ¦ LAST
    ¦ { ABSOLUTE ¦ RELATIVE } <simple value specification>

<simple value specification> ::=
      <parameter name>
    ¦ <embedded variable name>
    ¦ <literal>

<fetch target list> ::=
    <target specification> [ { <comma> <target specification> }... ]

<target specification> ::=
      <parameter specification>
    ¦ <variable specification>

<close statement> ::=
    CLOSE <cursor name>
```

```
<select statement: single row> ::=
    SELECT [ <set quantifier> ] <select list>
      INTO <select target list>
        <table expression>

<select target list> ::=
    <target specification> [ { <comma> <target specification> }... ]

<SQL data change statement> ::=
      <delete statement: positioned>
    ¦ <delete statement: searched>
    ¦ <insert statement>
    ¦ <update statement: positioned>
    ¦ <update statement: searched>

<delete statement: positioned> ::=
    DELETE FROM <table name>
      WHERE CURRENT OF <cursor name>

<delete statement: searched> ::=
    DELETE FROM <table name>
      [ WHERE <search condition> ]

<insert statement> ::=
    INSERT INTO <table name>
      <insert columns and source>

<insert columns and source> ::=
      [ <left paren> <insert column list> <right paren> ]
            <query expression>
    ¦ DEFAULT VALUES

<insert column list> ::= <column name list>

<update statement: positioned> ::=
    UPDATE <table name>
      SET <set clause list>
        WHERE CURRENT OF <cursor name>

<set clause list> ::=
    <set clause> [ { <comma> <set clause> }... ]

<set clause> ::=
    <object column> <equals operator> <update source>

<object column> ::= <column name>

<update source> ::=
      <value expression>
    ¦ <null specification>
    ¦ DEFAULT

<update statement: searched> ::=
    UPDATE <table name>
      SET <set clause list>
      [ WHERE <search condition> ]
```

```
<SQL transaction statement> ::=
      <set transaction statement>
    ¦ <set constraints mode statement>
    ¦ <commit statement>
    ¦ <rollback statement>

<set transaction statement> ::=
    SET TRANSACTION <transaction mode>
        [ { <comma> <transaction mode> }... ]

<transaction mode> ::=
      <isolation level>
    ¦ <transaction access mode>
    ¦ <diagnostics size>

<isolation level> ::=
    ISOLATION LEVEL <level of isolation>

<level of isolation> ::=
      READ UNCOMMITTED
    ¦ READ COMMITTED
    ¦ REPEATABLE READ
    ¦ SERIALIZABLE

<transaction access mode> ::=
      READ ONLY
    ¦ READ WRITE

<diagnostics size> ::=
    DIAGNOSTICS SIZE <number of conditions>

<number of conditions> ::= <simple value specification>

<set constraints mode statement> ::=
    SET CONSTRAINTS <constraint name list>
        { DEFERRED ¦ IMMEDIATE }

<constraint name list> ::=
      ALL
    ¦ <constraint name> [ { <comma> <constraint name> }... ]

<commit statement> ::=
    COMMIT [ WORK ]

<rollback statement> ::=
    ROLLBACK [ WORK ]

<SQL connection statement> ::=
      <connect statement>
    ¦ <set connection statement>
    ¦ <disconnect statement>

<connect statement> ::=
    CONNECT TO <connection target>
```

```
<connection target> ::=
      <SQL-server name>
        [ AS <connection name> ]
          correspondence with Tony Gordon)
        [ USER <user name> ]
    | DEFAULT

<SQL-server name> ::= <simple value specification>

<connection name> ::= <simple value specification>

<user name> ::= <simple value specification>

<set connection statement> ::=
    SET CONNECTION <connection object>

<connection object> ::=
      DEFAULT
    | <connection name>

<disconnect statement> ::=
    DISCONNECT <disconnect object>

<disconnect object> ::=
      <connection object>
    | ALL
    | CURRENT

<SQL session statement> ::=
      <set catalog statement>
    | <set schema statement>
    | <set names statement>
    | <set session authorization identifier statement>
    | <set local time zone statement>

<set catalog statement> ::=
    SET CATALOG <value specification>

<value specification> ::=
      <literal>
    | <general value specification>

<set schema statement> ::=
    SET SCHEMA <value specification>

<set names statement> ::=
    SET NAMES <value specification>

<set session authorization identifier statement> ::=
    SET SESSION AUTHORIZATION
        <value specification>

<set local time zone statement> ::=
    SET TIME ZONE
        <set time zone value>
```

```
<set time zone value> ::=
      <interval value expression>
    | LOCAL

<SQL dynamic statement> ::=
      <system descriptor statement>
    | <prepare statement>
    | <deallocate prepared statement>
    | <describe statement>
    | <execute statement>
    | <execute immediate statement>
    | <SQL dynamic data statement>

<system descriptor statement> ::=
      <allocate descriptor statement>
    | <deallocate descriptor statement>
    | <set descriptor statement>
    | <get descriptor statement>

<allocate descriptor statement> ::=
    ALLOCATE DESCRIPTOR <descriptor name>
       [ WITH MAX <occurrences> ]

<descriptor name> ::=
    [ <scope option> ] <simple value specification>

<scope option> ::=
      GLOBAL
    | LOCAL

<occurrences> ::= <simple value specification>

<deallocate descriptor statement> ::=
    DEALLOCATE DESCRIPTOR <descriptor name>

<set descriptor statement> ::=
    SET DESCRIPTOR <descriptor name>
        <set descriptor information>

<set descriptor information> ::=
      <set count>
    | VALUE <item number>
        <set item information> [ { <comma> <set item information> }... ]

<set count> ::=
    COUNT <equals operator> <simple value specification 1>

<simple value specification 1> ::= <simple value specification>

<item number> ::= <simple value specification>

<set item information> ::=
    <descriptor item name> <equals operator> <simple value specification 2>
```

```
<descriptor item name> ::=
      TYPE
    ¦ LENGTH
    ¦ OCTET_LENGTH
    ¦ RETURNED_LENGTH
    ¦ RETURNED_OCTET_LENGTH
    ¦ PRECISION
    ¦ SCALE
    ¦ DATETIME_INTERVAL_CODE
    ¦ DATETIME_INTERVAL_PRECISION
    ¦ NULLABLE
    ¦ INDICATOR
    ¦ DATA
    ¦ NAME
    ¦ UNNAMED
    ¦ COLLATION_CATALOG
    ¦ COLLATION_SCHEMA
    ¦ COLLATION_NAME
    ¦ CHARACTER_SET_CATALOG
    ¦ CHARACTER_SET_SCHEMA
    ¦ CHARACTER_SET_NAME

<simple value specification 2> ::= <simple value specification>

<item number> ::= <simple value specification>

<get descriptor statement> ::=
    GET DESCRIPTOR <descriptor name> <get descriptor information>

<get descriptor information> ::=
      <get count>
    ¦ VALUE <item number>
        <get item information> [ { <comma> <get item information> }... ]

<get count> ::=
    <simple target specification 1> <equals operator>
         COUNT

<simple target specification 1> ::= <simple target specification>

<simple target specification> ::=
      <parameter name>
    ¦ <embedded variable name>

<get item information> ::=
    <simple target specification 2> <equals operator> <descriptor item name>>

<simple target specification 2> ::= <simple target specification>

<prepare statement> ::=
    PREPARE <SQL statement name> FROM <SQL statement variable>

<SQL statement name> ::=
      <statement name>
    ¦ <extended statement name>
```

```
<extended statement name> ::=
    [ <scope option> ] <simple value specification>

<SQL statement variable> ::= <simple value specification>

<deallocate prepared statement> ::=
    DEALLOCATE PREPARE <SQL statement name>

<describe statement> ::=
      <describe input statement>
    ¦ <describe output statement>

<describe input statement> ::=
    DESCRIBE INPUT <SQL statement name> <using descriptor>

<using descriptor> ::=
    { USING ¦ INTO } SQL DESCRIPTOR <descriptor name>

<describe output statement> ::=
    DESCRIBE [ OUTPUT ] <SQL statement name> <using descriptor>

<execute statement> ::=
    EXECUTE <SQL statement name>
      [ <result using clause> ]
      [ <parameter using clause> ]

<result using clause> ::= <using clause>

<using clause> ::=
      <using arguments>
    ¦ <using descriptor>

<using arguments> ::=
    { USING ¦ INTO } <argument> [ { <comma> <argument> }... ]

<argument> ::= <target specification>

<parameter using clause> ::= <using clause>

<execute immediate statement> ::=
    EXECUTE IMMEDIATE <SQL statement variable>

<SQL dynamic data statement> ::=
      <allocate cursor statement>
    ¦ <dynamic open statement>
    ¦ <dynamic fetch statement>
    ¦ <dynamic close statement>
    ¦ <dynamic delete statement: positioned>
    ¦ <dynamic update statement: positioned>

<allocate cursor statement> ::=
    ALLOCATE <extended cursor name> [ INSENSITIVE ]
        [ SCROLL ] CURSOR
      FOR <extended statement name>
```

```
<extended cursor name> ::=
    [ <scope option> ] <simple value specification>

<dynamic open statement> ::=
    OPEN <dynamic cursor name> [ <using clause> ]

<dynamic cursor name> ::=
      <cursor name>
    ¦ <extended cursor name>

<dynamic fetch statement> ::=
    FETCH [ [ <fetch orientation> ] FROM ] <dynamic cursor name>
        <using clause>

<dynamic close statement> ::=
    CLOSE <dynamic cursor name>

<dynamic delete statement: positioned> ::=
    DELETE FROM <table name>
      WHERE CURRENT OF
          <dynamic cursor name>

<dynamic update statement: positioned> ::=
    UPDATE <table name>
      SET <set clause>
          [ { <comma> <set clause> }... ]
        WHERE CURRENT OF
            <dynamic cursor name>

<SQL diagnostics statement> ::=
    <get diagnostics statement>

<get diagnostics statement> ::=
    GET DIAGNOSTICS <sql diagnostics information>

<sql diagnostics information> ::=
      <statement information>
    ¦ <condition information>

<statement information> ::=
    <statement information item> [ { <comma> <statement information item> }... ]

<statement information item> ::=
    <simple target specification> <equals operator> <statement information item
    ➥name>

<statement information item name> ::=
      NUMBER
    ¦ MORE
    ¦ COMMAND_FUNCTION
    ¦ DYNAMIC_FUNCTION
    ¦ ROW_COUNT

<condition information> ::=
    EXCEPTION <condition number>
      <condition information item> [ { <comma> <condition information item> }...]
```

Part VI App C

```
<condition number> ::= <simple value specification>

<condition information item> ::=
    <simple target specification> <equals operator> <condition information item
➥name>

<condition information item name> ::=
      CONDITION_NUMBER
    | RETURNED_SQLSTATE
    | CLASS_ORIGIN
    | SUBCLASS_ORIGIN
    | SERVER_NAME
    | CONNECTION_NAME
    | CONSTRAINT_CATALOG
    | CONSTRAINT_SCHEMA
    | CONSTRAINT_NAME
    | CATALOG_NAME
    | SCHEMA_NAME
    | TABLE_NAME
    | COLUMN_NAME
    | CURSOR_NAME
    | MESSAGE_TEXT
    | MESSAGE_LENGTH
    | MESSAGE_OCTET_LENGTH

<embedded SQL host program> ::=
      <embedded SQL Ada program>
    | <embedded SQL C program>
    | <embedded SQL COBOL program>
    | <embedded SQL Fortran program>
    | <embedded SQL MUMPS program>
    | <embedded SQL Pascal program>
    | <embedded SQL PL/I program>

<embedded SQL Ada program> ::= !! <EMPHASIS>(See the Syntax Rules.)

<embedded SQL C program> ::=
      !! <EMPHASIS>(See the Syntax Rules.)

<embedded SQL COBOL program> ::= !! <EMPHASIS>(See the Syntax Rules.)

<embedded SQL Fortran program> ::=
    !! <EMPHASIS>(See the Syntax Rules.)

<embedded SQL MUMPS program> ::= !! <EMPHASIS>(See the Syntax Rules.)

<embedded SQL Pascal program> ::=
    !! <EMPHASIS>(See the Syntax Rules.)

<embedded SQL PL/I program> ::= !! <EMPHASIS>(See the Syntax Rules.)

<embedded SQL declare section> ::=
      <embedded SQL begin declare>
        [ <embedded character set declaration> ]
        [ <host variable definition>... ]
```

```
      <embedded SQL end declare>
    | <embedded SQL MUMPS declare>

<embedded SQL begin declare> ::=
    <SQL prefix> BEGIN DECLARE SECTION
        [ <SQL terminator> ]

<SQL prefix> ::=
      EXEC SQL
    | <ampersand>SQL<left paren>

<SQL terminator> ::=
      END-EXEC
    | <semicolon>
    | <right paren>

<embedded character set declaration> ::=
    SQL NAMES ARE <character set specification>

<host variable definition> ::=
      <Ada variable definition>
    | <C variable definition>
    | <COBOL variable definition>
    | <Fortran variable definition>
    | <MUMPS variable definition>
    | <Pascal variable definition>
    | <PL/I variable definition>

<Ada variable definition> ::=
    <Ada host identifier> [ { <comma> <Ada host identifier> }... ] :
    <Ada type specification> [ <Ada initial value> ]

<Ada type specification> ::=
      <Ada qualified type specification>
    | <Ada unqualified type specification>

<Ada qualified type specification> ::=
      SQL_STANDARD.CHAR [ CHARACTER SET
         [ IS ] <character set specification> ]
          <left paren> 1 <double period> <length> <right paren>
    | SQL_STANDARD.BIT
          <left paren> 1 <double period> <length> <right paren>
    | SQL_STANDARD.SMALLINT
    | SQL_STANDARD.INT
    | SQL_STANDARD.REAL
    | SQL_STANDARD.DOUBLE_PRECISION
    | SQL_STANDARD.SQLCODE_TYPE
    | SQL_STANDARD.SQLSTATE_TYPE
    | SQL_STANDARD.INDICATOR_TYPE

<Ada unqualified type specification> ::=
      CHAR
          <left paren> 1 <double period> <length> <right paren>
    | BIT
          <left paren> 1 <double period> <length> <right paren>
```

```
    | SMALLINT
    | INT
    | REAL
    | DOUBLE_PRECISION
    | SQLCODE_TYPE
    | SQLSTATE_TYPE
    | INDICATOR_TYPE

<Ada initial value> ::=
    <Ada assignment operator> <character representation>...

<Ada assignment operator> ::= <colon><equals operator>

<C variable definition> ::=
      [ <C storage class> ]
      [ <C class modifier> ]
      <C variable specification>
    <semicolon>

<C storage class> ::=
      auto
    | extern
    | static

<C class modifier> ::= const | volatile

<C variable specification> ::=
      <C numeric variable>
    | <C character variable>
    | <C derived variable>

<C numeric variable> ::=
    { long | short | float | double }
      <C host identifier> [ <C initial value> ]
            [ { <comma> <C host identifier> [ <C initial value> ] }... ]

<C initial value> ::=
    <equals operator> <character representation>...

<C character variable> ::=
    char [ CHARACTER SET
             [ IS ] <character set specification> ]
      <C host identifier>
        <C array specification> [ <C initial value> ]
        [ { <comma> <C host identifier>
          <C array specification>
                 [ <C initial value> ] }... ]

<C array specification> ::=
    <left bracket> <length> <right bracket>

<C derived variable> ::=
      <C VARCHAR variable>
    | <C bit variable>
```

```
<C VARCHAR variable> ::=
    VARCHAR [ CHARACTER SET [ IS ]
        <character set specification> ]
        <C host identifier>
            <C array specification> [ <C initial value> ]
          [ { <comma> <C host identifier>
              <C array specification>
                      [ <C initial value> ] }... ]

<C bit variable> ::=
    BIT <C host identifier>
        <C array specification> [ <C initial value> ]
      [ { <comma> <C host identifier>
        <C array specification>
                  [ <C initial value> ] }... ]

<COBOL variable definition> ::=
    {01¦77} <COBOL host identifier> <COBOL type specification>
      [ <character representation>... ] <period>

<COBOL type specification> ::=
      <COBOL character type>
    ¦ <COBOL bit type>
    ¦ <COBOL numeric type>
    ¦ <COBOL integer type>

<COBOL character type> ::=
    [ CHARACTER SET [ IS ]
          <character set specification> ]
    { PIC ¦ PICTURE } [ IS ] { X [ <left paren> <length> <right paren> ] }...

<COBOL bit type> ::=
    { PIC ¦ PICTURE } [ IS ]
        { B [ <left paren> <length> <right paren> ] }...

<COBOL numeric type> ::=
    { PIC ¦ PICTURE } [ IS ]
      S <COBOL nines specification>
    [ USAGE [ IS ] ] DISPLAY SIGN LEADING SEPARATE

<COBOL nines specification> ::=
      <COBOL nines> [ V [ <COBOL nines> ] ]
    ¦ V <COBOL nines>

<COBOL nines> ::= { 9 [ <left paren> <length> <right paren> ] }...

<COBOL integer type> ::=
      <COBOL computational integer>
    ¦ <COBOL binary integer>

<COBOL computational integer> ::=
    { PIC ¦ PICTURE } [ IS ] S<COBOL nines>
      [ USAGE [ IS ] ] { COMP ¦ COMPUTATIONAL }
```

```
<COBOL binary integer> ::=
    { PIC ¦ PICTURE } [ IS ] S<COBOL nines>
      [ USAGE [ IS ] ] BINARY

<Fortran variable definition> ::=
    <Fortran type specification>
    <Fortran host identifier>
        [ { <comma> <Fortran host identifier> }... ]

<Fortran type specification> ::=
      CHARACTER [ <asterisk> <length> ]
          [ CHARACTER SET [ IS ]
                <character set specification> ]
    ¦ BIT [ <asterisk> <length> ]
    ¦ INTEGER
    ¦ REAL
    ¦ DOUBLE PRECISION

<MUMPS variable definition> ::=
    { <MUMPS numeric variable> ¦ <MUMPS character variable> }
        <semicolon>

<MUMPS numeric variable> ::=
    <MUMPS type specification>
      <MUMPS host identifier> [ { <comma> <MUMPS host identifier> }... ]

<MUMPS type specification> ::=
      INT
    ¦ DEC
          [ <left paren> <precision> [ <comma> <scale> ] <right paren> ]
    ¦ REAL

<MUMPS character variable> ::=
    VARCHAR <MUMPS host identifier> <MUMPS length specification>
      [ { <comma> <MUMPS host identifier> <MUMPS length specification> }... ]

<MUMPS length specification> ::=
    <left paren> <length> <right paren>

<Pascal variable definition> ::=
    <Pascal host identifier> [ { <comma> <Pascal host identifier> }... ] <colon>
      <Pascal type specification> <semicolon>

<Pascal type specification> ::=
      PACKED ARRAY
          <left bracket> 1 <double period> <length> <right bracket>
        OF CHAR
          [ CHARACTER SET [ IS ]
                <character set specification> ]
    ¦ PACKED ARRAY
          <left bracket> 1 <double period> <length> <right bracket>
        OF BIT
    ¦ INTEGER
    ¦ REAL
    ¦ CHAR [ CHARACTER SET
                                   [ IS ] <character set specification> ]
    ¦ BIT
```

```
<PL/I variable definition> ::=
    {DCL ¦ DECLARE}
        {   <PL/I host identifier>
          ¦ <left paren> <PL/I host identifier>
                [ { <comma> <PL/I host identifier> }... ] <right paren> }
    <PL/I type specification>
    [ <character representation>... ] <semicolon>

<PL/I type specification> ::=
      { CHAR ¦ CHARACTER } [ VARYING ]
          <left paren><length><right paren>
          [ CHARACTER SET
                [ IS ] <character set specification> ]
    ¦ BIT [ VARYING ] <left paren><length><right paren>
    ¦ <PL/I type fixed decimal> <left paren> <precision>
          [ <comma> <scale> ] <right paren>
    ¦ <PL/I type fixed binary> [ <left paren> <precision> <right paren> ]
    ¦ <PL/I type float binary> <left paren> <precision> <right paren>

<PL/I type fixed decimal> ::=
      { DEC ¦ DECIMAL } FIXED
    ¦ FIXED { DEC ¦ DECIMAL }

<PL/I type fixed binary> ::=
      { BIN ¦ BINARY } FIXED
    ¦ FIXED { BIN ¦ BINARY }

<PL/I type float binary> ::=
      { BIN ¦ BINARY } FLOAT
    ¦ FLOAT { BIN ¦ BINARY }

<embedded SQL end declare> ::=
    <SQL prefix> END DECLARE SECTION
        [ <SQL terminator> ]

<embedded SQL MUMPS declare> ::=
    <SQL prefix>
      BEGIN DECLARE SECTION
        [ <embedded character set declaration> ]
        [ <host variable definition>... ]
      END DECLARE SECTION
    <SQL terminator>

<embedded SQL statement> ::=
    <SQL prefix>
      <statement or declaration>
    [ <SQL terminator> ]

<statement or declaration> ::=
      <declare cursor>
    ¦ <dynamic declare cursor>
    ¦ <temporary table declaration>
    ¦ <embedded exception declaration>
    ¦ <SQL procedure statement>
```

Part VI App C

```
<embedded exception declaration> ::=
    WHENEVER <condition> <condition action>

<condition> ::=
    SQLERROR ¦ NOT FOUND

<condition action> ::=
    CONTINUE ¦ <go to>

<go to> ::=
    { GOTO ¦ GO TO } <goto target>

<goto target> ::=
      <host label identifier>
    ¦ <unsigned integer>
    ¦ <host PL/I label variable>

<host label identifier> ::= !!<EMPHASIS>(See the Syntax Rules.)

<host PL/I label variable> ::= !!<EMPHASIS>(See the Syntax Rules.)

<preparable statement> ::=
      <preparable SQL data statement>
    ¦ <preparable SQL schema statement>
    ¦ <preparable SQL transaction statement>
    ¦ <preparable SQL session statement>
    ¦ <preparable implementation-defined statement>

<preparable SQL data statement> ::=
      <delete statement: searched>
    ¦ <dynamic single row select statement>
    ¦ <insert statement>
    ¦ <dynamic select statement>
    ¦ <update statement: searched>
    ¦ <preparable dynamic delete statement: positioned>
    ¦ <preparable dynamic update statement: positioned>

<dynamic single row select statement> ::= <query specification>

<dynamic select statement> ::= <cursor specification>

<preparable dynamic delete statement: positioned> ::=
   DELETE [ FROM <table name> ]
      WHERE CURRENT OF <cursor name>

<preparable dynamic update statement: positioned> ::=
   UPDATE [ <table name> ]
      SET <set clause list>
      WHERE CURRENT OF <cursor name>

<preparable SQL schema statement> ::=
      <SQL schema statement>

<preparable SQL transaction statement> ::=
      <SQL transaction statement>
```

```
<preparable SQL session statement> ::=
      <SQL session statement>

<preparable implementation-defined statement> ::=
    !! <EMPHASIS>(See the Syntax Rules.)

<direct SQL statement> ::=
    <directly executable statement> <semicolon>

<directly executable statement> ::=
      <direct SQL data statement>
    ¦ <SQL schema statement>
    ¦ <SQL transaction statement>
    ¦ <SQL connection statement>
    ¦ <SQL session statement>
    ¦ <direct implementation-defined statement>

<direct SQL data statement> ::=
      <delete statement: searched>
    ¦ <direct select statement: multiple rows>
    ¦ <insert statement>
    ¦ <update statement: searched>
    ¦ <temporary table declaration>

<direct select statement: multiple rows> ::=
    <query expression> [ <order by clause> ]

<direct implementation-defined statement> ::=
    !!<EMPHASIS>(See the Syntax Rules)

<SQL object identifier> ::=
    <SQL provenance> <SQL variant>

<SQL provenance> ::= <arc1> <arc2> <arc3>

<arc1> ::= iso ¦ 1 ¦ iso <left paren> 1 <right paren>

<arc2> ::= standard ¦ 0 ¦ standard <left paren> 0 <right paren>

<arc3> ::= 9075

<SQL variant> ::= <SQL edition> <SQL conformance>

<SQL edition> ::= <1987> ¦ <1989> ¦ <1992>

<1987> ::= 0 ¦ edition1987 <left paren> 0 <right paren>

<1989> ::= <1989 base> <1989 package>

<1989 base> ::= 1 ¦ edition1989 <left paren> 1 <right paren>

<1989 package> ::= <integrity no> ¦ <integrity yes>

<integrity no> ::= 0 ¦ IntegrityNo <left paren> 0 <right paren>

<integrity yes> ::= 1 ¦ IntegrityYes <left paren> 1 <right paren>
```

```
<1992> ::= 2 ¦ edition1992 <left paren> 2 <right paren>

<SQL conformance> ::= <low> ¦ <intermediate> ¦ <high>

<low> ::= 0 ¦ Low <left paren> 0 <right paren>

<intermediate> ::= 1 ¦ Intermediate <left paren> 1 <right paren>

<high> ::= 2 ¦ High <left paren> 2 <right paren>
```

# Index

## Symbols



## A

## B



## C

## D

## E

## F

## G

## H



## I

## M

## Q



## R

## S

## T

## U

## W



## X-Z

# Check out Que® Books on the World Wide Web http://www.quecorp.com

As the biggest software release in computer history, Windows 95 continues to redefine the computer industry. Click here for the latest info on our Windows 95 books

Make computing quick and easy with these products designed exclusively for new and casual users

Examine the latest releases in word processing, spreadsheets, operating systems, and suites

The Internet, The World Wide Web, CompuServe®, America Online®, Prodigy® —it's a world of ever-changing information. Don't get left behind!

Find out about new additions to our site, new bestsellers and hot topics

In-depth information on high-end topics: find the best reference books for databases, programming, networking, and client/server technologies

A recent addition to Que, Ziff-Davis Press publishes the highly-successful *How It Works* and *How to Use* series of books, as well as *PC Learning Labs Teaches* and *PC Magazine* series of book/disc packages

Stay on the cutting edge of Macintosh® technologies and visual communications

Find out which titles are making headlines

With 6 separate publishing groups, Que develops products for many specific market segments and areas of computer technology. Explore our Web Site and you'll find information on best-selling titles, newly published titles, upcoming products, authors, and much more.

- Stay informed on the latest industry trends and products available
- Visit our online bookstore for the latest information and editions
- Download software from Que's library of the best shareware and freeware

QUE®

Copyright © 1997, Macmillan Computer Publishing-USA, A Viacom Company

# Complete and Return this Card for a *FREE* Computer Book Catalog

Thank you for purchasing this book! You have purchased a superior computer book written expressly for your needs. To continue to provide the kind of up-to-date, pertinent coverage you've come to expect from us, we need to hear from you. Please take a minute to complete and return this self-addressed, postage-paid form. In return, we'll send you a free catalog of all our computer books on topics ranging from word processing to programming and the internet.

Mr. ☐ Mrs. ☐ Ms. ☐ Dr. ☐

Name (first) ☐☐☐☐☐☐☐☐☐☐☐ (M.I.) ☐ (last) ☐☐☐☐☐☐☐☐☐☐☐☐☐☐☐

Address ☐☐☐☐☐☐☐☐☐☐☐☐☐☐☐☐☐☐☐☐☐☐☐☐☐☐☐☐☐☐☐☐☐☐☐

☐☐☐☐☐☐☐☐☐☐☐☐☐☐☐☐☐☐☐☐☐☐☐☐☐☐☐☐☐☐☐☐☐☐☐

City ☐☐☐☐☐☐☐☐☐☐☐☐☐☐☐ State ☐☐ Zip ☐☐☐☐☐ ☐☐☐☐

Phone ☐☐☐ ☐☐☐ ☐☐☐☐ Fax ☐☐☐ ☐☐☐ ☐☐☐☐

Company Name ☐☐☐☐☐☐☐☐☐☐☐☐☐☐☐☐☐☐☐☐☐☐☐☐☐☐☐☐☐☐☐☐☐

E-mail address ☐☐☐☐☐☐☐☐☐☐☐☐☐☐☐☐☐☐☐☐☐☐☐☐☐☐☐☐☐☐☐☐☐

**1. Please check at least (3) influencing factors for purchasing this book.**

- Front or back cover information on book ☐
- Special approach to the content ☐
- Completeness of content ☐
- Author's reputation ☐
- Publisher's reputation ☐
- Book cover design or layout ☐
- Index or table of contents of book ☐
- Price of book ☐
- Special effects, graphics, illustrations ☐
- Other (Please specify): ________________ ☐

**2. How did you first learn about this book?**

- Saw in Macmillan Computer Publishing catalog ☐
- Recommended by store personnel ☐
- Saw the book on bookshelf at store ☐
- Recommended by a friend ☐
- Received advertisement in the mail ☐
- Saw an advertisement in: ________________ ☐
- Read book review in: ________________ ☐
- Other (Please specify): ________________ ☐

**3. How many computer books have you purchased in the last six months?**

- This book only ☐
- 3 to 5 books ☐
- 2 books ☐
- More than 5 ☐

**4. Where did you purchase this book?**

- Bookstore ☐
- Computer Store ☐
- Consumer Electronics Store ☐
- Department Store ☐
- Office Club ☐
- Warehouse Club ☐
- Mail Order ☐
- Direct from Publisher ☐
- Internet site ☐
- Other (Please specify): ________________ ☐

**5. How long have you been using a computer?**

- ☐ Less than 6 months
- ☐ 6 months to a year
- ☐ 1 to 3 years
- ☐ More than 3 years

**6. What is your level of experience with personal computers and with the subject of this book?**

| | With PCs | With subject of book |
|---|---|---|
| New | ☐ | ☐ |
| Casual | ☐ | ☐ |
| Accomplished | ☐ | ☐ |
| Expert | ☐ | ☐ |

Source Code ISBN: 0-7897-1015-3

**7. Which of the following best describes your job title?**

- Administrative Assistant ☐
- Coordinator ☐
- Manager/Supervisor ☐
- Director ☐
- Vice President ☐
- President/CEO/COO ☐
- Lawyer/Doctor/Medical Professional ☐
- Teacher/Educator/Trainer ☐
- Engineer/Technician ☐
- Consultant ☐
- Not employed/Student/Retired ☐
- Other (Please specify): ______________ ☐

**8. Which of the following best describes the area of the company your job title falls under?**

- Accounting ☐
- Engineering ☐
- Manufacturing ☐
- Operations ☐
- Marketing ☐
- Sales ☐
- Other (Please specify): ______________ ☐

**9. What is your age?**

- Under 20 ☐
- 21-29 ☐
- 30-39 ☐
- 40-49 ☐
- 50-59 ☐
- 60-over ☐

**10. Are you:**

- Male ☐
- Female ☐

**11. Which computer publications do you read regularly? (Please list)**

______________________________

***Comments***: ______________________________

Fold here and scotch-tape to mail.

NO POSTAGE NECESSARY IF MAILED IN THE UNITED STATES

**BUSINESS REPLY MAIL**

FIRST-CLASS MAIL PERMIT NO. 9918 INDIANAPOLIS IN

POSTAGE WILL BE PAID BY THE ADDRESSEE

ATTN MARKETING
MACMILLAN COMPUTER PUBLISHING
MACMILLAN PUBLISHING USA
201 W 103RD ST
INDIANAPOLIS IN 46290-9042